The Law of Loyalty

The Law of Loyalty

LIONEL SMITH

OXFORD
UNIVERSITY PRESS

Oxford University Press is a department of the University of Oxford. It furthers the University's objective of excellence in research, scholarship, and education by publishing worldwide. Oxford is a registered trade mark of Oxford University Press in the UK and certain other countries.

Published in the United States of America by Oxford University Press
198 Madison Avenue, New York, NY 10016, United States of America.

© Lionel Smith 2023

All rights reserved. No part of this publication may be reproduced, stored in a retrieval system, or transmitted, in any form or by any means, without the prior permission in writing of Oxford University Press, or as expressly permitted by law, by license, or under terms agreed with the appropriate reproduction rights organization. Inquiries concerning reproduction outside the scope of the above should be sent to the Rights Department, Oxford University Press, at the address above.

You must not circulate this work in any other form
and you must impose this same condition on any acquirer.

Library of Congress Cataloging-in-Publication Data
Names: Smith, Lionel, author.
Title: The law of loyalty / Lionel Smith.
Description: New York, NY : Oxford University Press, [2023]
Identifiers: LCCN 2023062191 (print) | LCCN 2023062192 (ebook) |
ISBN 9780197664582 (hardback) | ISBN 9780197664605 (epub) |
ISBN 9780197664599 (updf) | ISBN 9780197664612 (digital-online)
Subjects: LCSH: Duty of loyalty.
Classification: LCC K579.L69 S65 2022 (print) | LCC K579.L69 (ebook) |
DDC 340/.11—dc23/eng/20230208
LC record available at https://lccn.loc.gov/2022062191
LC ebook record available at https://lccn.loc.gov/2022062192

DOI: 10.1093/oso/9780197664582.001.0001

Printed by Integrated Books International, United States of America

Note to Readers
This publication is designed to provide accurate and authoritative information in regard to the subject matter covered. It is based upon sources believed to be accurate and reliable and is intended to be current as of the time it was written. It is sold with the understanding that the publisher is not engaged in rendering legal, accounting, or other professional services. If legal advice or other expert assistance is required, the services of a competent professional person should be sought. Also, to confirm that the information has not been affected or changed by recent developments, traditional legal research techniques should be used, including checking primary sources where appropriate.

(Based on the Declaration of Principles jointly adopted by a Committee of the American Bar Association and a Committee of Publishers and Associations.)

You may order this or any other Oxford University Press publication by visiting the Oxford University Press website at www.oup.com.

For my son Hugh
Who makes me proud

And for Steve Smith
My brother in the law

Preface

Since early in my academic career, I have been fascinated by the common law's concepts of fiduciary obligations and fiduciary relationships. How can we make sense of the idea that people are legally obliged to make decisions in the pursuit of the interests of other people? The basic elements of private law—contract, tort, and restitution—know nothing of this. Like many others, I was struck—'haunted' might be a better word—by the observation of a chief justice of Australia that '[t]he fiduciary relationship is a concept in search of a principle'.[1] That can be read as a warning; I took it as a challenge. This book is my response.

By 2000, I had become a comparative lawyer, thanks in no small part to Peter Birks and Michele Graziadei. I had begun to see in the civil law tradition a kind of parallel universe, a very different way of comprehending the realities I had hitherto known only through the concepts of the common law. When I came that year to McGill University, I continued teaching trust law and corporate law, a combination which already gives multiple perspectives on fiduciary relationships; but I also began to study and teach the civil law, which has its own language and concepts for the very same issues and problems. Not only does today's Civil Code of Québec regulate carefully the administration of the property of others, but without looking too hard one can find, in the texts preserved in the *Digest* of Justinian, rules against unauthorized profits and against exercising powers held for others while in a conflict of interest. And so the challenge widened into one that at McGill might be called 'transsystemic'. It became wider still as I became aware of a growing literature and case law exploring the question whether public powers can be understood as governed by principles that are similar to those that govern private powers held for others.

This expansion of the ambitions of my project was also accelerated and facilitated by being at McGill. My colleagues there had an immeasurable impact on the development of my work. Steve Smith was known for his lightning-quick analytical mind, profound legal and philosophical learning, and especially for his (almost notorious) gift for striking at the very heart of the matter with a simple but penetrating question. To the immense loss of us all, Steve passed away as this book was in press. Evan Fox-Decent is a global leader in thinking about how public power can be conceptualized and legitimized by understanding it as held

---

[1] Sir Anthony Mason, 'Themes and Prospects' in Paul D Finn (ed), *Essays in Equity* (Law Book Co 1985) 242, 246.

in a fiduciary capacity. In the depths of the pandemic, Evan organized an international online symposium to discuss my draft typescript, which generated a great deal of invaluable feedback. Madeleine Cantin Cumyn grasped long ago the fundamental and foundational conceptual divide in private law between acting for others and acting for ourselves; seeing beyond the black letter of Quebec's codification of the 'administration of the property of others', she showed that this is only a subset of a larger intellectual category, one that includes the holding of powers over the non-pecuniary interests of another.[2] Paul Miller, now at Notre Dame, helped not only me but many others through his leadership in the organization of intellectually stimulating events in private law theory, in Canada, the United States, and elsewhere. His scholarship has advanced the state of the art and has assisted me tremendously in the development of my ideas. Alexandra Popovici, now at the *Université de Sherbrooke*, helped me immeasurably with questions, comments, and observations that frequently caused me to rethink what was important and to restructure my arguments. Her scholarly generosity is limitless. All five of these were my colleagues at McGill's Faculty of Law, which was for a time the home of a transsystemic, public–private dream team of fiduciary thinking. They are often cited in my footnotes, but in fact their influence is on every page.

At more of a distance, the scholarship of Paul Finn was inspirational. He long ago saw that common principles underlie the legal regulation of other-regarding power, in private law and in public law.[3] My friend and former colleague Robert Stevens of Oxford University assisted me from beginning to end—indeed, from before the beginning, and no doubt after the end—with high-level insights that ultimately contributed to the structure and organization of the whole undertaking. While I felt pretty confident about what is common to acting for others across private and public law, he helped me to better articulate what is not.

Other friends have helped me to sharpen my ideas, avoid mistakes, and benefit from scholarship and court decisions of which I would otherwise have been unaware. I have had generous and invaluable assistance from Marie-Pier Baril, Kit Barker, Gerhard Dannemann, Simone Degeling, Joshua Getzler, Andrew S. Gold, Michele Graziadei, Birke Häcker, Matthew Harding, Lusina Ho, Adam

---

[2] See Madeleine Cantin Cumyn, *L'administration du bien d'autrui* (Éditions Yvon Blais 2000) (current edition: Madeleine Cantin Cumyn and Michelle Cumyn, *L'administration du bien d'autrui* (2nd edn, Éditions Yvon Blais 2014)); Madeleine Cantin Cumyn, 'Le pouvoir juridique' (2007) 52 McGill LJ 215 (translation: Madeleine Cantin Cumyn, 'The Legal Power' (2009) 17 Eur Rev Priv L 345); and Madeleine Cantin Cumyn, 'De l'administration des biens à la protection de la personne d'autrui' in Barreau du Québec – Service de la Formation continue (ed), *Obligations et recours contre un curateur, tuteur ou mandataire défaillant 2008*, vol 283 (Yvon Blais 2008) 205.

[3] For an overview of his contributions and the evolution of his thinking, see Paul D Finn, 'Fiduciary Reflections' (2014) 88 ALJ 127, 127–31.

Hofri-Winogradow, Jessica Hudson, Nicholas Kasirer, Nick McBride, Charles Mitchell, Joanne Murray, James Penner, Weiming Tan, and Remus Valsan. And like every scholar who produces a substantial project, I have been helped by others who are too numerous to name. I have also benefited from the gracious hospitality of a range of institutions which invited me to share my work in progress. As every academic knows, the benefits of such presentations are immeasurable. I was fortunate to hold visiting positions at All Souls College, Suor Orsola Benincasa University, *Roma Tre* University, the International Institute for the Unification of Private Law, and the Universities of Toronto, New South Wales, Oxford, Edinburgh, Queensland, and Florence. During the final stages, Jordan Halligan provided invaluable assistance with the index.

I thank also the Killam Trustees, who saw fit to award me a Killam Research Fellowship during 2014–16. It was at the end of that period of intensive reflection that I was able to start the book in earnest. I express my gratitude to the Social Sciences and Humanities Research Council of Canada and to McGill University and its Faculty of Law for their material support for my research. I have also been tremendously assisted—although I am not certain that thanks are in order in this respect—by developments in politics which have given me constant examples of how other-regarding power should and should not rightly be exercised.

LDS
Elvis Presley's birthday, 2023

Summary Contents

Table of Cases   xxv

PART I: INTRODUCTION

1. Foundations   3
   - I. Scope   3
   - II. Significance   5
   - III. Ambitions of the argument   12
   - IV. Concepts   18
   - V. Unity and diversity   33

PART II: ACTING FOR OTHERS IN PRIVATE LAW

2. Introduction   59
   - I. Significance and scope of this Part   59
   - II. Private law's regulation of acting for others   61
   - III. The constitution and termination of relationships of private administration   65

PART II.A: THE CORE CASES OF PRIVATE LAW ADMINISTRATION

3. Loyalty in the Exercise of Private Law Powers of Administration   79
   - I. Introduction   79
   - II. The role of loyalty   85
   - III. Who is required to exercise powers loyally?   100
   - IV. The content of loyalty: The proper use of other-regarding powers   109
   - V. Plurality of roles   138

4. Conflicts in Relation to Private Law Administration   141
   - I. Introduction   141
   - II. Overview of the rules against conflicts   141
   - III. Definition   152
   - IV. Justification for the rules against acting while in a conflict   154
   - V. Legal consequences of conflicts   163
   - VI. Apparent, potential, and trivial conflicts   167
   - VII. Managing conflicts   173

5. Attribution: Costs, Profits, and Information — 181
   I. Introduction — 181
   II. The attribution of profits — 183
   III. The relationship between the attribution of profits and the rules about conflicts — 200
   IV. Attribution applies to both authorized and unauthorized actions — 208
   V. Legal mechanisms of attribution: Accountability — 210
   VI. The scope of the rule against unauthorized profits — 216
   VII. Contractual accountability for unauthorized profits — 220
   VIII. Duties of disclosure — 228

6. Other Features of Private Law Administration — 239
   I. Introduction — 239
   II. Duty of commitment — 239
   III. Duty of care, skill and diligence; or, duties of prudence and diligence — 240
   IV. Good faith — 243

PART II.B: THE WIDENING REACH OF ADMINISTRATION IN PRIVATE LAW

7. The Widening Reach of Administration in Private Law — 247
   I. Introduction — 247
   II. Legal powers outside of established categories — 248
   III. Legal powers over non-financial or extrapatrimonial interests — 260
   IV. Factual powers — 264
   V. Parents — 276

PART II.C: THE ENFORCEMENT AND SUPERVISION OF PRIVATE ADMINISTRATION

8. The Enforcement and Supervision of Private Administration — 281
   I. Introduction — 281
   II. Rights and powers, and their enforcement and supervision — 281
   III. Mechanisms of enforcement and supervision — 283

PART III: ACTING FOR OTHERS IN PUBLIC LAW

9. Foundations of Public Law Administration — 299
   I. Structure, goals, and scope of this Part — 299
   II. The domain of public administration — 314
   III. Characteristics of public administration — 331

10. The Enforcement and Supervision of Public Law Administration — 335
   I. Introduction: Dimensions of the enforcement and supervision of public administration — 335
   II. Mechanisms of enforcement and supervision — 339
   III. Conclusion — 373

11. Spheres of Public Law Administration — 375
   I. Introduction — 375
   II. Non-State holders of public powers — 376
   III. The components of the State, and its emanations — 381
   IV. The State itself as holder of public powers — 412
   V. The widening reach of public administration: Professionals — 418
   VI. Conclusion — 428

PART IV: CONCLUSION

12. Conclusion — 431

Bibliography — 437
Index — 455

Detailed Contents

Table of Cases   xxv

PART I: INTRODUCTION

1. Foundations   3
   I. Scope   3
   II. Significance   5
       A. A survey of the field   5
       B. The invisibility of its unity   9
   III. Ambitions of the argument   12
       A. Methodology and objectives   12
       B. Justificatory principles   14
       C. The limits of this study   16
   IV. Concepts   18
       A. Power   18
          1. Introduction   18
          2. Ambiguity of 'power'   20
       B. Discretion   23
       C. Mission, assignment, function, task, charge   25
       D. Fiduciary relationships and relationships of administration   27
       E. Relationships of administration and obligations of administration   29
       F. Loyalty   30
       G. Status   32
   V. Unity and diversity   33
       A. Unity   33
       B. Diversity   36
          1. Diversity of contexts   36
          2. Diversity of conceptualizations   38
             a) Private law   38
             b) Public law   41
          3. Diversity of legal incidents   42
             a) Acting for persons or for a purpose   43
             b) Representation   44
                (1) Legal representation   44
                (2) Legal representation and mandate and agency   46
                (3) Political representation   49
             c) Subject to instructions, or not   51
             d) The administrator as office-holder, or not, and the court's
                supervisory jurisdiction   53

PART II: ACTING FOR OTHERS IN PRIVATE LAW

2. Introduction 59
   I. Significance and scope of this Part 59
      A. Significance 59
      B. Scope 60
   II. Private law's regulation of acting for others 61
      A. Background 61
      B. Overview of private law administration 63
   III. The constitution and termination of relationships of private
       administration 65
      A. Constitution 65
          1. Private assignment and acceptance of a mission 65
          2. Unilateral constitution of oneself as administrator 67
          3. By operation of law 68
          4. By court appointment 68
          5. The role of an undertaking by the administrator 69
          6. Conclusion 71
      B. Termination 71
          1. Resignation 71
          2. Recusal (temporary or partial resignation) 72
          3. Private removal 73
          4. End of term of office-holder 73
          5. Removal by the court 74
          6. Ad hoc replacement of private law administrators 74
          7. Conclusion 75

PART II.A: THE CORE CASES OF PRIVATE LAW ADMINISTRATION

3. Loyalty in the Exercise of Private Law Powers of Administration . . . 79
   I. Introduction 79
      A. Specifying the context 79
      B. Different meanings of 'loyalty' 79
      C. Manifestations of the legal requirement of loyalty in the exercise
         of powers of private administration 81
      D. Intention, purpose, and motivation 82
   II. The role of loyalty 85
      A. The necessity of a requirement of loyalty 85
      B. The necessity of a *subjective* requirement of loyalty 87
      C. Further limitations 93
          1. Objective limitations on authority that are separate from loyalty 93
          2. Narrower formulations of what loyalty requires 95
      D. Conclusion 99

III.	Who is required to exercise powers loyally?	100
	A. Introduction	100
	B. How is the power held?	100
	1. For the accomplishment of an other-regarding mission	101
	2. For oneself	102
	3. Conclusion	105
	C. Powers without discretion	106
IV.	The content of loyalty: The proper use of other-regarding powers	109
	A. The demands of loyalty in different situations	109
	1. A requirement to exercise powers in what the power-holder considers to be the best interests of a person	109
	2. A requirement to exercise powers in what the power-holder considers to be the best pursuit of an impersonal purpose	111
	B. Mixed purposes or motives	115
	1. The proper consideration of other interests in assessing the beneficiary's interests	115
	2. Mixed motives or purposes that include improper considerations	117
	C. Giving of reasons for the exercise of powers	122
	D. Is an administrator required to hear from those affected by an exercise of their power?	122
	E. Delegation of powers and fettering of discretion	124
	F. Consequences of misuse of powers	126
	1. Setting aside a legal act	126
	2. Nullity, voidness, and voidability	128
	3. Protection of third parties	130
	4. Who can set aside a legal act that is defective for disloyalty?	133
	5. Misuse by non-use	135
	G. Disloyalty in the use of powers is not necessarily a breach of duty	136
V.	Plurality of roles	138
4. Conflicts in Relation to Private Law Administration		**141**
I.	Introduction	141
II.	Overview of the rules against conflicts	141
	A. Examples of conflicts	141
	B. Some misunderstandings about conflicts	144
	1. Conflict of interest and conflict of interests	144
	2. Administrators and conflicts of interests	146
	3. The rules on conflicts of self-interest and duty (and conflicts of duty and duty) apply when an administrator is exercising the powers that they hold in that role	149
	4. Being in a conflict is not, as such, a breach of duty	151
III.	Definition	152

IV.	Justification for the rules against acting while in a conflict	154
	A. Conflict of self-interest and duty	155
	B. Conflict of duty and duty	159
V.	Legal consequences of conflicts	163
	A. Inability to use powers held as administrator	163
	B. Voidability of powers used while in a conflict	164
	C. Requirements of disclosure and duties of disclosure	166
VI.	Apparent, potential, and trivial conflicts	167
	A. Apparent conflicts	167
	B. Potential conflicts	168
	C. Trivial conflicts	171
VII.	Managing conflicts	173
	A. Prior authorization	173
	B. Informed consent	175
	C. Recusal	176
	D. Resignation or removal	179

5. Attribution: Costs, Profits, and Information — 181

I.	Introduction	181
II.	The attribution of profits	183
	A. Statement of the norm	183
	B. Justification for the norm	188
	1. Not based on deterrence	188
	2. Not based on conflict of interest	190
	3. Not even based on wrongdoing	191
	4. Based on attribution	196
III.	The relationship between the attribution of profits and the rules about conflicts	200
	A. The separateness of the principles	200
	B. Unauthorized profits without conflicts of interest or duty	204
	1. Ceasing to act	204
	2. Aligned interests	205
	3. Powers without discretion	206
	4. Conclusion	207
IV.	Attribution applies to both authorized and unauthorized actions	208
	A. Why this is so	208
	B. Taking an unauthorized profit is not ratification	209
V.	Legal mechanisms of attribution: Accountability	210
	A. Legal mechanisms of attribution	210
	B. Accountability	212
	1. Narrow and wide senses	212
	2. A very different sense	214
	3. Conclusion	215
VI.	The scope of the rule against unauthorized profits	216

	A.	Introduction	216
	B.	What can be attributed?	217
	C.	An allowance for the administrator?	219
	D.	Authorization	220
VII.	Contractual accountability for unauthorized profits		220
	A.	The problem stated	220
	B.	The problem solved	223
	C.	Other illustrations	225
	D.	Gain-based remedies for wrongdoing	227
VIII.	Duties of disclosure		228
	A.	The attribution of information creates duties of disclosure	228
	B.	General rules	229
		1. Information about the existence and state of the relationship	229
		2. Disclosure of conflicts and profits	230
		3. Disclosure of unlawful conduct	231
		4. Conclusion	232
	C.	Advisory administrators	233
	D.	The administrator who wishes to contract with their own beneficiary	233
	E.	The breach of an obligation to disclose is an unlawful act	236
	F.	Conclusion	237

6. Other Features of Private Law Administration 239
   I. Introduction 239
   II. Duty of commitment 239
   III. Duty of care, skill and diligence; or, duties of prudence and diligence 240
       A. Introduction 240
       B. Differences from duties in tort or general civil responsibility 240
       C. Breach 242
       D. Exemption 242
   IV. Good faith 243

PART II.B: THE WIDENING REACH OF ADMINISTRATION IN PRIVATE LAW

7. The Widening Reach of Administration in Private Law 247
   I. Introduction 247
   II. Legal powers outside of established categories 248
       A. Joint venturers (outside of partnership and corporation) 248
       B. Employees 252
          1. Employees can be in a relationship of administration 252
          2. The employment relationship itself is not a relationship of administration 254

          3. Similarities and false flags   256
       C. Trust protectors   259
   III. Legal powers over non-financial or extrapatrimonial interests   260
       A. Introduction   260
       B. Conflicts and unauthorized profits   262
       C. Doubts about the administration of non-financial interests   263
   IV. Factual powers   264
       A. Advisors   264
       B. De facto relationships   272
    V. Parents   276

PART II.C: THE ENFORCEMENT AND SUPERVISION OF PRIVATE ADMINISTRATION

8. The Enforcement and Supervision of Private Administration   281
    I. Introduction   281
   II. Rights and powers, and their enforcement and supervision   281
       A. Rights and their enforcement   281
       B. Powers and their supervision   282
  III. Mechanisms of enforcement and supervision   283
       A. Non-legal norms   283
       B. Criminal law   284
       C. Private law powers of enforcement and supervision   285
          1. Direct enforcement   285
          2. Representative enforcement   285
             a) Delegated representation of a capacitated person   286
             b) Delegated or appointed representation of an
                incapacitated person   286
             c) Appointed representation of a capacitated person   286
             d) Private law class action   288
             e) Supervision and enforcement by beneficiaries and
                others on behalf of the class of beneficiaries   290
       D. Private purpose trusts: Powers of enforcement without rights   293

PART III: ACTING FOR OTHERS IN PUBLIC LAW

9. Foundations of Public Law Administration   299
    I. Structure, goals, and scope of this Part   299
       A. Introduction   299
       B. Structure and goals of this Part   300
       C. Public trust and fiduciary government   301
          1. Introduction   301
          2. Limits of my argument   305

			a) Not a theory of the State or of the source of State power	305
			b) Not even a theory of any part of the State	308
			c) Does not demand or rule out particular exercises of State power	308
		3.	Dicey and 'common law constitutionalism'	309
	II.	The domain of public administration		314
		A.	Introduction	314
		B.	Beneficiaries of public administration	318
		C.	Examples of public administration	319
		D.	Some borderline cases	320
			1. Legal persons with private missions: Business corporations	321
			2. Legal persons with public missions: Universities	323
			3. Contractual powers held by public entities	326
			4. Public–private partnerships	327
	III.	Characteristics of public administration		331
		A.	The problems with which this study is concerned	331
		B.	Removal of public administrators	332
10.	The Enforcement and Supervision of Public Law Administration			335
	I.	Introduction: Dimensions of the enforcement and supervision of public administration		335
	II.	Mechanisms of enforcement and supervision		339
		A.	Non-legal norms	339
			1. Introduction	339
			2. Reasons to resist legal norms governing public administration?	340
			3. Problems with reliance on non-legal norms	344
		B.	Criminal law	346
		C.	Supervision with non-criminal denunciatory sanctions	347
		D.	Enforcement by the State	348
		E.	The problem of self-supervision	349
		F.	Enforcement by claims of non-State bodies acting in the public interest against their own administrators	351
		G.	Representative enforcement of claims of the State or its emanations	353
			1. Delegated or appointed representative actions to enforce rights of a legal person with a public mission	353
			2. Representative enforcement of the claims of the State	354
		H.	Private enforcement of undirected public duties and liabilities	356
			1. Where private rights are affected	356
			2. Where interests but not rights are affected	358
		I.	Private claims for compensation	361
			1. Harm inflicted by abuse of public powers	362
			2. Unintended infliction of loss	366

		a) Introduction	366
		b) Harm to persons or property caused by State action	367
		c) Pure economic loss caused by State action	369
		d) Harm to persons, property, or financial interests caused by State omission	371
	III.	Conclusion	373
11.	Spheres of Public Law Administration		375
	I.	Introduction	375
	II.	Non-State holders of public powers	376
		A. Trusts with public objects	376
		B. Legal persons, that are independent of government, with public objects	378
	III.	The components of the State, and its emanations	381
		A. The executive and its delegates	381
		1. Members of the executive	382
		a) The use of powers for proper purposes	382
		b) Reasons	385
		c) Procedural fairness	387
		d) Conflicts and unauthorized profits	388
		e) Liability for loss caused	392
		2. Delegates from the executive	392
		3. Conclusion	393
		B. Emanations of the State	394
		1. Scope of the term	394
		a) Legal persons controlled by the State	394
		b) Administrative tribunals	395
		c) Commissions of inquiry	396
		d) Local political units	396
		2. Legal norms of sound administration	397
		a) The use of powers for proper purposes	397
		b) Reasons and procedural fairness	398
		c) Conflicts	399
		d) Unauthorized profits	400
		e) Liability for loss caused	401
		f) Conclusion	402
		C. Legislators	403
		D. Judges	407
		1. Introduction	407
		2. Use of powers for proper purposes, and conflicts	408
		3. Unauthorized profits	410
		4. Duties of care and skill, or of prudence and diligence	411
		5. Conclusion	411

IV.	The State itself as holder of public powers	412
	A. Is the State an administrator towards all persons in it?	412
	1. Undirected, not directed duties	412
	2. Who acts unlawfully?	413
	B. The State's obligations towards Aboriginal persons	415
V.	The widening reach of public administration: Professionals	418
	A. Introduction	418
	B. Professionals in a strict sense	419
	C. Professionals in a wider sense	423
	1. Teachers and professors	423
	2. Journalists	426
	3. Conclusion	427
VI.	Conclusion	428

PART IV: CONCLUSION

12. Conclusion	431

Bibliography	437
Index	455

Table of Cases

For the benefit of digital users, page references are to the entire paragraph in which the case is cited. For this reason, where a page reference spans two pages (e.g., 52–53), the referenced case may appear on only one of those pages.

CASES (COMMON LAW)

Aas v Benham [1891] 2 Ch 244 (CA) 221–22
Aberdeen Ry Co v Blaikie Brothers (1854) 1 Macq 461, 1 Paterson 394 (HL)..........121
ADGA Systems International Ltd v Valcom Ltd (1999) 43 OR (3d) 101 (CA) 95
Ahmed Anguillia bin Hadjee Mohamed Salleh Anguillia v Estate and
    Trust Agencies (1927) Ltd [1938] AC 624 (PC) 95, 160
Ainsworth v Criminal Justice Commission (1992) 175 CLR 564 ..... 123–24, 312–13, 387
Akita Holdings Ltd v Attorney General of the Turks & Caicos
    Islands [2017] UKPC 7, [2017] AC 590 ....184–85, 195–96, 349, 391–92
Alberta v Elder Advocates of Alberta Society 2011 SCC 24,
    [2011] 2 SCR 261 ....28, 249–50, 289–90, 304, 417
Alkallay v Bratt 2002 CanLII 18363, EYB 2002-38861 (Que CS) 73
Ancient Order of Foresters in Victoria Friendly Society Ltd v Lifeplan
    Australia Friendly Society Ltd [2018] HCA 43 214–15
Annetts v McCann (1990), 170 CLR 596 .... 123–24, 387
Armitage v Nurse [1998] Ch 241 (CA) 242–44
Arthur v Attorney General of the Turks & Caicos Islands [2012] UKPC 30..... 349, 391–92
Atlantic Lottery Corp v Babstock 2020 SCC 19 257
Attorney-General v Edmunds (1868) LR 6 Eq 381...................... 349, 392–93
Attorney-General v London County Council [1901] 1 Ch 781 (CA) 354–55, 396–97
Attorney-General v De Keyser's Royal Hotel Ltd [1920]
    AC 508 (HL) 310, 312–13, 361–62
Attorney-General v Guardian Newspapers Ltd (No 2) [1990] AC 10.................248
Attorney-General v Blake [2001] 1 AC 268 (HL).................. 214–15, 227–28, 257
Attorney-General for Hong Kong v Reid [1994] 1 AC 324 (PC) 42, 211, 349, 392–93
Bamford v Bamford [1970] Ch 212 (CA) 133, 251
Banca Nazionale del Lavoro SPA v Playboy Club London Ltd [2018]
    UKSC 43, [2018] 1 WLR 4041 369
Bank of Montreal v Kuet Leong Ng [1989] 2 SCR 429 .... 186–87, 251, 253–54, 420–21
Bank of Nova Scotia v Thibault 2004 SCC 29, [2004] 1 SCR 758 ....45, 93–94
Bank of Upper Canada v Bradshaw (1867) LR 1 PC 479..........................173
Barron, In re 302 AD2d 81, 751 NYS2d 563 (App Div, 2002) 408
Bartlett v Barclays Bank Trust Co (Nos 1 and 2) [1980] Ch 515....................285
Barton v Armstrong [1976] AC 104 (PC).............................. 120–21, 268
Bateman's Bay Local Aboriginal Land Council v Aboriginal Community
    Benefit Fund Pty Ltd (1998) 194CLR 247........... 54–55, 301–2, 345–46, 349–50,
                                              352–53, 354–55, 358–59, 383
BCE Inc v 1976 Debentureholders 2008 SCC 69, [2008] 3 SCR 560.... 98–99, 115–17, 322

TABLE OF CASES

Beach Petroleum NL v Kennedy [1999] NSWCA 408, 48 NSWLR 1 250
Beatty, Re [1990] 1 WLR 1503 (ChD)..................................113–14
Beatty v North-West Transportation Co (1884) 6 OR 300 (ChD) 165
Bell v Lever Bros Ltd [1932] AC 161 258
Bell v Molson 2015 QCCA 583 242–43
Beloved Wilkes's Charity, Re (1851) 3 Mac & G 440, 42 ER 330 (LC) 377–78
Berkeley Applegate (Investment Consultants) Ltd, Re [1989] Ch 32................219–20
Bhullar v Bhullar [2003] EWCA Civ 424, [2003] 2 BCLC 241.....................223
Binsaris v Northern Territory [2020] HCA 22 .... 362, 367–68
Bishopsgate Investment Management Ltd (In Liquidation) v Maxwell (No 2)
 [1994] 1 All ER 261 (CA)..106
Black v Hollinger International Inc. 844 A2d 1022 (Del Ch, 2004) 82
Blackmagic Design Pty Ltd v Overliese [2011] FCAFC 24 230
Blumenthal v Trump 949 F3d 14 (DCCA, 2020).................................359
Boardman v Phipps [1967] 2 AC 46 (HL)................172–73, 184–85, 191, 206, 214,
 219, 226, 273, 275–76, 291
Bonham v College of Physicians (1610) 8 Co Rep 107, 77 ER 638 (KB)...............399
Boston Deep Sea Fishing and Ice Co v Ansell (1888) 39 ChD 339 (CA)...............211
Bowes v Toronto (City) (1858) 11 Moo PC 463, 14 ER 770............ 351–52, 354, 401
Bradford Corp v Pickles [1895] AC 587 (HL).................................9–10
Braganza v BP Shipping Ltd [2015] UKSC 17, [2015] 1 WLR 1661 103–4
Brandeis Brokers Ltd v Black [2001] 2 All ER (Comm), 2 Lloyd's
 Rep 359 (QB (Comm)) 207
Bray v Ford [1896] AC 44 (HL)..380
Breakspear v Ackland [2008] EWHC 220, [2009] Ch 32 122
Breen v Williams (1995) 186 CLR 71 ....23–24, 79–80, 151, 263–66, 272
Bristol & West Building Society v Mothew [1998] Ch 1 (CA)......................79–80
British Columbia (Minister of Forests) v Okanagan Indian Band 2003
 SCC 71, [2003] 3 SCR 371 373
Burger Estate, Re [1949] 1 WWR 280 (Alta SC) 88
Burland v Earle [1902] AC 83 (PC).......................................165
Burmah Oil Co v Lord Advocate [1965] AC 75 (HL).................. 312–13, 361–62
Burnell v Trans-Tag Ltd [2021] EWHC 1457 (Ch) 204, 216–17
Butler, Re [1951] 4 DLR 281 (Ont SC) 123–24
Butler-Sloss v Charity Commission [2022] EWHC 974 (Ch) 36–37, 96–97
Cadbury Schweppes Inc v FBI Foods Ltd [1999] 1 SCR 142, 167 DLR (4th) 577 257
Campbell v Hogg [1930] 3 DLR 673 (PC)..................................214
Canada (Minister of Citizenship and Immigration) v Vavilov 2019
 SCC 65... 341–42, 385–86
Canadian Aero Services Ltd v O'Malley [1974] SCR 592 ....204, 216–17, 220–21,
 252–53, 255
Canadian National Railway Co v McKercher LLP [2013] 2 SCR 649,
 2013 SCC 39 .... 153–54, 173
Canson Enterprises Ltd v Boughton & Co [1991] 3 SCR 534 .... 233, 270–71
Carltona Ltd v Commissioners of Works [1943] 2 All ER 560 (CA)..............341, 392
Carnie v Esanda Finance Corp (1995) 182 CLR 398 288
Case of Proclamations (1611) 12 Co Rep 74, 77 ER 1352 .... 310, 341–42
Cavendish Bentinck v Fenn (1887) 12 App Cas 652 (HL).......................236–37
Centre de santé et de services sociaux de Laval v Tadros 2015
 QCCA 351... 253–54, 420–21
Chan v Zacharia (1984) 154 CLR 178......................................191

TABLE OF CASES xxvii

Charron v Montreal Trust Co [1958] OR 597, 15 DLR (2d) 240 (CA)..............272
Cheney v United States Dist Court for the District of Columbia 541
   US 913 (2004) 157, 410
Cheng Wai Tao v Poon Ka Man Jason [2016] HKCFA 23..........................223
Cie immobilière Viger v Lauréat Giguère Inc [1977] 2 SCR 67 251
Citibank NA v MBIA Assurance SA [2007] EWCA Civ 11 102
Citizens for Responsibility & Ethics in Washington v Trump 939 F3d
   131 (2d CCA, 2019) 359, 360
Clay v Clay (2001) 202 CLR 410 277
Clayton v Clayton [2016] NZSC 29...259
Cobbs v Grant 8 Cal3d 229, 502 P2d 1 (SC, 1972) 233
Communities Economic Development Fund v Candian Pickles Corp [1991]
   3 SCR 388 326–27
Compagnie de pulpe de Métabetchouan v Paquet (1906) 3 CS 211 186–87
Coote v Whittington (1873) LR 16 Eq 534 272
Coster v UIP Companies Inc 255 A3d 952 (Del, 2021) 82, 165
Council of Civil Service Unions v Minister for the Civil Service [1985]
   AC 374 (HL) 341–42
Cowan v Scargill [1985] Ch 270................................... 36–37, 96–99
Criterion Properties plc v Stratford UK Properties LLC [2004]
   1 WLR 1846 (HL)..131
CS, Re [2015] NIQB 36.. 54–55, 324–25, 380
D v A [2022] NZCA 430...276
Dale v IRC [1954] AC 11 (HL)...197–98
Daly v Sydney Stock Exchange Ltd (1986) 160 CLR 371 .... 233, 234, 265–66, 267–68
Davis v Kerr (1890) 17 SCR 235 .... 54–56, 132, 164
Dean v MacDowell (1878) 8 ChD 345 (CA)......................................221–22
Deloitte & Touche v Livent Inc (Receiver of) [2017] 2 SCR 855, 2017 SCC 63 369
Department of Commerce v New York 139 S Ct 2551, 204 L Ed 2d 978 (2019).........386
Desimone v Barrows 924 A2d 908 (Del Ch, 2007)....................................95
Diplock, Re [1948] Ch 465, [1948] 2 All ER 318 (CA) 292–93
District of Columbia v Trump 930 F3d 209 (4th CCA, 2019).........................359
Dobbie v Arctic Glacier Income Fund 2011 ONSC 25 .... 43–44, 116–17
Doe v Metropolitan Toronto (Municipality) Commissioners of Police (1998)
   39 OR (3d) 487 (Gen Div) 371
Douglas/Kwantlen Faculty Assn v Douglas College [1990] 3 SCR 570................379
Downsview Nominees Ltd v First City Corp [1993] AC 295 (PC) 103
Droit de la famille – 13681 2013 QCCA 501 173–74
Dubai Aluminium Co v Salaam [2002] UKHL 48, [2003] 2 AC 366.................273
Duffy v Senate of Canada 2020 ONCA 536 405
Earle v Burland (1900) 27 OAR 540 (CA) 165
Eclairs Group Ltd v JKX Oil & Gas plc [2015] UKSC 71 ......82, 89–90, 105, 113–14, 119,
                                                                                                                                                                     120–21, 126
Edmonton (City) v Hawrelak [1976] 1 SCR 387................................ 351–52, 401
Edwards v Lee's Administrator 96 SW2d 1028 (Ky CA, 1936) 227–28, 257
Enbridge Gas Distribution Inc v Marinaccio 2012 ONCA 650......................255
English v Dedham Vale Properties Ltd [1978] 1 WLR 93 273
Entick v Carrington (1765) 19 St Tr 1029, 2 Wils KB 275, 95 ER 807 (KB).........367–68
Estate of Rothko 372 NE2d 291 (NY, 1977) 166
Evans v Eckelman 265 Cal Rptr 605 (Cal App 1 Dist, 1990)...................232, 276

xxviii TABLE OF CASES

F & C Alternative Investments (Holdings) Ltd v Barthelemy (No 2) [2011]
    EWHC 1731 (Ch), [2012] Ch 613 89–90
Fales v Canada Permanent Trust Co [1977] 2 SCR 302......................241, 285
Federal Republic of Brazil v Durant International Corp [2015] UKPC 35,
    [2016] AC 297 349
FHR European Ventures LLP v Cedar Capital Partners LLC
    [2014] UKSC 45, [2015] AC 250.................................... 192–93, 211
Financière Transcapitale inc c Fiducie succession Jean-Marc Allaire 2012
    QCCS 5733 132
Fiona Trust & Holding Corp v Privalov [2010] EWHC 3199 (Comm)...........170–71
Foster Bryant Surveying Ltd v Bryant [2007] EWCA Civ 200 71–72
Fox v Fox Estate (1996) 28 OR (3d) 496 (CA) 117–18, 123–24, 126, 132, 135
Frame v Smith [1987] 2 SCR 99, 42 DLR (4th) 81 .... 23–24, 110, 249–50
Friedmann Equity Developments Inc v Final Note Ltd [2000] 1 SCR 842 47–48
Furs Ltd v Tomkies (1936) 54 CLR 583 184–85
Galambos v Perez 2009 SCC 48, [2009] 3 SCR 247 249–50
Garrett v Attorney-General [1997] 2 NZLR 332 (CA) 362
GasTOPS Ltd v Forsyth 2012 ONCA 134......................................255
Geffen v Goodman Estate [1991] 2 SCR 353, 81 DLR (4th) 211..................267–68
Gibson v Jeyes (1801) 6 Ves Jun 266, 31 ER 1044 (LC) 235–36
Gibson v Barton (1875) LR 10 QB 329 (DC) 273–74
Glenn v Watson [2018] EWHC 2016 (Ch)............................... 172–73, 217
Goldcorp Exchange Ltd, Re [1995] 1 AC 74 (PC)................................250
Goose v Wilson Sandford & Co [1998] EWCA Civ 245...........................411
Gouriet v Union of Post Office Workers [1978] AC 435 (HL) 342–44, 345–46, 355,
                                                                        374, 382–84
Grand View Private Trust Co v Wong [2022]
    UKPC 47 .... 79–80, 86, 89–90, 105, 113–14, 129, 137, 291–92
Gravino v Enerchem Transport Inc [2008] RJQ 2178,
    2008 QCCA 1820..27–28, 186, 216–17
Gray v Global Energy Horizons Corp [2020] EWCA
    Civ 1668... 184–85, 191, 195–96, 219
Gray v New Augarita Porcupine Mines Ltd [1952]
    3 DLR 1 (PC)............................72, 166, 171, 175, 178–79, 195–96, 201, 207
Gresham Life Assurance Society, Re (1872) LR 8 Ch App 446 (CA)...............88, 122
Grosse v Grosse 2015 SKCA 68..259
Guerin v R [1984] 2 SCR 335, 13 DLR (4th) 321 .... 28, 304–5, 415–16, 417
Guinness plc v Saunders [1990] 2 AC 663 (HL) 219
Hall v Libertarian Investments Ltd [2013] HKCFA 93, [2014] 1 HKC 368..........23–24
Hardoon v Belilios [1901] AC 118 (PC) 45
Harmer v Armstrong [1934] Ch 65 (CA) 45, 292–93
Harries v Church Commissioners for England [1992] 1 WLR 1241 .... 36–37, 96–97
Hartigan Nominees Pty Ltd v Rydge (1992) 29 NSWLR 405 (CA)..................122
Haslam v Haslam (1994) 114 DLR (4th) 562 (Ont Gen Div)........................124
Hayim v Citibank NA [1987] AC 730 (PC) 74–75, 102, 113–14, 292–93
Hay's Settlement Trusts, Re [1982] 1 WLR 202 (ChD) 103–4, 105, 113–14, 124
Hedley Byrne & Co Ltd v Heller & Partners Ltd [1964] AC 465 (HL) 369
Heims v Hanke 93 NW2d 455 (Wis, 1958)......................................50–51
Helmet Integrated Systems Ltd v Tunnard [2006] EWCA Civ 1735...............254–55
Henderson v Johnston [1957] OR 627, 11 DLR (2d) 19 (CA).....................420–21

TABLE OF CASES xxix

Hill v Hamilton-Wentworth Regional Police Services Board 2007 SCC 41,
  [2007] 3 SCR 129 368–69
Hilton v Barker Booth & Eastwood (a firm) [2005]
  1 WLR 567 (HL).................................162–63, 166–67, 233, 328–29
Hodges, Re (1878) 7 ChD 754 135–36
Hodgkinson v Simms [1994] 3 SCR 377 ....69, 233, 265–66, 267–68, 270–71
Hogg v Cramphorn Ltd [1967] Ch 254 ....82, 83
Home Office v Dorset Yacht Co [1970] AC 1004 (HL).....................367–68
Hospital Products Ltd v United States Surgical Corp (1984) 156 CLR 41........23–24, 250
Houle v National Bank of Canada [1990] 3 SCR 122 103
How Weng Fan v Sengkang Town Council [2022] SGCA 72......................401
Howard v Federal Commissioner of Taxation [2014] HCA 21, 253 CLR 83 .....79–80, 222
Howard Smith Ltd v Ampol Petroleum Ltd [1974] AC 821 (PC) 82, 83–84, 86–87, 105,
                                                               120–21, 126, 129, 133
Hurstanger Ltd v Wilson [2007] 1 WLR 2351 (CA)................. 195–96, 207, 220
ICBC v Dragon Driving School Canada Ltd 2005 BCSC 1093 400–1
Imageview Management Ltd v Jack [2009] EWCA Civ 63, [2009]
  2 All ER 666... 172–73, 197, 198, 219
Industrial Development Consultants Ltd v Cooley [1972]
  1 WLR 443..221, 222–23, 224–25, 226–27
Island Export Finance Ltd v Umunna [1986] BCLC 460 (ChD) 216–17
Item Software (UK) Ltd v Fassihi [2004] EWCA Civ 1244, [2005] 2 BCLC 91......231–32
J (LA) v J (H) (1993) 13 OR (3d) 306, 102 DLR (4th) 177 (Gen Div) 276
James, Ex parte (1803) 8 Ves Jun 337, 32 ER 385 (LC) 236
Jamison v McClendon 476 F Supp 3d 386 (SD Miss, 2020)................. 362, 365–66
John v Rees [1970] Ch 345 (ChD) 356–57, 387–88
JSC Mezhdunarodniy Promyshlenniy Bank v Pugachev [2017]
  EWHC 2426 (Ch)... 250, 259, 260
Juliana v United States 217 FSupp3d 1224 (D Or, 2016)................. 303–4, 358–59
Kaufman v American Express Travel Related Services Co 877 F3d 276
  (7th CCA, 2017) 289–90
Keech v Sandford (1726) Sel Cas t King 61, 25 ER 223, 2 Eq Cas
  Abr 741, 22 ER 629 (LC) 184–85, 194–95, 209
Kelly v Cooper [1993] AC 205 (PC)..173
Kenny v Lockwood [1932] OR 141, [1932] 1 DLR 507 (CA) 270–71
King v Whitmer 556 FSupp3d 680 (ED Mich, 2021).........................419–20
*Kingstreet Investments Ltd v New Brunswick (Department of
  Finance)* [2007] 1 SCR 3, 2007 SCC 1..............................13–14, 400
Klug v Klug [1918] 2 Ch 67 (ChD) 74, 113–14, 135–36
Kyprianou v Kyprianou [2004] RJQ 293 (CS) 275
LAC Minerals Ltd v International Corona Resources Ltd [1989] 2 SCR 574... 248, 249–50
Lacey, Ex parte (1802) 6 Ves Jun 625, 31 ER 1228 (LC) 236
Lakeside Colony of Hutterian Brethren v Hofer [1992] 3 SCR 165..................103
Lamb, Re [1894] 2 QB 805 (CA) 151–52, 155, 163–64, 180, 400
Lapierre v Attorney General (Quebec) [1985] 1 SCR 241 368
Laurent v Buanderie Villeray Ltée [2001] JQ no 5796, JE 2002-3,
  2001 CanLII 158 (CS) 54–55, 352–53
Lavigne v Ontario Public Service Employees Union [1991] 2 SCR 211 379
Lefebvre v Filion [2008] RJQ 145 (CS) 186–87, 198, 209
Lehtimäki v Cooper [2020] UKSC 33, [2022] AC 155... 23–24, 79–80, 88, 89–90, 378, 380
Letterstedt v Broers (1884) 9 App Cas 371 (PC)...........................54–55, 74

TABLE OF CASES

Levy-Russell Ltd v Tecmotiv Inc (1994) 54 CPR (3d) 161 (Ont Gen Div) 174–75, 178
Lewis v Tamplin [2018] EWHC 777 (Ch). 122
Lister v Stubbs (1890) 45 ChD 1 (CA)..211
Lloyd, Ex parte (1882) 47 LT 64 (CA)..88
Lloyds Bank Ltd v Bundy [1975] QB 326 (CA) 267–68
Locabail (UK) Ltd v Bayfield Properties Ltd [2000] QB 451 (CA)................409
Loewen Funeral Chapel Ltd v Yanz (1999) 136 Man R (2d) 318 (QB)................272
London Loan & Savings Co v Brickenden [1934] 3 DLR 465 (PC)........... 233, 236–37, 269, 270–71
Londonderry's Settlement, Re [1965] Ch 918 (CA) 122
Louie v Lastman (No 1) (2002) 61 OR (3d) 449, 217 DLR (4th) 257 (CA) 277–78
Lujan v Defenders of Wildlife 504 US 555 (1992)...............................360
M, Re [1994] 1 AC 377 (HL) 415
M (K) v M (H) [1992] 3 SCR 6, 96 DLR (4th) 289..........................70, 232, 276
Magical Waters Fountains Ltd v Sarnia (City) (1992) 8 OR (3d) 689 (DC) 326–27
Maguire v Makaronis (1997) 188 CLR 449..................... 230, 233, 236–37, 272
Mahesan s/o Thambiah v Malaysia Government Officers'
  Co-operative Housing Society Ltd [1979] AC 374 (PC) 201, 211
Manisty's Settlement, Re [1974] Ch 17 .... 134–35, 383–84
Manitoba Fisheries Ltd v The Queen [1979] 1 SCR 101................. 312–13, 361–62
Mayer v Rubin 2017 ONSC 3498..156
M'Caig v University of Glasgow 1907 SC 231 293–94
McClurg v Canada [1990] 3 SCR 1020..98–99, 115
McInerney v MacDonald [1992] 2 SCR 138, 93 DLR (4th) 415...................264–65
McKenzie v McDonald [1927] VLR 134.................................... 233–34, 272
McKinney v University of Guelph [1990] 3 SCR 483 379
McPhail v Doulton [1971] AC 424 (HL).............................. 113–14, 135–36
McWilliam v Norton Finance (UK) Ltd (t/a Norton Finance
  (In Liquidation)) [2015] EWCA Civ 186 ....207, 220
Meinhard v Salmon 249 NY 458, 164 NE 545 (CA, 1928) 249, 250
Merchant Navy Ratings Pension Fund Trustees Ltd v Stena Line Ltd
  [2015] EWHC 448 (Ch)..44, 97
Merrill Lynch, Pierce, Fenner & Smith, Inc v Cheng 901 F2d 1124
  (DC Cir, 1990) 106–7, 108, 232, 270–71
Mettoy Pension Trustees Ltd v Evans [1990] 1 WLR 1587 (ChD) 135–36
Miazga v Kvello Estate 2009 SCC 51, [2009] 3 SCR 339 363
Mills v Mills (1938) 60 CLR 150..119
Minister for Immigration and Citizenship v Li [2013] HCA 18, 249 CLR 332 385–86
Ministry of Health v Simpson [1951] AC 251................................292–93
Mongeau v Mongeau [1973] SCR 529..186–87
Montréal (Ville) v Octane Stratégie Inc 2019 SCC 57...........................130
Moody v Cox [1917] 2 Ch 71 (CA) 161–62
Moore v Regents of University of California 51 Cal3d 120,
  793 P2d 479 (SC, 1990) 233, 270–71
Morice v Bishop of Durham (1805) 10 Ves Jun 522, 32 ER 947 (LC)................29
Movitex Ltd v Bulfield [1988] BCLC 104 (ChD) 151–52, 172–73, 177, 234–35
Murad v Al-Saraj [2005] EWCA Civ 959.......................................195–96
N v Poole Borough Council [2019] UKSC 25 372
Neel v Magana, Olney, Levy, Cathcart & Gelfand 6 Cal3d 176,
  491 P2d 421 (SC, 1971) 232
Nelson v Larholt [1948] 1 KB 339 .... 134–35, 292

TABLE OF CASES xxxi

New Zealand Maori Council v Foulkes [2015] NZCA 552, [2016] 2 NZLR 337........124
New Zealand Netherlands Society "Oranje" Inc v Kuys [1973] 1 WLR 1126 (PC) 220
Nicholson v Haldimand-Norfolk Regional Police Commissioners [1979] 1 SCR 311 356
Nocton v Lord Ashburton [1914] AC 932 (HL) 233, 236–37, 270–71
Norberg v Wynrib [1992] 2 SCR 226...266
North-West Transportation Co v Beatty (1887) 12 App Cas 589 (PC)................165
Northern Territory v Mengel (1995) 185 CLR 307...............................362
Nova Chemicals Corp v Dow Chemical Co 2022 SCC 43 214–15
Novoship (UK) Ltd v Nikitin [2014] EWCA Civ 908........... 191, 192, 195–96, 214–15
NZ Council of Licenced Firearms Owners Inc v Minister of Police
    [2020] NZHC 1456...............................341–42, 361–62, 384, 385–86
O'Donnell v Shanahan [2009] EWCA Civ 751 .... 191, 221–22
O'Reilly (No 2), Re (1981) 28 OR (2d) 481, 111 DLR (3d) 238 (HC).............274–75
O'Sullivan v Management Agency and Music Ltd [1985] QB 428 (CA) 219
Odhavji Estate v Woodhouse 2003 SCC 69, [2003] 3 SCR 263............... 362, 365–66
Oei v Hui 2020 BCCA 214...363
Ohio Casualty Insurance Co v Mallison 223 Ore 406, 354 P2d 800 (1960)............276
Ontario College of Teachers v Lewis 2017 ONOCT 94 (Disc Ctee, Ontario
    College of Teachers)..425
Oshlack v Richmond River Council (1998) 193 CLR 72..........................373
Otkritie International Investment Management Ltd v Urumov [2014]
    EWHC 191 (Comm) 193–94
Otkritie International Investment Management Ltd v Urumov [2014]
    EWCA Civ 1315 410
Padfield v Minister of Agriculture, Fisheries and Foods [1968]
    AC 997 (CA, HL) 344, 383–84, 385–86
Paradis Honey Ltd v Canada 2015 FCA 89, [2016] 1 FCR 446 .... 370–71, 392
Paragon Finance plc v Nash [2001] EWCA Civ 1466, [2002] 1 WLR 685...........103–4
Paramasivam v Flynn [1998] FCA 1711, 90 FCR 489, 160 ALR 203 (FCFCA).........276
Parker v McKenna (1874) LR 10 Ch App 96 (DC) 155, 183, 184–85
Parker-Tweedale v Dunbar Bank plc (No 1) [1991] Ch 12 (CA)..................292–93
People's Holding Co v Attorney-General of Quebec [1931] SCR 452 324–25
Pierson v Post 3 Cai R 175, 2 Am Dec 264 (NYSCJ, 1805) 303–4
Pilmer v Duke Group Ltd (in liq) (2001) 207 CLR 165 .... 79–80, 250, 263–64
Pinochet, Ex parte (No 1) [1998] UKHL 41, [2000] 1 AC 61 409
Pinochet, Ex parte (No 2) [1999] UKHL 1, [2000] 1 AC 119 ..... 42, 312–13, 357–58, 409
Pinochet, Ex parte (No 3) [1999] UKHL 17, [2000] 1 AC 147 ....360, 409
Pitt v Holt [2013] UKSC 26, [2013] 2 AC 108 .... 53, 79–80, 103–4, 106, 126, 128–29
Porter v Magill [2002] 2 AC 357 (CA, HL).................................350, 401–2
Pramatha Nath Mullick v Pradyumna Kumar Mullock (1925)
    LR 52 Ind App 245 (PC)..98–99
Proprietors of Wakatū v Attorney-General [2017] NZSC 17, [2017] 1 NZLR 423 ...415–16
Provigo Distribution Inc v Supermarché ARG Inc [1998] RJQ 47 (CA)..........27–28, 30
Prudential-Bache Commodities Canada Ltd v Placements Armand
    Laflamme Inc [1998] RJQ 765 (CA).....................................265–66
R v Governor of Brockhill Prison, Ex p Evans (No 2) [2000] UKHL 48,
    [2001] 2 AC 19 367–68
R v Tener [1985] 1 SCR 533................................... 312–13, 361–62
R v Tower Hamlets London Borough Council, Ex p Chetnik
    Developments Ltd [1988] AC 858 (HL) 383
R v Sparrow [1990] 1 SCR 1075..417

xxxii TABLE OF CASES

R v Stubbs [2018] UKPC 30, [2018] 1 WLR 4887 410
R (Gujra) v Crown Prosecution Service [2012] UKSC 52, [2013] 1 AC 484 ... 343, 354–55
R (Miller) v Secretary of State for Exiting the European Union [2017]
    UKSC 5, [2018] AC 61 357
R (Miller) v Prime Minister [2019] UKSC 41, [2020] AC 373 .... 341, 343–45, 357, 374,
                                                                               382–84, 385–86
R (Palestine Solidarity Campaign Ltd) v Secretary of State for Housing,
    Communities and Local Government [2020] UKSC 16 .... 79–80, 96–97
Ranson v Customer Systems plc [2012] EWCA Civ 841 .... 252–53, 254–55, 256, 258
Reading v Attorney-General [1951] AC 507 (HL) 349, 392–93
Recovery Partners GP Ltd v Rukhadze [2023] EWCA Civ 305 .... 191, 195–96, 219
Reference re Supreme Court Act, ss 5 and 6 2014 SCC 21, [2014] 1 SCR 433 344–45
Regal (Hastings) Ltd v Gulliver (1942) [1967] 2 AC 134 (HL) ... 183–85, 186–87, 190–91,
                                                                               192, 205–6, 214, 220–21
Regentcrest plc (in liquidation) v Cohen [2001] 2 BCLC 80 (ChD) 189
Ridge v Baldwin [1964] AC 40 (HL) 123–24
Ringuet v Bergeron [1960] SCR 672 124
Roberts v Hopwood [1925] AC 578 (HL) 402
Roberts v Gill & Co [2010] UKSC 22, [2011] 1 AC 240 292–93
Rolled Steel Products (Holdings) Ltd v British Steel Corp [1986] Ch 246 (CA) 128–29
Roncarelli v Duplessis [1959] SCR 121 .... 8–9, 363–64, 382–83, 384, 385–86, 392
Ryder v Osler, Wills, Bickle Ltd (1985) 49 OR (2d) 609, 16 DLR (4th) 80 (CA) 23
Sandford v Porter (1889) 16 OAR 565 (Ont CA) 229–30
Saulnier v Royal Bank of Canada 2008 SCC 58, [2008] 3 SCR 166 321
Saunders v Vautier (1841) Cr & Ph 240, 41 ER 482 (LC) 73
Schmidt v Rosewood Trust Ltd [2003] 2 AC 709 (PC) 229
Schnell v Chris-Craft Industries Inc 285 A2d 437 (Del, 1971) 82
Secretariat Consulting PTE Ltd v A Company [2021] EWCA Civ 6 .... 154–55, 247
Secretary, Department of Health and Community Services v JWB
    (1992) 175 CLR 218 276
Serious Fraud Office v Litigation Capital Ltd [2021] EWHC 1272 (Comm) 219–20
Shank v Daniels (2002) 57 OR (3d) 559 (DC) 324–25, 380, 423–24
Sharbern Holding Inc v Vancouver Airport Centre Ltd 2011 SCC 23,
    [2011] 2 SCR 175 172–73
Sheikh Tahnoon Bin Saeed Bin Shakhboot Al Nehayan v Kent [2018]
    EWHC 333 (Comm) 103
Sidaway v Board of Governors of the Bethlem Royal Hospital [1985]
    AC 871 (HL) 264–65
Sim Poh Ping v Winsta Holding Pte Ltd [2020] SGCA 35 .... 236–37, 269
Skeats' Settlement, Re (1889) 42 ChD 522 (ChD) 259
Smile Inc Dental Surgeons Pte Ltd v Lui Andrew Stewart [2012] SGCA 39 .... 254–55, 256
Smith v Canada (Attorney General) 2020 FC 629 408
Smith and Fawcett Ltd, Re [1942] Ch 304 (CA) 88, 89–90
Soulos v Korkontzilas [1997] 2 SCR 217, 146 DLR (4th) 214 .... 198, 209–10, 211
Southcott Estates Inc v Toronto Catholic District School Board 2012
    SCC 51, [2012] 2 SCR 675 136–37
Southwind v Canada 2021 SCC 28 .... 236–37, 269
Space Investments Ltd v Canadian Imperial Bank of Commerce
    Trust Co (Bahamas) Ltd [1986] 1 WLR 1072 (PC) 173–74
Stanford International Bank Ltd v HSBC Bank plc [2022] UKSC 34 99
Stevens v Canada (Attorney General) 2004 FC 1746 396

TABLE OF CASES xxxiii

Stoffman v Vancouver General Hospital [1990] 3 SCR 483 379
Strother v 3464920 Canada Inc 2007 SCC 24, [2007]
    2 SCR 177 .... 226–27, 233, 250, 264–65
Sun Indalex Finance, LLC v United Steelworkers [2013]
    1 SCR 271, 2013 SCC 6 .... 174–75, 178, 235, 329
Swain v The Law Society [1983] 1 AC 598 (HL) 28, 304, 318
Swindle v Harrison [1997] 4 All ER 705 (CA) 233, 236–37, 270–71
Szarfer v Chodos (1986) 54 OR (2d) 663, 27 DLR (4th) 388 (HCJ) 218
T Choithram International SA v Lalibai Thakurdas Pagarani [2001]
    1 WLR 1, [2001] All ER 492 (PC) 67
Tan Yok Koon v Tan Choo Suan [2017] 1 SLR 654, [2017] SGCA 13 (Sing CA) 68
Tasarruf Mevduati Sigorta Fonu v Merrill Lynch Bank and Trust
    Company (Cayman) Ltd [2011] UKPC 17, [2012] 1 WLR 1721 259
Tate v Williamson (1866) 2 Ch App 55 (LC) 233–34, 265–66, 272
Teck Corp v Millar (1972) 22 DLR (3d) 288 (BCSC) 83–84, 97–98
Telstra Super Pty Ltd v Flegeltaub [2000] VSCA 180 123–24
Thomas v University of Bradford [1987] AC 795 (HL) 54–55, 324–25, 380
Thompson v Sénécal (1894) 3 BR 455 186–87
Three Rivers District Council v Bank of England (No 3) [2003] 2 AC 1 (HL) 362
Tito v Waddell (No 2) [1977] Ch 106 .... 136–37, 151, 154–55
Toronto Party v Toronto (City) 2013 ONCA 327, 115 OR (3d) 694 401
Transvaal Lands Co v New Belgium (Transvaal) Land and
    Development Co [1914] 2 Ch 488 (CA) 162, 172–73
Trident Holdings Ltd v Danand Investments Ltd (1988) 64 OR (2d) 65,
    49 DLR (4th) 1 (CA) 45, 93–94
Trump, In re 958 F3d 274 (4th CCA en banc, 2020) 359
Trump v Committee On Ways And Means, United States House Of
    Representatives 143 SCt 476 (2022) 405–6
Trump v Deutsche Bank AG 943 F3d 627 (2d CCA, 2019) 405–6
Trump v Mazars USA LLP 940 F3d 710 (DCCA, 2019), rehearing
    denied 941 F3d 1180 (DCCA, 2019) 405–6
Trump v Mazars USA, LLP 140 SCt 2019, 207 LEd 2d 951 (2020) 405–6
Trump v Mazars USA LLP 39 F4th 774 (DCCA, 2022) 405–6
Tsilhqot'in Nation v British Columbia 2014 SCC 44, [2014] 2 SCR 257 ....416, 417
Turner v Turner [1984] Ch 100 (ChD) 49–50, 53, 86–87, 113–14, 127–29,
                                                                132, 134–35, 137, 292
Ultraframe (UK) Ltd v Fielding [2005] EWHC 1638 (Ch) 273
United Pan-Europe Communications NV v Deutsche Bank AG [2000]
    2 BCLC 461 (CA) 195–96
University of Nottingham v Fishel [2000] EWHC 221 (QB) 227–28, 254–55, 423
UPM-Kymmene Corp v UPM-Kymmene Miramichi Inc (2002)
    214 DLR (4th) 496 (Ont SCJ) 72, 174–75, 178
Upton v Hutchison (1899) 2 Què Practice Rep 300 (QB App Side) 54–55, 352–53
Valard Construction Ltd v Bird Construction Co 2018 SCC 8,
    [2018] 1 SCR 224 .... 79–80, 213, 229, 236–37
Varcoe v Sterling (1992) 7 OR (3d) 204 (Gen Div) 267–68
Varity Corp v Howe 516 US 489 (1996) 23–24
Vatcher v Paull [1915] AC 372 (PC) 103–4
Wall v Shaw 2018 ONCA 929 214
Walling v Walling 2012 ONSC 6580 244
Walters v Walters 2022 ONCA 38 .... 128, 135–36

*Wastech Services Ltd v Greater Vancouver Sewerage and
   Drainage District* 2021 SCC 7 103–4
Wayling v Jones [1995] 2 FLR 1029 (CA) 120–21
Webb v Webb 2020 UKPC 22 (PC) 259
Wewaykum Indian Band v Canada 2002 SCC 79, [2002] 4 SCR 245 .... 415–16, 417
Whitehouse v Carlton Hotel Pty Ltd (1987) 162 CLR 285 .... 83–84, 86–87, 105, 119,
                                                                                126, 128–29
Wight v Olswang [2000] EWCA Civ 310 .... 163–64, 180
Willcock v Muckle [1951] 2 KB 844 (DC) 8–9, 397
Willers v Joyce [2016] UKSC 44 363
Wingecarribee Shire Council v Lehman Brothers Australia Ltd (in liq)
   [2012] FCA 1028 .... 265–66, 267–68
Wohlgemuth v Meyer 139 Cal App2d 326, 293 P2d 816 (1st Dist, 1956) 264–65
Wong v Burt [2004] NZCA 174, [2005] 1 NZLR 91 81–82
Wood v Commercial First Business Ltd [2021] EWCA Civ 471 49
Woolwich Equitable Building Society v Inland Revenue Commissioners
   [1993] AC 70 400
Yared v Karam 2019 SCC 62, [2019] 4 SCR 498 105
York Buildings Co v Mackenzie (1795) 8 Brown PC 42, 3 ER 432 (HL) 154–55, 166
Young v Murphy [1996] 1 VR 279 (CA) 292
*Yukon Francophone School Board, Education Area #23 v Yukon
   (Attorney General)* [2015] 2 SCR 282, 2015 SCC 25 172–73

CASES (FRENCH)

Conseil d'État, 19 mai 1858, *Vernhes*, Rec 399 8–9
Conseil d'État, 25 février 1864, *Lesbats*, Rec 210 8–9
Conseil d'État, 14 janvier 1938, *Société anonyme des produits laitiers
   'La Fleurette'*, 51.704 361–62
Conseil d'État, 28 mai 1954, *Barel*, Rec 308 344
Cour de cassation, 1re civ, 13 avril 1983, Bull civ I 119, No 81-16.728 270–71
Cour de cassation, 1re civ, 6 juillet 2005, Bull civ I 302, No 01-15.912 275

PART I
INTRODUCTION

1
Foundations

I. Scope

This study is concerned with the law's regulation of a certain kind of relationship or juridical situation: the situation in which a person has been authorized and empowered to carry out a mission, an assignment, a function, a task, a charge for or on behalf of someone else. The word 'empowered' indicates that in the creation of such a relationship, the person has been granted certain powers in order to achieve that other-regarding end. 'Someone else' has to be read broadly; in the case of a corporate director, the someone else might be a single person; in the case of a charitable trustee, the someone else might be the pursuit of the charity's objects; in the case of a police officer, it might be the protection of the general public. In such a situation, the powers that the person acquires don't really belong to them, the way that their own money sitting in their pocket belongs to them. You can do whatever you want with your own money. If it's not your money, that's different.

When someone is given powers in order to carry out a mission, an assignment, a function, a task, or a charge—and hereafter I will use 'mission' to cover this idea compendiously—there are two consequences that follow naturally. The first arises from the fact that the person has acquired powers *in order to* equip them to carry out their other-regarding mission. Having been empowered in order to act for others, she has not been empowered in order to act for herself. In such a situation, the powers have to be used properly. Powers that were granted to allow a person to accomplish some other-regarding purpose can only rightly be exercised in the pursuit of the reason for which they were granted or created, not for some alien pursuit. Using them to pursue one's own interests is a pursuit alien to the purpose for which the powers were granted. It is this concern that gives rise to our apprehension about conflicts of interest, an apprehension that only ever arises when someone is required to exercise judgment in an other-regarding way. A conflict of interest gives us a strong reason to be concerned that the person, consciously or not, is using the power in their own interests.

The second consequence is that this type of situation requires us to distinguish between the different roles that the person plays in going about their life and interacting with others. When the person is acting for themself, they may

The Law of Loyalty. Lionel Smith, Oxford University Press. © Lionel Smith 2023.
DOI: 10.1093/oso/9780197664582.003.0001

incur costs, acquire property or information, or find out about opportunities; and all of this will be for their own account. On the other hand, when they are acting in the role of fulfilling their mission, it is not obvious that they should bear the costs personally; conversely, if they acquire information or property, or find out about opportunities, they should not be able to extract any of this for personal gain. That would be a diversion to themself of something that they acquired when acting for others. Thus both the costs and the benefits of acting in an other-regarding role will be attributed to the one on whose behalf they are acting. This attribution arises directly from the other-regarding role; it does not have a necessary link to the misuse of powers granted to enable a person to fulfil such a role.[1]

These are claims that certain norms should or will apply to the situation under consideration. In some contexts, they are implemented as legal norms; in other contexts, they may be implemented as non-legal norms. If John is playing backgammon against Mary, and John has to leave the room for a while in the middle of a game, John might ask Bill to play John's side of the game. Bill has been given powers to carry out an assignment on John's behalf, and Bill would not use those powers properly if he did not do his best for John with the dice rolls that he made. If John returns and Bill has learned something relevant to John's decision-making process, Bill should share that with John. And if, before John's return, Bill happens to win the game and there was a $5 bet riding on it, the money belongs to John, not to Bill (although they may have made an agreement as to Bill's compensation). Conversely, if Bill loses the game, on the face of things it will be John, not Bill, who has to pay the $5 to Mary, because Bill was playing *for* John.

In this study, the main concern is with the legal understanding of these situations and the legal norms that may be imposed in them. The law very often imposes norms in line with the scenario described above, although there is a great deal of variation depending on the context. At the same time, this study will sometimes make reference to parallel non-legal norms, since they often shed light on the problems that are under consideration. Moreover, it is not uncommon for the law to begin to regulate a situation that was originally governed by non-legal norms, and this is a development that needs to be analysed and assessed.

---

[1] In section IV.B below, and in Chapter 3, section III.C, we will see that is possible to act for and on behalf of another even without having been granted any discretion in relation to the powers that one holds. In such a case, the rules about the proper exercise of discretionary powers (including the rules about conflicts) can have no application, but the rules about the attribution of costs and advantages, and of information, can and do apply.

II. Significance

A. A survey of the field

The situations in which a person holds powers in order to act for others are numerous and diverse. They arise in both private law and in public law, and the similar concerns that they raise are recognized in both the common law and the civil law traditions.

In this section, I aim briefly to illustrate the importance and the pervasiveness of the situation with which this study is concerned.

In private law, a core example of a person having powers to act on behalf of another exists where a person has legal authority to manage the property or affairs of another person. This typically involves making contracts for the other person. These contracts may involve buying and selling investments or other rights, and can potentially reach to almost any kind of contract (services, leasing, insurance, and so on). Crucially, the power-holder is generally not a party to these contracts; their power is to bind someone else. This covers such well-known private law relationships as business partners, agents and mandataries, and guardians of property for children or incapacitated adults.

Another example is the case of directors of business corporations and other legal persons. Although such persons are sometimes described as agents or mandataries, this is a mistake in both common law and civil law.[2] This is because agents and mandataries act *under the direction and control* of their principals and mandators. Directors of a legal person are, inversely, the ones who control it.[3] But directorship is a clear case of persons who hold powers in order to act on behalf of another. In law, the other person is the legal person of which they are the directors.[4]

---

[2] It is a mistake as a *general* understanding of the role of a director. It is true that a director may also be, at the same time, an agent or a mandatary (often as 'managing director' or 'officer'); but that is a separate role and does not arise in virtue of being a director. See Caroline Pratte, 'Essai sur le rapport entre la société par actions et ses dirigeants dans le cadre du Code Civil du Québec' (1994) 39 McGill LJ 1; Susan Watson, 'Conceptual Confusion: Organs, Agents and Identity in the English Courts' (2011) 23 Singapore Academy of LJ 762; American Law Institute, *Restatement of the Law Third: Agency*, 2 vols, vol 1 (ALI 2006) 29.

[3] In other words, the board of directors is one of the decision-making organs of the corporation; the shareholders are another such organ in other settings. One illustration that directors (or shareholders) when so acting are not acting as agents or mandataries of the corporation is that one of the things they can do is to cause the corporation to appoint an agent or mandatary who may interact with the world.

[4] Economists, who are only concerned with natural persons, may look at the matter differently from lawyers and may say that directors act on behalf of shareholders or other relevant constituents (some legal persons, like universities, do not have shareholders). The legal analysis differs from the economic one, just as it differs from the moral analysis (which would also only be concerned with natural persons), because a legal person acts in law: it holds rights, bears duties, and has legally cognizable interests.

Trustees are another clear example. Civil law trusts may be conceptually different from common law trusts, but we can say generally that trustees manage rights for the benefit of the beneficiaries. Speaking generally again, trustees do not have any power to bind their beneficiaries in contract. They are not, however, acting for themselves, because they are not the ones who derive benefit from the trust assets. Trustees are empowered to act in law for the benefit of the beneficiaries.

One step beyond these examples is the case of the advisor, who may be a lawyer, a doctor, a financial advisor, or anyone who stands in an equivalent relationship. This person typically does not make contracts or perform other legal acts on behalf of his advisee, but because of the factual power that the advisor holds, the relationship may be treated as analogous by the law.

A step in a different direction takes us to the case of the guardian for medical care: the person who is legally authorized to make medical decisions on behalf of another. Like the trustee, the director, or the business partner, this person holds legal and not factual powers; his authority, however, is not over property and contracts, but rather over another person's body and its integrity. Parents stand in a similar relationship to their minor children.

Private law also has examples of persons who are empowered to act, not directly for another person, but for the pursuit of a purpose. In modern trusts, trustees are usually given what are often called 'dispositive discretions': the authority to dispose of trust property as they see fit.[5] For example, a testatrix may by her will establish a trust in which the trustee is to invest the trust property and pay the income to the testatrix's surviving spouse during that person's lifetime; and on the death of the spouse, to divide the capital among the spouses' children. But a dispositive discretion is often added to allow for unforeseen difficulties: the trustee will be given a power to encroach on the capital in favour of the surviving spouse during the latter's life, in case the income is not enough for his needs. In deciding whether and how to exercise this power, the trustee cannot be required to act solely in the interests of the children; if he were, he would probably never be able to use the power. But nor can he be understood as acting solely in the interests of the spouse; if he were, he would probably be required to hand over all the capital to the spouse. The legal solution is to say that the trustee's role is to aim to fulfil the *purpose* for which the power was granted: that is, to allow flexibility to look after the spouse, should the income be insufficient.[6]

---

[5] Similar (but less general terms) include 'power of appointment', 'power of advancement', and *faculté d'élire* (roughly, 'power of choice').

[6] Lionel Smith, 'The Motive, Not the Deed' in Joshua Getzler (ed), *Rationalizing Property, Equity and Trusts: Essays in Honour of Edward Burn* (LexisNexis Butterworths 2003) 53, 69–70, with citations to case law.

In the case of this particular power, the decision-maker's mission is not to act for and on behalf of the children, nor is it to act for and on behalf of the spouse. But it is still the case that the trustee must pursue this mission unselfishly: he must try to achieve the purpose, and in this sense, he is acting for others.[7] He is certainly not entitled to use the power to advance his own interests. The same kind of situation is seen even more clearly in relation to 'purpose trusts', of which the best-known example in the common law is the charitable trust.[8] This is a trust that does not have any persons as beneficiaries; it exists only to pursue a purpose, such as the relief of poverty in a particular area.[9] Here, even more clearly, the trustees have powers to fulfil a mission which is not about acting for another person, but is rather about aiming to fulfil a purpose.[10] Again, however, the trustees can be said to act for others. The pursuit of charitable objects is definitionally something that benefits some segment of the public, and the trustees must use their powers unselfishly, for the promotion of those objects.[11]

Charitable trusts are sometimes called public trusts, and the requirements that they impose on their trustees can help us to understand the public law manifestations of the situation with which we are concerned. Those who hold

[7] For the sake of variation I sometimes say 'unselfish' when I mean 'other-regarding', a term used in some fiduciary scholarship (Robert Cooter and Bradley J Freedman, 'The Fiduciary Relationship: Its Economic Character and Legal Consequences' (1991) 66 NYU L Rev 1045, 1048, 1049, 1051; Evan Fox-Decent, 'The Fiduciary Nature of State Legal Authority' (2005) 31 Queen's LJ 259, 267, 268, 280, 301; Paul B Miller, 'Regularizing the Trust Protector' (2018) 103 Iowa L Rev 2097, 2114, 2115). The latter term is however more precise. The reason is that I do not mean to imply that a trustee must act generously; gratuitous trustees give their efforts for nothing, but professional trustees are in business, and their being paid is not inconsistent with the proper use of their powers.

[8] In the law of Quebec, it is arguable that all trusts, even those with beneficiaries, are purpose trusts. This follows from the definition of the institution (Civil Code of Québec, art 1260: a trust arises when the settlor 'appropriates [property] to a particular purpose') and from the fact that enforcement can be by 'the settlor, the beneficiary or any other interested person...' (art 1290). There can certainly be non-charitable purpose trusts without beneficiaries (arts 1268, 1270). See Alexandra Popovici, *Êtres et avoirs: Les droits sans sujet en droit privé actuel* (Éditions Yvon Blais 2019).

[9] In many civilian systems, similar functions may be performed by particular kinds of legal persons, such as foundations. Here the constraint as to purpose will exist in the constitution of the legal person. We will return to this kind of constraint in Chapter 3, section II.C.1.

[10] Paul B Miller and Andrew S Gold, 'Fiduciary Governance' (2015) 57 Wm & Mary L Rev 513 is a thorough discussion of situations in the common law (including but not limited to charitable trusts) in which powers are held for other-regarding purposes, and how this differs from the situation where powers are held for the advancement of the interests of persons. The authors draw out many consequences, including implications for enforcement and for the holding of powers for public purposes. These issues, and others, will be addressed in different Parts of the present study (Chapter 3, section III.A (powers held for purposes in private law); Chapter 8, section III.C.3 (enforcement in private law); Chapter 9, section II.B (powers held for purposes in public law); and Chapter 10 (enforcement in public law)).

[11] In the case of non-charitable purpose trusts, it may be less clear that the trustee's mission can be said to act for others, in the sense of other people. This, indeed, is a substantial objection against the possibility of creating such trusts: they effectively allow property to be affected to a purpose that may benefit no one. But even in legal systems where such trusts are allowed, while it might be difficult to say that the trustees must act 'for others', it remains clear that the trustees must act in an other-regarding way; they must use their powers to pursue the purposes of the trust, and cannot use them to pursue their own interests. See Chapter 8, section II.C.2.e.

public powers of the State are not usually trustees in the technical sense: they do not hold particular assets subject to an enforceable obligation relating to the benefit of those assets.[12] But they do not hold their public powers to benefit themselves; they are granted those powers in order to fulfil their role or function. And, not surprisingly, they are required to exercise them for the purposes for which they were granted. Take the case of a judge, who has the power to decide lawsuits and prosecutions, and to pronounce as to remedies and sentences. It goes without saying that a judge would not act rightly if she used these powers in her own interest, but it is just as true that she may not use them in what she perceives to be the particular interests of the particular litigants before her.[13] On the contrary, the judge is required to exercise her judicial powers in the public interest, in the interests of the administration of justice according to law.[14] A judge who acted in another way would be disloyal to her oath and her office.[15]

The same is true in relation to holders of public powers in other branches of government. They acquire powers in order to pursue a function or role, and those powers can only be properly used in the pursuit of that mission. As a legal norm, this principle has come into focus relatively recently. There is a much longer history of asking what is the *scope* of a power: Does an official have the authority to regulate the use of a public beach? Does a police officer have the power to demand an identification card from a citizen? Does a licensing agency have the power to cancel a restaurant's license to serve alcohol? It was an important development for courts to ask the subsequent question: *Even if* you had the power, did you use it for the right purposes? Did you use it properly, or did you misuse it? This began in French law during the nineteenth century, and in the common law, during the twentieth century.[16] In principle, the holders of public powers in all

---

[12] It is legally possible for the State or an emanation of it to be a trustee in the technical sense. This is mentioned in Chapter 9, section II.A, while the 'public trust doctrine' is discussed in Chapter 9, section I.C.

[13] There is an important qualification to this: sometimes a judge is empowered in a supervisory role in relation to the interests of a person (below, section V.B.3.d). Here, the judge will indeed exercise powers (such as the power to appoint a guardian or tutor or trustee, or to decide which parent shall have custody of a child) in the interests of one or more persons.

[14] It is not enough to say that the judge must be neutral as between the parties. If that was all that was required, we would be content for her to flip a coin to decide the case. She must be neutral *while applying the law*; that is her mission.

[15] The oath of office of a judge of the Supreme Court of Canada is typical; the judge swears '... that I will duly and faithfully, and to the best of my skill and knowledge, execute the powers and trusts reposed in me...': *Supreme Court Act*, RSC 1985, c S-26, s 10.

[16] The example of regulating the beach comes from the French case Conseil d'État, 19 mai 1858, *Vernhes*, Rec 399: the power to regulate use of the beach could not be used to require people who lived nearby to pay fees to rent changing cabins to the profit of the town (also considered foundational is Conseil d'État, 25 février 1864, *Lesbats*, Rec 210). The example of the identity card comes from *Willcock v Muckle* [1951] 2 KB 844 (DC): the power to demand identity for security purposes could not be used as a matter of routine procedure. The example of the liquor licence comes from *Roncarelli v Duplessis* [1959] SCR 121: the power to revoke a liquor licence could not be used to take revenge on a political enemy. The last case is discussed in Chapter 10, section II.I.1.

three branches of government—executive, judicial, and legislative—hold their public powers to enable them to fulfil an other-regarding mission; all of them are examples of the situation with which we are concerned. This extends to those who may hold public powers by delegation, such as government functionaries, police officers, and those who make decisions in administrative bodies and tribunals.

This survey shows that there is a huge range of situations in which a person is empowered in order to allow the fulfilment of a mission to act for others. It also allows us to see the relationship between some of these situations. In discussions of the private law manifestations, it is typical to focus on the situations where one person is required, in making decisions or exercising judgment, to do so in what he perceives to be the best interests of another person or persons. Such a requirement is often considered to be the core of fiduciary law or of a duty of loyalty. But this brief overview shows that it is really a special case of a more general situation: the situation where a person is required to act, or to exercise judgment or decision-making power, in an other-regarding way. That requirement may, on further examination, require attention to the best interests of a person; alternatively, it may instead require attention to a more abstract purpose or mission.[17]

To avoid circumlocution, I will usually refer to powers held for otherregarding purposes, as a way to cover all of the possibilities that have been discussed: whether public or private; whether on behalf of a single person or many; or for the benefit of the public interest; or for some other abstract, impersonal purpose such as the relief of poverty.

B. The invisibility of its unity

In seeing this wide range of relationships as governed by common legal principles that do not apply elsewhere, I am following in the footsteps of many other scholars. Later in this chapter, I will say more about the unity of the field covered by this study.[18] Here it is useful to reflect on why this way of seeing the law has not been widely recognized, and why it is still in the process of being acknowledged.

There are two distinct but related tendencies in legal thinking that have tended to make it invisible. The first is perhaps more important, because it is systemic and may be largely unconscious. This is a presupposition that we are always free in law to pursue our own interests, unless or until there is some legal rule to the contrary. In the civil law this idea is embodied in private law in thinking about

---

[17] Fox-Decent (n 7), 261, 268, 276, 280. Miller and Gold (n 10) apparently reject the view that loyalty to persons is a special case of loyalty to purposes; their text systematically treats them as opposed rather than nested, and they note (578 n 229) their disagreement on this point with Fox-Decent.
[18] Section V.A.

'subjective rights', a vision of legal rights that carries with it the conviction that the right-holder is sovereign in their exercise of their rights, limited only by the doctrine of abuse of rights.[19] The common law is equally familiar with this idea, albeit without the language of subjective rights, particularly since any notion of abuse of rights may be difficult to find.[20] This atomistic conception of the legal regulation of human interaction can be seen to pose a tremendous barrier to finding any commonality with public law, unless, of course, one goes further and applies the same atomistic philosophy to public law. The result of such an approach would be in one sense to reduce the disparity between private and public law; but conversely, it would be also to expand into public law the presumption that we are always at liberty to act in our own interests. A jurist who looks at the law with that presumption may find it difficult to see the unity of the field that is addressed in this study. This is because it is a field in which that presumption simply does not hold, as a matter of positive law.[21]

The other tendency is another kind of legal atomism, which operates more at the level of legal rules and prerogatives, but that may well be of the first kind. This is a reluctance to see that all of the principles that are discussed in this book are aspects of a single juridical situation: that of acting for others in law. This reluctance may lead one to seek particular explanations for particular legal principles through the use of familiar toolboxes. In private law, this especially includes the law of contract, which everyone knows can explain many rights, duties, and obligations. In public law, the will of the legislator is a familiar and reliable guide.

Let me give some examples that are visible in the scholarship. When we act for others, we are accountable to them, and this naturally gives rise to a rule against extracting unauthorized profits.[22] But this will not occur to a scholar who supposes that we always act for ourselves. Accountability, in law and in ordinary language, means having to give an account of oneself and of one's actions and inactions; we are not accountable to anyone when we act for ourselves.[23] In order to make sense of the rule against profits, such a scholar is likely to construct a theory that the rule involves wrongdoing, and has a deterrent function. Such an account is in fact unnecessary. Moreover, when we act for others, we acquire powers that are affected to an other-regarding purpose, with the result that we cannot properly use those powers for our own purposes but only in the

---

[19] Michele Graziadei, 'Diritto soggettivo, potere, interesse' in Rodolfo Sacco (ed), *Trattato di diritto civile* (Utet 2001) 1.

[20] A famous case is *Bradford Corp v Pickles* [1895] AC 587 (HL). The rising recognition in the common law of a requirement to act in good faith is discussed in Chapter 3, section III.B.2.

[21] Ernest Weinrib observed of the fiduciary relationship that 'its underlying premises are not those of individualistic private ordering': Ernest J Weinrib, 'The Fiduciary Obligation' (1975) 25 UTLJ 1, 3; see also Ernest Weinrib, 'The Juridical Classification of Obligations' in Peter Birks (ed), *The Classification of Obligations* (Clarendon Press 1997) 37, 44–46.

[22] Chapter 5, where some of the theories alluded to in this paragraph are discussed.

[23] There are other legal senses of accountability: Chapter 5, section V.B.

pursuit of the relevant purpose.[24] The law thus allows the exercise of such powers to be set aside when they have been used for an improper purpose. A scholar who supposes that we always act for ourselves may not realize, or not accept, that a power can be affected in this way. Such a person may try to explain the law on the review of powers for 'proper purposes' in terms of objective features of the fact situation, because outside of acting for others, the law usually reacts to objective features. But this turns out to be impossible in this context. The power has been entrusted to the power-holder, and the law does not dictate any objective outcome in relation to its exercise. It only requires that the power-holder's purposes are suitable; this is a subjective inquiry. To take another example, the rules about conflicts of interest also protect the proper exercise of other-regarding powers; they do not depend on profit-making.[25] But again, and even less plausibly, deterrent theories may be invoked to explain them. The result of such efforts is inevitably an absence of coherence. These approaches lead to accounts in which the review and control of other-regarding power—which is at the heart of the subject—is placed in a different conceptual category from the rules about profits and contracts. Such approaches also tend to have a poor fit with the actual law, because they have misunderstood what the law is doing and why.

In short, much scholarship reveals an effort to explain the law on how we act for others within a framework that supposes that we always act for ourselves. This leads to a makeshift and disjointed account. Focusing on some of the trees, it fails completely to see the forest. The law about acting for others is different from the law about acting for ourselves. It is a different way of acting in law. It rests on relationships that do not exist when we act for ourselves. Once this is seen, it becomes clear that rights, duties, and other legal requirements grow directly out of these relationships, to give them effect in law.

In most legal systems, when people get married or otherwise establish a lasting affective relationship, there are certain legal effects (some of which may be variable by agreement). These are likely to include, for example, rights of inheritance, and obligations of support and of property division if the relationship ends. No one, so far as I know, argues that these are created to deter people from getting married or from getting divorced, or that any of them arise because anyone has committed an unlawful act. They are the legal effects of the relationship.

That is what has been missed in many accounts of the field of this study. Acting for others is different, in law, from acting for oneself, and a different understanding is needed. The clearest proof of this has not been mentioned yet. In private law, we hold many powers for ourselves: for example, in most long-term contracts, one or both parties often have a power to end the contractual

---

[24] Chapter 3, where again some of the arguments mentioned in this paragraph are discussed.
[25] Chapter 4.

relationship. That power may be subject to some legal regulation, but it belongs to the holder, who can use it to pursue their own interests.[26] When you act for others in law, your powers do not belong to you. On the contrary, they equip you to fulfil your other-regarding mission. They can *always* be taken away.[27]

III. Ambitions of the argument

It is important to say what I am aiming to do in this study, and what I am not aiming to do.

A. Methodology and objectives

In this study I adopt what my colleague Stephen A Smith has called an 'interpretive' methodology. This methodology aims to examine a body of law and to provide the best account of it in the following sense: 'by explaining why certain features of the law are important or unimportant and by identifying intelligible connections between those features—in other words, by revealing an *intelligible order* in the law, so far as such an order exists.'[28] This methodology is reflexive: examining the law allows one to articulate an intelligible order; that order, once understood and articulated, can be turned back towards the law in order to assess it. In this way, some elements of the body of law—some cases, or legislative rules—can be criticized as failing to respect the law's intelligible order. Within this methodology, such an interpretive reflexive critique can extend to some parts of the relevant body of law, but not all of it.[29] One criterion of success for an interpretive theory is whether it fits the body of law with which it engages.[30] Theories calling for fundamental law reform may, of course, be able to stand on their merits, but they will not be interpretive theories.

An interpretive account must therefore in some sense start with the what the law is. Like all comparative lawyers, I am a legal positivist as legal positivists

---

[26] Further discussion of such powers is in Chapter 3, section III.B.2.
[27] This is addressed in Chapter 2, section III.B in relation to private law; Chapter 9, section III.B. in relation to public law.
[28] Stephen A Smith, *Contract Theory* (OUP 2004) 5.
[29] If one concluded that a whole field of law was unprincipled, there would be no point in seeking an intelligible order in it; or to put this differently, if one concluded that, then it does not seem possible that the principles that one was applying to reach that conclusion were principles that were identified within the field of law itself.
[30] SA Smith (28), 7; other criteria mentioned there (and expanded, in relation to contract theory, at 7–32) are coherence, morality, and transparency.

understand that term.[31] Unless one is a legal positivist, it is not easy to understand how, by crossing an invisible and notional line on the surface of Earth, a person can pass from one to another legal order, with different legal rules, different legal principles, different people qualified to practise law and decide disputes, and so on.[32] Thus the interpretive methodology that I use starts from the positive law. This is perfectly consistent with taking a critical and evaluative perspective towards the law.[33]

The body of law that I aim to examine is large: it embraces elements of the common law and the civil law, of public law and private law. But naturally it does not include all of these fields; it includes only situations where one person acts for and on behalf of another, which involve the grant (in one of several possible ways) of powers to the person who is so acting. I will argue that this body of law reveals an intelligible order inasmuch as there are justificatory principles which apply in all of these situations, and only in these situations. In this way, I aim to show that acting for others is categorically different, in law, from acting for oneself, and brings with it a suite of juridical consequences. This argument of course builds on the work of others, reaching back for centuries. Making the argument through the articulation of justificatory principles—an expression explained in the next subsection—is not however so well-explored. It is this part of the methodology that makes possible the wide scope of this study.

It is no part of the argument to minimize the differences between common law and civil law, still less, those between private law and public law. The latter distinction is the *summa divisio* of this study. It is part of the argument, however, that the principles that apply when one is acting for others are common to public law and private law. They are manifested differently, because of the fundamental differences between public law and private law, just as they are manifested differently in common law and civil law.

Although the distinction between public law and private law is a fundamental one, there are other fundamental distinctions that may cut across that divide. Take, for example, the forms of justice famously identified by Aristotle.[34]

---

[31] John Gardner, 'Legal Positivism: 5½ Myths' (2001) 46 Am J of Jurisprudence 199; François Chevrette and Hugo Cyr, 'De quel positivisme parlez-vous?' in Louise Rolland and Pierre Noreau (eds), *Mélanges Andrée Lajoie* (Éditions Thémis 2008) 33.

[32] I owe this point to the late John Gardner who made it during a presentation at McGill University in 2012; so far as I know there is no published version but a later iteration of the presentation, entitled "What Is Legal Pluralism?", given at Osgoode Hall Law School in 2013, can be found on youtube.com and a version of this point is made at 27:00 ff.

[33] Gardner (n 31), 209–10: 'Agreeing that a norm is legally valid is not incompatible with holding that it is entirely worthless and should be universally attacked, shunned, ignored, or derided.' See also 215–17, showing that judicial law-making through the use of legal resources is not legislative in nature and is consistent with legal positivism.

[34] Aristotle, *Nicomachean Ethics* (T Irwin tr, 2nd edn, Hackett Publishing Co 1999), Book V, chs 3–4.

Distributive justice is justice in the allocation of some good, according to some criterion or criteria. Corrective or rectificatory justice is the reparation of a past bilateral injustice.[35] One might think that public law is the realm of distributive justice and private law is the realm of corrective justice; and this is largely true. But if a citizen pays a tax to the State that was not legally due, the State must make restitution;[36] this is a perfect example of Aristotle's corrective justice, even though it is a claim against the State and concerns State revenue. Conversely, systems of distribution on bankruptcy, and general average in maritime law, are systems designed to distribute assets according to a criterion of justice when a group of persons, strangers to one another, are faced with a common disaster. This is distributive justice, as also are non-voluntary systems for the distribution of the assets of a deceased person, which may apply on intestacy or which may, in some jurisdictions, override testamentary freedom.

My argument is that the principles applicable to acting for others are found in both public law and private law, and that this is true in the common law and the civil law. I do not say that when we act for others in private law, we are acting in a public law way or for public purposes; conversely, I do not say that the legal regulation of public power can be understood using private law concepts. My claim is rather that in both legal traditions, the fundamental distinction between acting for ourselves and acting for others cuts across the divide between public law and private law. In short, I aim to offer a trans-systemic theory of acting for others in law.[37]

B. Justificatory principles

These common principles which I claim to identify can be called justificatory principles. A justificatory principle is a principle that is not, itself, a legal rule that operates directly on facts that have occurred, but is rather a higher-level idea that explains and justifies one or more legal rules.[38] An example is that 'no one should retain an unjust enrichment at the expense of another'. This principle is not directly pleadable in court as a rule that creates a legal right or a legal liability, but it justifies a range of rules that are and do. It stands in a justificatory relationship to

---

[35] This seems to be the plainest reading of Aristotle, but his idea of corrective justice can also be understood more widely and may be rendered as 'commutative justice' to signal this: see Allan Beever, *Forgotten Justice: Forms of Justice in the History of Legal and Political Theory* (OUP 2013) 74–81.

[36] *Kingstreet Investments Ltd v New Brunswick (Department of Finance)* [2007] 1 SCR 3, 2007 SCC 1.

[37] Mathieu Devinat and Édith Guilhermont, 'Enquete sur les théories juridiques en droit civil québécois' (2010) 44 RJT 7, 13–21.

[38] Benoît Moore, 'La théorie des sources des obligations : éclatement d'une classification' (2002) 36 Rev Juridique Thémis 689; Lionel Smith, 'Sources of Private Rights' in Simone Degeling, Michael Crawford, and Nicholas Tiverios (eds), *Justifying Private Rights* (Hart 2020) 129.

those legal rules. Legal rules, whether derived from statute or from case law, do not typically advertise the justificatory principle or principles that underlie those rules. Justificatory principles must often be worked out by inference, although some may be less controversially present than others.

One of the justificatory principles that I will describe is this: a person who is granted a power for the pursuit of an other-regarding mission can only rightly use the power for that purpose. That general principle justifies or stands behind different legal rules in different contexts. Where it is violated, it may allow the improper exercise of power to be impugned. It may however be that in some contexts, the principle does not generate any *legal* rule, but only non-legal consequences: for example, political consequences. Related to this is the principle that so long as the person *does* use the power for the correct purpose, its exercise cannot be challenged as improper. This is a jurisdictional principle: the person holding the power is the empowered decision-maker.

Another justificatory principle is that a person who exercises judgment on behalf of others should not do so when their own self-interest is in play. This principle does not require proof of misuse, of the kind discussed in the previous paragraph. It arises because there is a danger of misuse.[39] This principle is particularly important when a person acting for others holds *discretionary* legal powers that affect the legal position of others, because in such cases the law does not give any single objective answer as to how that power must or must not be exercised. This freedom of action may make it difficult to tell misuse of the power from its proper use. The principle about conflicts is manifest in legal (and sometimes non-legal) rules that may disqualify a person from acting in that situation, and that may also allow the exercise of judgment or power in a conflict situation to be impugned after the fact. When we think deeply about our concerns about conflicts of interest, in all the situations where those concerns arise, we find that the common thread is that they arise only where a person is authorized to exercise judgment in an other-regarding way.

A related principle generates similar outcomes in relation to the exercise of other-regarding powers in a situation where the power-holder has a conflicting loyalty towards someone else. This conflict of duty and duty vitiates the exercise of powers just as much as does a conflict of self-interest and duty.

Another justificatory principle is that a person who is acting for and on behalf of others should not profit personally from so acting without specific authority, and thus should render any benefits derived from so acting to those for whom they were acting. This principle extends to the divulgation of relevant information acquired from so acting. It also has a corollary: in the same way, and for the same reasons, the person so acting should not bear the costs of so acting, which

---

[39] This is discussed in Chapter 4.

rather should be borne by the persons for whom they were acting. These principles, properly understood, are not activated by conflicts of interest. They can be applicable to a person who is acting for others even if that person does not hold discretionary other-regarding legal powers.

A further principle is that a person who is acting for and on behalf of others should do so with care and skill, with prudence and diligence. To do nothing in such a role would be wrongful as a complete abdication of the mission which one has been empowered to fulfil. Acting carelessly in the performance of the mission would not be a complete abdication, but if it causes loss to those on whose behalf one is acting, it would be a shortcoming in the fulfilment of the mission. The less grave nature of this shortcoming is visible in the legal rules that implement this justificatory principle; in particular, that liability for breach of this duty may be subject to exclusion, while the requirement to use a power for the purpose for which it was granted is not.

Finally, at least for this overview: powers held for others do not *belong* to the power-holder in the same way that our assets generally belong to us. The power-holder is entrusted with them for the purposes of a mission. There is always a way in which the power-holder can be relieved of them.

One of the advantages of proceeding through the identification of justificatory principles is that such principles can be sought in relation to any rule, whether it arises from statute law or case law. This makes this approach eminently suitable for a study that includes both common law and civil law, and both public law and private law.[40]

C. The limits of this study

In this section I aim to clarify what I am *not* aiming to accomplish in this study. There has been something of an explosion of literature over the last twenty years that relates, in different ways, to this project. I do not, in what follows, aim to engage with all of that literature, and in this section I give some of the reasons why.

This is a study at a high level of generality. No one should expect to find herein the solution to a particular legal problem. Citations to cases are intended to be illustrative, not exhaustive. Even within the common law, there are many variations in the law between jurisdictions and between fields. For example, even apart from jurisdictional variations, some scholars insist on the differences

---

[40] Indeed the approach through justificatory principles rests on the scholarship of a civilian, Benoît Moore (n 38; his system is explained in English in Smith (n 38)). Moore identifies four different senses of the 'source' of an obligation. Whether it is derived from statute or from case law is a question as to its 'formal source', but this is quite separate from the question of justificatory principles.

between corporate fiduciary law, agency fiduciary law, and trustee fiduciary law.[41] Differences there surely are, and I am as interested in these differences as anyone. This study, however, is not a legal encyclopaedia. The goal is to show that there are common justifying principles in multiple spheres of law. These principles can be manifested in different ways, and I will discuss examples of these diverse legal rules. Although I will not aim to be comprehensive in relation to the details of the law, it is my goal that the reader will not only understand the logic of the different justificatory principles, but will recognize the situations in which they apply.

Nor is this a work of legal history. I firmly believe that the law always makes more sense when you understand its history; and I will call on history from time to time, particularly in this role of illuminating the present law. Although I would dearly like to one day write a history of this area of law, this is not that book.

Some scholars have aimed to use concepts of fiduciary law to provide a justification for the power of the State.[42] In the present study, I do not engage closely with this important work. This is not because I disagree with it, but only because my objectives, set out above, are quite different. Similarly, some theorists aim to relate fiduciary law, or other aspects of private law, to a particular moral framework, as have done in some of my earlier work in this field.[43] The present project does not take a position on this. This is not because of any particular change in my own views, but is rather, and again, a question of defining the ambitions of the current project, which is not a work of philosophy. I am also influenced by an argument of Stephen A Smith, who contends that judges and scholars who aim to articulate justifications for the law should do so on the basis of 'intermediate principles', rather than on the basis of any 'comprehensive moral view'.[44] The reason is that in order for a justification to be acceptable in a pluralistic society, it should be one that speaks to citizens no matter what may be their comprehensive moral theory, and even if they have none. What Smith describes as 'intermediate principles' are, I believe, exactly what I have described as 'justificatory principles'.

---

[41] See for example the chapter headings in Evan J Criddle, Paul B Miller, and Robert H Sitkoff (eds), *The Oxford Handbook of Fiduciary Law* (OUP 2019).

[42] Evan Fox-Decent, *Sovereignty's Promise: The State as Fiduciary* (OUP 2011); Evan J Criddle and Evan Fox-Decent, *Fiduciaries of Humanity* (OUP 2016).

[43] I referred to Kant's discussion of which duties could rightly be legal duties in Lionel Smith, 'Can We Be Obliged to Be Selfless?' in Andew S Gold and Paul B Miller (eds), *Philosophical Foundations of Fiduciary Law* (OUP 2014) 141.

[44] Stephen A Smith, 'Intermediate and Comprehensive Justifications' in Simone Degeling, Michael Crawford, and Nicholas Tiverios (eds), *Justifying Private Rights* (Hart 2020) 63.

IV. Concepts

In this section my goal is to define more precisely some of the ideas that were used above to set out the ambitions of this study. This section will also discuss other concepts, either because they will be invoked frequently as the argument develops, or conversely to explain why they will not figure prominently in the argument.

A. Power

1. Introduction

We are concerned with situations where someone holds legal powers in order to accomplish some mission on behalf of others. These can be the powers of directors to control a legal person; the powers of a trustee over the trust property; the powers of an agent or mandatary to bind his principal or mandator to contracts; the power of a judge to order a defendant to pay damages; and so on. These powers have a range of sources. In some cases they come from a statute; in other cases they may be associated with an office or role as a matter of common law or *droit commun*; in many cases, the powers are granted consensually, by a private legal act.

An early understanding of the centrality of other-regarding power can be found in the work of Jeremy Bentham. Remus Valsan has shown that Bentham was perhaps the first person to articulate a definition of 'fiduciary power' in the sense known in the common law today.[45] In *An Introduction to the Principles of Morals and Legislation*, addressing powers to enforce legal duties, first printed in 1780 and first published in 1789, he wrote:

> [W]herever any such power is conferred, the end or purpose for which it was conferred... must have been the producing of a benefit to somebody: in other words, it must have been conferred for the *sake* of somebody. The person then, for whose sake it is conferred... must be either the superior [the one holding the power] or the inferior [the one subject to it]. If the superior,... the power may be termed a *beneficial* one. If it be for the sake of the inferior that the power

---

[45] Remus Valsan, 'Understanding Fiduciary Duties: Conflict of Interest and Proper Exercise of Judgment in Private Law', Doctor of Civil Law, McGill University, 2012, online at https://escholarship.mcgill.ca/concern/theses/wd376141g, 13. The phrase 'fiduciary power' appears, with less attempt at definition, in John Locke, *Two Treatises of Government:* [...] (A Churchill 1690) 369 (legislative power is 'only a Fiduciary Power to act for certain ends'), 376 (the executive's power to dismiss the legislature is a 'Fiduciary Trust placed in him for the safety of the People').

is established... the power, being thereby coupled with a trust, may be termed a *fiduciary* one.[46]

More recent common law scholarship has increasingly placed other-regarding power at the heart of the fiduciary relationship.[47] The rules controlling fiduciary powers dominate Finn's renowned monograph;[48] and JC Shepherd put 'encumbered power' at the heart of his argument in 1981.[49] More recent scholarship takes other-regarding power to be the central feature of fiduciary relationships.[50]

Although perhaps not quite as old as Bentham's work, the centrality of other-regarding power has also a long history in the French legal tradition. The notion of *pouvoir* has been part of the regime of public administration and administrative law for many years.[51] More recently, it has been increasingly deployed also in private law.[52] In civil law, the contract of mandate, and the powers of the mandatary, have often served as a core case from which a more general theory can be developed.[53] The mandatary who has the power to bind their mandator is said to have a 'power of representation';[54] for many years, a French legal term

---

[46] Jeremy Bentham, 'An Introduction to the Principles of Morals and Legislation' in JH Burns and HLA Hart (eds), *The Collected Works of Jeremy Bentham* (OUP 1995) 238.

[47] Weinrib, 'Fiduciary Obligation' (n 21), positing discretionary legal power as underlying fiduciary relationships.

[48] Paul D Finn, *Fiduciary Obligations* (Law Book Co 1977); Paul Finn, *Fiduciary Obligations: 40th Anniversary Republication with Additional Essays* (Federation Press 2016).

[49] JC Shepherd, 'Toward A Unified Concept of Fiduciary Relationships' (1981) 97 LQR 51; JC Shepherd, *The Law of Fiduciaries* (Carswell 1981).

[50] See Fox-Decent (nn 7 and 42) and the extensive work of Paul Miller, notably Paul B Miller, 'A Theory of Fiduciary Liability' (2011) 56 McGill LJ 235 and Paul B Miller, 'The Fiduciary Relationship' in Andrew S Gold and Paul B Miller (eds), *Philosophical Foundations of Fiduciary Law* (OUP 2014) 63. I share this view: Smith (n 6); Lionel Smith, 'Fiduciary Relationships: Ensuring the Loyal Exercise of Judgement on Behalf of Another' (2014) 130 LQR 608.

[51] The theory of *détournement de pouvoir*, which allows the annulment of an administrative act that was implemented for an improper motive, was born in the 1860s, but was preceded by recourses for *excès de pouvoir* (going beyond one's powers). What are now considered the earliest cases on *détournement de pouvoir* were themselves reasoned as cases of *excès de pouvoir*, before the separateness of *détournement* as a ground of review was fully theorized: Roger Vidal, 'L'évolution du détournement de pouvoir dans la jurisprudence administrative' (1952) 68 RD public et de la science politique 275, 277–86.

[52] Jean Dabin, *Le droit subjectif* (Dalloz 2008 [1952]), 246–68, discussing the powers of parents and corporate directors as examples.

[53] Michele Graziadei, 'Virtue and Utility: Fiduciary Law in Civil Law and Common Law Jurisdictions' in Andrew S Gold and Paul B Miller (eds), *Philosophical Foundations of Fiduciary Law* (OUP 2014) 287, 288, notes that in its Roman origin, mandate was the 'ideal type' of a loyalty-based relationship, being gratuitous and involving accountability. Just as in the common law trusteeship is often said to be the paradigm of the fiduciary relationship, so one might say that in the civil law, mandate is the paradigm of relationships of the administration of the rights of others.

[54] Michel Storck, *Essai sur le mécanisme de la représentation dans les actes juridiques* (LGDJ 1982) has a substantial discussion of powers (123–89); Adrian Popovici, *La couleur du mandat* (Les Éditions Thémis 1995) 195–97 and *passim*.

for a commercial mandatary has been *fondé de pouvoir*, one who is vested with powers.[55] Others, like corporate directors and testamentary executors, have long been seen as holding powers whose use may be scrutinized by the courts.[56] The next step has been the development of more general theories of how the law regulates all the situations in which one person acts for and on behalf of another in private law.[57] The Civil Code of Québec, which came into force in 1994, frequently uses the language of powers, and it has a Title on the administration of the property of others, which been used as the foundation of a more general theory of other-regarding powers.[58]

2. Ambiguity of 'power'

The word 'power' can have different connotations in different discourses and in different legal traditions. A burglar who breaks into a house armed with a knife has a kind of power over the sleeping occupants. This is brute, physical power. This is not the kind of power with which any study of relationships of administration is concerned.

More narrowly, sometimes it means an ability to bring about changes in *legal* relationships.[59] Even in this narrower sense, it has multiple shades of meaning. One person, by deliberately punching another, can create a liability to pay compensation. This kind of factual ability to change legal relationships is not usually contemplated when people talk about legal powers; rather, this a situation where the legal relationships respond to facts, and people have the physical power to make facts occur. A more suitable understanding of powers confines them to those that are implemented, at least in part, by manifestations of volition or consent to change legal relations. This means that legal powers are prerogatives that are activated by what civilians call a 'juridical act' or *Rechtsgeschäft*.[60] This narrower legal power could be defined as an ability to change legal relationships

---

[55] S Corniot (ed), *Dictionnaire de droit*, 2 vols, vol 2 (2nd edn, Dalloz 1966), sv 'pouvoir', noting also the public law and private law senses. The expression *fondé de pouvoir* is found in the French text of the Civil Code of Québec (arts 2692, 2799, 2995, 2999.2) for what in English is called a hypothecary representative (representing multiple secured creditors).

[56] Dabin (n 52); Madeleine Cantin Cumyn and Michelle Cumyn, *L'administration du bien d'autrui* (2nd edn, Éditions Yvon Blais 2014) 75–76, with citations going back to 1950.

[57] Emmanuel Gaillard, *Le pouvoir en droit privé* (Economica 1985).

[58] Cantin Cumyn and Cumyn (n 56), who show (9–31) how the rules of mandate long served as the general law of private other-regarding powers in the civil law, while arguing (87ff) that under the Civil Code of Québec, the rules on administration of the property of others now fulfil this role.

[59] Wesley N Hohfeld, *Fundamental Legal Conceptions as Applied in Judicial Reasoning* (Yale UP 1964) 50–60.

[60] A juridical act has been defined as the '[m]anifestation of intention of one or more persons in a manner and form designed to produce effects in law': France Allard and others, *Private Law Dictionary and Bilingual Lexicons—Obligations* (Les Éditions Yvon Blais 2003), sv 'juridical act'. All of the bilingual civil law dictionaries of the Crépeau Centre are available online at www.mcgill.ca/centre-crepeau/.

that has, as a necessary (but possibly not sufficient) element of its exercise, the manifestation of an intention to bring about the relevant change.

But even if we focus on legal powers that are activated by manifestations of volition, we can notice that everyone with full capacity has the legal power to make contractual offers, or to accept them. On one view, it is rather trivial to label these prerogatives as 'powers' because they are just part of the capacity of a legal subject.[61] A more focused sense of the word describes what might be called *particular* powers, that is, powers that not everyone holds.

A still further cut is needed. Many particular Hohfeldian powers can be used unlawfully. Take the case of a common law trustee who holds an interest in land in trust, and assume that the terms of the trust do not allow the alienation of that interest. The nature of the common law trust is to vest the trustee with management powers by ensuring that she *holds* the rights held in trust; this has always carried the risk of unlawful dealings with those rights. In Hohfeld's terms, the trustee has the power to alienate the interest in land, even though this act would be a breach of trust.[62] But when common lawyers ask what are the 'powers' of a trustee, they are not referring to all Hohfeldian powers; they are referring to Hohfeldian powers in relation to the trust property which the trustee is authorized to exercise.

Pouvoir or 'power' in civilian discourse is less ambiguous and less capacious than Hohfeld's notion. It does not include brute power, nor those powers that are inherent in legal capacity, nor powers unaccompanied by authority. Civilian scholars increasingly contrast 'power' with 'right' in a way that is quite different from Hohfeld. The distinction falls on the axis of whether the prerogative may be used selfishly, or must rather be used in an other-regarding way.[63] This usage arises from the long civilian tradition of the idea of a 'subjective right' as an aspect of a person's economic existence, as it is represented in the law. In this tradition, a subjective right is definitionally something that the holder can use as she wishes, controlled only by the doctrine of abuse of rights. On this approach, a power is defined in opposition to a right, a power being a legal prerogative that is definitionally *not* available for self-regarding applications.

---

[61] Frederick H Lawson, 'Rights and Other Relations In Rem' in Ernst von Caemmerer and others (eds), *Festschrift für Martin Wolff* (Mohr Siebeck 1952) 103.

[62] It may be possible to reverse this unlawful alienation, or not, depending on other facts; this is beside the current point.

[63] Gaillard (n 57); Madeleine Cantin Cumyn, 'Le pouvoir juridique' (2007) 52 McGill LJ 215; Madeleine Cantin Cumyn, 'The Legal Power' (2009) 17 European Rev of Private Law 345. Civil law in the French tradition also knows the *faculté d'élire* (see Civil Code of Québec, art 1282, rendered in English as 'power to appoint'); the relationship between this prerogative and the necessarily other-regarding *pouvoir* is currently the subject of doctoral research by Me Marie-Pier Baril. See John EC Brierley, 'Powers of Appointment in Quebec Civil Law' (1992–93) 95 Revue du Notariat 131 and 245.

The distinction between 'right' and 'power' is drawn differently in the common law world.[64] This is partly due to the influence of Hohfeld, although his scholarship largely aimed to develop and regularize usages that he found in existing sources. In Hohfeld's scheme, a right always corresponds to a duty owed by another, while a power does not. If you owe me $50, I have a right against you to be paid $50, because you owe me a duty to pay me $50. But I do not have a *right* to forgive the debt, because you owe me no duty in this respect; I have a power to forgive the debt.[65] A power *may* be held for other-regarding purposes, as in the power of a trustee to purchase investments. But it may also be held for oneself: I have a Hohfeldian power to give away my rights, and a power to bind myself to contracts. Similarly, in the common law, a right is not always held for oneself; indeed, it is quite common for a person to hold a right but not for his own benefit. This is the structure of the common law trust.

In this study we are mainly concerned with particular legal powers that are held for other-regarding purposes; since these powers are held for the accomplishment of a mission, they are necessarily accompanied by an authorization for their use (although this does not entail that every use of them is authorized). This subcategory of Hohfeldian powers corresponds to the civilian idea of *pouvoir*.

It is important to add, however, that we will sometimes be concerned with people who have only factual, and not legal, powers over others. The main case is that of the professional advisor. This is outside of both Hohfeld's idea of power, and the civilian idea of power. As we will see later on, in some situations the law—both the common law and the civil law—treats the holder of factual powers in a similar way to the holder of legal powers. This does not occur in cases of brute power, but some factual powers are assimilated by the law to legal powers of the kind described in the previous paragraph. Under the interpretive approach adopted here, the account I offer must incorporate this reality. The result is that while the holding of legal powers is *typical* or *characteristic* of the kinds of relationships with which this study is concerned, it is not *diagnostic* of them.[66] Specifically *legal* powers are not necessary features of these relationships. What

---

[64] Lionel Smith, 'Droit et pouvoir' in Anne-Sophie Hulin and Robert Leckey (eds), *L'abnégation en droit civil* (Éditions Yvon Blais 2017) 109. Here it is noted (128 n 55) that Jean Dabin (n 52) took a view more in line with the common law position described immediately below: that rights could be held in an other-regarding way.

[65] Conversely, according to the civilian distinction between rights and powers discussed in the previous paragraph, it would be said that I have a right to forgive the debt, exactly because I can do whatever I want with my rights in relation to the debt; what defines a right in this discourse is not whether there is a corresponding duty, but whether I can do exactly as I wish (subject only to the limit of abuse of right). In order to draw Hohfeld's distinction between rights and powers, a civilian may call the ability to forgive the debt a *droit potestatif* (Smith, ibid 127) which could be rendered as an 'enabling right'.

[66] I use the word in the sense familiar in biological taxonomy, of a feature that is distinctive of a species.

is diagnostic is that someone is in a role in which they hold a power—which may, in particular cases, be purely factual—in order to accomplish an other-regarding mission.[67]

B. Discretion

Like 'power', the word 'discretion' can be ambiguous. Etymologically it means 'judgment', and it is related in this sense to 'discreet' and even 'discrete', since the exercise of judgment involves drawing justifiable distinctions.

One sense of 'discretionary' is therefore 'involving the exercise of judgment'. In this sense, a discretionary power is one that can rightly be exercised in more than one way. Another sense focuses on the liberty that is connoted by 'discretionary', so that this second sense effectively means 'unconstrained'. There is still a third and technical sense that appears in relation to investment advisors, at least in the United States and Canada: to say that an advisor manages a 'discretionary' account means that the advisor not only gives advice but also has the legal power to buy and sell assets in the name of the client without specific authorization from the client.[68] Here it is the *account*, and not the power, that is characterized as discretionary or not.[69] In this book I adopt the first sense; to say that a power is discretionary is to say that it involves the exercise of judgment. The law does not direct any particular way in which the power is to be used. But this is *not* the second sense: a power may be discretionary and yet still be subject to legally enforceable constraints. Such constraints are a major focus of this book.

Much common law fiduciary discourse, in both scholarship and case law, asserts that discretion is a diagnostic and thus necessary feature of fiduciary relationships.[70] And yet, it is possible for a trustee or an agent to have no

---

[67] When we examine advisors in more detail in Chapter 7, section IV.A, we will examine whether 'acting for others' is an example of a cluster concept, meaning that it is not possible to provide a single definition that includes all instances.

[68] Arthur B Laby, 'Advisors as Fiduciaries' (2020) 72 Florida L Rev 953, 969–70, 989 n 250. For a Canadian example of this usage, see *Ryder v Osler, Wills, Bickle Ltd* (1985) 49 OR (2d) 609, 16 DLR (4th) 80 (CA).

[69] A discretionary account in this sense is necessarily accompanied by a legal power that is discretionary (probably in the first sense). But in the case of a non-discretionary account, the investment advisor must still use discretion (in the sense of judgment) in advising the client, and as Laby explains at length, may still be held to be a fiduciary in relation to the advice-giving role.

[70] See Weinrib 'Fiduciary Obligation' (n 21); Fox-Decent (n 7); Miller (n 50); James Penner, 'Distinguishing Fiduciary, Trust, and Accounting Relationships' (2014) 8 J of Equity 202, 219–23. I have also stated the position that discretion is essential (eg Smith (n 43)) and now retract it. For a review of literature on this point, see Laby (n 68) 980–6. Laby notes that Julian Velasco, Evan Criddle, and Robert Flannigan have denied or doubted that discretion is essential to fiduciary relationships; see also Deborah A DeMott, 'Fiduciary Principles in Agency Law' in Evan J Criddle, Paul B Miller, and Robert H Sitkoff (eds), *The Oxford Handbook of Fiduciary Law* (OUP 2019) 23, 31: fiduciary duties apply to an agent '. . . regardless of whether an agent has access to property of the principal and whether an agent's functions require the exercise of discretion'. Laby also denies it, but with some

discretion in their role, and rather to be confined to following the terms of the trust or the instructions of the principal. These persons are clearly in fiduciary relationships; trusteeship and agency are per se fiduciary relationships. When we turn to the civil law, we find that scholars are well aware that discretion may be held in relation to some, but not all, other-regarding powers.[71] The idea that discretion is essential may be related to the consideration that in the common law, difficult questions about *whether* someone is in a fiduciary relationship arise only in cases of alleged ad hoc fiduciary relationships. In dealing with those ad hoc situations, the courts have sometimes formulated tests expressed in language that includes some reference to discretion.[72]

Another explanation for the focus on discretion is that, as we will see in more detail in Chapter 4, the rules about conflicts of interest only apply to discretionary powers (including factual powers). Since the rules on conflicts are a characteristic feature of common law fiduciary relationships, it is natural to suppose that the discretionary powers to which those rules apply are an indispensable part of a fiduciary relationship. But, again, while the rules about conflicts are *characteristic* of fiduciary relationships, they are not *diagnostic* of them. There may be a relationship of administration in which those rules do not apply, even where there are discretionary powers. When a person is a trustee with dispositive discretions and is also, himself, one of the objects who may benefit from that discretion, the person is in a conflict of interest, but the creation of a trust of this kind is possible, and involves an implicit authorization of the conflict.[73] Although the rules

---

conflation of the question whether the advisor has legal powers and whether the advisor exercises discretion. In my view, the giving of advice (which is Laby's concern) always involves the exercise of discretion in the sense of judgment, even if there is no legal power involved.

[71] See Cantin Cumyn and Cumyn (n 56), 272–74, noting that a 'discretionary power' is still subject to juridical control (that is, rejecting the sense of 'discretion' that means 'unconstrained). They analogize private law constraints to those that operate in (public) administrative law, which (in France and Quebec) distinguishes discretionary powers from non-discretionary powers *(pouvoirs liés)*, both of which are subject to judicial review, on some grounds that are common to both and some *(détournement de pouvoir* or misuse of power) that are particular to discretionary powers.

[72] For example, the dissenting judgment of Wilson J in *Frame v Smith* [1987] 2 SCR 99, 42 DLR (4th) 81, 136 (SCR), which was very influential in Canadian law for many years (although she referred to 'discretion or power', implying that power without discretion is enough); *Varity Corp v Howe* 516 US 489 (1996), 504: '... the primary function of the fiduciary duty is to constrain the exercise of *discretionary* powers which are controlled by no other specific duty imposed by the trust instrument or the legal regime' (emphasis in original). This formulation leaves room, of course, for non-primary functions. Contrast *Breen v Williams* (1995) 186 CLR 71, 92–93, 113, 137; and *Lehtimäki v Cooper* [2020] UKSC 33, [2022] AC 155, [44]–[46] *per* Lady Arden, defining the fiduciary relationship in terms of one in which one person is obliged to act for the benefit of another, without reference to discretion. In *Hospital Products Ltd v United States Surgical Corp* (1984) 156 CLR 41, 96–97, Mason J defined it similarly and referred, like Wilson J, to power *or* discretion. See also *Hall v Libertarian Investments Ltd* [2013] HKCFA 93, [2014] 1 HKC 368, [110]: '... discretionary powers do not feature in many fiduciary relationships'.

[73] Common law: Lionel Smith, 'Parenthood Is a Fiduciary Relationship' (2020) 70 UTLJ 395, 446–51; civil law: Lionel Smith, 'A Tale of Two Patrimonies: Limits on the Flexibility of Trust Law' (2021)

on conflicts respond to one of the justificatory principles mentioned above,[74] a relationship of administration can be constituted in which that principle is not applicable either because it has been excluded or simply due to the absence of discretion; the other principles, and their legal implementations, will remain relevant.

Discretionary powers also make it much more challenging to know whether an administrator has complied with a different justifying principle: that powers granted for the pursuit of an other-regarding mission must be used for the right purposes. Where the power is non-discretionary, this question can be answered objectively, although it still must be answered; in other words, it is clear that non-discretionary powers can be misused. But where a power is discretionary, as we will see at length in Chapter 3, we must ask whether the power-holder acted in what *they thought* was the best pursuit of the mission. In relation to discretionary powers, the law does not command a particular course of action; the choice belongs to judgment of the power-holder. The proper exercise of powers of administration is a hugely important part of the subject, and that matter is far more complex where the power is discretionary than where it is not.

Discretionary powers run all through this book. Although discretion is not essential to the constitution of a relationship of administration, it is typical and characteristic of such a relationship, and generates many (but not all) of the unique features of this field of law.

C. Mission, assignment, function, task, charge

As we will see in more detail in Chapter 3, when we are seeking to identify whether a relationship is one of administration, the question is whether the power in question is held in order to allow the holder to fulfil a mission, an assignment, a function, a task, or a charge: in briefer form, a mission.

This question is answered by interpretation; in particular, by interpreting the grant of the power in issue. As has been mentioned, the power can have a range of possible sources: for example, a consensual grant in a private transaction, a statutory grant, or a grant arising by operation of law through the holding of a particular role (such as trustee or parent). If the proper interpretation of the grant of power is that it allows the recipient to use the power for their own benefit, then they can, and we would be outside of the scope of the present study. Conversely,

---

40 ETPJ 139, 148–50. The authorization of the conflict is not, of course, an authorization of misuse of the power.

[74] Section III.B.

the grant of the power, properly interpreted, may include a mission: a stipulation as to the reason for which the person was granted the power. When there is a mission that restricts the exercise of the power, this restriction is inherent in the grant of the power.[75] Typically, a person is not required to accept a power, or to accept a role that carries powers with it.[76] No one is compelled to be a director, a trustee, an agent or mandatary, a judge or an elected politician. At least in private law, there may be room for negotiation as the powers that one acquires. But if one accepts a power, one takes it as it comes, including the restrictions as to how it may be used.

The exercise of interpretation is often a simple one. It does not take much thinking to conclude that the powers of a judge, or of a member of the executive branch of the government, cannot properly be used selfishly and for private purposes. The same is true of the well-known roles in private law: director, trustee, agent or mandatary, and so on. It is simply obvious that in these roles, one acquires powers that are to be used for and on behalf of others.

More difficult cases are those outside the well-known roles. In the common law tradition, *any* relationship can potentially be classified as a fiduciary relationship. Courts and commentators have struggled to articulate exactly what is required for a relationship to be properly classified as fiduciary. In my view, the issue can be stated quite simply (although, as always, particular cases may be difficult to solve). The test is the one already described: Did the person acquire powers which, properly understood, were granted in order to allow that person to act on behalf of another (or, less likely in private law, for an impersonal other-regarding purpose)?

As we will see in more detail in Chapter 3, the relevant idea of acting on behalf of another does not mean, simply, acting for their benefit. A person who mows my lawn pursuant to our contract is acting, in a way, on my behalf, and in a way, is carrying out a mission; but although the person has been authorized to be on my land, they have not been granted any power to affect my legal position. This is not a relationship of administration. Conversely, acting on behalf of another does not occur in the case where someone *does* hold legal powers over another's interests, but does not hold them in order to accomplish a mission for that other person. Speaking generally, an employer can terminate an employment contract

---

[75] It would be possible, of course, to grant a person a wide power that they could use as they wished, and then later to reach an agreement with them that restricted what they could do with it. Naturally, this would require their consent to the later restriction. In this rather unlikely possibility, what is said in the text would be applicable to the later, restrictive agreement that replaces the earlier, wider grant and that now governs. A related example might be that a person is given $5,000 to do with as she chooses; later, she declares herself a trustee of this money for the benefit of a beneficiary. With the declaration of trust, she has voluntarily (though unilaterally, not by agreement) put herself in a position in which her powers over the money must be used unselfishly.

[76] 'Typically', because some relationships of administration are imposed by law: Chapter 2, section III.A.3.

without cause, so long as a period of notice is given. In general, that is a power that the employer can use in a selfish way.[77] The employer has a power *over* the employee, just as creditors may have powers over their debtors. This is not a relationship of administration as the power is not held *on behalf of* another nor, more generally, was it granted to allow the employer to fulfil some mission on behalf of others.

D. Fiduciary relationships and relationships of administration

The situations with which this study is concerned include what are known in the common law tradition as fiduciary relationships: trustee–beneficiary, lawyer–client, and so on. But it covers many other relationships and situations, including in civil law and in public law, on the view that the same justificatory principles are engaged (but this does not mean, and I do not argue, that all of the applicable legal principles will be the same). The word 'fiduciary' is contested in its scope, and has been for some time. Those who use the word in a wide sense might well say that my concern in this study is, very simply, with fiduciary law. This would be a view that effectively assigns to the label 'fiduciary law' the same content that I have staked out for the study: those situations in which a person acts for other-regarding purposes, usually via the grant of legal powers.

There are two distinct reasons why I do not use the concept of 'fiduciary law' to define the study. One is that the label 'fiduciary' does not resonate beyond the common law. There is some irony in this, because the root of the word is the Latin *fides* that also gives us such words as 'confidence' and 'fidelity', which have both legal and non-legal senses in multiple languages. Moreover, Roman law, which is the foundation of the modern civil law, knew (in different stages of its long life) the *fiducia*, the *fideicommissum*, fiduciary guardianship, fiduciary substitutions, and so on. And at least from the classical period (roughly the first two centuries CE), the Roman jurists were conscious of the issues surrounding duty-bound judgment, and the problems of conflicts of interest that can arise in this context. The civil law tradition has remained alive to these issues through the ages. And yet, in the modern world, it is a fact that the ideas of 'fiduciary obligations' and 'fiduciary relationships' are often seen as alien to the civilian tradition.[78] To

---

[77] The employer may be constrained by an obligation or a requirement of good faith, or other similar implied obligations. This does not, however, rise to the level of requiring that the employer cannot act selfishly, taking account of its own interests. This is a subject that will be discussed in more detail in Chapter 3, section III.B.2.

[78] For example, *Provigo Distribution Inc v Supermarché ARG Inc* [1998] RJQ 47 (CA), 58, stating that the concept of fiduciary relationship has no relevance Quebec civil law; see also *Gravino v Enerchem Transport Inc* [2008] RJQ 2178, 2008 QCCA 1820, [39], expressing doubt as to the appropriateness of the expression 'fiduciary duty' in Quebec law.

use such labels in a study that includes the civilian tradition would be a bit like writing a book about comparative property law which described both common law and civil law with the terminology of patrimonial and extrapatrimonial rights; or, a book about comparative contract law that discussed the civilian ideas of *cause* and *objet* as instantiations of the doctrine of consideration.

The other difficulty, already mentioned, is that the situations with which I am concerned go well beyond fiduciary relationships, as that expression has traditionally been understood even in the common law. Its traditional scope is limited to private law relationships; efforts to apply it to public law situations have a long pedigree but remain contested. Those who see the word as standing for a particular regime that is known to private law in the common law tradition would naturally say that discussions of fiduciary law or fiduciary principles in other contexts, including public law contexts, can only be analogical or metaphorical.[79] As we will see, some disagreements are substantive while others may be largely about what 'fiduciary' properly means.[80] It is very much the aim of this study to take a position on the substantive question; but it is not my aim to engage in a terminological debate, particularly if it conceals rather than clarifies the issues.

For these reasons I do not apply 'fiduciary law' to the whole scope of the present study, but only to private law relationships in the common law tradition. My goal is to show that a set of particular justificatory principles applies when people act for others, in all the contexts with which I am concerned, and to explore the extent to which these justificatory principles are manifested in legal rules. The generic term that I will use for all of these situations is 'relationships of administration'. The person holding other-regarding powers is called an 'administrator'.[81]

---

[79] See for example Len S Sealy, 'Fiduciary Obligations, Forty Years On' (1995) 1 J of Contract L 37, 35–37, doubting that a servant of the Crown (even a Director of Public Prosecutions) is properly called a fiduciary; Timothy Endicott, 'The Public Trust' in Evan J Criddle and others (eds), *Fiduciary Government* (CUP 2018) 306, arguing that fiduciary duties, properly understood, are necessarily in relation to a private interest; Samuel L Bray and Paul B Miller, 'Against Fiduciary Constitutionalism' (2020) 106 Virginia L Rev 1479, arguing that fiduciary concepts do not apply in the public sphere as a matter of law, but only as a matter of 'political morality'.

[80] In *Swain v The Law Society* [1983] 1 AC 598 (HL), Lord Brightman said (618): 'The duty imposed on the possessor of a statutory power for public purposes is not accurately described as fiduciary because there is no beneficiary in the equitable sense'. In *Guerin v R* [1984] 2 SCR 335, 13 DLR (4th) 321, the majority of the Supreme Court of Canada said (385 (SCR)): 'Public law duties, the performance of which requires the exercise of discretion, do not typically give rise to a fiduciary relationship ... the Crown is not normally viewed as a fiduciary in the exercise of its legislative or administrative function'. In *Alberta v Elder Advocates of Alberta Society* 2011 SCC 24, [2011] 2 SCR 261, the same Court unanimously confirmed this ([37]–[38]), and said ([49]–[50]): 'The government, as a general rule, must act in the interest of all citizens ... No fiduciary duty is owed to the public as a whole, and generally an individual determination is required to establish that the fiduciary duty is owed to a particular person or group'. The disagreement between these judicial approaches and a 'fiduciary government' approach may turn on the fact that any fiduciary duty to the public as a whole must be an undirected public duty (this idea is explained in Chapter 10, section I).

[81] In the common law tradition this word may also have a narrow and technical connotation, being (1) the person appointed by a court to administer the estate of a person who dies intestate or

The person for whom an administrator acts (if the administrator is not acting in pursuance of an abstract purpose) is called a 'beneficiary'.

One might object that this is no more neutral than 'fiduciary', since 'administration' is the term used in the law of France and Quebec. It is used in the public law context to refer to the powers of the State, but it has also been used for many years in private law to refer to those situations where one person is managing the property of another.[82] In the Civil Code of Québec, which came into force in 1994, this usage is evident in the Title on the administration of the property of others, which been used as the foundation of a more general theory that could extend, for example, to those authorized to make medical decisions for others.[83] Even so, in my view it covers exactly the needed ground. You do not 'administer' what belongs to you. Moreover, common law courts and scholars have often used the word in the sense in which I will use it.[84]

E. Relationships of administration and obligations of administration

An authoritative voice in recent common law scholarship is that of Paul Miller, in part because of his convincing arguments against the atomization of the juridical apprehension of acting for others which was mentioned earlier.[85] A current of common law scholarship in recent decades has insisted that fiduciary *relationships* are not the proper object of study, but that we should instead seek to justify individual fiduciary *duties*.[86] That was partly in reaction to the older usage that deployed 'fiduciary relationship' in a too-wide sense that included, for example, relationships involving protected confidential information and those

---

whose will does not name an executor; and (2) in some jurisdictions, an insolvency officer. As a result, my use of 'administrator' as a wide term encompassing all of the roles in which a person acts in an other-regarding role includes administrators in these narrow senses.

[82] Cantin Cumyn and Cumyn (n 56), 59–60. *Administrateur* is also often used for the director of a legal person, who is always an administrator in my broad sense.

[83] Madeleine Cantin Cumyn, 'De l'administration des biens à la protection de la personne d'autrui' in Barreau du Québec—Service de la Formation continue (ed), *Obligations et recours contre un curateur, tuteur ou mandataire défaillant 2008*, vol 283 (Yvon Blais 2008) 205.

[84] Fox-Decent (nn 7 and 42); see also Paul B Miller, 'Fiduciary Representation' in Evan J Criddle and others (eds), *Fiduciary Government* (CUP 2018) 21, referring frequently to 'private and public administration'. The language of 'administration' and 'mal-administration' was used by Lord Eldon in the foundational trust law case *Morice v Bishop of Durham* (1805) 10 Ves Jun 522, 32 ER 947 (LC), 539, 540, 542 (Ves Jun), 954, 955 (ER).

[85] Section II.B.

[86] Peter Birks, 'The Content of the Fiduciary Obligation' (2000) 34 Israel LR 3, 23–26; Matthew Conaglen, *Fiduciary Loyalty: Protecting the Due Performance of Non-Fiduciary Duties* (Hart 2010) 7–10.

involving presumptions of undue influence.[87] That too-wide usage made 'fiduciary relationship' an incoherent category, or at least one that could not be used in legal reasoning.[88] But abandoning the centrality of the relationship was an overreaction and a mistake, because the relevant duties and other legal incidents all grow out of and implement a particular kind of relationship.[89] In Quebec civil law, a similarly synthetic approach is taken by Madeleine Cantin Cumyn, who argues that the various consequences of acting for others in private law are all derived from the other-regarding role of the administrator.[90]

F. Loyalty

A great deal of judicial and academic writing on fiduciary law—whether in the private law setting or in public law contexts—treats loyalty as the central organizing concept, often in terms of a 'duty of loyalty'. Indeed, this is very often said to be the central feature of the common law's fiduciary relationship. Moreover, it is interesting to note that civilian jurists who reject the labels 'fiduciary relationship' or 'fiduciary obligation' may prefer to cast the relationships with which we are concerned in terms of a duty of loyalty.[91] This is not surprising, because loyalty is, at least in part, about acting in an other-regarding way; it is about being guided by the interests of others, and not by one's own interests.

Loyalty, however, is a concept with many shades of meaning, in ordinary language, in philosophy, and in law.[92] Indeed, it has so many meanings that some would suggest that it cannot usefully serve as an organizing concept in this field of law. A thief who is a stranger and who breaks into my house to steal something behaves wrongfully and unlawfully, but not disloyally. On the other hand, if my friend, who knows that I habitually leave a particular window unlocked, enters my house through that window and steals something, we might certainly say that

---

[87] Len S Sealy, 'Fiduciary Relationships' [1962] CLJ 69. It is thus not surprising that in his 1977 monograph (n 48), which covered all of these situations, Finn, like Sealy, deprecated reasoning in terms of fiduciary relationships (eg at 1: '. . . it is meaningless to talk of fiduciary relationships as such'). Finn's research that led to the monograph was written at Cambridge and he acknowledges Sealy in the Preface to the original edition. Much more recently, Finn concluded that he 'erred' in not seeking a unifying principle: Paul D Finn, 'Fiduciary Reflections' (2014) 88 ALJ 127, 131 (republished with the 2016 republication of the monograph (n 48), 362).
[88] William M Gummow, 'Review: *Fiduciary Obligations*' (1978) 2 UNSWLJ 408.
[89] This is a theme of Miller's work; among many examples, see the papers cited in n 50; see also Fox-Decent (nn 7 and 42).
[90] First in Madeleine Cantin Cumyn, *L'administration du bien d'autrui* (Éditions Yvon Blais 2000); see now Cantin Cumyn and Cumyn (n 56).
[91] ibid; *Provigo* (n 78).
[92] Andrew S Gold, 'The Loyalties of Fiduciary Law' in Andrew S Gold and Paul B Miller (eds), *Philosophical Foundations of Fiduciary Law* (OUP 2014) 176; Andrew S Gold, 'Purposive Loyalty' (2017) 74 Wash & Lee L Rev 881.

he has been disloyal. He has betrayed me. The possibility of betrayal presupposes a prior relationship that has created expectations; you can betray your friend, your spouse, or your country, but you cannot betray a stranger. And every betrayal is a kind of disloyalty.

Our concern is with those who hold powers that equip them to act for other-regarding purposes. When my friend breaks into my house, his disloyalty does not relate to the misuse of some authority; his conduct is clearly dishonest and unlawful, without any inquiry into how the friend made his decisions or used his authority (which, in any case, he did not have). This is the kind of example that leads some people to say that loyalty is too broad a concept to be useful in analysing the particular problem of the proper exercise of judgment and decision-making power that is held for other-regarding purposes.

Then again, it might be too narrow. Take the case of a professional trustee, who does her job properly and conscientiously. She fulfils all of her obligations, including her fiduciary obligations, but without feeling any personal concern for, or connection to, the many beneficiaries of the trusts she manages. Because of that lack of personal concern, some might say that she does not act in a way that is properly called 'loyal'. She merely does her job as a professional.[93]

But just as there is more than one kind of justice, we may ask whether there is more than one kind of loyalty. The observation that loyalty has many meanings can thus be turned around: if we are careful to clarify exactly what kind of loyalty we are concerned with, the concept, so circumscribed, may well be useful in our analysis, even though the word 'loyalty' can be used in other senses. An ordinary employee can be said to act disloyally, for example by facilitating a burglary; but an ordinary employee (I mean an employee who is not, for example, also an agent or mandatary) does not hold legal powers on behalf the employer. The employee acts under the instructions of the employer, but not for and on behalf of the employer, in the sense of making decisions that bind the employer in law. So we might say that the loyalty demanded of an employee, as such, is different from the loyalty demanded in relation to the exercise of powers held for others. Indeed, this is exactly what both the common law and the civil law do. They both make use the idea of a 'duty of loyalty' in relation to those who hold powers on behalf of others, but they also make use of a (different) duty of loyalty as owed by every employee. These are two distinct kinds of juridical loyalty.[94]

---

[93] Authors skeptical of the usefulness of loyalty in law include James Penner, 'Is Loyalty a Virtue, and Even If It Is, Does It Really Help Explain Fiduciary Liability?' in Andrew S Gold and Paul B Miller (eds), *Philosophical Foundations of Fiduciary Law* (OUP 2014) 159; Stephen A Smith, 'The Deed, Not the Motive: Fiduciary Law Without Loyalty' in Paul B Miller and Andrew S Gold (eds), *Contract, Status and Fiduciary Law* (OUP 2016) 213.

[94] This is discussed in detail in Chapter 7, section II B.

A central concern of this study is therefore with a particular kind of loyalty, namely loyalty in the exercise of judgment with respect to one's other-regarding powers. This is a way to describe the proper manner of exercising such judgment: according to the tenor of one's function or assignment.[95] And conversely, the particular failure that we are concerned with not just any betrayal, but the misuse of one's other-regarding powers, or the misuse of that other-regarding role. The friend who misuses his knowledge about my house betrays me, but does not commit a betrayal of *this* kind.

This is the idea of loyalty that I will use in this study.[96] I will aim to show that there are articulable legal rules governing the proper exercise of judgment in relation to powers held for others, and governing other aspects of the relationships in which such powers are held. I will argue that some, but not all, of these legal rules are properly called 'duties' in the strict sense of that word. In my view, it is perfectly defensible to use 'loyalty' as a word with a particular signification in law to refer to those rules. Indeed, since the judgments of courts in both common law and civil law use the 'duty of loyalty' as a central feature of this field of law, the interpretive methodology demands that we seek the internal logic of this juridical expression. This does not, in my view, imply any claim that one is talking about the same loyalty that applies, for example, between friends. The phrases 'duty of loyalty' or 'legal requirement of loyalty' are enough to avoid ambiguity.[97] This is a study of legal relationships of administration, and the loyalty with which I am concerned is the legal manifestation of loyalty in such relationships. It could be called loyalty in the exercise of authority.

G. Status

In the common law, those fiduciary relationships that are per se fiduciary—that is, automatically fiduciary—may be described as 'status-based'. Examples are trustee–beneficiary and agent–principal. These may be contrasted with the ad hoc fiduciary relationships that may be found in the absence of a relationship that has been previously classified as fiduciary. Like many of the words addressed in this section, 'status' is polysemous. In a wide sense, it may refer to a position or office that one holds, like being a trustee or being a director.[98] My usage of the

---

[95] Stephen Galoob and Ethan J Leib, 'Fiduciary Loyalty, Inside and Out' (2018) 92 S Cal L Rev 69, 91–117; Chapter 3, section II.B.
[96] It will be developed in Chapter 3.
[97] It has to be borne in mind, however, that even among those who do use the word 'loyalty', the meaning assigned to it may vary widely. See for example Conaglen (n 86), whose understanding of what fiduciary loyalty means is very different from mine, and from that of Galoob and Leib (n 95).
[98] James Edelman, 'The Role of Status in the Law of Obligations' in Andrew S Gold and Paul Miller (eds), *Philosophical Foundations of Fiduciary Law* (OUP 2014) 21; Paul B Miller, 'The Idea of Status in

word is much narrower than this. I take 'status' to refer to a feature of one's legal personality, that has some effects on one's legal capacities.[99] Examples of statuses in this sense are the states of being: a minor; a corporate entity; a citizen; a mentally incapacitated adult; an undischarged bankrupt.

On this usage, being in a relationship or being at one end of a relationship is not a legal status. Being an administrator or a fiduciary is not a legal status, any more than being party to a contract or being a debtor is a status. The idea of 'status' will not be much invoked in what follows.

V. Unity and diversity

A. Unity

Two themes in this study will be unity and diversity. The unity is what holds this study together. There is a conceptual unity in the juridical treatment of all of the situations in which a person is empowered to carry out a mission to act for other-regarding purposes. Across public law and private law, across common law and civil law, there are similar features, which make applicable the same justificatory principles. The diversity arises because the same justificatory principles may, for a range of reasons, give rise to different legal rules (or perhaps no legal rules at all) in different contexts.

Going into a little more detail on the unity, we can say again that such powers need to be exercised properly, and there need to be adequate responses if they are not. This will be explored in greater detail; here it is only necessary to say that the question whether the power has been exercised properly is answered by whether it has been exercised in the pursuit of the mission for whose achievement it was granted. When the power is discretionary, as it usually is, this requires an inquiry into whether the decision-maker acted for the right motives in exercising their judgment. This is not a wholly objective inquiry but is, at least in part, a subjective one. The reason is that the person holds the power, and also the authority, to make the relevant decision. This is another way of saying that there is no objective, juridical test as to what is the correct decision. The mission or task of such a person is inherently tied up with the exercise of judgment, discretion, and decision-making power. This means that, to do their job properly, they are required to exercise their judgment in a particular way, namely, with

Fiduciary Law' in Paul B Miller and Andrew S Gold (eds), *Contract, Status and Fiduciary Law* (OUP 2016) 25.

[99] Lionel Smith, 'Contract, Consent, and Fiduciary Relationships' in Paul B Miller and Andrew S Gold (eds), *Contract, Status and Fiduciary Law* (OUP 2016) 117, 120–23.

the goal of fulfilling the mission for which they were given their discretions and their powers. It follows that in deciding whether or not the person has done their job properly, we need to know not just what they did, but how they decided: did they exercise judgment in the pursuit of their assignment, or for some other (improper) reason? In making this subjective inquiry, we do not evaluate the decision as such, but the way that it was made. We ensure that the decision was made for the correct, unselfish, other-regarding reasons, which reflect a kind of loyalty: loyalty in the exercise of authority.

The subjective nature of the inquiry is subject, however, to a huge qualification. Those who are required to exercise judgment for other-regarding reasons are typically subject also to rules about conflicts of interest.[100] This is a large topic with many dimensions, but here it is worth mentioning that when the rules about conflicts apply, a decision is reviewable without inquiry into the subjective decision-making process. This is because in conflict situations it becomes impossible to be certain what were the operative reasons, even in relation to a decision-maker who is of perfect integrity. The reason is that the decision-maker herself may not be aware of them. Conflicts of interest create a universal danger when judgment must be exercised unselfishly, because power can be improperly used entirely unconsciously. Moreover, as we will see, there can be many other objective limitations with which a holder of other-regarding authority must comply.[101]

If there was a problem with the way the power was exercised—it was exercised for the wrong reasons, *or* it was exercised in a conflict situation, in which it may be impossible to know what were the operative reasons—then there are legal consequences: typically, the decision can be annulled or set aside. This may involve other consequences: if the decision involved, for example, the sale of property, then annulment may require the decision-maker to restore the property, or its value, if the purchaser cannot be made to restore it for one reason or another.

Decision-makers who hold powers for others may also, particularly in private law contexts, be subject to what is often called in the common law a duty of care and skill, and which in the civil law may be called a duty of prudence and diligence.[102] In this context, an objective standard is applied; this clearly differentiates this duty from the requirement to exercise powers for the right reasons. But in another way, this duty follows the same logic: it is about the decision-making *process*, not the decision itself. Differently from the ordinary law of extracontractual liability for carelessness or fault, in this context the

---

[100] Conflicts in the private law setting are addressed in Chapter 4; in public law, in various sections of Chapter 11 dealing with different public actors.

[101] Chapter 3, section II C.

[102] These duties in the private law setting are discussed in Chapter 6, section III; in public law, in Chapter 10, section II.I.2; and in various sections of Chapter 11 dealing with different public actors.

question is whether the decision-maker followed an objectively careful decision-making process.

As has been mentioned above, another important principle is that the person exercising powers for others is not acting in the way that people generally act in law. A legal actor can generally act for herself and as she chooses, in the pursuit of her own interests. The present study is concerned with situations where this is *not* case: the actor is acting for others, or for another, or on behalf of the public, or in the pursuit of some abstract purpose. One result of this acting for another is that the legal system will presumptively attribute the costs and benefits of so acting to the other.[103] When this principle operates, it brings about the result that the actor cannot extract personal gain from the role of acting for another; if they acquire rights from so acting, these rights should be made over to the other on whose behalf they were acting. Nor, however, should the actor suffer loss, if they have acted properly; if they incur expenses, they should be allowed to recover them. This attribution can also apply to valuable information: the person acting for another should no more be able to take the benefit of this, than to take the benefit of valuable rights. This result can be and is implemented by requiring that the information be disclosed. In other words, this principle involves the allocation of costs and benefits to the correct sphere. It is a direct consequence of the other-regarding nature of the relationship.

With variations according to context, the presence of these features is what unifies all of the situations discussed in this study. The most prominent division within the unity is probably that between private and public law, which will be addressed below. There is a long history in political theory of seeing public powers as held in trust, but this has often been understood as a kind of analogy or a claim about political theory, not as a claim about law.[104] One early exception is found in Jeremy Bentham's work. In a text published after his death, Bentham classified legal rights as either personal ('those which are exercised for the benefit of him who possesses them') or fiduciary ('those which are possessed to be exercised for the advantage of another only'); and, he noted, '[a]ll political power is fiduciary'.[105] The legal reality of the unity across public and private law is also seen in the 'public trust' doctrine of US law, which is very much a legal and not merely a political construct.[106] The concept of *pouvoir* (an other-regarding power) has been well-known in French administrative law since the nineteenth century; Jean Dabin may have been the first to argue that it also has a crucial role to play in private law, accompanied by a parallel legal recourse for misuse of

---

[103] This principle is discussed in Chapter 5.
[104] See Locke (n 45).
[105] 'A General View of a Complete Code of Laws' in Jeremy Bentham, *The Works of Jeremy Bentham*, John Bowring (ed), 11 vols, vol 3 (William Tait 1843) 155, 182; cited in Valsan (n 45), 13.
[106] This is discussed in Chapter 9, section I.C.

power.[107] Emmanuel Gaillard aimed to develop a general theory of legal powers in private law.[108] Paul Finn, going in the opposite direction, showed how aspects of private fiduciary law could be used to understand the law relating to public powers.[109] The latest developments have come from scholars including Evan Fox-Decent,[110] Evan Criddle,[111] and others.[112]

B. Diversity

1. Diversity of contexts

This study casts a wide net and covers a very wide range of situations. It is clear that the legal norms that apply are variable across contexts. It is not part of my argument that the law is the same in the common law and in the civil law, or that the same legal norms apply to judges as apply to trustees. The argument, rather, is that there are common justifying principles that explain and help us to understand why there are *so many* commonalities in the applicable legal norms. At the same time, the diversity of contexts draws our attention to the reasons for the differences that exist.

We can use the examples of the judge and the trustee to illustrate this. Take the case of a trustee who holds assets in trust for a single beneficiary. In exercising her administrative powers (such as the power to invest or the power to insure), the trustee must act in what she perceives to the best interests of her beneficiary. The judge, as we have seen, must use his powers in the pursuit of the administration of justice. Both are constrained to use their powers in the pursuit of their mission, but there are important differences in their mission, that lead to different articulations of the relevant norms. The contexts also mean that the question of who has standing to enforce the applicable legal norms may be answered quite differently in the two settings.[113]

Indeed, even within the relatively narrow setting of trustees' investment powers, there may be different ways to formulate the applicable norm: in a pension trust, an English court said that the trustees must act in what they perceive to be the best *financial* interests of the beneficiaries.[114] The pension trust was for

---

[107] Dabin (n 52), 248–54.
[108] Gaillard (n 57).
[109] Paul D Finn, 'The Forgotten "Trust": The People and the State' in Malcolm Cope (ed), *Equity: Issues and Trends* (Federation Press 1995) 131.
[110] Fox-Decent (n 42).
[111] Criddle and Fox-Decent (n 42).
[112] Evan J Criddle et al (eds), *Fiduciary Government* (CUP 2018); much other scholarship on aspects of 'fiduciary government' will be referred to in Part III of the present book.
[113] See Chapters 8 (private law) and 10 (public law).
[114] *Cowan v Scargill* [1985] ch 270.

coal miners; the trustees were not permitted to avoid investments in enterprises that were in competition with the coal industry. But the goal of maximizing financial return cannot be absolute: the trustees of a charitable trust cannot be expected to make investments, however profitable, that are inconsistent with the goals of the charity.[115]

Take another example: a person is often entrusted with making medical decisions on behalf of another person who is not capable of making them on her own. This is clearly a situation of holding powers to act for another, and very often the governing legislation makes it perfectly clear that the person holding the power must use it in what he perceives to be the best interests of the incapacitated person.[116] Now, as mentioned above, those who hold powers for others must generally avoid conflicts of interest, and are presumptively not able to exercise their powers when they are in such a conflict.[117] Very often the person holding the power to make medical decisions on behalf of an elderly person is their adult child, who frequently stands to inherit upon the death of the parent. Viewed from a financial perspective, a potential conflict of interest is inherent in the constitution of this relationship. It would become an actual conflict in the case of a decision about medical treatment that involved the possibility of the death of the parent. In this setting of personal care within a family, the conflicts rules that might be applicable in a context of purely financial management are not necessarily applicable.[118]

These small examples help to explain the structure of the book. The first context to be examined will be that of the private law relationships involving the management of property, or of patrimonial rights: mandataries and agents, trustees, guardians and curators, directors of legal persons, and so on. This is not because it is considered logically or historically prior to other contexts; it is only because private law contexts involving financial considerations have led to a detailed elaboration of the norms, rules, standards, and duties governing those who hold powers for others. Following that, other private law contexts will be examined, followed by the very wide range of situations in which public powers are held. The goal is to identify both the unities and the diversities that characterize the field of study.

---

[115] *Harries v Church Commissioners for England* [1992] 1 WLR 1241; *Butler-Sloss v Charity Commission* [2022] EWHC 974 (Ch). These cases, and some related developments in English law, are further discussed in Chapter 3, section II.C.2.

[116] Examples include the Civil Code of Québec, art 12; Ontario *Substitute Decisions Act, 1992*, SO 1992, c 30, s 66. In both cases, the decision-maker must take account of wishes expressed by the patient.

[117] A fuller definition and discussion of conflict of interest will be advanced in Chapter 3.

[118] It is suggested in Chapter 7, section III.B, that they may be implicitly excluded here.

2. Diversity of conceptualizations
a) Private law

The ambitions of this study cross a number of boundaries, as I aim to include both private law and public law, both common law and civil law. One challenge for such an enterprise is that across these different domains, not only may the legal norms differ (as discussed in the previous section), but the conceptual structures used to make sense of the legal norms may also differ.

We have already seen some examples of this, in the discussion of the meaning of 'power'. In the common law, to say someone has a power does not imply anything about whether they hold it for themselves, or for another. A settlor may have a power to revoke an inter vivos trust, recovering all the property for himself; a mortgagee may have a power of sale, which it can use on default by the mortgagor, in the mortgagee's own interest and for its own account (surrendering, of course, any surplus once the debt, interest, and costs of sale have been covered). Indeed, in this approach, anyone who holds property could be said to have a power to transfer it or encumber it, to whomever and on whatever terms he pleases.[119]

To identify a power held for others, the jurist of the common law is likely to say that he holds the power in a fiduciary capacity. The use of the concept of a 'capacity' that stands apart from the person's personal capacity is less precise than it might seem.[120] It may signal the presence of one or more of a range of juridical features. One of them, stressed in the common law by the adjective 'fiduciary', is that the person cannot use the power for his own ends. Another is that the power is tied to the fiduciary role: if the agency is ended or the director is removed from office or the trustee resigns, they no longer have these powers.[121] In some settings, but not all, acting in a capacity may imply that one acts in a representative capacity, and does not engage one's own responsibility but only that of the person represented.[122]

As we have already seen, in the civil law, to say someone has a 'power' may aim exactly to signal that they have a juridical prerogative that they do not hold for their own benefit. This usage derives from the idea that a 'right', particularly a 'subjective right', is, for many civilians, definitionally held for one's own benefit. As we have seen, this has the potential to create some terminological confusion when one is working in both traditions.[123] In French and Quebec civil law, when a person is exercising powers (necessarily for the benefit of others), we may again

---

[119] Hohfeld (n 59) 51–22.
[120] Some authors may use 'status' in a similar way but see above, section IV.G.
[121] Some but not all relationships of administration involve an office. This is discussed below, section V.B.3.d.
[122] Some but not all relationships of administration involve representation in this technical sense. This is discussed below, section V.B.3.b.
[123] Section IV.A.2.

refer to her as acting in the capacity or in the quality (in French, and sometimes in English, *ès qualités*) of mandatary, director, and so on.

In private law in the French tradition, some of the aspects of holding powers for others are conceptualized through the patrimony. Any thorough discussion of this important idea is beyond the scope of this study. Briefly, the patrimony is a legal concept that aims to account for individual economic freedom of action in a liberal economy, while also accounting for individual responsibility in a world in which execution on the body of a debtor is forbidden. The patrimony represents one's economic personality, as embodied in one's legal capacity: it is the fluctuating set, or 'universality of law', of all of a person's rights and obligations that are of economic value. The qualification 'that are of economic value' excludes, for example, a person's right to their reputation, or their right to vote. These are considered 'extrapatrimonial' rights.[124] Extrapatrimonial rights are part of what one *is*, not what one *has*. The patrimony may also be described as the container that holds patrimonial rights and obligations.[125] Everyone has a patrimony: this means in part that every person has the capacity to acquire rights and obligations. The assets in one's patrimony are available to answer to the obligations therein: this means that one is responsible as an economic actor via one's economic holdings.[126] And, in the classical theory, the patrimony is indivisible: this represents the idea that one cannot shield assets from creditors, or partition one's assets among one's creditors.[127]

In this way of looking at things, where a person holds powers on behalf of others, these powers cannot be seen as legal prerogatives in the patrimony of the one who holds them. They are not available to be freely used by that person, and they are not available to his creditors. At the same time, there is no tradition of describing them as 'extrapatrimonial', if only because that is a qualification that goes with 'rights', not with 'powers'. As we have seen, according to one civilian current of thought, rights cannot be held for others, while powers are always held

---

[124] These are called 'superstructural' rights in Peter Birks, 'Definition and Division: A Meditation on *Institutes* 313' in Peter Birks (ed), *The Classification of Obligations* (Clarendon Press 1997) 1, 11–12, 24–25.

[125] Legal writing frequently switches between the patrimony as a container and the patrimony as a universality; but it cannot be both container and contents. The two ideas anyway are conceptually different: a container can be empty, while a universality (like a flock of sheep or a library of books) ceases to exist when the last element is removed, if not before (can one sheep make a flock?). The universality of law can be seen however as a way of representing the continuity of a patrimony over time, despite its fluctuating *contents*; a theatre company retains its identity despite some comings and goings among the players. The patrimony as container, by contrast, represents the capacity to acquire, hold, and alienate legal prerogatives.

[126] This is captured by the concept of the assets of a debtor as the 'common pledge' of their creditors ('*gage commun des créanciers*'). It is not a pledge in the sense of the deposit of a thing as collateral, but in the sense that all the creditors have recourse to all of the assets.

[127] For some discussion of exceptions in modern French law, see Guillaume Wicker, *La notion du patrimoine* (Les Éditions Thémis 2015); in Sylvio Normand, 'Quebec Law' in *Introduction au droit des biens* (3rd edn, Wilson & Lafleur 2020) 28–34.

for others; on that view, powers cannot possibly be patrimonial. One might thus say that the dichotomy patrimonial/extrapatrimonial is one that is applicable to rights, not to powers.

Patrimonial concepts are often used in civilian systems to implement trust structures. A legal person has its own patrimony, but if the trust is to be implemented without legal personality, typically some modification of the classic theory of the patrimony is required. One approach is to modify the rule that each person can have only one patrimony. Where it is specifically authorized by statute, a person may have multiple patrimonies: for example, a 'business' patrimony and a 'personal' patrimony, as in the French *entreprise individuelle à responsabilité limitée* or EIRL. This allows limited liability without a legal person, because assets and liabilities are partitioned; business creditors can only execute against assets in the business patrimony, and vice versa. By the same logic, one can implement a trust by allowing a person (the trustee) to have a personal patrimony and a trust patrimony.[128] Personal creditors cannot touch the trust assets, while the beneficiaries are creditors of the trustee who can have access only to the assets in the trust patrimony. The difference from the EIRL is that in the trust, in relation to one of the patrimonies, the trustee is not free to use the assets as he wishes. But as with the common law trust, the trustee's powers are part and parcel of the trustee's holding of the rights that are the trust property. The trustee has full powers (in the Hohfeldian sense) to deal with those rights because the trustee *holds* those rights; but because he is a trustee, he is required to use them in accordance with the terms of the trust and for the benefit of the beneficiaries.

This structure has gained a great deal of popularity in civilian implementations of the trust.[129] For some, however, it is problematical because as we have seen, there is a school of thought that it is inherent in the concept of ownership, or of subjective rights more generally, that one is free to use one's subjective rights exactly as one wishes.[130] On this view, it may be thought to be impossible to say that the trustee holds *rights* as a trustee.[131] But nor can the beneficiaries be said to hold

---

[128] George Gretton, 'Trusts Without Equity' (2000) 49 ICLQ 599; Kenneth GC Reid, 'Patrimony Not Equity: the Trust in Scotland' (2000) 8 European Rev of Private Law 427. The Scots trust thus allows a patrimonial division without express statutory authority.

[129] Lusina Ho, 'Trust Laws in China' in Lionel Smith (ed), *Re-imagining the Trust: Trusts in Civil Law* (CUP 2012) 183, 212–14; François Barrière, 'The French *fiducie*, or the Chaotic Awakening of a Sleeping Beauty' in Lionel Smith (ed), *Re-imagining the Trust: Trusts in Civil Law* (CUP 2012) 222.

[130] Henri Motulsky, 'De l'impossibilité juridique de constituer un Trust anglo-saxon sous l'empire de la loi française' (1948) 37 Rev critique de droit international privé 451; Alexandra Popovici, 'La fiducie québécoise, re-belle infidèle' in Alexandra Popovici, Lionel Smith, and Régine Tremblay (eds), *Les intraduisibles en droit civil* (Thémis 2014) 129.

[131] The Scots law response (n 128) is to say that it is perfectly possible in civilian thinking to restrict one's liberty with respect to one's subjective rights (including the right of ownership) via the law of obligations. This is how the multiple-patrimony trust works, and also the common law trust, although the common law trust, not being a patrimony, has to find a way to say that the trustee's obligations may also bind creditors (Lionel Smith, 'Trust and Patrimony' (2009) 28 ETPJ 332).

those rights, or they would be entitled to demand their transfer from the trustee. This has led to an approach that implements the trust as a patrimony by appropriation: a free-standing patrimony, in the sense that the rights and obligations that are in it are not in any person's patrimony.[132] This has been adopted in the laws of Quebec and the Czech Republic. In this approach, the trustee is conceptualized as the administrator of another's property, empowered to manipulate the trust property rather like the guardian of an incompetent person. The consideration that the trust property is held by no legal person does, however, create difficult theoretical challenges.[133]

b) Public law

It goes without saying that the conceptualization of holding powers for others is typically understood differently in public law than in private law. Particularly in the common law, concepts like trust, agency, and fiduciary obligation may be invoked in public law settings; whether this invocation is juridical or a matter of political morality is a matter of debate, to which we will return in Part III.[134] The intellectual current may have travelled in the other direction in some civilian systems: the development in France and Quebec of the idea of 'power' as an other-regarding legal prerogative in private law was inspired by public law terminology.[135]

Many of the differences are obvious. In private law, the task of the power-holder is very often to attend to some interest, or the general interests, of another person or persons; this is why the norm for the exercise of powers is often expressed in terms of acting in what the power-holder perceives to be the best interests of another. Typically, this entails that the person to whom the duty is owed is also the one who can enforce it, or who can authorize exceptions to it (such as permitting a conflict of interest, or the extraction of a profit, that the law would otherwise forbid). That person may, in private law, also have the authority to issue instructions or to terminate the relationship, depending on the details of the situation.

In public law, the other-regarding mission is typically one that requires the power-holder to use the power in what she perceives to be the public interest or the public good, or some subsection of the public good (such as the administration of justice according to law in relation to the cases assigned to a judge). This does not engage the 'best interests' of any particularized person or persons. It

---

[132] Pierre Lepaulle, *Traité théorique et pratique des trusts en droit interne, en droit fiscale et en droit international* (Rousseau et Cie 1932); partial translation: Alexandra Popovici and Lionel Smith, 'Lepaulle Appropriated' in Remus Valsan (ed), *Trusts and Patrimonies* (Edinburgh University Press 2015) 13.
[133] Popovici (n 8).
[134] In particular, Chapter 9, section I.C.
[135] Gaillard (n 57), 97–99.

will be argued below, however, that this is not the definition of the boundary between private and public administration.[136] We have already seen that there can be administration for private purposes.[137] There can also be public administration that may require attention to the best interests of a person: for example, the administrators of a public university must use their powers in what they perceive to be the best interests of the university.

Public administration is distinguished because whether or not there is such a 'best interests' duty, there are (instead or in addition) *undirected* legal duties. Although these are legal duties, they do not correspond to a right held by another person; they are not duties *to* anyone in particular.[138] This makes no room for waiver, because only a right-holder can waive a right. Even though a public duty may not correspond to a right, this does not mean it cannot be enforced. In the case of undirected duties, however, because there is no right-holder, enforcement must operate differently. The Attorney General (or some other official) may be charged with enforcement, just as they may enforce directed duties owed to the State.[139] Members of the public, although they do not have a right in the sense known in private law, may nonetheless have standing to enforce undirected duties and in this way to protect the public interest in the performance of those duties. For example, a litigant in a lawsuit is not owed a duty directly by the judge, but the litigant naturally has standing to raise the question whether a judge is disqualified by a conflict of interest.[140]

Clearly, the framework and the context of public powers are different from those that obtain in private law. The important question for this study is whether there are shared normative foundations: whether there are similar features of the juridical situation that activate the same justificatory principles and thus lead to recognizably similar legal norms. To the extent that there are, we will find some unity among the diversity, and we will better understand both contexts.

3. Diversity of legal incidents

Relationships of administration are extremely variable. Above, I have tried to clarify what, on my account, is common to all of them: that a person holds powers in order to allow them to accomplish an other-regarding mission. These relationships may have other juridical features which, however, are not essential.

---

[136] The distinction between private and public administration is addressed in Chapter 9, Part II.
[137] Section II.A.
[138] An example is the duty not to commit crime. The idea of undirected duties is further explained in Chapter 10, section I.
[139] For example, in *Attorney-General for Hong Kong v Reid* [1994] 1 AC 324 (PC), the State was allowed to recover an unauthorized profit (a bribe) from its employee through the application of fiduciary principles.
[140] *Ex parte Pinochet (No 2)* [1999] UKHL 1, [2000] 1 AC 119. Enforcement of undirected duties by members of the public is discussed in Part III, particularly in Chapter 10, section II.H.

Since the book as a whole deals with such a wide range of situations, it is useful to set out some of the possibilities at the outset.

a) Acting for persons or for a purpose

As we have already seen, a person may hold powers to accomplish a mission for another person, or a set of persons. A trustee whose trust has three beneficiaries must generally be guided by what the trustee perceives to be their best interests. In other cases, an administrator's mission is the advancement of a purpose: this would be true of a trustee of a charitable trust which exists for the advancement of education. We have also seen above that it is possible to conceptualize acting for another person as simply a special case of acting for an other-regarding purpose.[141]

This relationship between the two possibilities is also emphasized when we note that the distinction is often blurred. One example we have seen is that of a private trustee who has a dispositive discretion. If the trustee who has three beneficiaries is also empowered, in her discretion, to allocate the trust property among them unequally as she sees fit, she must be guided in exercising that discretion by the purpose for which it was granted. Another example of this blurring can be seen in relation to administration that benefits a legal person, as opposed to a natural person. Whether it is a business corporation or a university, we may say that the powers of its directors or governors must be exercised in the best interests of the legal person; but in practical terms, this is not so different from saying that they must be exercised in the way that is thought best to advance the purposes of the legal person. A similar effect can be seen even in the case of a relationship of administration with natural persons, if there are a large number of them. A business enterprise might be conducted through a trust structure, so that the investors are trust beneficiaries and not shareholders. In principle, the trustees must act in what they perceive to be the best interests of those beneficiaries;[142] but this will be modulated through the purposes of the trust, as a vehicle for investors who seek to earn returns. In other words, the trustees will not need to know the individual circumstances of their beneficiaries before making decisions, as they might in a family trust. The beneficiaries of the business trust may be constantly changing, particularly if their interests are publicly traded. The 'best interests' calculation here will again amount to the trustees' assessment of the best way to advance the purposes of the trust, even though it is not a purpose trust as such.[143] A similar example mentioned above is that in

---

[141] Section II.A.

[142] *Dobbie v Arctic Glacier Income Fund* 2011 ONSC 25, [55].

[143] The only purpose trusts which the common law allows are charitable trusts; in non-charitable trusts, there must be persons (not purposes) who are beneficiaries, and this is often called the 'beneficiary principle'. Miller and Gold (n 10), although they are aware of the principle (522), claim that the common law is 'liberal' (525) in relation to the creation of what they call 'governance mandates',

a pension trust, the trustees may properly be guided by the goal of advancing the financial interests of the pension members.[144] In an English case concerning such a trust the judge held:

> It is necessary first to decide what is the purpose of the trust and what benefits were intended to be received by the beneficiaries before being in a position to decide whether a proposed course is for the benefit of the beneficiaries or in their best interests. As a result, I agree with [Lord Nicholls'] conclusion that '... to define the trustee's obligation in terms of acting in the best interests of the beneficiaries is to do nothing more than formulate in different words a trustee's obligation to promote the purpose for which the trust was created.[145]

That is how the interests of beneficiaries are assessed in this kind of trust, and it means that the trustees' mission is not that different from advancing a purpose.

There are, however, fundamental legal differences, and these are evident when it comes to enforcement and supervision of the relevant duties and powers.[146] Duties owed to persons—whether the many members of a pension trust, or a corporation that is a legal person—are enforceable by those persons. They may also be enforceable by the legal representatives of those persons, which in corporate law includes the possibility of representative (or derivative) actions. Duties that are genuinely in respect of a purpose, however, cannot be directed duties that are owed to any person.[147] They are usually public, but they may be private (where the law specifically authorizes it); either way, enforcement will not be by a right-holder, because none exists. It may be by an official of the State, in the case of public duties, and in either public or private law, it may also be by a member of the public, necessarily involving an inquiry into standing.

b) Representation

(1) Legal representation The legal sense of 'representation' is the legal power to bind another person in law, acquiring rights (personal or property rights)

---

meaning that powers are held for purposes and not for the benefit of persons. They give pensions and commercial trusts as examples, but in the common law these non-charitable trusts are always trusts for persons, even if there are purposes underlying them (as of course there are purposes behind all trusts: see James Penner, 'Purposes and Rights in the Common Law of Trusts' (2014) 48 RJT 579).

[144] See the text at n 114.
[145] *Merchant Navy Ratings Pension Fund Trustees Ltd v Stena Line Ltd* [2015] EWHC 448 (Ch), [228], citing Lord Nicholls, 'Trustees and Their Broader Community: Where Duty, Morality and Ethics Converge' (1995) 9 Trust Law International 71, 74.
[146] The matters outlined in this paragraph are discussed in more detail in Chapters 8 (private law) and 10 (public law).
[147] Miller and Gold (n 10).

on their behalf that are thereupon vested in them, or alienating their rights, or binding them to contractual obligations.[148] In civilian terminology, we may say that a person with the power of representation has powers that allow her to intervene in the patrimony of the other.

Some relationships of administration are also relationships of representation, but some are not. An agent–principal relationship generally includes representation, as does generally the relationship between mandatary and mandator in Quebec and France. But a common law trustee is not in this relationship with her beneficiaries, and nor is a trustee in Quebec law or in French law.[149] A trustee's actions may of course affect the wealth of the beneficiaries; successful investments will improve their position, while unsuccessful ones will worsen it. But this does not happen through a process in which the trustee transfers rights held by the beneficiaries, or causes them to acquire new rights; rather, the trustee modifies the rights held in trust, with a consequent impact on the (separate) rights of the beneficiaries. Nor does the trustee represent 'the trust', because in none of these systems is the trust a legal person.

It was mentioned above that the language of 'capacity' is ambiguous. In a Quebec trust, the trustee does not represent the trust because the trust is not a person; but a trustee who expressly acts in his capacity as a trustee will not bind himself. The binding effect is on the separate trust patrimony, which though not a person, contains rights and obligations. The case is different in the common law, where the trust is neither a person nor a patrimony.[150] In the common law, all the liabilities assumed by a trustee are personal liabilities, even when he is acting 'as trustee'. If a trustee signs a contract stating that he is acting 'in my capacity as trustee and not personally', this may have some effect as a contractual limitation on the rights of the other party, but it does not affect non-parties, such as the beneficiaries or the trustee's other creditors.[151]

---

[148] Storck (n 54); Wolfram Müller-Freienfels, 'Legal Relations in the Law of Agency: Power of Agency and Commercial Certainty' (1964) 13 Am J of Comp Law 193 and 341. The ability to make someone liable extracontractually is not understood to be a power of representation. The term 'representation' is sometimes, but not systematically, used in common law. See Rachel Leow, 'Understanding Agency: A Proxy Power Definition' (2019) 78 CLJ 99, referring to 'proxy powers'.

[149] Care must be taken here: a common law trustee *as such* is not a representative; but it is legally possible that a trustee is also the agent of the beneficiary: *Harmer v Armstrong* [1934] Ch 65 (CA); *Trident Holdings Ltd v Danand Investments Ltd* (1988) 64 OR (2d) 65, 49 DLR (4th) 1 (CA). This helps explain the feature of such cases, which is not present in other trusts, that the beneficiary is personally liable to indemnify the trustee for expenses properly incurred (*Hardoon v Belilios* [1901] AC 118 (PC)). Quebec civil law does not recognize trusts in which the trustee is under the control of the beneficiary: *Bank of Nova Scotia v Thibault* 2004 SCC 29, [2004] 1 SCR 758.

[150] Smith (n 131).

[151] An exception to this is posited by recent developments in US trust law, which (consciously or not) has adopted a civilian model for at least some trusts: Lionel Smith, 'Scottish Trusts in the Common Law' (2013) 17 Edinburgh L Rev 283.

The distinction between relationships with representation and those without has led some Quebec authors to propose a fundamental division in other-regarding private law powers: some are powers of representation, and some—those outside of legal representation—are autonomous powers.[152] For them, this division generally falls on exactly the same line as the one between acting for persons (in the case of representation) and acting for purposes (when the powers are autonomous). This does not transpose directly into common law, because a common law trustee or executor does not legally represent their beneficiaries, but they are bound to act in what they perceive to be their best interests, rather than in the pursuit of a purpose.[153] In both traditions, however, the distinction between powers of representation and autonomous powers falls along an important distinction relating to enforcement and supervision, because in the case of powers of representation the power-holder is subject to control and direction by the represented person, which is not the case in relation to autonomous powers.[154]

(2) Legal representation and mandate and agency The relationship between legal representation, on the one hand, and agency (in common law) or mandate (in civil law), on the other hand, is a complex one. In the common law, agency is often defined as a relationship involving legal representation.[155] The definition of mandate in Quebec law is similar; there can be no mandate without representation.[156]

In Roman law, there was the contract of mandate but no legal institution of representation for the making of contracts.[157] A mandatary acted for and on behalf of the mandator, but did not have the legal power to represent the mandator.

---

[152] Cantin Cumyn and Cumyn (n 56), 95–99. 'Autonomous powers' is Madeleine Cantin Cumyn's own translation of her expression *pouvoirs propres* (Cantin Cumyn, 'The Legal Power' (n 63), 356–57).

[153] In the law of Quebec, it is arguable that all trusts, even those with beneficiaries, are purpose trusts: see n 8. For French law, the matter is debatable (*Code civil*, art 2011).

[154] Alexandra Popovici, 'Droits de regard : la fiducie dans le *Code civil du Québec*' in Christine Morin and Brigitte Lefebvre (eds), *Mélanges en l'honneur du professeur Jacques Beaulne* (Wilson & Lafleur 2018) 225. Whether or not the administrator is subject to instructions is addressed below, section V.B.3.c. Mechanisms of enforcement in private law are addressed in Chapter 8; in public law, in Chapter 10.

[155] Peter Watts and Francis MB Reynolds, *Bowstead and Reynolds on Agency* (22nd edn, Sweet & Maxwell 2020), ¶ 1-001(1): 'Agency is the fiduciary relationship which exists between two persons, one of whom expressly or impliedly manifests assent that the other should act on his behalf so as to affect his legal relations with third parties, and the other of whom similarly manifests assent so to act or so acts pursuant to the manifestation.'

[156] Civil Code of Québec, art 2130: 'Mandate is a contract by which a person, the mandator, confers upon another person, the mandatary, the power to represent him in the performance of a juridical act with a third person, and the mandatary, by his acceptance, binds himself to exercise the power.' See Popovici (n 54), 17–19.

[157] It did develop representation in relation to litigation: William W Buckland, *A Text-Book of Roman Law* (3rd edn, CUP 1963) (revised by Peter Stein), 708–11.

Rather, the mandatary dealt with third parties in his own name—say, acquiring goods—and then a separate legal step was needed in order to transfer the rights to those goods to the mandator (and probably to be reimbursed for the price). All modern systems have an institution of representation, which is extremely useful in commerce and other contexts. German law, however, carefully maintains the distinction between mandate and representation.[158] Representation can be added to mandate, and to other analogous relationships (the latter point is especially important since in that system, as in Roman law, mandate is definitionally gratuitous).

But in German law there can clearly be mandate without representation, as was always the case in Roman law. What is interesting in this setting, in a comparative light, is that the relationship of mandate (and analogous non-gratuitous relationships) has many of the characteristics of a relationship of administration, even in the absence of representation.[159] This may seem puzzling, but a mandatary even without representation still has legal powers held for the accomplishment of an other-regarding mission. If (to repeat the earlier example) the mandatary goes out and purchases goods for the mandator, the goods (for the time being) belong to the mandatary. But assuming he has acted properly, the mandatary has created obligations binding the mandator: to reimburse the mandatary and to take ownership of the goods. And the mandatary has the power to create those obligations in order to accomplish their mission, for and on behalf of the mandator.

Some legal systems view mandate or agency as including cases in which the mission to be carried out is purely factual and not legal.[160] This obviously makes room for the relationship to exist without being accompanied by representation. There is a type of agency without representation known to English law, that may be called 'commission agency'.[161] Commentators may struggle with whether this is really agency, since often they have defined agency as including representation; they may call it 'incomplete agency'.[162] And yet, like mandate without representation in German law, it is a relationship of administration; it is a fiduciary

---

[158] Gerhard Dannemann and Reiner Schulze (eds), *German Civil Code: Bürgerliches Gesetzbuch (BGB)*, 2 vols, vol I (CH Beck 2020), §§ 164–81 (representation); §§ 662–75b (mandate and paid management of another's affairs).

[159] This includes duties to account and provide other information (§§ 666–68) and rights to recover expenses (§§ 669–70). The rule that power of representation cannot be used in a conflict situation, however, is part of the law on the power of representation (§ 181).

[160] This seems to include Swiss law (Franz Werro, *Le mandat et ses effets* (Éditions Universitaires Fribourg 1993), 14–28) and US law (American Law Institute, *Restatement of the Law Third: Agency*, 2 vols, vol 1 (ALI 2006), §1.01). As a result, in US law, all employees are considered agents (ibid comment c, 19: 'The elements of common-law agency are present in the relationships between employer and employee...'). This is not true in other common law jurisdictions (see Chapter 7, section II.B).

[161] *Bowstead and Reynolds* (n 155), ¶1-022.

[162] ibid.

relationship in common law.[163] Another type of agency without representation may exist in the case of the 'bare trust': a common law trust in which the trustee is bound to follow the instructions of the beneficiary. Courts may conclude that the trust relationship coexists with an agency relationship, since the trustee is under the control of the beneficiary.[164] And yet, it is possible to structure the relationship so that the trustee/agent does not hold the power of legal representation of the beneficiary/principal.[165]

The claim that it is mandate or agency, and not representation as such, that creates a relationship of administration can be made from the other side as well. In different ways, there can be representation in a relationship that is *not* a relationship of administration.[166] A secured creditor often has the legal power to sell the collateral, thus alienating the rights of the debtor; but the creditor does so in his own interest, and is not required to take account of the interests of the debtor in exercising this power.[167] Security arrangements sometimes take the form of mandate or agency, in which the 'agent' or 'mandatary'—the creditor—is empowered by the 'principal' or 'mandator'—the debtor—to deal in some way with the latter's rights in the event of default. An example would be an authority given to the creditor to transfer shares held by the debtor to the creditor, in the event of default by the debtor. Such arrangements lack the general feature of mandate or agency that the mandator or principal can usually terminate the arrangement at will.[168] This is because these security arrangements serve the interest, not of the nominal principal or mandator, but the nominal agent or mandatary. One could thus question whether they are properly called mandate or agency at all.[169] They are not relationships of administration; the creditor is not empowered to

---

[163] ibid and ¶ 1-001(4). Also described as incomplete agency (ibid ¶ 1-020) are 'introducing' agents like real estate agents. These persons, however, may have the power to make and receive legally effective communications, which can be seen as a kind of representation (Popovici (n 54), 217–21; Leow (n 148), 118). Note that these persons may also be advisors, which can give rise to a relationship of administration in the absence of legal powers (see Chapter 7, section IV.A).

[164] See n 149.

[165] *Friedmann Equity Developments Inc v Final Note Ltd* [2000] 1 SCR 842.

[166] An example from Roman law is the *procurator in rem suam*: roughly, the agent acting for himself. In the absence of a general law of assignment, the would-be assignor of a claim could bring about a similar result by making authorizing the 'assignee' to collect the debt, so that the latter could take proceedings in the name of the 'assignor', keeping the proceeds recovered: Buckand (n 157), 520–21.

[167] The creditor will be under a duty of care and a duty of good faith, but neither of these require that the sale be made in the best interests of the debtor. Other actions of a secured creditor may involve administration; for example, in the common law the creditor will be a trustee of any surplus remaining after it has paid itself out of the proceeds of sale. Cf Cantin Cumyn and Cumyn (n 56), 114–18.

[168] For a comparative study of European systems on this point, see Michele Graziadei, Ugo Mattei, and Lionel Smith, *Commercial Trusts in European Private Law* (CUP 2005), 103–217 (Case 1, Alternative 1); see also Deborah A DeMott, 'The Fiduciary Character of Agency and the Interpretation of Instructions' in Andrew S Gold and Paul B Miller (eds), *Philosophical Foundations of Fiduciary Law* (OUP 2014) 321, 333; Civil Code of Québec, art 2179, para 3.

[169] *Bowstead and Reynolds* (n 155), ¶ 10-007.

carry out a mission in the interests of the debtor, but is empowered only as a mode of giving security for a debt.

All of this underlines that while mandate and agency generally go with legal representation, it is the other-regarding nature of mandate and agency that make these relationships of administration; it is not the power of representation as such. This fits with the observations that many other relationships of administration (like trusts) do not involve legal representation, and many cases of legal representation (like some secured lending arrangements) are not relationships of administration. It also fits with the consideration that there can be relationships of administration that are purely advisory; this consideration shows that a power of legal representation is not necessary for a relationship of administration.[170]

(3) **Political representation** In defending a view that private relationships of administration are of a similar kind to relationships of public administration, Paul Miller has argued that all involve representation, but not the legal representation that is discussed above.[171] His argument is that what is common to all relationships of administration, private and public, is that '... each is carried out on a *representative* basis through mandates under which one or more persons personate others in the authorized exercise of other-regarding legal powers'.[172] This idea of representation as personation I will call, following Miller, 'political representation' (although it has legal consequences).

This kind of representation is obviously an extremely important idea in understanding the legitimacy of the exercise of public power. Most obviously in democracies, but not necessarily only in them, the justification for the rightful holding and exercise of public power may rest on different articulations of the idea that the holders of power represent the people. And it may well be that every relationship of public law administration does, or should, correspond ultimately to a relationship of political representation. That is a question of political theory.

In my view, however, private law shows that legally, the relationship of political representation to relationships of administration is similar to the relationship between legal representation and relationships of administration: political representation is not essential to relationships of administration, and it can

---

[170] Advisory relationships of administration are discussed in Chapter 7, section IV.A. Such relationships are well established in the common law and are also known in the civil law. This means that it is very puzzling that the Court of Appeal of England and Wales recently held that an advising agent can be subject to the same obligations as would apply to a fiduciary agent, without the need to decide that they are in a fiduciary relationship with the principal: *Wood v Commercial First Business Ltd* [2021] EWCA Civ 471. This decision approximates to a holding that an animal has all the characteristics of an elephant, even while we do not have to decide that it is an elephant.

[171] Miller is well aware that some, but not all, relationships of administration include legal representation: Miller (n 84), 37–39.

[172] ibid 23 (emphasis in original). Miller uses 'mandate' to refer to what I call a mission, assignment, function, task, or charge; he is not referring to the civilian contract of mandate.

exist in the absence of a relationship of administration. Miller himself notes one problem: a person can make himself into a trustee, creating a relationship of private administration with the beneficiaries; but a person cannot represent himself.[173] Moreover, cases where relationships of administration arise by operation of law cannot easily be seen as involving political representation.[174] But the problem exists even in a paradigmatic three-party trust: the settlor appoints the trustee who acts for the benefit of the beneficiary; the relationship of (political) representation is between settlor and trustee, since the trustee carries out the mission assigned by the settlor, and in this way 'personates' the settlor. But the relationship of administration is between the trustee and the beneficiary.[175] The trustee does not represent the beneficiary, legally or politically;[176] and in this three-party trust, the beneficiary is not the author of the trustee's mission.[177] This becomes clear when we bear in mind that the beneficiary may be a purpose, or may be a person who is incapacitated; neither one can be the author of the trustee's mission. So a relationship of private administration can exist that does not correspond to a relationship of political representation. In the case of relationships of administration arising by operation of law, the relationship of administration does not even arise from a relationship of political representation.

As with legal representation, this lack of co-extension between administration and political representation is also visible in the opposite direction. A secured creditor who sells the asset of the debtor can be said to 'personate' the debtor, since the creditor is dealing with the debtor's rights, and this, via the earlier-granted authority of the debtor. Moreover, we can consider the case of an employee who is not in a relationship of administration with the employer (and thus is not a fiduciary in common law terminology). The employee can still make the

[173] ibid 39 n 53. It is possible in Quebec law also for a settlor to create a trust of which he is a trustee, although in Quebec law a second trustee is needed (Civil Code of Québec, art 1275; Jacques Beaulne, *Droit des fiducies* (3rd edn, Wilson & Lafleur 2015), 192–94).

[174] These are discussed in Chapter 2, section III.A.3. Briefly, they include some resulting and constructive trusts, and parenthood of a minor child.

[175] In the common law, the settlor presumptively has no rights of supervision or enforcement at all. In *Turner v Turner* [1984] Ch 100 (ChD), the trustees followed the instructions of the settlor and were found to have acted unlawfully. Even though he had assigned the trustees' mission, so that they were representing him politically, they were required to exercise judgment independently and in what they considered to be the best interests of the beneficiaries. In Quebec law, the settlor does have rights of supervision and enforcement; but in administering the trust, the trustee must be guided by the purposes embodied in the trust, not by consideration of the settlor's wishes or interests.

[176] It is noted above (n 149) that in the common law, it is possible (but not usual) for there to be a relationship of legal representation between a trustee and her beneficiaries.

[177] Miller sometimes suggests the opposite (eg n 84, 39); but overall his argument is that the trustee represents or personates the person who assigned other-regarding powers to the trustee for the accomplishment of a mission designed by that person. This is the settlor, not the beneficiary. If both relationships—carrying out the settlor's assignment, and acting for and on behalf of a beneficiary—were considered different kinds of political representation, then it would follow that not all relationships of political representation are relationships of administration (or fiduciary relationships), which is one of the points I am making here.

employer vicariously liable for wrongs committed by the employee in the course of employment.[178] A common way of understanding this vicarious liability is that it arises because the employer controls the employee and can be said to *act through* the employee.[179] One could say that it is based on the presence of political representation: the employee personates the employer in carrying out the mission that was assigned by the latter.

It is true that the majority of relationships of administration may involve political representation in their creation; but only in some cases is that relationship of political representation coterminous with the relationship of administration itself. Moreover, as with legal representation, political representation can exist and can generate legal consequences outside of relationships of administration. Even if I do not agree with all of it, Miller's argument helps us to understand why the law allows us to act through others, in private law and in public law, and why it attaches different characteristics to different ways of acting through others. These legal characteristics may include vicarious liability and legal powers of representation, as well as the incidents that arise in relationships of administration, whether those relationships be for the benefit of the one who created the assigned mission or for another. Some relationships will have *all* of those characteristics (as in the case of an agent or mandatary); others may generate the possibility of vicarious liability without a relationship of administration; and many relationships of administration lack any kind of representation in the relationship between administrator and beneficiary, and thus any possibility of vicarious liability.

c) *Subject to instructions, or not*
Some, but not all, administrators are required to follow the instructions of their beneficiaries. This can be seen in both private and public administration. The requirement to follow instructions is most clearly present in agency and mandate.[180] This characteristic underlies the general feature of such relationships that the principal/mandator can usually terminate the relationship at will, even if it was agreed to be for a fixed term or irrevocable.[181]

Not long ago, in both common law and civil law, such a relationship ended automatically if the principal/mandator lost legal capacity. Now it is generally

---

[178] Robert Stevens, *Torts and Rights* (OUP 2007), 257–64; Civil Code of Québec, arts 1463–64; Popovici (n 54), 20. As mentioned above (n 160), US law seems to consider all employees (even gratuitous helpers) to be agents (*Heims v Hanke* 93 NW2d 455 (Wis, 1958)), which makes it harder to see non-agency vicarious liability.

[179] Storck (n 54), 202; Stevens, ibid, noting that some recent decisions are difficult to square with this traditional view; Daniel Harris, 'The Rival Rationales of Vicarious Liability' (2021) 20 FSU Business L Rev 49, noting that the traditional control view remains dominant in US law outside of California.

[180] BGB (n 158), §665 *a contrario*; Werro (n 160), 179–86; DeMott (n 168).

[181] This may create liability in breach of contract; see above n 168.

possible to create an authorization that will survive the loss of capacity. Typically, this is possible in relation to property management and also decisions about personal care. Courts have always had the authority to name persons to take on those roles, where no such designation was validly made by the now-incapacitated person. Even though these relationships are on behalf of an incapacitated person, they include legal representation, since the administrator is authorized to manage the legal position of the incapacitated person, performing legal acts on their behalf.

Even where capacity has been lost, however, there is a sense in which this relationship is one in which the administrator is subject to instructions. The reason is that while they have decision-making authority, their authority is almost certainly constrained by wishes that were validly expressed by the now-incapacitated person while they still had capacity, or wishes that they are still be able to express. Thus the Civil Code of Québec provides, in art 12:

> A person who gives his consent to or refuses care for another person is bound to act in the sole interest of that person, complying, as far as possible, with any wishes the latter may have expressed.[182]

In a similar way, an Ontario guardian of property should generally not alienate property of the incapacitated person if the person has made a specific bequest of that property in a valid will.[183]

Many administrators, however, are not subject to instructions. As was mentioned above, leading Quebec authors have proposed a fundamental division in other-regarding private law powers, between powers of representation and autonomous powers.[184] A holder of autonomous powers, such as a trustee, is not subject to instructions or direction.[185] On this view, there is a subcategory of autonomous powers that can be called 'organic powers'.[186] These are powers held by the decision-making 'organs' of legal persons and unincorporated associations. Directors of a corporation are not (as directors) its agents or mandataries. Agents and mandataries act under instructions. Directors, on the contrary, control and decide what the corporation will do. When the board of directors decides, for example, that the corporation shall issue a dividend, this is a decision of the corporation that the board is empowered to make for it.[187]

---

[182] Cf the Ontario *Substitute Decisions Act, 1992*, SO 1992, c 30, s 66(3) and *Health Care Consent Act, 1996*, SO 1996, c 2, Sched A, s 21.

[183] *Substitute Decisions Act*, ibid s 35.1. Under s 36, if such disposition is necessary, the intended legatee is entitled to a monetary equivalent from the estate where possible.

[184] Cantin Cumyn and Cumyn (n 56), 95–99.

[185] Unless it is a common law bare trust: see n 149.

[186] ibid 125–38.

[187] Not all organic powers, however, involve a relationship of administration. Corporate law allocates some decisions to a different organ, namely the shareholders, who generally can vote in

Holders of public powers of administration may or may not be subject to instructions. Some of them, in addition to holding public powers, are in a relationship of employment. This might be true of a police officer or an employee who processes applications for business licences; it might also be true of the CEO of a large State-controlled enterprise, such as a public pension fund. The employment relationship itself will require that lawful instructions be followed. The same may be true without an employment relationship in the strict sense. The armed forces are always under the direction of the executive, even if the most senior officer holds a commission which does not constitute a typical employment relationship.

Legislators, however, do not act under instructions as a matter of law, although they may be subject to more or less discipline from their own party. Judges certainly act under no one's instructions, even if they are elected. The same is true of those holding undelegated executive power. In a democracy, at least, they are periodically accountable at the ballot box; more frequently and more often in some democracies than in others. But the power of the voters does not amount to the giving of legally binding instructions, although political norms can rightly constrain executive power in relation to matters that were, or were not, publicly announced goals or promises.

An administrator who is not subject to instructions has been entrusted with powers that they are required to exercise themself, in the pursuit of the purpose for which the powers were granted. Thus if a trustee does take instructions, even from the settlor who gave the trustee the relevant powers, the trustee will find that they have not used their powers properly and what they have done is liable to be set aside.[188]

d) *The administrator as office-holder, or not, and the court's supervisory jurisdiction*

Some administrators hold an office, but some do not. The word 'office' does not have a fixed legal meaning but in this context, it captures the idea of a role that stands apart from the identity of the occupant from time to time. It implies that someone needs to be in the role at any given time, and that certain powers are held by the current holder of the office in virtue of holding it.[189]

If an agent or mandatary quits or dies or is fired, it is not necessary to have a new one; that is a decision for the principal or mandator. The same is usually true

their own interests. They may be subject however to some legal constraints, as is the case in relation to certain other powers that are held outside of relationships of administration: see Chapter 3, section III.B.2.

[188] *Turner v Turner* (n 175); *Pitt v Holt* [2013] UKSC 26, [2013] 2 AC 108, [66]–[67].
[189] See the papers in the special issue 'The Idea of An Office' (2020) 70 UTLJ Supp 2 163–314.

in a business partnership, subject to the partnership agreement; the agreement can provide for the departure of partners, without requiring their replacement. But if the executor of an estate, the trustee of a trust, or the director of a corporation quits or dies or is removed, in general they must be replaced.[190] The same is true for parents, and those who care for the property and care of incapacitated persons. And we could say the same about a judge of the Supreme Court of the United States, the President of the French Republic, or the Mayor of Flin Flon. These administrators hold offices.

Those roles that are offices are, in a sense, impersonal: the role stands apart from the person who occupies it from time to time. This is not true of relationships that do not involve offices, such as agency or mandate. Those latter roles are held by a particular person, and while it is always possible to create a new mandate or agency, this is not understood as involving the replacement of a prior office-holder. It is important to say, however, that the idea that an office is impersonal can be misleading. The reason is that in an important sense, every administrative role is personal, whether it constitutes an office or not. It is personal in the sense that the relevant powers are held by a person who holds it at any given time, and that person, as long as they are in the role, holds the decision-making power and authority, within the limits of the law. To the extent that the power is discretionary, it belongs to that person to decide how the power shall be used.[191]

In private law as in public law, there is likely to be legal machinery for the appointment of a new office-holder where needed. The terms of a trust or the corporate constitution should provide such machinery; if they do not, the general law may provide a solution. If it fails to do so, or if for some reason the machinery is non-functional, the courts can usually assist. This is because the presence in private law of offices in this sense coexists with a supervisory power of the court, of a kind that is not found in contractual arrangements like agency, mandate, or partnership. Although many aspects of the supervisory jurisdiction may be found in the Civil Code or in statute law, the courts may also have inherent powers of this kind.

Under this jurisdiction the court has the power to remove an office-holder, and to appoint a new one, if there is no other available machinery or if the machinery is non-functional. These powers are well-known in the law of trusts.[192]

---

[190] In some trusts and many corporate constitutions, the number of trustees or directors is not fixed but set as a range with a minimum and maximum. In this case, the removal of one will not necessarily require replacement by another so long as the minimum is still in place.

[191] This is explored in more detail in Chapter 3, section II.B.

[192] Daniel Clarry, *The Supervisory Jurisdiction Over Trust Administration* (OUP 2019); Clarry explains how in the common law of trusts, the supervisory jurisdiction has evolved to include an advisory jurisdiction. On removal of trustees, see Donovan WM Waters, Mark Gillen, and Lionel Smith, *Waters' Law of Trusts in Canada* (5th edn, Thomson Reuters 2021) 945–53; Austin W Scott,

Trustees can be removed for dishonesty or other grave breach of trust, but they may also be removed if they are unfit to act, or in an unmanageable conflict of interest. But the court's powers are wider; it can remove a trustee or executor from office simply if it considers that this course is in the best interests of the beneficiaries.[193] Although it may be less used and less well-known, the court also has a supervisory jurisdiction over legal persons.[194] There is also supervisory jurisdiction over the affairs of children, and of adults who lack full legal capacity.[195] In the common law at least, some aspects of this are derived from the Crown's role as *parens patriae*.[196]

It is plausible therefore to infer that while a supervisory jurisdiction is not needed in relation to administrators holding powers of legal representation, it may well be necessary in relation to those holding offices, where the powers are autonomous and the power-holder is not subject to instructions or direct control.[197] In Quebec civil law, it has been argued that even in the absence of explicit statutory authority, the courts can remove office-holding administrators because this is an indispensable tool of supervision.[198]

When acting in a supervisory role, a judge's role and authority are sensibly different from what they are when a judge is resolving a dispute between litigants. The judge as supervisor ceases to be a neutral arbiter between litigants. Instead, she needs to consider the interests of one or more persons as she exercises powers

---

William F Fratcher, and Mark L Ascher, *Scott and Ascher on Trusts*, vol 1 (4th edn, Aspen Publishers 2006), §11.10; Civil Code of Québec, art 1290.

[193] *Letterstedt v Broers* (1884) 9 App Cas 371 (PC).

[194] For Quebec law, see *Code of Civil Procedure*, CQLR c 25.01, s 34; *Upton v Hutchison* (1899) 2 Que Practice Rep 300 (QB App Side), 304; *Laurent v Buanderie Villeray Ltée* [2001] JQ no 5796, JE 2002-3, 2001 CanLII 158 (CS). In the common law the courts have always had this supervisory jurisdiction over corporations, at least those created by letters patent: Franklin W Wegenast, *The Law of Canadian Companies* (Burroughs and Co 1931), 775–76; Roscoe Pound, 'Visitatorial Jurisdiction Over Corporations In Equity' (1936) 49 Harv L Rev 369; *Bateman's Bay Local Aboriginal Land Council v Aboriginal Community Benefit Fund Pty Ltd* (1998) 194 CLR 247, [26]. The jurisdiction may be subject to the jurisdiction of a Visitor where the legal person has one, which may be the case for charitable corporations; this person's role is to resolve internal disputes (see *Thomas v University of Bradford* [1987] AC 795 (HL); *Re CS* [2015] NIQB 36).

[195] Parents of minor children can also be deprived of their parental authority by the court; the holding of parental authority is an office and the application of the supervisory jurisdiction is natural. More detail on this is in Chapter 7, section V, and in Smith (n 73), 445–46. The supervisory jurisdiction may not be confined to appointing and removing administrators. For example, in *Davis v Kerr* (1890) 17 SCR 235, under the Civil Code of Lower Canada, the tutor who wished to borrow money in the name of the minor child had to secure the approval of the court.

[196] John Seymour, 'Parens Patriae and Wardship Powers: Their Nature and Origin' (1994) 14 OJLS 159. For an argument that the detailed regulation in the Civil Code makes it unnecessary to rely on *parens patriae* in Quebec law, see Michel Morin, 'La compétence parens patriae et le droit civil québécois : un emprunt inutile, un affront à l'histoire' (1990) 50 Rev du Barreau 827.

[197] On the distinction between powers of representation and autonomous powers, see above, section V.B.3.b.1.

[198] Cantin Cumyn and Cumyn (n 56), 349–53, arguing that codal references to the occasion of 'replacement' of an administrator imply a curial power of removal.

for the benefit of that person or persons.[199] In appointing or removing trustees, these are the interests of the beneficiaries, or otherwise the pursuit of the purpose of the trust. In appointing a guardian or tutor, the interests of the incapable person will be paramount, as they are when the court is deciding who shall have custody of a minor child. In a corporate matter, it would be the interests of the corporation. Thus the supervisory judge is acting less like a resolver of disputes, and more like an administrator of the affairs of one or more persons.[200] The supervisory judge, however, is still exercising powers of public administration.[201]

---

[199] Supervisory jurisdictions in private and public law are discussed in Dawn Oliver, *Common Values and the Public-Private Divide* (reprint edn, CUP 2010) 25–27. Oliver, however, uses the phrase in a wide sense to cover all legal oversight of relationships of administration (and even some other situations). I am using it more narrowly to refer to situations where the judge steps out of the usual neutral judicial role and acts to protect the interests of one or more identified persons.

[200] As in all human affairs, the processes do not always unfold as they should. In *Davis* (n 195), Taschereau J said of the prothonotary (244): 'In utter disregard of the duties assigned to him in the matter and seemingly unconscious of the responsibility attached to his functions, he contented himself with relying upon the notary's proceedings, and granted the authority to borrow a large sum in this minor's name without any attempt whatever to exercise his own judgment on the merits of the application or on the necessity of the loan. A more iniquitous proceeding, a more glaring fraud against the law, is hardly conceivable...'

[201] In other words, even though the judge is legally bound to exercise their powers in what they perceive to be the best interests of one or more persons, the judge's duty is an undirected public duty (see above, section V.B.2.b).

PART II
ACTING FOR OTHERS IN PRIVATE LAW

2
Introduction

I. Significance and scope of this Part

A. Significance

The exercise of powers held on behalf of another is highly regulated in private law. This regulation, however, has proceeded unevenly over the centuries. In many ways, it has stood apart from the basic tools of private law thinking: the law of property, of contracts, of private wrongs, of unjust enrichment. This is why attempts to theorize it in a unified way are relatively recent, in both the common law and the civil law.[1] It is also why many such attempts proceed reductively, attempting to explain acting for others in private law through the use of concepts that are found among these well-known basic tools. In other words, such commentators attempt to use other private law categories, particularly contract law, to make sense of acting for others. These attempts have never succeeded, and as we will see, never can succeed because different tools and concepts are needed.

There are two reasons for this. The first is that powers held on behalf of another have many sources, not a single source.[2] They *may* be created by agreement, but they can also be created by the law; one can even turn one's own powers into powers held for another, as in the case where a person declares themself to be a trustee. A *general* account needs to rise above the particular, and a contractual or agreement-based explanation of acting for others can only be particular.

The second reason is more profound. In order to understand the law's regulation of acting for others, it has to be appreciated that different justificatory principles apply from those that apply when one is acting for oneself. Speaking generally, private law allows us to act selfishly and to take account only of our own interests in making our decisions and in using our legal prerogatives. Many attempts to understand the legal principles examined in this study have been compromised by a failure to understand that the regulation of acting for others is categorically different. A simple example comes from the legal norm that presumptively allocates to the beneficiary any rights that the manager extracts from acting as manager.[3] From the perspective that private law starts from selfishness,

---

[1] See also Chapter 1, section II.B.
[2] Modes of creation of relationships of administration are explored below, in section III.A.
[3] This is explored in detail in Chapter 5.

and that one is free to pursue one's own interests within the limits of the law, this norm has to be understood as one triggered by a *breach of duty*. Moreover, it must be a breach that generates a recourse measured by the defendant's gain, instead of the ordinary measure of loss caused to the plaintiff. This in turn has led to the emergence of a range of more or less contrived deterrence theories that aim to explain the rule but which never fit the actual law. A paradigm shift changes everything: when you are acting for another, any unauthorized benefit that you extract is held for that other. This is not about wrongdoing, but about the implementation of the other-regarding nature of the relationship.

The importance of this Part is not only to address the inner logic and importance of the regulation of these relationships in private law; it is also to show how the basis of such regulation transcends contractual ideas. Indeed, this Part aims—in combination with Part III—to show that the basis of such regulation transcends any ideas that are particular to private law.

B. Scope

The scope of this Part is confined to private law, and indeed most of it is confined to a subset of those private law relationships in which one person holds legal powers on behalf of another. Part II.A, which includes Chapters 3 through 6, examines those relationships in which one person holds powers to manage the property (in a wide sense of that term) of other persons. In civilian terms, we are concerned with powers to intervene in the patrimony of another.[4] In common law terms, we might say that we are concerned with the management of pecuniary interests, or of assets.[5] We therefore leave aside (until Part II.B., that is, Chapter 7) some private law relationships that are governed by related principles.[6] Part II.A is concerned with pecuniary relationships including agent–principal, mandatary–mandator, director–legal person, trustee–beneficiary, guardian–ward, and tutor–pupil.[7] It includes partners in a business partnership,

---

[4] For discussion of the patrimony, see Chapter 1, section V.B.2.a.

[5] In earlier work, I defined 'asset' to include both personal and proprietary rights, but only those rights that are not held by everyone, thus excluding rights such as one's right to bodily integrity (Lionel Smith, *The Law of Tracing* (Clarendon Press 1997) 49–54, discussing also the wide and narrow senses of 'property').

[6] These include relationships involving the administration of non-pecuniary interests, such as parenthood, or the case where a person is legally empowered to make health-care decisions for another. They also include some advisory relationships, where the administrator does not hold legal powers.

[7] To the extent that a lawyer is an agent or mandatary, or a trustee, the lawyer–client relationship is thus included. Even if the relationship is purely advisory, so that there is no mandate or agency or trust, the lawyer–client relationship is still a relationship of the kind with which this book is concerned. This kind of purely advisory relationship, however, is discussed in Chapter 7, section IV.A.

since they are mutual agents or mandataries. In the common law, it also includes the personal representative (executor or administrator) who acquires the assets and liabilities of the estate of a deceased person, in order to distribute it according to the will or to the applicable intestacy rules.[8] I will call this the core private law context of acting for others.

This definitional move is designed to give Part II.A a relatively narrow scope for the purposes of exposition, while allowing it to retain a comparative regard, across both of the legal traditions with which I am concerned. I do not mean to imply that this core private law context has any kind of priority over other contexts in which we act for others. On the contrary, I will argue later that in all contexts, the same justifying principles underlie the parallel legal norms that are applicable. The core private law context does, however, present a clear case, which can serve as a starting point for the analysis. It allows us to identify a range of features of the legal regulation of these relationships, and to understand why the law imposes the norms that it does. This in turn will allow us to see which of these norms are characteristics of the very idea of acting for others.

II. Private law's regulation of acting for others

A. Background

For many jurists, particularly those of the common law tradition, the fiduciary relationship developed in the English Court of Chancery represents a distinctive creation.[9] Some of its features emerged in cases involving trustees in the eighteenth century, although the label 'fiduciary relationship' arose only in the nineteenth, and only really caught on in the late twentieth. Many of the elements of this suite of norms, however, are much older—older, indeed, than the common law itself.[10] Centuries ago, Roman law had norms against the exercise of other-regarding legal powers in conflict situations. Around 200, the jurist Paul published a commentary that built on the work of earlier jurists. Part of it was later extracted into the *Digest* of Justinian:

---

[8] Succession in the civilian tradition does not characteristically operate via a trustee-like executor inasmuch as the deceased's rights vest directly in the heirs. The succession is administered by them, or possibly by a liquidator who is not an heir. To the extent that any such person is managing the assets of others, they are an administrator within this Part II.A. (Madeleine Cantin Cumyn and Michelle Cumyn, *L'administration du bien d'autrui* (2nd edn, Éditions Yvon Blais 2014) 113–14).

[9] Leonard I Rotman, *Fiduciary Law* (Thomson/Carswell 2005) ch 4, discussing also equity as known in ancient law and philosophy.

[10] For an argument that Equity's contribution is historically contingent and path dependent, but nonetheless includes a highly evolved set of legal norms that regulate how we act for others in private law, see Lionel Smith, 'Equity Is Not a Single Thing' in Dennis Klimchuk, Irit Samet, and Henry Smith (eds), *Philosophical Foundations of the Law of Equity* (OUP 2020) 144.

A *tutor* cannot buy a thing belonging to his ward; this rule extends to other persons with similar responsibilities, that is, curators, procurators, and those who conduct another's affairs.[11]

Interestingly, this stricture covers quite exactly the scope of Part II.A of this book: those who conduct another's pecuniary affairs. In the early common law, the relationship between guardian and ward was also the site of intervention in relation to some characteristics that are now seen as attaching to fiduciary relationships, namely the obligation to account and the corresponding inability to extract personal profit. In 1215 the Magna Carta, which in many respects was understood to confirm existing law, provided that a feudal guardian could take only reasonable and customary revenues from the land belonging to the ward.[12] What exactly was reasonable and customary, of course, was a separate question, but this text recognizes that the guardian did not hold his powers simply as pecuniary assets to be exploited as he should wish; they were held *for* the ward. Excess profits had to be surrendered.[13] The common law soon developed the requirement of the rendering of an account, which is an obligation to provide information; this information allowed (among other things) the ascertainment of liability for the extraction of unauthorized profits. These developments preceded the later evolution of the Court of Chancery and its accounting machinery.

It would be a mistake, therefore, to think that when the fiduciary relationship, as it is now understood, emerged from the Chancery decisions of the eighteenth and nineteenth centuries; it was cut out of whole cloth.[14] It would also be a mistake to think that the rules about conflicts, and about unauthorized profits, were the creation of Chancery or are unique to the fiduciary relationship of the common law tradition. There was plenty of precedent, centuries old and from inside and outside English law, for the application of these norms to relationships of this kind.

It would also be a mistake, of course, to consider these rules as relevant only in private law relationships. If we think about a judge, for example, we apply

---

[11] D.18.1.34.7; translation from Alan Watson (ed), *The Digest of Justinian*, 4 vols (rev edn, U of Pennsylvania Press 1998). The extract is from Paul's *Libri ad edictum*. 'Tutor' is a civil law term for the guardian of a minor or other person lacking full capacity. 'Curator' may also be applied and the relationship between the two terms depends on the system. The meaning of 'procurator' can depend on the time and context but here refers to a mandatary, who would be an agent in the common law.
[12] Clause 4. This clause also provided for liability of the guardian for what came to be called waste, that is, harming the capital value of the land.
[13] In relation to the extent to which the guardian was authorized to extract profits, distinctions were drawn between different kinds of feudal tenures, a matter that long ago lost significance. See John H Baker, *An Introduction to English Legal History* (5th edn, OUP 2019) 261.
[14] Joshua Getzler, 'Rumford Market and the Genesis of Fiduciary Obligations' in Andrew Burrows and Lord Rodger of Earlsferry (eds), *Mapping the Law: Essays in Memory of Peter Birks* (OUP 2006) 577, finding also origins in the regulation of public power.

recognizably similar norms. We do not want judges to extract unauthorized gains from their official role, and we do not want them to act while in a conflict.[15] The goal of this Part II.A is not to identify something that is *unique* to private law, but rather to identify the legal rules that characterize the core private law *relationships* with which we are concerned. This will allow us to understand the normative foundations of these rules. And this, in turn and perhaps reflexively, will allow us to think about the extent to which the same rules properly apply in other contexts, due to the presence in those contexts of relationships with relevantly similar features.

B. Overview of private law administration

In the previous chapter, I explained why I use the label 'administrator' for a person who is charged with an other-regarding mission.[16] This includes the various categories of private law relationships that were mentioned above.[17]

After centuries of development and refinement, we can find the following characteristics in the core private law cases with which we are concerned.

First, the administrator holds *powers* to administer the financial interests of the other. But there is more to say about this, because there is a crucial difference between holding powers *over* another person, and holding powers *on behalf of* another person, to allow one to act for their benefit. An employer has powers over its employees; it has the power to terminate the contract of employment, albeit this is likely subject to various constraints. But the employer does not generally act for and on behalf its employees; it is not charged with a mission on their behalf. So a crucial feature of the relationships with which we are here concerned is that the powers are held by the administrator *for and on behalf of* the other or others.[18]

The administrator may be required, by the terms of his mission, to do or not to do various things. She must abide by these terms. But it is a common feature of all the relationships with which we are concerned that the mission is not typically exhaustively defined in advance. It may be subject to constant supervision and instruction giving by the beneficiary of the administration, but this is not true in a wide range of cases.[19] For this reason, the powers that the administrator holds

---

[15] See Chapter 11, section III.D.
[16] Chapter 1, section IV.D.
[17] Section I.B.
[18] This may or may not mean that the administrator has the power bind the beneficiary in law: Chapter 1, section V.B.3.b.1.
[19] Chapter 1, section V.B.3.c.

are typically discretionary powers, which allow her to do certain things, but that do not require her to do those things.

Not surprisingly, we find that in all these relationships, there is legal regulation of how these powers (discretionary or not) are used. Since the powers exist to allow the administrator to carry out a mission, they must be so used. It is often said, in the context of the situations under discussion in Part II.A, that the administrator must act in the best interests of the person for whom she acts: more precisely, in what she perceives to be the best interests of the person for whom she acts.[20] There are typically other constraints as well, which depend on the nature of the relationship. If these discretionary powers are used improperly, there are consequences: typically that the exercise of the power can be set aside.[21]

Speaking generally, the administrator is not allowed to use his powers when he is in a conflict of interest. This requires a great deal of qualification: there are important exceptions, and a good definition of 'conflict of interest' is required. We will return to this, and we will explore why the rules about conflicts are especially needed where the powers held by the administrator are discretionary.[22]

Again speaking generally, the administrator is not allowed to extract unauthorized personal profit from his role. The scope of this principle may be difficult to draw in particular cases. Importantly, it stands apart from the rules about conflicts. There can be conflicts without unauthorized profits, and, once conflicts are properly defined, it is clear there can also be unauthorized profits without conflicts.[23]

The administrator is required to provide information to those for whom he acts. Depending on the nature of the relationship, this may involve a requirement to provide a formal accounting. But such an accounting is just one kind of information; it is a special, detailed case of the more general requirement that the administrator, who is acting for others, be transparent towards those others in relation to how he has acted and is acting.[24] Finally, the administrator is presumptively required to use some degree of objective care, skill, diligence, or prudence in carrying out his assignment or mission. A breach of this duty potentially leads to liability for loss caused by the breach.[25]

Every one of these characteristics will be discussed in turn. It is my argument that all of them can be understood as the legal consequences of the creation of

---

[20] Even in this private law setting, however, it is sometimes more accurate to say that the administrator must use the powers for the pursuit of the purpose for which they were granted: Chapter 1, section II.A. That formulation, which includes the 'best interests' formulation but is more general, is much more important in public law administration.

[21] Chapter 3, particularly section IV.E.
[22] Chapter 4.
[23] Chapter 5.
[24] Chapter 5, section VIII.
[25] Chapter 6, section III.

a situation in which one person is authorized and empowered to act for and on behalf of another. They form a unity inasmuch as every one of them finds its normative foundation in the nature of the relationship between the parties. A clear understanding of the foundation of each of these norms will allow their limits to be better understood, as well as their relevance to other relationships, in private law and in public law.

III. The constitution and termination of relationships of private administration

A. Constitution

There are a number of modes by which relationships of private law administration are constituted. One reason to spend time distinguishing them is in order to be sure of being able to distinguish what is *diagnostic* of such relationships from what is *typical* or *characteristic* of them. This is important because understanding what is diagnostic of such relationships helps us to recognize them in other contexts. This includes the wider range of private law relationships of administration that are discussed in Part II.B, and the public law relationships of administration discussed in Part III.

1. Private assignment and acceptance of a mission

Many relationships of administration are typically constituted in this way: business partnerships, agency and mandate, trusteeship, executorship, and directorships of legal persons (although most of these can be constituted in other ways as well).

The creation of relationships of administration in this way can be seen as an example of 'political representation', which was introduced in the previous chapter.[26] This is the idea that one can act through another person. The law in various ways makes it possible to act through others, and the law attaches consequences to acting though others. If one person A proposes to another person B that B should take on certain powers in order to pursue some other-regarding mission that is defined by A, and if the law allows this (subject to B's agreement), then the law is enabling the political representation of A by B in respect of this mission defined by A.

Straightforward examples are found in the relationships of mandate (in civil law) and agency (in the common law). Here, the relationship embodies political representation and it typically also involves legal representation: the mandatary

---

[26] Chapter 1, section V.B.3.b, where it was contrasted with legal representation.

or agent is able to alter the legal position of the mandator or principal vis-à-vis third parties, through legal acts like making contracts. We have seen, however, that even in the absence of a grant of legal representation, B as agent or mandatary can be in a relationship of administration towards A.[27] With or without legal representation, there is a relationship of private administration that is coterminous with the relationship of political representation: B is an administrator in relation to A.[28] Modern legal systems also allow a person to appoint an agent or mandatary to administer either or both of their property and their health-care decisions, in such a way that the appointment will endure even if the appointing person loses their legal capacity.[29] This can lead to the creation of a relationship of administration by private assignment by the beneficiary, even though the beneficiary is now incapacitated.

On one view, a similar constitution occurs where a director of a legal person is elected by shareholders or members of the legal person, or, as may be possible, is appointed by the board. In either case, the appointing or electing persons are exercising powers they hold as a decision-making organ of the legal person. In this sense, the legal person itself appoints the new director, vesting her in turn with organic powers, which may come from the corporate constitution, the general law, or both.[30] The director, as such, does not have a power of legal representation, but on this way of looking at the appointment, one could say that the relationship between the legal person and the new director is one of political representation, and that it is coterminous with a relationship of administration. Another way of looking at these situations is that the relationship of political administration is between those who vote and the director who is chosen.[31] Here, however, the relationship of political representation would not be coterminous with the relationship of administration, because the relationship of administration is between the director and the legal person.

Other cases show even more clearly that political representation may be the source of a relationship of administration, but the relationship of administration so created may be between different persons. If A proposes to B that B should

---

[27] Chapter 1, section V.B.3.b.2.

[28] This applies by extension to the relationships between and among business partners, who are mutual agents or mandataries. The discussion in the text omits cases in which the so-called mandate or agency is constituted in the interest of the mandator/agent. These were mentioned in Chapter 1, section V.B.3.b.2, where it was suggested that the labels of mandate and agency are not appropriate in these cases.

[29] Until a few decades ago, the loss of capacity would end the authority of any mandatary or agent.

[30] This term was introduced in Chapter 1, section V.B.3.c. The powers held through being (or being part of) a decision-making organ are one type of autonomous powers, that is, powers not subject to instructions from another.

[31] It would be difficult, however, to apply this directly to cases in which a board is empowered to appoint persons to that same board, which is not unusual in not-for-profit entities and sometimes arises for business corporations. That is because the board, so acting, is itself acting in a representative role and is deploying other-regarding powers in a relationship of administration.

become a trustee for the benefit of C, and B accepts, then this is again a case in which B is in a relationship of political representation towards A, carrying out the mission that A has designed. In this case, however, B will be in a relationship of administration with C, not with A. Moreover, there is by default no legal representation in such a case. The same thing occurs if A, in A's will, names B as executor of the will, with legacies to C and others. To take another case, A's proposal (in his will or while alive) may be that B should be the trustee of a trust that is defined by purposes set by A.[32] If B accepts, then B is representing A in the political sense; but B's mission is not guided by the interests of A, but rather by the purpose that A assigned.

Thus many relationships of administration are created through the law's implementation of political representation. In all these cases, the law facilitates the granting by one person of an other-regarding mission to another person. But only sometimes is the relationship of administration with the person who created the mission—the one who is being represented. Moreover, not all occurrences of political representation give rise to relationships of administration. The employment relationship, as such, allows the employer to assign a factual mission to an employee. Because of the control retained at all times by the employer, this is a kind of political representation that has legal consequences: namely, the employee can make the employer liable for extracontractual wrongs committed by the employee. But employment as such is not a relationship of administration in most systems.[33]

2. Unilateral constitution of oneself as administrator

A person can unilaterally place himself in a relationship of administration. The clearest example is the person who makes herself a trustee: that is, she is both the settlor of the trust and the trustee.[34] Here, a relationship of administration is created with the trust beneficiary, or the purpose of the trust; but this arises without political representation.[35]

---

[32] In the common law, except where modified by statute, this must be a charitable purpose to be possible.

[33] For more detail, including exceptions, see Chapter 7, section II.

[34] An example in the common law: *T Choithram International S.A. v Lalibai Thakurdas Pagarani* [2001] 1 WLR 1, [2001] All ER 492 (PC). This is possible in Quebec trust law, but in Quebec law a second trustee is needed (Civil Code of Québec, art 1275; Jacques Beaulne, *Droit des fiducies* (3rd edn, Wilson & Lafleur 2015) 192–94.

[35] Miller argues that in these cases, a person represents (in the political sense) the beneficiaries: Paul B Miller, 'Fiduciary Representation' in Evan J Criddle and others, *Fiduciary Government* (CUP 2018) 21, 39 n 53. This however seems to be inconsistent with the bulk of his argument, in which the one who is represented politically is the one who creates the assignment: see Chapter 1, section V.B.3.b.3. Another example of the unilateral constitution of oneself as an administrator is the case of the de facto trustee, agent, or executor: Chapter 7, section IV.B. It is argued there, however, that this possibility is based on different reasoning.

3. By operation of law

When a minor child holds property, someone may need to be authorized to manage it for and on behalf of the child. This may be called guardianship in the common law and tutorship in the civil law. In some jurisdictions this relationship may be created automatically by law, often making the parent or parents the administrators. Sometimes a court proceeding is needed, as is likely in the case of incapacitated adults; this mode of constitution is discussed in the next section.

Even where the child does not hold patrimonial rights or assets, I will argue in Chapter 7 that the parent of a minor child is in a relationship of private administration with the child. This is because the parent holds a range of legal powers over the child, but holds them for and on behalf of the child. These are powers over non-pecuniary interests, such as decisions regarding medical treatment.

A parent could be said to have unilaterally placed herself in this relationship of administration, as discussed in the previous section. However, the parent is in a relationship of administration even if she had no knowledge of or understanding of the parental authority that she would acquire as a parent. It seems clearer, and more general, to say that this relationship is constituted by the law.

Another example arises in the common law, when trusts come into existence by operation of law. If a person innocently receives trust property transferred donatively in breach of trust, there is a sense in which the property remains subject to the trust;[36] but that innocent recipient will not owe any personal obligations to the beneficiaries.[37] On the other hand, if that person, while still holding the property, becomes aware that it was transferred in breach of trust—or, a fortiori, if they knew that all along—they will be subject to personal obligations owed to the beneficiaries. This includes fiduciary obligations; in other words, that person will be in a relationship of administration with the trust beneficiaries.[38] This trust, and the duties and obligations that go with it, are imposed by operation of law.

4. By court appointment

Where the role of administrator is an office, the court generally has the power to appoint someone to the office. This possibility exists alongside other modes of

---

[36] There is a trust in this sense, that if the recipient were to re-transfer the property, including by dying or becoming bankrupt, any recipient would also be liable to return the property to a proper trustee, unless they could establish a defence.

[37] In other words, if the recipient has innocently dissipated the property before learning of the trust, they will not be liable.

[38] Robert Chambers, 'The End of Knowing Receipt' (2016) 2 CJCCL 1. A detailed discussion of the principles, case law, and academic writing is in *Tan Yok Koon v Tan Choo Suan* [2017] 1 SLR 654, [2017] SGCA 13 (Sing CA), [188]–[210]. The case deals with resulting trusts, some of which are like constructive trusts in the sense relevant to this discussion. (Some resulting trusts, by contrast, bind property in the hands of trustees who agreed to be trustees of express trusts; these trustees are always in a relationship of administration, and the resulting trust changes only who are their beneficiaries.)

constituting such a relationship. For example, we have already seen that a trustee may become a trustee through private appointment; by unilateral constitution; and, in the common law, by operation of law. On top of all those possibilities, a common law court has an inherent jurisdiction to appoint a trustee, now typically placed on a statutory footing; and this is also true in Quebec law.[39] It was suggested earlier that relationships in which the administrator is seen as occupying an office attract a supervisory jurisdiction of the court.[40]

Where a person lacks or loses capacity, the court may be empowered to appoint a guardian, tutor, curator, or other such person. These persons will also hold a kind of office, although in this case the office may be constituted by the court's initial decision that such an administrator is needed, as where an adult loses legal capacity. The need for this office may be temporary, as the relevant person may acquire or regain full legal capacity. The link between offices of administration and the court's supervisory jurisdiction can be seen here as well, since the courts have a supervisory and protective jurisdiction over natural persons who lack full capacity, which may of course be regulated by legislation.[41]

5. The role of an undertaking by the administrator

There is a long history in common law scholarship of taking the view that fiduciary relationships—which are relationships of private administration—depend upon the giving by the fiduciary of an 'undertaking' to act in the interests of another.[42] This is a view with which I have expressed agreement.[43]

Although fiduciary relationships *may* arise in this way, I no longer think that fiduciary relationships *necessarily* arise in this way. The first reservation is one that I have expressed before: the incidents of a fiduciary relationship arise when one accepts to act in a role to which those incidents are attached.[44] One must

---

[39] Civil Code of Québec, art 1277.
[40] Chapter 1, section V.B.3.d.
[41] See the discussion of *parens patriae*, ibid. At the end of that section it is noted that a judge who acts in a supervisory role must, unusually, be guided by the interests of one or more persons (such as the person who lacks capacity); however, although the judge is empowered to create a relationship of private administration by appointing an administrator, the judge herself is not in a relationship of private administration with the incapacitated person. The distinction between private and public administration is addressed in Chapter 9, Part II.
[42] Austin W Scott, 'The Fiduciary Principle' (1949) 37 Cal L Rev 539, 540: 'A fiduciary is a person who undertakes to act in the interest of another person.' See also James Edelman, 'When Do Fiduciary Duties Arise?' (2010) 126 LQR 302.
[43] Lionel Smith, 'Fiduciary Relationships—Arising in Commercial Contexts—Investment Advisor: Hodgkinson v Simms' (1995) 74 Can Bar Rev 714; Lionel Smith, 'Constructive Fiduciaries?' in Peter Birks (ed), *Privacy and Loyalty* (Clarendon Press 1997) 249, 263–64.
[44] Smith, 'Fiduciary Relationships', ibid 725 n 47: 'Rather than finding a presumed or fictional version of the undertaking which is required for fact-based fiduciary relationships, it is clearer to say that no undertaking is required for institutional fiduciary relationships'; Smith, 'Constructive Fiduciaries?', ibid 263: 'Voluntarily undertaking certain offices or relationships is enough to attract [fiduciary] obligations'. See also Lionel Smith, 'The Motive, Not the Deed' in Joshua Getzler (ed),

undertake the role, because relationships of administration are typically voluntary. But one is not required to undertake, individually, each of the obligations and incidents that the law attaches to the role. This means that the incidents of such relationships do not correspond with what we normally mean when we talk about voluntarily assumed obligations. That label is typically applied to cases in which the existence but also the *content* of the obligation is referable to our consent.[45] When a person gets married, they must do so voluntarily or the marriage will not be valid. It does not follow, however, that all of the obligations that ensue are what we mean by voluntary obligations. Those obligations come as a package once one is married. The same is true, as we will see, of the incidents of relationships of administration.[46]

So the undertaking theory is incorrect if it is taken to assert that all of the legal incidents of a fiduciary relationship arise and take their content from the volition of the fiduciary. Those incidents are voluntary in a much weaker sense: speaking generally, you can take them or you can leave them.

The second reservation is that I now argue that even this weaker sense is not pertinent to *all* relationships of administration. In those cases where the relationship arises by operation of law, some of which were discussed above, there is not even the voluntary undertaking of some role to which the incidents of the relationship are attached by law. Take the case of a trustee who becomes so by operation of law and with knowledge that he has so become; he will be in a relationship of administration even though he never wished to be a trustee at all. Parents may become parents without intending to become parents.[47]

In the constitution of *some* fiduciary relationships, as relationships of administration, it may be important to find an undertaking on the part of the fiduciary to relinquish their self-interest. This may be particularly true in relation to relationships that are not in an established category of administration, including

Rationalizing Property, Equity and Trusts: Essays in Honour of Edward Burn (LexisNexis Butterworths 2003) 53, 61.

[45] Joseph Raz, 'Voluntary Obligations and Normative Powers' (1972) 46 Proceedings of the Aristotlean Society, Supplementary Volumes 79, 97; Benoît Moore, 'La théorie des sources des obligations : éclatement d'une classification' (2002) 36 Rev Juridique Thémis 689, 722-24; see also Adrian Popovici, *La couleur du mandat* 23-24 (Les Éditions Thémis 1995), 23-24: '... l'acte juridique est doublement volontaire: il faut la volonté de l'agent de le poser et celle de vouloir les effets prévus par la loi: il est volitif et voulu'.

[46] And just as in marriage, some elements of the package are subject to modification in individual cases.

[47] Parenthood was recognized as a fiduciary relationship by the Supreme Court of Canada in *M (K) v M (H)* [1992] 3 SCR 6, 96 DLR (4th) 289; La Forest J said, for the majority (at SCR 63) that an undertaking by the fiduciary is not always essential. In later cases, the court has used the word 'undertaking' to refer to the conclusion that there is a fiduciary relationship, rather than to refer to an act or manifestation on the part of the fiduciary; references and explanation are at Lionel Smith, 'Parenthood Is a Fiduciary Relationship' (2020) 70 UTLJ 395, 404.

advisory relationships.[48] In relationships involving the creation of legal powers, it will always be possible to *construe* those powers to determine whether they were granted for the pursuit of an other-regarding mission. In advisory relationships, there are no such juridical powers. The finding of a genuine undertaking may be essential to the conclusion that the advisor is bound to act in the sole interest of the advisee.

6. Conclusion

It is an important conclusion that relationships of administration show no unity, but rather diversity, in the modes of their constitution. What is diagnostic of such relationships is not related to how they are created, but is related to the juridical situation that has been created. This will be explored in detail in the next chapter.

B. Termination

Every administrator can, in one way or another, cease to act in this role. This can happen in several different ways.[49] Sometimes, but not always, the relationship of administration continues with one or more other administrators.

This is a fundamentally important characteristic because it differentiates relationships of administration from other parts of private law in which people act for themselves.[50] In particular, the many ways in which an administrator can be removed even if they do not wish to be helps us to see more clearly that the powers of administration that they hold do not really belong to them, the way our rights normally belong to us.

1. Resignation

In general an administrator can quit—although if the relationship is governed by an employment or other contract, this withdrawal may be a breach of the contract.[51] And as it was put in an English case on corporate directors, '[a] director's power to resign from office is not a fiduciary power'.[52] In our terms, the power

---

[48] These are discussed in Chapter 7, sections II.A and IV.A.

[49] The situations discussed below are those where someone—the administrator, the beneficiary, or another—decides that the administrator should cease acting. Not mentioned are situations arising from other events, such as the death of the administrator, or their ceasing to be qualified to act (for example, a person who becomes bankrupt may cease to be qualified to be a director of a business corporation). Mandate and agency are terminated by the death of the of the mandator or principal, and directorship of a legal person will end if the legal person is dissolved.

[50] See also Chapter 1, section II.B.

[51] In the unreformed common law, the executor of an estate, once he or she accepts to act, cannot withdraw from the role. Some jurisdictions have modified this by statute.

[52] *Foster Bryant Surveying Ltd v Bryant* [2007] EWCA Civ 200, [8], quoting with approval an earlier decision.

to resign is not held for the achievement of the other-regarding mission. On the contrary, it is one that the administrator can use in her own interests—subject to her other obligations, of course. A director does not, in deciding whether to exercise the power to resign, have to act in what she considers to be the best interests of the corporation; she can act exactly as she chooses. As the court went on to say, '[h]e is entitled to resign even if his resignation might have a disastrous effect on the business or reputation of the Company'.[53]

This statement about directors is a general one. The power to resign can be exercised by an administrator in their own interest. It is important to remember, however, that while the person will thereby cease to be an administrator, they will *not* cease to be accountable for benefits they acquired while they were an administrator; and this includes information so acquired, even if the former administrator only turns the information to their own advantage after resigning.[54]

2. Recusal (temporary or partial resignation)

An administrator may not be in a position to act in relation to some decision, for example, because of a conflict of interest. Complete resignation may not be desired by anyone. In some contexts, it may be possible for the administrator to recuse herself in relation to the decision. In private law, this is usually feasible only where the administrator is one of a group, such as being one director on a board, or one of multiple trustees.[55] This is because it leaves others in place to make the relevant decision.[56] Very often the recusal procedure is regulated by corporate law, the corporate constitution, securities law, or a trust instrument.[57] Where recusal is possible, the recusing administrator does not act in the particular situation, but otherwise remains in the relevant role.[58]

---

[53] ibid.

[54] In attempting to understand the cases on accountability for profits after resignation, I once suggested that the power to resign was held in an other-regarding capacity: Smith, 'The Motive, Not the Deed' (n 44), 78. I now retract this position. My explanation of these cases is in Chapter 5, section VI.A.1.

[55] A trial judge typically acts alone in any particular case, but is a member of a court and can thus be replaced in relation to any particular case if recusal is necessary. There is no parallel to this institutional structure in private law.

[56] Thus it also depends for its feasibility on the capacity of the remaining administrators to act without the recusing administrator; this is a question of quorum and the rules vary between trust law and corporate law. If (as is the default rule in common law trusts that are not charitable) trustees must act unanimously, recusal is impossible.

[57] For an example in corporate law: Canada Business Corporations Act, RSC 1985, c C-44, s 120; for examples in trust law: New Brunswick Trustees Act, SNB 2015, s 54(6); Society of Trusts and Estates Practitioners, *STEP Standard Provisions*, 2nd edn (2011), cl 9 (online at step.org).

[58] If the recusing person is personally contracting with the beneficiary or with the non-recusing administrators, the person must still make a full disclosure of their relevant self-interest; this shows that the positive obligation to disclose is independent of the inability to exercise administrative powers in a conflict situation. See *Gray v New Augarita Porcupine Mines Ltd* [1952] 3 DLR 1 (PC), 14–15; *UPM-Kymmene Corp v UPM-Kymmene Miramichi Inc* (2002) 214 DLR (4th) 496 (Ont SCJ), [120], aff'd (2004), 250 DLR (4th) 526 (CA) and the discussion of duties to disclose in Chapter 5, section VIII.

3. Private removal

Administrators can also be removed by others, in different ways. In a principal-agent or a mandator-mandatary relationship, the principal or mandator can generally terminate the relationship at any time, even if it was agreed to be irrevocable during a period of time (although again, this may give rise to a claim for breach of contract).[59] The only apparent exception to this is where the arrangement exists for the interest of the 'agent'/'mandatary', but it is questionable whether in such a case the relationship is properly called agency or mandate.[60]

Corporate law usually provides procedures for the removal of directors; a trust may provide machinery for the removal of a trustee. In these cases, a new administrator may need to be installed, privately or by the court, as discussed in the section above on how relationships of administration are constituted.

The common law also knows a different kind of private removal in the context of trusts. If the beneficiaries of the trust are all fully capacitated and in agreement, they can override the terms of the trust, and require the trustees to dispose of the trust property in whatever way they are instructed by the beneficiaries.[61] The logic of this is that the common law trust always exists for the benefit of the beneficiaries, and this fundamental principle is capable of overriding the trust terms.[62] If the beneficiaries are fully capacitated, this means that they are taken to be the judges of what is in their best interests, and so if they are unanimous, they can override the trust terms. This principle does not exist in Quebec law, because all Quebec trusts are purpose trusts, not trusts that must benefit the beneficiaries.[63]

4. End of term of office-holder

We have noticed that some, but not all, administrative roles are offices.[64] In some cases, such as directors of legal persons, appointment to the role may be for a defined term which will eventually come to an end. This will typically activate some procedure for a new election or appointment, possibly of the same person.

---

[59] See Chapter 1, section V.B.3.c.
[60] Chapter 1, section V.B.3.b.2.
[61] This is known as the rule in *Saunders v Vautier* (1841) Cr & Ph 240, 41 ER 482 (LC).
[62] J Langbein, 'Mandatory Rules in the Law of Trusts' (2004) 98 Northwestern U L Rev 1105.
[63] *Alkallay v Bratt*, 2002 CanLII 18363, EYB 2002–38861 (Que. C.S.) It also does not exist in most states of the United States, although this harder to understand since the general rule (as in other common law jurisdictions) is that a purpose trust is invalid (unless it is charitable). Thus it is not clear why the non-charitable purposes of the settlor should override the mandatory principle that the trust must benefit the beneficiaries. Some states now have legislation allowing non-charitable purpose trusts; as in *Quebec*, the rule in *Saunders* could never apply to such a trust.
[64] See Chapter 1, section V.B.3.d.

5. Removal by the court

In the case of a role that is an office, the court may well have the power to remove an office-holder, if there is no other available machinery for private removal, or if the machinery is non-functional. This comes up most often in trusts and estates, because corporate law almost invariably has procedures for the removal of directors, whereas trusts and wills may not. In these contexts, the court has an inherent jurisdiction to remove an administrator from office if it considers that this course is in the best interests of the beneficiaries.[65] In the common law, trustees can be removed for dishonesty or other grave breach of trust;[66] they may also be removed if they are in some way unfit to act or in an unmanageable conflict of interest.[67] But they can also be removed simply because the court believes that removal would be in the best interests of the beneficiaries, as for example where there is ongoing friction.[68]

The same type of jurisdiction is almost certain to exist in offices such as guardian, curator, or tutor, to anyone (child or adult) lacking full legal capacity. It exists also in relation to parents, who hold an office in relation to their minor children; in very grave cases they can be stripped of their parental authority.

6. Ad hoc replacement of private law administrators

The law also recognizes examples of a kind of ad hoc replacement of private law administrators who are office-holders. Trustees are administrators for the benefit of their beneficiaries. They may hold in trust rights (such as rights of action) against third parties. If they refuse to perform their duties, beneficiaries may be allowed to enforce the rights of the trustees against third parties.[69] In this setting, unusually, the beneficiaries are given standing to enforce rights that do not belong to them, but that rather belong to the trustees. Where this is permitted, it is for the benefit of the beneficiaries as a group, to fill the gap created by the inaction of the trustees themselves. The trustees might not actually be removed,

---

[65] Austin W Scott, William F Fratcher, and Mark L Ascher, *Scott and Ascher on Trusts*, vol 2 (4th edn, Aspen Publishers 2006) §11.10; Donovan WM Waters, Mark Gillen, and Lionel Smith, *Waters' Law of Trusts in Canada* (5th edn, Thomson Reuters 2021) 945–53.

[66] Not every action that is later characterized as a breach of trust will necessarily justify removal. This is partly because the common law's rules on breach of trust are very strict when it comes to dealing with the trust property, with the result that some breaches of trust can be committed by a person in perfectly good faith.

[67] In *Klug v Klug* [1918] 2 Ch 67 (ChD), one trustee wished to exercise a dispositive discretion in favour of the beneficiary who was in need of money. The other trustee refused; this trustee was the beneficiary's mother, who disapproved of her daughter's marriage. The court was of the view that the mother was acting improperly; it did not remove her as trustee but directed that the advance should be made. One could say that the mother was recused against her will from the particular decision.

[68] *Letterstedt v Broers* (1884) 9 App Cas 371 (PC).

[69] Civil Code of Québec, art 1291, also mentioning the settlor 'or any other interested person'; *Hayim v Citibank N.A.* [1987] AC 730 (PC), 748. In the common law, the same ad hoc standing may be afforded to beneficiaries, including creditors, of the estate of a deceased person: Chapter 8, section II.D.5.

but they are in a sense temporarily displaced in terms of decision-making authority. In a similar way, in the case of legal persons, those holding powers of administration may be temporarily displaced; a shareholder, for example, may be authorized to bring a legal proceeding asserting the rights of the corporation. This possibility is especially important when the rights being asserted are rights against the administrators who, in the ordinary course of events, make decisions about whether the legal person should take legal proceedings against anyone.[70]

7. Conclusion

Administrators can resign from their role; this is hardly surprising and reflects the liberty of the individual. What is perhaps more interesting is that it is universally true that administrators can be removed from their role, even against their will, when this is judged to be in the best interests of the beneficiary of the administration. Sometimes that removal power belongs to the beneficiary herself, where she is fully capacitated, and thus is taken to be the best judge of her own interests. In other contexts, it may be that the court makes this decision, or some other constituency that is empowered to make it (such as voting shareholders in relation to corporate directors).

This helps us to see that acting for others is categorically different from acting for oneself. Generally, no one can take away another person's rights, or the powers that they hold for their own benefit. But powers that a person holds for the accomplishment of an other-regarding purpose do not belong to that person in the same way that their own assets belong to them. This is why they cannot be sold, or left in a will, and why they can always be taken away. The best accomplishment of the mission can thus rightly prevail over the administrator's wishes.

---

[70] Discussed in more detail in Chapter 8, section II.D.3.

PART II.A
THE CORE CASES OF PRIVATE LAW ADMINISTRATION

3
Loyalty in the Exercise of Private Law Powers of Administration

I. Introduction

A. Specifying the context

This chapter examines why and how the law enforces loyalty in relation to the exercise of the powers that are held by an administrator who acts for others in private law. The loyal exercise of powers is one requirement of sound administration, but it is not the only aspect of the legal regulation of such administration.[1]

These powers cover a very wide range of situations. A commercial agent or mandatary typically has powers to make contracts on behalf of his principal or mandator. A director of a corporation has the power to decide how that legal person will behave: what lines of business it will pursue or abandon, what strategies it will adopt, when it will pay dividends, and so on. A trustee usually has powers in relation to investments and dispositive discretions that allow her to distribute trust property to various persons. A guardian or tutor has powers over the property of his ward or pupil, which again may involve investment, or the sale of assets to cover expenses for education or other needs. The executor, administrator, or liquidator who administers the estate or succession of a deceased person has powers to enable her to fulfil her task of distributing the property according to the wishes of the deceased, or according to the rules of intestacy; particularly in the common law tradition, these powers may be quite extensive, partly because they may involve management of assets over a period of time, but also because a will may expressly grant various discretionary authorities to an executor.

B. Different meanings of 'loyalty'

Many decided cases, and a great deal of scholarship, make reference to the 'duty of loyalty' or sometimes to 'duties of loyalty'. There is little consensus, however,

---

[1] An overview of other aspects is in Chapter 1, section I.

The Law of Loyalty. Lionel Smith, Oxford University Press. © Lionel Smith 2023.
DOI: 10.1093/oso/9780197664582.003.0003

as to what precisely these terms mean. Earlier, we set aside different meanings of loyalty that lie outside of the law governing relationships of administration.[2] Even with that done, however, there is ambiguity. Sometimes the duty of loyalty is confined to the rules against exercising powers while in a conflict of interest, and against extracting unauthorized profits.[3] A wider usage extends the term to include the rules that govern the proper exercise of other-regarding powers.[4] A still wider sense extends it to include the duty of good faith that is owed by administrators.[5] This is complicated, in the common law, by a cross-cutting disagreement about which duties are properly called 'fiduciary'.[6] On one view, 'fiduciary duty' *means* the duty of loyalty which itself, as we have just seen, has different meanings for different people. Thus some may confine 'fiduciary duties' to the rules against unauthorized profits and against exercising fiduciary powers while in a conflict;[7] others may treat the term as covering all of the legal constraints on the exercise of fiduciary powers.[8] Another view is that 'fiduciary duties' refers to those duties that grow out of and give legal effect to a fiduciary relationship, which is a relationship of administration. On this view, therefore, a fiduciary's duty of care, skill, and diligence is rightly called a fiduciary duty, even though it is not a duty of loyalty.[9]

---

[2] Chapter 1, section IV.F.

[3] Eg Matthew Conaglen, *Fiduciary Loyalty: Protecting the Due Performance of Non-Fiduciary Duties* (Hart 2010) 59–61; Deborah A DeMott, 'Breach of Fiduciary Duty: On Justifiable Expectations of Loyalty and Their Consequences' (2006) 48 Arizona L Rev 925, 926; Paul B Miller, 'Justifying Fiduciary Remedies' (2013) 63 UTLJ 570, 607.

[4] Lionel Smith, 'The Motive, Not the Deed' in Joshua Getzler (ed), *Rationalizing Property, Equity and Trusts: Essays in Honour of Edward Burn* (LexisNexis Butterworths 2003) 53; Lionel Smith, 'Fiduciary Relationships: Ensuring the Loyal Exercise of Judgement on Behalf of Another' (2014) 130 LQR 608; in Quebec civil law, see Caroline Le Breton-Prévost, 'Loyalty in Québec Private Law' (2014) 9 J of Civil Law Studies 329.

[5] Eg *Bristol & West Building Society v Mothew* [1998] Ch 1 (CA), 18; Leo E Strine Jr and others, 'Loyalty's Core Demand: The Defining Role of Good Faith in Corporation Law' (2010) 98 Georgetown LJ 629.

[6] For a detailed discussion of different views, see Lionel Smith, 'Parenthood Is a Fiduciary Relationship' (2020) 70 UTLJ 395, 401–18.

[7] This is the view of Conaglen (n 3), following case law of the High Court of Australia: *Breen v Williams* (1995) 186 CLR 71, 113; *Pilmer v Duke Group Ltd (in liq)* (2001) 207 CLR 165, [74]; *Howard v Federal Commissioner of Taxation* [2014] HCA 21, 253 CLR 83, [31], [56].

[8] This was the view taken in Paul D Finn, *Fiduciary Obligations* (Law Book Co 1977); see also Paul D Finn, 'Fiduciary Reflections' (2014) 88 ALJ 127, 140; both reprinted in Paul Finn, *Fiduciary Obligations: 40th Anniversary Republication with Additional Essays* (Federation Press 2016). It is also evident in the case law of the UK Supreme Court: *Pitt v Holt* [2013] UKSC 26, [2013] 2 AC 108, [1], [10], [40]–[41]; *Lehtimäki v Cooper* [2020] UKSC 33, [2022] AC 155; *R (Palestine Solidarity Campaign Ltd) v Secretary of State for Housing, Communities and Local Government* [2020] UKSC 16, [44]. See also *Grand View Private Trust Co v Wong* [2022] UKPC 47 and G Thomas, *Powers* (2nd edn, OUP 2012) 573.

[9] This is the dominant view in the US (see eg Strine and others, n 5) and has been adopted by the Supreme Court of Canada (eg *Valard Construction Ltd v Bird Construction Co* 2018 SCC 8, [2018] 1 SCR 224, [2], [13], [18]–[20], [24], [34]); see also discussions of the fiduciary duty of care in Paul B Miller, 'A Theory of Fiduciary Liability' (2011) 56 McGill LJ 235, 281–85, and Lionel Smith, 'Prescriptive Fiduciary Duties' (2018) 37 UQLJ 261, 268 (also citing case law from Canada, Australia, and England and Wales in nn 5 and 10).

It is important to clarify therefore that the primary concern of this chapter is with the way in which the exercise of other-regarding powers is constrained by a requirement of loyal exercise. This requirement is not a duty in the strict sense: it does not require or forbid any defined conduct.[10] This will be clear by the end of this chapter, when the workings of the requirement of loyalty have been explored in more detail; in short, fulfilment of the requirement of loyalty is needed to make the exercise of a power unimpeachably valid. In a later chapter we will discuss the legal duties that an administrator *does* owe, some of which are implementations of aspects of loyalty.[11] But the focus of this chapter is to show how and why loyalty is a precondition for the fully effective exercise of other-regarding legal powers (and only other-regarding legal powers). When such powers are exercised disloyally, they are defectively exercised and their exercise may be set aside.[12]

C. Manifestations of the legal requirement of loyalty in the exercise of powers of private administration

The interpretive methodology of this book starts from the law as it exists and as it understands itself, in order to develop a theory of how we act for others in law.[13] The legal requirement of loyalty in relation to the exercise of powers of private administration is found in both the civil law and the common law. In the common law, it is often called the 'proper purposes' doctrine.[14] In the civil law it is called *détournement de pouvoir*, or misuse of power.[15] In both cases, it rests on '... the fundamental juristic principle that any form of authority may only be exercised for the purposes conferred.'[16] Both traditions presumptively forbid the

---

[10] Lionel Smith, 'Can We Be Obliged to be Selfless?' in Andrew S Gold and Paul B Miller (eds), *Philosophical Foundations of Fiduciary Law* (OUP 2014) 141; see also Charles Mitchell, 'Stewardship of Property and Liability to Account' [2014] Conveyancer and Property Lawyer 215, 219 (under the rubric of the 'proper purposes' doctrine which is a central concern of this chapter). The point is further discussed below, section IV.G.

[11] Chapter 6.

[12] Below, section IV.E.

[13] Chapter 1, section III.A.

[14] Another label is 'fraud on a power' but this is misleading as fraud in any ordinary sense is not required. The common law 'proper purposes' doctrine has more than one manifestation, and one manifestation of it is applicable to powers that are not held in an administrative capacity: below, section III.B.2. The requirement of loyalty to a purpose does not, however, apply in that context.

[15] Jean Dabin, *Le droit subjectif* (Dalloz 2008 [1952]), 248–54; Emmanuel Gaillard, *Le pouvoir en droit privé* (Economica 1985), 95–124; Madeleine Cantin Cumyn, 'Le pouvoir juridique' (2007) 52 McGill LJ 215, 229–36; Madeleine Cantin Cumyn, 'The Legal Power' (2009) 17 European Rev of Private Law 345, 359–64; Madeleine Cantin Cumyn and Michelle Cumyn, *L'administration du bien d'autrui* (2nd edn, Éditions Yvon Blais 2014), 328–29; Le Breton-Prévost (n 4), 347–51.

[16] *Wong v Burt* [2004] NZCA 174, [2005] 1 NZLR 91, [27]. Many other authorities will be cited in what follows.

exercise of other-regarding powers in conflict situations; this is discussed in the next chapter.

D. Intention, purpose, and motivation

When asking whether a power held for an other-regarding purpose has been rightly used, courts and commentators may speak of intention, purpose, motive or motivation, or some combination of them.[17] Much litigation in the common law world about 'proper purposes' has involved the power of directors of legal persons to issue shares in the corporation of which they are directors. If they do so because the corporation needs more capital, they probably act lawfully. Where shares are issued as a defensive tactic in the face of a takeover, litigation may result as to whether they are using the power for proper purposes or rather misusing it. For the ends of discussion, let us assume that the directors decide to use their power to issue shares to a friendly shareholder, Amelia, because the directors wish to make it more difficult for a hostile shareholder, Barkha, to gain effective control of the corporation.[18]

If we ask about the *intentions* of the board, as we often do in criminal law, we usually focus on a particular outcome or outcomes that the board desired to bring about, or alternatively that they knew would come about whether or not they desired it.[19] Actions are often performed with multiple intentions in this sense. In the criminal law, the only intentions that are relevant are the ones that are elements of a relevant offence. The board's *purposes* could similarly be described by reference to more or less precisely articulated outcomes that were intended: to increase the shareholding of Amelia; to dilute the shareholding of Barkha; to change the control situation; to protect the corporation against an attack perceived as harmful; to keep their jobs. Purposes are similar to intentions—at least, to the primary sense of intention, meaning something that is desired. But in criminal liability, if there is a criminal intention to bring about a forbidden action, any other purposes that may exist are usually irrelevant.

---

[17] For examples of discussion in terms of motive, see *Hogg v Cramphorn Ltd* [1967] Ch 254, 263, 269; *Howard Smith Ltd v Ampol Petroleum Ltd* [1974] AC 821 (PC), 831–32, 834–35; *Eclairs Group Ltd v JKX Oil & Gas plc* [2015] UKSC 71, [15], [18]; Gaillard (n 15), 98–99, 101–2 and *passim*.

[18] The authorities I cite in this corporate law context are generally from Commonwealth courts, but the same principles exist in Delaware corporate law: *Schnell v Chris-Craft Industries Inc* 285 A2d 437 (Del, 1971); *Black v Hollinger International Inc* 844 A2d 1022 (Del Ch, 2004), aff'd 872 A2d 559 (Del, 2005); *Coster v UIP Companies Inc* 255 A3d 952 (Del, 2021); see Strine and others (n 5), 640–44.

[19] Jeremy Horder, *Ashworth's Principles of Criminal Law* (9th edn, OUP 2019), 189–93. Thus a person who puts on a new pair of shoes and wears them on the street intends to degenerate their condition, even if he does not wish to. This less intuitive sense of intention is sometimes called 'oblique' or 'indirect' intention.

The *motive* or *motives* or *motivation* of the board could also be described in different ways. Motives are not the goals of actions but rather reasons for actions, and they are also typically irrelevant in criminal liability. Sometimes, motives are articulated quite generally as a way of giving a context for decision-making; a person might be said to have been motivated by greed, spite, or indeed loyalty.[20] But often, 'motive' and 'motivation' are used in a way very similar to 'purpose': all of the different purposes of the board, mentioned in the previous paragraph, could also be described as motives of the board. This is because although motives are not the goals of actions but rather reasons for actions, if the action is described as the issuing of the shares, then all of those different purposes could also be described as motives for *that* action, the issuing of the shares.[21]

This is why motives, as well as purposes, can be relevant in relation to whether administrative powers have been used loyally.[22] This is particularly so in cases where the purpose for which a power was granted is capable of articulation only in a general way. Assume that it was decided that the purpose for which the board of directors is given the power to issue shares is in order that the board may issue shares when it is, in the view of the board, for the benefit of the corporation. The issuing of shares to Amelia could be described as having the purpose of frustrating Barkha's takeover bid; but if the motive for that purpose could be described as protecting the best interests of the corporation, then the power would have been exercised properly.[23] But this is not the only possible interpretation of the power. A more constrained interpretation of its purpose might restrict the relevance of motives. If it were decided that the purpose for which the board of directors is given the power to issue shares was only to raise capital, then any use of the power to affect control could be said to be for an improper purpose, whatever might be the motive.[24]

Indeed, in some cases motives may be more important than purposes, when purposes are defined as intended outcomes. In one case on share issues, the Privy Council refused to say what exactly was the purpose for which the power to issue shares was granted to directors; they said only that a use of it

---

[20] Richard K Scheer, 'Intentions, Motives, and Causation' (2001) 76 Philosophy 397, 399–401, also distinguishing other senses.
[21] *Oxford English Dictionary*, www.oed.com, sv 'motive, *noun*', 3.a.: '... a contemplated end the desire for which influences or tends to influence a person's actions'.
[22] To quote Maurice Cullity, 'Judicial Control of Trustees' Discretions' (1975) 25 UTLJ 99, 115: 'In this context it is unnecessary to draw any distinction between improper purpose and improper motive.'
[23] *Teck Corp v Millar* (1972) 22 DLR (3d) 288 (BCSC).
[24] This is one reading of *Hogg* (n 17), in which the share issue was invalidated.

solely to affect control was improper.[25] But every issue of shares is likely to affect control.[26] That can be said to be the purpose, or one of the purposes, behind the share issue.[27] In this sense, the only way to tell a proper use of the power from an improper one will be by looking at the motives of the board, and what the Privy Council actually identified was an improper motive for a purpose that might, with a different motivation, have been proper. In its review of the case law, the Privy Council concluded that the cases where the power was used properly were the ones in which the board was motivated by managerial considerations, being considerations other than the balance of control.

A hypothetical example from trust law also illustrates this. Take the case of a trust with beneficiaries A, B, and C, who at some future time will presumptively share the trust property equally. Now assume that the trustee is given a power to allocate the property unequally at that moment of distribution. What is the purpose for which this power was granted? Probably, to allow the trustee to respond to unforeseen events, and to different needs and resources of the beneficiaries that may be evident at the time of distribution. If the trustee makes any unequal division, then his purpose—or one of his purposes—is to make an unequal division. But that is authorized by the power. To tell whether the purpose is improper, we must look at the reasons for forming that purpose. Assume that the trustee has given more to A and B than to C. If it is also true that the trustee so acted because he thought that C had no need of resources while A and B did have need, then the trustee has acted properly; but this describes a motive, not a purpose. If, on the other hand, the same unequal division were made and the evidence showed that the trustee was motivated by spite towards C, there would obviously be a problem even though, articulated in terms of the financial result of the unequal division, the trustee's purpose is the same as in the first case. The proof of spite would lead us to reassess whether the trustee had exercised the power loyally: that is, whether he was guided only by his judgment as to what was the best way to implement the purpose for which it was given.

---

[25] *Howard Smith* (n 17). The Board opined that its holding was consistent with the result in *Teck* (n 23). *Howard Smith* was followed in *Whitehouse v Carlton Hotel Pty Ltd* (1987) 162 CLR 285.

[26] This is not the case where new shares are issued to existing shareholders in precisely the proportions of their prior holdings. Although some corporate constitutions may require that this offer be made, they do not forbid the issuance of shares to others in the case that one or more existing shareholders choose not to subscribe for new shares. Thus even in the presence of such a rule, it never guaranteed that control will be totally unchanged, and if the shares are held widely such a result is quite improbable.

[27] Even if it is not desired, still if it is known to be what will result, it is intended in an important sense (n 19).

II. The role of loyalty

A. The necessity of a requirement of loyalty

The administrator has a mission and has powers to carry it out. This section answers the following question: Why do we need 'loyalty', or some idea like it, to understand the legal regulation of the exercise of those powers?

The reason is directly tied to the fact that in the situations with which we are concerned, the administrator's powers are almost invariably discretionary.[28] This means that the administrator has a certain authority, an authority to make her *own* choices as to how to pursue the mission at hand. In making those choices, the administrator will be deciding whether and how to use her powers. She will exercise her judgment.

Some commentators who have sought to understand the legal regulation of these situations without recourse to any free-standing idea of loyalty have assumed that there can be an objective answer to the question whether the administrator has lawfully carried out his or her mission.[29] On this view, if an administrator never violates any objectively defined duties, then necessarily they have done nothing unlawful. It seems to be true that *if* it were possible to spell out the administrator's task in the ordinary language of obligations—he must do or not do some defined thing, or list of things—then it would indeed be unnecessary to ask whether he had acted loyally.

But it is not possible, and the idea that there is a purely objective answer to the question whether the administrator has fulfilled his mission is a misunderstanding. The administrator is empowered to pursue a mission which is *not* defined by any particular result. The administrator's powers are usually discretionary: they do not require any particular set of actions. They authorize a range of actions and inactions; but within the range of what they authorize, these powers must be used for the right reasons, or (to say the same thing in different words) in pursuit of the right goal. They cannot be used for selfish purposes; this is clear on a moment's reflection. An agent or mandatary holds powers, including usually a power to bind her principal or mandator to contracts. Can we suppose that the agent or mandatary could rightly use that power for her own selfish ends, rather than to promote the interests of the principal or mandator? If she could, we would not consider her to be an agent or mandatary, but rather to be in some other relationship. It is the same with all of the other cases with which we are concerned: it simply does not make sense to imagine that a director of a legal

---

[28] On the rare cases in which the powers are not discretionary, see section III.C.
[29] Conaglen (n 3); Stephen A Smith, 'The Deed, Not the Motive: Fiduciary Law Without Loyalty' in Paul B Miller and Andrew S Gold (eds), *Contract, Status and Fiduciary Law* (OUP 2016) 213.

person, or a tutor or guardian, or a trustee, could rightly use their powers in the pursuit of their own self-regarding ends. Those powers only exist to allow the administrator to serve the ends of the beneficiary, and for this reason, they can only be used rightly when they are used for that end. Take the case of a trustee who complies with all of the objective duties that apply to him, but who has dispositive discretions that allow him to distribute the trust property unequally among the beneficiaries. He uses the power to give all the trust property to one of the beneficiaries because he likes that beneficiary the most. This is not a proper use of the power, but this cannot be revealed by reference only to objective duties; the trustee's power authorized him to do what he did. He acted badly because he did something he was authorized to do but did it for the wrong reasons.

Another example comes from agency (or mandate). An agent is empowered to buy land for the principal. There may be objective limits on the power: a limit of price, and limits as to the area in which land can be bought.[30] There is also an objective duty to use reasonable care and skill. But imagine that the agent complies with all this: he binds the principal to a contract to buy an interest in land that is within the objective limits of place and price, and at a price that any reasonable person would agree is a good one. However, the agent does so for the wrong reasons: unlike most people, he believes that land in this area is overpriced and he believes prices will collapse soon. Surely this agent has not acted properly or lawfully in making the contract.[31] And this is true whether or not prices do, in the end, collapse. And yet, if another agent with the same powers made the same contract for the right reasons—thinking, along with everyone else, that the investment was a good one—then this would be a proper use of those powers. On the basis of objectively articulated obligations judged in terms of outcomes, these two cases cannot be distinguished.

Someone might say that all these examples show a diversion of the power for selfish purposes; but even setting aside the *selfish* use of the powers, a

---

[30] Objective limits are discussed further below, section II.C.1.

[31] Civil law: Gaillard (n 15); Madeleine Cantin Cumyn, 'De l'administration des biens à la protection de la personne d'autrui' in Barreau du Québec—Service de la Formation continue (ed), *Obligations et recours contre un curateur, tuteur ou mandataire défaillant 2008*, vol 283 (Yvon Blais 2008) 205, 215–16; Cantin Cumyn and Cumyn (n 15). Common law: Cullity (n 22); Smith, 'The Motive, Not the Deed' (n 4); Richard Nolan, 'Controlling Fiduciary Power' (2009) 68 CLJ 293; Strine and others (n 5), 633, 655, 672–73 and *passim*; Stephen Galoob and Ethan J Leib, 'Fiduciary Loyalty, Inside and Out' (2018) 92 S Cal L Rev 69, 91–96. In my view, Nolan fails (at 297–304) to appreciate the subjective nature of the inquiry, which I elaborate in the next section of the text (and which is discussed briefly in Smith, 'The Motive, Not the Deed' (n 4), 71–72). In construing a power, courts may find not only its objective limits but also the purposes for the achievement of which it was granted; but whether an administrator has used the power loyally requires an inquiry into whether the administrator's subjective purpose matched the purpose for which it was granted (see the explication of this in *Grand View Private Trust Co v Wong* (n 8), [61], [72]). Nolan's discussion (at 304) of the difficulty of applying the 'proper purposes' doctrine to boards of directors shows, however, that he is somewhat aware that it involves a subjective inquiry.

requirement of loyal exercise is still needed.[32] Take the case of a trustee who has a discretionary investment power. Imagine that the trustee satisfies the objective standard of the duty of care, skill, and diligence by producing, through research and work, lists of potential investments that are objectively reasonable in terms of a sound assessment of the balance of risk and return. Then assume that this trustee makes the final decision as to which investments should be acquired by flipping coins or rolling dice. It would be wrong to say this person has complied with their mission or mandate, even though they have satisfied all the applicable objective standards. On the contrary, they have misused their power, because it could only rightly be used in the pursuit of what the trustee thought were the best interests of the beneficiaries. The trustee must exercise judgment, not flip coins.[33]

This is one of the reasons why relationships of administration cannot be fully understood according to the standard tools of private law. I do not claim that the only inquiry is the one now under discussion; there are many aspects of the legal regulation of these situations that are purely objective. These will be addressed in what follows.[34] But I do claim the following: even if the administrator complies with all of the objective requirements that apply to the exercise of his powers, nonetheless if he uses those powers for the wrong purposes, he uses them improperly. The powers are only used properly when they are used in what the administrator believes is the best pursuit of his or her mission. This requirement of subjective loyalty in the exercise of powers is an essential (but not exhaustive) part of understanding the legal regulation of acting for others.

B. The necessity of a *subjective* requirement of loyalty

In the previous section, I suggested that the requirement of loyalty is subjective. It is not quite right to say that an agent (for example) must, in exercising his powers, act in the best interests of his principal. The agent must act in what *he perceives to be* the best interests of his principal.[35]

---

[32] 'Self-interest is only one, though no doubt the commonest, instance of improper motive': *Howard Smith* (n 17), 834, *per* Lord Wilberforce; see also *Whitehouse* (n 25), 293: 'In this as in other areas involving the exercise of fiduciary power, the exercise of a power for an ulterior or impermissible purpose is bad notwithstanding that the motives of the donee of the power in so exercising it are substantially altruistic.'
[33] Not that different is the case of *Turner v Turner* [1984] Ch 100 (ChD), in which trustees exercised their discretionary powers as instructed by the settlor. In one sense the trustees clearly and objectively carried out the assignment that the settlor had given them, having done exactly what he wanted; but these exercises were held to be invalid. The case is discussed below, section IV.E.1.
[34] Objective constraints, below, section II.C; objective rules about conflicts, in Chapter 4; objective rules about unauthorized profits, in Chapter 5; and other objective duties, in Chapter 6.
[35] Authority is cited immediately below after the argument is presented. Speaking more generally across contexts, an administrator must use her powers in what she perceives to be the best pursuit of the mission that was assigned to her. We will return to this generalization below (section IV.A).

Why is this important? It captures an essential aspect of the juridical situation, which is that the discretionary powers are *held by* the administrator, who exercises *his* judgment in their use. Although he does not hold them for his personal benefit, he is the one who holds them. This is part of what it means to say that they are discretionary; there is no objective answer given by the law as to how they must be exercised. But it has the further implication that the discretion that belongs to the administrator does not belong to anyone else. In relation to the objective limits on the powers, there is a legally correct answer as to whether any particular use of the power is permissible.[36] But within the range of options that are objectively legally permissible, the administrator exercises personal judgment. Within that range, if the administrator uses their judgment loyally, then no one else—not even a court—can say, in this context, that the administrator's decision was incorrect. If a court could—if there was always a legally determined correct course of action—then there would not be a discretionary power.

> The principles to be applied in cases where the articles of a company confer a discretion on directors . . . are, for the present purposes, free from doubt. They must exercise their discretion bona fide in what they consider—not what a court may consider—is in the interests of the company, and not for any collateral purpose.[37]

The fact that the decision *belongs* to the administrator applies across contexts, albeit under different names. In trust law, the courts may speak of a principle of non-intervention;[38] in corporate law, of the 'business judgment rule'.[39] These are effectively jurisdictional principles: unless the administrator has done something unlawful, the decision is theirs, not the court's.[40]

This is another reason why relationships of administration cannot be fully understood according to the standard tools of private law, such as the law of obligations. The relevant power both belongs to the administrator, and does not.

---

[36] Discussed below, section II.C.
[37] *Re Smith and Fawcett Ltd* [1942] Ch 304 (CA), 306.
[38] *Lehtimäki* (n 8); see also *Ex parte Lloyd* (1882) 47 LT 64 (CA) and *Re Burger Estate* [1949] 1 WWR 280 (Alta SC), 285–86, in which the Court simply refused to answer the trustees' question, on an application for directions, whether they should sell a particular investment, on the ground that the decision belonged to them and not the Court. This is quite a strict decision, as usually courts are willing to give advice and direction when it is sought, on the view that this does not infringe on the principle of non-intervention.
[39] In the words of Amir Licht, the business judgment rule '. . . boils down to a requirement that in exercising their powers, corporate fiduciaries fulfill their duties of loyalty and care. Or, put even more simply, that they act lawfully': Amir N Licht, 'Farewell to Fairness: Towards Retiring Delaware's Entire Fairness Review' (2020) 44 Del J Corp L 1, 13.
[40] The inability of the court to interfere with properly made decisions of corporate directors was said to be a matter of jurisdiction in *Re Gresham Life Assurance Society* (1872) LR 8 Ch App 446 (CA), 449.

It *belongs* to the administrator jurisdictionally: the relevant decision is theirs alone, and the law does not dictate what they must do. It is a fundamental mistake to think that the law gives a single right answer to how an administrator must act.[41] But in another sense the power *does not* belong to the administrator; this is true not only in the sense that they cannot use the power however they wish, but also in the sense that it can always be taken away from them in one way or another.[42]

It is because the discretionary power belongs jurisdictionally to the administrator that the requirement of loyal exercise is subjective in nature. It is not the case that a trustee must act in what is, objectively, the best interests of the beneficiary; if it were, then he would not really have any discretion at all. Indeed, in many contexts it makes little sense to ask what is objectively in the best interests of the beneficiary. Take the case of trustee investing: what a particular trustee thinks is in the best interests of the beneficiaries will depend on a range of assumptions which that trustee makes about the future, and on the trustee's exercise of judgment in relation to present facts, including the needs of the beneficiaries. Prudence, or objectively reasonable care, will impose certain limits, but prudence alone cannot exhaustively determine which investments should be made.[43] Within a range of objectively reasonable possibilities, what the trustee thinks is in the best interests of the beneficiaries will depend on the individual trustee, including his or her assessment of the balance between risk and reward, and between the short term and the long term.

This is why the correct formulation is the subjective one: the administrator must act in what he perceives to be the best interests of the beneficiary, or more

---

[41] It is arguable that some versions of 'shareholder primacy' theory fall into this 'one right answer' fallacy: Edward Iacobucci, 'Indeterminacy and the Canadian Supreme Court's Approach to Corporate Fiduciary Duties' (2009) 48 CBLJ 232; Jeffery MacIntosh, 'BCE and the Peoples' Corporate Law: Learning to Live on Quicksand' (2009) 48 CBLJ 255. These authors are uncomfortable with the wide range of decision-making independence that corporate law gives to directors, but this is how almost all relationships of administration operate (the exception being those where the administrator is obliged to follow the instructions of the beneficiary: Chapter 1, section V.B.3.c). An investor who does not want the person managing the invested funds to have any discretion should not choose the corporate form unless the investor controls the corporation.

[42] Chapter 2, section III.B.7.

[43] Objective limits on loyalty are discussed in the next section. In an extreme case of a tightly restricted investment power, a trustee might not have any discretion as to investments; there would then be nothing for trustee loyalty to regulate. In a trust, however, such terms are liable to be struck out on application to the court, as they are often liable to defeat the purposes of the trust (see John H Langbein, 'Mandatory Rules in the Law of Trusts' (2004) 98 Northwestern U L Rev 1105). This is one of several reasons why 'contractarian' views of trust law are unconvincing. Where the general mission assigned to the trustee by the settlor—in this case, to further the best interests of the beneficiaries—conflicts with some particular wish of the settlor, the former may prevail where the particular provision is judged to be a badly designed attempt to implement the general mission. In a contract it would be the other way around. As we have seen, the same logic explains beneficiaries' ability to terminate trusts in the common law (Chapter 2, section III.B.3).

generally the best pursuit of the purpose for which the power was granted.[44] This has the consequence that if we imagine two different administrators in identical situations, they might be required, by their own individual assessments of the situation, to act differently. If Agent 1 believes that it is in the best interests of her principal to accept an offer to buy an interest in land, then loyalty requires her to do so. If Agent 2, in the identical situation, has a different subjective assessment and believes that the price being asked is too high, then loyalty requires him to reject the offer. Loyalty does not necessarily dictate a single right answer.

Note that the interpretive exercise of deciding what was the purpose for which the power was granted to the administrator is itself an objective exercise; very often in private law, the answer will be, 'for the protection and promotion of the interests of the beneficiary'.[45] It is the inquiry into whether the administrator used the power loyally that must necessarily be subjective, because we must compare that administrator's subjective state of mind to the objectively assessed purpose for which the power was granted. It is important to remember that the subjective standard does not mean that an administrator can do whatever they wish and then simply claim that they thought it was in the best interests of the beneficiary. A subjective inquiry does not imply that anyone has to believe everything that the administrator says.[46] Note too that just because the administrator acted loyally, it does not follow that their action was lawful; they may have breached another legal norm, such as the duty of prudence and diligence, or of care and skill.[47] And separately again, their actions, even if they were loyal, may have exposed them to removal from their role.[48]

One response to my argument would be the following: the requirement of loyalty could be formulated objectively, without necessarily being understood as pointing to a single authorized course of action. In general, administrators in

---

[44] *Re Smith and Fawcett Ltd* (n 37); *Regentcrest plc (in liquidation) v Cohen* [2001] 2 BCLC 80 (ChD), [120]; *F & C Alternative Investments (Holdings) Ltd v Barthelemy (No 2)* [2011] EWHC 1731 (Ch), [2012] Ch 613, [253]; *Eclairs Group Ltd* (n 17), [15]; *Lehtimäki* (n 8), [29], [100], [180], [187] (the majority judges add a nuance to this (at [232]) but here they refer precisely to the matters discussed below in section II.C ('Further limitations')); *Grand View Private Trust Co v Wong* (n 8), [72]; see also the many cases cited in Smith, 'The Motive, Not the Deed' (n 4), Strine and others (n 5), and David Pollard, 'The Short-Form "Best Interests Duty"—Mad, Bad and Dangerous to Know' (2018) 32 Trust Law International 106 and 176, 184–87. For an argument that the subjective approach to loyalty should be accepted in Japanese law, see Eriko Taoka, 'Shaping and Re-shaping the Duty of Loyalty in Japanese Law' (2019) 14 Asian J of Comp Law S119.

[45] *Grand View Private Trust Co v Wong* (n 8); for the objective exercise of finding the purpose, see [61]; for the subjective inquiry as to the administrator's actual purpose, see [72]. It is not, however, always the case in private law that the purpose is the promotion of someone's interests (below, section III.B); still less is this the case in public law (see Chapter 9).

[46] Subjective mind states (such as a subjective intention to bring about an outcome) are routinely required in criminal law, and are proven by evidence every day all over the world; and this, in common law jurisdictions, to the standard of 'beyond a reasonable doubt'.

[47] Chapter 6, section III.

[48] Chapter 2, section III.B.

private law are subject to a duty to use reasonable care and skill, in the common law formulation, or to be prudent and diligent, in the civilian formulation. This duty is formulated objectively; but it does not point to a single authorized course of action. Care, skill, diligence, and prudence are, in this context, matters relating to the process by which decisions are made. Hence the duty (which I will call simply the duty of care for the remainder of this section) qualifies a range of possible decisions as unlawful, because they are reached in ways that are unreasonably careless or unreasonably unskilful; but the duty also qualifies as lawful a whole range of possible decisions, being reached both carefully and with reasonable skill. Within that range of lawful activity, the duty of care does not point to any particular decision. Why could loyalty not work in the same way?

This approach suggests that we could make loyalty into an objective inquiry, by asking whether a decision could reasonably (but objectively) be understood as one that was in the best interests of the beneficiary. On this approach, the requirement of loyalty, like the duty of care, would qualify a range of possibilities as ones which could *objectively* be seen as being in the best interests of the other.

There are three reasons, or three aspects of the same reason, why this approach does not work. The first problem is that this would have the effect that loyalty would not really be any different from the duty of care. The duty of care applies an objective control to all the possible courses of action and qualifies some of them as unlawful. The objective version of loyalty would be nothing but another objective duty of care, formulated slightly differently. The only difference might be in relation to the recourses generated.[49] But it is universally recognized, in case law and commentary, in common law and in civil law, that what is required by the duty of care is different from what is required by loyalty.

Conversely, this objective formulation would permit the misuse of powers. This is illustrated by the example, given above, of the agent who contracts in the name of the principal in a way that is objectively reasonable but where the agent subjectively believes that loss to the principal will result. It is not enough for an administrator to act objectively reasonably; if he acts for what are subjectively the wrong reasons, he misuses his powers. That is precisely why a subjective requirement of loyalty is essential to the regulation of these situations. It adds a separate and necessary standard to the objective requirement of the duty of care.

Third, it would not be possible to make sense of the rules about conflicts if loyalty were entirely objective. If it were wholly objective, there would be no need for a separate regulation of conflicts, because it would always be possible to determine, objectively, whether a person had acted in accordance with loyalty. The

---

[49] The disloyal exercise of a power can generally be set aside (below, section IV.E); a breach of the duty of care and skill does not allow this but presumptively allows the recovery of loss caused, including pure economic loss (Chapter 6, section III).

rules about conflicts exist precisely because loyalty is subjective: the conflict rules mark out the dangerous situations in which it is impossible to be sure that the administrator has acted with (subjective) loyalty.[50] If loyalty were purely objective, there would be no such situations.

Of course, the rules about conflicts are themselves objective. The reasons for this will be discussed in the next chapter. But so far from undermining the need for a subjective standard of loyalty, this actually supports it. As I have just explained, there would be no need for the conflicts rules if the requirement of loyal exercise was objective. If someone were to argue that the objective rules about conflicts *are* the objective standard that is applied to loyalty regarding the exercise of powers, the argument would fail, for two distinct reasons. First, this argument fails completely to explain why the law says that the subjectively disloyal exercise of a power can be set aside even in the absence of any conflict.[51] The second problem can be illustrated by comparing two scenarios, A and B. In both, a mandatary makes a contract for the purchase of goods in the name of her mandator, within the authority granted to her. In both scenarios, the price paid is objectively a fair and reasonable price. But in scenario A, the mandatary is in a conflict of interest, say due to having a financial interest in the company that is the seller of goods; in scenario B, there is no conflict. The law is clear that the exercise of the power of representation is improper in scenario A but not in scenario B.[52] On my view, this makes sense because the conflict in scenario A means that we cannot be certain whether the mandatary used the power with the right motives; her self-interest, an improper motive, may have influenced her exercise of judgment. But if we tried to say that the question whether she used the power properly is answered entirely objectively, we would be left with no reason to distinguish between the two scenarios, since the same objective contract was made in each case. There is no logical way to tie the objective rule about conflicts to the validity of the exercise of the power, except on the basis that the propriety of the exercise of the power depends upon the subjective integrity of the mandatary's exercise of her judgment.[53]

Nor should this be at all surprising. An administrator is given discretionary authority to make decisions, and it follows necessarily that different administrators

---

[50] This is elaborated in Chapter 4.
[51] See the sources of positive law in n 31.
[52] The contract may be liable to be set aside: below, section IV.E.
[53] Some authors have argued that the way to link them is by assigning a deterrent function to the conflict rules. Because it relies on profit-stripping as the primary deterrent, this approach depends upon conflating the rule against unauthorized profits with the rules about conflicts. This conflation is demonstrably inconsistent with the law, because the exercise of powers in conflict situations can be set aside whether or not there is a profit, and unauthorized profits must be surrendered even in the absence of a conflict. This is explained in Chapters 4 and 5, where it is shown that the rules on conflicts have different foundations from the rule about unauthorized profits, and that deterrent accounts of the rule about unauthorized profits are inadequate.

may use that authority differently, each of them acting lawfully and properly. Every one of them is subject not only to objective constraints, but to the subjective constraint that they must use the powers in what they believe to be the best pursuit of their mission.

C. Further limitations

1. Objective limitations on authority that are separate from loyalty

Although loyalty involves a subjective inquiry, there may be many limitations on the administrator's authority that can be articulated objectively. These limitations are *in addition* to the legal requirement that the powers of the administrator be exercised loyally.

Some examples have been mentioned already. For one thing, there is an overarching requirement that all decisions made by an administrator comply with a general duty of care and skill, which is objective in nature and which governs the process by which decisions are reached.[54]

In addition to this, the particular mission can set out any number of objective limitations. A trustee can be given a list of authorized investments; an unauthorized investment is not permitted, regardless of the trustee's subjective opinion. Similarly, a trustee may have the discretionary authority to distribute trust property among a class of persons, such as the settlor's children; a distribution to the settlor's nephew would be unlawful. An agent or mandatary may be given objective limitations on price or subject matter, in relation to the contracts that she may make. A director of a legal person may well be constrained by limitations on the activities that the legal person can carry out. Activities outside those limitations would be unlawful, regardless of whether the director thought that they were in the best interests of the legal person. Similarly, directors of legal persons may have the power to issue new shares, but in modern corporate law statutes, typically they may only do so if the full price of the shares is paid to the corporation. They have the power to declare dividends of income, but typically only out of profits.

All of these objective limitations identify the limits of the administrator's powers. Attempts to act outside of them typically involve simply an absence of power, rather than a disloyal use or misuse of a power. These limitations can have many sources. In a trust, they can either be in the trust deed or other instrument that constitutes the trust; or, they can be imposed by the general law. Rules on authorized investments may be imposed by the general law as default rules that will apply unless they are disapplied by the trust instrument. So too in the setting of

---

[54] Discussed further in Chapter 6, section III.

legal persons: limitations may be in the corporate constitution, or in the general law governing legal persons or the kind of legal person in question. For an agent or mandatary, such objective limitations may well be in the original mandate or grant of authority; moreover, unlike in most trusts, the terms of a mandate or agency can be modified from time to time.[55] We have already seen that it is an important feature of this kind of administration that the authority of the agent or the mandatary—in other terms, his or her powers—are always subject to modification or revocation by the principal or mandatary.[56]

In fact the wholly 'open' case, in which there are no objective limitations at all, probably does not exist. By this I mean the case in which the administrator can do anything he wishes with the powers that he holds as such, subject only to the requirement of loyalty that he act in what he perceives to be the best interests of the beneficiary. Rare would be a trust in which the trustee can do whatever he or she wishes with the trust property, or an agency which allows the agent to make any contract at all in the name of the principal, so long as they are acting in what they perceive to be the best interests of the beneficiary. The most unconstrained relationships of administration in private law may be in relation to the management of the financial affairs of incapacitated persons. Whether the authority was given by the incapacitated person while still capacitated, or was given by a court order, the authority of the guardian in such a case is typically very wide. Even here, however, some objective limits apply. Take the case of Ontario law; when the court appoints a guardian:

> A guardian of property has power to do on the incapable person's behalf anything in respect of property that the person could do if capable, except make a will.[57]

The limitation as to will-making reflects a general principle, arising from the idea that a will must be authored by the testator.[58] The legislation confirms that the guardian is in a fiduciary relationship;[59] but it also imposes some further objective restrictions on what the guardian can do. These include the requirement to take account of wishes that were validly expressed by the now-incapacitated

---

[55] In the common law, the categories of agency and trust are not analytically distinct inasmuch as an agent may hold property on a bare trust, whose terms are amendable on the fly by the principal/beneficiary (see *Trident Holdings Ltd v Danand Investments Ltd* (1988) 64 OR (2d) 65, 49 DLR (4th) 1 (CA)). Quebec civil law does not recognize trusts in which the trustee is under the control of the beneficiary: *Bank of Nova Scotia v Thibault* 2004 SCC 29, [2004] 1 SCR 758.
[56] Chapter 1, section V.B.3.c.
[57] *Substitute Decisions Act, 1992*, SO 1992, c 30, s 31(1); for an attorney appointed by private act, s 7(2).
[58] Lionel Smith, 'What Is Left of the Non-Delegation Principle?' in Birke Häcker and Charles Mitchell (eds), *Current Issues in Succession Law* (Hart 2016) 209.
[59] *Substitute Decisions Act* (n 57), s 32(1).

person while they still had capacity, or wishes that they are still be able to express.[60] It may also require that attention be paid to how property decisions will affect the comfort of the incapacitated person, and coordination with the decisions being made as to health care.[61] Moreover, if the incapacitated person has made a will leaving specific property to someone, the guardian should not dispose of that property unless it is necessary.[62] Again, while it is possible for the guardian to make gifts of the property of the incapacitated person, these are subject to certain objective restraints.[63]

And in every case, the administrator is precluded from choosing courses of action that are contrary to the general law.[64] This includes infringing the private rights of others. The Privy Council once held that a testamentary executor is under no duty to breach a contract, even if he thinks it would be in the best interests of the estate beneficiaries to do so.[65] A private law administrator cannot commit or procure the commission of an extracontractual wrong simply because he thinks this would be in the best interests of his beneficiary.[66] The case is even clearer for criminally unlawful conduct.[67]

2. Narrower formulations of what loyalty requires

Thus the normal situation of acting for another in private law involves a combination of constraints. Certain objective limits on the administrator's powers will be combined with an overriding requirement of loyalty: a requirement that the administrator use her powers in what she perceives to be the best interests of the beneficiary.

There are situations in which these combinations are more subtle. It was mentioned above that the exercise of interpreting the grant of the relevant power, to decide for what purpose it may rightly be used, is itself an objective exercise. The required subjective inquiry is into how, and for what purposes, the power *was actually used* in the particular case.

---

[60] Civil Code of Québec, art 12; *Substitute Decisions Act*, ibid s 66(3).
[61] *Substitute Decisions Act*, ibid ss 32(1.1)–(1.2).
[62] ibid s 35.1.
[63] ibid ss 37(3)–(5).
[64] *Desimone v Barrows* 924 A2d 908 (Del Ch, 2007), 934–35: '. . . it is utterly inconsistent with [a director's] duty of fidelity to the corporation to consciously cause the corporation to act unlawfully. The knowing use of illegal means to pursue profit for the corporation is director misconduct'.
[65] *Ahmed Anguillia bin Hadjee Mohamed Salleh Anguillia v Estate and Trust Agencies (1927) Ltd* [1938] AC 624 (PC).
[66] *ADGA Systems International Ltd v Valcom Ltd* (1999) 43 OR (3d) 101 (CA), leave to appeal to Supreme Court of Canada dismissed (April 6, 2000, File No. 27184).
[67] Bruce Welling, 'Individual Liability for Corporate Acts: The Defence of Hobson's Choice' in Lionel Smith (ed), *Ruled by Law: Essays in Memory of Mr Justice John Sopinka* (LexisNexis Butterworths 2003) 55; Andrew S Gold, 'The New Concept of Loyalty in Corporate Law' (2009) 43 UC Davis L Rev 457, 475–77.

But the interpretation of the power may lead to a narrower formulation of its purpose. Rather than a conclusion that the administrator must use it in what he perceives to be the best interests of the beneficiary, the purpose of the power may be articulated more specifically. And the subjective inquiry into whether the power was used properly will be measured against this narrower formulation of the power's purpose. A well-known example comes from the English trusts case *Cowan v Scargill*, and the developments that have followed from it.[68] *Cowan* involved trustees' powers of investment, in a pension trust for beneficiaries who worked in the coal industry. The issue was whether the trustees could follow an investment policy that involved avoiding investment in industries that competed with the coal industry, on the grounds that protecting the coal industry would be in the best long-term interests of the beneficiaries, including those who were not yet retired. In a well-known judgment, Megarry V-C said:

> [Trustees] must, of course, obey the law; but subject to that, they must put the interests of their beneficiaries first. When the purpose of the trust is to provide financial benefits for the beneficiaries, as is usually the case, the best interests of the beneficiaries are normally their best financial interests. . . . In considering what investments to make trustees must put on one side their own personal interests and views. . . . Powers must be exercised fairly and honestly for the purposes for which they are given and not so as to accomplish any ulterior purpose, whether for the benefit of the trustees or otherwise.[69]

This is an example of a phenomenon we have already seen: loyalty to 'best interests', particularly of a large number of persons, may be capable of articulation as loyalty to a purpose: the purpose which led them to participate in the relevant enterprise.[70] Pension members participated in the pension plan to invest and save for their retirements. The result in *Cowan* was that the purposes for which the investment power could properly be used were defined more specifically than in terms of a general 'best interests' standard. The formulation in terms of 'best financial interests' also relieves the trustees from any requirement to address the particular circumstances of individual beneficiaries, which would generally be impossible in a trust of this kind.

Of course, in line with what was said in the previous section about objective limitations on an administrator's powers, it is quite possible for a trust or other structure to include investment criteria or restrictions which the general law would not apply. These might involve avoiding certain investments, or favouring

---

[68] *Cowan v Scargill* [1985] Ch 270.
[69] ibid 287, 288.
[70] This was discussed in Chapter 1, section V.B.3.a.

others, for a whole range of reasons. In cases where there were no such norms, *Cowan* was read by many as making it impossible for trustees to adopt a policy of 'ethical investment'; but later developments suggest that this was mistaken.[71] Such a policy could not be supported if it existed merely to indulge the trustees' own personal preferences; that would involve a disloyal use of the investment power. Quite different is the case of trustees who subjectively believe that some investment policy is in the best interests—perhaps the best long-term interests—of the beneficiaries; or, that the policy aligns with the known or presumed wishes of beneficiaries, without having any material effect on investment returns.[72]

Perhaps the best way to reconcile *Cowan* with later developments is simply to understand it as imposing a qualification to the basic 'best interests' standard: a qualification which requires administrators to take account of the purpose of the structure in question, which structure inevitably exists to support the interests of its members.[73] In the case of a pension fund, then, one might say that in considering what is in the best interests of the member beneficiaries, trustees *must* consider their financial interests. Trustees thus could not make investment decisions solely on the basis of considerations related to (say) the unhealthiness of the lawful products of a business (as in the case of tobacco). But, subject to any contrary indication in the trust instrument, such considerations could be taken into account, so long as it was in the context of considering the best interests of the beneficiaries, and so long as that consideration included their financial interests. As is usually the case with investment powers and with many other powers of administration, it lies within the authority of pension trustees to balance risk and return, and to decide whether to take a longer-term or a shorter-term perspective.

There have been developments in corporate law which could be understood in the same light. Over several decades, Canadian cases confirmed the principle that corporate directors must make their decisions in what they considered to be the best interests of the corporation, which is a legal person and therefore has interests of its own in legal analysis.[74] By refusing to constrain that test in any narrower terms, courts left directors with a wider range of lawful possibilities in the use of their powers than would otherwise be the case. Conversely, English

---

[71] For charitable trusts, see *Harries v Church Commissioners for England* [1992] 1 WLR 1241 and *Butler-Sloss v Charity Commission* [2022] EWHC 974 (Ch); for pension trusts, see *R (Palestine Solidarity Campaign Ltd)* (n 8), [43], suggesting that non-financial factors may be considered by pension trustees if they have good reason to think that members would also wish those factors to be considered, and that taking account of the factors does not involve a risk of significant financial detriment.

[72] Lord Nicholls, 'Trustees and Their Broader Community: Where Duty, Morality and Ethics Converge' (1995) 9 Trust Law International 71.

[73] See *Merchant Navy Ratings Pension Fund Trustees Ltd v Stena Line Ltd* [2015] EWHC 448 (Ch), [228], quoted in Chapter 1, section V.B.3.a.

[74] An example is the decision in *Teck Corp* (n 23).

and Australian cases held that was not enough that directors used their power to issue shares in what they thought were the best interests of the corporation; that power was further constrained inasmuch as it could not be used to alter the control situation.[75] Here they arguably took an approach that one could compare to *Cowan*: in addition to requiring loyalty according to the general standard of using the power in what the directors thought was the corporation's best interests, they further narrowed the range of permissible uses of the power. This narrowing was based on their view of the correct interpretation of the purpose for which the power was granted.

In more recent Canadian litigation, it was argued that at least in the context of a change-of-control transaction, even the basic 'best interests' test has only one possible meaning: it means that directors must take the course of action that leads to the highest possible share price.[76] The Supreme Court of Canada rightly rejected this approach, which is flawed for several reasons. First, by proposing that the directors be required to look *only* at the interests of shareholders, this approach ignores the legal personality of the corporation, which is the most fundamental principle of corporate law.[77] If the corporation is a person in law, it necessarily has interests cognizable in law.[78] Second, by proposing that directors are constrained to a single course of action, this approach ignores the basic character of the role of the director, which is to make discretionary decisions aimed at promoting the well-being of the corporate entity. It is up to the directors to decide, for example, whether to take a longer-term or shorter-term approach, and how to balance risks and rewards in relation to business opportunities as well as change-of-control proposals.[79] The law does not give a single, correct answer; if it did, being a director would be like being a computer.[80] But in fact, a director or

---

[75] These cases were discussed in section I.D.

[76] *BCE Inc v 1976 Debentureholders* 2008 SCC 69, [2008] 3 SCR 560.

[77] In any event, shareholder interests may not be uniform. Many corporations have multiple share classes; the interests of some of them (those historically called 'preferred' or 'preference' shares) may well align more with the interests of creditors than with the interests of shareholders of other classes. Moreover, in the context of dividends, the interests of the corporation do not align with those of shareholders. For a clear statement that the interests of shareholders are only a factor in the directors' overall assessment of the best interests of the corporation, see also *McClurg v Canada* [1990] 3 SCR 1020, 1040–41, 1044–46.

[78] *Pramatha Nath Mullick v Pradyumna Kumar Mullock* (1925) LR 52 Ind App 245 (PC). Although it is not necessary, inasmuch as every legal person has legally cognizable interests, statutes that enact corporate personality often also enact that corporations have interests, eg Canada Business Corporations Act, RSC 1985, c C-44, ss 121(1)(a), 121(1.1), 124(3)(a), 239(2)(c). Iacobucci (n 41) suggests (235) that it is 'nonsensical' that a corporation has interests, but this seems not only to ignore the positive law but also to confuse economic analysis with legal analysis. It is clear that the legal rights and legal duties of a corporation are separate from those of its shareholders, and the same is true for legally cognizable interests.

[79] It seems clear that corporate law has always allowed directors to make decisions for the long as well as the short term; following the decision in *BCE Inc* (n 76), this was made explicit in the *Canada Business Corporations Act*, RSC 1985, c C-44, ss 121(1.1)(c).

[80] In other words, this approach adopts the 'one right answer' fallacy (n 41). Martin Gelter and Geneviève Helleringer, 'Constituency Directors and Corporate Fiduciary Duties' in Andrew S Gold and Paul B Miller (eds), *Philosophical Foundations of Fiduciary Law* (OUP 2014) 302, 319, noting the

any other administrator is a person charged with a mission involving the exercise of their judgment.

But an analogy with what was said above about *Cowan* could be formulated in this way: although it belongs to the directors to decide what course of action they believe is in the best interests of the corporation, there is an objective constraint on their decision-making: they must take account of the financial interests of the shareholders. Just as a pension trust exists to provide financial benefits to its beneficiaries, a business corporation exists to provide financial benefits to its shareholders.[81] At the same time, in both contexts, decision-making authority has been entrusted to an administrator (trustee or director), and this cannot be ignored. Moreover, the choice of the corporate form is the choice of a legal form that makes shareholders into interested third parties in the relationship of administration between the directors and the corporation. Of course, when the corporate entity prospers, so do the shareholders; but it would be a fundamental mistake to think that it follows from this that they, the shareholders, are directly owed the duties that the directors owe to the corporation, any more than shareholders are the creditors when someone owes money to the corporation, or shareholders are landowners when the corporation holds an interest in land.[82]

D. Conclusion

It is universally the case that there are objective limitations on the decisions that an administrator can make in private law. Despite these objective limitations, however, the requirement of loyalty that applies to the exercise of an administrator's powers cannot be entirely objective. For one thing, this would make the law helpless to restrain badly motivated decision-making: decisions in which the administrator complies with all of the objective limitations that apply, but misuses the power in the sense of using it for some improper reason. The subjective core of the requirement of loyalty demands that the power be used for

---

agenda-setting autonomy of directors, suggest that directors can themselves 'determine the content of the duty of loyalty'. The implication is that the law should tell directors exactly what to do. Directors do not determine what the law requires of them, but they do have the authority to decide what is in the corporation's best interests.

[81] This of course is not true of other legal persons (like government investment funds or universities).

[82] The interested status of shareholders is what may give them, in certain circumstances, powers to enforce rights that belong to the corporation (Chapter 8, section II.C.2.c). Representative enforcement does not demonstrate that the rights are rights of the shareholders; creditors may also be rightly given the power to enforce rights of the corporation. See the discussion in *Stanford International Bank Ltd v HSBC Bank plc* [2022] UKSC 34: although the dissenting judgment of Lord Sales rightly notes that the interests of creditors may be a proper consideration in relation to the directors' assessment of the corporation's best interests, it does not follow (as his reasoning would seem to imply) that a loss suffered by a creditor is a loss suffered by the corporation.

the pursuit of the administrator's mission. Equally importantly, the subjective aspect of loyalty helps us to understand the rules about conflicts, which would otherwise present an insoluble puzzle. Those rules, however, are the subject of the next chapter.

III. Who is required to exercise powers loyally?

A. Introduction

This study is of situations in which a person has acquired powers in order to carry out a mission. But the word 'power' has to be understood in a particular way. We have already seen that it is a word with many meanings.[83] To recap what was said there: our concern here is with legal powers, being powers to change legal relations that are implemented by manifestations of volition or consent. Moreover, we are concerned with particular powers—that is, powers that not everyone holds—and within those, with such powers as carry with them lawful authority to use the power.

B. How is the power held?

Even with all those restrictions in place, the most important one is still to come. Once we are within the field of particular legal powers coupled with authority, we have to ask how the power is held. There are very many situations in which one person holds legal powers, which they may lawfully use, but without being bound to use them loyally; that is because they were not acquired by the holder in order to allow that holder to carry out an other-regarding mission.

For example, both parties to an employment contract can terminate the relationship on giving appropriate notice. This is a legal power and it may very seriously affect the other party. The balance of power almost always lies on the side of the employer, although in rare cases the opposite may be true, as in the case of the 'star' employee. But it is quite obvious that the power held by each party to terminate the contract is not like the powers that a trustee has over the trust property. Each party to the employment contract holds a power to terminate that contract as part of their own wealth; they may use it, quite properly, for themselves. The power is thus held in the way that rights and other prerogatives are generally held: for the use and benefit of the holder. The same is true of the power that a secured creditor may have, to sell the property of her debtor if there has been a

---

[83] Chapter 1, section IV.A.2.

default. This is a particular legal power, to transfer the debtor's rights to a third party; but the creditor can use it for his own benefit.

1. For the accomplishment of an other-regarding mission

Loyalty in the exercise of powers is required where those powers have been given to a person in order to equip them to carry out an other-regarding mission.[84] In all of the relationships covered by this Part II.A—the core cases of private law administration—the administrator is required to use their powers with loyalty. This is because the powers granted to the administrator to equip them to pursue their mission are not held by that person as a kind of asset that they can exploit for their own benefit.

In the common law, the core cases—trustees, agents, business partners, directors of legal persons, executors, and administrators of estates—are often called per se fiduciary relationships. Corresponding relationships in the civil law are also clearly ones in which the administrator must act with loyalty: mandataries (including partners and other non-gratuitous management relationships), directors, and everyone who manages the property of another. Often this is expressly provided by a text of law, such as a civil code.[85] In other cases, it may depend on case law or doctrine, but there is still categorical recognition of these relationships as ones of administration. Not every civilian system is codified, and even in codified systems, the requirement loyalty in the exercise of powers may be applicable without direct codal support.[86] Determining whether or not that is the case requires the construction of the power and the characterization of the relationship.[87] The civilian tradition tends to set great store in the process of characterizing relationships, with each defined relationship attracting a range of incidents.[88]

---

[84] The earliest observation to this effect seems to be that of Jeremy Bentham: Chapter 1, section IV.A.1.

[85] For example, Civil Code of Québec, arts 322 (directors), 1309 (administrators of the property of others, including trustees), 2088 (employees), 2138 (mandataries, including business partners). The French text refers to *loyauté* while the English text usually says 'faithfully' (but 'with . . . loyalty' in art 322). As in common law, the loyalty required of employees is importantly different: see Chapter 7, section II.B.

[86] Cantin Cumyn (n 31); Stefan Grundmann, 'Trust and Treuhand at the End of the 20th Century—Key Problems and Shift of Interests' (1999) 47 Am J Comp Law 401, 412–22; Holger Fleischer, 'Legal Transplants in European Company Law—The Case of Fiduciary Duties' (2005) 2 Eur Co & Financial L Rev 378; Martin Gelter and Geneviève Helleringer, 'Fiduciary Principles in European Civil Law Systems' in Evan J Criddle, Paul B Miller, and Robert H Sitkoff (eds), *The Oxford Handbook of Fiduciary Law* (OUP 2019) 583; Thilo Kuntz, 'Transnational Fiduciary Law: Spaces and Elements' (2020) 5 UC Irvine J Int'l Transnational & Comp L 47, 62–63. Other examples outside of the core cases of private law administration arise in the case of advisors: Chapter 7, section IV.A.

[87] Cantin Cumyn and Cumyn (n 15), 81–82.

[88] ibid 34–35. At 9–31 the authors show how, since Roman law, the contract of mandate was often used very widely in civilian analysis to characterize a whole range of relationships of administration which were not actually mandate, because mandate was the relationship of administration that was regulated in the most detail by the law. Just as in the common law trusteeship is the paradigm of the

The unifying feature of all of these relationships is that it is clear as a matter of positive law, and obvious as a matter of logic, that the powers of the administrator are held for an other-regarding mission, and are only exercised properly (and validly) if they are exercised in the pursuit of that mission. For the relationships dealt with in this Part, that generally means they must be exercised in what the administrator believes are the best interests of some other person or persons.[89] Sometimes, however, loyalty requires that the powers be exercised in the pursuit of an abstract purpose.[90]

Some of the features of acting for others in law will be difficult to understand, or even to see, for someone who does not agree that a power, from the moment of its creation, can be affected to the achievement of a mission so that it is only properly used when it is used in the pursuit of that mission.[91] Within the interpretive method of this study, however, that challenge is impossible. The law is full of examples of the exercises of powers being invalidated because they were used for an improper purpose.[92]

In both the civil law and the common law, there are situations where relationships of administration may be found outside of the established categories. Courts have often struggled to articulate tests to determine when this is rightly the case. That issue lies outside of this Part II.A and is dealt with later.[93]

2. For oneself

Outside of relationships of administration, a person holding a power may well hold it for their own benefit. Even here, there are likely to be some legal limits

---

fiduciary relationship, so one might say that in the civil law, mandate is the paradigm of relationships of administration: Michele Graziadei, 'Virtue and Utility: Fiduciary Law in Civil Law and Common Law Jurisdictions' in Andrew S Gold and Paul B Miller (eds), *Philosophical Foundations of Fiduciary Law* (OUP 2014) 287, 288. The Civil Code of Québec, which came into force in 1994, has a Title on Administration of the Property of Others with detailed regulation, apart from the rules on the contract of mandate, and the regime of administration is now more suited to the role of providing the general law of relationships of administration.

[89] It may be possible for a person to be in one of the relationships covered by this Part, but for the requirement of loyalty to be disapplied from some particular power that they hold, so that they can exercise that power in an unconstrained manner while the incidents of the relationship of administration otherwise apply. It was so held in the controversial decision in *Citibank NA v MBIA Assurance SA* [2007] EWCA Civ 11, discussed in Charles Mitchell, 'Good Faith, Self-Denial and Mandatory Trustee Duties' (2018) 32 Trust Law International 92, 103–5. In an earlier case, it was held to be possible to exempt an executor from any duty in relation to a particular named asset (but not its proceeds), creating a mixed situation in which the executor was in a relationship of administration except in relation to its powers over that asset: *Hayim v Citibank NA* [1987] AC 730 (PC).

[90] Some and arguably all Quebec trusts are private purpose trusts: Chapter 1, section II.A.

[91] See Chapter 1, section II.B.

[92] In addition to the discussion in this chapter (above, sections I.C and I.D; below, section IV.E), it will be argued in Chapter 4 that the setting aside of the exercise of powers in conflict situations rests on the same foundation.

[93] Chapter 7, sections II, IV.A.

on how it can be used. These may be imposed by the general law, or by the terms of the power, or by particular contractual arrangements. Loyalty in our sense is not relevant or applicable, because in these situations, it is not the case that the power must be used for an other-regarding purpose, to achieve some mission that is external to the holder. The power may be limited, but it belongs to the one who holds it. The goal of this section is to differentiate these legal limits from the requirement of loyalty.

In the civil law, such limits are likely to be imposed by the general law of good faith, or perhaps more precisely through the idea of abuse of rights. This notion starts from the proposition that even rights (and powers) that one holds for oneself may not be used abusively.[94]

Common law courts are also increasingly likely to say, even in purely contractual relationships, that a person is restricted as to how they may rightly use their contractual powers. Sometimes, this is through the express adoption of a duty to act in good faith.[95] But using different language, similar constraints have been developed in relation to contractual powers to change interest rates,[96] or to make factual decisions that have implications for contractual entitlements.[97] There is a longer history of constraints on powers to expel a person from a voluntary association.[98] Some common law commentators resist seeing these developments as the arrival of a duty of good faith in contractual performance, and would say that these cases turn merely on contractual interpretation.[99] Others might think that the march towards a general requirement of good faith is probably unstoppable.

But wherever these constraints apply, and whatever they require, they do not require loyalty: they do not require a party to use the powers in what they perceive to be the interests of another, or an other-regarding mission. This is because these powers are not held for and on behalf of another, but rather for the holder's own benefit. There are three distinct but related proofs of this. One is that the standard of review tends to be much higher than the one that applies in the review of other-regarding powers. As we have seen, other-regarding powers are not properly exercised if they are not used in what the holder believes to be the

---

[94] A crucial case in Quebec civil law is *Houle v National Bank of Canada* [1990] 3 SCR 122, on the abuse by a secured creditor of its rights to realize on the security. These are powers in the Hohfeldian analysis (Lionel Smith, 'Powership and Its Objects' in Andrew Steven, Ross Anderson, and John MacLeod (eds), *Nothing So Practical as a Good Theory: Festschrift for George L Gretton* (Avizandum 2017) 223), but rights in Quebec law (Chapter 1, section IV.A.2).

[95] *Downsview Nominees Ltd v First City Corp* [1993] AC 295 (PC), recognizing a duty of good faith on a secured creditor; *Sheikh Tahnoon Bin Saeed Bin Shakhboot Al Nehayan v Kent* [2018] EWHC 333 (Comm), [167]–[176], discussing good faith in relational contracts; *Wastech Services Ltd v Greater Vancouver Sewerage and Drainage District* 2021 SCC 7, requiring good faith in the exercise of a contractual power of termination.

[96] *Paragon Finance plc v Nash* [2001] EWCA Civ 1466, [2002] 1 WLR 685

[97] *Braganza v BP Shipping Ltd* [2015] UKSC 17, [2015] 1 WLR 1661.

[98] *Lakeside Colony of Hutterian Brethren v Hofer* [1992] 3 SCR 165, citing earlier English cases.

[99] Michael Bridge, 'The Exercise of Contractual Discretion' (2019) 135 LQR 227.

best advancement of the mission for which the powers were granted. By contrast, in the context of powers not held in an administrative or fiduciary capacity, courts may say that the exercise of a power cannot be attacked unless it has been exercised capriciously, or arbitrarily, or in a way in which no reasonable person, acting reasonably, could have exercised it.[100] The UK Supreme Court has invoked *Wednesbury* unreasonableness: not unreasonableness as such, but rather an action so unreasonable as to compel the inference that the decision was irrational, arbitrary, capricious, or perverse.[101] Thus, the legal standards for the judicial review of powers held for oneself are quite different from the standards of loyalty that apply to other-regarding powers. The use of the common label 'proper purposes' in both contexts is potentially quite misleading.[102]

The second proof that the legal inquiries are quite different in the two contexts is that persons exercising contractual powers are not disqualified from exercising them when they are in a conflict of interest; that stricture only applies to decision-makers who are forbidden from consulting their own interests in making their decision. In other words, it only applies to administrators.[103] The third proof is that, as we have seen, powers held by an administrator for the purpose of accomplishing an other-regarding mission can always be taken away from them.[104] This is precisely because those powers do not belong to them for their own benefit. In the purely contractual context, the powers do indeed belong to the one who holds them, with the result that while the exercise of those powers can be subjected to legal controls, the powers cannot be taken away from the one who holds them.[105]

---

[100] *Nash* (n 96), [42]; cf *Re Hay's Settlement Trusts* [1982] 1 WLR 202 (ChD), 209.

[101] *Braganza* (n 97). In *Wastech* (n 95) there are suggestions that the standard is simply one of reasonableness ([5], [62], [71], [76]–[78], [88]), but other passages ([5], [62], [71], [86]–[88]) suggest that the decision is reviewable only if it was 'arbitrary or capricious'. In Quebec civil law, the codified norm of abuse of rights requires conduct that intends to injure (a subjective standard) or that is '*excessive and* unreasonable' (Civil Code of Québec, art 7, emphasis added).

[102] The phrase 'proper purposes' may be used where powers created under a trust are not held by the trustees, but by others who are not administrators (see eg *Vatcher v Paull* [1915] AC 372 (PC), 378; *Pitt v Holt* (n 8), [61]); also, in relation to the voting power of shareholders (eg Sarah Worthington, 'Corporate Governance: Remedying and Ratifying Directors' Breaches' (2000) 116 LQR 638, 646–51). As in the case of contractual powers, and despite the language of proper purposes, the control of these powers is not based on loyalty but can be understood through good faith (Nolan (n 31), 312; Worthington, ibid 646–47). The discussion in *Vatcher* addresses the use of the power to benefit indirectly someone who is not even an object of the power (eg by making a collateral agreement). This can easily be characterized as bad faith, since the power-holder is attempting to do something secretly that would be absolutely void if done openly.

[103] The logic of this is explored in the next chapter.

[104] Chapter 2, section III.B.

[105] Philip Sales, 'Use of Powers for Proper Purposes in Private Law' (2020) 136 LQR 384 argues that 'proper purposes' in these very different contexts (relationships of administration, and contracts which do not include such a relationship) can be explained by the consideration that the interpretation of the power is fundamental in both settings. This is true; indeed, interpretation is required even in order to decide into which category a power falls (above, section III.B; see also Chapter 7). But as shown by the three proofs in the text, despite this shared feature there are nonetheless important differences in the legal rules that apply in the two contexts.

3. Conclusion

Any legal power can be accompanied by restrictions on its use. Of course, it has a scope, which defines the authority of its holder. But even within that authority, the power can be misused. In the case of power-holders who are not administrators, proof of this misuse must meet a relatively high threshold. Irrationality, bad faith, intent to injure, and capriciousness are examples of the requirements that have been used in different contexts.

When administrators hold other-regarding powers, the threshold for review is lower. Such a power can only be rightly used in the pursuit of the mission for which the administrator was granted it. Any other exercise is improper and may lead to the setting aside of the relevant legal act.[106] Another difference is shown by the possibility of release, or renunciation, of a power. Generally a non-administrator, who is not required to pursue any mission, can release a power; an administrator, however, may not release a power (except by resigning, which is not a release as the power will be held by the successor).[107] A release cannot be seen as the proper pursuit of the mission for which the power was granted. Indeed, the disloyal refusal to exercise a power by an administrator is grounds for disqualification from the role.[108]

Although in the common law the label 'proper purposes' may be used in relation to both administrators and non-administrators, the difference in the applicable legal standard is clear.[109] When the 'proper purposes' doctrine is invoked in relation to administrators—in the common law, those who hold powers in a fiduciary capacity—the courts are clear that the doctrine involves a failure to comply with peculiarly *fiduciary* standards: namely, loyalty to the assigned mission.[110] As Hoffmann LJ said:

---

[106] In a thorough study, Cullity (n 22) concluded that while many courts have said that the exercise of fiduciary powers can be set aside where there was *mala fides*, this term was quite inappropriate in this context as it suggests that the threshold for misuse is much higher than the cases actually reveal. In this respect the expression is as misleading as 'fraud on a power' (n 14).

[107] On the two contexts in the common law, see Thomas (n 8), 804–18; on the inability of an administrator to release a power in the civil law, Cantin Cumyn and Cumyn (n 15), 89. In the Quebec case *Yared v Karam* 2019 SCC 62, [2019] 4 SCR 498 a trustee purported to release a power while arguing that he held his powers in an administrative capacity. The ultimate decision in the case was however that he held his powers for his own benefit (see Lionel Smith, 'A Tale of Two Patrimonies: Limits on the Flexibility of Trust Law' (2021) 40 ETPJ 139). The inability of an administrator to release a power could be tied to the principle that an administrator may not decide in advance how they will exercise their discretion (above, section IV.E).

[108] Below, section IV.F.5.

[109] Thus I disagree with those (eg Conaglen (n 3), 44–50) who argue that since 'proper purposes' can apply to those who are not administrators, it has no connection to loyalty.

[110] For example, *Howard Smith* (n 17), 834–35; *Whitehouse* (n 25), 292–93, 300, 309–10; *Re Hay's Settlement Trusts* (n 100), 209; *Eclairs Group Ltd* (n 17), [16], [23], [30], [37], [39] (the last three paragraphs were concurred in by all members of the Court); *Grand View Private Trust Co v Wong* (n 8), [1]: 'It is a fundamental principle of equity that a fiduciary power may be exercised only for a purpose for which the power has been conferred.' In the same way, Delaware courts hold that that the rules on review for proper purposes are sourced in the fiduciary duties of directors (n 18).

If a director chooses to participate in the management of the company and exercises powers on its behalf, he owes a duty to act bona fide in the interests of the company. He must exercise the power solely for the purpose for which it was conferred. To exercise the power for another purpose is a breach of his fiduciary duty.[111]

This also includes the case in which administrators act unlawfully in failing to consider matters that they were legally required to consider, or in considering matters that they were not required to consider. As we have seen, the interpretation of the power sometimes leads to the addition of further specifications to the basic 'best interests' standard.[112] A failure to comply with those further specifications is still a failure to use the power in the pursuit of the purpose for which it which was granted.[113]

It follows that the 'proper purposes' doctrine as it applies to non-fiduciaries depends on different standards. Such persons are not required to pursue an other-regarding mission; in this context, the doctrine involves a different test despite the shared label.[114]

C. Powers without discretion

Generally the authority of an administrator includes some room for discretion, which is why the phrases 'power or discretion' or 'discretionary power' are so often seen. This, however, is not strictly necessary.[115] In the common law, the relationship between trustee and beneficiary is a per se fiduciary relationship, because trustees' powers are always held to allow the trust to be performed. And yet, in a 'bare trust', as that term is often used in the common law, the trustee's duty is to do with the trust property exactly as she is told by the beneficiary.[116]

---

[111] *Bishopsgate Investment Management Ltd (In Liquidation) v Maxwell (No 2)* [1994] 1 All ER 261 (CA), 265.

[112] Section II.C.2.

[113] In *Pitt v Holt* (n 8), [40]-[41], [73], [96]-[97], it was held that exercises of fiduciary powers can be set aside for breach of fiduciary duty, and that one such breach involves making decisions on the basis of 'inadequate deliberation' ([62]). There is no reason to distinguish this from a failure of loyalty in the exercise of the power (use for an improper purpose); this is discussed below, at the end of section IV.F.1.

[114] See n 102.

[115] Non-discretionary powers were introduced in Chapter 1, section IV.B.

[116] This includes many resulting or constructive trusts, excepting many constructive trusts binding persons who are otherwise express trustees (who will hold on the terms of the express trust). Since, in a bare trust, the trustee must follow the instructions of the beneficiary, such a trust relationship is probably also therefore a kind of agency relationship. Although the characteristics of trusts and agency are quite different, they are not mutually exclusive in the common law, and agents often hold property in trust for their principals (n 55).

Even in a trust in which the trustee is not under the control of the beneficiary, it is possible that a trustee has no room for discretion.[117] In the same way, it is possible to contemplate an agency relationship without discretionary powers: an agent might be empowered to contract on behalf of the principal without having any discretion at all as to the terms of the contract.[118] Such an arrangement could exist also in a civilian mandate. The role of a real estate agent is, apart from a crucial advisory function, effectively to communicate their client's offer or acceptance; typically they hold no discretion.[119] In these situations, even though the terms of the administrator's mission are non-discretionary, the powers held by the administrator (trustee, agent or mandatary) are crucial to carrying out their mission. For example, if the beneficiary of a bare trust directs the trustee to convey the property to the beneficiary, the trustee must do so; the beneficiary himself cannot bring about the transfer.[120]

There might seem to be a paradox here, inasmuch as it is the discretionary nature of private powers that demands regulation through a subjective requirement of loyalty.[121] In other words, where there is no discretion, one might think that there is always an *objective* answer to the question whether the power was exercised properly or not. This objectivity could be seen to bring these situations into line, for example, with the general law of contractual obligations: we do not need a legal concept of loyalty to regulate contractual performance, because the question whether the contract was performed or not is answered objectively. Indeed, one might go so far as to say that a non-discretionary power *cannot be* misused in the sense of being used disloyally. The absence of discretion forecloses the possibility of a use that is permitted by the power but that is disloyal. In the case of a non-discretionary power, any use is either authorized or not; there is

---

[117] Experience has shown that such trusts may be unwise as they leave trustees unable to address unforeseen situations; but the rise of trustee discretions is a matter of prudence, not law.

[118] Eg *Merrill Lynch, Pierce, Fenner & Smith, Inc v Cheng* 901 F2d 1124 (DC Cir, 1990), in which the stockbroker of a 'non-discretionary' account was an agent even though their authority was limited to carrying out the instructions of the client.

[119] Advisory relationships are discussed in Chapter 7, section IV.A. There is always an element of discretion in the giving of advice, and an advisory relationship may, itself, justify the characterization of a relationship as one of administration.

[120] Courts of Equity could only *order* the defendant to make the transfer, on pain of imprisonment (unless the property in question was itself an Equitable interest). In *Attorney-General v Day* (1748) 1 Ves Sen 218, 27 ER 992, 224 (Ves Sen), 996 (ER), Lord Hardwicke LC mentioned an extreme case: the Court of Chancery could order a party to convey an interest in land; '[b]ut if he will not, choosing to lie all his life in prison, as Mr. *Savil* did, the court cannot carry it into execution...'. Today, in some jurisdictions, the court may have a statutory power to bring about the transfer by its own order, but even where these powers exist, they may not apply to all kinds of property and they may only apply in particular situations. For discussion of Canadian law with citations to statutes, see Donovan WM Waters, Mark Gillen, and Lionel Smith, *Waters' Law of Trusts in Canada* (5th edn, Thomson Reuters 2021), 545–46.

[121] Above, sections II.A–II.B.

no room for a use that is within the scope of the power, and so authorized in that sense, but that is improperly motivated and so disloyal.[122]

Because of the absence of discretionary powers in bare trusts, it has been argued that the relationship between the trustee and the beneficiary of a bare trust is not a fiduciary relationship.[123] The best way to understand this is as an observation that in the absence of discretionary powers, the rules about the proper exercise of such powers have little or no role to play. These are the rules on the requirement of loyalty in the exercise of powers, discussed in this chapter, and the rules on conflicts, discussed in the next chapter. As we have just seen, the requirement of loyalty seems superfluous in non-discretionary powers. As for conflicts, as we will see, an administrator should not exercise their discretionary powers while in a conflict of self-interest and duty; but if they have no such discretionary powers, the situation does not arise in that form. Thus where powers are non-discretionary, the rules about loyalty and about conflicts seem to have no work to do.

It remains true, however, that the cases of the bare trust, or the non-discretionary agency or mandate, are indeed relationships of administration. A non-discretionary power is held exactly to allow the performance of a mission: it is held for and on behalf of another, not for the benefit of the holder. And the rules on loyalty and on conflicts are not the only legal rules governing relationships of administration. A non-discretionary relationship of administration will attract the usual norms governing the attribution of benefits acquired through acting as an administrator.[124] The logic of these norms extends to information and so can create duties of disclosure, again in the absence of discretion.[125]

It can also be observed that even in a so-called non-discretionary situation, the administrator must in some contexts exercise personal judgment in relation to the powers that he holds.[126] Take this case: the principal has made a

---

[122] One possible response to this would be that, for example, a trustee without discretion can misuse his powers by conveying trust property to someone, without authority to do so. This, however, seems to play on the ambiguity of 'power' (see Chapter 1, section IV.A.2). The trustee has a Hohfeldian power to make the unauthorized transfer, but they do not have that power under the terms of trust. As we saw in Chapter 1, our general concern is with powers that are coupled with authority. In that sense, the trustee simply does not have the (authorized) power to make the transfer.
[123] Lionel Smith, 'Constructive Fiduciaries?' in P Birks (ed), *Privacy and Loyalty* (Clarendon Press 1997) 249, at 263–65; James Penner, 'Distinguishing Fiduciary, Trust, and Accounting Relationships' (2014) 8 J of Equity 202.
[124] These are the subject of Chapter 5.
[125] DeMott (n 3), 941; Deborah A DeMott, 'The Fiduciary Character of Agency and the Interpretation of Instructions' in Andrew S Gold and Paul B Miller (eds), *Philosophical Foundations of Fiduciary Law* (OUP 2014) 321, 326; *Merrill Lynch* (n 118) (duty on agent to disclose its own unlawful conduct). On the conceptual link between duties of disclosure and the attribution of benefits, see Chapter 5, section VIII.
[126] See also DeMott, 'Fiduciary Character', ibid 322–26.

contract to sell the principal's property to X, and the principal directs their (non-discretionary) agent to transfer the property to X. Assume that X has not yet paid the price; the agent learns, unknown to the principal, that X is insolvent. Would the agent use his powers loyally if he carried out his principal's instruction and made the transfer, without communicating with the principal, so ensuring that the principal would be exposed to making an unsecured claim for the price in the insolvency of X? Assuming that the applicable contract law afforded some discretion to the principal as to whether to transfer the property in such a case, the answer to that question is 'no': the agent would not use his powers loyally in making such a transfer.[127] The conclusion is that even an apparently non-discretionary power, being an authority held on behalf of another, can be subject to a subjective requirement of loyalty. This is because it may require judgment to be exercised by the one holding authority, even if the power-holder's course of action seems to be dictated by instructions and non-discretionary. That judgment must be exercised loyally.

IV. The content of loyalty: The proper use of other-regarding powers

A. The demands of loyalty in different situations

1. A requirement to exercise powers in what the power-holder considers to be the best interests of a person

In this chapter, the requirement of loyalty in the exercise of powers is generally articulated as a requirement that the administrator use the relevant powers in what she judges to be the best interests of another person or persons. This is because in private law, the relevant powers are usually held in order to protect and advance the interests of that other person. But loyalty as the pursuit of the best interests of one or more persons is, in fact, not the general case, but only a special case of what loyalty requires.

The point of a legal requirement of loyalty in relation to the exercise of powers to act for others is simply to require that those powers be used properly. Generally when the mission is to look after the financial or pecuniary affairs of another person or persons, what loyalty requires in the exercise of powers is that the powers be used to best promote the interests of that other person or persons. In the context of the patrimonial or pecuniary decisions with which we are concerned in this Part II.A, this typically requires that the administrator

---

[127] The agent on these assumptions also owes a duty to disclose this material information to the principal (n 125), but this is a separate point.

consider their *financial* interests, even if it may be permissible to also consider other factors in deciding what is in their interests.

Where the administrator's powers are required to be exercised in what the administrator considers to be the best interest of another person, the relationship of administration is between the administrator and that person. In some cases, confusion arises because the exercise of the power may *affect* other persons.[128] *Frame v Smith*[129] concerned a custodial parent, who had parental authority over the children of the now-ended marriage, and a non-custodial parent whose relationship with the children had been harmed by the exercise of parental authority by the custodial parent. Wilson J, in dissent, would have held that there was a fiduciary relationship between the custodial parent and the non-custodial parent, since the latter was vulnerable to the former's power. A parent holding parental authority is indeed an administrator; but the relationship of administration is with the children, for whose benefit the authority is given, and in whose interests the power must be exercised.[130] It is not with the estranged spouse, even though that person may be affected by the use of the power. Particular duties or other jural relationships may be needed between the former spouses to address this vulnerability (such as a stipulation that the children may not be moved to a distant place without the consent of the non-custodial parent or the court).

A similar observation arises in corporate law. Corporate directors have powers over the corporation and they hold these powers, not for themselves, but for and on behalf of the corporation. Loyalty requires them to use these powers in what they perceive to be the best interests of the corporation.[131] The way the directors exercise their powers may have tremendous effects on others, such as corporate employees; but although the directors are administrators who are bound to be loyal, they are not administrators of the property or affairs of the employees, but rather of the corporation. Only if we were to conclude that directors are empowered in order to act for the benefit of the employees would we constitute a relationship of administration towards them. Such a structure is not legally impossible, but it would mean (among other things) that the employment relationship was quite differently organized in law depending on whether the employer was a corporation or a natural person.[132]

In a similar way, the decisions of the directors will also of course affect the interests of the shareholders, but that does not itself constitute a relationship of

---

[128] This is one of the problems with focusing on vulnerability, which is not enough on its own to identify a relationship of administration; see Chapter 7, section II.

[129] *Frame v Smith* [1987] 2 SCR 99, 42 DLR (4th) 81, corrected by an erratum published at [2011] 1 SCR, Part 3, iv.

[130] Chapter 7, section V.

[131] Above, section II.C.2.

[132] Rosemary T Langford, 'Best Interests: Multifaceted but Not Unbounded' (2016) 75 Cambridge LJ 505, 521–27.

administration between directors and shareholders, any more so than in the case of employees. We have already seen, however, that directors may consider the interests of employees and shareholders when assessing what are the interests of the corporation, and I have suggested that the consideration of shareholder interests could be mandatory rather than optional.[133] Moreover, there may be good reasons to allow shareholders, and even perhaps employees, to enforce rights belonging to the corporation.[134] This does not mean that the rights belong to the shareholders or employees, nor that they are in a direct relationship of administration with the directors, but it is a way of recognizing that they are deeply interested in its welfare.

2. A requirement to exercise powers in what the power-holder considers to be the best pursuit of an impersonal purpose

We have already noticed that sometimes a requirement to advance the best interests of persons may be articulated in terms of advancing a purpose.[135] When people pool their resources in contributing to pension trusts or in investing in corporations, they are trying to increase their financial well-being. Individually, they may have an infinite number of purposes in mind, whether short- or long-term; and their individual circumstances may also be infinitely variable. But a common purpose can be articulated, and in these circumstances, the pursuit of that common purpose is largely indistinguishable from the pursuit of the best interests of the relevant persons. Even so, these are cases in which the administrators are required to act in what they perceive to be the best interests of the relevant persons, even if those interests are articulated in a way that captures the common purpose. We have also noticed that objective limitations may apply to restrict what would otherwise be the freedom of the relevant administrators to choose how best to pursue the interests of the beneficiaries.[136]

These situations, then, can be understood as relationships of administration in which the administrators are required to use their powers in what they perceive to be the best interests of the beneficiaries, as is usually the case in private administration. This not changed either by the addition of objective limitations (such as forbidding certain investments or lines of business), or by a narrower formulation of best interests (such as 'best financial interests').

So too, in the corporate law context, the mission of the directors in their administration is to pursue the best interests of the corporation. Again, there are

---

[133] Section II.C.2.
[134] Unpaid employees are creditors of the corporation and as such may have this standing (eg *Canada Business Corporations Act*, RSC 1985, c C-44, ss 238 'complainant' (d); 241(2)). This kind of representative enforcement is discussed in more detail in Chapter 8, section III.C.2.c.
[135] Above, section II.C.2.
[136] Above, section II.C.1.

some objective constraints on their latitude in this respect. I have argued above that they are required always to consider the financial interests of shareholders; and it may be that some of their powers can only be properly used for more precisely articulated corporate purposes.[137] Within those constraints, directors have a wide range of authority to decide how best to promote the best interests of the corporation.[138] In some corporate law scholarship, it is assumed that directors must be loyal to 'corporate purposes', but in my view this is just a different way of articulating the requirement of loyalty to the corporation's interests.[139]

There are, however, situations that arise in private law where the loyalty required of administrators is best articulated as being towards a purpose rather than towards the interests of a person. A good example is provided by the case of dispositive discretions held within a trust structure. These discretions qualify and modify the default rights of the beneficiaries of the trust. For example, the trust may require that on the death of one beneficiary, the capital shall be distributed equally among that person's surviving children. But someone may hold a discretionary power to distribute some or all of the capital before that death. Such powers allow some responsiveness to situations that were not and could not be foreseen when the trust was created. It is a separate question who are the 'objects' of this power; the objects may be the trust beneficiaries, or other people, or a mix of both. When such a power exists, there is a question of interpretation as to how it is held. Sometimes the conclusion is that the holder of the power is only bound to act in good faith and to respect the terms of the power; this might be a suitable interpretation if, for example, the power was held by family member who was not otherwise involved in the trust's administration. Another possible interpretation is that, in the language of the common law, the power is held in

---

[137] Both points are made above, section II.C.2. Below, section IV.B.1, I argue that it is lawful for corporate directors to consider other interests in assessing the best interests of the corporation. This does not require express statutory authorization and indeed may be true in relation to other administrators.

[138] Above, section II.B.

[139] In this regard I disagree with Paul B Miller and Andrew S Gold, 'Fiduciary Governance' (2015) 57 Wm & Mary L Rev 513 when they suggest (580–85) that the requirement of loyalty in ordinary business corporations can be understood, in at least some cases, as requiring the pursuit of both the best interests of the corporation and one or more impersonal purposes. In such corporations (unlike in the case of 'benefit corporations', mentioned briefly below in section IV.B.1), directors' actions must always be referable to the pursuit of the best interests of the corporation. Miller and Gold acknowledge that this basic standard of loyalty to the corporation's interests gives directors a great deal of latitude (above, section II.C.2; and this, whether or not there is explicit statutory authority to consider various interests: below, section IV.B.1); this seems to make it unnecessary to postulate that directors have a second, potentially conflicting, loyalty to an impersonal purpose. Indeed, Andrew S Gold, 'Purposive Loyalty' (2017) 74 Wash & Lee L Rev 881 argues that loyalty to a corporation's purposes may point in a different direction to loyalty to its best interests (there is a trace of this in Miller and Gold, 561). He uses lexical and philosophical arguments built on the multiple meanings of 'loyalty' (on which see Chapter 1, section IV.F), but I do not understand him to argue that existing business corporation law ever requires director action in the pursuit of corporate purposes as opposed to the pursuit of the corporation's best interests.

a 'fiduciary capacity'; this is the natural interpretation if the power is held by a trustee. By this it is meant that not only must the power-holder act in good faith and respect the terms of the power; moreover, he is treated as an administrator (in the language of the present study) with respect to the exercise of the power. This means that he must use it loyally, just as he must use his other trustee powers loyally.

This conclusion, however, brings with it a particular version of the requirement of loyalty. Such powers are *not* necessarily required to be exercised in what the holder considers to be the best interests of any particular person or persons; this would be inconsistent with their nature. Consider the case in which the beneficiaries A, B, and C will get equal shares of the capital on the death of D, but the trustee has a power to give capital to any of A, B, and C during D's lifetime. Any such disposition will benefit the recipient, but will reduce the shares of the other two. So if the trustee was required to use the power in what he thought was the best interests of *all* of the objects—A, B, and C—then probably he could not use the power, or could only use it to make equal distributions to all of them. But this would frustrate the point of the power, which authorizes unequal dispositions and which is designed to allow responsiveness to unforeseen events. The point is even clearer in the case of a power in favour of an object (say X) who is not otherwise a beneficiary of the trust. To say that the power must be used in what the trustee considers the best interests of the trust beneficiaries (A, B, and C) would seem to prevent the trustee from using such a power, since its use will impoverish all of them. Conversely, to say that the power must be used in what the trustee considers the best interests of the object of the power (X) would seem to *require* the trustee to use the power; but the whole point of the power is that it is a discretionary authority, which the trustee may or may not use as his judgment determines.

The law, therefore, formulates the requirement of loyalty differently in cases of this kind. It does not say that the trustee must act in what he perceives to be the best interests of one or more persons. Rather, such powers are required to be exercised in what the holder considers to be the best manner of fulfilling the purpose for which the power was granted.[140] As we have already seen, a version of this reasoning may appear even when the powers *are* held to allow the administrator to pursue the best interests of the beneficiaries; the courts may qualify that

---

[140] There are many cases in the common law that confirm this principle: *Klug v Klug* [1918] 2 Ch 67 (ChD), 71; *McPhail v Doulton* [1971] AC 424 (HL), 449, 457; *Re Hay's Settlement Trusts* (n 100), 209; *Turner* (n 33), 109–10; *Re Beatty* [1990] 1 WLR 1503 (ChD), 1506; *Hayim* (n 89), 746; *Eclairs Group Ltd* (n 17), [15]–[16], citing authorities reaching back to the eighteenth century; *Grand View Private Trust Co v Wong* (n 8). It is therefore strongly arguable that a power to which no purpose can sensibly be assigned cannot be created as an administrative (fiduciary) power, as it would be impossible to say whether it had been misused: P Matthews, C Mitchell, J Harris, and S Agnew, *Underhill and Hayton: Law Relating to Trusts and Trustees* (20th edn, LexisNexis 2022) ¶ 10.90—¶ 10.100.

open-ended purpose with further constraints, based on their interpretation of the purpose for which the power was granted.[141]

The trust of Quebec civil law provides a more general example of powers that must be used in the best pursuit of an impersonal purpose. The Quebec trust does not need to have beneficiaries; it can instead be constituted for a purpose.[142] Indeed, it is arguable that all Quebec trusts, even if they have beneficiaries, are purpose trusts.[143] In the unreformed common law, the only permissible purpose trusts are charitable trusts; these, as we will see, are an example of public administration.[144] But the purpose of a Quebec trust need not satisfy the common law definition of charity, which indeed is foreign to Quebec law. Trustees of a Quebec trust, therefore, are bound by a requirement of loyalty that requires them to use their powers in the way that they think will best achieve the purposes assigned to the trust by the settlor.

These cases of powers held for purposes imply that the 'best interests' formulation of loyalty is actually a special case. The most general formulation of the requirement of loyalty is that powers that are held to allow someone who acts as an administrator to fulfil his or her mission must be used for what the administrator considers to be the best way to fulfil that mission.[145] As Paul Miller and Andrew Gold have explained, the supervision and enforcement of relationships in which powers are held for purposes needs to be understood differently. When powers are held for persons, those persons—beneficiaries—are presumptively empowered to supervise and enforce the administrator's actions; but where powers are held for purposes, there is no person who is a beneficiary in this sense.[146] Mechanisms of enforcement are addressed later.[147]

---

[141] Above, section II.C.2.

[142] Civil Code of Québec, arts 1266–70.

[143] This follows from the definition of the institution (Civil Code of Québec, art 1260: a trust arises when the settlor 'appropriates [property] to a particular purpose') and from the fact that enforcement can by 'the settlor, the beneficiary or any other interested person . . .' (art 1290). See Alexandra Popovici, *Êtres et avoirs: Les droits sans sujet en droit privé actuel* (Éditions Yvon Blais 2019); Alexandra Popovici, 'Droits de regard: la fiducie dans le *Code civil du Québec*' in Christine Morin and Brigitte Lefebvre (eds), *Mélanges en l'honneur du professeur Jacques Beaulne* (Wilson & Lafleur 2018) 225.

[144] Chapter 9, section II.A. In many offshore jurisdictions, non-charitable purpose trusts are permitted by legislation, and this kind of legislation is starting to appear in places that are not usually considered offshore, like Delaware: Lionel Smith, 'Give the People What They Want? The Onshoring of the Offshore' (2018) 103 Iowa L Rev 2155.

[145] Evan Fox-Decent, 'The Fiduciary Nature of State Legal Authority' (2005) 31 Queen's LJ 259, 261, 268, 276, 280. Miller and Gold (n 139) explore in detail the conceptual differences between powers granted for the pursuit of the interests of persons (which they call 'service mandates') and powers granted for the pursuit of impersonal purposes (which they call 'governance mandates'). They agree (523, 549) that all powers of administrators are ultimately held for purposes, but they resist Fox-Decent's suggestion that one is a special case of the other (578 n 229).

[146] Miller and Gold (ibid).

[147] Chapter 8, sections III.C.2.e (powers held for purposes in trusts for persons) and III.D (private purpose trusts); Chapter 10 (powers held for public purposes).

B. Mixed purposes or motives

Assume we are in a situation where the 'best interests' standard does apply, modified as it always is by objective constraints.[148] Can the administrator take other interests into account, so long as, in the end, he does what he thinks is best for the beneficiary?

One important case is that in which the administrator is also a member of the class of beneficiaries. The same person, for example, may be the trustee of a trust and also one of the beneficiaries of that trust. The general principle is that when he is acting as a trustee, he must not take account of his own personal interests; he must act in what he thinks are the best interests of the beneficiaries. But in this case, he is also one of the beneficiaries. We will analyse this situation in more detail later on in this chapter.[149] Here we merely note that such a trustee occupies multiple roles, and when he is acting as trustee it is proper for him to take account of his own interests as a beneficiary, along with the interests of the other beneficiaries.[150]

1. The proper consideration of other interests in assessing the beneficiary's interests

Sometimes, however, it makes perfect sense for an administrator to consider the interests of persons other than the beneficiary, in assessing what is in the best interests of the beneficiary. This is not the same as acting in the interests of those other persons, which would be improper. Take the case of directors of a business corporation. In the Canadian decision in *BCE Inc v 1976 Debentureholders*, it was held that:

> In considering what is in the best interests of the corporation, directors may look to the interests of, *inter alia*, shareholders, employees, creditors, consumers, governments and the environment to inform their decisions.[151]

---

[148] Above, section II.C.
[149] Section V.
[150] Gaillard (n 15), 21, classifies a legal prerogative as a power (in the French and Quebec sense of an administrative power: Chapter 1, section IV.A.2) if it must be used for an interest that is at least partially distinct from that of the holder; in other words, if the holder is not free to use it just as he wishes, subject only to the principle against abuse of rights. This is the case where the administrator is also a member of the beneficiary class.
[151] *BCE Inc* (n 76), [40]; see also *McClurg* (n 77) and now *Canada Business Corporations Act*, RSC 1985, c C-44, s 122(1.1), adding other interests that may be considered and specifying that the list is not exhaustive. Corporate statutes in many US states are similar and are generically called 'stakeholder' statutes. It is arguable that in the case of a business corporation, the directors *must* take account of the financial interests of shareholders in assessing the interests of the corporation: above, section II.C.2.

Directors must exercise their powers in what they consider to be the best interests of the corporation, but this pronouncement articulates a range of factors (including other interests) that directors may rightly decide are relevant in assessing the interests of the corporation. A business corporation is typically constituted for the financial benefit of its shareholders; it depends upon its employees; it has need of creditors, consumers, and governments; and, like all of us, it requires a healthful environment. Its interests are typically intertwined with the interests of some or all of those others.[152]

The 'benefit corporation' is a relatively recent form of business association that makes it obligatory (not merely lawful) for directors to take account of interests beyond the financial interests of shareholders.[153] In assessing the limited uptake of this form, one author comments, in relation to ordinary business corporations:

> in the absence of bad faith or unreasonable behavior, directors typically enjoy tremendous latitude. It is rare that a board cannot successfully justify a decision as rational and in the benefit of the shareholders. Consequently, directors are rarely found to have acted outside of their fiduciary duties. This holds true with respect to decisions regarding corporate social responsibility as well. Further, few corporations are immune to the pressures of public opinion. As such, the same sentiments that have led to the promulgation of benefit corporation statutes across the nation have long pushed corporations to embrace some measure of social responsibility.[154]

This latitude on the part of corporate directors is an example of a general principle that the proper assessment of the interests of the beneficiary of a relationship of administration may rightly involve, because of the context and the juridical situation, the consideration of the interests of persons other than the beneficiary. Some might argue that this is particular to the case of corporate law, where the beneficiary is a legal and not a natural person. There is no reason to think this is so. If BCE Inc had been organized as a trust structure rather than a corporation, the investors would not be shareholders but beneficiaries of a trust, and the fiduciary duties of the director/trustees would be owed directly to those beneficiaries.[155] But there is no reason to think that what was said in the passage quoted above would cease to be applicable in that setting. Although the reference to shareholders would be otiose, the interests of other stakeholders would

---

[152] See Michael Kerr, Richard Janda, and Chip Pitts, *Corporate Social Responsibilty: A Legal Analysis* (LexisNexis 2009).

[153] Benefit corporations are not analyzed in the present study but they are mentioned in the brief discussion of public–private partnerships in Chapter 9, section II.D.4.

[154] Ronald J Colombo, 'Taking Stock of the Benefit Corporation' (2019) 7 Texas A&M L Rev 73, 108.

[155] *Dobbie v Arctic Glacier Income Fund* 2011 ONSC 25, [55].

be still be a potentially relevant consideration in assessing the best interests of the beneficiaries; and this, even though on this hypothesis the beneficiaries would be natural persons. Another illustration is that in the case of the parent–child relationship of administration, a parent may, in assessing the interests of the child, consider the interests of other family members, such as those of the parent.[156]

2. Mixed motives or purposes that include improper considerations

More difficult is the case in which it is shown that the administrator took into account, or was motivated by, some consideration that was improper in the sense that it was irrelevant to the proper assessment of the beneficiary's interests. One approach would be to say that the exercise of the power is proper if, in the end, it is shown that the administrator actually exercised his judgment properly, in the pursuit what he thought were the best interests of the beneficiary, even if he might have considered some improper factor or factors. A stricter view would say the opposite: that the exercise in these circumstances is treated as disloyal and improper. This would be based on the idea that it is probably impossible to know, either in advance or in hindsight, whether and to what extent the improper factors affected the administrator's decision. I will argue that the law is committed to the stricter view, because of the impossibility of unravelling human decision-making processes.[157]

The point came up in an Ontario case, *Fox v Fox Estate*.[158] A trust was created by will, in which the sole trustee (and executrix of the will) was the testator's widow, Miriam Fox. She was also entitled to 75% of the income generated by the trust property during her life, while the other 25% of the income was payable to Walter Fox, the adult son of the marriage. Walter would also receive the trust capital if he were to survive his mother. Miriam Fox, however, had a power of appointment by which she could encroach on the trust capital for the benefit of Walter's children—her own grandchildren. Therefore she held a discretionary dispositive power, in an administrative capacity; as we have seen, she was required to exercise the power in what she thought was the best way to accomplish the purpose for which it was granted. Walter had two children by his first marriage, and he and the children's mother were later divorced. Walter then married another woman, who was of a different faith from Walter and his mother Miriam. Miriam reacted by using her power of appointment to transfer all of the trust capital directly to her grandchildren, now young adults. This eliminated not only Walter's right to 25% of the income during Miriam's life (since there was

---

[156] The parenthood relationship is discussed in Chapter 7, section V; for the proper consideration of the parent's own interests, see also Smith, 'Parenthood' (n 6), 446–51.
[157] This will be explained below.
[158] *Fox v Fox Estate* (1996) 28 OR (3d) 496 (CA); application for leave to appeal dismissed, [1996] SCCA No. 241.

no longer any capital to generate income), but also his contingent interest in the capital upon her death. The Court set aside the appointments on the basis that Miriam had used her power improperly. It also removed Miriam Fox as a trustee, as she had repeatedly acted as if there was no difference between the estate assets and her own.

There was some discussion of the question of mixed motives. The trial judge had held that the mother may have considered the interests of the grandchildren, but her primary motivation was her disapproval of her son's marriage. In the Court of Appeal, Galligan JA held, with reference to the arguments of Maurice Cullity, that so long as an improper motive or desire was part of the decision-making process, the decision was improper and could be set aside.[159] McKinlay JA agreed in the result: 'I agree with Galligan JA that a capital encroachment made because of [Walter Fox]'s involvement with a person not of the Jewish faith does not constitute a bona fide exercise of discretion. . . . If the discretion of [Miriam Fox] was exercised in this case because of her religious bias, then the decision of Galligan JA, in my view, is decisive.'[160] She suggested, however, that if Miriam Fox had had other and valid reasons, the case might be different.[161] On her view, a proper interpretation of the will meant that Miriam Fox could have had no good reason for the encroachment, and indeed McKinlay JA seemed to conclude that what Miriam purported to do was not authorized by the terms of the will trust.[162] McKinlay JA added that Miriam Fox did not consider the will at all, and had always acted as if the estate assets were her own. The implication is that even if Miriam had reasons apart from expressing disapproval of Walter's marriage, they could not possibly have been proper ones.

The third judge, Catzman JA, agreed that Miriam's exercise could be set aside on the basis that she treated the assets as her own, or on the basis that what she did was not authorized by the will. He said:

> I incline to the view, however, that if an executrix exercises her discretion to encroach for a 'good' reason, clearly within the contemplation of the power conferred upon her by the will, we should be reluctant to interfere on the ground that she was, additionally, motivated by a 'bad' reason.[163]

---

[159] At 499–502, citing Cullity (n 22). Galligan JA agreed with Cullity that the term 'mala fide', often used in the cases, is satisfied by the presence of improper motives or purposes. In other words, bad faith in the sense of intention to harm is not required in the case of powers held in a fiduciary or administrative capacity.

[160] At 509, 510.

[161] At 503.

[162] At 510–12. This, however, is hard to justify from the terms of the will that are set out in the judgment, and the judge may have been unfamiliar with the wide discretions that increasingly appear in trust instruments.

[163] At 517.

More recently, in *Eclairs Group Ltd v JKX Oil & Gas plc*,[164] a board of directors had a fiduciary power to issue notices that restricted shareholders from voting or transferring their shares. The board had used this power, and the issue was whether that use was invalid as having been made for an improper purpose. Lords Sumption and Hodge said, following *dicta* of the High Court of Australia, that the exercise of a power by a board of directors might be valid where both proper and improper purposes were shown to have been operating.[165] In such a case, they said, it is necessary to filter out the improper purpose by asking whether the same decision would have been reached even without the presence of that improper purpose. If it would have been, then the exercise was valid:

> A director may be perfectly conscious of the collateral advantages of the course of action that he proposes, while appreciating that they are not legitimate reasons for adopting it. He may even enthusiastically welcome them. It does not follow without more that the pursuit of those advantages was his purpose in supporting the decision. All of these problems are aggravated where there are several directors, each with his own point of view.... if there were proper reasons for exercising the power and it would still have been exercised for those reasons even in the absence of improper ones, it is difficult to see why justice should require the decision to be set aside.[166]

This however was a position expressed in *obiter dicta* by a minority.[167] The majority of the Court refused to express any view on the question whether a case of mixed proper and improper purposes can be resolved through this kind of causal analysis. The exercise of the power was set aside as improper.

The position of Galligan JA in *Fox*, which is also that of Maurice Cullity, seems correct in principle. A decision cannot be considered proper when it is known that it was reached, even in part, for extraneous and improper reasons.[168] That strict approach to mixed motives is supported by the law's rules on conflicts, which we will examine in more detail in the next chapter. When a power is exercised by the administrator in a situation of conflict between self-interest and duty to the beneficiary, the exercise is liable to be set aside simply because of the

---

[164] *Eclairs Group Ltd* (n 17).
[165] ibid [17]ff, citing *Whitehouse* (n 25). They suggested at [17] that the proper purposes principle in corporate law is less demanding than in public law, and at [18] cited *Mills v Mills* (1938) 60 CLR 150 for the proposition that corporate law is less demanding than trust law in this regard.
[166] ibid [20]–[21].
[167] A similar causal approach was suggested by the majority in *Whitehouse* (n 25), 294, also in *obiter dicta*.
[168] This is also the position taken in Gaillard (n 15), 120–24, for French private law, though he notes that in French public law the presence of a good motivation may be enough to save the exercise of a power even in the presence of a bad motivation.

conflict.[169] It is not necessary to show that the administrator was *actually* improperly influenced by his own self-interest; the mere possibility is enough to make the decision improper. As we will see, this is because it is impossible (even for the administrator, let alone the beneficiaries or the court) to know whether the administrator was improperly favouring his own interests. The law insists on excluding even that possibility. If, therefore, it is *known* that an improper reason went into the decision-making process, it is difficult to see how the decision can be seen as properly made.[170]

Thus while the causal analysis proposed by Lord Sumption is possibly theoretically justifiable, the rules on conflicts imply that it is impossible to apply in practice.[171] Lord Sumption expressly said that he was not dealing with the case in which a personal interest of the decision-maker was one of the factors in the decision.[172] However, the logic of the legal rule that applies in the case of conflicts—that improper considerations cannot be untangled from proper ones—seems rightly applicable to any case of partially improper purposes.[173] One might argue that only cases involving the self-interest of the decision-maker make it impossible causally to untangle mixed purposes. This, however, will not do, because the law is equally strict in cases where a power is exercised by the administrator in a situation of conflict between his duty to the beneficiary and his duty owed to some other party.[174] The presence of that strict norm, even if the absence of self-interest, shows that the established position of the law—at least, of the common law—is that it is impossible to untangle the causal effects of multiple factors in a

---

[169] Nor is this, as is sometimes thought, a principle that originated in the Court of Chancery; as we will see in Chapter 3, it is well-known in the civil law.

[170] It is sometimes suggested in the common law that there is a tension between two formulations of loyalty, as requiring that the fiduciary exercise their powers (1) in what they perceive to be the *sole* interests of the beneficiary, or rather (2) in what they perceive to be the *best* interests of the beneficiary (eg John H Langbein, 'Questioning the Trust Law Duty of Loyalty: Sole Interest or Best Interest?' (2005) 114 Yale LJ 929; for a rebuttal, Melanie B Leslie, 'In Defense of the No Further Inquiry Rule: A Response to Professor John Langbein' (2005) 47 William and Mary L Rev 541). In my view it is a mistake to see these as alternatives. The basic requirement of loyalty is the best interest standard (but see section IV.A.); the requirement of 'sole interest' is not an alternative, but is cumulative to that requirement, or else is a different way of articulating it. The 'best interest' requirement is an articulation in positive terms of how the power must (generally) be exercised; the 'sole interest' requirement is an articulation in negative terms, excluding all other considerations (and forbidding action in conflict situations). In fact, the 'sole interest' formulation is often inaccurate (section IV.B.1). Langbein's argument for law reform is compromised by a failure to see that the more relaxed standards that apply in corporate law are not an abolition of the traditional law, but are rather based on procedures for *authorizing* conflicted transactions in advance (on which see Chapter 4, section VII.B).

[171] But see, supporting Lord Sumption's analysis, Remus Valsan, 'Directors' Powers and the Proper Purposes Rule' (2016) 27 KCLJ 157.

[172] *Eclairs Group Ltd* (n 17), [17].

[173] 'Self-interest is only one, though no doubt the commonest, instance of improper motive': *Howard Smith* (n 17), 834, *per* Lord Wilberforce.

[174] Chapter 4, section IV.B.

human decision-making process. Indeed, quite outside of any kind of conflict, the law is likely to treat a decision as tainted if there was any improper influence on the decision-maker, without attempting to isolate the multiple factors and without requiring the decision-maker to prove that the improper factor was decisive.[175]

In the passage quoted above, Lord Sumption mentioned that the corporate law context brings in the problem of multiple decision-makers, who may have different motivations, since a board of directors usually has more than one member and makes decisions by majority vote. He suggested that this consideration makes it impracticable to treat as improper those exercises of power that are based in part on improper considerations. This problem arises in other contexts as well, including trust law, where there may be multiple trustees. Again, the rules on conflicts undermine Lord Sumption's argument. In a situation in which one of multiple administrators was in a conflict when a decision was made, the decision is liable to be set aside as a result of the conflict of that single administrator. This is because, in trust law and in corporate law, a conflicted decision-maker is considered to be disqualified and thus the collective decision-making process is tainted by their participation.[176] Multiple administrators, including corporate boards, must deal with the disqualification of conflicted directors, possibly through full disclosure and recusal from the decision.[177] Again, directors acting partly for improper purposes are at least equally disqualified as those in conflicts, and arguably more so, if it is possible to speak of degrees of disqualification.[178]

---

[175] Examples can be found in *Barton v Armstrong* [1976] AC 104 (PC), in the context of duress; and *Wayling v Jones* [1995] 2 FLR 1029 (CA), in the context of proprietary estoppel. Elise Bant, 'Causation and Scope of Liability in Unjust Enrichment' [2009] Restitution L Rev 60 argues that 'decision causation' is governed by principles different to those governing physical causation. For a similar argument from a philosophical perspective, see Scheer (n 20).

[176] In the common law, trustees (except of charitable trusts) must act unanimously unless the trust instrument provides otherwise. Where multiple administrators act by a majority, it is possible that a decision in which a conflicted administrator was in the losing minority would be immune from attack on the ground of the conflict. But where someone participated in the majority or unanimous decision who should not have (or did so for improper reasons), there is no authority allowing the decision to be upheld on the basis that it could have been made without that person's vote, even where unanimity is not required (see *Aberdeen Ry Co v Blaikie Brothers* (1854) 1 Macq 461, 1 Paterson 394 (HL), 473 (Macq), 400 (Paterson)). Just as the decision-making processes of the human mind cannot be picked apart so as to isolate the causal effects of different considerations, nor can the collective decision of a group be assessed for how it would have proceeded in the absence of the participation of someone who did actually participate in it.

[177] The ways in which conflicts may be managed are discussed in Chapter 4, section VII.

[178] It may be possible to speak of the intention or the purposes of the collective (eg the board of directors), as distinct from those of the individuals who compose it (see John Gardner, *Law as a Leap of Faith* (OUP 2012), 59–65); but this does not efface the intentions or purposes of the individuals in casting their votes.

C. Giving of reasons for the exercise of powers

If administrative powers can only be used for the right purposes, one might think that administrators should be obliged to give reasons for their exercise of such powers. In this way, those who have powers of supervision could assess whether the power was exercised properly. Since the administrator is by definition acting for others, not for herself, it does not seem like any kind of imposition to require her to give an account of her reasons. As we will see, the accountability of administrators imposes positive obligations on them, including obligations to provide information; and the reasons for the exercise of powers are nothing but a kind of information. One commentator has noted that an obligation to give such reasons would be no more onerous than the obligation to render accounts which falls on many private law administrators.[179]

Indeed, it might seem paradoxical that an administrator is *not* obliged to provide reasons, when the law is clear that the exercise of a power can be set aside if that exercise was made for an improper purpose. The law has not traditionally imposed such an obligation. In the common law, the justification in the context of trust law has generally been related to the consideration that trusteeship is often gratuitous and that persons would be discouraged from acting as trustees by the imposition of such an obligation, which might require them openly to take sides in intra-familial disagreements.[180] Some courts and commentators, however, have wondered whether this consideration is sufficient.[181] Not only are many trustees and other private law administrators professionals; but all of them are administering the assets of others, so it hardly seems inappropriate to require them to give some account of their actions in relation to their powers.

D. Is an administrator required to hear from those affected by an exercise of their power?

This question seems to arise only in relation to trust law. An administrator who acts under instructions (such as an agent or mandatary) may or may not be obliged to seek instructions before exercising their power, say to make a contract

---

[179] Gaillard (n 15), 117.

[180] *Re Londonderry's Settlement* [1965] Ch 918 (CA); *Breakspear v Ackland* [2008] EWHC 220, [2009] Ch 32. See also *Re Gresham Life Assurance Society* (n 40), upholding the refusal of corporate directors to give their reasons, to a would-be transferee of shares, for their decision to disallow the share transfer. It was held in *Lewis v Tamplin* [2018] EWHC 777 (Ch) that this principle of immunity from the disclosure of reasons applies to dispositive discretions but not to administrative ones.

[181] See the dissenting judgment of Kirby P in *Hartigan Nominees Pty Ltd v Rydge* (1992) 29 NSWLR 405 (CA); Gaillard (n 15), 117–24; Lionel Smith, 'Massively Discretionary Trusts' (2017) 70 CLP 17, 48–51.

binding on the principal or mandator.[182] If they are not obliged then they are not obliged and no further question arises. The guardian or tutor who manages the property of an incapacitated person is required to pay attention to the wishes of that person to the extent that the person is able to communicate them.[183] This may require communication with the incapacitated person, as their wishes are controlling.

Other administrators do not act under instructions, and in many cases no question of hearing from the beneficiary will arise. Corporate directors could not seek input from the corporation, because it is incapable of providing instructions and the directors, as a body, are in fact the corporation's decision-making organ.

Trustees, however, often have dispositive discretions. These, if they are exercised, will usually benefit the chosen objects, but will impoverish, to a greater or lesser extent, the beneficiaries of the trust (or the other beneficiaries, if the chosen object is also a beneficiary).[184] The case of *Fox v Fox Estate*, discussed above,[185] provides an example (although the exercise of the power there was set aside). By advancing the trust capital to her grandchildren, the trustee would have ended the income and capital interests of her son, Walter. It is in this type of situation that it has sometimes been asked in the common law whether the trustee should first give someone in the position of Walter a chance to be heard. The general answer is 'no'.[186] Although the right to be heard has been described in public administration as part of the requirements of natural justice,[187] this is not seen to be applicable in private administration. The reasons for this are not entirely clear, as justice is as important in private law as it is in public law.[188] A majority of the High Court of Australia has said that a right to be heard arises in public law where '... the power involved is one which may "destroy, defeat or prejudice a person's rights, interests or legitimate expectations". Thus, what is decisive is the nature of the power, not the character of the proceeding which attends its exercise'.[189] Certainly the dispositive

---

[182] On the question of which administrators act under instructions, see Chapter 1, section V.b.3.c.
[183] Above, section III.2.C.1.
[184] This is discussed above, section IV.A.2. Executors, liquidators, or other administrators of the estate of a deceased person may have similar dispositive discretions; this will often, but not necessarily, be under the terms of a trust established pursuant to the will.
[185] Section IV.B.2.
[186] Some judicial pronouncements to this effect are collected in Raymond Davern, 'Impeaching the Exercise of Trustees' Distributive Discretions: "Wrong Grounds" and Procedural Unfairness' in D Hayton (ed), *Extending the Boundaries of Trusts and Similar Ring-Fenced Funds* (Kluwer Law International 2002) 437, 452–54; and in Toby Graham and Thomas Beasley, 'Trust the State: The Relevance of Principles of Public Law in Trust Law and Practice' (2019) 25 Trusts & Trustees 841.
[187] *Ridge v Baldwin* [1964] AC 40 (HL).
[188] Dawn Oliver, *Common Values and the Public-Private Divide* (reprint edn, CUP 2010), 95–99, 191–92.
[189] *Ainsworth v Criminal Justice Commission* (1992) 175 CLR 564, 576, quoting *Annetts v McCann* (1990), 170 CLR 596, 598.

powers of trustees and some other private administrators would often meet that test.[190]

Perhaps the only thing that can be said is that the question is in general a matter of construction and interpretation. In public law, even if the right to heard arises from the general law, it may be excluded by legislation. In private law, it is a trust instrument that needs to be interpreted. Thus perhaps the explanation is that a trust instrument which gives an unqualified dispositive power to the trustee is usually best interpreted as excluding any requirement that the holder of that power should hear from those affected before making their decision.[191]

E. Delegation of powers and fettering of discretion

In order for a private law administrator to use a power properly, she must turn her mind to the purpose for which the power was given, and how best that purpose can be achieved. This can be understood to underlie two general principles that are often seen in private law administration. One is that delegation may be prohibited.[192] An administrator who delegates a power is not in a position to turn *her* mind to the question of how to use the power, and to exercise *her* judgment accordingly. The law may allow the delegation of ministerial functions, such as collecting on a cheque, but these are precisely functions that do not require the exercise of other-regarding judgment.[193] The other principle is that an administrator may not 'fetter' her discretion, which means purporting to decide ahead of time how her judgment will be exercised at some point in the future.[194] Doing this would disable her from exercising her judgment at the crucial time, the moment in the future when the relevant decision needs to be made.

The principle against delegation, however, is far from absolute. In the modern world it has become evident that some functions are better

---

[190] Graham and Beasley (n 186) review the cases to conclude that natural justice does not apply, but neither they nor the courts provide any justification for this; the same is true of *Underhill and Hayton* (n 140), ¶60.16. See also *Telstra Super Pty Ltd v Flegeltaub* [2000] VSCA 180, [30], suggesting that 'bona fide inquiry and genuine decision making' (and not natural justice) may require a trustee to seek input from a person affected by the pending decision (here related to questions of fact); see also *Re Butler* [1951] 4 DLR 281 (Ont SC).

[191] Some of the cases cited by Davern (n 186) and by Graham and Beasley (n 186) involve charities; these are in fact cases of public, not private administration (Chapter 11, section II.A). In this sense, it is a mistake to oppose (as those authors do) 'trust law' and 'public law'. Although a charitable trust is a public trust, it is true that it is a creature of the trust instrument, not of legislation.

[192] Some examples from the common law: *Re Hay's Settlement Trusts* (n 100); *Haslam v Haslam* (1994) 114 DLR (4th) 562 (Ont Gen Div); *New Zealand Maori Council v Foulkes* [2015] NZCA 552, [2016] 2 NZLR 337. For the civil law, see Cantin Cumyn and Cumyn (n 15), 274–75.

[193] *Waters' Law of Trusts in Canada* (n 120), 968–72; cf Civil Code of Québec, art 1337.

[194] The principle and its limits are discussed in *Ringuet v Bergeron* [1960] SCR 672.

performed by experts, and that some tasks of administration (such as large corporations, in business or not) are so complex that delegation is essential. Hence in trust law, statutory interventions generally allow delegation for the investment function, under various conditions of monitoring, and possibly for other functions as well.[195] Corporate law may specify that the directors must 'manage, or supervise the management of' the business and affairs of the corporation.[196] In the common law, an agent cannot delegate his functions (except ministerial acts);[197] interestingly, the Quebec law of mandate explicitly allows a mandatary to engage a sub-mandatary, who is a delegate of the mandatary, unless the contract of mandate provides otherwise.[198] In all of these cases, the administrator who delegates remains responsible for the administration.[199]

Even though the principle against delegation has many exceptions, it still has, along with the principle against fettering discretion, a strong hold in many contexts of private administration. Where these principles apply, they represent a manifestation of the requirement of loyalty inasmuch as they require the administrator to turn his or her own mind to the decisions that must be made in the pursuit of the purpose for which the relevant powers were granted.[200] The general law of contract, including contractual powers that a person holds for their own benefit, has no general principles against delegation or fettering because one who exercises such powers is not constrained to use those powers in the furtherance of an other-regarding mission. The principle against delegation also reflects the personal nature of administration: the particular administrator has been chosen to exercise the relevant powers. As we have seen, this personal dimension is closely related to the subjective nature of the inquiry into loyalty.[201] If there was an objective answer to what the administrator must do, it would not matter whether it was done by delegation to another.

---

[195] *Waters' Law of Trusts in Canada* (n 120), 972–87.
[196] This is the language of *Canada Business Corporations Act*, RSC 1985, c C-44, s 102(1).
[197] Peter Watts and Francis MB Reynolds, *Bowstead and Reynolds on Agency* (22nd edn, Sweet & Maxwell 2020), ¶ 5–001(1).
[198] Civil Code of Québec, art 2142. The Code also contemplates the appointment by a mandatary of a substitute mandatary who replaces the original mandatary, but this must be expressly authorized (art 2140). See generally Adrian Popovici, *La couleur du mandat* (Les Éditions Thémis 1995), ch II.
[199] The details of this responsibility are variable by context. In the case of the Quebec sub-mandate, the original mandatary is fully liable for all acts of the sub-mandatary. In most contexts of authorized delegation, the original administrator is liable only for careless choice or supervision of the delegate.
[200] Cantin Cumyn and Cumyn (n 15), 274–78; Smith, 'Fiduciary Relationships' (n 4), 612.
[201] Above, section II.B.

F. Consequences of misuse of powers

1. Setting aside a legal act

Loyalty imposes a required way of using the powers that are subject to it; that is, powers held for an other-regarding mission. When the powers are not used with loyalty to the purpose for which they were granted, they have been misused. What is the consequence? The general consequence, subject to exceptions that exist for good reasons, is that the legal act that resulted from the improper exercise of the power by the administrator can be set aside.[202]

A legal act is what is called a 'juridical act' in France and Quebec, or a *Rechtsgeschäft* in German law; it does not have an established name in the common law tradition, but the idea is clear enough. It is an action that has legal effects that depend in part on the manifestation of an intention (in our case, the intention of the administrator) to bring about those legal effects.[203] Thus it includes making or accepting a contractual offer, issuing shares of a corporation, making a gratuitous transfer whether or not that is considered a contract in the relevant legal system, transferring property or rights of any kind, and so on.[204]

Even when one is acting for oneself, a legal act can be set aside when the manifestation of intention by which it was realized is vitiated in some way. Mistake and illegitimate pressure (called 'force and fear' in Scots law) are well-known vitiations. The ability to annul or rescind what one has done as a result of these vitiations is not absolute. If one has accepted a contractual offer based on a mistake that was caused by other party's untruth, or based on illegitimate pressure exercised by that other party, then one can almost certainly set aside the acceptance (and thus the contract). But if one has made a contract due to such a mistake or pressure and the other contracting party, *not* being the source of the vitiating factor, was entirely unaware of it, then the result may well be different. The manifestation of consent is equally vitiated, but in this variation the other contracting party has a relevant interest that is legally protected.

This framework helps us to understand why it is possible to set aside legal acts that arose from the disloyal exercise of a power by an administrator. Consent is constitutive of a legal act, and consent is undermined by mistake and by duress.

---

[202] Civil law: Gaillard (n 15); Cantin Cumyn and Cumyn (n 15). Common law: eg *Howard Smith* (n 17); *Whitehouse* (n 25); *Fox v Fox Estate* (n 158); *Pitt v Holt* (n 8); *Eclairs Group Ltd* (n 17).

[203] In fact, German law is more careful than the French tradition to distinguish the legal act (*Rechtsgeschäft*) from the declaration of intention (*Willenserklärung*). The legal act is that which results from one or more declarations of intention (possibly combined with other requirements). See Gerhard Dannemann and Reiner Schulze (eds), *German Civil Code: Bürgerliches Gesetzbuch (BGB)*, 2 vols, vol I (CH Beck 2020), 138–40.

[204] In Chapter 1, section IV.A.2, we noted that we are concerned with (a subset of) legal powers, which were defined as those powers the exercise of which requires a manifestation of intention. Thus the manifestation of intention is a necessary (but perhaps not sufficient) condition for the exercise of a legal power, and the legal act is the result of that if all necessary conditions are present.

Where a power is held by an administrator, it is by assumption held not for the benefit or the purposes of the administrator, but for the accomplishment of a mission; thus it can only be rightly used in the pursuit of that mission. In this case, loyalty to the purpose is constitutive of the legal act that is the exercise of that other-regarding power. Conversely, the law treats disloyalty in the exercise of such a power as a defect in the manifestation of intention that is necessary to exercise the power. The result is that the legal act resulting from the exercise of the power can be set aside, again subject to protection for those who have interests worthy of a countervailing legal protection (a topic to be discussed shortly).[205]

There is another parallel between loyalty on one hand, and mistake and duress on the other: all of these defects are internal to the subjective reasoning process of the legal actor. Of course, protections available to innocent third parties will often arise because such persons relied on objective appearances; but these protections will typically be withdrawn where the third party was subjectively aware of the relevant defect. The defect itself is subjective in nature, and its effect may be constrained when other interests need to be protected.

A good example of setting aside an improper legal act by an administrator, from the field of trust law, is the English case *Turner v Turner*.[206] The trustees had discretionary powers to appoint (or fix) beneficial interests, and to transfer property out of the trust to named persons. The trustees used these powers in various ways, but each time they merely did what the settlor (the creator of the trust) asked; the trustees did not actually turn their minds to the appointments that they made. They did not read or understand the documents that they signed. We could say that they were acting for improper purposes: they did not use their powers in the way that they were required to use them, exercising their own judgment for the accomplishment of their mission.[207] Later the trustees became concerned whether they had acted properly, and it was they who brought proceedings to determine the validity of what they had purportedly done. The court held that the appointments should be set aside, and that a person to whom property had been transferred had to re-transfer it. It did not matter that the trustees had been in good faith, nor did it matter that what they had done was within the scope of their authority; innocently perhaps, they had misused their powers.[208]

---

[205] Section IV.F.3.
[206] [1984] Ch 100.
[207] ibid 110: '... the trustees exercising a power come under a duty to consider. It is plain on the evidence that here the trustees did not in any way "consider" in the course of signing the three deeds in question'.
[208] Mervyn Davies J said (at 111) that one appointment was 'wholly void' and some commentators argue that the appointments were void, not voidable. But on the same page he said twice that all three appointments were 'set aside' retroactively (and used that phrase twice more); this is the language of voidability, since in the case of a wholly void act there is nothing to set aside.

It has been suggested in English law that although both cases involve the breach of fiduciary duties, there may be a difference between (1) exercising a power for an improper purpose and (2) exercising a power while either ignoring factors that one was legally required to consider, or considering factors that one was legally required to ignore.[209] Except perhaps as a matter of descriptive subdivision of the idea of disloyalty, there is no pressing reason to draw this distinction.[210] *Turner* shows that both problems are example of the overarching problem of disloyalty to the mission for which the power was granted, and so the distinction seems unnecessary. The trustees breached their fiduciary duties by ignoring the beneficiaries' interests, the very factor which should rightly have guided them. One could call this inadequate deliberation, or the use of the power for an improper purpose, or its disloyal use. There is no substantive difference between failing to consider factors that you were legally bound to consider and considering factors which the law classifies as improper considerations.

Thus, a legal act entered into for the wrong reasons—in violation of the requirement of loyalty to the purposes of the relevant power—can be set aside, at least potentially.[211]

2. Nullity, voidness, and voidability

When a legal power has been exercised defectively, there are several possible legal consequences. The civil law may consider it null, but there is absolute nullity and relative nullity.[212] Civilian authors tend to the view that the legal act arising from the disloyal exercise of a private administrative power is relatively null.[213] In the common law the act may be void or voidable, with the further complication that it may be fully valid 'at common law' while being void or voidable 'in Equity'.[214]

---

[209] *Pitt v Holt* (n 8), apparently distinguishing ([60]–[80]) between (1) using a power for an improper purpose and (2) using it with 'inadequate deliberation', and ([62]), suggesting that the former case leads to voidness (in Equity), while the latter only to voidability.

[210] See *Walters v Walters* 2022 ONCA 38, [45] and Lionel Smith, 'Can I Change My Mind? Undoing Trustee Decisions' (2009) 27 ETPJ 284.

[211] The same consequence does not follow where there has been a breach of the duty of care, skill and diligence, or prudence and diligence, that is owed by an administrator. That duty, which is discussed in Chapter 6, section III, requires careful administration and may lead to personal liability for loss caused by its breach. It is a duty in the strict sense but it is not a constitutive element of the proper exercise of a power. The requirement of loyalty, by contrast, is not a duty in the strict sense and is, rather, a required way of exercising powers (see below, section IV.G). This is why the exercise of a power can be set aside where there is a failure of loyalty. An extreme case (like *Turner*) may reveal both problems, but the legal responses to the two problems generate quite different remedies.

[212] Absolute nullity arises in the public interest, can be invoked by anyone including the court, and cannot be waived. Relative nullity arises to protect a particular interest, and can generally be invoked or waived only by the person or persons protected (note however Civil Code of Québec, art 1420: 'The relative nullity of a contract may be invoked only by the person in whose interest it is established or by the other contracting party, provided he is acting in good faith and suffers serious injury therefrom...').

[213] Gaillard (n 15), 114; Cantin Cumyn and Cumyn (n 15), 334–36.

[214] Thus a trustee may have a power under the trust to dispose of legal rights that she holds. If the power is exceeded or misused, its exercise may be void or voidable in Equity; but the transfer of legal

The dominant view in the common law is that an Equitable power used by a fiduciary for an improper purpose is voidable in Equity.[215]

It is sometimes said by common law commentators that when a fiduciary power is misused, the exercise is entirely void because it was unauthorized and so was outside the scope of the power.[216] This, however, seems to play on an equivocation in the concept of 'unauthorized'.[217] A power held by directors to issue shares does not authorize them to cancel shares; there is no authority for this (purported) act and it would be ineffective in law. But if the directors do issue shares, but do so for an improper purpose, this is not a case of the absence of power, but of the misuse of power. The consequences of misuse of power *could* be the same as the consequences of absence of power. But the cases are conceptually different inasmuch as a misuse of power supposes that the person misusing the power possessed the power that was misused.[218]

The responses of voidability, or relative nullity, make sense inasmuch as the exercise of the power was within the authority of the administrator, but the authority was exercised improperly and so misused. As with legal acts vitiated by mistake or duress, so it is with disloyalty: the act is imperfect, but it has some existence in law. As in those cases, the act can be set aside at the instance of the person whose interests are protected by the rule that makes the act defective. Moreover, as in those cases, the setting aside of the legal act operates retroactively. This is because the defect in the legal act was present at the moment it was made; it is not something that happened later. This retroactivity is the reason that in most cases, the distinction between relative nullity or voidability, on one hand, and complete voidness, on the other, makes no practical difference.

Again, however, there is protection for third parties, as discussed in the next section. For example, if the disloyal act was the making of a contract by the administrator with a third party who had no way of knowing of the administrator's

---

rights is probably effective even though there will be a right to have it reversed (*Turner* (n 206), 111; *Rolled Steel Products (Holdings) Ltd v British Steel Corp* [1986] Ch 246 (CA), 303).

[215] Eg *Whitehouse* (n 25), 293–94; *Pitt v Holt* (n 8), [43], [93]; Watts (n 224), 5; Michael Ashdown, *Trustee Decision Making* (OUP 2015), ch 6; see, arguing for a more complex understanding, Jessica Hudson, 'One Thicket in Fraud on a Power' (2019) 39 OJLS 577.

[216] Ross Grantham, 'The Powers of Company Directors and the Proper Purpose Doctrine' (1994–95) 5 KCLJ 16, 32–39; *Underhill and Hayton* (n 140), ¶¶ 60.33–60.36, 60.57. This analysis is explicitly rejected in leading cases such as *Howard Smith* (n 17), 834, and *Grand View Private Trust Co v Wong* (n 8), [59].

[217] Nolan (n 31), 300, calls it 'entirely artificial ... simply a sleight of hand'.

[218] *Underhill and Hayton* (n 140), ¶ 60.39 puzzlingly suggest that if a trust deed stipulates that powers can only be exercised following proper deliberation, then cases of improper deliberation will no longer lead to voidability but to voidness, apparently on the theory that such a clause would convert a misuse of power into an absence of power. That distinction, however, is not a creation of the trust deed. The deed is capable of articulating the trustees' authority, but not of converting the misuse of authority into its absence, since misuse arises from the subjective reasoning process of the trustees (see *Grand View Private Trust Co v Wong* (n 8) [61], [72]).

disloyal use of the power, then the third party can probably resist any attempt to have the contract set aside.

3. Protection of third parties

As we have already mentioned, the law often protects third parties who rely in good faith on appearances. Such protections exist not only in relation to problems of disloyalty, but also in relation to problems of mistake and duress, which are not explored here. Indeed, they may also exist in relation to problems of absence of authority.

Assume that an agent has authority to bind his principal to contracts, as a buyer, up to a price of $10,000. The agent purports to make a contract binding his principal to buy property for the price of $15,000. This is a purported legal act but one made without authority.[219] In principle, it is an absolute nullity, as much as would be a contract for a price of $10 million.[220] The limit on the agent's authority is objective. Why is it a nullity only 'in principle'? The reason is that rules exist to protect third parties who rely, in good faith, on appearances. These rules take different forms in different legal systems. Even within the same system, their contours may be different in different contexts. But in our example, these rules may well have the consequence that the third party, if they were unaware of the price limit on the agent's authority, can enforce the contract for $15,000 against the principal.[221] Although the absence of authority means that the legal act could not be created, the innocent third party is entitled to be treated *as if* the relevant legal act had been performed.[222]

---

[219] I leave aside the possibility of retroactive ratification.

[220] Here I do not mean 'absolute nullity' in the sense that this expression has in French and Quebec law, and in related civilian systems. In those systems the expression means a nullity that can be invoked by anyone, and that cannot be waived by anyone, but that still requires a court order. What I mean here is that the contract has no existence in law at all. In the French/Quebec tradition this is sometimes called a 'non-existent contract', which is as much a contradiction in terms as the common law expression 'void contract': *Montréal (Ville) v Octane Stratégie Inc* 2019 SCC 57, [61], [118]–[120].

[221] Civil Code of Québec, art 2163; Popovici (n 198), 107–18; Henri De Page and René Dekkers, *Traité élémentaire de droit civil belge*, vol 5 (2nd edn, Bruylant 1975), 443–45; Jérôme Huet and others, *Les principaux contrats spéciaux*, Jacques Ghestin (ed), *Traité de droit civil* (3rd edn, LGDJ 2012), 1078–82.

[222] Adrian Popovici, 'Le mandat apparent, une chimère?' in Anne-Sophie Hulin, Robert Leckey, and Lionel Smith (eds), *Les apparences en droit civil* (Éditions Yvon Blais 2015) 3. In the common law the usual explanation is that the contract binds the principal where the latter is estopped from denying his agent's authority, so that again the third party is treated as if there was a contract; but other theories exist (*Bowstead and Reynolds* (n 197), ¶¶ 8-027–8-028). Some of them entail that the unauthorized contract is a genuine contract, and this is also the position in German law (Dannemann and Schulze (n 203), 230–31) although the matter is debated (Basil S Markesinis, Hannes Unberath, and Angus Johnston, *The German Law of Contract: A Comparative Treatise* (2nd edn, Hart Publishing 2006), 113).

Almost every administrator has objective limits on their authority, limits which operate cumulatively with the subjective requirement of loyalty.[223] In respect of any act in excess of those objective limits, however, third parties may be protected in one way or another. Consider trust law: a trustee's power of investment can be restricted to certain investments by the trust instrument. If a trustee purchases an unauthorized investment, is the contract invalid? Not if the counterparty relied on in good faith on the objective appearance of authority. In Quebec civil law, this may be through the application of the general 'theory of appearances' that also applies in the context of mandate and in other settings.[224] In a common law trust, third parties are protected in a more complicated and historically contingent way, by the differing principles of common law and Equity. The trustee's lack of authority to acquire an investment is a matter for Equity; at common law, as the phrase goes, the trustee is the owner of the asset with which the unauthorized investment was purchased. The third party who gives value in good faith for that asset will not be affected by the Equitable limitations on the trustee's authority, unless the third party knew or should have known about them.

Thus these protections for third parties can operate even in cases where the administrator lacked, in an objective sense, the authority to perform the relevant legal act. They can operate a fortiori where the administrator had that authority but misused it, in the sense of using it in a way that did not comply with the requirement of loyalty.

In German law, the issues arise primarily in the context of the legal power of representation, which may be held by mandataries or others. This legal system and those following it in this respect are perhaps the most careful to distinguish between the scope of the administrator's power to bind the beneficiary to transactions with third parties, and any contractual or other limitations imposed between the beneficiary and the administrator who holds the power.[225] Limitations of the latter kind are unlikely to affect the third party, perhaps even if the third party is aware of them. This approach means that the protection of the third party is less likely than in other systems to turn on particular facts, such as

---

[223] For the cumulative nature of loyalty in addition to authority, see *Criterion Properties plc v Stratford UK Properties LLC* [2004] 1 WLR 1846 (HL), [4]; Peter Watts, 'Authority and Mismotivation' (2005) 121 LQR 4.

[224] Cantin Cumyn and Cumyn (n 15), 342–47. The theory is understood to arise from general principles even though these principles are exemplified in codal rules only in particular cases (eg in the Civil Code of Québec, art 447 (spouses), arts 1323 and 1362 (administration of the property of another), arts 2162–63 (mandate). As noted above (n 88), the rules of mandate have long and often been used to articulate general principles of administration in civilian systems.

[225] For the background and subsequent influence on other systems, see Wolfram Müller-Freienfels, 'Legal Relations in the Law of Agency: Power of Agency and Commercial Certainty' (1964) 13 Am J Comp Law 193, 197–200, and 341.

the knowledge of the third party or their reliance on appearances.[226] One might think that this would make it very difficult for a third party to be adversely affected by disloyalty in the use of a power of representation. There are however limit cases. The third party who knows that he is dealing with a representative always knows that the power of legal representation is held for the benefit of the represented beneficiary, and will not be able to enforce contracts which are obviously inconsistent with that mission.[227]

The invalidation of the exercise of administrative powers for disloyalty is perhaps seen more often in the law of trusts than in other settings of administration. One reason is that in many legal systems and contexts, the protection of third parties in good faith may not extend to one who receives a transfer of rights gratuitously (although this is by no means a universal principle). This is true of the Equitable principle mentioned above, which protects someone who acquires from a trustee a legal interest, for value, in good faith, and without notice of the trustee's lack of authority. That principle simply does not apply to one who receives gratuitously, and this is why it makes no appearance in cases like *Turner v Turner*[228] or *Fox v Fox Estate*.[229] The persons who benefited from the trustees' exercises of their powers were not protected by that principle.

A third party who needs to show that they relied on appearances must show that they did so in good faith; whether or not it is necessary that they made a bargain, it is necessary that they neither knew, nor should have known, of the defect that later comes to light. The defects that we have discussed in this section are want of authority and disloyalty, which means misuse of authority within its limits.[230] It follows that even in a commercial context of a bargain made for value, if the third party knew or should have known that the power was being misused by an administrator, that third party will not be able to claim to have relied in good faith on appearances.[231]

---

[226] Reasonable reliance is, however, a relevant factor in relation to apparent authority including in the sense of actual authority that has been revoked (Dannemann and Schulze (n 203), 230–31). Birke Häcker, *Consequences of Impaired Consent Transfers* (Mohr Siebeck 2009; Hart 2013) 216–26 discusses the strong protection of third parties in German law; her analysis focuses on transfers of rights rather than powers of legal representation.

[227] Dannemann and Schulze (n 203), 225; Matthias Weller, 'Who Gets the Bribe?—The German Perspective on Civil Law Consequences of Corruption in International Contracts' in Michael J Bonell and Olaf Meyer (eds), *The Impact of Corruption on International Commercial Contracts* (Springer 2015) 171, 180–81; see also the discussion in Müller-Freienfels (n 225) 207–15, 341–46.

[228] N 206.

[229] N 158.

[230] For an example of a third party who could not rely on appearances, see the Quebec case *Davis v Kerr* (1890) 17 SCR 235. Cantin Cumyn and Cumyn (n 224) treat the theory of appearances as equally applicable to an absence of power and a misuse of power; a lack of capacity, however, may not be curable by the theory of appearances (*Financière Transcapitale inc c Fiducie succession Jean-Marc Allaire* 2012 QCCS 5733). For the common law, see for example *Bowstead and Reynolds* (n 197), ¶¶8-220–8-221.

[231] See Watts (n 223), noting that a third party may be unable to rely on a contract made by an administrator within the administrator's authority, if the third party was aware that the administrator

4. Who can set aside a legal act that is defective for disloyalty?

Speaking generally, the act can be set aside at the instance of the person in whose interests the administrator was supposed to be acting: the principal, the mandator, the trust beneficiary, or other person as the case may be. This person may be a party to the legal act in question, but in many cases they are not a party. Take the case of a corporation whose directors cause it to issue shares for an improper purpose, which is a disloyal use of their administrative powers. In principle, the allotment of shares is voidable by the corporation, subject to protections for third parties that may be in order.[232] This case has some relationship to the situation in which a person who enters a legal act while under a mistake can set aside that legal act, to which they are a party, subject to protections that may be available to the other party.

The person in whose interests the administrator is supposed to act might not, however, be a party to the problematic legal act. An example would be a disloyal sale of trust property, by a trustee, to some third party. The beneficiaries are not in any sense parties to the contract.[233] They, however, are the ones in whose interests the trustee was supposed to be acting, and they can set aside the legal act (subject to protections for innocent third parties). This is further from the case of setting aside a contract for mistake, inasmuch as we are now looking at the setting aside of a contract by someone who is not a party to that contract. Some might find it difficult to contemplate the idea of a juridical act's being set aside by a non-party.[234] This concern, however, seems misplaced. When a defect in the formation of a legal act makes that act voidable, it is voidable in order to protect someone. In the case of mistake or duress, the person protected is a party to the transaction whose consent was vitiated. In the case of disloyalty, the person

---

was using their powers disloyally. Nolan (n 31), 318, makes a similar point but in my view incorrectly treats a disloyal use of authority as unauthorized (which seems contrary to his own argument at 300, where he notes that the proper purposes doctrine is conceptually different from the scope of authority). Recall that in German law a third party may be able to rely on an administrator's outward-facing authority without the need to show that they actually relied on appearances; but even here, a third party who is aware of misuse is unlikely to be protected (above, n 227).

[232] As is typical in corporate law, particularly where the directors whose conduct is impugned are still in control of the corporation, the courts may allow shareholders to assert the power of the corporation to set aside the allotment of shares. This is what happened in *Howard Smith* (n 17). This kind of representative enforcement is discussed in Chapter 8, Ssction III.C.2.c. This also means that the corporation, acting through another organ such as the shareholders, may be able to ratify an otherwise voidable allotment of shares: *Bamford v Bamford* [1970] Ch 212 (CA).

[233] Although some legal systems permit trusts in which the beneficiaries are the owners of the trust property (South African and Chinese law). Other systems would definitionally disqualify such structures as trusts.

[234] Ying-Chieh Wu, 'Trusts Reimagined: The Transplantation and Evolution of Trust Law in Northeast Asia' (2020) 20 Am J of Comp Law 1, 20–21, discussing the trust laws of Japan, South Korea, and Taiwan, which give beneficiaries a right of rescission exigible against third parties in relation to some unauthorized dispositions of trust property. Wu suggests that it is indefensible to say that the beneficiary has only personal rights and yet holds such a right of rescission.

protected may or may not be a party; but either way, they are the one whom the requirement of loyalty aims to protect, and so they are the one who can set aside the legal act if they so choose.

In an earlier section, it was noted that loyalty does not always operate as a requirement that powers be used in the best interests of some person or persons. Sometimes, loyalty requires an administrator to act in what he or she considers to be the best manner of fulfilling the *purpose* for which the power was granted.[235] In these cases, the question of who can intervene when the powers have been used improperly is more difficult. In Quebec law, arguably every trust, even if it has beneficiaries, is a purpose trust.[236] It is perhaps not surprising to see that a Quebec trust can be enforced not only by the beneficiaries, but also, since there may be none, by the settlor or his heirs, or by 'any interested party'.[237] The law thus gives standing to challenge the exercise of 'purpose powers' to an open-ended class of persons, a possibility much more typical in public law than in private law.[238]

In the common law, in the absence of legislation, the only purpose trusts are charitable trusts. The power of enforcement belongs to the Crown, which may delegate it by statute; a concerned citizen may be able to deploy that power, possibly via the relator action, possibly in their own name.[239] Within a private trust structure, even in the common law where private trusts must generally have persons as beneficiaries, it is not surprising to find that the objects of those powers (even if they are not beneficiaries of the trust) can rightly be understood to have the standing to challenge improper exercises, even though, as objects of powers, they have no rights at all that any benefit be conferred upon them.[240] Moreover, the trustees themselves may have that standing. *Turner v Turner*[241] was such a case: the trustees themselves questioned the validity of what they had done. In the same way, a trustee can challenge the actions of his or her co-trustee.[242] In these cases, of course, the administrators are not pressing claims of their own; they are doing what they think is best for the beneficiaries, and their standing comes from their being interested, not for themselves, but for the best interests

---

[235] Above, section IV.A.2.
[236] See n 143.
[237] Civil Code of Québec, arts 1287, 1290.
[238] See Chapter 10, section II.H.
[239] The relator action is discussed in Chapter 10, section II.G.2; the possibility of public law standing to enforce claims against charitable administrators is discussed in Chapter 11, section II.A.
[240] *Re Manisty's Settlement* [1974] Ch 17, 25. Beneficiaries of the trust also have standing. It is important that not only the beneficiaries have standing, since their own interest may well be in the direction that the powers never be exercised (see above, section IV.A.2).
[241] N 206.
[242] *Nelson v Larholt* [1948] 1 KB 339 (one plaintiff was co-executor with the defendant executor). It seems also that successor trustees could bring proceedings in relation to actions of their predecessors: see *Waters' Law of Trusts in Canada* (n 120), 1059–61.

of the beneficiaries as a whole. In the end, one might think, the common law is not that different from Quebec law: a range of persons are considered 'interested parties' and granted standing to protect the proper use of trustees' powers.

We will return later to this question of representative supervision.[243] The conclusion here is that the disloyal exercise of a power can be set aside at the instance of persons who are not parties to the legal act that resulted from that exercise. This includes the person or persons whose interests should have been the guiding consideration in the exercise of the power. Moreover, in different ways, other persons may have standing to challenge the exercise of the power for disloyalty.

5. Misuse by non-use

What if a power is *not* used for improper purposes? Above I drew an analogy between setting aside the exercise of a power for disloyalty and setting aside other legal acts arising from manifestations of consent that are defective on the ground of mistake or duress. If, due to a mistake, a person did *not* accept a contractual offer, there would be nothing to set aside. It is possible that someone is liable for wrongfully causing any harm which results, but that is a quite separate inquiry from one into defects of consent.

Klug v Klug[244] bears some resemblance to *Fox v Fox Estate*[245] and was cited in that case. In *Klug*, a young woman was an income beneficiary under a trust created by her father's will. She owed a substantial amount of tax arising out of this inheritance, and could not pay it out of the limited income she was receiving. The trustees were her mother and the Public Trustee, and they had a discretionary power to advance to the daughter up to one-half of the capital that was held for her. The Public Trustee wished to use this power to pay the tax, but the mother refused to consent because her daughter had married without the mother's consent. In the common law, the default rule in non-charitable trusts is that trustees must act unanimously in exercising discretionary powers; thus the mother was able to block the exercise. The daughter took proceedings and the Court ordered that the course of action desired by the Public Trustee should take place. The mother's improper non-exercise could not be set aside. What the Court did, in effect, was to temporarily remove her from participating in a decision, where she had acted disloyally in making her decision against the use of the power.

Traditionally, courts did not *order* administrators to exercise their powers, even if the court was of the view that there had been an improper non-

---

[243] Chapter 8, section III.C.2.
[244] N 140.
[245] N 158.

exercise.[246] This relates to the jurisdictional point discussed above.[247] Whether and how an administrative power should rightly be used is not a purely legal question that is within the knowledge of the court; it is a matter for the judgment of the administrator, the one who holds the power. Improper non-exercise may be a reason to remove an administrator, either temporarily (as in *Klug*) or permanently. If the court were to order that the power be used in a particular way, it would effectively be taking over the administrator's role. The court may well be able to do that, taking on an advisory or supervisory role, but usually only if the administrator requests it or resigns.[248]

G. Disloyalty in the use of powers is not necessarily a breach of duty

In this chapter, I have often referred to a 'requirement' of loyalty rather than the more common phrase, a 'duty of loyalty'. There is a reason for this: loyalty, when it is understood as a required way of using powers held for others, is not a duty in a strict sense.[249] By a 'duty in the strict sense', I mean a situation where one person owes a duty and someone else has a corresponding right. If I have a duty to pay you $100, you have a right against me to be paid $100.

But not every legal rule that generates legal consequences is a duty in the strict sense that it corresponds to a right held by another person; and not every case of non-compliance with a legal rule is a breach of duty that attracts a sanction.[250] Courts often say that plaintiffs have a 'duty to mitigate' when they have been wronged, especially (but not only) in the context of breach of contract. They must conduct themselves reasonably, so as to minimize the loss suffered, rather than to act in such a way that the loss is magnified. But although this is a way in which the law requires such plaintiffs to behave, it is not a duty in a strict sense.[251]

---

[246] *McPhail v Doulton* [1971] AC 424 (HL), 456 (Lord Wilberforce): '... although the trustees may, and normally will, be under a fiduciary duty to consider whether or in what way they should exercise their power, the court will not normally compel its exercise.'

[247] Section II.B.

[248] For a discussion of courts acting like administrators when they are in a supervisory role, see Chapter 1, section V.B.3.d. In *Walters v Walters* (n 210), the Court ordered trustees to exercise their dispositive discretions but apparently without removing them (although their removal had been sought). It is not clear that the Court was made aware that this is not a usual order. See also *Re Hodges* (1878) 7 ChD 754 and *Mettoy Pension Trustees Ltd v Evans* [1990] 1 WLR 1587 (ChD), 1617–18.

[249] Smith, 'Can We Be Obliged to be Selfless?' (n 10); Mitchell (n 10).

[250] See the discussion of 'power-conferring rules' in Herbert LA Hart, *The Concept of Law* (3rd edn, 2012) 27–35, noting that the failure to comply with all of the requirements of a power-conferring rule is not a breach of duty.

[251] *Southcott Estates Inc v Toronto Catholic District School Board* 2012 SCC 51, [2012] 2 SCR 675, [72]: 'A plaintiff is not contractually obliged to mitigate, and in this sense the term "duty to mitigate" is misleading.'

The plaintiff who fails to mitigate has not committed a legal wrong, an infringement of another's right. That plaintiff will merely find that his claim to damages is reduced.[252]

So it is with loyalty in the manifestation that is addressed in this chapter: it is a required way of exercising powers.[253] If it is not complied with, there are consequences: legal acts can be set aside. But the requirement of loyalty in the exercise of powers is not a duty in the strict sense.[254] Again, *Turner v Turner* is a good illustration. This was not in any sense a claim for compensation or damages. The trustees were not being sued for having breached a duty; indeed, they were the ones who commenced the proceeding. The conclusion of the court was that their powers had been improperly used, and so their exercise was set aside. No monetary liability was claimed or arose.

We can again draw an analogy with mistake. Consider the case in which a person, A, has entered into a contract under some serious mistake that was brought about by the other party, B. Even if B was acting perfectly innocently, A can probably set the contract aside. This right or power or ability on the part of A does not arise because B did something unlawful; it arises because consent is constitutive of a legal act, and consent is undermined by a serious mistake. Thus mistake may allow a legal act to be set aside because the act is not unimpeachably constituted. But when that happens, it does not follow that there has been a breach of duty by anyone. There may have been, as there would be in a case of deliberate deceit, but the ability to set aside a legal act does not depend on that.

In the same way, a disloyal exercise of a power *may* involve a breach of duty in the strict sense. A trustee generally has a power to dispose of trust property for appropriate purposes. If a trustee simply embezzles the trust property, disposing of it to himself, then of course there is a breach of duty, perhaps several breaches of several duties, in this misuse of the power. Some of these will be examined later.[255] But the fundamental point is that a disloyal and thus improper exercise of a power can be set aside, without the *need* to show that a duty, in the strict sense, has been breached.

---

[252] Another example, given by Megarry J in *Tito v Waddell (No 2)* [1977] Ch 106, 249, is that if a trustee becomes personally bankrupt, they may be subject to removal (and the same is true of a corporate director); but the operation of this legal rule does not reveal a breach of duty in the strict sense.

[253] See Hudson (n 215), 579–82, referring to 'fraud on a power' as involving a standard and not a duty. *Grand View Private Trust Co v Wong* (n 8) was concerned with loyalty in the exercise of fiduciary powers, and refers twice ([51], [52]) to the 'duties *and restrictions*' that govern the exercise of such powers (emphasis added).

[254] See Gaillard (n 15), 109–13; Cantin Cumyn and Cumyn (n 15), 328, distinguishing nullity for misuse of powers from liability for wrongful conduct (fault). Both sources note that in French and Quebec law, liability for fault requires proof of loss caused by the fault, while nullity for misuse of powers does not.

[255] Chapter 6.

This distance from duties in the strict sense underlines once again that in the context of an other-regarding power, loyalty to the purpose of that power is constitutive of its proper exercise. Disloyalty means that the power has not been unimpeachably exercised.

In discussing private law administrators, commentators and courts may say that the administrator owes a duty to *act* in the best interests of the beneficiary. As a general proposition, this is inaccurate and potentially misleading.[256] Usually, what is meant is that the exercise of administrative powers is subject to the requirement (not duty) of loyalty. The administrator does typically have some legal duty to act, so that if he or she does nothing at all, this will be unlawful. The administrator is presumptively subject to a duty of care, skill and diligence, or in civilian terminology, duties of prudence and diligence.[257] But the formulation of an open-ended duty to *act* in the best interests of the beneficiary is clearly wrong. If the administrator were under such a duty, would he not be under a duty to give all his wealth to the beneficiary, and to spend all his time trying to advance the interests of the beneficiary? This is obviously not right. The duty of care, skill, and diligence; or duties of prudence and diligence, tell the administrator, in objective terms, how much effort he or she must expend on the affairs of the beneficiary. The requirement of loyalty tells the administrator how to use their administrative powers properly.

V. Plurality of roles

In the right circumstances, a person can be both an administrator and a beneficiary of that administration. Normally a person cannot be in a juridical relationship with himself or herself. But this is possible when the person plays multiple roles and where at least one other person is involved on at least one side of the relationship.

Some examples will illustrate this. In the common law, a person cannot hold property on trust for the benefit of himself; that would amount to saying that he simply owns the property in the normal, non-trust way. There would be no point in trying to distinguish when he is acting 'as a trustee' from when he is acting otherwise, since the only one concerned with how he acts as a trustee is himself. But it is possible for a person to hold property on trust for a group of people (being at least two in number), of which he is a member.[258] In this situation, we

---

[256] David Pollard, 'The Short-Form "Best Interests Duty"—Mad, Bad and Dangerous to Know' (n 44).

[257] Chapter 6, section III. There may also be contractual duties to act.

[258] In Quebec, this is also possible except that a beneficiary cannot be the sole trustee (Civil Code of Québec, art 1278).

have to play close attention to when he is acting as a trustee. The reason is that when he does so, he must act in what he perceives to be the best interests of the beneficiaries, and this means of *all* the beneficiaries. And the other beneficiaries, of course, have the legal standing to hold him to account for his use of his administrative (trustee) powers. Conversely, it is also possible for a group of trustees (being at least two in number) to hold property in trust for a beneficiary who is one of the trustees. Here again, it is important to know when that person is acting as a trustee, because in that role he must act along with the other trustees. And combining both possibilities, it is possible for a person to be a member of a group of persons who are trustees for a group of beneficiaries, while also being a member of that group of beneficiaries.

Such situations are everyday fare in the law of business partnerships. A partnership is not a legal person in most legal systems.[259] In law, it is simply a group of persons, typically doing business under a common name. Each partner is in a relationship of administration with, we may say, 'the partnership'; but since the partnership is not a person in law, what we actually mean is that each partner is in such a relationship with each and all of the partners. But he or she is one of the partners. It is because there are multiple partners that this is legally and conceptually possible. A person who can use a power however he wishes is not an administrator in relation that power. But a person who must use the power in what he perceives to be the best interests of a group is an administrator, even if he is a member of that group.[260] This is because he must take account of interests other than his own; he cannot do just as he wishes; and he can be held to account by other persons in relation to how he exercised the power.

It is also common that an administrator, in assessing what are the best interests of the beneficiary, may be able to consider the interests of others.[261] In corporate law, this is called a 'stakeholder' approach, although it is not obvious why such persons need to be characterized as stakeholders. In that context, the directors owe their duties to the corporation that they administer, but they are permitted, in assessing the interests of the corporation, to consider (for example) the interests of the corporation's employees. Corporations all over the world provide benefits to their employees that they are not legally required to provide, and the expenditure of corporate resources in this way can easily be justified on the basis that the directors believe that it is in the best interests of the corporation. This is simply because most corporations need their employees and most corporations flourish when their employees are well treated. The corporate law context shows that an administrator may even rightly be able to consider their own interests

---

[259] Scots law is an exception: Partnership Act 1890, s 4(2).
[260] Gaillard (n 15), 21 defines an (administrative) power as one that must be exercised in the pursuit of an interest that is at least partially distinct from that of the holder.
[261] This was discussed above, section IV.B.1.

in deciding what is in the best interests of the corporation. The reason is that a corporate administrator may be an employee (as in the case of an officer or managing director) and may also be a shareholder. In assessing the interests of the corporation, the administrator may consider the interests of employees and shareholders, of which she may be well be one.

Thus even when an administrator is not technically in the class of beneficiaries (as they are in the trust and partnership examples given earlier in this section), they may be able to consider their own interests in exercising their powers. This is simply a consequence of the fact that beneficiaries are not atoms living in separate worlds, but are functioning in the actual world in which people interact and are interdependent. When we say that an administrator cannot consider his or her own interests, we say something that is generally true, but to which there may be exceptions, because the contexts of legal relationships of administration are so varied.

4
Conflicts in Relation to Private Law Administration

I. Introduction

This chapter examines the norms relating to conflicts, in the context of private law administrators. After outlining those norms, it aims to provide a sound definition of them, and a justification for them that is tied to the requirement of loyalty that was discussed in the preceding chapter. It then explores the consequences that may be attached when these norms are violated. Finally, it considers the wide range of ways in which it may be possible to manage conflicts when they arise. All of this follows the interpretive methodology described in Chapter 1.[1]

II. Overview of the rules against conflicts

A. Examples of conflicts

One of the oldest legal norms regulating the use of legal powers in a conflict situation is found in the *Digest* of Justinian; the text is an extract from a book written around 200 CE:

> A *tutor* cannot buy a thing belonging to his ward; this rule extends to other persons with similar responsibilities, that is, curators, procurators, and those who conduct another's affairs.[2]

We see almost the same norms in art 1596 of the French *Code civil*, which provides in part:

---

[1] Chapter 1, section III.
[2] Alan Watson (ed), *The Digest of Justinian*, 4 vols (revised edn, U of Pennsylvania Press 1998), 18.1.34.7 (Paul). A tutor is the civil law term for the guardian of a minor. A procurator in this context can be understood as a litigation representative.

The Law of Loyalty. Lionel Smith, Oxford University Press. © Lionel Smith 2023.
DOI: 10.1093/oso/9780197664582.003.0004

The following persons cannot be buyers, either directly or through an intermediary, or else the contract will be null:

Tutors, of the property of their wards;
Mandataries, of the property that they are mandated to sell; ...
Trustees, of the trust property.[3]

These texts speak to the kind of conflict known as a conflict of self-interest and duty. They address the case in which the tutor, or other administrator, is proposing to buy, for himself, a thing belonging to his ward or other beneficiary. The conflict exists because the tutor is on both sides of the same transaction. He proposes to buy the thing, for himself; but he is also selling it, not for himself, but through the exercise of the powers that he holds in an administrative capacity to allow him to manage the affairs of the beneficiary. His self-interest favours a sale at a low price; his duty to his beneficiary, which governs the exercise of his other-regarding powers, favours a sale at a high price.[4] This is the conflict. As we will see, in the modern law there is not necessarily an absolute prohibition on such a sale. It might be possible to manage the conflict in such a way that the sale can go ahead. Identifying the conflict is a separate step from deciding what are its consequences.

This situation is often generically referred to as 'self-dealing' and it is perhaps the archetype of a conflict situation. It is not by chance that it was well-known to the Roman jurists. There are, however, other types of conflicts. First, the self-interest that conflicts with the administrator's duty need not be financial or pecuniary self-interest, nor need it be a legally protected interest. It only needs to be a self-interest, that is, something that would be beneficial to the administrator. If the administrator proposed to sell the property of his ward to the spouse of the administrator, this would be a conflict of self-interest and duty. If the administrator was a convicted criminal, and was selling the property of the ward to a buyer who had the power to grant a pardon to the administrator, this would be

---

[3] My translation of: 'Ne peuvent se rendre adjudicataires, sous peine de nullité, ni par eux-mêmes, ni par personnes interposées: Les tuteurs, des biens de ceux dont ils ont la tutelle; Les mandataires, des biens qu'ils sont chargés de vendre; ... Les fiduciaires, des biens ou droits composant le patrimoine fiduciaire.' I have omitted the provisions dealing with public officers. Cf Civil Code of Québec, art 1709. The civilian idea of 'nullity' does not refer absolute voidness. In its guise of 'relative nullity' which is relevant here, it means that a contract or other legal act is vulnerable to being set aside retroactively by a judicial declaration, which generally speaking may be sought only by the party who is protected by the nullity.

[4] In the previous chapter we saw that the requirement of loyalty that applies to all other-regarding powers of administrators is not actually a duty but a required manner of exercising the powers. In line with that, the problem described here is that self-interest conflicts with the requirement of loyalty. Since the administrator does owe duties to the beneficiary (see Chapters 5 and 6), and since the expression 'conflict of self-interest and duty' is established, I use it.

a conflict of self-interest and duty because this administrator has a special personal interest in pleasing this particular buyer.

The *Digest* extract quoted above is in a section dealing with sale—as is art 1596 of the French civil code—and both texts say that the conflicted administrator cannot be a buyer of the administered property. It is obvious, of course, that the problem is more general; the conflicted administrator also cannot be a seller who will be paid his price out of the property he is administering.[5] Nor is the principle confined to sale; a lease in either direction would be equally problematic.[6]

There can also be conflicts that do not involve self-interest. Consider the case in which a guardian proposes to sell property belonging to his ward to a corporation. If the guardian had a financial interest in the corporation, this would be another simple example of a conflict of self-interest and duty. Now assume that the guardian does not have any financial interest in the corporation, but the guardian is a director of the buying corporation. As such, the guardian is an administrator vis-à-vis the corporation, and he owes duties to the corporation. This is not a conflict of self-interest and duty, inasmuch as the guardian's self-interest is not directly in play; he does not stand to benefit from the transaction no matter what happens. It is not a case of self-dealing in the ordinary sense. Rather, this is a conflict of duty and duty. The guardian is, again, on both sides of the transaction; but in this variant, it is not the case that he is on one side personally and on the other side as an administrator; rather, he is on both sides as an administrator.[7]

This might be thought to be, in some sense, less serious than a conflict of self-interest and duty, inasmuch as the administrator cannot extract any benefit from the situation. But it may be treated by the law as an equally serious problem. A case which is frequently problematical, and often litigated, is that in which a lawyer or a law firm acts for two clients whose interests are opposed. This is treated, by the law and by professional ethical standards, as a serious problem that must be regulated, regardless of whether the lawyer's self-interest is implicated.[8] The problem would be a serious one even if the lawyer was working pro bono for both clients. Although the administrator does not stand to profit in such a case, from the beneficiary's point of view, the problem is as serious as a conflict of self-interest and duty: the beneficiary wants the administrator to be concerned solely with the best interests of the beneficiary in exercising the

---

[5] This is made explicit in Civil Code of Québec, art 1709, para 2.

[6] The Civil Code of Québec has more generic norms forbidding the exercise of administrative powers in a conflict situation: arts 324–26 (directors of legal persons), 1310–12 (administrators of the property of others (which includes trustees); 2138, 2143, 2147 (mandataries).

[7] As with conflicts of self-interest and duty (see n 4), the problem here is the conflict between opposing requirements of loyalty; but the administrator does owe duties to each beneficiary, and the phrase 'conflict of duty and duty' is well established in law.

[8] On conflicts of duty and duty, below, section IV.B; on professionals as public administrators; and Chapter 11, section V.

administrator's other-regarding powers, and the beneficiary is rightly concerned if the administrator's decision-making is affected by inappropriate factors, whether those factors concern the welfare of the administrator himself, or that of some other beneficiary.[9]

This helps us to understand the rationale of the conflicts rules, because it helps us to see that it is too simplistic to think that the conflicts rules are just about trying to stop administrators from wrongly taking advantage of their function or role. Rather, the rules aim to stop administrators from using their powers in situations where their judgment is liable to be affected, in unknowable ways, by improper considerations. We will return presently to this.

Later, we will distinguish conflicts of interest from potential conflicts of interest and from apparent conflicts of interest. We will also introduce the idea that conflicts can be of varying degrees of severity.

B. Some misunderstandings about conflicts

1. Conflict of interest and conflict of interests

Before that, it is important to say what is *not* a conflict for the purposes of this analysis. There are many situations in which a person may feel 'torn' and 'conflicted'. A person may feel conflicted when she is deciding how much of her wealth to spend on her own ends, and how much to pass on to her children, or to give to charity. But this kind of 'conflict' has nothing to do with this study. Subject to her legal obligations relating to support and so on, these decisions can be made however the person wishes. They may feel, and be, difficult, but they do not involve powers held in an administrative capacity.

Moreover, a 'conflict between interests' or a 'conflict of *interests*' is not a 'conflict of interest'.[10] When two independent parties are negotiating a contract, their

---

[9] If we draw a distinction between conflicts of self-interest and duty, on the one hand, and conflicts of duty and duty, on the other, there may be cases which are difficult to classify as one or the other: see Lionel Smith, 'Conflict, Profit, Bias, Misuse of Power: Dimensions of Governance' in PB Miller and Matthew Harding (eds), *Fiduciaries and Trust: Ethics, Politics, Economics and Law* (CUP 2020) 149, 161. However, since both kinds are problematical, nothing generally turns on this overlap.

[10] Michael Davis, 'Conflict of Interest' in Ruth Chadwick (ed), *Encyclopedia of Applied Ethics* (2nd edn, Elsevier 2012) 571, 571, 576; Remus Valsan, 'Fiduciary Duties, Conflict of Interest, and Proper Exercise of Judgment' (2016) 62 McGill LJ 1, 16; David Kershaw, 'Corporate Law's Fiduciary Personas' (2020) 136 LQR 454, 471–77. See also Remy Cabrillac, 'Les conflits d'intérêts en droit civil' in Centre français de droit comparé (ed), *Les conflits d'intérêts: fonction et maîtrise* (Société de législation comparée 2013) 236, 237: 'Surely then conflicts of interests are everywhere and thus nowhere? Is not every rule of private law promulgated in order to resolve a conflict of interests?' (my translation of: 'Mais alors le conflit d'intérêts n'est-il pas partout et par conséquent nulle part? Toute règle de droit civil n'est-elle pas édictée pour arbitrer un conflit d'intérêts?'). Cabrillac goes on to say that 'conflict of interest' must be confined to a conflict between the interests of one person and those of another person for whom the first person is responsible; this corresponds closely to the definition I will offer below.

interests are opposed and therefore in conflict. This is normal and not inherently problematic. There are norms that protect the integrity of the bargaining process, relating to undue influence, duress, misrepresentation, and so on. But this situation of conflicting interests is not what we mean by a conflict of interest. When parties conclude a contract, their interests remain in conflict, but their rights and obligations are crystallized in the valid contract. Again, this is not what we mean by a conflict of interest.

This is important because of the volume of scholarship relating to what economists call 'agency costs', using 'agency' not in its juridical nor in its philosophical sense but to mean acting through others.[11] The important point is that the economist's agency costs arise not only in the context of legal powers held in an administrative capacity, but in a much wider range of relationships. They arise in many simple employment relationships, and also in relationships with an independent contractor which are not employment relationships.[12] Agency costs include 'looting' and 'shirking'. Take the case of an employee in a large retail store. If the employee disappears into a back room whenever a customer needs assistance, this is shirking. It is an agency cost because it is a cost, imposed on the store owner, that arises through the use of other persons in his or her business; if the store owner could do everything himself or herself, this cost would not arise. If the employee were to misappropriate merchandise belonging to the store owner, this would be looting: another agency cost. If the employee were to work a shorter shift than that for which he is paid, one might say he is shirking (doing less than that for which he is paid) or looting (taking assets of the store owner to which the employee has no right: wages that he has not earned). But although these actions are breaches of contract, and possibly torts and crimes, none of them creates a conflict of interest. The problems do not arise because the employee is exercising a legal power which they must use, according to their judgment, in the interests of another; this employee has no such powers. The problems arise simply because the employee's interests are opposed to those of the employer, and the employee's self-interest may lead him to favour his own interests at the expense of the employer. This is a conflict of *interests*. Because this employee has no legal powers held in a managerial capacity, there can be no conflict of interest in the sense of that term that is relevant to this study. If

---

[11] In Chapter 1, section V.B.3.b.3, this was characterized as political representation.

[12] In other words, there may be 'agency cost' problems in the economic sense in a contractual relationship that is not, in the legal sense, an agency (or mandate) relationship, and not a relationship between an administrator and a beneficiary. These problems arise whenever 'when one party (the agent) has discretionary and unobservable decision-making authority that affects the wealth of another party (the principal)': Robert H Sitkoff, 'An Agency Costs Theory of Trust Law' (2004) 69 Cornell L Rev 621, 636. I am aware that in US law, every employment relationship is an agency relationship, which is not true in other common law jurisdictions; however, even in US law, a relationship between independent contractors is not legally an agency relationship, but it can give rise to agency costs in the economic sense.

an employee steals, or shows up late for work, there are of course legal and non-legal sanctions, but they are not relevant to this book. The conflict of *interests* between employer and employee is regulated entirely by contract law, property law, and so on. There is no need, and no occasion, to call on the principles governing conflicts of interest. The economist's category of agency costs is not one that is confined to relationships of administration.[13]

2. Administrators and conflicts of interests

Of course, people who *are* administrators may also be in conflicts of *interests*, and this can create confusion because these people are indeed subject to the rules about conflicts of interest. One could say, in fact, that every administrator is constantly in a situation of conflict of *interests*: this is because his or her interests are in some ways opposed to those of the beneficiary for whom he or she acts. The administrator's self-interest, narrowly construed, is to do as little as possible for the beneficiary, leaving the administrator with more time for their own activities. This conflict is present whether or not the administrator yields to it in any way: to identify a conflict, whether a conflict of interests or a conflict of interest, is not the same as saying that anyone has been affected by the conflict.[14] And it is present whether the administrator is remunerated or not, because however well or poorly one is paid, it is in one's self-interest to finish the job as quickly as possible.[15]

This is enough to show us that there is no *general* rule against being in a conflict of interests; there could not be. Thus any account of this area of law that is premised on a prohibition against conflicts of interests must be misconceived. So too must be an account that says that administrators are disqualified from exercising their fiduciary powers when they are in a conflict of interests: every administrator is always in a conflict of interests, and it would not make sense to suggest that they are therefore always disqualified from exercising their powers. There can be no prohibition against being or acting in a conflict of interests; if there were, relationships of administration could not lawfully exist. The principle is that an administrator is disqualified from exercising their fiduciary powers

---

[13] This, incidentally, shows that it is unworkable to develop a theory of relationships of administration (or, in common law terms, of fiduciary relationships) that posits that the function of such relationships is to control agency costs. If that were right, the category of such relationships would be much wider than it is in the actual law. For example, bakers and mechanics would be administrators (or fiduciaries) towards their customers: see the description of the scope of agency costs in n 12, and Lionel Smith, 'Parenthood Is a Fiduciary Relationship' (2020) 70 UTLJ 395, 409–10.

[14] See generally Smith (n 9).

[15] This may not be true of an administrator paid by time; but this only underlines the point that the conflict of *interests* is ubiquitous. If this administrator's self-interest lies in the direction of spending *more* paid time on the work that the beneficiary will pay for, that obviously conflicts with the beneficiary's interests just as much as in the case of an administrator whose interest lies in spending less time on the work.

when they are in a conflict of interest, or a conflict of duty and duty. In those situations, their exercise of other-regarding judgment stands to be influenced by an improper consideration: their own interest, or that of a person extraneous to the relationship. It follows that any definition of 'conflict of interest' that merely looks for conflicting interests is unhelpful and confusing.[16]

The reason that the administrator's self-interest in relation to how much effort she expends does *not* create a conflict of self-interest and duty is simply that there is no particular reason to worry that it will have an adverse effect on the manner in which she exercises her judgment in relation to her discretionary powers. Imagine again that we are dealing with a guardian, selling the property of the ward. Laziness might cause the guardian to do nothing, and a legal sanction might be in order if there is a breach of the duty of care and skill, or of diligence and prudence. But there is no reason to think that laziness will lead to the *misuse* of the guardian's powers in relation to any particular sale that the guardian makes or has made, in the sense of the use of those powers for an ulterior or improper purpose. As we saw earlier, the rules about conflicts exist for a precise reason: to protect against the misuse of the administrator's powers, in the sense of protecting against the use of those powers for improper purposes. It is the role of other norms to protect against simple inaction. The administrator's self-interest in relation to how much work they do is regulated, not by the rules on conflicts of interest, but by the duty that in the common law is known as the duty of care, skill, and diligence, and in the civil law may be called the duty of diligence and prudence. This is a legal duty that tells the administrator, objectively, how much work they are required to do.[17]

One author has suggested that a conflict of interest arises when a person is exercising powers as an administrator, but at the same time her decision-making may be influenced by her desire to advance her own career, by doing her job well.[18] In fact, this is another example of a conflict of interests (or another way of describing the same conflict of interests that we have already looked at). It is true that considerations relating to career advancement are not proper considerations in relation to the exercise of judgment by an administrator. But the crucial point is that there is no particular reason to think that this extraneous consideration will influence the administrator's judgment in their use of their

---

[16] This is one reason that the argument in Matthew Conaglen, *Fiduciary Loyalty: Protecting the Due Performance of Non-Fiduciary Duties* (Hart 2010) does not, in my view, succeed. Conaglen supposes that fiduciary law forbids a fiduciary from being in a situation in which their self-interest is in conflict with their non-fiduciary duties towards the beneficiaries. In fact, every fiduciary is always in a conflict of that kind, since what he describes is a conflict of *interests*, not a conflict of interest.

[17] Chapter 6, section III. There may also be positive contractual obligations.

[18] Stark calls this an in-role conflict: Andrew Stark, 'Comparing Conflict of Interest Across the Professions' in Michael Davis and Andrew Stark (eds), *Conflict of Interest in the Professions* (OUP 2001) 335, 336 and *passim*. Other cases of what Stark calls in-role conflicts are conflicts of duty and duty in legal terminology.

powers. The person wishes to do a good job and to be personally successful as a result; they have a self-interest in that. But this consideration, if anything, points in the direction of causing her to do a *better* job of considering proper factors in exercising her judgment as an administrator. A conflict of interest would arise only if the administrator's personal interest was *opposed* to (in conflict with) the requirements of loyalty that apply to the exercise of her powers.

Compensation strategies are often designed to try to eliminate the conflicts of interests that are inherent in employment and other bilateral relationships. Any financial incentive to do a good job falls into this category. A simple example would be commissions or bonuses for salespersons; these may align their interests more closely with their employer's interests. An example from relationships of administration, however, shows some of the dangers: the attempt to address a conflict of interests may create a conflict of interest. Consider the case of the grant to a corporate officer of options to acquire corporate shares. Again, the goal is to align the financial interests of the administrator with the interests of the corporation; in other words, to minimize the conflict of interests. Such systems may fail by introducing a conflict of interest in the strict sense. As we have seen, the mere fact that it is in an administrator's self-interest to be successful does not create a conflict of interest because it does not typically introduce an improper (selfish) consideration into her exercise of her other-regarding powers. But variable compensation can generate the opposite effect. It is notorious that option plans may lead to inappropriately short-term thinking. The director's financial self-interest may be in the direction of an immediate rise in the share price. And unlike in the case of the typical salesperson, the director holds other-regarding powers of administration over the corporation. The requirement of loyalty demands that these powers be exercised in what the director thinks are the best interests of the corporation, but to the extent that their exercise is tied to the share price, there is a genuine conflict of self-interest and duty.[19] There are other situations in which conflicts of interests coexist with conflicts of self-interest and duty.[20]

Particularly in the common law, the problem of unauthorized profits acquired by administrators is often conflated with the problems of conflicts of interest. The rule against unauthorized profits, however, is a separate norm from the

---

[19] Whether the creation of such a compensation plan implicitly authorizes this conflict is a separate question (below, section VII.A).

[20] Although this lies outside of the current Part II.A, a lawyer's advisory function is treated by the law as an administrative power that should not generally be exercised in a conflict-of-interest situation (Chapter 7, section IV.A). Most lawyers are generally paid by time, which is a simple example of a conflict of interests between lawyer and client. In advising a client to (for example) pursue a lawsuit rather than doing nothing, the lawyer is also in a conflict of self-interest and duty, since the lawyer's self-interest has the potential to affect the advice they give. This is a typical scenario and can be understood to be acceptable inasmuch as the client is perfectly aware of this conflict (below, section VII.B).

rules against exercising powers while in a conflict; each has a separate justification, and each can operate separately from the other even though they often overlap. We will explore this more in the next chapter. Here I will say only a few words to show why the two sets of rules are separate. The acquisition of a benefit (authorized or not) does not, as such, put the administrator on both sides of a transaction in two separate roles; it does not, as such, create a conflict of interest. Consider that if the administrator acquires an authorized benefit, it is lawful; it is not a violation of the rule against *unauthorized* benefits. But a conflict is a conflict, whether it is authorized or not. If every benefit created a conflict of interest, then simply being paid would create a conflict of interest, albeit an authorized one, which cannot be correct. So, it is a mistake to think that every benefit, or even every unauthorized benefit, is or creates a conflict of interest.[21]

3. **The rules on conflicts of self-interest and duty (and conflicts of duty and duty) apply when an administrator is exercising the powers that they hold in that role**

The common law of trusts distinguishes between rules on 'self-dealing' and 'fair-dealing' and applies similar norms to other administrators who are not trustees. The rules on self-dealing address core examples of conflicts of interest: they cover situations in which a trustee is exercising his powers to deal with trust property, but also holds a personal interest on the other side of the same transaction. A simple example is the trustee who sells land that he holds in trust to a corporation in which he is financially interested.[22] That is an archetypal conflict of self-interest and duty. Applied to other relationships of administration, this covers cases in which the administrator is exercising the other-regarding powers that they hold as such, in a transaction in which they are also personally interested on the other side. Again, if an agent to buy were to make, as agent, a contract of purchase with a company controlled by the agent, this would be self-dealing. The agent is using their other-regarding power of representation to bind the principal on one side of the contract, and the agent is also personally interested on the other side.

The rules on fair-dealing, by contrast, do not involve the exercise of the trustee's powers as a trustee. They apply where the trustee acquires, in his personal capacity, the rights of a beneficiary in the trust. Here, the trustee is not exercising any of the powers that he holds as a trustee; he is acting for his own account as the buyer, in dealing with the beneficiary. The beneficiary is the seller of her own rights; the trustee is not selling trust property as a trustee. Indeed, none

---

[21] As we will see later in this chapter, however (below, section VI.B.), an unauthorized benefit may create a *potential* conflict of interest.
[22] For discussion of some details, see Toby Graham, David Russell, and Tom Williams, 'Is the Genuine Transaction Rule Really So Genuine?' (2022) 28 Trusts & Trustees 156.

of the trust property is being sold when the beneficiary sells her own interest in the trust. Moreover, the trustee is not on both sides of the transaction in two different roles, as he is in the case of self-dealing. The beneficiary is acting personally, in selling her interest; she does not need the trustee to do that. The trustee is acting personally, in acquiring it. The principles of fair-dealing also apply in any relationship of administration, such as if (for example) an agent to sell were to propose to the principal that the agent herself would buy the property that needed to be sold. As in the trust case, this agent is not selling or buying as an agent; he is not exercising his powers as an agent to sell the principal's property. He is simply buying it from his principal.

Transactions of this fair-dealing kind are fraught with concerns about undue influence; they also generate duties of disclosure that would not apply if there were not a relationship of administration.[23] These duties, however, are different from rules about conflicts of interest in the strictest sense, which are rules governing the exercise of an administrator's powers. This is clear when we recognize the different grounds on which a transaction may be set aside in the two contexts. When a transaction is set aside because an administrator exercised their powers while in a conflict (self-dealing), it is because that person did not properly use the powers that she held as an administrator. When a transaction is set aside under the fair-dealing rules, it is because of a concern that the *beneficiary* did not properly agree to the transaction: she was unduly influenced or did not have all the relevant information. This is not a case of setting aside an exercise of an administrator's power due to a conflict of interest. The administrator acted personally and did not use their administrative powers; and there is no cause to set aside their exercise of their own personal powers. Again, the defect in this case is to the consent on the beneficiary's side.

The rules self-dealing and fair-dealing are often lumped together as related somehow to conflicts of interest. When they are analysed carefully, they help to clarify that the rules about conflicts, properly understood, are rules that disqualify an administrator from unimpeachably exercising their other-regarding powers. Those rules are not called upon in fair-dealing cases, because the administrator has not exercised their other-regarding powers. Only when exercising other-regarding powers is an administrator bound by the requirement of loyalty that governs such powers. The requirement of loyalty does not apply when the administrator is not using such powers. But, as we will see in more detail below, duties of disclosure—duties in the strict sense—do apply.[24]

---

[23] On these and other duties of disclosure, see Chapter 5, section VIII.
[24] ibid.

4. Being in a conflict is not, as such, a breach of duty

It is a mistake of a reductionist kind to suppose that if the law regulates something, it does so through legal duties. Not every legal rule that generates legal consequences is a duty in the strict sense that it corresponds to a right held by another person; and not every case of non-compliance with a legal rule is a breach of duty that attracts a sanction.[25] As Megarry V-C once pointed out, if a trustee becomes bankrupt, he or she may be removed from office; it does not follow that the trustee is under a duty not to become bankrupt.[26]

It is sometimes said that an administrator has a duty not to be in a conflict.[27] This, however, does not seem accurate, as an example will show.[28] Assume that a trustee rightly decides to sell a valuable asset held in trust and makes a public call for written offers. When she opens the offer letters, she finds to her surprise that the only offer is from her brother. This trustee is in a conflict, but she has not done anything wrong (at least, yet).

We saw in the last chapter that the requirement of loyalty that applies to other-regarding powers is not a duty in the strict sense.[29] It is rather a requirement for the fully valid exercise of those powers. The same thing is true of the rules about conflicts: they stipulate requirements for the fully valid exercise of other-regarding powers.[30] If they are not complied with, the exercise of the power is likely impeachable.[31]

Conflicts may have other consequences. Even in advance of the exercise of their other-regarding judgement, an administrator may be disqualified by conflicts, either generally or in relation to the particular decision. In *Re Lamb*,[32] a person was disqualified from appointment to a fiduciary role by foreseeable

---

[25] Herbert LA Hart, *The Concept of Law* (3rd edn, 2012), 27–42. This point was made also in Chapter 3, section IV.G, in relation to disloyalty in the use of powers.

[26] *Tito v Waddell (No 2)* [1977] Ch 106, 249. The same could be said about corporate directors, who may be disqualified by personal bankruptcy.

[27] In *Breen v Williams* (1995) 186 CLR 71, 113 (Gaudron and McHugh JJ); Conaglen (n 16), 39–40 and *passim*; Man Yip and Kelvin FK Low, 'Reconceptualising Fiduciary Regulation in Actual Conflicts' (2021) 45 Melbourne UL Rev 1. Although I now consider it to be mistaken, I also used this language in earlier work (Lionel Smith, 'The Motive, Not the Deed' in Joshua Getzler (ed), *Rationalizing Property, Equity and Trusts: Essays in Honour of Edward Burn* (LexisNexis Butterworths 2003) 53).

[28] For more detail, see Lionel Smith, 'Prescriptive Fiduciary Duties' (2018) 37 UQLJ 261, 281–84.

[29] Chapter 3, section IV.G.

[30] It was so held by Vinelott J in *Movitex Ltd v Bulfield* [1988] BCLC 104 (ChD), 116–20, 125b. As is typical in the United Kingdom, a company's constitution provided (in the articles of association) for the management of conflicts in relation to its directors through disclosure and recusal. Vinelott J observed that if there was a *duty* not to be in a conflict, then under the terms of the governing statute, that duty could not be varied by the articles. He concluded that it was not a duty, but only a requirement for unimpeachable decision-making by the board; the articles were competent to modify such a requirement.

[31] We can add that, again as with the requirement of loyalty, it is of course *possible* to breach a duty in the strict sense while being in a conflict.

[32] *Re Lamb* [1894] 2 QB 805 (CA).

conflicts. Had the person been appointed without the potential conflicts being known, those conflicts would have been grounds for removal.[33] In corporate law, a director may be disqualified from a particular decision of the board by a conflict.[34] The relationship between both of these examples and the general effect of a conflict—to disqualify the conflicted administrator from exercising an administrative power while in the conflict—is obvious. Both examples are also tied to the observation made earlier that a person who holds administrative powers does not, by hypothesis, hold them as a personal asset and so can always be relieved or removed, temporarily or permanently.[35]

III. Definition

Having sketched out the shape of the norms on conflicts, it is possible to provide a definition that captures these insights. An excellent general definition has been given by an ethicist, Michael Davis:

> A person has a conflict of interest if a) he is in a relationship with another requiring him to exercise judgment in that other's service and b) he has an interest tending to interfere with the proper exercise of judgment in that relationship.[36]

This definition precisely delimits the concept. It shows how the concern about conflicts is closely and directly tied to the object of this study: situations in which an administrator holds other-regarding powers that are generally discretionary and so generally involve the exercise of judgment. In those situations, the

---

[33] On the removal of common law trustees for conflict of interest, see Donovan WM Waters, Mark Gillen, and Lionel Smith, *Waters' Law of Trusts in Canada* (5th edn, Thomson Reuters 2021), 949–50; of administrators of the property of others (which includes trustees) in Quebec law, Madeleine Cantin Cumyn and Michelle Cumyn, *L'administration du bien d'autrui* (2nd edn, Éditions Yvon Blais 2014), 351–52; cf Civil Code of Québec, art 265 (authority to act as delegated curator subject to revocation for conflict of interest).

[34] *Movitex Ltd* (n 30); *Canada Business Corporations Act*, RSC 1985, c C-44, s 120(5); Civil Code of Québec, arts 325–26.

[35] Chapter 2, section III.B.

[36] Michael Davis, 'Conflict of Interest' (1982) 1 Business & Professional Ethics Journal 17, 21, with a fuller statement at 24; the shorter statement is also in Michael Davis, 'Conflict of Interest Revisited' (1993) 12 Business & Professional Ethics Journal 21, 21. For similar definitions in other contexts, see Hon William D Parker, *Commission of Inquiry into the Facts of Allegations of Conflict of Interest Concerning the Honourable Sinclair M Stevens* (Minister of Supply and Services Canada 1987) 35 (ministers of the Crown); Stephen R Latham, 'Conflict of Interest in Medical Practice' in Michael Davis and Andrew Stark (eds), *Conflict of Interest in the Professions* (OUP 2001) 279, 283 (medical practitioners); Law Society of Alberta, *Code of Conduct* (2020), 1.1–1 'conflict of interest' (lawyers; referring to potential effects on 'loyalty to or representation of a client' deriving from the lawyer's own interests, or from his or her duties to others). Davis's approach is also adopted in Valsan (n 10), 29–30.

administrator is required to use their powers to accomplish an other-regarding mission, with the result that the administrator can only rightly use their powers in the pursuit of that mission. Moreover, the definition makes clear that a conflict is generated not by *any* factor which simply makes the exercise of judgment difficult or challenging or complicated; nor is it generated by any factor that adds a different motivation, as in the case of the administrator who wishes to be seen as good at his or her job. A conflict is only generated by the presence of a factor which should *not* be taken into account by the administrator *and* which, if it were, would tend to interfere with the proper exercise of the administrator's other-regarding judgment.

Davis summarized important elements of his position in a later paper:

> I used 'judgment' to refer to that aspect of intelligent activity requiring more than mechanical rule-following, and 'interest' for any special influence, loyalty, or other concern capable of biasing otherwise competent judgment (under the circumstances in question).[37]

We have already seen that judgment of this kind is crucial to the kinds of situations with which we are concerned.[38] Davis defines 'interest' in a wide way so as to as to include both self-interest and duties owed to persons other than the beneficiary; his definition includes both conflicts of self-interest and duty and conflicts of duty and duty, examples of which were given above.[39]

In my view, Davis's definition of conflict of interest is accurate and succinct. He produced his general definition by starting from the analysis of conflicts in the context of the professional obligations of lawyers. In that setting, it is routine to describe the problem of conflicts of interest in terms of inappropriate influences on the lawyer's judgment.[40] A decade later, Davis stated that his generalized analysis had become standard in business and professional ethics.[41] He also responded to some criticisms that had been made of his analysis. I agree with Davis that although some situations raised by his critics—for example, disloyalty and abuse of authority—may be referred to by some commentators as 'conflicts of interest', it is inappropriate to take a technical term of this kind and to use it loosely to cover a range of other problems.[42] As we will see in more

---

[37] Davis, 'Conflict of Interest Revisited' (n 36), 21.
[38] Chapter 3, sections II.A and II.B.
[39] Above, section II.A.
[40] He discussed the American Bar Association's *Code of Professional Responsibility* in Davis, 'Conflict of Interest' (n 36), 18–21. For other examples, see *Canadian National Railway Co v McKercher LLP* [2013] 2 SCR 649, 2013 SCC 39, [38]; Law Society of Alberta, *Code of Conduct* (2020) (n 36).
[41] Davis, 'Conflict of Interest Revisited' (n 36), 21.
[42] See generally Smith (n 9).

detail in the next section, the problem that generates the legal norms governing conflicts of interest is a particular one; and the legal remedies for contravening those norms are tied to directly to that problem. Moreover, as will be explored at the end of this chapter, there are various ways to manage conflicts of interest, even though this is not possible in every situation. Conversely, there is no way to 'manage' an abuse or misuse of authority; there are only recourses and remedies that may be available in response to such actions.

IV. Justification for the rules against acting while in a conflict

Having adopted Davis's definition of conflict, let us examine his explanation of why conflicts are problematical. He says that the problem in a conflict-of-interest situation is analogous to the problem caused by a piece of foreign material that has gotten into a sensitive mechanical gauge. The dirt may affect the accuracy of the gauge. However, we cannot know whether it does or not; and if it does, we cannot know how much, or in which direction. It throws the gauge off in unknowable ways. In the same way, an extraneous interest can affect the exercise of judgment. In the terms used in the preceding chapter, we are dealing with judgments that must be made loyally. The extraneous interest that is present in a conflict *may* lead to an improper, disloyal exercise of judgment; but we cannot know whether judgment was affected, or how much.

What loyalty requires is that the administrator shall use her powers in what she believes to be the best interests of the beneficiary.[43] In a conflict, however, no one can be certain that the powers have been or will be exercised loyally. This is not merely a question of aiming to exclude corruption, although the norms about conflicts, if they are followed, will have that effect. The law's norms about conflicts cover more ground than that. The reason for this is that even an administrator in perfectly good faith cannot be certain of excluding the effect, on her decision-making process, of extraneous considerations. She may think, in good faith, that she has done so and has made the decision that is best for the beneficiaries. It may well be the case, however, that in the absence of the conflict she would have decided differently. This is why the law's starting point is that an administrator's powers should not be exercised in a conflict situation.[44]

---

[43] Or, in some contexts, in what the administrator believes is the best way to achieve a purpose: Chapter 3, section IV.A.

[44] This is the default rule in relationships of administration, which can be varied by authorization (below, section VII). It is possible, of course, for parties who are not in a relationship of administration to agree contractually to abide by rules which are like those applied by the law in such relationships; see D Gordon Smith, 'Contractually Adopted Fiduciary Duty' [2014] U Ill L Rev 1783; Smith (n 28), 268–69; *Secretariat Consulting PTE Ltd v A Company* [2021] EWCA Civ 6.

It is sometimes said that the administrator is disabled by the conflict from acting as such, unless the conflict can be managed so as to allow her to act.[45] In fact, the administrator is not completely disabled, but the exercise of administrative powers in a conflict situation is liable to be set aside.[46] Moreover, conflicts may be managed in various ways; to take one important example, both conflicts of self-interest and duty, and conflicts of duty and duty, can be authorized in advance.[47]

Leaving aside that possibility for the moment, the general disqualifying effect of a conflict is tied directly to the subjective nature of the requirement of loyalty.[48] If there was an objective answer as to whether the administrator had exercised their powers properly, there would be no need for a subjective requirement of loyalty, and there would be no need for rules about conflicts; we could always determine objectively whether the administrator had acted properly. But there is no objective answer; each administrator must exercise his or her own judgment.[49] Different administrators can do different things with their powers in identical situations, and all be acting properly. That is why loyalty is subjective; and the inscrutability of human decision-making, even to the decision-maker, requires disqualification in conflict situations, because in those situations it becomes impossible to know whether an administrator has exercised their powers with loyalty.

A. Conflict of self-interest and duty

In 1894, an English judge, AL Smith LJ, expressed the matter this way:

> It is obvious—everybody knows it who has any knowledge of life—that when a man has a pecuniary interest, his mind is naturally warped in favour of his own interest. It is human nature, and no one can doubt it.[50]

---

[45] For example, this was the way the case was argued for the pursuers, on the basis of civil law, in the Scottish case *York Buildings Co v Mackenzie* (1795) 8 Brown PC 42, 3 ER 432 (HL), 66 (Brown PC), 447 (ER): 'This conflict of interest is the rock, for shunning which, the disability under consideration has obtained its force by making that person, who has the one part entrusted to him, incapable of acting on the other side . . .'. Among other sources, counsel cited the text from Justinian's *Digest*, 18.1.34.7, set out at the start of this chapter. See also *Tito* (n 26), 248–49, and C Mitchell, 'Equitable Compensation for Breach of Fiduciary Duty' [2013] CLP 307, 314–17, discussing together the rules about conflicts, about unauthorized profits, and about duties of disclosure arising in fiduciary relationships.
[46] Below, section V.
[47] Management of conflicts is discussed in more detail below, section VII.B.
[48] Chapter 3, section II.B.
[49] This is why the mistaken view that loyalty is objective was earlier called the 'one right answer' fallacy: ibid.
[50] *Re Lamb* (n 32), 820. See also *Parker v McKenna* (1874) LR 10 Ch App 96 (DC), 118: '. . . it was utterly impossible for the [conflicted] directors, after the transaction upon which they themselves had entered, to exercise an independent and unbiassed judgment upon the subject of these relaxations.'

The same approach was taken by a US judge, writing extrajudicially.[51] Much more recently in Ontario, FL Myers J said:

> Such is the insidiousness of conflict of interest that people with no doubt as to their own bona fides can allow themselves to commit significant wrongdoing without thinking that they are doing anything wrong. . . . It is not an insult to anyone's integrity to understand that conflicts of interest are insidious. Conflicts of interest play havoc with peoples' judgment of their own capacity to maintain neutrality and a fiduciary stance.[52]

There is psychological research that supports the law's norms.[53] Experimental evidence shows not only that a conflict of interest affects judgment, but also that those who are affected are not aware of the effect. One paper notes that 'the violations of professionalism induced by conflicts of interest often occur automatically and without conscious awareness.'[54] Among the conclusions of another paper:

> Although people may be aware of their vulnerability to bias, they tend to underestimate it, and do not adequately correct for it when called on to do so.[55]
>
> Although economic models of rationality would assume that people can switch between roles without one influencing the other, evidence suggests that actual people have somewhat more trouble doing so. . . . This 'economic' account of conflict of interest is challenged by psychological research which suggests that biased information processing is not only pervasive, but is typically unconscious and unintentional—ie, seldom a matter of deliberate intentional choice [citations omitted]. As the results we present in this paper suggest, professionals who face conflicts of interest may find it difficult, if not impossible, to simply choose objectivity. This view is compatible with what Chugh *et al* (2005) call bounded ethicality: people routinely do things that dispassionate observers would regard as unethical without intending to behave unethically or even considering the possibility that their behavior has ethical implications.[56]

---

[51] Earl R Hoover, 'Basic Principles Underlying Duty of Loyalty' (1956) 5 Cleveland-Marshall L Rev 7, 10: 'Conflict destroys an essential ingredient without which a fiduciary relation cannot function—disinterested judgment.' See also US case law cited by Valsan (n 10), 24–25.
[52] *Mayer v Rubin* 2017 ONSC 3498, [13], [16].
[53] See also Valsan (n 10), 28–33.
[54] Don A Moore and George Loewenstein, 'Self-Interest, Automaticity, and the Psychology of Conflict of Interest' (2004) 17 Social Justice Research 189, 199.
[55] Don A Moore, Lloyd Tanlu, and Max H Bazerman, 'Conflict of Interest and the Intrusion of Bias' (2010) 5 Judgment and Decision Making 37, 43.
[56] ibid 46–47. The reference is to Dolly Chugh, Max H Bazerman, and Mahzarin R Banaji, 'Bounded Ethicality as a Psychological Barrier to Recognizing Conflicts of Interest' in Don A Moore

The paper concludes with a story about the late Antonin Scalia. Although it arose in the public law context, the psychological analysis is the same. Scalia was asked to recuse himself from a case involving Vice President Dick Cheney on the grounds that there was a personal friendship between the two and that Cheney had used a government aircraft to bring Scalia to a duck-hunting trip while the litigation was under way. Scalia refused, implying that it was ridiculous to suggest that he could be 'bought' so cheaply.[57] The story is indeed illustrative. Those who are challenged for being in a conflict frequently feel the challenge as a direct attack on their personal integrity. Their own conviction as to their integrity thus leads them to rebut the challenge to their fitness to act. From both a legal and a psychological perspective—and, I would add, a moral perspective—it is not necessarily the case that a complaint of conflict of interest is a challenge to integrity. The conflict is dangerous, and it is dangerous not only because of the risk of deliberate corruption but because the human mind is unable reliably to exclude certain influences.[58]

One mechanism by which this works—again, typically unconsciously and therefore not deliberately—is that when a person has a desired outcome for an exercise of judgment that they have to make, they will generate arguments in favour of that result: 'Thanks to what Perkins (1989) called the "myside" bias, people quite naturally think of arguments that favor the position they have taken or the outcome they desire.'[59] This is surely exacerbated by the consideration that

---

and others (eds), *Conflicts of Interest: Challenges and Solutions in Business, Law, Medicine, and Public Policy* (CUP 2005) 74.

[57] *Cheney v United States Dist Court for the District of Columbia*, 541 US 913 (2004), 929. The judgment is preoccupied with factual arguments in which Scalia J aims to show that he was not *actually* influenced by Cheney and (on somewhat contrived reasoning) that he did not personally benefit from the flight in Air Force Two. Both of these are entirely beside the point. Somewhat ironically, according to the practise of the US Supreme Court in recusal challenges, Scalia J was judge in his own cause without possibility of appeal.

[58] See also Vernon V Palmer and John Levendis, 'The Louisiana Supreme Court in Question: An Empirical and Statistical Study of the Effects of Campaign Money on the Judicial Function' (2008) 82 Tul L Rev 1291. Like earlier work in other states, this paper showed a correlation (which does not establish causation) between campaign contributions to elected judges and their judicial decision-making. The paper caused an uproar, as discussed in Vernon V Palmer, 'The Recusal of American Judges in the Post-Caperton Era: An Empirical Assessment of the Risk of Actual Bias in Decisions Involving Campaign Contributors' (2010), https://ssrn.com/abstract=1721665, 5. In this second paper, Palmer corrected some errors in the data but his conclusions remained intact. Again, although the judges (and others) may have felt this was an attack on their integrity, it can on the contrary be seen as evidence that conflict of interest can affect the exercise of judgment even of those who are in good faith and who seek to exclude any effect of the conflict. See also Morgan LW Hazelton, Jacob M Montgomery, and Brendan Nyhan, 'Does Public Financing Affect Judicial Behavior? Evidence from the North Carolina Supreme Court' (2015) 44 American Politics Research 587; Neel U Sukhatme and Jay Jenkins, 'Pay to Play? Campaign Finance and the Incentive Gap in the Sixth Amendment's Right to Counsel' (2020) 70 Duke LJ 775.

[59] Moore and others (n 55) 38. The reference is to David N Perkins, 'Reasoning as It Is and Could Be: An Empirical Perspective' in Donald M Topping, Doris C Crowell, and Victor N Kobayashi (eds), *Thinking Across Cultures: The Third International Conference on Thinking* (L Erlbaum Associates 1989) 175.

people have been shown to have an exaggerated and inaccurate belief in their own ability to be objective.[60]

If everyone was aware of these tendencies and their relative strengths, then perhaps they could be excluded or counteracted in the exercise of judgment. But the matter is more complicated. First, people are typically unaware of their own cognitive processes.[61] Moreover, it appears that there are separate neurological mechanisms in play. Psychologists distinguish between decision-making processes that may be called 'automatic', and which are relatively effortless and unconscious, and those that may be called 'controlled', which are more analytical, and which involve conscious effort.[62] A person deciding how to invest another's money will weigh various factors, using a controlled analytical process of which the person is very much aware. By contrast, for an experienced driver, driving a car under ordinary conditions involves mental processing and decision-making that is mostly automatic. When we consider an administrator who must exercise judgment in what she perceives to be the best interests of a beneficiary, we are likely to assume that this involves a controlled process: a conscious weighing and consideration of various factors. And it almost certainly does. There is reason to believe, however, that the influence of self-interest on reasoning proceeds by an automatic process.[63] This is why it can influence the reasoning process without impinging on the consciousness of the reasoner. And this is why conflicts may affect even those who try consciously not to be affected.

Conclusions reached by an automatic process are likely to be reached much more quickly than those that depend on a controlled process; and if self-interest activates an automatic process, and a conclusion that favours self-interest, the justification may be produced only later:

> contrary to the common view both among lay people and social scientists that decisions are made by weighing costs and benefits, the reality is that many decisions are made on the basis of impulse and intuition. This is not to say that

---

[60] Chugh and others (n 56), 81–83.

[61] Moore and others (n 54), 38: 'Such lack of insight into their own cognitive processes makes it difficult for people to purge biasing influences from their judgments even when they desire to do so.' See also Chugh and others (n 56), 77, speaking of psychological research over the last century: 'Conscious will is consistently given more credit than is due, despite robust evidence about its limitations. In parallel, the power of the unconscious mind in everyday life has become evident.'

[62] This distinction is most famously popularized in Daniel Kahneman, *Thinking, Fast and Slow* (Farrar, Straus & Giroux 2011). Although the book does not discuss conflicts of interest, the unconscious effect of conflicts on reasoning can be attributed to many of the phenomena described in this book, including 'framing' effects (see esp ch 34). Chugh and others (n 56), 77: '... automaticity has been found to play some role in virtually every cognitive process studied, and its inevitability has been cleverly termed the "unbearable automaticity of being".' (citation omitted).

[63] Moore and Lowenstein (n 54). Kahneman (ibid), in ch 3 and *passim*, shows that in general people are more likely to accept an answer suggested by 'fast thinking' than to invest the effort required to produce an answer through 'slow thinking'.

conscious deliberation is not important—it is. However, it is often relegated to the role of rationalizing and justifying decisions that have been made for other reasons.[64]

Finally, even if a person was able to pay full attention to their cognitive processes, and was fully aware of the possible effect on their judgment of some improper consideration and sought to exclude it, there would be no way for them, or anyone else, to know whether they had succeeded. This is what I meant when I referred earlier to the inscrutability of human decision-making. In another paper, Davis gives the example of the conflict of interest involved in being the referee of a soccer match in which his son is a player:

> I would find it harder than a stranger to judge accurately when my son had committed a foul. (After all, part of being a good father is having a *tendency* to favour one's own child.) I do not know whether I would be harder on him than an impartial referee would be, easier, or just the same. What I do know is that ... [a conflicting interest] is sufficient to make me less reliable in the role of referee than I otherwise would be.[65]

The law, just like ethics, has good reason to be very vigilant about the exercise of other-regarding judgment in conflict-of-interest situations, even in relation to people in perfectly good faith.

B. Conflict of duty and duty

As was mentioned above, the law is not only concerned with conflicts between an administrator's self-interest and the other-regarding requirements that govern the exercise of the administrative powers that they hold. It is also concerned with conflicts of duty and duty. Davis's definition of 'conflict of interest' uses 'interest' to refer to any improper consideration, and his definition therefore includes conflicts of duty and duty.[66] But the law—at least, the common law—typically puts conflicts of duty and duty in a separate category.

A conflict of duty and duty arises when the administrator's exercise of other-regarding judgment in relation to one beneficiary is liable to be affected by the

---

[64] Moore and Lowenstein (n 54), 194.
[65] Michael Davis, 'Introduction' in Michael Davis and Andrew Stark (eds), *Conflict of Interest in the Professions* (OUP 2001) 3, 16 (emphasis in original).
[66] Above, text at n 36. Davis's definition also reaches the case of a person who should not be involved in a decision-making process because of some prior involvement; for some discussion of how this problem relates to my narrower definition of 'conflict of self-interest and duty', see Smith (n 9), 168–70. For discussion of this problem in relation to judges, see Chapter 11, section III.D.2.

loyalty that the administrator owes to another beneficiary in relation to the exercise of the administrator's judgment. Thus, for example, a lawyer or a real estate agent who acts for two clients, whose interests are opposed to one another, is in a conflict of this kind.

An administrator is not in a conflict of this kind only because her duties as an administrator, that are owed to a beneficiary in relation to the exercise of the administrator's judgment, are in conflict with *any* legal duty that the administrator owes to another person. Both of the conflicting duties (more precisely, requirements of loyalty) have to be in relation to the exercise of judgment. The reason is that other kinds of duties demand performances that are objectively ascertainable. Take this example: the testamentary executor of a deceased person is in a relationship of administration with the creditors and beneficiaries of the estate. Now imagine that the executor is bound (in that capacity), by a contract made by the deceased, to render some performance to a third party. The executor may think that it would be in the best interests of the creditors and beneficiaries of the estate to breach that contract. This is not an example of the legal concept of a conflict of duty and duty, as one of the duties—the contractual one—does not relate to the exercise of other-regarding judgment. Legally, it simply has to be performed. The third party to whom that contractual duty is owed does not have to worry about whether the administrator's judgment was affected by improper considerations; that third party has a simple right to performance. Conversely, the creditors and beneficiaries of the estate have no particular reason to worry that the administrator's exercise of his powers as administrator were improperly affected by the mere presence of the contractual duty. There is no particular reason to think that that duty would tend to have an improper influence on the administrator's other-regarding judgment. It is simply an objective constraint, and the administrator must, in exercising his powers, abide by the law.[67]

Now take the hypothetical case—hypothetical, as forbidden by lawyers' codes of conduct—of a lawyer acting for both parties to a contested divorce. Here the lawyer's self-interest is not liable to affect the exercise of their judgment in acting for, or advising, either client.[68] If there is no conflicting self-interest, we might think that this situation is less morally problematic than a conflict of self-interest and duty. The lawyer, in exercising her professional judgment, is not drawn to promote her own interests above those of either client. But the problem is that since the clients' interests are opposed, it does not seem possible for the *same person*—the lawyer—to always act in what she believes to be the best interests of

---

[67] *Ahmed Anguillia bin Hadjee Mohamed Salleh Anguillia v Estate and Trust Agencies (1927) Ltd* [1938] AC 624 (PC); see also Chapter 3, section II.C.1.
[68] Whether acting *pro bono* or billing by time or in any other way, the lawyer's self-interest does conflict with the interests of both clients; there is a conflict of *interests*, not a conflict of interest (ie, not a conflict of self-interest and duty): above, section II.B.1.

both clients at the same time. It is rather like the person who tries to play a game of chess against herself. Eventually, consciously or not, you have to pick a side.[69]

In a leading English case, the defendants were a lawyer and his managing clerk, who held an interest in land as trustees.[70] They sold this interest to the plaintiff, who was the client of the defendant lawyer in the sale transaction. The defendant lawyer did not disclose to the plaintiff information that the defendants possessed, to the effect that the value of the land was less than the plaintiff was paying. This breach of the defendant lawyer's fiduciary duty of disclosure to the plaintiff allowed the plaintiff to set the contract aside. The lawyer's argument that he had an overriding duty to the beneficiaries of the trust was not accepted. Lord Cozens-Hardy MR said:

> A man may have a duty on one side and an interest on another. A solicitor who puts himself in that position takes upon himself a grievous responsibility. A solicitor may have a duty on one side and a duty on the other, namely, a duty to his client as solicitor on the one side and a duty to his [trust] beneficiaries on the other; but if he chooses to put himself in that position it does not lie in his mouth to say to the client 'I have not discharged that which the law says is my duty towards you, my client, because I owe a duty to the beneficiaries on the other side.' The answer is that if a solicitor involves himself in that dilemma it is his own fault. He ought before putting himself in that position to inform the client of his conflicting duties, and either obtain from that client an agreement that he should not perform his full duties of disclosure or say—which would be much better—'I cannot accept this business'. I think it would be the worst thing to say that a solicitor can escape from the obligations, imposed upon him as solicitor, of disclosure if he can prove that it is not a case of duty on one side and of interest on the other, but a case of duty on both sides and therefore impossible to perform. I do not desire to draw any distinction between the simple case where he has one client who is selling his own property to him and a case like the present, where he has a client and as trustee is selling to that client.[71]

The logic of this position is that from the point of view of the client, it is not relevant whether the administrator's loyalty is potentially compromised by

---

[69] And when an administrator in such a situation chooses a course of action, they are likely to construct a perfectly plausible justification for doing so, just as in conflicts of self-interest and duty; see n 64 and text.

[70] *Moody v Cox* [1917] 2 Ch 71 (CA). To complicate matters, the defendant clerk had taken bribes from the plaintiff. This was held not to disentitle the plaintiff from relief, and two judges observed (at 82, 85) that he was accountable to the trust beneficiaries for these amounts (a matter discussed in the next chapter).

[71] ibid 81–82.

self-interest or by the administrator's loyalty towards some other person. Both possibilities are equally problematic. As Warrington LJ said:

> It seems to me that [the defendant] has placed himself in a position in which he might possibly have been open to attack by his *cestuis que trust* [the beneficiaries of the trust] if he had done his duty to [the plaintiff], but that is no answer to [the plaintiff], who says, 'You have not done your duty to me'.[72]

This decision allowed the plaintiff to rescind the contract on the ground of non-disclosure, but it is clear that it embodies the view that a conflict of duty and duty is treated by law in the same way as a conflict of self-interest and duty.

It is true that some of the psychological issues mentioned in the previous section would be less applicable here. If people unconsciously favour their self-interest through an 'automatic' non-deliberative process, this complication would not arise in a conflict of duty and duty. We can imagine that an administrator with two clients whose interests conflict would be in a position to use 'controlled' deliberative reasoning in relation to both, and might not unconsciously favour one via the operation of an 'automatic' reasoning process.[73] But some of the other problems remain, including the illusion of being able to exercise judgment free of all improper influences, and the tendency to construct justifying arguments after jumping to a conclusion. More importantly, the requirements of loyalty towards both beneficiaries involve the exercise of judgment; they are not objective duties, to do or not do some objectively described thing. Thus it is never objectively clear whether the administrator has acted as they would have done in the absence of the conflict. It will always be unclear whether one beneficiary was favoured over the other.

The problem of conflict of duty and duty is sometimes described, often with a Christian scriptural reference, as an injunction that one cannot serve two masters.[74] As a statement of private law, this is not correct. Lawyers, real estate agents, trustees, and corporate directors can rightly and lawfully have multiple beneficiaries: not just two, but in some cases dozens or hundreds. But the point of the injunction is that one cannot serve two masters equally loyally if one is forced to choose between them in serving; that is an 'impossible position'.[75] And that

---

[72] *Moody*, ibid 85; see also *Transvaal Lands Co v New Belgium (Transvaal) Land and Development Co* [1914] 2 Ch 488 (CA); *Hilton v Barker Booth & Eastwood (a firm)* [2005] 1 WLR 567 (HL).

[73] Although it is possible that if the administrator has unconsciously chosen to favour one client, automatic reasoning in favour of that client may take place.

[74] Matthew 6:24, which ends with the injunction 'You cannot serve both God and money' (New International Version). That is actually an injunction against conflicts of self-interest and (religious) duty.

[75] *Hilton* (n 72), [44]. The conflict of duty and duty is not legally problematical where it is authorized, as for example in the case of a trust with different classes of beneficiaries whose interests may be opposed; see below, section VII.A.

is what an administrator must do, in the exercise of their other-regarding discretionary powers, because he must make a decision as to how to exercise those powers. In relation to both of the beneficiaries, there is no objective legal answer as to whether the administrator has or has not used the powers correctly; they are used correctly only if they are used, in each case, in what the fiduciary considers to be the best interests of that beneficiary. It will always be impossible to know whether the administrator acted in the same way, towards one or the other beneficiary, that the administrator would have acted if that beneficiary had been his or her sole beneficiary and sole concern.

Thus, for similar if slightly different reasons, such a conflict creates the same kind of problem as a conflict of self-interest and duty: namely, it is impossible to know whether a power exercised in either kind of conflict was exercised properly.[76]

V. Legal consequences of conflicts

What happens when a conflict of interest or a conflict of duty and duty arises? If an administrator were to use her powers in a conflict situation, her exercise of judgment might be affected by the extraneous influence: her own self-interest or the interests of another beneficiary. Since that interest is extraneous—that is, it is not something that should properly inform the administrator's exercise of judgment—any such effect would be problematical. It would entail a misuse of the power, as discussed in the preceding chapter. The previous section showed that the challenge about conflicts is that even the administrator herself may not realize, despite good faith efforts, that she has misused her power. This leads to a set of legal consequences.

A. Inability to use powers held as administrator

The first and most obvious is that the administrator cannot properly use her powers while in the conflict situation. She is presumptively disabled from exercising them. Speaking generally, only prior authorization, or the fully informed consent of the beneficiaries, can address this.[77]

As a result, foreseeable future conflicts may mean that a potential administrator is disqualified from appointment.[78] In the same way, actual conflicts that

---

[76] Conflicts of duty and duty, like conflicts of self-interest and duty, can be authorized in various ways, including in advance. This is discussed in more detail below, section VII.B.
[77] Again, management of conflicts is discussed below, section VII.
[78] *Re Lamb* (n 32).

have arisen may be grounds for the removal of an administrator.[79] In some contexts, particularly in corporate law, it may be possible for an administrator to be disqualified from a particular decision without being relieved permanently; where the administrator himself is able to do this, it is called recusal.[80]

B. Voidability of powers used while in a conflict

If the administrator *has* used their powers while in a conflict, the legal effect of that use can be set aside at the instance of any beneficiary.[81] It is significant that this is exactly the same redress that the law gives when powers have been shown to be *misused*, that is, used disloyally.[82] This is because the conflict creates an unassessable risk that the power *has been* misused, as explained in the previous section on the justification for the rules on conflicts. As was shown there, the risk that the power has been misused is impossible of assessment even by a fiduciary in good faith.

Any exercise of legal powers in such a situation is therefore treated by the law as improper. As with actual misuse, it is generally the beneficiaries who have the legal standing to set aside such exercises.[83] Like the requirement of loyalty, the norm about not using administrative powers in a conflict situation is not an obligation in the strict sense; rather, it defines the way in which the power can be used properly and unimpeachably. If the norm is not complied with, the power has not been used properly and its exercise is impeachable, although this is subject to the protection of third parties.[84] One result of this is that, just as with a proven disloyal exercise of a power, the beneficiary does not need to establish that any loss has been suffered; nor, conversely, is it relevant whether the administrator made any profit.[85] The claim is that the power was used in a situation when it should not have been used, and this is enough to allow it to be set aside.

---

[79] Above, n 33. Thus although the mere occurrence of the conflict is not itself a breach of duty, a trustee (for example) may commit a breach of trust by failing to deal with a situation in which he is unable to act due to a conflict; see *Wight v Olswang* [2000] EWCA Civ 310.

[80] Below, section VII.C.

[81] Common law: Conaglen (n 16), 76–79; Quebec law: *Davis v Kerr* (1890) 17 SCR 235, 246–47; Civil Code of Québec, arts 326, 1312, 1709, 2143, 2147; Cantin Cumyn and Cumyn (n 33), 287–88.

[82] Chapter 3, section IV.F.1.

[83] Chapter 3, section IV.F.4. Others, including objects of dispositive discretions and successor trustees, may also have standing.

[84] A matter discussed in Chapter 3, section IV.F.3.

[85] In the common law cases, this is made clear because the courts will set aside contracts and other legal acts without regard to their substantive fairness: Conaglen (n 16), 76–77. In the civil law, this is evident from the consideration that the claim is one of nullity, not civil liability: Cantin Cumyn and Cumyn (n 33), 328–30. Of course, in both legal traditions, it is possible that alongside the conflicted exercise of a legal power, the administrator has committed a legal wrong which may give rise to a claim for compensation, or has acquired an unauthorized profit which must be given up.

This is not as such a claim for loss wrongfully caused, nor is it a claim that the administrator has acquired an unauthorized profit. The latter situation is governed by a separate norm, addressed in the next chapter.

In some jurisdictions, the matter may be different in the context of corporate law, for governance reasons arising in that context. If the general law were applied to conflict-of-interest contracts made between a corporation and one of its administrators, then it would be the corporation as beneficiary which would have the right to set aside such a contract, or alternatively to give informed consent to permit it to stand. Since the administrators prima facie control the corporation, this creates a governance problem: those being supervised are prima facie also controlling the supervising legal person. This may be addressed through requiring disclosure and recusal of the conflicted directors.[86] Separately or in addition to that, however, shareholders may be given standing to challenge or to approve such a transaction. But shareholders are unlikely to be unanimous. If they are able to decide by a majority, the vote may be carried by the same people (voting as shareholders) who are the conflicted administrators.[87] But if the shareholders had to consent unanimously, any one shareholder could demand the unravelling of such a contract.[88] This is why the law in this context may combine a director or shareholder approval requirement with the possibility for testing the contract against a standard of fairness, whether as a matter of case law, as in Delaware's 'entire fairness' doctrine,[89] or pursuant to a statutory rule, as in Canada.[90] This does not mean that the fairness of the transaction on its own serves as a defence of it in the face of a conflict; it means that *even if* all the disclosure, recusal, and voting procedures are followed correctly for conflict management, the transaction may still be vulnerable to a fairness challenge.[91] Moreover, shareholder approval votes may require a special majority or may involve the disqualification of those shareholders whose self-interests are in conflict with the interests of the corporation.[92]

---

[86] Below, section VII.C.

[87] As in the well-known case of *North-West Transportation Co v Beatty* (1887) 12 App Cas 589 (PC).

[88] As indeed courts in Ontario once held, presumably applying trust law by analogy: *Beatty v North-West Transportation Co* (1884) 6 OR 300 (ChD), overruled on appeal, ibid; *Earle v Burland* (1900) 27 OAR 540 (CA), overruled *Burland v Earle* [1902] AC 83 (PC).

[89] Amir N Licht, 'Farewell to Fairness: Towards Retiring Delaware's Entire Fairness Review' (2020) 44 Del J Corp L 1.

[90] *Canada Business Corporations Act*, RSC 1985, c C-44, s 120(7)–(7.1). In the case of publicly traded corporations, securities law may also have requirements for what are often called in this context 'related-party transactions'.

[91] Still less does 'entire fairness' insulate a transaction in which the directors acted for an improper purpose: *Coster v UIP Companies Inc* 255 A3d 952 (Del, 2021).

[92] For some examples, see Lionel Smith, '*North-West Transportation Co Ltd v Beatty*' in C Mitchell and P Mitchell (eds), *Landmark Cases in Equity* (Hart 2012) 393, 411–18.

Setting aside a transaction may well lead to a money award in favour of the beneficiary, but in itself this does not depend on the proof of a consequential loss. Take a simple example of an agent who brings about a purchase of land on behalf of his principal from a corporation, where the agent is financially interested in the corporation. The principal can set the sale set aside if he wishes, without having to establish that the sale price was unfair in any way. The principal simply demonstrates that the purchase—an exercise of the agent's powers as an administrator—should not have occurred, due to the conflict. Upon setting the contract aside, he will have the right to recover the price that he paid (and the property will have to be returned to the seller). This is not a damages claim for a consequential loss; it is merely the result of setting aside the transaction.[93]

C. Requirements of disclosure and duties of disclosure

An administrator who seeks authorization to act in a conflict situation must necessarily disclose all aspects of the conflict to the beneficiaries, in order to secure an effective consent. This means not only the existence of the conflict, but its extent and nature.[94] That will be necessary in order to allow the administrator to use their powers unimpeachably.[95]

But it is a mistake to think that there is never a duty of disclosure in the strict sense, and to argue that the *only* role of disclosure is to allow the administrator to act in a situation in which they otherwise could not act due to the conflict. It will often be the case that the administrator owes a duty of disclosure in the strict sense, meaning not merely that disclosure is needed for the valid exercise of a power, but rather that the administrator will commit a wrongful act if they do not disclose, whether or not they seek to exercise their powers. The general principle is that the law requires disclosure where an administrator has information about the relationship that is relevant to the *beneficiary's* decision-making processes.[96] The obligation of disclosure may reach to other information if the administrator is in an advisory relationship to the beneficiary or wishes to contract with the beneficiary, or both. In these cases, we are not dealing with the

---

[93] The same thing could happen in reverse, if the conflicted agent brought about a sale by the beneficiary principal. In that case, the beneficiary is not claiming money but rather claiming to recover the property. This is what happened in, for example, *York Buildings Co* (n 45). If the property itself could no longer be recovered from the contractual counterparty, that person may be liable to restore its value (as in *Estate of Rothko* 372 NE2d 291 (NY, 1977)). Even this is not a damages claim, strictly speaking, as the beneficiary is not proving a loss consequential upon a wrongful act, but merely insisting on the reversal of the improper sale, and the return of the sold property is being effected by the payment of its value since it cannot be done *in specie*.
[94] Cf *Gray v New Augarita Porcupine Mines Ltd* [1952] 3 DLR 1 (PC), 14.
[95] See below, section VII.
[96] Chapter 5, section VIII.

conflict as something that potentially disables the administrator from exercising their other-regarding powers. The breach of one of these duties of disclosure generates liability for pure economic loss caused by the non-disclosure.[97]

VI. Apparent, potential, and trivial conflicts

A. Apparent conflicts

The subject of apparent and potential conflicts of interest is somewhat murky. Conflicts in general are sometimes said to be about appearances. This is because discussion in those terms provides a way of understanding why people should not act in conflicts, even though they have not necessarily done anything wrong, and even though no one is necessarily accusing them of having done anything wrong. One might say that it simply looks bad for them to act in such a case, which seems to be a claim about appearances.

In my view, this is not a good way of understanding the norms on conflicts. As discussed above, they are better understood as tied to the requirement of loyalty, and to the inability of the human mind to exclude extraneous influences on the exercise of judgment. That explanation is not about appearances at all; it is about reality. In general the law is concerned with reality, not appearances.

But the understanding that conflict norms are founded on appearances often leads to the idea that we need also to be concerned about 'apparent' conflicts. This is often reflected in policies regarding conflicts, which may have legal effect as contractual terms or otherwise. One such set of norms[98] contains a good definition of an 'actual' conflict of interest, which supposes that a person 'has a personal interest' of the relevant kind. It then provides a definition of an 'apparent' conflict, which is the same except that it applies where a person 'appears, in the opinion of a reasonably informed and well-advised Person, to have a personal interest' of the relevant kind.

The idea of apparent conflicts needs careful attention. Apparent conflicts need to be distinguished from potential conflicts, which are discussed in the next section. Private law does not directly regulate apparent conflicts of interest, and for good reason. I agree with Michael Davis:[99] 'Apparent conflicts of interest (strictly so-called) are no more conflicts of interest than counterfeit money is money'.

---

[97] For example, in *Hilton* (n 72) the failure to disclose a conflict of duty and duty, and a conflict of self-interest and duty, led to substantial compensatory damages. Many other examples are given in Chapter 5, section VIII.

[98] McGill University *Regulation on Conflict of Interest*, www.mcgill.ca/secretariat/files/secretariat/conflict-of-interest-regulation-on_0.pdf.

[99] Davis, 'Conflict of Interest' (n 10), 576. See also Bernard Lo and Marilyn J Field (eds), *Conflict of Interest in Medical Research, Education, and Practice* (National Academies Press 2009) ch 2.

Take the case of a trustee named John Smith who is selling land held in trust. He proposes to sell it to a corporation called John Smith Ltd. This could certainly create an apparent conflict of interest. But imagine that the trustee can prove that he has no financial or familial or other interest in John Smith Ltd; it is simply a coincidence, and he has absolutely no connection to this corporation. At that point, it would be clear that there is no conflict at all.

But I also agree with Davis when he goes on to say that an apparent conflict can be objectionable, by creating uncertainty in the beneficiaries. This might be one reason for a policy relating to conflicts to make particular regulation for apparent conflicts, although the most appropriate regulation is likely to involve disclosure and investigation. As Davis observes, 'An apparent conflict of interest is resolved by making available enough information to show that there is no actual or potential conflict'.[100] Of course, if the further information goes in the opposite direction and confirms that there is an actual conflict, this also dispenses with any separate treatment of apparent conflicts. Apparent conflicts are either conflicts, potential conflicts, or nothing. Private law, as we will see, imposes on administrators obligations to provide information regarding their role, including in relation to conflicts.[101] This is why it does not separately regulate apparent conflicts. Through the rules about information, the law requires private law administrators to ensure that their beneficiaries know whether there is a (genuine) conflict or not.

B. Potential conflicts

Davis also usefully discusses the idea of a 'potential' conflict of interest:

> A conflict of interest is potential if and only if P has a conflict of interest with respect to a certain judgment but is not yet in a situation in which he must make that judgment. Potential conflicts of interest, like time bombs, may or may not go off. A conflict of interest is actual if and only if P has a conflict of interest with respect to a certain judgment and is in a situation in which he must make that judgment.[102]

Again, private law does not have separate norms for potential conflicts of interest. The norms about not using powers in conflicts, and the possibility of setting aside acts done in contravention of those norms, naturally apply to actual

---

[100] ibid.
[101] Chapter 5, section VIII.
[102] Davis, 'Conflict of Interest' (n 10), 575. See also *Commission of Inquiry into the Facts of Allegations of Conflict of Interest Concerning the Honourable Sinclair M Stevens* (n 36), 29.

conflicts. But the obligations to provide information are wider, just as they are in the case of apparent conflicts. If there is a potential conflict and it is reasonably foreseeable that it may or will turn into an actual conflict, and if the beneficiary has a decision-making role in relation to the administrator, then the potential conflict is relevant information about the administrator's managerial role that relates to the beneficiary's decision-making processes; all such information must be disclosed to the beneficiary.[103]

In the strict sense of conflict of interest, as it was defined above, conflicts of interest do not exist 'in the air'. A conflict arises in relation to a particular exercise of a particular other-regarding power. Recall that the definition says that a person has a conflict of interest if (a) he is in a relationship with another requiring him to exercise judgment in that other's service and (b) he has an interest tending to interfere with the proper exercise of judgment in that relationship.[104] Now take the case of a trustee of a trust that holds land as an investment. Imagine that the trustee is, himself, an experienced investor in land. He has many friends and family members who are investors and real estate agents. The beneficiaries might well be concerned about this situation, and think that their trustee is in a conflict. Here again, the language of 'apparent' conflict might be used, although the label 'potential' is more precise. This is because it may be perfectly possible for this trustee to avoid ever being in a conflict. If he is careful how he sells the trust land, and to whom, he need never be conflicted in the strict sense. If his duties to his beneficiaries lead him to think that what would be best for them would be a sale that *would* create a conflict of interest, then this conflict should be managed (as discussed in the final section of this chapter) so as to secure the maximum benefit for the beneficiaries. This may be via fully informed consent, or possibly through the approval of the court.

Some administrators act under the instructions of their beneficiaries.[105] Take the case of a mandatary who is charged with selling in interest in land belonging to the mandator. The mandatary receives offers from three potential buyers, but one of them is a relative of the mandatary; this creates a potential conflict. Here the mandatary already has a duty to inform the mandator/beneficiary of the offers, as it is the mandator who will make the final decision. This duty will inevitably extend to disclosure of the potential conflict. The mandatary could not simply suppress that offer, as it might be the most attractive one. The decision belongs to the mandator, but the mandatary must disclose information in his possession that is relevant to that decision.

---

[103] Chapter 5, section VIII.
[104] Above, section III.
[105] Chapter 1, section V.B.3.c.

People sometimes treat all unauthorized profits as related to, or arising from, conflicts of interest. This is clearly a mistake on the definition of conflict of interest given above. A conflict of interest arises in the context of the exercise of an other-regarding power; the acquisition of profits does not necessarily do so. Moreover, a conflict of interest remains a conflict of interest even if it is authorized. It follows that if all profits were conflicts of interest, then even an administrator's agreed remuneration would be a conflict of interest, but one that was authorized. This is not correct. It is an error that arises from conflating conflicts of interest with conflicts of interests, and conflating conflicts with unauthorized profits.[106] There is no conflict of interest in receiving agreed remuneration.

One of the reasons that people may conflate unauthorized profits and conflicts of interest is that profits may create potential conflicts.[107] Imagine that a trustee manages a large investment portfolio. One day he receives a valuable gift from a stockbroker, with whom he currently does no business. This is, on its face, an unauthorized profit that must be surrendered.[108] If we stop the story here, however, immediately after the receipt of the gift, there is no conflict; not yet, at least. The trustee is not in the situation where he must exercise other-regarding judgment— such as, in deciding which stockbroker should he engage for trust investment business. If the stockbroker who gave the gift never sought any stockbroking business from the trustee, or anything else, then the trustee would never be in a conflict as such. But the unauthorized profit certainly creates a *potential* conflict. Gifts call for reciprocation and this is one way that we establish relationships with other people.[109] Less positively, the line between a gift and a bribe may be difficult to draw.[110] Even leaving aside any concern with corruption, if the trustee did have to decide which stockbroker to employ, his self-interest would be in conflict with his duty to the beneficiaries, because, having accepted the gift, he now has a kind of personal relationship with the gift-giving stockbroker and so

---

[106] Above, section II.B.1. The confusion of conflict and profit is further discussed in the next chapter, section III.

[107] *Fiona Trust & Holding Corp v Privalov* [2010] EWHC 3199 (Comm), [73], [1389]–[1392].

[108] Assuming that the gift was received by the trustee in the course of his performance of his administrative role: Chapter 5, section II.A.

[109] Jacques Godbout and Alain Caillé, *The World of the Gift*, trans Donland Winkler (McGill-Queen's University Press 1998). One study showed that trivial gifts from pharmaceutical companies to medical students led to more positive attitudes of those students towards the products of those companies: David Grande and others, 'Effect of Exposure to Small Pharmaceutical Promotional Items on Treatment Preferences' (2009) 169(9) Arch Intern Med 887. A more recent study showed that gifts from pharmaceutical companies to physicians are associated with more prescriptions per patient, more costly prescriptions, and more prescriptions of brand-name products as opposed to generics: Susan F Wood and others, 'Influence of Pharmaceutical Marketing on Medicare Prescriptions in the District of Columbia' (2017) 12(10) PLoS ONE e0186060, online at https://doi.org/10.1371/journal.pone.0186060 . See also Ashley Wazana, 'Physicians and the Pharmaceutical Industry: Is a Gift Ever Just a Gift?' (2000) 283(3) JAMA 373.

[110] Doug Rendleman, 'Commercial Bribery: Choice and Measurement Within a Remedies Smorgasbord' (2017) 74 Wash & Lee L Rev 369, 372–74.

he has an interest in choosing that stockbroker. It is in a person's interest to benefit those with whom that person has a personal relationship.

The difference between the profit and the conflict can be underlined by noting that even an *authorized* profit can create a potential conflict that may ripen into a conflict. Imagine that the gift from the stockbroker was disclosed to the trust beneficiaries, and that they, with full information and being fully capacitated, authorized the trustee to accept the gift. That would make the profit lawful. But it would not definitively resolve the conflict analysis: if, later, the gift-giving stockbroker were being considered by the trustee for trust business, this would create a conflict of interest in the sense I have articulated.[111] This transaction would have to be separately authorized or otherwise managed, or else it would be subject to being set aside.

Profits, whether authorized or unauthorized, are not the same as conflicts of interest. They can create potential conflicts, and any potential conflict can become an actual conflict. Again, private law addresses these problems by requiring disclosure. Full disclosure is essential to secure informed consent to a conflict, allowing the unimpeachable exercise of other-regarding powers.[112] Duties of disclosure, in the strict sense, arise in contexts where the administrator has information that is relevant to the beneficiary's decision-making process. This may require the disclosure of potential or actual conflicts, of unauthorized profits, or of breaches of duties.[113]

C. Trivial conflicts

Some conflicts may satisfy the definition but be trivial. Take the case of an agent, Mary, who is selling her principal's land; the buyer is the ABC Corporation. Now if Mary were a principal shareholder of the ABC Corporation, this would be an obvious and classic conflict. Imagine instead that the ABC Corporation is a publicly traded and widely held corporation. Mary holds various retirement investments, including units of a mutual fund, and 0.1% of the assets of the mutual fund are invested in shares of the ABC Corporation. This of course is by the choice of the investment manager of the mutual fund, not by the choice of Mary. In a sense, that is irrelevant: Mary has a financial interest in the success of the ABC Corporation, and so there is a conflict. But let us assume that in this indirect way, the value of Mary's stake in the ABC Corporation is $100. What are we to make of this, if the land is worth say $1,000,000?

---

[111] Cf *Gray* (n 94), 13: consent to a contract made in a conflict of interest does not automatically constitute consent to any profit acquired from that contract by a fiduciary.
[112] Management of conflicts is discussed in the final section of this chapter.
[113] Chapter 5, section VIII.

There are different ways to address this. Of course, the conflict can be managed; if Mary informed him, the principal would probably dismiss this minor conflict with a wave of the hand. That, however, is informed consent, by which any conflict can be managed. If a beneficiary is not capacitated, it may not be feasible. Thus the more interesting question, which is also a practical one, is whether there is a threshold of significance, below which conflicts can be dismissed as trivial. The answer is not obvious. On one view, that should be a judgment to be made by the beneficiary, which could mean that no conflict is classified as trivial by the law itself. Leaving it to the administrator to decide whether the conflict is trivial would be to give the administrator a power in relation to which she would always be in a conflict of interest (or, perhaps, a conflict of duty and duty).

On the other hand, the difficulty with the view that only the beneficiary can decide is that conflicts requiring management (such as informed consent) would proliferate exponentially. Moreover, when one's savings are in collective investments, the investments may be constantly changing; but unless one deploys a 'blind trust' structure, one typically always has the means of acquiring knowledge as to how the funds are invested.

Since the administrator cannot have the power to decide whether a conflict is trivial, the only way to avoid attaching the same consequences to all conflicts, however trivial, would be through the adoption of a legal rule that some conflicts are *de minimis*: too minor to engage the normal rules. Some courts have suggested that this is the law.[114] In relation to whether a judge has disqualified himself by conduct that suggests that he is not entirely impartial, it has been held that the legal norm is whether a reasonable and informed person would have cause for concern.[115] If an issue were to arise in private law as to whether a conflict was so trivial that it should be ignored, a similar test would probably be applied. Another approach would be to limit disclosure

---

[114] See *Movitex Ltd* (n 30), 122 (an interest 'may be so small that that it can as a practical matter be disregarded'); *Imageview Management Ltd v Jack* [2009] EWCA Civ 63, [2009] 2 All ER 666, [6], [38] (there must be a 'realistic possibility of a conflict of interest'); *Glenn v Watson* [2018] EWHC 2016 (Ch), [419] (citing earlier *dicta* for a limit of triviality). In *Boardman v Phipps* [1967] 2 AC 46 (HL), there was some discussion by the dissenting judges of which conflicts of interest were not juridically relevant. These speeches are compromised, however, by the misunderstanding that a conflict of interest was necessary in that case for the plaintiffs to succeed. As the majority judgments show, it was not; the case was about the rule against unauthorized profits (see Chapter 5, section III.A). Note that in *Transvaal Lands Co* (n 72), the conflict of one director (Harvey) arose because he held (in trust) 5% of the issued shares of the corporation on the other side of the transaction.

[115] *Yukon Francophone School Board, Education Area #23 v Yukon (Attorney General)* [2015] 2 SCR 282, 2015 SCC 25. In the McGill *Regulation* (n 98), the definition of conflict of interest requires that the person's interest be such that 'in the opinion of a reasonably informed and well advised Person', it is sufficient to affect their exercise of other-regarding judgment.

to matters judged 'material'.[116] Some corporate law statutes reflect a similar standard.[117]

VII. Managing conflicts

A. Prior authorization

It is possible that some conflicts of interest may be authorized in advance, by a corporate constitution or corporate law, or by the instrument that constitutes a trust, or by the contractual relationship that constitutes a mandate or an agency. In the case of mandate or agency, this would amount to prior consent by the same person— the mandator or the principal—who anyway is empowered to give informed consent to a conflict. An employee who is given the authority, as agent or mandatary, to engage other employees may say at the outset to the employer/mandator, 'my brother is looking for a job in this field', and might be told, 'if you think he is the best candidate, go ahead and hire him'. Where agents are known to have multiple clients, some conflicts of duty and duty may be implicitly authorized.[118]

A common example of prior authorization from trust law arises where one of the trustees is also one of the beneficiaries. In this situation, the person when acting as a trustee is required to consider their own interests, as beneficiary. The mere naming of one of the beneficiaries as trustee is understood to authorize the conflict implicitly.[119] A less common example comes from trustee investment. Just as it is a classic conflict of interest for a trustee to buy or sell trust property to a party related financially or personally to the trustee, so too a trustee who is empowered to invest would be in a conflict of interest if they proposed to invest trust assets with a related party. But where the trust instrument permits it, it is possible for the trustee to borrow the trust property itself, thus turning the trust relationship into a relationship of debtor and creditor and leaving the beneficiaries unprotected on the insolvency of the trustee/creditor.[120] In such a

---

[116] *Sharbern Holding Inc v Vancouver Airport Centre Ltd* 2011 SCC 23, [2011] 2 SCR 175, [150]–[151].

[117] *Canada Business Corporations Act*, RSC 1985, c C-44, s 120 provides a regime to regulate cases in which a corporation contracts with its own administrators. It applies only to a 'material' contract; also, if the conflict arises because the administrator has a financial interest in the other party to the contract, the section applies only if that interest is 'material'.

[118] *Kelly v Cooper* [1993] AC 205 (PC). The elaboration of how this reasoning applies to lawyers is likely to involve a range of considerations (see *CNR v McKercher* (n 40)). Implicit authorization is one way to read the surprising passage in *Bank of Upper Canada v Bradshaw* (1867) LR 1 PC 479, 489–90, that an agent was not in a relevant conflict when he contracted on his principal's behalf with a company in which the agent was a shareholder.

[119] For an example from Quebec law, see *Droit de la famille—13681* 2013 QCCA 501.

[120] *Space Investments Ltd v Canadian Imperial Bank of Commerce Trust Co (Bahamas) Ltd* [1986] 1 WLR 1072 (PC).

case, the prior authorization comes not from the beneficiaries but rather from the settlor who put that authorization in the trust instrument, which is effectively the constituting document of the trust.

Similarly, pre-authorized conflicts of duty and duty are quite common in trust law, because they are built in to any trust in which the trustees have discretionary powers but the interests of the beneficiaries are not aligned exactly with one another. For example, a trust may require that income from the investments be paid to A while A is alive, and on A's death that the capital be paid to B. The trustees usually have some discretion as to the choice of investments. While both A and B are alive, A's interest is in investments that generate the most income, while B's interest is in investments that promote the maintenance or growth of capital value. In a real sense, the trustees are in a conflict of duty and duty; but the terms of the trust authorize it. Trust law's solution to this is to impose another requirement, that the trustees maintain an 'even hand' among the beneficiaries.[121] Where the trustees hold wide dispositive discretions, the interests of the objects of those discretions are also potentially in conflict, inter se or with the interests of beneficiaries or both. Again, that conflict is authorized by the terms of the trust. As we have noted, in this context the law requires that the powers be exercised in what the power-holders believe to be the best advancement of the purpose for which the powers were granted.[122]

In some cases, the legislator may also authorize conflicts in advance. In Canadian law, an employer may be authorized to act as the administrator of the pension plan of its employees. The employer's self-interest may well conflict with its duties as administrator that are owed to the employees, but the conflict is implicitly authorized by the statutory regime.[123] Other examples of pre-authorized conflicts may exist in corporate law.[124]

In any case, prior authorization of a conflict is likely to be construed strictly. It may allow the conflicted administrator to exercise their other-regarding powers in a situation where the rules on conflicts would otherwise apply and would disable them from doing so. The underlying norms as to the proper use of those powers, of course, continue to apply in full force, as do any applicable duties of disclosure.[125] Authorizing the use of administrative powers while in a

---

[121] For civil law, see Civil Code of Québec, art 1317, and Cantin Cumyn and Cumyn (n 33), 289–91; for common law, including the complicated ramifications of the even hand principle that have evolved over many years, see *Waters' Law of Trusts in Canada* (n 33), 1090–1189.

[122] Chapter 3, section IV.A.

[123] *Sun Indalex Finance, LLC v United Steelworkers* [2013] 1 SCR 271, 2013 SCC 6, [64], [193]–[194], [198], [215].

[124] *Canada Business Corporations Act*, RSC 1985, c C-44, s 120(5), whose content is mentioned in the next section on recusal.

[125] *Sun Indalex* (n 123), [66], [217]–[218]; *Levy-Russell Ltd v Tecmotiv Inc* (1994) 54 CPR (3d) 161 (Ont Gen Div), [605]–[626]; *UPM-Kymmene Corp v UPM-Kymmene Miramichi Inc* (2002) 214 DLR (4th) 496 (Ont SCJ), [116]–[126], affirmed (2004), 250 DLR (4th) 526 (Ont CA).

conflict does not authorize the disloyal use of those powers, nor does it change obligations of disclosure.

B. Informed consent

In private law, an administrator almost always acts for and on behalf of one or more beneficiaries.[126] Those beneficiaries are the only ones who are interested, in the legal sense, in what the administrator does. It follows from this that if they give fully informed consent to a transaction that would otherwise be vulnerable due to a conflict, then the problem generated by the conflict is solved.[127]

The requirement that their consent be fully informed is crucial. The beneficiaries must be able to understand fully the nature and extent of the conflict; otherwise, their consent is not meaningful and will not be effective.[128] In some settings, the administrator's obligation to provide information about the conflict is independent of the question of consent; in other words, the beneficiaries must be fully informed even if their consent is not sought, or not given. The justification and scope of such obligations to inform beneficiaries are discussed in the next chapter.[129]

If the beneficiaries, or even one of them, do not wish to give consent, then this solution is of course not available. There may be other difficulties. One or more of the beneficiaries may lack full legal capacity. This does not generally arise in the law of business partnerships; similarly, a business corporation is always fully capacitated. But it is certainly possible in trusts, and in the administration of the estate of a deceased person; it is also possible in the kind of agency or mandate that endures after the grantor of authority loses their legal capacity. By definition, such persons are unable to give a valid consent. Where someone loses capacity, there may be another person—who will also be an administrator and required to act with loyalty—who can give consent on their behalf, but in the case of enduring mandates, this is probably the very same person who may be seeking authorization to act in a conflict situation. In such cases of incapacity, the court in its supervisory jurisdiction may be able to approve the transaction.[130] It would

---

[126] Where the administrator acts for an impersonal purpose, as in the Quebec trust, the issue of consent by beneficiaries may be immaterial and consent by the court may be the only solution.

[127] There is a difficult question that can arise in trust law where the trustees have dispositive discretions, since those may allow distributions to persons who are not beneficiaries of the trust. In the common law they are called 'objects' of the power, and the common law allows enormous classes of such objects (indeed, the class of objects can be everyone in the world): see Lionel Smith, 'Massively Discretionary Trusts' (2017) 70 CLP 17. If the trustee is in a conflict in relation to the exercise of such a power, do only the beneficiaries need to consent (as is implied in that text)? If all of the objects need to consent, then obviously consent will be impossible.

[128] Eg *Gray* (n 94).

[129] Section VIII.

[130] This jurisdiction is briefly discussed in Chapter 1, section V.B.3.d.

of course be necessary for the incapacitated parties to be represented before the court.

Corporate law may present its own difficulties in this context. Where the principle of corporate personality applies, the beneficiary for whom the directors (or corporate officers) must act is the corporation itself; it follows, as a matter of general principle, that informed consent must be given by the corporation. The next question becomes, who speaks for the corporation in this respect? Corporate law typically assigns some decision-making powers to the board of directors, and some to the shareholders. If a decision-making power is not specifically assigned, then different models of corporate constitution may give different answers as to where 'residual' authority lies.[131]

The problems of conflicts involving corporate directors and officers is, however, of such long standing that corporate constitutions and background corporate law often provide specific procedures for dealing with them. In the modern law, generally the governing statute (or perhaps the corporate constitution, or both) will set out procedures that must be followed to obtain informed consent in this context.[132] These procedures are discussed in the next section.

C. Recusal

Recusal refers to the ad hoc disqualification of an administrator, in relation to a particular decision. Usually it refers to the case in which the person disqualifies themself. The person stands aside as regards a particular matter but does not withdraw completely from their role; they do not resign.

As a way of managing conflicts, recusal can only work if there is someone else who can act in relation to the matter in question. In private law, this is most relevant where there are multiple administrators, as is very often the case with boards of directors. It may also be relevant in trusts and estates, which can have multiple trustees, executors, or liquidators. It can work so long as the non-recusing administrators constitute a quorum and are able to decide without the recusing administrator.

In corporate law, the regulation of conflicted transactions in the statute or the corporate constitution is likely to stipulate that a director who is in a conflict situation as regards a particular transaction is deprived of his or her vote in relation to the approval of that transaction.[133] Such regimes have in some cases been

---

[131] Smith (n 92), 409–14.

[132] Above, text at nn 89–92, where it is noted that securities law may be also be relevant in publicly traded corporations.

[133] In the *Canada Business Corporations Act*, RSC 1985, c C-44, s 120(5), it is specifically provided that a director *can* vote on a resolution to approve a contract for his or her own remuneration. The

adopted into trusts, to provide a way to manage similar conflicts where there are multiple trustees.[134]

These regimes uniformly provide that the recusing director or trustee must make full disclosure of their interest. One might ask exactly why this should be: the recusing administrator is no longer exercising their powers as a director, and so cannot be exercising such powers while in a conflict. If disclosure is part of getting approval for the disclosing administrator to exercise such a power *while in a conflict*, why should the recusing director have to disclose? It is sometimes said that the corporation is entitled to the unbiased judgment of all its directors.[135] But it is lawful for a director to not attend a particular meeting, and as long as there is a quorum, the board will still have decision-making power. The better explanation is that despite the recusal, a recusing director remains a member of the board and so in a relationship of administration with the corporation. And if one views the board as a single decision-making organ, the board itself is in a conflict if one of its members is in a conflict.

There is another reason for full disclosure by the recusing director, which we have already noticed: it is incorrect to think that disclosure is only an aspect of securing informed consent to the exercise of other-regarding power in a conflict.[136] There are true duties of disclosure that are part of the accountability of the administrator. Moreover, an even wider obligation of disclosure may arise to protect the decision-making processes of the beneficiary, where an administrator proposes, not to exercise their administrative powers, but rather to deal in their personal capacity with their beneficiary.[137] That is exactly what is happening in cases of this kind.[138] The recusing director remains a director, and is contracting personally (or via an intermediary) with their beneficiary, the corporation. Here the law requires the fullest disclosure.[139] Non-disclosure would

disclosure requirements still apply. The reason for disapplying the recusal rule in this case is not obvious.

[134] See for example Clause 9 of the Standard Provisions of the Society of Trust and Estate Practitioners, available at www.step.org. Similar provisions could be included in a will if there were multiple testamentary executors. In neither case is there an exact analytical match with corporate law regimes, because the corporation is a legal person provided with decision-making organs (the board and the shareholders) while neither a trust nor the estate of a deceased former person is a legal person.
[135] Eg *Movitex Ltd* (n 30), 118–19.
[136] Section V.C.
[137] Above, section II.B.3, this was described as the domain of the fair-dealing rules, as opposed to the self-dealing rules.
[138] In fact, these related-party transactions by corporations can be seen as a combination of the fair-dealing and the self-dealing scenarios. The board is exercising other-regarding powers which is the domain of self-dealing; the conflicted director(s) are dealing personally (or via an intermediary) with the beneficiary corporation, which is the domain of fair-dealing.
[139] This is more fully explained in Chapter 5, section VIII.

allow the corporation to impugn *its own* consent to the transaction and set it aside, separately from setting aside the exercise of administrative powers by its other directors.[140]

Following disclosure, the recusing director and the other directors remain bound by their duties as administrators; although the recusing director does not participate in the particular decision, she remains a director. Thus the underlying norms as to the proper use of their powers continue to apply in full force.[141] It goes without saying that the remaining directors, in exercising their powers, must act with undivided loyalty towards the corporation: that is, in what they believe to be the best interests of the corporation, unswayed by any consideration of the interest of the recusing director. This may be difficult; some might say, impossible. Only if one thought it possible could the recusal regime be considered useful. Any director who had a personal relationship with the recused director might think that this generated a separate conflict, possibly also requiring recusal.

The recusal regime is designed as a way of managing, not eliminating, the conflict. It builds on informed consent, and adds individual recusal to that in an attempt to mitigate the conflict, while also allowing the conflicted director to remain on the board for future business. In some cases, whether due to a lack of director quorum or perhaps some failure of disclosure, decision-making authority for the approval of the transaction may pass to the shareholders; this may also be regulated in different ways by statute or the corporate constitution, possibly requiring a special majority or the disqualification of those shareholders whose self-interests are in conflict with the interests of the corporation.[142] Even if the shareholders or the directors or both have approved the transaction, dissenting shareholders or others may have standing to question the transaction for fairness.[143] This is particular to this context, because of problems arising from majority rule. If unanimous consent by the beneficiaries is required, as in trust law, there is no need for the courts to test the fairness of the transaction.

Statutory or corporate constitutional regimes usually allow the conflicted director to retain any profit acquired from the transaction if the correct procedures are followed. This is important because otherwise, even if the corporation does not set aside the transaction, the administrator would be accountable for any

---

[140] In an analogous situation involving a trust, the recusing trustee is probably not contracting directly with the beneficiaries, but rather with the other trustees; but they in turn are acting for the beneficiaries, so it is logical that a duty of disclosure that would be owed to the beneficiaries is instead owed to those who are empowered to act in their interests. It is quite typical in trust law that trustees are empowered to enforce the rights of the beneficiaries, including rights to information, for the better administration of the trust: *Waters' Law of Trusts in Canada* (n 33), 1059–61.

[141] *Sun Indalex* (n 123), [66], [217]–[218]; *Levy-Russell Ltd* (n 125), [605]–[626]; *UPM-Kymmene Corp* (n 125), [116]–[126], affirmed (2004), 250 DLR (4th) 526 (Ont CA).

[142] For some legislative examples, see Smith (n 92), 411–8.

[143] See nn 89 and 90.

such profit that satisfies the rule against unauthorized profits.[144] This must be so, because even an administrator who has resigned can be accountable for profits.

In the absence of a specific regime, in statute law or a corporate constitution or a trust instrument, the possibility of recusal is not easily adopted in private law. Multiple trustees may be required to act unanimously, which excludes recusal; even if they may act by a majority, this does not necessarily permit a trustee to recuse themself in relation to a single decision, although it might if the trust specifically provided for a quorum, and if that quorum could be reached by the remaining trustees. But a lone administrator, whether trustee, executor, liquidator, agent, or mandatory—or indeed, director—cannot contemplate recusal as such.

In such a case, a court with supervisory jurisdiction might approve some improvised recusal solution, just as the court might be able to approve a proposed transaction on behalf of one or more beneficiaries who are incapacitated or otherwise unable to act. If, however, it be necessary to go to court, then it may make more sense to seek the court's approval of the transaction itself. In the absence of express statutory authority, however, the court will be extremely unlikely to override the withholding of consent by a capacitated beneficiary. Since the relevant norms apply for the benefit and protection of the beneficiaries, those with capacity will be allowed to make their own decisions.

D. Resignation or removal

The administrator can of course resign, or be removed by the court, or, depending on the circumstances, by the beneficiaries.[145] The conflict will be removed, because the administrator will no longer hold the relevant managerial powers. Depending on the situation, this step obviously may require the nomination of a replacement.

Administrators rarely wish to resign as a way of dealing with conflicts that have arisen. If it is a good solution, they will probably adopt it in anticipation of the conflict. Conversely, if the administrator chooses not to resign, it is presumably because he or she wishes to remain in the role. This may be because they wish to retain any compensation from the role, or it may be because they perceive that remaining in the role is the only way of bringing about the conflict-affected transaction that is the source of the problem. As we have seen in the previous section, in many private law contexts, recusal for a specific transaction is not feasible. If informed consent or court approval are not forthcoming, the

---

[144] *Gray* (n 94), 14–15. The rule is discussed in Chapter 5 and the test for its scope, in section II.A of that chapter.
[145] Chapter 2, section III.B.

administrator's options may be reduced to resignation or abandonment of the problematical transaction.

The beneficiaries, as we have seen, have remedies if the administrator goes ahead with the transaction.[146] If they become aware of the problem in advance, they need not wait, since there are mechanisms to remove an administrator. Courts have an inherent jurisdiction to remove prospectively a trustee or executor who is in a serious conflict, for that reason alone.[147] Agents and mandataries can always be removed by their capacitated principals or mandators.

---

[146] Section V.B. Conversely, an administrator cannot allow himself to be frozen into inaction by the conflict and a failure to manage a known conflict is a breach of duty: *Wight* (n 80).

[147] Above, n 33. In the same way, a foreseeable potential conflict may lead a court to conclude that an administrator should not be appointed to the role: *Re Lamb* (n 32).

5
Attribution: Costs, Profits, and Information

I. Introduction

In the common law, discussions of fiduciary law sometimes centre around norms that are said to be characteristic of that field: the rules against acting in conflicts and the rule against unauthorized profits. The previous chapter addressed conflicts, and this chapter addresses unauthorized profits. But it addresses more than that, and this is part of the argument. Administrators cannot reap unauthorized profits because of the very nature of their role, and the very nature of their role gives rise to a suite of norms, including but not limited to the rule against unauthorized profits (which I will sometimes call the 'no-profit rule'). Properly understood, the rule against unauthorized profits is not a rule activated by breach of duty or wrongdoing. Moreover, it is distinct, in its normative justification and in its consequences, from the rules against conflicts. The rule against unauthorized profits is not a creature of the Court of Chancery; it is found also in the civil law, dating back to its origins in Roman law.

Let us start with an example. Imagine that your neighbour is going away, camping in the wilderness for a couple of weeks. She asks you to keep an eye on her house; you agree, and she leaves you a key. Now imagine that one day you discover that there is a hole in her roof and the rain is leaking in. You cannot contact your friend. You pay a roofer to fix the roof. Can you recover this expense from your friend? It seems obvious that you can: although you might have made a contract with the roofer, and be liable to the roofer, still, as between you and your friend, the cost should fall on her. The reason is that even if you were not acting in her name, still you were acting on her behalf. You used your money to fix her house. The law will almost certainly implement this intuition. Even in the absence of any express authority from your friend to incur such an expense, legal tools such as implied authority, agency of necessity, or *negotiorum gestio* will probably allow a claim.[1]

---

[1] The Civil Code of Québec, which aims to eliminate Latin terminology, uses the phrase 'management of the business of another' as the English equivalent of the civilian institution, dating back to Roman law, that is often called, even in English, *negotiorum gestio* (arts 1482–90). On agency

---

The Law of Loyalty. Lionel Smith, Oxford University Press. © Lionel Smith 2023.
DOI: 10.1093/oso/9780197664582.003.0005

Now take a fanciful variation of the same story. One day there is an emergency with some overhead wires, and city workers have to occupy your friend's garden for a period of time. They do not cause any damage, but when they depart, seeing you in the house, they hand you an envelope with $200 in it, a payment from the city as compensation for the inconvenience. Can you keep it? In my view, the answer is 'no', and the reason is exactly the same: you were acting on her behalf. You were looking after her house, for her; you were not the occupant of the house, not even in the limited sense of a tenant or residential visitor. If you incur expenses when acting as a manager, they fall on the person for whom you are acting; if you reap benefits when acting as a manager, they fall to the person for whom you are acting. And indeed, the same legal relationships that will create a right of reimbursement will also create an obligation to account for profits.[2]

These are rules—or perhaps aspects of a single rule—of attribution of costs and benefits. They are not rules about the consequences of wrongdoing. It is not because your friend has done anything wrong that she has to repay the cost of having the roof fixed; it is because the cost was properly incurred on her behalf.[3] Conversely, and more importantly for this chapter, it is not because you have done anything wrong that you have to hand over the $200. It is simply because you acquired that profit while acting on her behalf; thus, as between you and your friend, she has the better claim to it.[4]

This idea of attribution therefore explains both claims to recover expenses and duties to turn over benefits. In an extended sense, it also covers information. While looking after your friend's house, you might acquire different kinds of information. Some might be good, and some might be bad. For example, you might hear sounds that make you think there are vermin in the house. Alternatively, you might find out that a movie is being filmed in the area and that your friend has the possibility to make a large sum of money if her house is to be used as a set. And then there is also information about your own management. For example, once you have received the $200 in the example given earlier, your friend does not know anything about it yet. I would say—and again, for the same reason—that you must share the information in each case. In the cases of costs and profits mentioned above, the law brings about attribution by assigning rights

---

of necessity and its relationship to implied authority, see Peter Watts and Francis MB Reynolds, *Bowstead and Reynolds on Agency* (22nd edn, Sweet & Maxwell 2020) ch 4.

[2] An argument for accountability that is framed in terms of unjust enrichment can only work if it is first concluded that as between you and your friend, she has a better right than you do to the $200. And once that conclusion is reached, unjust enrichment is superfluous.

[3] Of course, being obliged to repay you, she will do something wrong if she fails to do so. But that wrong cannot be what created the obligation.

[4] The same point can be made here as in the previous note: if you keep the money, you will be doing something wrong; but that wrong cannot be the source of your duty to hand it over.

of reimbursement and duties to hand over profits. Information as such is not a right, but the law can and does assign rights to information, which are duties of disclosure when seen from the other side. The information 'belongs' to your friend, not legally but colloquially; legally, the way to address this is to attribute to her a right to receive it. Whether the law *would* assign duties of disclosure in each of these three hypothetical cases is a separate point, but it certainly does so in private law relationships of administration.

There is nothing unusual in private law in duties that are created by law to give effect to a relationship. Parents are obliged to feed and clothe their children, and spouses are usually obliged to divide their property fairly when their relationship ends. Those positive duties are not remedies for wrongs; they are legal incidents of relationships. The same is true of the attribution of profits and expenses in the relationship between an administrator and a beneficiary. The administrator acts for and on behalf of the beneficiary, and the law gives effect to this.

II. The attribution of profits

A. Statement of the norm

Canonical statements of the rule against unauthorized profits, as it applies to private law administrators, are in line with the analysis above. They are not in terms of wrongdoing, still less in terms of deterrence. Rather, the obligation to account for—and then to surrender—the profit exists because of the nature of the relationship. In the terminology of the common law, all that is needed is that the profit be acquired through a fiduciary position. In one well-known case involving corporate directors, Lord Cairns LC said:

> All that the Court has to do is to examine whether a profit has been made by an agent, without the knowledge of his principal, in the course and execution of his agency.[5]

In the famous case of *Regal (Hastings) Ltd v Gulliver*,[6] the defendants were directors of a corporation, which became the plaintiff. To expand the plaintiff's business, a subsidiary corporation was created. That corporation needed to acquire a lease of land, and the future landlord was worried about security for the rent. The landlord wanted the defendants to give personal guarantees; of course

---

[5] *Parker v McKenna* (1874) LR 10 Ch App 96 (DC), 118. Directors are not, as such, agents; but they may additionally be agents, and they were in this case.
[6] *Regal (Hastings) Ltd v Gulliver* (1942) [1967] 2 AC 134 (HL).

they had no obligation to their corporation (the parent and the plaintiff) to do that. Alternatively the landlord wanted the new corporation to have more share capital. The defendants concluded, in their role as directors of the plaintiff corporation, that that corporation could not invest more than initially planned. It was then decided that the defendants would invest money of their own to acquire shares in the subsidiary (which, of course, they had no obligation to do). The subsidiary was successful and eventually its shares were sold at a profit to all shareholders, including both the plaintiff and the defendants.

The parent corporation sued to take away the defendants' personal profits, even though it was clear that the defendants had acted in good faith and the parent had profited by their actions. The Court of Appeal denied the claim, noting first that the directors were under no duty to obtain the shares (that they had acquired personally) for the parent corporation of which they were directors; and second, that the defendants could not have secured the benefit that was acquired by the parent without themselves personally acquiring shares in the subsidiary. The House of Lords held that both points were irrelevant to the operation of the rule against unauthorized profits, as was the consideration that the defendants had been in good faith throughout. Lord Russell said:

> The rule of equity which insists on those, who by use of a fiduciary position make a profit, being liable to account for that profit, in no way depends on fraud, or absence of bona fides; or upon such questions or considerations as whether the profit would or should otherwise have gone to the plaintiff, or whether the profiteer was under a duty to obtain the source of the profit for the plaintiff, or whether he took a risk or acted as he did for the benefit of the plaintiff, or whether the plaintiff has in fact been damaged or benefited by his action... The liability arises from the mere fact of a profit having, in the stated circumstances, been made.[7]

There are two distinct points to make here. The first point is that it is irrelevant whether the plaintiff suffered any loss at all as a result of the defendant's conduct.[8] This is why it was irrelevant in *Regal (Hastings)* whether the company

---

[7] ibid 144–45. The 'stated circumstances' are that the profit was acquired 'by use of a fiduciary position'. For other formulations: Viscount Sankey (139): the 'general rule' is that a person 'acting in a fiduciary capacity, is liable to account for the profits made by him from knowledge acquired when so acting'; Lord Macmillan (153): a fiduciary is accountable for any profit acquired 'by reason and in virtue of their fiduciary office'; Lord Wright (156): 'a director must account to his company for any benefit which he obtains in the course of and owing to his directorship'; Lord Porter (159): 'Their liability in this respect does not depend upon breach of duty but upon the proposition that a director must not make a profit out of property acquired by reason of his relationship to the company of which he is director.'

[8] Other important cases on this point include *Keech v Sandford* (1726) Sel Cas t King 61, 25 ER 223, 2 Eq Cas Abr 741, 22 ER 629 (LC); *Parker* (n 5); *Furs Ltd v Tomkies* (1936) 54 CLR 583; *Boardman v Phipps* [1967] 2 AC 46 (HL); *Akita Holdings Ltd v Attorney General of the Turks & Caicos*

could or might have secured the benefit itself, or whether the defendants were under a duty to obtain it for the company (since if they were, that could support a finding that a loss was caused). In other words, the application of the rule against unauthorized profits may well make the plaintiff beneficiary better off than if the administrator had never extracted the unauthorized profit. The second point is that it is irrelevant whether the plaintiff did anything legally wrongful in acquiring the benefit.[9] This is why it was also immaterial whether there was fraud or bad faith, or whether the defendants acted for the plaintiff's benefit or not, or (again) whether the defendants had been under a duty to obtain the benefit for the company (since if they had, the breach of that duty would have been wrongful). The rule is not about bad faith, loss, harm, or even wrongdoing. Nor is it about conflicts of interest, which were hardly mentioned in the speeches in *Regal (Hastings)*. It is a rule of attribution arising out of the relationship. It creates *primary* rights, not sanctions for wrongdoing.[10]

Although it might be less prominent, the same principle can be seen in the civil law tradition, particularly in the context of the contract of mandate.[11] Where such systems allow a mandator to recover from her mandatary profits acquired by so acting, scholars may sometimes see the remedy as arising from the proper interpretation of the contract, or from a breach of duty, or both.[12] But many systems have a norm that is not based on contractual interpretation and that does not depend on wrongdoing. The *Digest* of Justinian contains a text from the jurist Paul that reads: 'Nothing obtained as a result of a mandate ought to be left in the hands of the person who undertook the mandate, just as he ought not to suffer

Islands [2017] UKPC 7, [2017] AC 590, [17]; *Gray v Global Energy Horizons Corp* [2020] EWCA Civ 1668, [126].

[9] This was explicitly stated by Lord Porter (quoted in n 7) and by Lord Macmillan (153): the issue was not 'whether they had acted in breach of their duty. They were not said to have done anything wrong.'

[10] Here I use 'primary right' to mean a right that does not arise from wrongdoing, contrasted with a 'secondary right' (such as a right to damages) that arises from wrongdoing. Examples of primary rights in this sense are a right to contractual performance; a right to recover a payment of money made by mistake; a right of a child to the support of its parent.

[11] It was noted earlier (Chapter 1, section IV.A.1) that in the civil law, the contract of mandate has often been treated as the source of rules that apply generally to relationships of administration. Like trusteeship in the common law, in the civil law mandate is a paradigm relationship of administration: Michele Graziadei, 'Virtue and Utility: Fiduciary Law in Civil Law and Common Law Jurisdictions' in Andrew S Gold and Paul B Miller (eds), *Philosophical Foundations of Fiduciary Law* (OUP 2014) 287, 288.

[12] Michele Graziadei, Ugo Mattei, and Lionel Smith, *Commercial Trusts in European Private Law* (CUP 2005), Case 3, Alternative 1 (247–84), with comparative conclusions at 282–84. In civil law, wrongdoing generally leads to a compensatory measure and where a gain has been acquired by the mandatary, there may be a temptation to view it as a loss to the mandator, by arguing that the mandator had a right to it. This however will sometimes be fictitious. One reaction may be to argue that civil law should recognize gain-based damage awards (see Ewoud Hondius and André Janssen (eds), *Disgorgement of Profits: Gain-Based Remedies Throughout the World* (Springer 2015) 478–83, 499–504).

loss . . .'[13] That text was well-known to Jean Domat and Robert-Joseph Pothier, and a version of it has been in the French *Code civil* since it first came into force in 1804.[14] The text remains unchanged today:

> Every mandatary is bound to render an account of his management, and to transfer to the mandator everything that the mandatary received in virtue of his mandate, *even when what he received was in no way owing to the mandator*.[15]

The German Civil Code provides:

> The mandatary is obliged return to the mandator everything he receives to perform the mandate *and what he obtains from carrying out the transaction*.[16]

The Swiss Code of Obligations has a similar provision.[17] In Quebec, a comparable article was in the Civil Code of Lower Canada that was in force 1866–1993; art 2184, para 1 of the Civil Code of Québec now provides:

> Upon termination of the mandate, the mandatary is bound to render an account and hand over to the mandator everything he has received in the performance of his duties, *even if what he has received was not due to the mandator*.[18]

In different ways, these provisions have common ground with the principle in *Regal (Hastings)*. None of them requires the breach of a duty, or the proof of a loss, for the mandatary to be obliged to hand over unauthorized profits. As

---

[13] D.17.1.20, translated Alan Watson (ed), *The Digest of Justinian*, 4 vols (revised edn, U of Pennsylvania Press 1998). See also D.17.10.2 (Ulpian), written from the point of view of a mandator: 'Indeed, if he has lent my money out at interest and has obtained interest, we hold in consequence that he must pay [me] whatever profit he has made, whether I gave him a mandate [to lend] or not.' The insertions are not mine but are in the translation of Watson and others.

[14] Julien-Michel Dufour, *Code civil des français, avec les sources où toutes ses dispositions ont été puisées*, 4 vols, vol 3 (Lenormant 1806) 542.

[15] Art 1993 (emphasis added); my translation of: 'Tout mandataire est tenu de rendre compte de sa gestion, et de faire raison au mandant de tout ce qu'il a reçu en vertu de sa procuration, *quand même ce qu'il aurait reçu n'eût point été dû au mandant*.' To some eyes, the italicized words would seem intended to cover unauthorized profits. Interestingly, as a result of some well-known cases, French doctrine is also preoccupied with whether they cover mistaken overpayments to the mandatary of amounts which were not actually owed to the mandator.

[16] Gerhard Dannemann and Reiner Schulze (eds), *German Civil Code: Bürgerliches Gesetzbuch (BGB)*, 2 vols, vol I (CH Beck 2020) § 667 (emphasis added). This provision is applied to some other relationships of administration outside of mandate (ibid comment A.II).

[17] Code of Obligations, art 400¹.

[18] Emphasis added. See also art 2146, requiring the surrender of gains acquired by the use of information, discussed in *Gravino v Enerchem Transport Inc* [2008] RJQ 2178, 2008 QCCA 1820; an unofficial English translation of the judgment by the present author is in Bruce Welling, Lionel D Smith, and Leonard I Rotman, *Canadian Corporate Law: Cases, Notes & Materials* (4th edn, LexisNexis Canada 2010) 377.

in the common law, the obligation to surrender unauthorized profits is not a sanction for wrongdoing, but a primary obligation growing out of the relationship. The German law has been described as requiring the mandatary to give up benefits that arise from the mandate that are connected to the interests of the mandator, so including secret commissions and kickbacks.[19] This is also the law in Quebec: the mandatary cannot defend by saying that the bribe was not received on behalf of the mandator.[20] Many cases of unauthorized profits involve wrongdoing causing loss.[21] But often there is no loss to the mandator; recovery has been allowed nonetheless, measured by the unauthorized profit.[22] French courts have sometimes interpreted art 1993 more restrictively, but there is jurisprudence and doctrine interpreting it as having a similar scope to the *Regal (Hastings)* principle.[23] One nineteenth-century French author described a fundamental principle that the mandatary can retain no unauthorized profit, whether or not it was acquired illicitly.[24] This position was supported by other French jurists,[25] and is also supported by more recent scholarship.[26]

The civil law also shows a willingness to generalize from the contract of mandate, and to find that these principles rightly apply to other relationships of administration. One author argues that there is a general principle in German law requiring the surrender of unauthorized gains acquired in such relationships.[27] In Quebec, there are now multiple codal articles outside of the contract of

[19] Dannemann and Shulze (n 16), ibid comments B.III and B.IV. There is an unusual rule in Austrian law: although ABGB §1009 provides (as in other codes) that profits must be surrendered to the mandator, ABGB §1013 *in fine* provides that an unauthorized gift to a mandatary is forfeit to charity (see the decision interpreting this provision in OGH 1992/09/16 9ObA206/92; 9ObA292/92).

[20] *Thompson v Sénécal* (1894) 3 BR 455, applied in *Compagnie de pulpe de Métabetchouan v Paquet* (1906) 3 CS 211.

[21] *Mongeau v Mongeau* [1973] SCR 529; *Lefebvre v Filion* [2008] RJQ 145 (CS)

[22] That it was unnecessary to prove any loss was explicitly held in *Thompson* (n 20) and *Bank of Montreal v Kuet Leong Ng* [1989] 2 SCR 429.

[23] Jérôme Huet and others, *Les principaux contrats spéciaux*, Jacques Ghestin (ed), *Traité de droit civil* (3rd edn, LGDJ 2012), 1095. See also, for Belgian law, Henri De Page and René Dekkers, *Traité élémentaire de droit civil belge*, vol 5 (2nd edn, Bruylant 1975) 419–20. De Page and Dekkers say that the mandatary's dealings with third parties can never be a source of profit for the mandatary.

[24] Louis V Guillouard, *Traités des contrats aléatoires et du mandat* (2nd edn, A Durand & Pedone-Lauriel 1894) 424, 449. Guillouard also took the view (at 426) that liability for unauthorized profits could not be set off to reduce liability for losses caused by wrongdoing to reduce the latter. This is also the rule of Civil Code of Québec, art 2146. This is correct if, as I argue, the mandator's entitlement to the unauthorized profit is a primary right, and not a sanction for wrongdoing.

[25] Raymond-Théodore Troplong, *Du mandat* (Charles Hingray 1846) 406–10, 413; Paul Pont, *Commentaire-traité des petits contrats et de la contrainte par corps*, 2 vols, vol 1 (Cotillon 1864) 514–15.

[26] Franz Werro, *Le mandat et ses effets* (Éditions Universitaires Fribourg 1993), 176–78 (on Swiss law).

[27] Tobias Helms, 'Disgorgement of Profits in German Law' in Ewoud Hondius and André Janssen (eds), *Disgorgement of Profits: Gain-Based Remedies Throughout the World* (Springer 2015) 219, 223 (albeit phrasing the principle in terms of breach of duty).

mandate which provide comparable remedies.[28] These include the rules for directors and business partners.[29] Most important are those in the regime for administration of the property of others, because this regime can be seen as having replaced the contract of mandate as the general law of relationships of administration.[30] The Civil Code of Québec, after providing for the rendering of accounts and the return of the administered property, states:

> An administrator shall hand over all that he has received in the performance of his duties, even if what he has received was not due to the beneficiary or to the trust patrimony; he is also accountable for any personal profit or benefit he has realized by using, without authorization, information he had obtained by reason of his administration.[31]

It goes on to provide in the next article that the expenses of administration are borne by the beneficiary, underlining the link between expenses and unauthorized profits that was drawn above.

B. Justification for the norm

1. Not based on deterrence

A popular view among common law scholars is that the no-profit rule has a deterrent function. There are several problems with this account.[32] One is that any well-designed deterrent would have to do more than simply take away benefits.[33] You would not try to deter fraud by a sanction that only took away the profits of

---

[28] Michelle Cumyn, 'L'encadrement des conflits d'intérêts par le droit commun québécois' in Denis Mazeaud, Benoît Moore, and Blandine Mallet-Bricout (eds), *Les conflits d'intérêts* (Dalloz 2013) 49, 60–62; Lionel Smith and Jeff Berryman, 'Disgorgement of Profits in Canada' in Ewoud Hondius and André Janssen (eds), *Disgorgement of Profits: Gain-Based Remedies Throughout the World* (Springer 2015) 281, 287–88.

[29] Civil Code of Québec, arts 326, 2238. Business partners are mutual mandataries (art 2219), as they are mutual agents in the common law.

[30] Madeleine Cantin Cumyn and Michelle Cumyn, *L'administration du bien d'autrui* (2nd edn, Éditions Yvon Blais 2014), 87ff.

[31] Art 1366.

[32] A fuller argument: Lionel Smith, 'Deterrence, Prophylaxis and Punishment in Fiduciary Obligations' (2013) 7 J of Equity 87.

[33] If we are seeking a justification for the norm, it must be based on an argument that the norm has a deterrent *function*, that is, that it exists in order to deter; not merely that it has or may have a deterrent *effect*. Lots of things have a deterrent effect in some cases; for example, people may be deterred from trying to walk across a busy highway by the vehicular traffic, but it does not follow that the traffic exists in order to deter. Effects alone do not explain why things exist, and certainly not legal rules that have been created by people.

successful frauds; deterrence must do more than this if it is to have any chance of being effective.[34]

The second problem is that the deterrent argument supposes that the law is unjust. What is supposed to be deterred? Authors are not always clear, but they typically claim or assume that the law is trying to deter either harm to, or misappropriation from the beneficiary.[35] One author argues that the law aims to deter breaches of legal obligations by the administrator.[36] The problem is that, as we have seen, the rule against unauthorized profits can be activated without any of these things being present; all of them—harm, loss, breach of some other obligation—are irrelevant. Any deterrence theory therefore has to suppose that sanctions (in the form of taking profits) are applied to someone, as a deterrent, regardless of whether that person has done anything wrong, or has done the thing that we are trying to deter. It is simply implausible that the law is so unjust.[37]

Sometimes it is said that the law aims to deter or sanction 'opportunism', a word which to some may suggest laudable initiative while to others may suggest some lack of principles.[38] If these accounts are to be different from the ones just mentioned, it seems necessary to define 'opportunism' as referring to conduct that is lawful.[39] This however makes the problem even worse: How could the law rightly apply deterrent or confiscatory sanctions to lawful behaviour?[40]

Another problem bedevils the majority of deterrence theories, namely those that argue that the rule aims to deter misappropriation or harm to the beneficiary.

---

[34] Some authors note that the deterrent effect is multiplied by the costs of litigation and so on, but this is only an admission that the argument does not work as a justification for the rule against unauthorized profits as it exists in law, combined with an ad hoc attempt to prop it up.

[35] Peter Birks, *An Introduction to the Law of Restitution* (Clarendon Press 1985) 340–43 (harm); Robert Cooter and Bradley J Freedman, 'The Fiduciary Relationship: Its Economic Character and Legal Consequences' (1991) 66 NYU L Rev 1045, 1048–53 (misappropriation; similar is R Sitkoff, 'The Economic Structure of Fiduciary Law' (2011) 91 BU L Rev 1039 at 1043).

[36] Matthew Conaglen, *Fiduciary Loyalty: Protecting the Due Performance of Non-Fiduciary Duties* (Hart 2010).

[37] Remus Valsan, 'Fiduciary Duties, Conflict of Interest, and Proper Exercise of Judgment' (2016) 62 McGill LJ 1, 3–4.

[38] R Flannigan, 'The Boundaries of Fiduciary Accountability' (2004) 83 *Can Bar Rev* 35, 37 and in other writings uses 'opportunism' to refer to misappropriation, which has already been addressed.

[39] D Gordon Smith, 'The Critical Resource Theory of Fiduciary Duty' (2002) 55 Vanderbilt L Rev 1399, noting (at 1402 n 10) the ambiguity of 'opportunism'; none of the definitions he cites refers to unlawful conduct; Henry E Smith, 'Why Fiduciary Law Is Equitable' in Andrew S Gold and Paul B Miller (eds), *Philosophical Foundations of Fiduciary Law* (OUP 2014) 261, 265–68, defining 'opportunism' (at 267) as 'behavior that is undesirable but that cannot be cost-effectively captured—defined, detected, and deterred—by explicit ex ante rulemaking... It often consists of behavior that is technically legal but is done with a view to securing unintended benefits...'.

[40] Although HE Smith, ibid, defines opportunism as lawful conduct, his argument ultimately (273–75) seems to be that fiduciary law gives remedies for *unlawful* behaviour, in the form of misappropriation or other wrongdoing, and provides 'proxies' and presumptions that aid the beneficiary in proving these wrongs. It would seem to be impossible to argue that lawful opportunism becomes unlawful simply in virtue of being difficult to define, detect, or deter; but even if these were arguments for classifying the conduct as unlawful, then it would cease to be opportunism as defined.

As we will see in more detail in the next section, this gets the reasoning the wrong away around. If the administrator acquires a profit from a third party, why is this misappropriation *from the beneficiary*? It can only be such if we have already decided that the profit, or the occasion of its making, somehow belonged to the beneficiary. That is the logically prior question. But once we decide that, we have a reason for saying that the administrator cannot keep it, and that reason has nothing to do with deterrence. The administrator cannot keep it because it belongs to the beneficiary.[41]

Arguments based on deterring or sanctioning opportunism, defined as lawful conduct, may be founded partly on the realization that misappropriation or other wrongdoing cannot be invoked unless and until the benefit in question is allocated by the law to the beneficiary. But again, once that is done, arguments based on opportunism (defined as lawful conduct) become otiose.[42]

2. Not based on conflict of interest

The following section of this chapter expands in more detail on the distinctness of the rules about conflicts from the rule against unauthorized profits.[43] It shows that there are conflicts of interest in which there is no unauthorized profits, and there are unauthorized profits in which there is no conflict of interest.

A crucial issue in understanding this point, which has too long been ignored by common lawyers writing on conflicts, is the definition of conflict of interest. The definition of conflict of interest defended in the last chapter is that a conflict arises when an administrator is exercising or considering the exercise of a power held as an administrator (an other-regarding power, that must be exercised loyally), and that administrator has a self-interest (or a loyalty to some other) that conflicts with the proper (that is, loyal) exercise of the power.

With this definition, it becomes obvious that the rule against unauthorized profits can operate in the absence of any conflict of interest. Take the leading case of *Regal (Hastings)*, the facts of which were given above.[44] The defendant

---

[41] I use 'belongs' here in a loose sense of 'is attributed by law'. The benefit may belong as a matter of property law to the administrator, who owes an obligation to render an equivalent amount of money. But this loose sense of belonging, that the attribution to the beneficiary occurs through an obligation to account, is enough to make deterrence arguments otiose. It cannot be the case that we attribute the benefit to the beneficiary to deter the administrator from misappropriation, because there would be no misappropriation without the (prior) attribution. The attribution does all the explanatory work.

[42] One reading of at least some of the opportunism discourse in law and economics is as part of a prescriptive argument as to what the law should be; thus, it aims to identify conduct that *should be* unlawful (although I do not read Flannigan (n 38), DG Smith (n 39), or HE Smith (39) in that way). The interpretive methodology of the current study (Chapter 1, section III.A) starts from the positive law, in which opportunism analysis does not figure. The frequent discussions of opportunism in prescriptive law and economics seems, from the outside, to be an admission that it is not possible to produce an account of what the law should be on the basis solely of wealth maximization, without any input of morality.

[43] Below, section III.

[44] Text at n 6.

directors of the plaintiff company subscribed their own money to buy shares in the new subsidiary company, while the plaintiff company also subscribed its money for shares. The defendants were accountable for their profits. But when they bought the shares in the subsidiary, they were not exercising the other-regarding powers that they held as directors; they were exercising their own personal contractual capacities. They did not act while in a conflict of interest in the proper sense of that term. Indeed one might well say that their personal interests were *aligned* with the interests of the plaintiff company: both the plaintiff company and the defendant directors had invested in the same enterprise.

Some might disagree and say that these defendants were in a conflict. The difficulty is that the only definition of 'conflict of interest' which makes this true is a definition that corresponds to a conflict of *interests*: one that drops the crucial link to the exercise of administrative powers, and looks only to whether the interests of the administrator are opposed to those of the beneficiary.[45] But that definition, as we have seen, is unworkable. The reason is that every administrator is *always* in a conflict of that kind. That definition is therefore not only unhelpful but positively confusing to clear analysis.

The formulations of the rule against unauthorized profits by the members of the House of Lords make no mention of conflicts.[46] The relevant norms in the civil law in relation to mandate also make no mention of conflicts.[47] The source of the confusion between the rule against unauthorized profits and the rules about conflicts of interest may be attributable to a later decision of the House of Lords.[48] Subsequent scholarship and case law, plagued by poor definitions of conflicts of interest (and especially by confusing them with conflicts of interests), has often failed to notice that the rule on unauthorized profits is quite independent from the rules on conflicts.[49]

3. Not even based on wrongdoing
In much scholarship and some case law, it is simply assumed that if someone is liable to give up a gain, they must have done something wrong.[50] This is another

---

[45] For a more thorough discussion of conflict of interest vs. conflict of interests, see Chapter 4, section II.B.1.

[46] See the quotations in n 7. Some of the judgments do refer to conflicts, often in quotations from other cases. The English Court of Appeal also stated the rule without reference to conflicts in *O'Donnell v Shanahan* [2009] EWCA Civ 751, [52], [60]; *Novoship (UK) Ltd v Nikitin* [2014] EWCA Civ 908, [104]; *Gray v Global Energy* (n 8), [126]; *Recovery Partners GP Ltd v Rukhadze* [2023] EWCA Civ 305, [34]–[36].

[47] Above, text at nn 13–31.

[48] *Boardman* (n 8), discussed below, section III.B.2.

[49] Deane J insisted on their separateness in *Chan v Zacharia* (1984) 154 CLR 178, 199; see also Charles Harpum, 'Fiduciary Obligations and Fiduciary Powers—Where Are We Going?' in P Birks (ed), *Privacy and Loyalty* (Clarendon Press 1997) 145, 146–48. I conflated the two in Lionel Smith, 'The Motive, Not the Deed' in Joshua Getzler (ed), *Rationalizing Property, Equity and Trusts: Essays in Honour of Edward Burn* (LexisNexis Butterworths 2003) 53, 60 n 31, 75 n 94.

[50] This is an assumption that I have made in the past (eg ibid), which I now consider to be incorrect.

example of the persistent failure to see that acting for others in law is governed by principles that are different to those that apply when one acts for oneself.[51] Because someone is made liable to give up a gain, it is *assumed* that this is a sanction attached to some wrongful act. Since the sanction is not compensatory, this may lead to accounts based on deterrence.

But the assumption is incorrect.[52] Although there may be differences in the scope of the relevant norms, the civilian norms have this in common with the common law rule: they present a rule of primary attribution arising out of the relationship, not a sanction for wrongful conduct.[53] An administrator is not accountable because he has done something wrong, but because he acts for and on behalf of another.[54] Being accountable means not only *producing* an account, in relation to those administrators who are so obliged; their obligation to produce an account is clearly a primary obligation. Additionally, the primary obligation of accountability, I will argue, includes the obligation to render up unauthorized profits; these profits must be entered into the account, in favour of the beneficiary.[55]

In arguing that the rule about unauthorized profits does not respond to a breach of duty, some might charge me with deviating from the interpretive method I have adopted, since common law courts now routinely refer to 'breach of fiduciary duty' in the context of unauthorized profits.[56] Here I would make

---

[51] See Chapter 1, section II.B.

[52] Lord Millett made this point in a different way, arguing that a fiduciary is treated as if he acted lawfully in acquiring the profit, and cannot plead his own wrongful conduct: Peter Millett, 'Bribes and Secret Commissions' [1993] RLR 7; Lord Millett, 'Bribes and Secret Commissions Again' (2012) 71 CLJ 583. It was put in the same way a hundred years earlier by Guillouard (n 24), 449. I think it is clearer to say that the rule creates a primary right in the beneficiary (which has the consequence that the beneficiary has no need to prove wrongdoing by the administrator). Paul Miller has argued that the beneficiary's entitlement is a primary liability of the administrator: Paul B Miller, 'Justifying Fiduciary Remedies' (2013) 63 UTLJ 570. However, as I understand him, he uses 'primary liability' to mean liability for a wrong (eg (585): 'Primary liability turns on breach of a duty owed by the defendant to the plaintiff . . .'); this is not what I mean by a primary right (n 10). Miller's account makes the liability for unauthorized profits turn on *disloyalty*, and he uses the language of wrongdoing throughout. My account is that wrongdoing is no part of the explanation for the beneficiary's entitlement. There are however passages in Miller's article which can be read as arguing that the beneficiary's right to an unauthorized profit does not depend on wrongdoing.

[53] Two of the judges in *Regal (Hastings)* said this expressly (see n 9). The *Digest* texts and codal articles set out above (text at nn 13–31) make no reference to wrongdoing.

[54] It is true that he may do something wrong by failing to account, but that is a different point. A person is bound to perform a contract because they made it, not because they did anything wrong. Not performing the contract is a wrong; but it is not the source of the pre-existing obligation to perform. As the Court of Appeal of England and Wales put it in *Novoship (UK) Ltd* (n 46), [104]: '. . . the breach of duty does not consist in the making of a profit by the fiduciary, but in the keeping of it for himself'.

[55] For earlier discussions showing that the operation of legal rules does not necessarily involve any breach of duty in the strict sense, see Chapter 3, section IV.G (in relation to disloyalty in the use of administrative powers); and Chapter 4, section II.B.4 (in relation to the rules against the use of administrative powers in conflict situation).

[56] To take one example, *FHR European Ventures LLP v Cedar Capital Partners LLC* [2014] UKSC 45, [2015] AC 250.

three points. First, we have already seen that judges and commentators often use the language of 'duty' for anything that generates a legal consequence, even if it is not a duty in the strict sense, whose breach constitutes an unlawful act.[57] The aspect of the 'duty of loyalty' that requires other-regarding powers to be used for the purposes for which they were granted is not a duty in the strict sense.[58] The rule that other-regarding powers cannot be unimpeachably exercised in conflict situations is also not a duty in the strict sense.[59] Second, this itself may be tied to a habit of thought that fails to notice that acting for others is categorically different in law to acting for ourselves.[60] If we assume that everyone acts for themself, and the law makes someone liable to give up a gain, we may unreflexively assume that the person must have done something wrong to warrant this response. But this chapter will demonstrate that many primary duties arise in relationships of administration. It is uncontroversial that a trustee's duty to render an account, for example, does not arise from wrongdoing. Third, if we pay close attention to what courts *do*, we find that certain legal rules relating to liability for unauthorized profits only make sense when that liability is seen as primary.[61] In this regard, my account fits better with the law than accounts that argue or assume that liability for unauthorized profits arises from wrongdoing.[62]

Of course, there may be lots of wrongful conduct in relation to the extraction of profits by an administrator. For example, an agent or mandatary who demands or receives bribes from the people he deals with is obviously acting wrongfully. In private law he is acting wrongfully towards his principal or mandator, and possibly also towards those from whom he seeks bribes.[63] In public law, he may well also be committing a crime. Much public law regulation aimed at corruption is concerned to implement criminal and regulatory offences surrounding the improper use of both public law and private law administrative powers, and the

[57] In his groundbreaking and influential monograph, Paul Finn referred to a whole range of legal rules as duties or obligations, even though only some are duties in the strict sense, and many are requirements for the unimpeachable exercise of other-regarding powers: Paul D Finn, *Fiduciary Obligations* (Law Book Co 1977); reprinted Paul Finn, *Fiduciary Obligations: 40th Anniversary Republication with Additional Essays* (Federation Press 2016).

[58] Chapter 3, section IV.G; that section notes that the so-called duty to mitigate is not a legal duty in the strict sense.

[59] Chapter 4, section II.B.4; that section gave other examples of legal consequences that do not relate to duties in the strict sense.

[60] Discussed in Chapter 1, section II.B.

[61] One demonstration of this is later in this section, being the third of three reasons I will give as to why the rule is not based on wrongdoing. The legal rules discussed in the following section (II.B.4) also demonstrate this.

[62] Since interpretive accounts aim to make sense of the law as it is, an account that has a better fit with the law is, all else being equal, a better account than one with a worse fit: Chapter 1, section III.A.

[63] For discussion of the civil consequences of bribery in the common law, see Paul M Perell, 'Remedies for the Victims of a Bribe' (1999) 22 Advocates' Q 198; *Otkritie International Investment Management Ltd v Urumov* [2014] EWHC 191 (Comm), [67]–[73]; Doug Rendleman, 'Commercial Bribery: Choice and Measurement Within a Remedies Smorgasbord' (2017) 74 Wash & Lee L Rev 369.

development of this field of law is important for local, national, and international governance.[64]

My argument in terms of attribution rules does not aim to question the importance of identifying civil and criminal wrongdoing in these contexts. My point, however, is this: the basic norm against unauthorized profits cannot be fully explained through the concerns that are in play in these extreme cases. There are several reasons.

One reason is that the norm is wider than the extreme case. We have already seen that it extends to people who have acted in good faith and who have not done anything wrong. There is a parallel with the rules about conflicts that were discussed in the previous chapter: they apply to corrupt people, but they apply more widely than that, and so they cannot be properly explained by reference to our concerns about corruption.

A second reason is that the rules of attribution grow directly out of the characterization of the relationship, and that characterization must be logically *prior* to the characterization of the administrator's conduct as corrupt or wrongful (whether civilly or criminally). Take the case of a bribe paid to an agent or mandatary to conclude a contract between the briber and the principal or mandator. It is clearly caught by the basic attribution rule, but it is almost certainly also a civil wrong, and a crime as well. But it is only through the prior characterization of the relationship that we can characterize the conduct as corrupt. The administrator who takes a bribe has purported to sell something that is not his to sell: namely his authority that is held for another, or in other words, his decision-making powers that he is bound to use for the benefit of the beneficiary.[65] If the administrator was selling something that belonged to him to do with as he pleased, he would not be doing anything wrong. But other-regarding powers are not assets that belong to the person who holds them.[66] Thus, before we characterize conduct as wrongful corruption, we must make a prior decision about what belongs to whom.[67] That decision is based on the characterization of the

---

[64] For one study of private law sanctions for corruption, with some discussion also of criminal sanctions, see Michael J Bonell and Olaf Meyer (eds), *The Impact of Corruption on International Commercial Contracts* (Springer 2015).

[65] I do not suggest that only those acting for others can commit a crime by receiving a bribe; an employee who takes a bribe to let burglars into the employer's shop commits a crime, because the shop does not belong to him. I am saying that where a person takes a payment to conclude a contract, we have to decide whether what he purported to 'sell' belonged to him personally or not *before* we can know whether that payment was a corrupt bribe, or just the price of a contract.

[66] See Chapter 2, section III.B.7.

[67] Of course, the rules can change over time. King LC was the judge who decided *Keech* (n 8), considered a foundation of the rule against unauthorized profits in the common law. Before being appointed Lord Chancellor, he presided over the trial of his predecessor, Macclesfield LC, who was tried for corruption (which included the misappropriation of money paid into court, for purposes of speculation in the stock market). One biographer reports that when King was appointed Lord Chancellor, his salary was made £1,200 higher than his predecessor's, on the ground that the sale of offices in Chancery, which had previously been treated as part of the Lord Chancellor's remuneration, was now

relationship. It is not because the administrator has done something wrong that his authority is not for him to sell; that is the case for every administrator, even one who never does anything wrong. It's because his authority is not for him to sell that he would do something wrong if he purported to sell it.

Similarly, the attribution rules grow, not out of wrongdoing, but directly out of the characterization of the relationship. This can be illustrated by a slightly more complicated case. Imagine an administrator whose job it is to buy goods for and on behalf of his beneficiary: he is an agent or mandatory, acting for a principal or mandator. This administrator arrives at work one day and finds, sitting on his desk, a giant fruit basket. A note reveals that it comes from one of the enterprises that sells goods to the administrator's beneficiary. To make the case more interesting, imagine that conspicuously tucked under a pineapple there is $5,000 in cash. The whole thing is a complete surprise to the administrator. He never asked for it. The question is, as he walks into his office and sees all this, has he done anything wrong? It would seem not; if he immediately informed his beneficiary of what had happened, and sought instructions, surely he is behaving exactly as he should. If he does not do that, when would we consider that the administrator *has* done something wrong, civilly or criminally or both? If he started to eat the fruit, that would be a problem. If he pocketed the cash, that would certainly be a problem. But that is only because we have decided already that the fruit and the money are not available to him. That attribution must logically come before the decision about wrongdoing, since if they were his, he could take them.

I have already suggested that duties to provide information are also founded on the same idea of attribution. In the fruit basket example, if the administrator does not tell his beneficiary within the first ten seconds, he has probably not done anything wrong, yet. If after some days he has still not told his beneficiary about the gift, we must begin to ask why, and unless there is some difficulty of communication, we might think that this non-disclosure amounts to wrongdoing.[68] Again, this is because we have decided already that the beneficiary has the right to relevant information arising out of the management relationship.

A third reason that the rule about unauthorized profits is not based on wrongdoing relates to the way claims for such profits are measured. This measurement is inconsistent with a theory that the claim arises from wrongdoing. It is not a good defence for a defendant to say that although he acquired a gain that is caught by the no-profit rule, he *could have* acquired the gain, or part of it, in

---

illegal: Lord Campbell, *Lives of the Lord Chancellors*, John A Mallory (ed), 13 vols, vol 6 (R Carswell 1876) 3. See Joshua Getzler, 'Rumford Market and the Genesis of Fiduciary Obligations' in Andrew Burrows and Lord Rodger of Earlsferry (eds), *Mapping the Law: Essays in Memory of Peter Birks* (OUP 2006) 577, 584–85.

[68] Duties of disclosure are discussed below, section VIII.

a different way that would not have been caught by the rule.[69] If the rule were about taking away wrongful gains, a defendant could rightly reduce his liability by showing that he could have acquired some or all of the gain non-wrongfully. This would falsify any causal link between the wrong and the gain. But because the no-profit rule attributes the gain actually made as a matter of primary right to the beneficiary, the counterfactual defence that the gain *could have* been made in a different way is irrelevant. In exactly the same way, the defendant cannot keep the gain by showing that if he had made full disclosure to the plaintiff, the plaintiff would have consented.[70] This is another attempt to argue that the defendant *could have* lawfully acquired the gain. Such an argument *would* be valid if the claim to the gain had to be linked causally to a wrongful act.

But the law says that because the administrator did not get informed consent, as soon as he acquired the gain, he was obliged to render it to the plaintiff as a matter of primary right. A claim based on a primary right does not depend on showing wrongdoing, and therefore it does not depend on showing a causal link between wrongdoing and gain. An analogy from contract law, which also creates primary rights, illustrates this. Assume that Albert and Belinda have an agreement that they will share equally the profits extracted by Albert from some undertaking to which Belinda has contributed an investment. Albert extracts £100 of profit and Belinda claims her £50. There is clearly no room for Albert to argue that Belinda's claim should fail because there was some alternative way in which Albert *could have* lawfully acquired the whole profit for himself. Belinda has a primary right to her share; counterfactuals are irrelevant in this setting, because she only has to prove her right. She does not have to link it to a wrong.[71]

4. Based on attribution

The law treats both loss or harm, and wrongdoing, as irrelevant. It is not possible to make sense of this if the rule is aimed at protecting the beneficiary against loss or harm, or against wrongdoing. It makes perfect sense, however, when the rule

---

[69] Such an argument was rejected in *Murad v Al-Saraj* [2005] EWCA Civ 959 and in *Novoship* (n 46), [96]: 'A fiduciary's liability to account for a secret profit does not depend on any notion of causation. It is sufficient that the profit falls within the scope of his duty of loyalty to the beneficiary.' The gain must be linked to the administrator's role; it need not be linked causally to any breach of duty. The same point was made in *United Pan-Europe Communications NV v Deutsche Bank AG* [2000] 2 BCLC 461 (CA), [47]; *Akita Holdings Ltd v Attorney General of the Turks & Caicos Islands* (n 8), [17]; *Gray v Global Energy* (n 8), [128]; and *Recovery Partners GP Ltd* (n 46), [38].

[70] *Gray v New Augarita Porcupine Mines Ltd* [1952] 3 DLR 1 (PC); *Hurstanger Ltd v Wilson* [2007] 1 WLR 2351 (CA).

[71] To the same effect is the observation of Guillouard mentioned earlier (n 24), also found in Civil Code of Québec, art 2146: liability for unauthorized profits cannot be set off to reduce liability for losses caused by wrongdoing. If both arose from wrongdoing, set-off might be possible, but this is not the case where the beneficiary's right to the profit is a primary right.

against unauthorized profits is understood a rule of attribution arising out of the nature of the parties' relationship.

How can this be understood? In their treatise on the Belgian law of mandate, Henri De Page and René Dekkers discuss the mandatary's duty to account to the mandator for everything the mandatary received, not just in virtue of the mandate, but as a result of the mandate. They say that the mandate can never be a source of profit for the mandatary, apart from the mandatary's authorized compensation from the mandator. Why?

> When he is carrying out the mandate, the mandatary is the mandator. He is not allowed to be the mandator and himself at the same time, to the detriment of the one who has entrusted him as a representative.[72]

In 2009, Jacob LJ said for a unanimous Court of Appeal:

> If you undertake to act for a man you must act 100%, body and soul, for him. You must act as if you were him.[73]

The first passage speaks, of course, in metaphor. The administrator and the beneficiary are not the same person. Each has their own juridical sphere: their own personal rights and obligations. But the administrator, acting in that role, is acting for and on behalf of the beneficiary; the administrative powers of the administrator do not belong to him personally, and when acting in his administrative role, he is not acting for himself. When the administrator acquires rights through acting for and on behalf of the beneficiary, the law attributes those rights to the sphere of the beneficiary. It says that as between the administrator and the beneficiary, those rights belong to the beneficiary.[74] This is another way of saying that the administrator is accountable for those rights. That is how the law gives effect to the metaphor set out above, without recourse to an idea of breach of duty. This principle can also be seen to be one foundation of the common law's rules on 'automatic' resulting trusts. If a trust, or some interest within a trust structure, fails to take effect, the law allows the trustee to derive no benefit from the rights they hold in trust, and stipulates instead that they be held in trust for the settlor.[75]

---

[72] De Page and Dekkers (n 23), 419 ('Lorsqu'il exécute son mandat, le mandataire est le mandant. Il ne lui est pas permis d'être à la fois le mandant et lui-même, au détriment de celui qui l'a chargé de le représenter.')

[73] *Imageview Management Ltd v Jack* [2009] EWCA Civ 63, [2009] 2 All ER 666, [6].

[74] As it is sometimes put in the civil law, when acting for another you cannot become *auctor in rem suam*, creator of your own rights: see *Dale v IRC* [1954] AC 11 (HL), 26–27, *per* Lord Normand, discussing common law and civil law.

[75] R Chambers, *Resulting Trusts* (Clarendon Press 1997). Quebec trust law does not know resulting trusts by that name, but has a similar principle to ensure that trustees acquire no unauthorized profit (Civil Code of Québec, art 1297, para 2).

That is a primary right of the settlor, which does not arise from wrongdoing and has not, so far as I know, been said to have a deterrent function.

This account can be illustrated by a further example from the common law, as well as by some texts of the civilian tradition.

Paradoxically, in the common law at least, the rule against unauthorized profits does not even require a profit. In *Soulos v Korkontzilas*,[76] a principal wanted to buy a particular estate in land. The agent deliberately failed to communicate an offer to the principal, and bought the estate himself. The principal successfully claimed that the estate was held for his benefit. One defence was that the land was now worth less than when the agent had bought it; there was no profit, in the economic sense, nor was there harm to the principal. But the principal succeeded; it was decided that he was entitled to have the estate transferred to him, although he would have to reimburse the price paid by the agent. He would be buying the estate for less than it was now worth, but he had reasons for wanting it, and he was entitled to have it.

The same requirement of reimbursement would have been imposed if the estate had been worth much more than the agent paid; the principal would be entitled to the estate, but he would always have to reimburse the agent for what he had paid.[77] What *Soulos* shows is that the rule is not only about profits in an economic sense. Any right that accrues to the agent in acting as such is attributed to the principal, if he wants to take it.[78] That is because the agent's role was to act for and on behalf the principal (even though the agent sought to act selfishly). But if the principal wants to take it, he has to pay for it; that is also because the agent's role was to act for and on behalf of the principal.[79] The idea cuts both ways.

As we have suggested already, the logic of seeing the rule against unauthorized profits as a rule of attribution ties it to other features of the relationship between an administrator and her beneficiary. First, the feature that the administrator is presumptively entitled to recover her expenses: one might say that there is a 'no-loss' rule just as there is a 'no-profit' rule. No one ever suggested that the beneficiary must do something wrongful in order for the administrator to be able to recover the expenses of her management; in the same way, wrongdoing is not

---

[76] *Soulos v Korkontzilas* [1997] 2 SCR 217, 146 DLR (4th) 214.

[77] For an example in Quebec civil law, see *Lefebvre* (n 21), [93]–[94].

[78] If the agent was acting within his authority, the principal does not have a choice, and must accept what the agent has done. We will return to this below, section IV.

[79] However, in the common law at least, such an agent may forfeit their right to agreed compensation, which is thus treated differently from their right to recover expenses incurred. *Imageview Management Ltd* (n 73) confirmed that this forfeiture occurs where the agent takes a bribe or secret profit from the other side in a contract that the agent makes for the principal. Some of the cases there cited (eg at [43]) imply that any non-trivial breach of fiduciary duty may disentitle the agent from claiming their compensation. For US law, see Deborah A DeMott, 'Disloyal Agents' (2007) 58 Alabama L Rev 1049, 1059–61; American Law Institute, *Restatement of the Law Third: Agency*, 2 vols, vol 2 (ALI 2006) §8.01, comment (d)(2).

necessary to understand why the beneficiary is able to take the benefits acquired through other-regarding administration. Both possibilities arise from the nature of the relationship. Both profits and expenses are attributed by the law to the correct sphere.

This analysis has deep roots in the civilian tradition. As we already noted, the *Digest* of Justinian contains an influential text: 'Nothing obtained as a result of a mandate ought to be left in the hands of the person who undertook the mandate, just as he ought not to suffer loss . . .'[80] By its terms, this text is confined to the particular context of mandate, although other texts can be found that are relevant to other situations of administration.[81] But just as trusteeship is taken as the paradigm relationship of administration in common law, so mandate is taken as the paradigm in civil law.[82] This *Digest* text is precisely in line with the argument in this chapter, not only in articulating a no-profit rule that does not depend on wrongdoing, but in finding that the managerial nature of the relationship explains at once both the rule against unauthorized profits and the recovery by the administrator of her proper expenses.

Seeing the no-profit rule as a rule of attribution also ties it to the feature that the administrator must disclose relevant information to the beneficiary: although information does not consist of rights that can be transferred, the law reaches a similar result by imposing duties of disclosure.[83] These obligations also arise from the nature of the relationship, and not from wrongdoing.

When someone commits a wrongful act, or infringes another's rights, private law is usually more concerned about compensation for the plaintiff's losses than it is with taking away gains realized by the defendant. In recent years, this has changed, with a great deal of interest focused on the possibility of taking away the profits of wrongful conduct.[84] In the common law world, some of this scholarship started from the rule of fiduciary law that makes fiduciaries accountable for unauthorized profits. This rule, it was said, shows that the common law is open to gain-based remedies for wrongdoing, and the question became whether the same remedies were available for other wrongs. The paradox is that in the context of acting for others, the no-profit norm is not one that attaches a sanction to wrongdoing.

---

[80] D.17.1.20 (n 13).
[81] D.3.5.7(8) (Ulpian), in the context of *negotiorum gestio*, states (in the translation of Watson (ed) n 13): '. . . if, while acting as administrator for you or the state, I made a fraudulent claim for land as yours or the state's and obtained more of the fruits than I should have, all this will have to be handed over to you or the state, even though I had no right to make the claim'.
[82] Chapter 1, section IV.A.1.
[83] Below, section VIII.
[84] For a comparative study, see Hondius and Janssen (n 12).

For decades, much analysis of fiduciary law in the common law has been blind to this.[85] The reason, once again, seems to be a presupposition that we always act for ourselves, which makes it difficult to perceive the different legal principles that apply when we act for others. This leads to the view that unless I do something wrongful, I am at liberty to accumulate such profits as present themselves to me. This in turn has led to complex and artificial attempts to formulate the rule against unauthorized profits in terms of wrongdoing, which usually necessitates an argument about deterrence. But the presupposition is false.[86] The law knows many positive duties that do not grow out of wrongdoing, but rather out of the relationships that people are in. This does not only include contractual duties. Parents have duties to feed and clothe their children, and spouses are obliged to divide their property fairly when their relationship ends. Those are primary duties, not remedies for wrongs. The same is true of the attribution of profits and expenses as between an administrator and a beneficiary. The administrator acts for and on behalf of the beneficiary, and the law gives effect to this.

III. The relationship between the attribution of profits and the rules about conflicts

A. The separateness of the principles

The rules about conflicts are separate from the rule that attributes profits. They have different justifications, and they lead to different remedies when they are activated. Both are related to the same underlying idea: that the administrator is not acting for himself, but holds powers to carry out a mission for and on behalf of another person. But the two sets of norms are related to different aspects of that fundamental idea. The conflict rules exist to ensure that the administrator's judgment is properly exercised when she is using her other-regarding powers. That is why, when those rules are violated, the exercise of such powers can be set aside. The attribution rules that are discussed in this chapter exist to allocate benefits to the beneficiary, simply because the administrator acquired them through acting for and on behalf of the beneficiary. They do not lead to anything being set aside.[87] They lead to the beneficiary's having a right to recover those

---

[85] In the nineteenth and most of the twentieth centuries, however, courts and commentators often described the rule against unauthorized profits as a 'disability' which implied that it was not a remedy for wrongdoing; see C Mitchell, 'Equitable Compensation for Breach of Fiduciary Duty' [2013] CLP 307, 314–17, discussing together the rules about conflicts, about unauthorized profits, and about duties of disclosure arising in fiduciary relationships. See also the scholarship cited above at n 52.
[86] See also Chapter 1, section II.B.
[87] Where the administrator has profited through some dealing with a third party, the beneficiary will probably not wish to set *that* dealing aside, since that would entail restitution and the administrator will be left without the unauthorized profit that the beneficiary is entitled to claim.

benefits, or their value, from the administrator. They can also attribute *costs* to the beneficiary, giving the administrator a right to recover her expenses; and they can attribute *information* to the beneficiary, creating obligations of disclosure owed by the administrator to the beneficiary.[88]

It follows from this that the two sets of norms operate independently of one another. In order to rely on the rule that attributes profits, the beneficiary does not need to identify a conflict; and in order to rely on the rules about conflicts, the beneficiary does not need to identify an unauthorized profit. The two sets of norms can, of course, overlap. Many cases will make both sets relevant. For example, an agent is authorized to sell the principal's land; the agent takes a bribe from a third party in order to sell to that third party. Since this third party is the one who paid the bribe, the third party is not protected by the rules for good faith dealings; the result is that the principal can have the sale set aside, as it was made through the use of an administrator's powers while that administrator was in a conflict situation. This would require mutual restitution of the interest in land on one side, and of the price paid on the other. The principal could also recover the bribe from the agent, since it represents an unauthorized profit.[89] The principal could pursue both of these recourses, or it could pursue one without pursuing the other.[90] This shows that the norms operate independently, even when the same fact pattern activates both of them.[91]

This independence is shown more clearly by cases in which only one is in play and the other is not. It is clear that the conflict rules can apply in the absence of profit. We know this because the conflict rules operate to allow a transaction to be set aside without any inquiry into the fairness of that transaction, in both the common law and the civil law.[92] This means that they do not require the

---

[88] The principle about expenses was mentioned above; on information, see below, section VIII.

[89] In the common law at least, the agent in such a case forfeits their right to agreed compensation, even if the principal chooses to let the conflicted contract stand (n 79).

[90] In a case like this, involving corruption, there are even more possibilities, along with presumptions that assist the beneficiary; see n 63. The common law allows the recovery of the bribe not only from bribee but also from the *briber*, which can be very useful if the agent is insolvent or unavailable. Moreover, both the agent and the third party have committed fraud, and this allows a claim for loss suffered, if the sale cannot be set aside (for example if it was with some other entity that was unaware of the corruption). Not all of these possibilities can be cumulated; see *Mahesan s/o Thambiah v Malaysia Government Officers' Co-operative Housing Society Ltd* [1979] AC 374 (PC). The agent also forfeits their right to commission (n 79). The civil law would also, of course, allow claims based on fault in a case of corruption, as well as allowing annulment of any contract entered by an administrator while in a conflict. In any tradition, it is also quite possible that there will be criminal consequences.

[91] In *Gray v New Augarita* (n 70), 13, it was said that consent to a contract made in a conflict of interest does not automatically constitute consent to any profit acquired from that contract by a fiduciary.

[92] Chapter 4, section V.B, noting that fairness evaluation may take place in the corporate law context. However, substantive unfairness there gives an additional reason to set aside a transaction even if conflict management processes are correctly followed. If they are not followed, the transaction is liable to be set aside without inquiry into fairness.

beneficiary to show that she has suffered a loss, nor do they require the beneficiary to show that the administrator has acquired an unauthorized profit.

The same thing is true in the other direction. An unauthorized profit must be surrendered even if there was no conflict. This proposition may be resisted by some, simply because there are so many ways to use the idea of 'conflict'.

It is true that if one defines 'conflict' so widely as to capture every profit or advantage, then one could say that the rule against unauthorized profits is only a part of the rule against conflicts. But this leads to an understanding of the idea of 'conflict' that is so very wide as to become analytically unhelpful, as we saw in the previous chapter.[93] It confuses conflict of interest, in the technical sense of a conflict liable to affect other-regarding judgment, with conflicts of interests, which are merely situations in which the interests of different people are opposed. Such a wide meaning could surely cover unauthorized profits, but it covers too much. It supposes that merely in being paid or remunerated, the administrator is in a conflict, and is allowed to keep their pay only because the conflict was authorized. This contradicts any common-sense understanding of conflict of interest. Lawyers must be sensitive to conflicts of interest, but no lawyer (and no professional code of conduct which regulates conflicts of interest) supposes that merely getting paid is a conflict of interest, authorized or not.

The real defect of such a wide understanding of 'conflict of interest' is that every administrator is always in such a conflict so defined: their personal interests are opposed to those of their beneficiary. Since administrators are presumptively disabled from exercising their powers while in a conflict, this would make it impossible for them to act in their role, and it makes a nonsense of the idea of conflict of interest.

There could be another version of the argument that aims to make the rule against unauthorized profits into a kind of subcategory of the rules on conflicts. One might argue that any time an administrator receives a profit or advantage, this creates a potential conflict, because it creates a possibility that some future exercise of duty-bound judgment will be affected by self-interest.[94] Recall that a conflict in the strict sense can only arise when judgment is being exercised in relation to the use of an administrative power (and this is why such an exercise can be set aside). A potential conflict is a situation in which the exercise of such a power at some point in the future may be affected by some conflicting and improper consideration.

There is some truth in this analysis, but it shows that there is a more serious problem with seeing the rule against unauthorized profits as one based on the prohibition of conflicts. Such a view does not provide a sound link between the

[93] Chapter 4, sections II.B.1 and II.B.2.
[94] Discussed in Chapter 4, section VI.B.

rule and the remedy. It seems to link two very different remedies to the same rule: the remedy of setting aside a transaction and the remedy of capturing unauthorized profits. It also supposes that profits must be surrendered not only when they are acquired in a conflict in the strict sense, that allows a conflicted exercise of a power to be set aside, but even when they are acquired in a situation that creates a potential conflict (that may never mature into an actual conflict). This account does not advance our understanding at all. As far as the actual scope of the rule about profits, it seems to be exactly the same as one that is defined without any reference to conflicts: that is, unauthorized profits must be surrendered whenever they are acquired through acting in an administrative role. But by tying the liability to surrender unauthorized profits to conflicts of interest, this account not only makes itself more contrived and complicated than it needs to be; it is also forced back to arguments which we have seen are doomed to fail. This is because it must answer the question why the creation of an only potential conflict should lead to a remedy of surrendering profits. And the only way it can do this is by adopting a deterrent understanding of the rule against profits. We have already seen that such an understanding, though common, is unsuccessful as part of an interpretive account of the law.[95]

The more precise definition of conflict that was developed in the previous chapter covers a *particular* problem. It covers a problem that is always characterized by a conflict, and it covers a problem that arises only in relation to those who hold powers in an administrative or other-regarding capacity. A conflict is a problem that exists *in relation to* such a power; it exists when the administrator has a self-interest, or another duty, that tends to interfere with the proper exercise of their other-regarding judgment in relation to the use of the power. And, quite naturally, when that problem exists and is not managed, it allows the exercise of that power to be annulled.

When conflicts are defined in this more precise way, it is easier to understand the foundation for the norms about conflicts, and the remedies that arise. Conversely, it becomes necessary to see the no-profit rule as having a separate foundation. This is because it *is* possible for an administrator to acquire a profit or advantage in a way that does not involve a conflict, when that concept is carefully defined. Any profit that is acquired where there is only a potential conflict is actually an example. For example, an administrator takes a bribe, but has not done anything (by action or inaction) as a result. Some people might say this is a conflict of interest, but more precisely, this creates only a potential conflict. It is, however, a situation that clearly activates the rule against unauthorized profits, as defined without reference to conflicts.[96]

---

[95] Above, section II.B.1.
[96] It is also probably a breach of a duty to disclose and probably criminally unlawful.

B. Unauthorized profits without conflicts of interest or duty

We have seen that there can be conflicts without profits. By showing that there can also be unauthorized profits without conflicts, we will demonstrate that the two norms are separate, even if some facts will activate both.

I will give three examples of cases in which there is an unauthorized profit but no conflict in the strict sense.

1. Ceasing to act

One important example is the case in which there is no conflict because the administrator has ceased to act as such. Imagine that John manages the investments of Mary. Not merely an advisor, he buys and sells her investments, with her authority to do so. In doing so, he deals with various financial institutions. Imagine that one of these confers some valuable benefit on John: for example, season tickets to the matches of a sports team. This is done as a gift, but there is no personal relationship between the John and the giver. This gift is clearly caught by the no-profit rule, since John acquired the benefit through his position as an administrator. On my approach, it is not necessary or relevant to identify a conflict to reach that result. As mentioned above, someone who wants to subsume the no-profit rule within the rule against conflicts might say that there is a conflict here, although in my terminology, this is only a potential conflict.

But now change the case: imagine that John has resigned for unrelated, innocent, and valid reasons. The giver sent the tickets earlier, not knowing about the pending resignation. They arrive after John has stopped working for Mary. The benefit is still caught by the rule and belongs properly to Mary.[97] Moreover, the reason is the same: John acquired the benefit through his position as an administrator. In order to explain this result, it is only necessary to apply the basic rule against unauthorized profits which looks at whether the benefit was acquired through the role. Even though John has ceased to act in the role, it remains true that this later-acquired benefit was acquired by him through so acting.[98]

But is there a conflict? Here, there is not even a potential conflict. John has left the role. All the decisions that he is going to make in relation to Mary's

---

[97] Cf *Canadian Aero Services Ltd v O'Malley* [1974] SCR 592. Whether the giver might be able to recover the gift, as having been made by mistake, is a separate question which is left aside here.

[98] It is unexceptional that some juridical aspects of a relationship may survive the termination of the relationship in the full sense. In this context, it is not necessary even to say that obligations survive, but only liabilities (or disabilities, as they are sometimes called in the common law: n 85) that are founded in part on events that took place while the relationship was in existence. See *Burnell v Trans-Tag Ltd* [2021] EWHC 1457 (Ch), [406(c)], [410].

investments lie in the past. He has no administrative powers, and so by definition he can no longer be in a conflict or even a potential conflict. The gift cannot possibly influence John in this respect. So the approach that wants to understand the liability to give up profits through the concept of conflict of interest must fail, unless it would allow John to keep this benefit. In my view, that would be the wrong result.

2. Aligned interests

The independence of the two norms can also be illustrated by the case in which the profitable transaction *aligns* the self-interest of the administrator with that of the beneficiary.

The most famous example is *Regal (Hastings)*, the facts of which were already given.[99] The defendant directors caused their corporation, the plaintiff, to acquire shares in a new subsidiary corporation, and the defendants personally acquired shares in the same subsidiary. Both the plaintiff and the defendants profited. In short, the defendants embarked on a joint venture with the plaintiff. Their interests were aligned. It is no accident that executive compensation frequently involves compensation in the form of shares (or options) of the corporation: the idea is to align the interests of the executive with those of the corporation and its shareholders, so that financial success for the latter will be profitable for the executive.[100] Alignment is the opposite of conflict. Unlike in the case of an authorized compensation package, the profits acquired in *Regal (Hastings)* were unauthorized; but they did not arise from a conflict of interest. When the House of Lords held that the directors were accountable for their profits, it was with almost no mention of conflicts of interest.[101] The plaintiffs were not attacking the exercise of a fiduciary power in a conflict situation; the defendants had exercised their own personal contractual capacities. The case is a perfect illustration of the operation of the rule against unauthorized profits, and of its independence from the rules on conflicts.[102]

---

[99] N 6.

[100] It is notorious that doing this well may be more complicated than it may seem, and that the use of options in particular can encourage short-term management focused on the share price rather than long-term value-building. Thus an apparent alignment of interests may not be one after all (see Chapter 4, section II.B.2 and DeMott (n 79), 1055). This does not however touch the main point, that executive compensation may *aim* to align interests.

[101] Viscount Sankey mentioned conflicts (137), but formulated the liability (139) without reference to conflicts. Lord Wright mentioned conflicts (154) but seemingly in *obiter* and only to dismiss an argument that the profits could be retained. The other judges did not mention conflicts in their reasoning. Two judges noted that the liability did not depend on any breach of duty (n 9).

[102] Eilís Ferran, *Company Law and Corporate Finance* (OUP 1999) 190. Nolan argues that there were conflicts of interest in the case, but does not explain how he defines that term; it seems that he is thinking of conflicts of *interests*, which as we have seen are systematically present in every relationship of administration: Richard Nolan, '*Regal (Hastings) Ltd v Gulliver*' in Charles Mitchell and Paul Mitchell (eds), *Landmark Cases in Equity* (Hart 2012) 499.

A similar case is the equally well-known *Boardman v Phipps*.[103] The defendants in that case were in an agency relationship with the trustees of a trust.[104] One defendant was a beneficiary of the trust, and the other was solicitor to the trustees. The defendants were of the view that a company in which the trustees held shares could be made more successful through certain changes, via what might today be called shareholder activism. The trustees were not able to purchase any more shares of the company. The defendants bought some for themselves. The defendants were right: by their participation in the governance of the company, it was turned around, and the value of the shares went up. As in *Regal (Hastings)*, this benefitted both the trust beneficiaries and the defendants. Also as in *Regal (Hastings)*, this benefit to the trust beneficiaries did not exclude the rule against unauthorized profits, and the defendants were required to give up their profits.

Two of the judges in the House of Lords dissented, on the ground that they could not identify any relevant conflict.[105] The three majority judges realized that this was quite unnecessary under the law laid down in *Regal (Hastings)*. No one was attacking the exercise of powers held in an administrative capacity. One of judges in the majority, Lord Guest, did not even mention conflicts, noting that liability arose because the profits were derived from acting in an administrative role.[106] Just as in *Regal (Hastings)*, so far from being a conflict of self-interest and duty, the defendants aligned their interests with those of the beneficiaries. But if one understands the rule against unauthorized profits as one that operates separately from the rules about conflicts, *Boardman* becomes quite simple: it was a clear case of an unauthorized profit that was acquired through acting in an administrative role.

3. Powers without discretion

A third example shows that the rule against unauthorized profits is independent of the rules about conflicts. This is the situation in which there is a relationship of administration—of acting for and on behalf of another—but *without* the presence of any discretionary powers.

---

[103] N 8, which was the occasion for the belated reporting, in the (official) Appeal Cases of 1967, of *Regal (Hastings)*, which had been decided in 1942.

[104] The defendants were not trustees of the trust, but were treated as de facto agents of the trustees: Michael Bryan, '*Boardman v Phipps*' in Charles Mitchell and Paul Mitchell (eds), *Landmark Cases in Equity* (Hart 2012) 581, 586–69. On this kind of relationship of administration, see Chapter 7, section IV.B.

[105] *Boardman* may be the first decision in which liability under the rule against unauthorized profits was characterized (by Viscount Dilhorne, dissenting, 93–94) as a 'breach of fiduciary duty' rather than in terms of being accountable. In *Regal (Hastings)*, one judge (Lord Wright, 154) called it a breach of the fiduciary relationship, but that is a different idea (see n 9).

[106] The other judges in the majority, Lords Cohen and Hodson, both made it clear that the rules on conflicts were not necessary to decide the case, although they went on to discuss them.

These situations are less typical, but are not uncommon in private law.[107] Examples include the common law's 'bare trust', and the case of an agent or mandatary who does not have discretionary authority but must (like the bare trustee) follow instructions from the principal or agent for whom he is acting. Trusts can also be created that are not bare trusts but in which trustees do not have any discretion. In these situations, the administrator has administrative powers, but the only way the powers can be exercised is in accordance with the instructions given or the terms of the trust. As a result, this person cannot be in a conflict of interest as it was defined in the previous chapter.[108] The reason is that the definition is engaged only when someone has to exercise other-regarding judgment, and in these examples, there is no judgment involved in the exercise of the administrator's powers.

There is, however, every reason to think that the rule against unauthorized profits applies in full force. If such an agent were bribed or paid an undisclosed commission, the agent would be accountable to the principal.[109] If a bare trustee or other non-discretionary trustee were able to turn to profit some information acquired while acting in that role, the trustee would be accountable to the beneficiaries.

Thus, we see again that the rule against unauthorized profits operates independently from the rules regulating the exercise of administrative powers in conflict situations.

4. Conclusion

There can be accountability for unauthorized profits even in the absence of conflict of interest. In *Gray v New Augarita Porcupine Mines Ltd*,[110] it was said that consent to a contract made in a conflict of interest does not automatically constitute consent to any profit acquired from that contract by a fiduciary. This also shows that the rule on profits is not merely an aspect of the rules about conflicts.

---

[107] Chapter 3, section III.C.
[108] Chapter 4, section III.
[109] *McWilliam v Norton Finance (UK) Ltd (t/a Norton Finance (In Liquidation))* [2015] EWCA Civ 186, [35]–[48]; cf Deborah A DeMott, 'Breach of Fiduciary Duty: On Justifiable Expectations of Loyalty and Their Consequences' (2006) 48 Arizona L Rev 925, 941.
[110] N 70, 13. Similar on this point is *Hurstanger Ltd* (n 70): disclosure by an agent that it might be paid a commission by the party on the other side was not sufficient to constitute informed consent to an unauthorized profit. The principal was made aware of the *conflict*, but did not give informed consent to the profit. In *Brandeis Brokers Ltd v Black* [2001] 2 All ER (Comm), 2 Lloyd's Rep, 359 (QB (Comm)), cited by DeMott (ibid), an agent's contract with its principal authorized conflicts of interest (at [10]) but this was not held to oust the rule against unauthorized profits (at [49], although also basing the liability on misuse of confidential information).

IV. Attribution applies to both authorized and unauthorized actions

A. Why this is so

The attribution of costs and benefits to the principal is obvious where the administrator acts within her authority. Take the case of a mandatary who is authorized to buy land for the mandator. If she does so, within her authority, then she will be entitled to be reimbursed for the expenses that she properly incurs, and the mandator will be entitled to the land that the mandatary acquires.[111] This is so whether the bargain that the mandatary made is a good one, an indifferent one, or a bad one. We do not analyse the case in terms of the acquisition of a profit; it is simply the normal operation of the mandate relationship.

It is less obvious where the administrator acts without authority. There are a number of variations. Assume that the mandatary has made a purchase of land, but without authority, because the contract price was higher than authorized. If the beneficiary (the mandator in this case) wishes to approve the administrator's actions despite her exceeding her authority, most systems allow a form of ratification, that will operate retroactively and cause the situation to be treated just is if the administrator acted with authority all along. This, however, will not be possible in some cases. For example, it will not be possible if the beneficiary lacks full legal capacity, as in a case of guardianship. Another factual variation, that mainly applies to mandate and agency, is one in which although the administrator exceeded her authority, the principal bears some responsibility for the creation of a misleading appearance of authority. In this case, the law often gives protection to third parties who reasonably rely on the appearance so created.[112] Neither of these situations is usually relevant in the context of the rule against unauthorized profits: ratification is a facilitative and corrective institution that allows the principal or mandator to align the legal situation with what the agent or mandatary wanted to do all along, while the rules on appearances aim to protect third parties, not to regulate the relationship between the administrator and beneficiary.

The rule against unauthorized profits comes into its own when the administrator has purported to secure a benefit for herself by some unauthorized action, since it is a rule against unauthorized profits. A typical example is the administrator who takes a bribe, or a gift or secret payment, from some third party in relation to the administrator's role. Another typical example is the administrator

---

[111] In many cases, if the mandatary acts in the name of the mandator, the right to the land will pass directly from the seller to the mandator. This is called '(legal) representation' in the civil law: Chapter 1, section V.B.3.b.

[112] Chapter 3, section IV.F.3.

who takes advantage of some information acquired from his role in order to secure a profit.

In line with the argument above, the rule against unauthorized profits clearly covers these examples. It does not matter that the action was not authorized; the attribution rule pays no attention to that. The administrator *tried* to act for and on behalf only of himself, but the law does not allow him to step out of his role unilaterally. Because the administrator is in an other-regarding role, a role of accountability, the law attributes the gain to the beneficiary, regardless of the wishes of the administrator.

B. Taking an unauthorized profit is not ratification

The beneficiary's ability to take the profit is not an example of ratification that grants authority retroactively. This is shown by the fact that a profit can be taken by a beneficiary who is not fully capacitated and thus not in a position to ratify.[113] Again, if we consider the case of a trust, there may be no one who can modify or extend the trustee's authority; but if the trustee is forced to account for unauthorized profits, this will benefit the beneficiaries. It is also clear that an administrator commits a wrongful act against his beneficiary in taking a bribe without disclosing it, and stripping the bribe does not retroactively cure this wrongfulness.

Taking the unauthorized profit might seem like ratification inasmuch as the administrator gives up his *net* profit; he is entitled to his expenses.[114] But this is only because of the logic of the idea of attribution, which as we have seen cuts both ways, covering both costs and benefits. It would be a penal rule, not an attribution rule, that took the profit without noticing the cost incurred to acquire it.

Taking the unauthorized profit is not ratification but rather the enforcement of a primary right. It is, however, the result of a choice. When the administrator acts with authority, the beneficiary has no choice as to whether the profits and losses shall be attributed to him. But when there was no authority, the beneficiary can simply ignore the unauthorized action. In a case like *Soulos*,[115] where the administrator has acquired something by paying more than it is now worth, a beneficiary would normally leave things where they lie (apart from surely wanting to dismiss the administrator or have him removed). But if the administrator has secured some profit, the beneficiary can choose to invoke the attribution rule

---

[113] This is illustrated by *Keech* (n 8), where the proceeding was brought after the beneficiary reached adulthood but in respect of profits acquired earlier.

[114] *Soulos* (n 76) and *Lefebvre* (n 21); although in some cases, the administrator may forfeit any agreed compensation (n 79).

[115] ibid.

to capture that profit—and, as in *Soulos*, this option is also available where the opportunity was loss-making, if for some reason the beneficiary wishes to have that asset.

V. Legal mechanisms of attribution: Accountability

A. Legal mechanisms of attribution

How does attribution work in legal terms? There are several dimensions. Where the administrator has acted properly, say in acquiring rights for her beneficiary, it may well be that the rights so acquired are transferred directly to the beneficiary. This will occur where the relationship includes what the civil law calls representation.[116] In some cases, such as in mandate without representation, it may be that the rights are first acquired by the mandatary; thus, a second step is required in which the mandatary transfers the rights to the mandator. But from the moment the rights are acquired by the mandatary, the mandatary has an obligation to transfer the rights to the mandator. In this sense, the attribution occurs, via an obligational mechanism, from the outset. That obligation is fulfilled when the rights are transferred to the mandator. In a trust, unless the trust is to come to an end, the rights are not transferred to the beneficiary either directly or in two steps. For example, if the trustee acquires certain rights to be held in trust as an investment, this may affect the value of the rights of the beneficiaries, but the rights acquired by the trustee are not transferred to the beneficiaries.[117]

When the administrator is acting improperly, the analysis is likely to be different. For example, the administrator takes a bribe. I have said that the law attributes this to the beneficiary. What does this mean in law? That depends in part on the legal system. In the civil law, even in the case of a mandate with representation, it is almost certain that the bribe belongs, as a matter of property law, to the mandatary. But, as is the case with lawful conduct in mandate without representation, attribution can occur by way of an obligation. The law creates an obligation on the mandatary to transfer the bribe to the mandator. The attribution rule operates with patrimonial effects from the moment that the bribe is received, but the mandator's claim is initially one that lies in the law of obligations. There are also obligations of information. The mandatary's obligation to render an account will require that the bribe be disclosed, and the account itself, as a means of disclosing information, provides a way of attaching an amount to the

---

[116] Chapter 1, section V.3.b. As discussed there, common law agency generally includes a power of representation.
[117] The precise details depend on the legal system and on the structure of the trust in question.

mandatary's obligation to surrender the bribe to the mandator. The same analysis can work in a civilian analysis of the whole range of administration situations, including trusts, tutorship, and the administration of legal persons.

Since the beneficiary's claims are only obligational until such time as the administrator actually transfers the bribe, there is an insolvency risk in the intervening time. If the administrator were to become insolvent before transferring the bribe, the beneficiary would be merely an unsecured creditor for the amount of the bribe.

The common law has seen some controversy on this point. If we look at the common law in the narrow sense of the phrase that excludes the principles of Equity, the analysis is similar to that of the civil law (as is often the case): attribution operates via the law of obligations. In agency, the common law gives the beneficiary a claim against the administrator to transfer the profit to the beneficiary.[118] In this context, however, the common law was allowing the enforcement of a right which was sourced in Equity and in Equity's principles governing fiduciary relationships.[119] The next question is whether the bribe, or other profit, is held by the administrator on a constructive trust for the beneficiary, from the moment that it is received. The general rule is that whenever a person holds property and also has an unconditional obligation to hold the benefit of that property for another, there is a trust for that other.[120] If the profit were held in trust, this would reduce for the beneficiary the risk of insolvency of the administrator (at the expense of the unsecured creditors of the administrator), because a trust claim is not an unsecured claim. A nineteenth-century English case held that in the case of commercial agency, there is no trust of an unauthorized profit, but only an obligation.[121] To the contrary, many cases in other spheres have held, or assumed, that a trust arises. In recent years there has been academic debate, sometimes (but not always) on the assumption that there should be a single rule, either in favour of a trust solution or an obligational solution. The recent case law has been in favour of the constructive trust.[122]

---

[118] *Mahesan* (n 90).

[119] ibid 380, quoting *Boston Deep Sea Fishing and Ice Co v Ansell* (1888) 39 ChD 339 (CA), 367–68 (with a transcription error where 'implied contract' in the older case is rendered as 'applied contract') for the proposition that although the claim was enforceable at common law as a claim in money had and received, its basis was in Equity. Long before the fusion of the courts, common law courts would allow claims in money had and received for Equitable claims to ascertained sums of money: Lionel Smith, 'Simplifying Claims to Traceable Proceeds' (2009) 125 LQR 338.

[120] When the obligation arises by consent, it is an express trust; when it arises by operation of law, the trust is called constructive (or resulting, where the beneficiary is the one who transferred the property to the trustee).

[121] *Lister v Stubbs* (1890) 45 ChD 1 (CA).

[122] *Attorney-General for Hong Kong v Reid* [1994] 1 AC 324 (PC); *FHR European Ventures LLP* (n 56). In Canada the law seems to be that the court has a discretion whether or not a trust arises: *Soulos* (n 76). It is suggested in James Penner, 'Distinguishing Fiduciary, Trust, and Accounting Relationships' (2014) 8 J of Equity 202, 226–28, that there should be no constructive trust if the administrator was authorized by the beneficiary to operate on a debtor–creditor relationship with the

Thus the idea of attribution does not always work in the same way. It does not operate simply through a direct vesting of the unauthorized profit in the beneficiary. This is the mechanism that may operate when the administrator operates properly and lawfully. When an unauthorized profit is acquired, the profit belongs, as a matter of property law, to the administrator. Attribution typically takes place via an obligation: the administrator is obliged to transfer the profit to the beneficiary. In the common law tradition, this obligation is likely to be construed as a trust. In a constructive trust, the profit still belongs, as a matter of property law, to the administrator, but the trust has a number of property-like effects; in particular, it protects the beneficiary against insolvency risk.

The attribution of information has already been mentioned and will be discussed further below.[123] It works in exactly the same way: by the creation of obligations. When an administrator acquires information relevant to her role as administrator, she comes under an obligation of disclosure, to share that information with the beneficiary.

B. Accountability

The language of 'accountability' is used very often in relation to private law administrators, in both the common law and the civil law. The idea of accountability, however, has many senses, both inside and beyond administration. One very wide sense corresponds roughly to 'responsibility'. We might say that criminal punishment is a way of holding people accountable for their actions; some commentators understand the law of torts as existing largely in order to hold people accountable for the private wrongs they have committed.[124] What follows focuses on a narrower set of meanings, that are inside or at least related to relationships of administration.

1. Narrow and wide senses

First, many administrators are required to keep formal accounts and to produce them to the beneficiary. In the common law world these are sometimes called 'accounting parties'. The details of what accounts must be kept and on what intervals or notice they must be produced are variable from one jurisdiction to another and from one relationship to another. Generally, however, anyone who administers property that does not belong to her, or does not belong to her

beneficiary. It is not obvious, however, why an authority granted in relation to lawful receipts and disbursements should extend to bribes.

---

[123] In the very next section, and in more detail in section VIII.
[124] John Goldberg and Benjamin Zipursky, *Recognizing Wrongs* (HUP 2020) 9 and *passim*.

except as an administrator, will be required to produce accounts of this kind.[125] The idea of 'accountability' here stands for the obligation to keep the accounts, and the obligation to produce them. These, of course, are obligations to disclose information of a particular kind, as well as an obligation to retain evidence to substantiate that information. Accountability also carries with it the obligation to settle any balance that the account may reveal to be owing one way or the other. Accountability is a primary obligation that grows out of the relationship: it does not arise from misconduct of any kind.[126] Some who are accountable in this sense are not in a relationship of administration, because they do not hold powers for and on behalf of another.[127]

There is a wider sense of 'accountability', which applies to every private law administrator. It means, not that they have to produce accounts in a particular form, but that they have to 'give an account' of what they have done with the assets and the powers that they hold. They will have to provide information about what they are doing, and what they have done, that helps the beneficiary to understand what the administrator has done, and why. It is routine, in both common law and civil law, for the idea of accountability to cover both the narrow and the wide sense.[128]

Every administrator who is accountable in the narrow sense is also accountable in the wide sense. A trustee or an executor must produce accounts in the required form; but that is not the limit of their obligation to produce information. Trustees, for example, must tell the beneficiaries about the trust.[129] Administrators are obliged to disclose their own wrongdoing.[130] Administrators are accountable in this wider sense whether or not they are accountable in the narrow sense.

---

[125] James A Watson, *The Duty to Account: Development and Principles* (Federation Press 2016) [456]. The book provides a sweeping history of accountability, noting that the common law developed many relationships of accountability before the merger of the courts of common law and Chancery in the nineteenth century. Some, but not all, of these are now relationships of administration.

[126] Although Watson (ibid) argues that some kinds of wrongdoing generate a duty to account. I deal with this below, in the next subsection.

[127] A secured creditor who realizes on the security will be accountable in this sense to the debtor; the enforcing creditor is not an administrator inasmuch as the powers of enforcement are held by the creditor for its own benefit. The creditor may however (with variation among legal systems) be an administrator in relation to any surplus held for the debtor after enforcement. Some parties, like banks and other credit card issuers, maintain accounts without being accounting parties in the sense discussed here. These 'running accounts' simply keep track of a debtor-creditor relationship as it evolves over time.

[128] Philippe Pétel, *Les obligations du mandataire* (Litec 1988), 233–366; 56.24; P Matthews, C Mitchell, J Harris, and S Agnew, *Underhill and Hayton: Law Relating to Trusts and Trustees* (20th edn, LexisNexis 2022), ¶ 59.24; see also the Hague Convention on the Law Applicable to Trusts and on their Recognition (1 July 1985), art 2 (c).

[129] *Valard Construction Ltd v Bird Construction Co* 2018 SCC 8, [2018] 1 SCR 224.

[130] Section VIII below deals with obligations to disclose information; section VIII.B.3, with the obligation to disclose unlawful conduct.

The narrower and the wider senses have two things in common. First, the obligations that are described by the idea of accountability do not arise out of any wrongdoing. They are, rather, primary obligations that arise out of the relationship. It is because the administrator is looking after the affairs of the beneficiary that the administrator is required to provide relevant information to the beneficiary. Second, both senses often include an idea that goes beyond the provision of information, and include also the obligation to surrender unauthorized profits. In the civil law, often a single codal text covers both of these obligations.[131] In the common law, an administrator is often said to be 'accountable' for a gain or 'liable to account' for it; this means both that they must bring it into account, and ultimately that they are liable to surrender it.[132]

It is not at all surprising that courts and commentators often use the idea of 'being accountable' or 'liable to account' to cover all of these things. The obligation to keep accounts, the obligation to inform, and the obligation to surrender profits all arise out of the same consideration: that the administrator is looking after the affairs of the beneficiary.

2. A very different sense

There is a third sense of 'accountable' that can arise in the common law, but that is related only by procedural and historical analogy to the two senses already mentioned. The Court of Chancery developed a system for verifying the accounts of those who were required to keep them, including the use of judicial officers (who may now be called masters or prothonotaries) with expertise in accounting procedures. The procedural aspect of this survives, so that a trustee or executor can be required to 'pass her accounts', which means, to have them approved by the court—again, without any allegation of wrongdoing.[133]

In some contexts, this accounting machinery was borrowed in order to produce a particular kind of recourse for certain kinds of wrongdoing. One example is the infringement of a patent. In the nineteenth century, the Court of Chancery began to use the 'account of profits' as a remedy for infringement of patents.[134] In

---

[131] See the texts of the French Civil Code (n 15), the Swiss Code of Obligations (n 17), and the Civil Code of Québec (nn 18 (mandataries) and 31 (administrators of the property of others)), all of which provide in a single article for the obligation to produce accounts and the obligation to surrender unauthorized profits. In the BGB (n 16), the first is in § 666 and the second is in § 667.

[132] *Regal (Hastings)* (n 6); *Boardman* (n 8).

[133] *Campbell v Hogg* [1930] 3 DLR 673 (PC); *Wall v Shaw* 2018 ONCA 929. Not everyone who can be made to pass accounts is made to pass accounts. If those who are interested are content with the accounts that are produced privately, they may not demand a judicial proceeding, and this will save expense. A trustee or executor may be unable to secure a formal approval of their accounts outside of court, due to the incapacity of one or more beneficiaries; this administrator may himself seek to pass accounts, since judicial approval of the accounts protects the administrator.

[134] Stephen Watterson, 'An Account of Profits or Damages? The History of Orthodoxy' (2004) 24 OJLS 471.

general, of course, the defendant who infringed the plaintiff's patent was not an administrator of assets of the plaintiff; they were probably a stranger to the plaintiff. But if the defendant had made substantial profits, while the plaintiff could not prove significant loss, an account of profits could be awarded. The Court took advantage of its accounting machinery, and ordered the defendant (who, again, was not otherwise an 'accounting party') to produce its business records so that a conclusion could be reached about how much profit it had made from its wrongful infringement; and that profit would have to be surrendered. This is a practise that continues today.[135] An account of profits has been ordered as a remedy in some other cases where the courts wished to take away the profits of wrongdoing.[136] What is important is that this kind of 'accountability' is quite different from the other two kinds. Those kinds of accountability grow out of the relationship between the parties, not from any wrongdoing. In this third case, the opposite is true: it is no more nor less than a remedy for unlawful conduct.[137] This third sense is not relevant for the purposes of this study.[138]

3. Conclusion

In the context of private law administration, accountability is part of the proper interpretation of the relationship between the administrator and the beneficiary. The administrator is always accountable in the wide sense and may be accountable in the narrow sense, depending on case and statute law, and on the parameters of the particular relationship. Both senses include the rule about unauthorized profits, and this is why it is common to use the word 'accountable' to signify not only the keeping of accounts, and not only the provision of other information, but also the liability to surrender unauthorized profits.[139]

---

[135] For example, *Nova Chemicals Corp v Dow Chemical Co* 2022 SCC 43.
[136] It was ordered for a breach of contract in *Attorney-General v Blake* [2001] 1 AC 268 (HL).
[137] This is why, in the context of this third sense, it *is* necessary to prove a causal link between the wrongful act and the claimed profit: *Nova Chemicals* (n 135). In this context, the claim to a profit is not via a primary rule of attribution, but is entirely based on the consequences of wrongdoing.
[138] Common law courts may hold that a non-trustee is 'liable to account as a constructive trustee' in two situations. One is when he acquires trust property in a situation where he knew, or should have known, that the trustee was not authorized to transfer that property to the non-trustee; the other is where he knowingly assists the trustee to commit a breach of trust. Since the non-trustee is not in a relationship of administration with the beneficiary, the liability to account of the non-trustee may be seen as another example of this third, purely remedial sense of accountability. This was the position of the Court of Appeal of England and Wales in *Novoship* (n 46), [105]. However, if the courts aim to impose on such a person the same obligations that would apply *if* they were in a relationship of administration, this may not follow. See Steven B Elliott and Charles Mitchell, 'Remedies for Dishonest Assistance' (2004) 67 MLR 16; Charles Mitchell and Stephen Watterson, 'Remedies for Knowing Receipt' in Charles Mitchell (ed), *Constructive and Resulting Trusts* (Hart 2010) 115; Robert Chambers, 'The End of Knowing Receipt' (2016) 2 CJCCL 1, and the discussion in Chapter 7, section IV.B. This may be one way to understand the decision in *Ancient Order of Foresters in Victoria Friendly Society Ltd v Lifeplan Australia Friendly Society Ltd* [2018] HCA 43.
[139] It would be a mistake to think that the liability to surrender profits arises only because a person is required to keep accounts. Lawyers and real estate agents, for example, are clearly subject to the

VI. The scope of the rule against unauthorized profits

A. Introduction

We have seen that an administrator is accountable for profits acquired through acting in their role as administrator. When the rule is formulated in this way, there may be questions about its scope.

Take this example. A person works as a lawyer for forty years and sees scores of interesting things: dysfunctional families, spoiled rich children, backstabbing, and betrayal. In relation to all the people he meets, he is in the role of an administrator: as a lawyer, as a trustee, as an executor. On his retirement he writes a novel, *My Life as a Lawyer*, based on his experiences, which (despite its boring title) is made into a major motion picture. The lawyer makes millions.

This is a caricature, but it forces us to think about the scope and limits of the rule. This person's profit was, in a sense, derived from acting as an administrator. There is a causal link; if he had never been a lawyer, he could not have written the book.[140] But this kind of profit is not covered by the rule. The rule looks for more direct links than this. It is concerned with allocating profits to the correct patrimony or juridical sphere. We have already seen that in order for profits to be allocated to the beneficiary's sphere, it is *not* necessary that the beneficiary had a right to it or that the administrator was obliged to secure it for the beneficiary. All that is needed is that the profit arose from the administrator's acting in that role. This means that it was acquired by the use of the information, the opportunities, or the possibilities that came to the administrator as a result of acting as such.

But with all norms, legal or non-legal, we sometimes have to draw lines. Every administrator is a person, with their own skills, life experience, intellectual capital, and with their own assets and their own life to live. This points us in the direction of the limits of the rule.

Many disputes are about whether administrators (usually, former administrators) can compete with their former employer.[141] In such cases, the distinctions that the courts must draw can be understood as relating to whether the benefit was extracted from the administrator's role, or rather from the administrator's own human capital. If the person has learned of a *particular* opportunity while acting in their role as administrator, and after resignation they

---

rule against unauthorized profits, whether or not they handle client money. Corporate directors are an even clearer case.

[140] Above it was noted that the rule against unauthorized profits does not depend on showing a causal link between the profit and a *wrongful act*: section II.B.3. But the profit must be derived from the administrator's other-regarding role.

[141] Such cases may also raise issues of breach of contract and of misuse of confidential information, but for this discussion I assume no such claims are available.

profit from that, they will be accountable.[142] But this is not necessarily the case if, on the contrary, the former administrator chooses to exercise their own contractual capacity and their own human capital, even if their knowledge about a particular industry was enhanced by the experience they acquired as an administrator.[143] Valid contractual stipulations and confidential information apart, every person must be allowed to earn a living using their own knowledge and expertise.

In these terms, the case of the tale-telling lawyer can be framed as follows. The experiences that he acquired, and turned to profit, were too general to be caught by the rule against unauthorized profits. They contributed to his experience, knowledge, and human capital. Although one could say that his profits arose of out of information acquired while acting as an administrator, that information lacked the specificity needed to attract the operation of the rule.

B. What can be attributed?

Most cases about unauthorized profits are about the acquisition of rights: money, or valuable shares, or an interest in land. But we have already mentioned, and we will explore further below, that information as such can also be attributed to the beneficiary, creating duties of disclosure.

Unauthorized benefits can be of other kinds. In one case, an agent was bribed by the securing of a job for the agent's adult child.[144] This case was not directly about the rule against unauthorized profits. When an administrator uses their powers to execute a legal act (such as making a contract) while in a conflict of interest and duty, the legal act is voidable by the principal, and this was the legal outcome in this case. But this can lead us to ask what would be the outcome if the principal demanded that the agent account for this 'profit'?

As the judge noted, it may be extremely important for a parent to see their child started on the child's chosen career; the judge dismissed arguments that the benefit was trivial, and that it was of no value to the agent (as opposed to the child who got the job). It would be difficult, although perhaps not impossible, to put a pecuniary value on the benefit so as to quantify a liability to account. This,

---

[142] *Canadian Aero Services Ltd* (n 97).

[143] A case in Quebec law in which the line may have been difficult to draw, but in which it was held that accountability did not arise, is *Gravino* (n 18); for an English example, see *Island Export Finance Ltd v Umunna* [1986] BCLC 460 (ChD). The required balancing of interests is discussed in *Burnell* (n 98), [406], [410].

[144] *Glenn v Watson* [2018] EWHC 2016 (Ch), [427]-[431]. Like cash bribes, this kind of bribe may attract criminal sanctions: A Gara, 'JP Morgan Agrees to Pay $264 Million Fine for "Sons and Daughters" Hiring Program in China', *Forbes*, 17 Nov 2016 https://www.forbes.com/sites/antoinegara/2016/11/17/jpmorgan-agrees-to-pay-264-million-fine-for-sons-and-daughters-hiring-program-in-china/#d6d287356881.

however, may not be true in relation to other cases where the profit was not in the form of an acquired right. Consider the example of an agent who owed a third party $1,000; instead of bribing the agent with money, the third party bribes the agent by forgiving the debt. This agent does not acquire rights but rather is relieved of an obligation, but the benefit is wholly pecuniary and easy to quantify. If it is possible to attribute information to the beneficiary, and to give legal effect to that attribution by the imposition of duties of disclosure, it seems perfectly possible to attribute this negative benefit of the forgiveness of a debt to the beneficiary, and to give legal effect to that by the imposition of an obligation on the administrator to pay an equivalent amount of money.[145]

In an Ontario case, the plaintiff instructed his lawyer, the defendant, in relation to the plaintiff's bringing of a claim for wrongful dismissal.[146] The defendant learned that the plaintiff's marriage was in difficulty and began a sexual affair with the plaintiff's wife. The plaintiff's discovery of this affair caused severe psychiatric illness. The plaintiff sued the lawyer successfully for damages. The judge based his reasoning partly on breach of fiduciary duty, holding that the defendant had extracted personal advantage from the fiduciary relationship. The damages, however, were compensatory; this was not a case of the attribution of a gain. It is difficult to imagine how one could bring into account a benefit of this kind. However, the judge also based the claim on the misuse of confidential information. That is a sound basis for the decision, because the plaintiff had a legally protected interest in confidential information; its misuse was a legal wrong, one which can uncontroversially generate a claim for compensatory damages.

The rule attributes to the correct legal sphere the consequences of what the administrator has done. Its operation is most obvious when it attributes to the beneficiary the benefit of rights acquired by the administrator, whether the administrator's action was lawful or unlawful, authorized or unauthorized. I have also suggested that the same principle, or perhaps its mirror image, attributes to the beneficiary the costs of proper action by the administrator. One commentator took me to say that the rule against unauthorized profits could *force the administrator to act* in a certain way if that would generate a benefit for the beneficiary, and even if the administrator otherwise thought that action would be ill-advised.[147] It was never my intention to suggest that. The rule does not attribute

---

[145] It would not, however, be possible to impose a constructive trust, since a common law trust is always a trust of identified legal rights or other legal prerogatives.

[146] *Szarfer v Chodos* (1986) 54 OR (2d) 663, 27 DLR (4th) 388 (HCJ), affirmed (1988) 66 OR (2d) 350, 54 DLR (4th) 383 (CA).

[147] Penner (n 122), 233. I do not entirely understand Penner's reading of my argument but it seems to be founded on mixing my articulation of the rule against unauthorized profits with an understanding of 'conflict of interest' that I reject; namely one that includes all conflicts of *interests*, and that imagines that accountability arises from conflicts. It is not possible for administrators to avoid all conflicts of *interests* (Chapter 4, section II.B.1), and the rule about unauthorized profits does not depend on the presence of a conflict of interest (above, sections II.B.2, III).

possible futures; it does not tell the administrator how to act in their role. The administrator's proper use of their other-regarding powers is controlled by the requirement of loyalty and the rules about conflicts;[148] the effort that they are required to expend is regulated by the duty of care, skill and diligence, or of diligence and prudence, possibly supplemented by contractual obligations.[149]

C. An allowance for the administrator?

In one well-known English case, the defendants were found liable for unauthorized profits that they extracted while acting as administrators, being de facto agents.[150] They had improved the share value of a company, enriching both the plaintiff and themselves. The trial judge, however, stipulated that in addition to recovering their expenses, the defendants should be allowed a 'liberal' allowance for the work they had done.[151] His reasons were that the plaintiff could not have realized the benefit without employing a skilled professional who would have had to be paid. In the Court of Appeal, Lord Denning MR agreed, on the basis that the plaintiff would otherwise be unjustly enriched.[152] In the House of Lords, two of the three judges in the majority expressed their agreement with the trial judge on this point.[153] More recent decisions, however, have refused such allowances.[154]

The justification for the allowance is not obvious. If the argument from unjust enrichment worked, then every person acting as an administrator would be entitled to be remunerated for their work. But speaking generally, the opposite is true: in the absence of agreed remuneration, or statutory authority, such a person is entitled only to their expenses.[155] Moreover, it is a necessary result of the operation of the rule against unauthorized profits that the beneficiary may end up better off than if the administrator had not extracted the unauthorized profit.

---

[148] Chapters 3 and 4, respectively.
[149] Chapter 6, section III.
[150] *Boardman* (n 8); the facts are set out above in more detail (n 103).
[151] [1964] 1 WLR 993, 1018.
[152] [1965] Ch 992, 1020–21. The other judges did not address the point. The relevance of unjust enrichment to this issue was doubted in *Gray v Global Energy* (n 8), [127] and in *Recovery Partners GP Ltd* (n 46), [112].
[153] [1967] 2 AC 46, 105 (Lord Cohen), 112 (Lord Hodson); see also *O'Sullivan v Management Agency and Music Ltd* [1985] QB 428 (CA).
[154] *Guinness plc v Saunders* [1990] 2 AC 663 (HL); *Imageview Management Ltd* (n 73), [54]–[61]; *Gray v Global Energy* (n 8), [237]–[239]. An allowance was permitted in *Recovery Partners GP Ltd* (n 46), where it was said ([113]) to be appropriate 'only in exceptional circumstances'.
[155] See the discussion in Harpum (n 49), 154–60, noting that in relation to common law trusts the courts have claimed a discretion to award compensation as part of their inherent jurisdiction over the administration of trusts (see *Re Berkeley Applegate (Investment Consultants) Ltd* [1989] Ch 32; *Serious Fraud Office v Litigation Capital Ltd* [2021] EWHC 1272 (Comm), [478]).

This consideration cannot therefore justify the reduction of the very obligation that the rule imposes.

D. Authorization

The rule is one that captures unauthorized profits. Where the benefit was authorized in advance, it can of course be claimed and retained by the administrator. This includes the compensation that is payable to many administrators. The authorization may be contractual, as in the case many agents and mandataries, or it may be in the terms of a trust or of a will, or it may be in a corporate constitution in the case of directors. It may also be ad hoc: if some profitable opportunity presents itself which the administrator is not authorized to take, it will be possible for her to do so with the fully informed consent of the beneficiary.[156] This in turn requires that the beneficiary have full legal capacity. It also requires that they have full information on which to decide. This includes not just the fact of the profit, but the amount of it.[157]

If the administrator has already extracted a profit and holds rights that are subject to the rule, then the rule attributes those rights to the beneficiary. That person, if fully capacitated and fully informed, can of course still authorize the profit to remain with the administrator. In this setting, they are effectively waiving a right that they hold.[158]

VII. Contractual accountability for unauthorized profits

A. The problem stated

Those familiar with the common law will know that a rule against unauthorized profits sometimes seems to operate even more widely than I have suggested in this chapter. But a moment's reflection tells us that just because we have a similar legal remedy, it does not follow that the two remedies must arise from the same rule.

In this chapter, I have been discussing a rule that attributes to the beneficiary those profits acquired by an administrator through the latter's role as such. There are common law cases in which an administrator is accountable even for profits

---

[156] *New Zealand Netherlands Society "Oranje" Inc v Kuys* [1973] 1 WLR 1126 (PC).
[157] *Hurstanger Ltd* (n 70), [44]; *McWilliam* (n 109), [51]. See the discussion of both cases in Remus Valsan, 'Fiduciary Duties of Credit Brokers' (2016) 20 Edinburgh L Rev 99.
[158] Robert Stevens, 'Not Waiving but Drowning' in Andrew Dyson, James Goudkamp, and Frederick Wilmot-Smith (eds), *Defences in Contract* (Hart 2017) 125.

that do not fit that description. This type of case typically arises in a what are often called 'corporate opportunities' cases; more particularly, in a subclass of those cases. One type of corporate opportunity case is the one in which an administrator (in this context, a director or officer) learns of some profitable opportunity through acting in their administrative role, and then attempts to exploit that opportunity to secure a personal profit.[159] This case is within the rule as it has been discussed up to now.

But there is another type of corporate opportunity case in which the information is acquired independently, and yet, sometimes at least, the fiduciary is held to be accountable for the resulting profit. In *IDC Ltd v Cooley*,[160] the defendant was the managing director of the plaintiff, an engineering company. This meant that he was both a director and a very senior employee, with authority as an agent; thus, he was doubly an administrator.[161] An external party wanted services of the kind provided by the plaintiff, but did not want to deal with the plaintiff for reasons relating to its corporate organization. A representative of the external party therefore approached the defendant privately and discussed the matter with him. The defendant resigned his position with the plaintiff on a pretext of ill health, and took a position with the external party which would result in large profits for him, in relation to work of exactly the kind that was the business of the defendant. The plaintiff sued for an accounting of profits.

The defendant resisted on the basis that the information had come to him independently; he had been approached in his personal capacity. To the extent that this was true, one could say that the profitable opportunity (and thus the profits) did not fall within the formulation of the norm that has been discussed so far in this chapter. On his argument, it was as if he found money in the street, or bought a lottery ticket with his own money: the benefit did not come to him through his role as an administrator. And it is true that not every administrator is obliged to provide to his beneficiary everything the administrator knows, however it was learned, that the beneficiary might wish to know or might consider relevant. It is easy to show that such a proposition would be far too wide. Many such roles are part-time: the roles of trustees, directors, and executors, as such, are not full-time jobs.[162] A director can be director of multiple corporations, and usually has

---

[159] Eg *Regal (Hastings)* (n 6); *Canadian Aero Services Ltd* (n 97).
[160] *Industrial Development Consultants Ltd v Cooley* [1972] 1 WLR 443.
[161] The term 'managing director' is not routinely used in Canada and the United States. In those places, Cooley would probably be called an 'officer', and perhaps (since he was also a director) an 'executive director'. An 'officer' is a senior employee who is in a relationship of administration with the corporation. Officers may or may not be directors; but officers have wide powers as agents or mandataries of the corporation and so are administrators whether or not they are directors (see Deborah A DeMott, 'Corporate Officers as Agents' (2017) 74 Wash & Lee L Rev 847). The roles of director and of agent/mandatary are juridically distinct even if they are often combined (as mentioned in Chapter 1, section II.A).
[162] The same may also be true of partners in a business partnership, although much would turn on the partnership agreement. The older cases of *Dean v MacDowell* (1878) 8 ChD 345 (CA) and *Aas v*

a full-time job with (only) one of them. It cannot be correct that everything she finds out, by whatever means, must be disclosed to *all* of them, just because it would be relevant for them to know it. That would put the director in an impossible position. A lay (non-professional) trustee usually does other things apart from his trusteeship, as does a lay executor. They are not obliged to disclose to their beneficiaries everything they learn, however they learn it, that might benefit their beneficiaries. A trustee or an agent who, while looking for ways to invest his own money, learns of a promising opportunity, is not obliged to disclose this to his beneficiary, nor are they obliged to account for the profits made by pursuing it.

Professional administrators, as much as lay ones, are also allowed to keep some things to themselves. They cannot be obliged to disclose information simply because it would benefit their beneficiaries. Again, such a rule would be too wide. A professional trustee is typically trustee of multiple trusts, perhaps dozens or hundreds; it does not work full-time for any one of them, and it is not correct that everything it finds out, by whatever means, must be disclosed to *all* beneficiaries just because it would be advantageous for them to know it. A real estate agent or a lawyer may have dozens of clients; he is not obliged to tell all of them everything he learns that the clients might consider relevant or wish to know. And even these professionals have their own lives, and information that they discover on their own time generally does not have to be disclosed to *any* of their clients.

All of this merely underlines something we have already noticed: as a general rule, an administrator is not required to subordinate herself completely to her beneficiary. The suggestion that an administrator must always 'act' in the best interests of the beneficiary is too widely phrased.[163] As a general rule, an administrator is allowed to take advantage, for herself, of things that she discovers for herself.[164] If she comes across a valuable investment opportunity, she can take it, just as if she finds money in the street, she can pick it up and keep it. In relation to the conduct of her managerial task, the positive obligations she has towards the beneficiary—obligations to take action—are those arising from the duty of care, skill and diligence, or in civilian terminology the duty of prudence and diligence. Other positive obligations may arise by contract, and this will solve the puzzle of *IDC v Cooley*.

Benham [1891] 2 Ch 244 (CA) which allowed a partner to keep a profit acquired using information from the partnership, might not be decided the same way today; but see the discussion in *O'Donnell* (n 46), [67]–[68], explaining *Aas* as a case in which the partnership agreement effectively authorized the profit.

[163] Chapter 3, section IV.G.
[164] A clear statement is in *Howard v Federal Commissioner of Taxation* [2014] HCA 21, 253 CLR 83, [37].

B. The problem solved

The solution to the puzzle is that the rule that was applied in *IDC v Cooley* and similar cases is *not* the general attribution rule. It is a different rule, one that only applies to *some* administrators and not to all of them. Cooley was not merely a director; as we noticed, he was the managing director, and thus a full-time and senior employee of the company. This changes the analysis in a very important way, because such a person has a much wider range of positive obligations towards the corporation than someone who is *only* a director.[165] These extra obligations are not obligations that arise from her role as an administrator, but rather obligations that arise from her position as a senior employee.[166] If a person is a senior and full-time employee, she will have a number of positive obligations arising from the explicit and implicit terms of her contract of employment. These positive obligations go well beyond the positive obligations owed by someone who is merely or simply a director or other kind of private law administrator. For instance, if a senior, managerial employee of a corporation learns independently of a business opportunity that is potentially of interest to the corporation, he is obliged to disclose this. He is obliged by the terms of his employment, not by the general law of fiduciaries or those who act for others. That was the case with the defendant Cooley.

We can confirm that there are two different norms in play by noticing the differences between them. The general attribution rule applies to profits or opportunities arising from the administrator's role. It catches all such profits, *whether or not* the administrator was obliged to acquire them for the beneficiary, thus whether or not the advantage was 'in the line of business' of the beneficiary. But for the contractual rule under discussion here, exactly the opposite is true. It is *not* necessary that the advantage was acquired by the administrator through acting in their role as administrator; the advantage may have been acquired independently. On the other hand, it *is* necessary that the advantage be one that was 'in the line of business' of the beneficiary; otherwise, the person would have been

---

[165] *IDC v Cooley* (n 160) was applied in *Bhullar v Bhullar* [2003] EWCA Civ 424, [2003] 2 BCLC 241. In the latter case, it was never expressly said that the defendant directors were managing directors. If however they were only independent directors, the result would be indefensible. It would amount to saying that an independent director cannot pursue his own personal interests even when outside the boardroom, which is inconsistent with the fact that being an independent director is not a full-time occupation. This crucial distinction appears also to have been lost sight of in *Cheng Wai Tao v Poon Ka Man Jason* [2016] HKCFA 23, where accountability was correctly imposed because it is perfectly clear that the defendant director was also the managing director; he ran the entire operation (and his status as managing director is mentioned at [10]). But it is incorrect to imply, as the majority does, that the principles that govern such a case apply to all directors, even independent directors.

[166] Bruce Welling, *Corporate Law in Canada: The Governing Principles* (3rd edn, Scribblers 2006), 402–6; Smith (n 49), 58–59; David Kershaw, 'Corporate Law's Fiduciary Personas' (2020) 136 LQR 454.

free to keep it for themself. The defendant in *Cooley* would not have been liable if he had found a profitable opportunity that had nothing to do with the business of the plaintiff company.

Thus the reason that Mr. Cooley was accountable for the profits he acquired, even though he learned of the opportunity independently, is very simple: he was contractually obliged to turn that opportunity, when it arose, to the advantage of the defendant company.[167] Many administrators who were *not* full-time senior employees would not be so obliged in a comparable case. This contractual rule is therefore wider than the general rule, inasmuch as it can capture profits that would not be captured by the general rule. But it is also narrower, in two ways. First, it only bites on those opportunities which the administrator was already bound to turn to the advantage of the beneficiary; the general rule by contrast captures everything acquired in the administrator's role, whether or not the administrator was obliged to render that profit to the beneficiary. The other way in which the contractual rule is narrower is that it is only relevant to some administrators: those who have positive obligations, arising usually from a contract, to confer on the beneficiary a range of positive benefits that go far beyond what administrators must normally do for their beneficiaries. The general rule applies to all administrators.

This is *not* a claim that Mr Cooley was liable to give up the profit he made from a breach of contract.[168] Although the claim depended upon a contractual obligation, Mr Cooley was a fiduciary, in common law terminology; he was an administrator, who was accountable in the wide sense of that term even if not in the narrow sense.[169] The holding in *IDC v Cooley* is effectively that one who is accountable must account for gains derived from information that he was contractually obliged to disclose to the plaintiff beneficiary. This is hardly surprising given the nature of accountability, as an aspect of a relationship in which one acts for and on behalf of another. The logic of this would seem to apply as much in the civil law as in the common law; in the common law, however, there is the added consideration that the gain may be held on constructive trust.[170]

---

[167] The fact that this contractual obligation could trigger accountability even in relation to gains acquired after the contract was otherwise at an end is not extraordinary: see n 98.

[168] Below, in section VII.D, we will discuss gain-based remedies for wrongdoing, including breach of contract.

[169] Ie, even if not required to keep accounts: above, section V.B.1.

[170] Above, section V.A. In fact, constructive trusts can arise directly out of contractual obligations even in the absence of a fiduciary relationship or relationship of administration. A constructive trust only requires that one person is obliged unconditionally to confer on another the benefit of particular property that the first person holds (Lionel Smith, 'Philosophical Foundations of Proprietary Remedies' in Robert Chambers, Charles Mitchell, and James Penner (eds), *Philosophical Foundations of Unjust Enrichment* (OUP 2009) 281). For example, when one person becomes unconditionally obliged to transfer particular property to another (outside of the sale of goods, since that is governed by statute), the first person will hold the property on trust, even if the obligation is purely contractual.

In such cases, the contractual duty to disclose information leads to a duty to bring into account a gain acquired from the information; but the duty to account is (like the contractual duty) a primary duty. As with accountability arising from the general rule of attribution, the claim to the gain is one to enforce a primary duty. There is no need to frame the case in *breach* of contract. One consequence of this is that in the same way as under the general rule, it is irrelevant for the defendant to argue that no loss was caused because the plaintiff could not have acquired the gain itself.[171] That argument was rejected in *IDC v Cooley*. It would also be equally irrelevant for the defendant to argue that he could have made the gain lawfully. Both of those arguments suppose that the plaintiff's case is built on linking a wrong to the gain, but the claim to the gain is a claim to enforce primary right, so those arguments have no relevance.

In the common law corporate opportunity cases, the defendants are always fiduciaries, and the tendency is to assume that the explanation for accountability for profitable business opportunities must in all cases be the general fiduciary no-profit rule, which is the common law's name for the attribution rule that applies to administrators. That rule applies to gains acquired through acting in the fiduciary role. Those administrators who have positive duties to seek out opportunities for their beneficiaries can, however, be accountable in respect of opportunities which they acquire independently. In both situations—accountability arising from the attribution rule for all administrators, and accountability arising out of an administrator's positive contractual obligation—accountability arises as a primary obligation. It is not a remedy for the breach of an obligation.

C. Other illustrations

The principle of *IDC v Cooley* as I have articulated it is in fact codified in most common law jurisdictions in partnership legislation, as in Ontario:

> Every partner must account to the firm for any benefit derived by the partner without the consent of the other partners from any transaction concerning the partnership or from any use by the partner of the partnership property, name or business connection.[172]

That statutory rule includes the general rule that has been discussed at great length above, but by extending it to benefits derived 'from any transaction

---

[171] For the irrelevance of this in relation to the general attribution rule, see above, section II.B.3.
[172] *Partnerships Act*, RSO 1990, c P.5, s 29(1). Partners are mutual agents and so fiduciaries, just as in the civil law they are mutual mandataries.

concerning the partnership' the rule incorporates any benefit which the partner acquired independently, while being obliged by the partnership agreement to render that benefit to the partnership.

This analysis helps us to understand a Canadian case which divided the Supreme Court of Canada. *Strother v 3464920 Canada Inc*[173] concerned a lawyer called Strother who, like Cooley, had a contractual relationship with his client, the plaintiff, while also being in a fiduciary relationship with the plaintiff. Strother's role was to give advice on a valuable business that was driven by tax shelters; due to changes in the law, these opportunities disappeared. A few months later, Strother (along with a former employee of the plaintiff) hit upon a way to revivify this business. Strother was now doing routine corporate work for the plaintiff under a non-exclusive retainer, and so was still in a lawyer-client relationship with it, when he began working with the new client. Strother did not tell the plaintiff of the new opportunity but profited handsomely from it himself. In an echo of *Boardman v. Phipps*,[174] the Supreme Court of Canada divided 5-4 on the question whether there was, or was not, a conflict of interest. There was; but just as in *Boardman*, that was not the crucial issue.[175] The authors of both judgments also realized that the crucial issue was what were Strother's *contractual* obligations to the plaintiff. The dissenting judges held that he was not obliged to disclose the new opportunity; the majority held that he was:

> if Strother knew there was still a way to continue to syndicate US studio film production expenses to Canadian investors on a tax-efficient basis, the 1998 retainer entitled [the plaintiff] to be told that Strother's previous negative advice was now subject to reconsideration.[176]

This is effectively just what happened in *IDC v Cooley*. To make the point even clearer, the majority also looked to the contract to delimit Strother's liability. They denied a claim by the plaintiff for legal fees that it had paid to Strother; the *Cooley* principle did not touch those fees. As for his business profits, the majority required him to surrender them, but only to the point in time when he ceased acting for the plaintiff. This was said to be because at that point, 'the conflict was spent'.[177] But Cooley was liable for benefits acquired long after he had ceased

---

[173] *Strother v 3464920 Canada Inc* 2007 SCC 24, [2007] 2 SCR 177.
[174] N 8, discussed in more detail in n 103.
[175] When I co-authored a note on *Strother*, I and my co-author expressed the view that the dissenting judges were incorrect in the narrow view they took of conflicts of interest: Remus Valsan and Lionel Smith, 'The Loyalty of Lawyers: A Comment on *3464920 Canada Inc v Strother*' (2008) 87 Can Bar Rev 247. I still believe that, but I now think that the conflict was not what created the plaintiff's entitlement to the profit.
[176] N 173, [43]. This conclusion was based partly on the fact that Strother was a professional and not in business ([42]).
[177] ibid [95].

working with IDC, as have been other administrators;[178] this shows the error in tying this principle to the conflict as such. Still, the limitation in the award could be justified on the basis that before the lawyer-client relationship came to an end, the plaintiff knew all about what Strother had done, and about the new version of the business that he was conducting. In both cases, the plaintiff's claim to the gain was to the gain derived from information that should have been disclosed to the plaintiff; gains otherwise acquired were not within the principle. In *IDC v Cooley*, the defendant could not have been made liable for all remuneration he ever received for the rest of his life, even if he had continued to work with the external party who had 'poached' him. So in *Strother*, once the lawyer-client relationship was over *and* the plaintiff was aware of all relevant information, it ceased to be true that subsequent gains were derived from information that should have been disclosed to the plaintiff.

D. Gain-based remedies for wrongdoing

There may be other private law remedies that look somewhat similar to the general attribution rule and to the contractual extension of it that is discussed in this section. Take the case of a low-level employee who has no legal powers, so that he is not an agent or a mandatary; thus, the attribution rule for administrators simply does not apply to him. Such an employee is not, *generally*, liable to hand over every profit that he may acquire in connection with his employment.[179] Now imagine that for a bribe, he lets a robber into the employer's premises after business hours, when no one is there. The employer might have a claim against the employee for the bribe, but this is not by application of the attribution rule. We might say that the employee has committed a profitable wrong. This argument could be based on his breach of contract.[180] It could also be based on his facilitation of the wrongful infringement of the employer's right of property; in a sense, the employee profited by purporting to sell access to something that did not belong to him.[181] But just because the employer might have a legal recourse measured by the defendant's profit, it does not follow that this is an example of

---

[178] See n 98.
[179] *University of Nottingham v Fishel* [2000] EWHC 221 (QB). Employees are discussed in Chapter 7, section II.B.
[180] The employee is said to owe a duty of loyalty, in both common law and civil law, but this does not have the same content as the duty of loyalty of an administrator: Chapter 1, section IV.F; Chapter 7, section II.B.3. In *Blake* (n 136) the House of Lords held that courts could order a gain-based remedy for breach of contract; this was not because the defendant was an administrator, but through the use of accountability as a remedy for a wrong (above, section V.B.2).
[181] This is exactly the configuration that led to a famous gain-based recovery in *Edwards v Lee's Administrator* 96 SW2d 1028 (Ky CA, 1936).

the attribution rule that applies to private law administrators. It is a similar result but reached through other legal principles.

VIII. Duties of disclosure

A. The attribution of information creates duties of disclosure

In the context of private law administration, the law attributes benefits and profits acquired by the administrator to the beneficiary, simply because the administrator is acting for and on behalf of the beneficiary. It also attributes the costs of proper management to the beneficiary, for the same reason, thus giving the administrator a presumptive right to recover his expenses.

We have already touched several times on the idea that the same logic works for information. Information does not consist of rights; the formula for a soft drink is not a right, nor is the composition of a mineral layer underground, or a list of clients. But information can be very valuable and can be used to acquire rights of great value. Moreover, there can certainly be rights and obligations with respect to information. In the context of private law administration, it is through the idea of attribution that the law creates such rights and obligations.

The administrator is acting for and on behalf of the beneficiary, and so it is natural to say that information acquired by the administrator is held for and on behalf of the beneficiary. This generates duties of disclosure because the beneficiary cannot act on the information until they are aware of it. Such duties do not generally apply to everything that the administrator ever finds out: rather, the general rule about information operates in parallel to the general rule against unauthorized profits. It applies to information that the administrator acquires when acting as such. If the information is turned into actual profits, as in the case of a profitable business or investment opportunity, then of course those profits are caught by the rule against unauthorized profits, as we have already seen.

We have seen, however, that some administrators may have much wider duties relating to information, typically arising from their contract of employment.[182] Again, if that information is turned into actual profits, such an administrator will be accountable for those profits. We will see wider duties relating to information also arise when the administrator enters into a bargain of some kind with their beneficiary.

We have already noticed that the idea of 'accountability' speaks as much, or more, to the provision of information as it does to a liability to surrender or 'account for' rights.[183] A duty to account in the narrow sense—to render an

---

[182] Section VII.
[183] Above, section V.B.1.

account—is nothing but a duty to provide information. Accountability also imposes other duties to provide information, as well as a duty to pay over any balance that the account shows is owed, which may involve the surrendering of unauthorized profits. This helps us to see that all of these liabilities arise from the same source: from the relationship of administration, understood as a relationship in which one person acts for another.

B. General rules

The general rule requires an administrator to disclose to the beneficiary all and any information held by the administrator and relating to the administration. In some cases, the general rule may be qualified by considerations of confidentiality.[184] It may of course be qualified or modified by the law, or by particular terms of the particular relationship.[185]

1. Information about the existence and state of the relationship

Not surprisingly, it has been held that a trustee has an obligation, arising out of their accountability, to tell the beneficiary of the existence of the trust.[186] A trustee cannot be accountable in a meaningful sense to a beneficiary who does not know about the trust. This obligation was not framed in absolute terms; rather it was said that the duty arises where it would be 'to the unreasonable disadvantage of the beneficiary' not to be told of the trust's existence.[187] As to the strictness of this duty once it arose, it was held that 'the standard to be met in respect of this particular duty is not perfection, but rather that of honesty, and reasonable skill and prudence'.[188]

Trustees and many other administrators are accountable in the narrow sense, that they are required to keep, and to produce, accounts. This is because they hold assets in their administrative role and must always be able to explain and justify the current state of those assets. Here also, the administrator's duties are

---

[184] *Schmidt v Rosewood Trust Ltd* [2003] 2 AC 709 (PC), which addresses also the standing to obtain information of objects of trustees' dispositive discretions, where those objects are not beneficiaries with a right to any trust property. Because of the rise of such discretions, the question of access to such information is increasingly important: see Lionel Smith, 'Massively Discretionary Trusts' (2017) 70 CLP 17, 33–39. In the current chapter, the aim is to discuss principles that apply to private law administration generally.

[185] It is probably not possible, however, to extinguish all obligations to provide information while preserving the relationship as one of administration. This is because accountability is a definitional part of such a relationship. See, in the trust context, David Hayton, 'The Irreducible Core Content of Trusteeship' in Anthony Oakley (ed), *Trends in Contemporary Trust Law* (OUP 1996) 47, 49–52.

[186] *Valard Construction Ltd* (n 129).

[187] ibid [19].

[188] ibid [26].

not absolute. They are not what civilians call 'obligations of result', being duties to bring about a particular outcome regardless of difficulty; rather, they are 'obligations of means', being duties to make reasonable efforts to bring about the result.[189]

2. Disclosure of conflicts and profits

It has been argued by some courts and commentators that disclosure by an administrator of a conflict or potential conflict, or of a profit that has or may arise in the course of the administrative role, is never required by a positive duty; on this argument, disclosure is only necessary to avoid breaching the rules about conflicts or unauthorized profits.[190] There is some truth in this, but it fails to address important situations in which there are indeed genuine duties of disclosure.

Take the case of a trustee, T, who is going to invest trust property. Among many suitable investments, the trustee considers acquiring an interest in commercial office space that will generate rents. T happens to know that T's brother, S, is aiming to sell just such an interest in land. If the trustee wished to purchase S's interest in land as a trustee investment, then obviously there would have to be fully informed consent of the beneficiaries (and possibly of the court, if one or more beneficiaries lack full legal capacity). But if T simply disregards that particular investment because there are many other equally good or better opportunities, then the potential conflict disappears and there is no obvious reason that it needs to be disclosed. This situation may be seen to support the idea that there is no duty to disclose conflicts or potential conflicts.

But what if, on investigation, T honestly believes that the investment opportunity represented by S's interest in land is the best investment opportunity that is available? T has to use the investment power in what he perceives to be the best interest of the beneficiaries, and any other use of it would be a misuse. In these changed facts, T cannot simply discard this opportunity. To do so would be a breach of the duty of care, still and diligence, or in civilian terms the duty of prudence and diligence. Indeed, ignoring the interests of the beneficiaries—the very thing that should guide T's decision-making—would be a breach of the duty of good faith.[191] In this scenario, the right thing to do is to pursue the opportunity, seeking the fully informed consent of the beneficiaries, of the court, or both.

---

[189] In relation to an accounting party's duties to keep and produce accounts, a leading Canadian case describes that party's obligation as requiring reasonableness in providing the information: *Sandford v Porter* (1889) 16 OAR 565 (Ont CA); see also, discussing French and Swiss law, Werro (n 26), 177 n 29.

[190] This is a common view among those who think that there is a duty, in the strict sense, not to be in a conflict and not to acquire an unauthorized profit; see for example *Maguire v Makaronis* (1997) 188 CLR 449, 466 and *Blackmagic Design Pty Ltd v Overliese* [2011] FCAFC 24. For argument that these are not duties in the strict sense, see Chapter 4, section II.B.4, above, and section II.B.

[191] These duties are discussed in Chapter 6, sections III and IV.

Thus T will be obligated to make full disclosure of the conflict in the course of seeking approval.[192] Again, we see that disclosure is required when necessary to allow the beneficiaries to make their decisions.[193]

3. Disclosure of unlawful conduct

The general principle is that the beneficiary is entitled to information that allows her to understand her legal position and to make informed decisions about it. This principle requires an administrator to disclose their own unlawful conduct. In an English case, the defendant was a director and senior employee of the plaintiff corporation.[194] While the company was trying to renegotiate one of its most important contracts with a third party, the defendant was secretly negotiating with that party to set up a new company and thus misappropriate the business opportunity. This conduct was obviously a breach of contract and a breach of fiduciary duty, including the duty of care and skill and the duty of good faith.[195] The plaintiff failed to renegotiate the contract and suffered a loss. The interesting feature of the case is that the trial judge found that the defendant's disloyal conduct did not cause the non-renewal of the contract on the terms that the plaintiff had been seeking; the plaintiff had taken an aggressive negotiating strategy and sought very advantageous terms, and the third party would not in any event have renewed on those terms. However, the judge also found that if the defendant had told the plaintiff of the defendant's unlawful actions, then the plaintiff would have adopted a different negotiating strategy, and would have accepted the third party's offered terms. This meant that the defendant's non-disclosure of his own unlawful conduct *did* cause the loss of the contract, albeit its loss on terms less favourable to the plaintiff. Hence the legal question became whether the non-disclosure of his unlawful conduct was a separate legal wrong to the original disloyal conduct. The holding was that it was indeed. The implication is that an administrator's obligations of disclosure extend to an obligation to disclose his own unlawful conduct.

---

[192] If there was any potential profit to T in taking the opportunity (eg if the seller was a corporation in which T was interested) then this, of course, would also create conflict of self-interest and duty which would have to be disclosed. Moreover, if T was in a conflict of duty and duty (as where the S was a corporation in which T was not financially interested but of which T was a director), this would also have to be disclosed.

[193] As we have seen (Chapter 1, section V.B.3.d), if the court is involved in the approval of such a transaction, it is not adjudicating a lawsuit; it is rather acting in a supervisory role and needs to be guided by the beneficiaries' interests in making the decision. Just like a capacitated beneficiary, it needs full information in order to decide.

[194] *Item Software (UK) Ltd v Fassihi* [2004] EWCA Civ 1244, [2005] 2 BCLC 91. The decision followed earlier first-instance holdings to the same effect which are cited in the judgment.

[195] These duties are discussed in Chapter 6, sections III and IV.

Some may find this strange, but it follows perfectly the logic of accountability.[196] As we saw above, duties of disclosure arise when information about the administrator's management is needed by the beneficiary in order to make decisions that belong to the beneficiary. That was exactly what happened here. In a way, an obligation on the administrator to disclose their own wrongdoing is not that different from a trustee's basic obligation to tell the beneficiaries of the trust.[197] People need to know what their rights are in order to know what to do with them. It is important to say that the recognition of this duty does not imply some absurdly optimistic view that administrators will rush to report their own wrongdoing. It is rather the careful identification of a separate juridically wrongful act, which may attract different remedies.[198] This is exactly why it was relevant in *Item Software*. Other courts have held that even if a limitation period might have otherwise expired on the original wrong, the failure to disclose that wrong is a separate wrong that may suspend the running of time on the original claim:

> Thus the fact that a client lacks awareness of a [fiduciary lawyer's] malpractice implies, in many cases, a second breach of duty by the fiduciary, namely, a failure to disclose material facts to his client. Postponement of accrual of the cause of action until the client discovers, or should discover, the material facts in issue vindicates the fiduciary duty of full disclosure; it prevents the fiduciary from obtaining immunity for an initial breach of duty by a subsequent breach of the obligation of disclosure.[199]

4. Conclusion

In all of these situations, we see that the administrator cannot keep relevant information relating to the administration from the beneficiary. This is hardly surprising, since by assumption the administration is being carried on for that person's benefit. As the Supreme Court of California once put it: 'The duty of a fiduciary embraces the obligation to render a full and fair disclosure to the beneficiary of all facts which materially affect his rights and interests.'[200] This is true in the civil law as well as in the common law.[201]

---

[196] For similar holdings in US law, see *Neel v Magana, Olney, Levy, Cathcart & Gelfand* 6 Cal3d 176, 491 P2d 421 (SC, 1971) and *Merrill Lynch, Pierce, Fenner & Smith, Inc v Cheng* 901 F2d 1124 (DC Cir, 1990), 1128–9, discussed in DeMott (n 109), 941.

[197] Above, section VIII.B.1.

[198] Al Capone was imprisoned for tax evasion.

[199] *Neel* (n 196), 189 (Cal3d), 429 (P2d); followed in *Evans v Eckelman* 265 Cal Rptr 605 (Cal App 1 Dist, 1990) and *M (K) v M (H)* [1992] 3 SCR 6, 96 DLR (4th) 289.

[200] *Neel* (ibid), 188–89 (Cal3d), 429 (P2d); see also *Merrill Lynch* (n 196). Compare a typical provision of common law partnership legislation: 'Partners are bound to render true accounts and full information of all things affecting the partnership to any partner or the partner's legal representatives.': *Partnership Act*, RSO 1990, c P.5, s 28.

[201] Writing on the French law of mandate, Pétel (n 128) argues that the mandatary must disclose (without being asked) any fact that will affect the mandator's decisions: 253, 288–89.

C. Advisory administrators

Purely advisory administrators fall outside the scope of this Part;[202] but many private law administrators who are within this Part also have an advisory role. The most obvious example of these multiple functions is the case of a lawyer, who is almost always an advisor but is also an agent or mandatary, and may be also a trustee.

On the face of it, advice given by an advisory administrator is necessarily given in what the administrator believes to be the best interests of the beneficiary. For this reason, it must always be accompanied by the fullest disclosure. This includes conflicts of self-interest and duty,[203] as well as conflicts of duty and duty.[204]

The governing principle is similar. Advice is given to allow the beneficiary to make a decision. Information relevant to that decision must be included, and conflicts are obviously relevant information.[205] In a jurisdiction in which physicians are treated as advisory fiduciaries, the Supreme Court of California has said that '[t]he scope of the physician's communications to the patient ... must be measured by the patient's need, and that need is whatever information is material to the decision.'[206]

D. The administrator who wishes to contract with their own beneficiary

Perhaps the most burdensome duties of disclosure fall on the administrator who wishes to contract with their own beneficiary.[207] For example, an agent, B, who is charged with selling the land of his principal, A, receives several offers. B then tells A that he, B, will offer a higher price than any of them. There is nothing impossible about such a transaction. However, B will be required to disclose to A any information that B has acquired about the value of the land, regardless of how that information was acquired (eg, even if B secured a valuation at his own

---

[202] Chapter 7, section IV.A.
[203] *Nocton v Lord Ashburton* [1914] AC 932 (HL), 964–65, 969; *London Loan & Savings Co v Brickenden* [1934] 3 DLR 465 (PC); *Daly v Sydney Stock Exchange Ltd* (1986) 160 CLR 371, 377, 385–86; *Moore v Regents of University of California* 51 Cal3d 120, 793 P2d 479 (SC, 1990); *Hodgkinson v Simms* [1994] 3 SCR 377; *Maguire* (n 190); *Swindle v Harrison* [1997] 4 All ER 705 (CA).
[204] *Canson Enterprises Ltd v Boughton & Co* [1991] 3 SCR 534; *Hilton v Barker Booth & Eastwood (a firm)* [2005] 1 WLR 567 (HL).
[205] If the relationship is governed by a contract, it is possible that the advisor will be obliged by that contract to disclose information that the advisor acquired quite independently; see for example *Strother* (n 173), discussed above, section VII.C.
[206] *Cobbs v Grant* 8 Cal3d 229, 502 P2d 1 (SC, 1972), 244 (Cal3d), 28 (P2d), cited and followed in *Moore* (n 203), 129 (Cal3d), 483 (P2d).
[207] There is an overlap with the cases mentioned in the previous section, if the contracting administrator is also an advisor, which is often the case.

expense).[208] This is not an obligation that falls on any other potential buyer. Nor is it merely an obligation to disclose a conflict of interest: the simple fact of the conflict is probably obvious, as the parties are dealing contractually with one another.[209] In fact, there is a conflict of *interests* between A and B, but this conflict of interests is not specific to B and arises in relation to any potential buyer. B is not proposing to use his powers as an agent, which would generate a conflict of interest in the strict sense.[210] If A contracts with B, A will be acting personally, not through B's agency.

Because of the role he is in—of acting for and on behalf of A—B is obliged to disclose to A everything relevant that is known to B; this includes information that no other buyer would be obliged to disclose.[211] If he fails to do so, the contract will be voidable by A, as much as if B had misled A during contract formation.[212] It is important to see that this is not the setting aside by A of B's use of B's duty-bound administrative powers, which is what can happen when B's administrative powers are exercised in a conflict.[213] In the case under discussion, B acts personally and does not exercise his administrative powers. There is nothing defective about B's consent to the transaction. What A can do, if B did not disclose fully, is set aside the contract on the basis that A's *own* consent to it was vitiated by the non-disclosure. B breached a duty of disclosure. The result is that A can point to a mistake of A's own for which B was legally responsible; this makes the case parallel to one in which B had actively misled A by a misrepresentation.[214] Just as in that case, A can set the contract aside.[215]

We noticed earlier that an administrator who learns *independently* of some beneficial information is generally permitted to take advantage of it for themself

---

[208] *Tate v Williamson* (1866) 2 Ch App 55 (LC); *McKenzie v McDonald* [1927] VLR 134. In the common law's terminology, this is an example of what is called the 'fair-dealing' rule: the administrator is contracting in his personal capacity with the beneficiary (so that no administrative powers are being used). See Chapter 4, section II.B.3.

[209] If B were acting through an intermediary, or the conflict was not be obvious for some other reason, then it would indeed have to be disclosed along with all other relevant information held by the administrator, however acquired.

[210] On the distinction, see Chapter 4, section II.B.1.

[211] In *Daly* (n 203), it was said that the advisory administrator was under a duty to disclose its own near-insolvency before borrowing money from the client beneficiary.

[212] For a similar result in French law (1re civ, 13 April 1983), see Chapter 7, section IV.A.

[213] One example of such a conflict attracts what, in the common law, is called the 'self-dealing' rule: Chapter 4, section II.B.3.

[214] A similar analysis arises in insurance: the insured is obliged to disclose everything material to the risk, and non-disclosure, even innocent, allows the insurer to avoid the contract. See Lionel Smith, 'Prescriptive Fiduciary Duties' (2018) 37 UQLJ 261, 283–84.

[215] It was noticed earlier (Chapter 4, section VII.C) that when a corporate director contracts (personally or through an intermediary) with the corporation, that director is within these fair-dealing rules but also, since she has not resigned from the board even if she has recused herself, she and the board of which she is a member are within the self-dealing rules, which address conflicts of interest in the strict sense.

(unless they are contractually bound to secure that kind of information for the beneficiary or turn it to the profit of the beneficiary).[216] This type of case, however, is different. This is because the administrator wishes to step out of their role as an administrator, and to transact personally with the beneficiary. The conflict of *interests*, which is always present in the relationship, now becomes central, because any advantage obtained by the administrator will come at the expense of the beneficiary.[217] In this respect, the administrator is, in one sense, *not* acting for and on behalf of the beneficiary in relation to the transaction. And yet, they are so acting, because they have not resigned their position as administrator. The transaction is fraught with the possibility of advantage-taking by the administrator.[218]

The very wide duty of disclosure that arises here is aimed at ensuring that no advantage is taken through this mixing of roles. The law refuses to allow the administrator to say, 'for this transaction, I am to be treated as a stranger and have no more duties than a stranger'.[219] Instead, it requires the administrator to subordinate their personal interest and to give prevalence to their other-regarding role. Thus, although an administrator may in general be able to benefit personally from independently acquired information, it does not follow that they can use that independently acquired information to acquire a benefit *at the expense of their beneficiary*. A stranger could so use the information, but the administrator is hardly a stranger. As Lord Eldon said:

> It has been truly said, an attorney [an agent who is an administrator] is not incapable of contracting with his client. He may for a horse, an estate &c. A trustee may also may deal with his *Cestuy que trust;* but the relation must be in some way dissolved: or, if not, the parties must be put so much at arm's length, that they agree to take the characters of purchaser and vendor....

---

[216] Above, section VII.
[217] For the demonstration that the relationship is always characterized by a conflict of interests, see Chapter 4, section II.B.1.
[218] See *Movitex Ltd v Bulfield* [1988] BCLC 104 (ChD), 121. In the common law, fiduciary relationships import a presumption of undue influence when the fiduciary deals personally with the beneficiary. The positive obligations to disclose information under discussion here are juridically separate from that doctrine, although both bodies of modern law grew out of a general concern of Chancery with inappropriate advantage-taking: see Julius Grower, 'From Disability to Duty: From Constructive Fraud to Equitable Wrongs', Doctor of Philosophy, University College London, 2021.
[219] In *Sun Indalex Finance, LLC v United Steelworkers* [2013] 1 SCR 271, 2013 SCC 6, a corporation was both the employer and the fiduciary administrator of the employees' pension plan. It was suggested by counsel that in assessing its behaviour, the Court should ask which of the two 'hats' it was wearing at the relevant time. The Court refused to accept this mode of analysis; the simultaneous inconsistent roles of an administrator cannot be ignored in this way. Deschamps J said ([65]): 'Where interests do conflict, I do not find the two hats metaphor helpful.' See also [201], [269].

Therefore I say, he might contract: but then he should have said, if he was to deal with her for this, she must get another attorney to advise her as to the value: or, if she would not, then out of that state of circumstances this clear duty results from the rule of this Court, and throws upon him the whole *onus* of the case; that, if he will mix with the character of attorney that of vendor, he shall, if the propriety of the contract comes in question, manifest, that he has given her all that reasonable advice against himself, that he would have given her against a third person. It is asked, where is that rule to be found. I answer, in that great rule of the Court, that he, who bargains in matter of advantage with a person placing confidence in him is bound to shew, that a reasonable use has been made of that confidence; a rule applying to trustees, attorneys, or any one else.[220]

In this category of case, the duty to disclose does not derive directly from the administrator's accountability, but rather from their desire to act simultaneously in two inconsistent roles. One role must necessarily be prioritized, and it is not surprising that the law stipulates that it is the unselfish role that must take precedence.

E. The breach of an obligation to disclose is an unlawful act

The attribution rules, in respect of profits and of information, do not arise from wrongdoing; they create primary obligations, including duties of disclosure. But the breach of a duty of disclosure itself amounts to wrongdoing.

In the previous section, it was noted that a breach of a duty to disclose all relevant information to the beneficiary when the administrator contracts with the beneficiary will allow the beneficiary to set aside their own consent to the transaction. That result implies that there is a duty to disclose, because such a duty makes non-disclosure the legal equivalent of a positive misrepresentation. However, it does not necessarily follow that a breach of this duty supports a claim for loss caused by the breach. For example, an innocent misrepresentation may allow its victim to set aside their consent to a contract, while it will not support a claim for damages for loss suffered.

But the law is clear that when a loss is caused to the beneficiary by an administrator's breach of a duty of disclosure, the loss is recoverable against the administrator.[221] This is perhaps most evident in the cases on advisors,

---

[220] *Gibson v Jeyes* (1801) 6 Ves Jun 266, 31 ER 1044 (LC), 277, 278 (Ves Jun), 1049, 1050 (ER). See also his well-known judgments in *Ex parte Lacey* (1802) 6 Ves Jun 625, 31 ER 1228 (LC) and *Ex parte James* (1803) 8 Ves Jun 337, 32 ER 385 (LC).
[221] Eg *Valard Construction Ltd* (n 129).

where there has been a breach of a duty to disclose a conflict.[222] In this context, it is sometimes said that this shows that being in a conflict of interest is a legal wrong.[223] This is not quite right. The advisor typically gives advice without disclosing the conflict, and the beneficiary suffers a loss due to some fall in the market, or a business failure, or the action of some third party.[224] Then the beneficiary discovers the conflict. She can potentially recover her loss against the advisor. But the loss was not caused by the administrator's simply being in a conflict. If we imagine the facts occurring in the same way, but without any conflict, the loss would have still been suffered, because its cause was external. The actual complaint of the beneficiary is not, 'you were in a conflict', but rather, 'you were in a conflict *and you did not tell me when you advised me*'. Hence the plaintiff's case is that, if the plaintiff had known about the conflict, she would not have followed the advice.[225] It was the non-disclosure that caused the loss. And because there was a duty to disclose, non-disclosure is a legal wrong that generates a claim for compensation for loss caused.[226]

F. Conclusion

The logic of attribution explains many of the obligations, and indeed some of the rights, of an administrator. It explains also many of the obligations of disclosure that fall on an administrator. Like the no-profit rule, those obligations do not arise from wrongdoing. They do, however, create genuine obligations, and the breach of those obligations may itself amount to wrongdoing. Getting the logical sequence right unlocks all of the mysteries of this area of the law.

The logic of attribution does not reach far enough to explain the wide obligations of disclosure that fall on advisory administrators; it is the very nature of advice that imports a requirement of full disclosure. Nor does it explain

---

[222] See for example the cases cited in nn 203 and 204 (although *Maguire* (n 190)) did not involve a claim for damages). These cases refer systematically to non-disclosure as the basis of the claim.

[223] Mitchell (n 85).

[224] The kind of case discussed here is not argued on the theory that the advisor gave objectively bad advice, but on the failure to disclose. These cases tend to be defended by the advisor in blaming the loss on the external event.

[225] There is authority that breach of the duty of disclosure will reverse the burden of proof in relation to whether the loss was caused by the breach: *Brickenden* (n 203). This was doubted in *Swindle* (n 203); see now *Southwind v Canada* 2021 SCC 28, [82], suggesting that *Brickenden* is good law in Canada. The most thorough discussion of the treatment of *Brickenden* all over the common law world is in *Sim Poh Ping v Winsta Holding Pte Ltd* [2020] SGCA 35, accepting ([240]) that the burden of proof should be reversed.

[226] It is arguable that until *Nocton* (n 203) or possibly *Cavendish Bentinck v Fenn* (1887) 12 App Cas 652 (HL), the breach of a duty to disclose did not permit recovery of losses caused: J McCamus, 'Prometheus Unbound: Fiduciary Obligation in the Supreme Court of Canada' (1997) 28 CBLJ 107; Mitchell (n 85), 31236; Grower (n 218), ch 6.

the even wider obligations that fall on administrators who wish to contract personally with their own beneficiary. Here the law takes the position that the administrator cannot simultaneously keep and shed that role, and purport to interact with the beneficiary as a stranger could. Since they wish to act in both roles, they must allow the other-regarding role to prevail, and must disclose everything they know that is reasonably relevant to the decision-making process of the beneficiary.

6
Other Features of Private Law Administration

I. Introduction

This chapter completes Part II.A by describing other important features of relationships of private law administration. These are different duties that arise in such relationships. All of these duties are linked to the character of the relationship, as one in which one person is authorized and empowered to manage the affairs of another person.

II. Duty of commitment

This phrase stands for the duty to comply with the particular obligations of the particular mission entrusted to the administrator. There are always some obligations that are particular to each relationship. A trustee must abide by the terms of the particular trust, and an executor or liquidator of an estate must follow the instructions in the particular will. An administrator who is in a contractual relationship with his or her beneficiary must abide by the terms of the contract, and an agent or mandatary must follow instructions. A director must abide by the corporate constitution, and of course the governing corporate law statute. These obligations may be enforced by injunctions and may give rise to compensatory claims if loss is caused by a breach.[1]

Both the civil law and the common law differentiate obligations by 'intensity' or 'strictness'. Some obligations require the one who owes them to make reasonable efforts to bring about a result, while some require that person to bring about the result, without any excuse of having made a reasonable effort. Duties of commitment to the terms of the particular relationship might be of either kind.[2]

---

[1] See also Chapter 3, section III.C.1, discussing limits on an administrator's authority that do not derive from the requirement of loyalty.

[2] In the common law of trusts and estates, duties regarding the disposition of the trust or estate property were absolute, or were duties of result in civilian terms. This was implemented through trustee accounting: trustees could not claim to be discharged of liability to hold in trust any property if they lacked the authority to disburse that property, regardless of whether they had taken reasonable care. This led to the rise of exculpatory clauses in trust instruments and wills, and ultimately in

The Law of Loyalty. Lionel Smith, Oxford University Press. © Lionel Smith 2023.
DOI: 10.1093/oso/9780197664582.003.0006

III. Duty of care, skill and diligence; or, duties of prudence and diligence

A. Introduction

One who administers the affairs of another is presumptively bound to do so with reasonable care and skill. In the common law, this is called the duty of care and skill, or sometimes the duty of care, skill and diligence. In Quebec civil law, administrators have duties of 'prudence and diligence'.

What both kinds of duties impose is a general regime for the taking of care in the administrator's managerial role. These duties can apply to any activity of the administrator that is not otherwise regulated by some more specific norm. Examples may include investment decisions, the employment of agents or mandataries or employees, and decisions about any other matter related to contracts or property that might arise.

These duties impose an objective standard, which is different from what the law demands in relation to the loyal exercise of the powers of an administrator.[3]

B. Differences from duties in tort or general civil responsibility

This objective standard might seem to make these duties similar to the general duties, that we all owe one another, not to cause harm or damage by careless conduct. And in a lot of common law scholarship, the administrator's 'duty of care' is treated as merely an example of the duty of care that underlies the ordinary law of negligence or of civil responsibility.[4]

This is a mistake because the duties are different, in some important ways. They are different as to source and they are different as to content.[5]

---

most jurisdictions to a general jurisdiction in the court to excuse breaches of trust where the trustee behaved reasonably. The overall result, therefore, is something like what a civilian would call an obligation of means: an obligation to take reasonable steps to bring about the correct result. Some courts, perhaps misunderstanding the traditional rules, have also started to relax those rules, but this is controversial. See Lionel Smith, 'The Duties of Trustees in Comparative Perspective' (2016) 6 European Rev of Private Law 1031, 1032–36.

[3] Chapter 3, section II.B.
[4] Matthew Conaglen, *Fiduciary Loyalty: Protecting the Due Performance of Non-Fiduciary Duties* (Hart 2010) 35–39, notes carefully the variation among different duties of care, but takes the position that the fiduciary's duty of care is not a fiduciary duty because it is not peculiar to fiduciaries.
[5] I have made the argument that follows in earlier writing, partly as a response to Conaglen, ibid (eg Lionel Smith, 'Prescriptive Fiduciary Duties' (2018) 37 UQLJ 261, 268). Paul Miller earlier made the same points in greater detail: Paul B Miller, 'A Theory of Fiduciary Liability' (2011) 56 McGill LJ 235, 282–85. See also Weiming Tan, 'Peering Through Equity's Prism: A Fiduciary's Duty of Care or a Fiduciary Duty of Care?' (2021) 15 J of Equity 181.

As to source, the administrator's duties are not owed to the world at large, but to the particular beneficiaries. They do not grow out of the general relationship of one stranger to another; they grow rather out of the particular relationship between an administrator and the person or persons whose affairs the administrator is managing. They do not govern accidental interactions between persons, or the appropriation by one person of the assets of another; they govern rather the standards demanded in relation to the management of another's assets. In this respect, they have more in common with the duties that presumptively apply when one person is entrusted with another's physical thing than with the duties that we all owe to one another. Such a relationship, which may be called bailment in the common law or deposit in the civil law, is not a relationship of administration, but it presumptively imposes an objective duty of care.

This brings us to differences as to content. The general law of liability for careless harm requires us to take reasonable care as we go about our own lives. The duties now under discussion relate to the management of another's affairs. One immediate difference that this reveals is that the general law of liability for careless harm does not require us to act, but only to avoid causing harm by our actions. If I stay home and watch television, I will not breach the duties of the general law. But the objective duties that are owed by a private law administrator cannot be satisfied by inaction.[6] This is one reason why we see the words 'diligence' and 'prudence' in many formulations, in both common law and civil law. This is another manifestation of the fact that it is a duty relating to management, a duty which requires one to manage carefully. This is quite different from a general duty to be careful to respect the interests of other citizens in the world, as one goes about one's daily life.

The nature of the administrator's duty as a duty relating to management helps to explain why the courts may seem to take a more deferential attitude to administrators who are accused of breaching it than they do in relation to those who have caused physical accidents.[7] The liability question does not present itself in the same way as in the case of an accident involving personal injury or property damage. In the case of an accident, we may ask whether the defendant made reasonable decisions in relation to whatever she did that was causally implicated in the accident. In relation to the duty of careful management, it is the whole management process that must be evaluated. This management process typically includes the gathering of information and may involve the assessment of multiple factors such as risk versus reward, and whether to focus on the longer term or the shorter term. If, for example, the value of trust investments has gone

---

[6] *Fales v Canada Permanent Trust Co* [1977] 2 SCR 302.
[7] A difference seen as puzzling, for example, by FR Easterbrook and DR Fischel, *The Economic Structure of Corporate Law* (Harvard UP 1991) 94.

down, the beneficiaries may feel aggrieved. But this is not like a road accident where someone has been hurt. The difference is that (exceptional cases aside) no one is *authorized* to injure another person or cause damage to their things, even though a defendant may not be liable if he took reasonable care. The value of investments, by contrast, can go down in value without any wrongdoing at all. The mere loss of value in an investment portfolio cannot be treated as the infringement of a protected interest, as are personal injury and property damage. This is why, if the beneficiaries wish to complain, they cannot necessarily point to a particular decision and demand that it be reviewed as to whether it was careful. Their protected interest is not that they should never lose money; it is that care should be taken in designing and implementing the managerial process. To succeed, they have to show that the administrator's process was defective, which requires a more holistic evaluation by the court. This may have the appearance of being more deferential.

C. Breach

The breach of these duties leads to a liability to compensate the beneficiary for loss caused by the breach. This can be—indeed, in the cases under study in this Part II.A, it will be—a purely financial or economic loss, since we are dealing with a management duty, rather than a duty to be careful in our interactions with other people and their thing. A breach does not lead to the setting aside of legal acts, as is possible when administrators use their powers improperly.[8] That is because an improper use of the power generates a defect in the constitution of the legal act that results from the exercise of the power. In the case of unlawfully careless decision-making, the legal acts are properly constituted as legal acts. The carelessness amounts to the breach of an objective duty and creates a liability to compensate.

D. Exemption

In the common law, it has generally been accepted that it is permissible to exempt administrators, in advance, from liability for breach of these duties.[9] This is commonplace in trust law and in corporate law, although professional trustees may in some places and in some contexts be subject to different rules that do not permit such exemption. Quebec civil law, by contrast, treats the duties of

---

[8] Chapter 3, section IV.F; Chapter 4, section V.
[9] One leading case is *Armitage v Nurse* [1998] Ch 241 (CA).

prudence and diligence as inherent to the relationship of administration, so that an exemption clause apparently cannot exclude them.[10]

IV. Good faith

In the civil law, good faith is a general requirement for conducting oneself as an actor in the law.[11] In the common law it is, of course, more controversial and traditionally was understood to be imposed only in particular relationships.[12] However, it is universally accepted in the common law that a person who owes fiduciary obligations owes a duty of good faith, and this includes all relationships of private administration. In this sense, everyone with whom this Part II.A is concerned must conduct themselves in good faith, in both common law and civil law.

What this actually means is a more difficult question. What does such a duty require of the person who owes it? And is the answer different for an administrator than it is for someone else who owes a duty of good faith?

Private law administrators stand apart from other private law actors inasmuch as they are legally empowered and legally bound to act for and on behalf of another person. In relation to discretionary powers that typically hold for the pursuit of this mission, they are legally required to exercise judgment in what they perceive to be the best interests of another. This points us in the direction of understanding that good faith requires more of an administrator than it might require of someone else, in just the same way as a 'duty of loyalty' means something different in the context of an administrator than in the context of an employee who is not an administrator.[13]

Since every administrator must exercise their powers in what they perceive to be the best interests of the beneficiary, an administrator is in bad faith when they consciously disregard those interests.[14] If they engage in such conduct, they ignore the very interests that should be guiding them. That action is fundamentally

---

[10] Or at the very least, such a clause will be interpreted extremely restrictively: *Bell v Molson* 2015 QCCA 583, [88]–[103].
[11] Civil Code of Québec, art 6.
[12] For some discussion of common law developments in relation to contractual powers, see Chapter 3, section III.B.2.
[13] Chapter 7, section II.B.3.
[14] Richard Nolan and Matthew Conaglen, 'Good Faith: What Does It Mean for Fiduciaries and What Does It Tell Us about Them?' in Elise Bant and Matthew Harding (eds), *Exploring Private Law* (CUP 2010) 319, 332; Leo E Strine Jr and others, 'Loyalty's Core Demand: The Defining Role of Good Faith in Corporation Law' (2010) 98 Georgetown LJ 629, esp 647–48, 673; Lionel Smith, 'Parenthood Is a Fiduciary Relationship' (2020) 70 UTLJ 395, 432–35. For the civil law, see Michel Storck, *Essai sur le mécanisme de la représentation dans les actes juridiques* (LGDJ 1982), 163–64, arguing that a conscious misuse of powers of administration constitutes a fault and thus generates civil liability.

inconsistent with the role they are in, which justifies characterizing it as bad faith. And it also explains why it is impossible for an exemption clause to dispense with the duty of good faith.[15] Like the requirement of loyalty in relation to the exercise of powers, it is definitionally essential to the other-regarding relationship of administration.

Thus, serious wrongdoing like misappropriation will always amount to a breach of the duty of good faith. Such misappropriation is almost certainly a breach of other duties: the duty of commitment and the objective duties of care and skill, to name only those. Those duties, however, can be breached innocently and in good faith. Identifying bad faith, as in cases of misappropriation, may be very important inasmuch as in some jurisdictions, it may attract punitive damages.[16] Even in the absence of deliberate misappropriation, it is arguable that grosser forms of carelessness can be understood to amount to bad faith. This will be the case where the administrator is subjectively aware that they are not being guided by the best interests of the beneficiary.[17] Since this will amount to bad faith, it is likely to take the administrator out of the protection of any exemption clause. Indeed, serious wrongdoing of this kind may attract criminal liability.[18]

---

[15] Eg *Armitage* (n 9).
[16] *Walling v Walling* 2012 ONSC 6580.
[17] Joshua Getzler, 'Duty of Care' in P Birks and A Pretto (eds), *Breach of Trust* (Hart 2002) 41, 51–53; Strine and others (14), 693.
[18] Storck (n 14), 160–63; Madeleine Cantin Cumyn and Michelle Cumyn, *L'administration du bien d'autrui* (2nd edn, Éditions Yvon Blais 2014), 355–56, mentioning criminal breach of trust among other possibilities.

PART II.B
THE WIDENING REACH OF ADMINISTRATION IN PRIVATE LAW

7
The Widening Reach of Administration in Private Law

I. Introduction

Part II of this study addresses relationships of private law administration; Part II.A looked at an important subset of such relationships. In civilian terms, they were relationships in which an administrator holds legal powers to intervene in the patrimony of another. A common lawyer might say that Part II.A dealt with administration of financial or pecuniary interests.

In this chapter, the only one in Part II.B, we will stay within private law, but we will consider how similar principles apply to regulate a wider range of relationships. This widening can be seen to operate in three dimensions. First, the law may treat a relationship as a relationship of private law administration even if it does not belong to one of the established, nominate categories of such relationships, such as trustee–beneficiary or director–corporation. Second, some people hold legal powers for and on behalf of other persons, but powers that are non-patrimonial. An example is a person who has the authority and power to decide what medical treatment shall be received by another person. This creates a relationship of administration. Third, some people do not hold legal powers at all, but may only have factual powers over another person's interests. One example is certain kinds of advisors.

All three of these dimensions have contributed to enormous increase since the 1970s in the importance of the applicable legal principles. Since that time, those principles have been applied to a greater and greater range of private law relationships. So long as the core of the relationship of holding power for and on behalf of another is present, we should not be surprised to find that the legal regulation is the same. But different contexts may call for differences as well.

It should be remembered that even outside of a relationship of administration, parties are at liberty to agree contractually to abide by rules which are like those applied by the law when such a relationship is found.[1]

---

[1] See D Gordon Smith, 'Contractually Adopted Fiduciary Duty' [2014] U Ill L Rev 1783; Lionel Smith, 'Prescriptive Fiduciary Duties' (2018) 37 UQLJ 261, 268–69; *Secretariat Consulting PTE Ltd v A Company* [2021] EWCA Civ 6.

II. Legal powers outside of established categories

One way in which the law of fiduciary relationships has become much more prominent in the common law world has been through the courts' applying that characterisation to relationships that do not fall into an established category. Established categories include such relationships as director–corporation, agent–principal, and trustee–beneficiary. These categories, thoroughly explored in Part II.A, always involve holding powers for and on behalf of another person. Common law courts, however, through a process of reasoning by analogy which has been as dramatic as it has been occasionally unguided, have been increasingly willing to characterize other relationships as fiduciary and therefore as attracting the same legal regulation. These are sometimes called 'ad hoc' fiduciary relationships. In the nature of things, ad hoc fiduciary relationships could arise in a very wide range of legal situations. In this section, we will look at three examples: joint venturers, employees, and trust 'protectors'.[2] We will also consider the extent to which the experience of the common law has been, or could be, mirrored in the civil law.

A. Joint venturers (outside of partnership and corporation)

Many cases have involved joint venturers. Typically, these disputes involve the appropriation by one party of some opportunity arising in the course of the joint venture. If the relationship is one of administration—in the common law, a fiduciary relationship—then this appropriation will not be permitted, being contrary to the rule against unauthorized profits, and probably also involving breaches of obligations of disclosure. If it is not such a relationship, then on the face of it the parties are free to pursue their own interests.[3]

'Joint venture' does not have a fixed meaning in law and can refer to a range of juridical situations. For example, although not every joint venture is a partnership, some might be. A partnership is an established category of administration. In the common law, partners are mutual agents of another, and so a partnership

---

[2] Another example of such expansion is the case of advisors, discussed in section IV below. While some advisory relationships have been found to be ad hoc fiduciary relationships, there are some advisory relationships (such as lawyers and real estate agents) that are considered to belong to an established category of fiduciary relationship.

[3] Of course there may be liability for breach of contract. There may also be liability for the misuse of confidential information. Although older cases may use the label 'fiduciary relationship' in the context of confidential information, it has now been clarified that the misuse of such information creates a free-standing ground of liability, which in no way depends on the finding of a fiduciary relationship in the modern sense of a relationship of administration. Examples of this recognition include *LAC Minerals Ltd v International Corona Resources Ltd* [1989] 2 SCR 574 and *Attorney-General v Guardian Newspapers Ltd (No 2)* [1990] AC 10.

always involves fiduciary relationships. The same is true in the civil law: partners are mutual mandataries of one another, and this is equally an established relationship of administration. In both traditions, whether or not a partnership exists is a legal question of characterization; in part because it has effects on third parties, the characterization of the relationship is not left to the will of the partners.

But there can be joint ventures that do not satisfy the definition of partnership. What a business person calls a joint venture may be implemented through a corporate structure with the joint venturers as shareholders. Shareholders, of course, are not as such in a relationship of administration, but corporate directors and officers are in such relationship, vis-à-vis the corporation.

Now consider a joint venture that involves neither a partnership nor a corporation. Common law courts have sometimes characterized the parties' relationship as fiduciary, which, in the terms of this book, means that is a relationship of administration.[4] It attracts the legal incidents that have been explored in Part II.A, including duties of disclosure and the rule against unauthorized profits.

Over the years and over many cases, the courts have used a range of legal tests for answering the question whether a relationship should be characterized as an ad hoc fiduciary relationship.[5] The Supreme Court of Canada, for example, used to focus on whether the beneficiary was 'vulnerable' to the alleged fiduciary.[6] This was not quite the correct inquiry, because people are vulnerable to brute power, as the pedestrian crossing the street is vulnerable to a motorist. The inquiry evolved into asking whether the alleged fiduciary had power in the sense of authority to affect the position of the beneficiary; such a power, of course, always carries with it a particular kind of vulnerability, simply as the correlative of the power.[7] What has often been missing from the analysis is that the power must be held *for and on behalf of* the other person.[8] It is possible to hold legal or factual authority over another person in such a way that this authority is not held for the

---

[4] A well-known example is *Meinhard v Salmon* 249 NY 458, 164 NE 545 (CA, 1928).

[5] For a detailed study, see Gerard MD Bean, *Fiduciary Obligations and Joint Ventures* (Clarendon Press 1995).

[6] *LAC Minerals* (n 4).

[7] Vulnerability as a free-standing requirement was abandoned in *Galambos v Perez* 2009 SCC 48, [2009] 3 SCR 247, [67]–[68] and *Alberta v Elder Advocates of Alberta Society* 2011 SCC 24, [2011] 2 SCR 261, [28], [33], in favour of the view that the only relevant vulnerability is that which arises from the holding of lawful power by the fiduciary.

[8] This was not noticed in the set of criteria set out in the frequently cited dissenting judgment of Wilson J in *Frame v Smith* [1987] 2 SCR 99, 42 DLR (4th) 81, 136 [SCR], corrected by an erratum published at [2011] 1 SCR, part 3, iv; but it explains the result in that case. The parties were divorced parents and the defendant mother had custody of their children. She held juridical powers over the children, and she held those powers for their benefit; she was in a fiduciary relationship with her children (below, section V). But the plaintiff father failed in his claim that she owed fiduciary duties *to him*: although she had some factual power over him, and juridical powers over the children, in neither case did she hold that power for *his* benefit, in order to manage *his* affairs.

benefit of that person.[9] But a relationship of administration depends on finding that the administrator's authority is held *for and on behalf of* the beneficiary.

This has sometimes been addressed by looking for an undertaking by the power-holder to act in the other person's interests. In the context of joint ventures, and other ad hoc relationships, especially contractual ones, this makes sense, because the terms of the parties' relationship are set by their agreement.[10] But even where an undertaking is an important part of concluding that there is a relationship of administration, it does not follow that the undertaking explains the applicability of the legal norms governing that administration.[11] Marriage is a voluntary undertaking, but the precise legal rights and duties that arise from marriage owe much more to the law than to any undertaking that was given. So too in relationships of administration, any undertaking does not define the precise contours of the parties' legal relationship once it is constituted as a relationship of administration.[12]

When it is found that the nature of the arrangement is that one joint venturer has power over the other but holds that power for and on behalf of the other, or for the benefit of the joint venture, then a common law court will find a fiduciary relationship.[13] As an English judge put it in a different context: '... the question is: for whose benefit, as a matter of construction of the [document], has the power been given?'[14]

---

[9] Examples that show this: an employer has authority over the employer; a principal or mandator has authority over the agent or mandatary (but the relationship of administration is in the other direction); a military commander has authority over those under his command. See further Chapter 9, section I.C.2.a.

[10] The requirement of an undertaking to act on another's behalf is not necessarily general, however, since some powers of administration are not acquired by agreement but rather by law (as, for example, in the case of a testamentary executor).

[11] For more detailed analysis of the relationship of undertakings to fiduciary relationships, see Chapter 2, section III.A.5, and Lionel Smith, 'Parenthood Is a Fiduciary Relationship' (2020) 70 UTLJ 395, 402–04.

[12] *Re Goldcorp Exchange Ltd* [1995] 1 AC 74 (PC), 98: '... the essence of a fiduciary relationship is that it creates obligations of a different character from those deriving from the contract itself'; *Beach Petroleum NL v Kennedy* [1999] NSWCA 408, 48 NSWLR 1, [192]: '... a fiduciary responsibility is an imposed not an accepted one, one concerned with an imposed standard of behaviour' (citing Paul D Finn, 'The Fiduciary Principle' in Timothy G Youdan (ed), *Equity, Fiduciaries and Trusts* (Carswell 1989) 1, 54); *Strother v 3464920 Canada Inc* 2007 SCC 24, [2007] 2 SCR 177, [34]: 'When a lawyer is retained by a client, the scope of the retainer is governed by contract. . . . The solicitor-client relationship thus created is, however, overlaid with certain fiduciary responsibilities, which are imposed as a matter of law'. See also Lionel Smith, 'Contract, Consent, and Fiduciary Relationships' in Paul B Miller and Andrew S Gold (eds), *Contract, Status and Fiduciary Law* (OUP 2016) 117.

[13] In *Meinhard* (n 4), for example, the arrangement was contractual and one party was described as the 'manager' of the enterprise. A person is not a manager of that which belongs entirely to them. The interpretive question may of course be difficult; it was held by a bare majority that the relationship was not fiduciary in *Hospital Products Ltd v United States Surgical Corp* (1984) 156 CLR 41 and in *LAC Minerals* (n 4); see also *Pilmer v Duke Group Ltd (in liq)* (2001) 207 CLR 165.

[14] *JSC Mezhdunarodniy Promyshlenniy Bank v Pugachev* [2017] EWHC 2426 (Ch), [203]. The context there was whether a 'trust protector' was or was not an administrator. This is addressed below, section II.C.

The civil law can be as flexible and innovative as the common law, but it tends to proceed conceptually and it is unlikely to label a category of relationships as 'ad hoc'.[15] The question will be to identify the crucial features that make a relationship one of administration, and to ask whether those are found in the relationship being examined.[16] Not all of the civil law is found in the civil code, and the recognition that specific codal provisions are only examples of general principles can allow for substantial flexibility.[17] In the civilian tradition, mandate has generally been seen as the paradigm relationship of administration.[18] In a decision of the Supreme Court of Canada under the previous Civil Code of Lower Canada, it was held that the codal rule against unauthorized profits, set out as part of the contract of mandate, was not confined to that contract; it 'attaches rather to the underlying function and relationship between the parties to the contract'.[19] In a similar way, civilian authors may argue that relationships of administration arise whenever one person acts for and on behalf of another, and thus rather than being tied to particular named contracts or legal relationships, they should be codified in a general part of the civil code.[20]

The Civil Code of Québec now has a Title on the Administration of the Property of Others, and it has been argued that this has become the foundation for a general regime governing relationships of administration.[21] But the conceptual analysis is apt to make that regime even wider than the administration of property interests. Civilians in the French and Quebec traditions will ask whether one person holds 'powers' in the sense known in those traditions: legal prerogatives which the holder is not free to use as they wish, but rather must use in a the pursuit of an interest that is at least partly different from their own.[22] Rather like the common law's 'ad hoc' fiduciary relationship, this can allow

---

[15] Lionel Smith, 'Civil and Common Law' in Andrew S Gold and others (eds), *Oxford Handbook of the New Private Law* (OUP 2020) 228.

[16] This, of course, is ultimately also what the common law has done, albeit starting with analogical extension rather than conceptual reasoning.

[17] Eg *Cie immobilière Viger v Lauréat Giguère Inc* [1977] 2 SCR 67, 76: 'The Civil Code does not contain the whole of civil law. It is based on principles that are not all expressed there, which it is up to case law and doctrine to develop...'

[18] Madeleine Cantin Cumyn and Michelle Cumyn, *L'administration du bien d'autrui* (2nd edn, Éditions Yvon Blais 2014), 9–31; Michele Graziadei, 'Virtue and Utility: Fiduciary Law in Civil Law and Common Law Jurisdictions' in Andrew S Gold and Paul B Miller (eds), *Philosophical Foundations of Fiduciary Law* (OUP 2014) 287, 288.

[19] *Bank of Montreal v Kuet Leong Ng* [1989] 2 SCR 429, 436; in the French text, the obligation 'se rattache plutôt à la fonction et aux rapports sous-jacents entre les parties au contrat'. The decision has been criticized; this will be discussed, and the decision defended, in more detail in the next section, on employees.

[20] Franz Werro, *Le mandat et ses effets* (Éditions Universitaires Fribourg 1993), 170–73.

[21] Cantin Cumyn and Cumyn (n 18).

[22] Madeleine Cantin Cumyn, 'De l'administration des biens à la protection de la personne d'autrui' in Barreau du Québec—Service de la Formation continue (ed), *Obligations et recours contre un curateur, tuteur ou mandataire défaillant 2008*, vol 283 (Yvon Blais 2008) 205; for more on the civilian terminology of powers, see Chapter 1, section IV.A.2.

courts to treat private law relationships as relationships of administration because of their legal characteristics, even without explicit codal support.

B. Employees

In the common law, many cases have struggled with the question whether an employee was in a fiduciary relationship with his or her employer. Such disputes often turn on the appropriation of opportunities by an employee after they have left, but they may also turn on unauthorized profits acquired during the employment relationship. A fiduciary employee may be unable to acquire such benefits lawfully, under the rule against unauthorized profits, while a non-fiduciary employee might be at liberty to pursue an opportunity of which she learned through the employment relationship.[23]

1. Employees can be in a relationship of administration

A first point is that just as with joint venturers, some employees are uncontroversially in a relationship of administration. This is because, although they are employees, they *also and simultaneously* belong to an established relationship of administration. In US law, every employee is considered to be an agent of the employer, and agency is a relationship of administration.[24] In other common law systems, employees are not necessarily administrators, but they may be. Directors are always in a relationship of administration with their corporation; and some directors are also employees.[25] These people will be administrators in their role of director; the fact that they are also employees does not change this. In the same way, employees who are not directors can be administrators, probably because they are also agents.[26] One Canadian common law case is well-known for holding that senior management employees are fiduciaries, even if they are not on the board of directors.[27] In common law terms, however, senior management employees are almost inevitably agents of the corporation, with wide authority to

---

[23] Of course, as with joint venturers there are many other grounds of liability, including misuse of confidential information (for example, about contacts or business plans) and breach of contract (such as contractual promises not to compete, or the implied contractual duty of fidelity, mentioned below).

[24] American Law Institute, *Restatement of the Law Third: Agency*, 2 vols, vol 1 (ALI 2006) §1.01, comment *c*, discussed in chapter 1, section V.B.3.b.2.

[25] On the distinctness of the two relationships, see *Ranson v Customer Systems plc* [2012] EWCA Civ 841, [21]: 'The appointment of a person as a company director does not make that person an employee of the company. A director is the holder of an office. Nor does appointment as a company director of itself bring into existence any contract between the director and the company'.

[26] Aline Van Bever, 'When Is An Employee A Fiduciary?' (2014) 18 Canadian Lab & Emp LJ 39, 49–50.

[27] *Canadian Aero Services Ltd v O'Malley* [1974] SCR 592; this is now in Canadian statutes (eg *Canada Business Corporations Act*, RSC 1985, c C-44, s 122(1)(a)).

make contracts and to perform other legal acts (such as terminating contracts or paying debts or transferring property) on behalf of the corporation. In this sense, there is nothing difficult about realizing that they are in a relationship of administration, in virtue of the relationship of agency.[28] But even employees who are not management employees can be agents of their employer, and in this case they will be in a relationship of administration with the employer.

Exactly the same is true in the civil law. The civilian tradition is characterized by individually defined, nominate contracts, but it does not follow that a person must be *either* an employee *or* a mandatary.[29] Modern civilian systems have generally abandoned the old rule of Roman law that mandate is definitionally gratuitous, thus making it possible for a person to be a mandatary even though she is remunerated.[30] The definitions of the two contracts, employment and mandate, are different, but they are not incompatible: a doctor is not a painter, but the same person can be a doctor and a painter. This is one way to read the decision of the Supreme Court of Canada, applying Quebec law under the Civil Code of Lower Canada, in *Bank of Montreal v Kuet Leong Ng*.[31] The defendant was an employee and the Court applied the rule against unauthorized profits that was applicable to mandataries; but the employee could bind his employer to contracts, so he was a mandatary as well as an employee.[32] The definitions of these two contracts in the Civil Code of Québec certainly make it possible that a person can be an employee and a mandatary at the same time, and in relation to the same employer/

---

[28] Deborah A DeMott, 'Corporate Officers as Agents' (2017) 74 Wash & Lee L Rev 847.

[29] Jérôme Huet and others, *Les principaux contrats spéciaux*, Jacques Ghestin (ed), *Traité de droit civil* (3rd edn, LGDJ 2012), 1007–08, 1020–21; cf Werro (n 21), 26–28. See also Raymonde Crête, 'Les manifestations du particularisme juridique des rapports de confiance dans les services de placement' in Raymonde Crête and others (eds), *Courtiers et conseillers financiers: encadrement des services de placement* (Éditions Yvons Blais 2011) 275 (discussing more generally the possibility that a relationship involves more than one codal regime).

[30] German law has retained the principle that mandate is gratuitous by definition (Gerhard Dannemann and Reiner Schulze (eds), *German Civil Code: Bürgerliches Gesetzbuch (BGB)*, 2 vols, vol I (CH Beck 2020) § 662; but this is potentially misleading in two ways. First, German law also has a named contract for nongratuitous management of the affairs of another (§ 675), to which many of the provisions relating to mandate are legislatively applied by cross-reference. Secondly, German law separates analytically the bilateral contract of mandate (or nongratuitous management of the affairs of another) from the power of legal representation, which itself can be attached to a range of relationships, and which brings with it some of the regulation of private law administration (Chapter 1, section V.B.3.b.2).

[31] N 19.

[32] The reasoning has sometimes been questioned because it could be read as suggesting that there is a duty to account in all contracts (Adrian Popovici, *La couleur du mandat* (Les Éditions Thémis 1995) 224 n 574), or as suggesting that the duty to account arises from good faith (Michelle Cumyn, 'L'encadrement des conflits d'intérêts par le droit commun québécois' in Denis Mazeaud, Benoît Moore, and Blandine Mallet-Bricout (eds), *Les conflits d'intérêts* (Dalloz 2013) 49, 60–62; this is a similar criticism since in Quebec law all contracts must be performed in good faith). If however the decision is read as holding that those employees who are also mandataries must comply with the obligations of mandataries, then it seems entirely defensible. In *Centre de santé et de services sociaux de Laval v Tadros* 2015 QCCA 351, [27], the Quebec Court of Appeal unanimously described *Kuet Leong Ng* as a case in which the defendant was a mandatary.

mandator.[33] It is an approach that has also been adopted by the Quebec legislature in relation to corporate officers, who are always employees, but who are declared to be mandataries as well,[34] just as was discussed above in relation to the common law.

Indeed this must be true for a whole range of employees, in both common law and civil law, even though the labels may differ across legal systems. Consider a large retail establishment. The employees who are dealing with purchasing customers are making contracts on behalf of their employer, taking payment and transferring ownership. Some may have the authority to negotiate, say in the case of damaged goods, but even those who do not are agents or mandataries. Somewhere else in the organization, other employees are making contracts to buy goods or to have them manufactured, to have them shipped and so on, and still other employees have the authority to hire employees and to terminate them. In the case of junior employees, these relationships of administration may have a narrow scope since the employee may have little or no discretion.[35] It may therefore be quite unlikely that issues relating to the improper use of legal powers, or to conflicts or unauthorized profits, would arise in respect of these employees who are also agents or mandataries.

Another possibility is that an employee could be in a relationship of administration even if the employee is not an agent or mandatary, or a director. This is because the employee, while outside those established relationships, nonetheless holds some power or powers for and on behalf of their employer, a situation that was discussed above.[36]

2. The employment relationship itself is not a relationship of administration

Thus many employees fall into an established relationship of administration. It was mentioned earlier that in US law, all employees are considered agents.[37] Outside of that system, however, the employment relationship itself is not a relationship of administration.[38] It is only through the superposition of some other

---

[33] Art 2085: 'A contract of employment is a contract by which a person, the employee, undertakes, for a limited time and for remuneration, to do work under the direction or control of another person, the employer'. Art 2130: 'Mandate is a contract by which a person, the mandator, confers upon another person, the mandatary, the power to represent him in the performance of a juridical act with a third person, and the mandatary, by his acceptance, binds himself to exercise the power'.

[34] Quebec *Business Corporations Act*, RSQ c S-31.1, s 116: 'The officers are mandataries of the corporation'. / 'Les dirigeants de la société sont mandataires de la société'.

[35] The question of administrators with no discretion is discussed in Chapter 3, section III.C.

[36] Section II.A. For discussion of this possibility for employees, see Van Bever (n 26), 50–57.

[37] N 24 and text.

[38] The leading English holding to this effect is *University of Nottingham v Fishel* [2000] EWHC 221 (QB); approved, *Helmet Integrated Systems Ltd v Tunnard* [2006] EWCA Civ 1735; *Ranson* (n 25); *Smile Inc Dental Surgeons Pte Ltd v Lui Andrew Stewart* [2012] SGCA 39. See also Samuel J Stoljar, *The Law of Agency: Its History and Present Principles* (Sweet & Maxwell 1961) 268, cited in the civil law context by Werro (n 21), 171–72.

relationship that an employee may be an administrator. Even so, employers are always potentially vicariously liable for the wrongs of their employees; that conclusion arises from control, and does not require the presence of a relationship of administration.

This means that it is not possible to conclude in the common law that an employee is a fiduciary simply on the basis that they are a very important employee. This reasoning has unfortunately become rather typical in Canada.[39] In one case, the Ontario Court of Appeal said:

> The trial judge reached his conclusion that Cass and Vandenberg were fiduciaries after a detailed review of their roles at GasTOPS. He found that along with the other two personal appellants '[t]hey were responsible for developing a significant commercial component of GasTOPS' business, and achieved that through the use of sensitive technological information that they helped develop and which was at the very core of GasTOPS' corporate identity': see para 270. They worked with little if any supervision but with a high degree of responsibility. They had integral knowledge of and involvement with the design, development and future of GasTOPS' family of products. GasTOPS was in essence a technology company. In this respect, Cass and Vandenberg were crucial to its direction and guidance. The trial judge specifically concluded that all four personal appellants were part of GasTOPS' senior management.[40]

The Court upheld the trial judge's decision on this point. But in fact, none of these issues is directly relevant to finding a relationship of administration, or, as it is called in the common law, a fiduciary relationship. The rules about conflicts, unauthorized profits, and accountability for information do not apply *simply* because someone is really important or really senior, or even crucial to the enterprise. They apply because the person holds powers for and on behalf of another. Usually, senior employees do hold such powers, and it may be the case that junior employees do as well.[41]

---

[39] Possibly as a result of the *Canadian Aero* case (n 27), which referred to 'senior employees'. Another explanation is that for a time, Canadian common law incorrectly used a 'vulnerability' test to decide whether a relationship was fiduciary: above, section II.A. The Canadian case law is criticized on this point in Douglas Brodie, 'The Employment Relationship and Fiduciary Obligations' (2012) 16 Edinburgh L Rev 198 and Van Bever (n 26), 57–68.

[40] *GasTOPS Ltd v Forsyth* 2012 ONCA 134, [82]. See also *Enbridge Gas Distribution Inc v Marinaccio* 2012 ONCA 650, confirming a decision that an employee was a fiduciary with some discussion of seniority and vulnerability. The employee, however, was authorized to make contracts and approve payment of invoices, and so was clearly an agent, who is always a fiduciary.

[41] See also Van Bever (n 26), 58–60, noting that some employees may function as de facto directors; again, this is an independent reason to conclude that they are administrators. See below, section IV.B.

3. Similarities and false flags

There are some false flags that may make the employment relationship look like a relationship of administration. The most prominent of these is that employees may be said, by courts or even by legislation, to owe duties of fidelity or duties of loyalty; and this is true in both common law and civil law.[42] But in both traditions, this refers to a juridical relationship that is different to a relationship of administration.[43] Although it might not always be clear whether the employee has fulfilled his or her obligations, it remains the case that in principle, whether or not he has done so is answered objectively. Employees as such (that is, employees who are not administrators) cannot be subject to the subjective requirement of loyalty as we have defined it for administrators,[44] because they do not hold the powers of an administrator to which that requirement of loyalty applies. It may be said that an employee must act in the interests or even the best interests of the employer, but in this context, this is not a legal norm that governs the exercise of other-regarding judgment; it is merely a way of describing the fact that the employee's obligations towards the employer must be fulfilled. The employee, in performing his or her contractual obligations, will further the interests of the employer and in that sense is obliged to advance those interests. But this goes beyond employment and could be said of a wide range of contracts.[45] We can also notice that some employees may be able lawfully to extract profit from their employment role or from information so acquired; in order to determine whether such conduct was lawful, the courts have to interpret the terms of the employment contract, express and implied. An administrator, by contrast, can never derive an unauthorized profit from her role, and as discussed in Chapter 5, this rule does not depend on showing wrongdoing.

The confusion, in effect, has gone in two opposing directions. As we saw in the preceding section, lots of employees, and not just senior ones, are administrators. Even a delivery driver who must collect payment from the recipient of the goods is necessarily a kind of mandatary or agent, since he is performing a legal act in the name of his employer that binds the employer. In the other direction, some courts have been too willing to see employees as fiduciaries merely on the basis of seniority. Seniority alone does not create a relationship of administration.

---

[42] Civil Code of Québec, art 2088: 'The employee is bound . . . to act faithfully and honestly' / 'Le salarié . . . doit agir avec loyauté et honnêteté'; *Tunnard* (n 38), [26].

[43] Madeleine Cantin Cumyn, 'L'obligation de loyauté dans les services de placement' (2012) 3 Bulletin de droit économique 19; Cantin Cumyn and Cumyn (n 18), 281–83; A Frazer, 'The Employee's Contractual Duty of Fidelity' (2015) 131 LQR 53; *Ranson* (n 25), [41]–[43]; *Smile Inc* (n 38), [51]–[55].

[44] Chapter 3, section II.

[45] If I buy goods, the seller, being obliged to deliver them, is in a sense obliged to act in the furtherance of my interests.

Other false flags relate to the rule against unauthorized profits. For example, it is sometimes observed that an employee cannot lawfully take a bribe, and must give it up if he does. This, it may be suggested, shows that employees are administrators. But this does not follow. There are other explanations for why a person cannot lawfully take a bribe, and why that person might have to give it up if he does take one. Consider the case of a security guard who accepts a bribe in order to leave a door unlocked, or to let someone in to the premises, or to provide information about the security system. Every one of these acts is a breach of the contract of employment. The first two moreover involve the misuse of the employer's property, and the third, of confidential information. In other words, each of these possibilities is doubly unlawful, as constituting a breach of contract and an extracontractual wrong or fault.[46] In fact, in the common law bribery (including of an employee) is a named tort, committed by both the briber and the bribee.[47] We should not be very surprised that the employee is liable. Nor should we be surprised if the law makes him liable to surrender the amount of the bribe. In the common law, such a gain-based measure is possible for the profitable misuse of confidential information[48] and possibly for a profitable breach of contract.[49] It is certainly available when a defendant has profited by misusing the plaintiff's property.[50] Such gain-based remedies for wrongdoing are increasingly recognized in the civil law as well.[51]

What is characteristic about a relationship of administration is that the administrator must surrender unauthorized profits even *without* having done anything wrong.[52] In that context, accountability for the profit is not a sanction or remedy for doing something wrong. The rule against unauthorized profits is what *creates* a new primary obligation, to hand over the profit. As a result, the security guard bribe case, if it is based on breach of contract, tells us nothing about whether the employment relationship is fiduciary. More relevant is an inquiry

---

[46] In some civil law systems, all of the wrongs would be classified as contractual as they arise in the course of a contractual relationship. Even so, it is true to say that each of the three possibilities would give rise to extracontractual liability were it to be committed outside of a contractual relationship.

[47] Paul M Perell, 'Remedies for the Victims of a Bribe' (1999) 22 Advocates' Q 198. Other ways in which the bribing non-employee may be liable in the common law are for conspiracy and inducing breach of contract; if the employee is a fiduciary, then another possibility is knowing assistance in a breach of fiduciary duty (see *Enbridge Gas* (n 41). All of these could constitute fault in the civil law.

[48] *Cadbury Schweppes Inc v FBI Foods Ltd* [1999] 1 SCR 142, 167 DLR (4th) 577.

[49] *Attorney-General v Blake* [2001] 1 AC 268 (HL); see also *Atlantic Lottery Corp v Babstock* 2020 SCC 19.

[50] The defendant in the well-known case *Edwards v Lee's Administrator* 96 SW2d 1028 (Ky CA, 1936) was liable for profits made by charging third parties to trespass on the plaintiff's land, which seems directly relevant to the case of a bribe for physical access.

[51] Ewoud Hondius and André Janssen (eds), *Disgorgement of Profits: Gain-Based Remedies Throughout the World* (Springer 2015).

[52] Chapter 5, section II.B.

of this kind: What if the security guard, while doing his job, learned from a conversation that his employer was going to buy a plot of land in another part of the city, and the guard, correctly foreseeing that this would raise land values, made a profit by acquiring some land in that neighbourhood? Unless this was a misuse of confidential information, it seems that he could keep the profit. An administrator could not.

It is also true that a fiduciary or other administrator is accountable, and this creates primary and ongoing obligations to disclose anything relevant to the administration, including his own breaches of duty, the acquisition of an unauthorized profit, or the presence of an actual or potential conflict in relation to the proper use his administrative powers or that is relevant to the beneficiary's decision-making.[53] These obligations do not arise in the case of employees.[54]

Another false flag also leads to potential confusion with the rule against unauthorized profits. As we saw in an earlier chapter, employees may have positive contractual obligations to seek out and to secure certain opportunities for the employer.[55] If such an employee instead takes the opportunity for himself, that is a breach of contract. Moreover, the primary obligation, to hand over or at least offer the opportunity or its fruits to the employer, might be specifically enforceable, in civil law or in common law. This would lead to the result that the profit is taken away (rather than leading to a claim in damages for loss caused).[56] This looks somewhat like the rule against unauthorized profits, but as we have seen, it is not. The rule that prevents an administrator from keeping an unauthorized profit applies regardless of whether the profit or opportunity should have been, or even could have been, obtained for the beneficiary. The employment-based rule is almost the opposite: it applies only to opportunities that were 'in the line of business' of the employer, and only if the employee was independently obliged (usually by contract) to procure that advantage for the employer. It is also true that the employees who are going to have the most wide-ranging *contractual* obligations to seek out opportunities for the employer are senior employees, like officers, who are likely to be administrators in any event. This may be part of the confusion that leads to the thought that seniority itself creates a relationship of administration or a fiduciary relationship.

---

[53] Chapter 5, section VIII.
[54] The clearest example is *Bell v Lever Bros Ltd* [1932] AC 161, discussed in Brodie (n 39), 201; see also *Ranson* (n 25), [44]–[58].
[55] Chapter 5, section VII.
[56] Although even a claim framed as a claim for loss may be assessed at the value of the gain extracted by the employee, if the employee was obliged to ensure that the gain accrued to the employer.

C. Trust protectors

Common law trusts now often have one or more persons in the role of 'protector'. This term does not have a fixed meaning but speaking generally, the protector is given certain powers in relation to the trust that, in the absence of a protector, would be held by the trustee. For this reason, US law may refer to this as a case of 'directed trusteeship'.[57] Examples of powers held by protectors include a power to remove and appoint trustees; a power to approve some exercises of powers by trustees in order for them to be effective; and a power to add or remove beneficiaries. Inevitably the question arises whether the protector holds these powers as an administrator, or not. In the language of the common law, the question will be whether the protector holds the powers in a fiduciary capacity. If they do, then all of the principles discussed in Section II.A will presumptively apply, including the requirement of loyalty, the rules about conflicts, and the rules about the attribution of profits. Moreover, in this case the role of protector will almost certainly be construed as an office, meaning that the court will have a supervisory jurisdiction potentially allowing it to remove or appoint protectors, just as it can remove or appoint trustees.[58] On the other hand, if the protector does not hold their powers in a fiduciary capacity, then the presumptive consequences are the opposite.[59] The only controls will be imposed by the limits of the power and by the requirement of good faith. Moreover, since the protector in this alternative holds the power for their own benefit, it may be accessible by their creditors, which may give the creditors access to the trust property via exercise of the non-fiduciary power.[60]

In one well-known English case, the power was to remove and appoint trustees. The judge tested the case by asking whether the person holding that power could sell the office of trustee to the highest bidder. Concluding that the answer was obviously negative, he held that the power was held in an administrative capacity.[61] In a more recent case, the judge said:

---

[57] The Uniform Directed Trust Act, promulgated in 2017 by the US Uniform Law Commission, may be found at https://www.uniformlaws.org/.

[58] Chapter 1, section V.B.3.d.

[59] Some suggest that there is an intermediate position of a 'qualified fiduciary power': see David Russell and Toby Graham, 'Protector Questions' (2020) 26 Trusts & Trustees 709, where the power-holder is also explicitly a member of the class who can benefit from the exercise of the power. It seems easier to say that this is a fiduciary power, and that the principles that would therefore *presumptively* apply may be disapplied in part, to give effect to the terms of the power and the express authorization for the power-holder to benefit himself. See chapter 3, section V.

[60] *Tasarruf Mevduati Sigorta Fonu v Merrill Lynch Bank and Trust Company (Cayman) Ltd* [2011] UKPC 17, [2012] 1 WLR 1721; *Pugachev* (n 14). Indeed this consequence may follow where even a trustee holds a non-fiduciary power in relation to the trust property: *Grosse v Grosse* 2015 SKCA 68; *Clayton v Clayton* [2016] NZSC 29; *Webb v Webb* 2020 UKPC 22 (PC). These cases show courts may ignore an attempt to dress a power up as fiduciary (or 'qualified fiduciary' (see n 59)); if the reality is that the power-holder can do whatever they wish with the power, it cannot be fiduciary.

[61] *Re Skeats' Settlement* (1889) 42 ChD 522 (ChD), 526.

The task of construction is to consider objectively what the purpose is for which the power has been conferred. Putting it another way, the question is: for whose benefit, as a matter of construction of the trust deed, has the power been given?[62]

In other words, the question is the same one that is always determinative when asking whether a power is held in an administrative capacity or not: Does the person hold the power as an asset and for their own benefit, or were they granted it in order to pursue an other-regarding mission?[63]

III. Legal powers over non-financial or extrapatrimonial interests

A. Introduction

Another dimension of the widening reach of administration in private law relates to powers over non-financial interests. The best example of this situation is where one person has the power to make decisions on behalf of another person relating to medical treatment or health care. Such a relationship fits precisely the description of a relationship of administration. One person holds a discretionary legal authority or power that affects another, but the first person holds the power not *over* the second person, but *for and on behalf* of the other person. The first person has been given the power in order to allow them to pursue the task or mission of taking care of the health of the other person. The result is that the first person does not hold the power to do with as they please. The difference from the kinds of relationships that we have been considering up to this point is that the power is not a power to acquire or alienate assets, or to make or break contracts, but to make decisions relating to a person's body and their health.

There are many examples of these relationships. Parents, or those with parental authority, hold such powers over minor children, although in this context the details of the legal relationship are likely to evolve as the child approaches the age of majority.[64] A person who has reached the age of majority may lack capacity to make their own health-care decisions. Either as a result of a formal document that they executed earlier, or as a result of some judicial or administrative

---

[62] *Pugachev* (n 14), [203].
[63] For a detailed analysis in this sense, see Paul B Miller, 'Regularizing the Trust Protector' (2018) 103 Iowa L Rev 2097.
[64] Parents are discussed specifically below in section V.

procedure, one or more persons may then acquire the authority to make health-care decisions for the incapacitated person. In a medical emergency, a person may be unconscious or otherwise incapable of giving consent to medical treatment, and here the law often grants one or more other persons the authority to make those decisions. When the emergency is extreme, it may be the case that a health-care practitioner can treat without consent, which effectively means that the practitioner has the authority to make the relevant decisions on behalf of the patient.

Just as in relationships of administration over financial interests, this power is acquired in order to permit the accomplishment of a mission, assignment, function, or charge: in this case, to look after the health of the other. As a result, just as in those cases, the power must be exercised in the pursuit of this mission. In this context, this means that the decision-maker must use the power in what he or she believes to be the best interests of the other person. But, as in some other relationships of administration, the wishes of the beneficiary are controlling.[65] Hence the decision-maker must also take account of any relevant wishes of the other person that have earlier been validly expressed. Thus the Civil Code of Québec provides, in art 12:

> A person who gives his consent to or refuses care for another person is bound to act in the sole interest of that person, complying, as far as possible, with any wishes the latter may have expressed.[66]

The need to take account of expressed wishes is exactly consistent with what is seen when a relationship of administration of financial interests is created by a capacitated beneficiary, typically through agency or mandate.[67] Moreover, just as in that context, delegation will not generally be permissible.[68] When a patient, or the legal system, grants substitute decision-making power to a person, that person is being authorized to use their own judgment to do what they think is best for the patient; this is not consistent with delegation.

The interests at stake here—health, well-being, life itself—are obviously just as important as pecuniary interests, if not more so. The law protects these interests as legal rights, with corresponding duties, just as it protects pecuniary interests. Legal relationships involving the administration of these non-pecuniary interests are legal relationships of private administration.[69]

---

[65] Chapter 1, section V.B.3.c.
[66] Cf the Ontario *Health Care Consent Act, 1996*, SO 1996, c 2, Sched A, s 21.
[67] Chapter 1, section V.B.3.c.
[68] Chapter 3, section IV.E.
[69] See Cantin Cumyn (n 22); Paul B Miller, 'A Theory of Fiduciary Liability' (2011) 56 McGill LJ 235, 276.

B. Conflicts and unauthorized profits

What of the rules about conflicts? If these powers can only be properly exercised in the best interests of the beneficiary, the logic of the conflicts rules would seem to require that these powers cannot rightly be exercised in a conflict situation. Take the case of an elderly person who has lost the capacity to make care decisions, but who, being single, has named her adult son as her substitute decision-maker. As would often be the case, assume that the son will benefit under the parent's will when the parent dies. Now if the full rigour of the conflicts rules were to apply here, we might think that this child would be disqualified from acting as substitute decision-maker, at least if treatment or non-treatment involves any risk of death. This is because the child stands to gain financially on the death of the parent, and that interest could interfere with the exercise of his judgment in relation to treatment decisions.

The rules on conflicts of interest are not, however, typically invoked in these situations. The explanation is that the conflict is implicitly authorized in advance. The parent, naming her son as substitute decision-maker, is aware that the son will benefit from her estate but she names him nonetheless. Thus we might say that there has been an implicit authorization for decision-making in a conflict situation, and informed consent by the beneficiary is sufficient to disapply the rules about conflicts.[70] If a settlor creates a trust in which the trustee is also one of the beneficiaries, there is an implicit but effective advance authorization for the trustee/beneficiary to exercise powers while in a conflict. In the same way, a court in authorizing a person to make care decisions will know, if they are a family member, that it is quite likely that they will stand to benefit from the death of the patient. We might say something similar about the rule against unauthorized profits: there is implicit authorization for the advantage that will be acquired should the patient die.[71] But the applicability otherwise of that rule remains: if the decision-maker were to take a bribe from someone in order to make a care decision in a certain way, the rule against unauthorized profits should certainly apply.[72]

---

[70] Chapter 4, section VII.A.

[71] That profit is in any event not obviously linked directly to the managerial role, since it arises from the death of the patient, not from acting as a decision-maker, although the link is arguably present in some cases. For example, the decision-maker might refuse some potentially life-saving intervention, for the (proper) reasons that this is what the parent would have wanted, or that it is not in her best interests to prolong suffering. In such a case one could say that the inheritance arises quite directly out of the decision-making function and thus that it might be caught by the rule against unauthorized profits, were the profit not implicitly authorized.

[72] The decision-maker would be accountable to the incapacitated person for the bribe. Were the incapacitated person to die in such a case, it is possible that the decision-maker would be incapacitated from inheriting via the principles of unworthy heirs in civil law, or, in the terminology of the common law, some variation of the law of forfeiture (called in the United States the 'slayer rule') that

C. Doubts about the administration of non-financial interests

It may not be obvious that relationships involving the administration of non-financial interests can attract the same kind of regulation that applies to the administration of financial interests. In the common law, a person holding the power to make medical decisions on behalf of another may not routinely be classified as being in a fiduciary relationship with that person. This section aims to make sense of this reluctance.

At one level, it seems uncontroversial that non-financial interests can be subject to fiduciary regulation. If a person is engaged in a legal dispute with another person about custody of their joint children, then each litigant's lawyer will uncontroversially be in a fiduciary relationship with their own client. It does not matter that there is no money claim involved in the litigation, and that these lawyers are protecting non-pecuniary interests. Thus there is no rule against seeing fiduciary relationships as confined only to the administration of property, money, or pecuniary interests.

In the common law, some courts and scholars take the view that the only rules that are properly called 'fiduciary' are the rules about conflicts and about unauthorized profits.[73] For the reasons discussed in the previous subsection, these rules are less likely to appear in the context of the administration of non-financial interests, and this might lead some to take the view that such relationships are therefore not fiduciary. Conversely, for one who holds that view about which rules are properly called 'fiduciary', the presence and operation of one of those rules will overcome any reluctance to find a fiduciary relationship.

In *Breen v Williams*,[74] the High Court of Australia is understood to have adopted that narrow view of which duties are 'fiduciary'.[75] The case concerned the physician–patient relationship, in relation to a demand by a patient for physical possession of items in her doctor's files. The relationship in question was not one in which the physician was empowered to make care decisions; it was an advisory relationship, discussed in the subsection immediately below. Gummow J stated that the advisory doctor–patient relationship is fiduciary, while four of the other five judges accepted that some aspects of the relationship are or might be

---

prevents inheritance through illegal acts. Those principles however do not depend on the existence of a relationship of administration.

[73] Chapter 3, section I.B.
[74] (1995) 186 CLR 71.
[75] This was confirmed in *Pilmer* (n 13) and is often referred to as the 'proscriptive only' view: fiduciary duties are only proscriptive, not prescriptive, being the 'duty' not to acquire unauthorized profits and the 'duty' not to *be* in a conflict. For arguments that these rules are not duties as such, see Chapter 4, section II.B.4; Chapter 5, section II.B. For a full argument that the 'proscriptive only' view is based on a misapprehension, see Smith, 'Prescriptive Fiduciary Duties' (n 1).

fiduciary in nature.[76] Interesting for the present point is the statement of Dawson and Toohey JJ:

> it is conceivable that a doctor may place himself in a position with potential for a conflict of interest—if, for example, the doctor has a financial interest in a hospital or a pathology laboratory—so as to give rise to fiduciary obligations.[77]

The reasoning seems to be the wrong way around; unless there was a fiduciary relationship, the doctor would be free to act while in a conflict, and to extract profits. But what this shows is that as soon as the rules about conflicts and unauthorized profits make a clear appearance with financial consequences, the scepticism about finding a relationship of administration in relation to non-financial interests drops away.

The problem is that those proscriptive rules, as we have seen, are not definitive of a relationship of administration. They are ways in which the law supports the requirement of loyalty, and gives effect to the other-regarding nature of a relationship of administration. It is the holding of powers for and on behalf of another person that generates such a relationship. It is clear that such powers can be held in relation to non-pecuniary interests.

IV. Factual powers

A. Advisors

There are many settings in which people are treated as administrators, even though they do not hold *legal* powers on behalf of another person. The common law is very clear that a fiduciary relationship can sometimes be found in a purely advisory relationship, and this appears to be possible in the civil law as well.

Many lawyers are in this relationship with each of their clients. If there is litigation under way, or even certain kinds of negotiation, then the lawyer may be the client's agent or mandatary, holding a legal power of representation, and that is always a relationship of administration.[78] But the lawyer is *always* treated as being in such a relationship, even if there is no communication or dealing with third parties. In those cases, the lawyer is only advising the client, and so not exercising legal powers on behalf of the client.[79] We might also think of real

---

[76] *Breen* (n 74), 134 (Gummow J), 93–94 (Dawson and Toohey JJ), 107–08 (Gaudron and McHugh JJ). Even in a fiduciary relationship, rights to information do not as such give rise to rights to physical possession of particular things belonging to the fiduciary, which was the actual claim in *Breen*.
[77] ibid.
[78] On legal representation, see Chapter 1, section V.B.3.b.
[79] Eg *Strother* (n 12).

estate agents or agents in the entertainment industry: they advise their clients, but (speaking generally) they do not make contracts in their name and on their behalf. They do not hold a power of legal representation, and are rather advisors. In at least some jurisdictions, the relationship between a medical doctor and her patient is treated as a relationship of administration.[80] This is so even though the doctor does not usually have the power to give consent to treatment on behalf of the plaintiff.[81] In other words, the aspect of the relationship that attracts the norms of administration is the advisory aspect, which includes the prescription of medication and all other recommendations relating to treatment.[82]

Thus lawyers and agents, and in some jurisdictions physicians are treated as administrators even if the relationship is purely advisory. This is not a conclusion reached on an ad hoc analysis, but is rather based on the characteristics of the category of relationship.

In addition to this, other advisory relationships may be classified as fiduciary based on the characteristics of the particular relationship.[83] An investment advisor who actually manages the client's assets, in the sense of buying and selling investments, is clearly an administrator, being an agent or a mandatary.[84] Civilian authors have noted that investment advisors may be in a contract of service with their client, but in some cases, there may also be a contract of mandate or a relationship of the administration of the property of another, both of which are relationships of patrimonial administration.[85] But some investment advisors only give advice, leaving the client to make the actual decisions. Here, common law courts have held that the relationship may or may not be fiduciary. The courts will examine the particular relationship and if it reveals

---

[80] *Wohlgemuth v Meyer* 139 Cal App2d 326, 293 P2d 816 (1st Dist, 1956); *McInerney v MacDonald* [1992] 2 SCR 138, 93 DLR (4th) 415; see also *Breen* (n 74), discussed in the preceding subsection. In *Sidaway v Board of Governors of the Bethlem Royal Hospital* [1985] AC 871 (HL), 884, one judge opined in *obiter dicta* that the physician–patient relationship is not fiduciary. For an argument that English law should recognize this relationship as fiduciary, see Suzanne Ost, 'Breaching the Sexual Boundaries in the Doctor-Patient Relationship: Should English Law Recognize Fiduciary Duties?' (2016) 24 Medical L Rev 206.

[81] *Wohlgemuth* (ibid); *McInerney* (ibid); see also *Breen* (n 74), discussed in the preceding subsection. Characterizing a physician as a fiduciary in relation to the giving of advice (including the prescription of medication) does not necessarily extend to the physician's obligations in respect of treatment, which is not an advisory function. This has arguably been a source of confusion.

[82] Many have argued for extending this to the relationship between those who conduct medical research and the persons who are participating as subjects in the research: Madeline Motta, 'Fiduciary Obligations of the Physician Scientist in a Post Hippocratic Era', Doctor of Civil Law, McGill University, 2008, online at https://escholarship.mcgill.ca/concern/theses/1r66j143r.

[83] This 'ad hoc' analysis was discussed above in section II.A.

[84] The typical industry terminology, in Canada and the United States, is to describe such an account as 'discretionary' (eg *Prudential-Bache Commodities Canada Ltd v Placements Armand Laflamme Inc* [1998] RJQ 765 (CA)). This is somewhat misleading inasmuch as the giving of advice involves discretion in the sense of exercising judgment, and yet a purely advisory relationship is described as a 'non-discretionary' account.

[85] Crête (n 29); Cantin Cumyn and Cumyn (n 18), 119–21.

certain characteristics, a fiduciary relationship will be found.[86] This shows that as a matter of positive law, advisory relationships are frequently classified as relationships of administration.

How is the case of the advisor as administrator to be understood, when the paradigm case of administration involves legal powers? There are two possibilities, but only one seems to work. One possibility would be to say that upon closer inspection, these relationships *do* reveal legal powers. In some civil law jurisdictions, the relationship between mandator and mandatary is understood to require that the mandator have the power to represent the mandatary in the performance of a juridical act with a third party.[87] In those systems, one might say that a real estate agent (for example) is not really a mandatary, if he only gives advice to the client. But this would be to go too fast: even in an advisory relationship, where the advisor does not have the power to make contracts for the advisee, nonetheless the advisor may have the power to perform *some* juridical acts. It has been pointed out that communicating a contractual offer to the offeree is itself a juridical act, so in this sense the real estate agent can be a mandatary in Quebec law.[88] In the same way, investment advisors and lawyers are likely to have some authority in relation to communicating with third parties in ways that have juridical effects. A 'non-discretionary' investment advisor who leaves all of the decisions to the client may well execute the client's instructions once the decision is made, acting in this respect as an agent or mandatary. Physicians have a legal power to prescribe medications which itself can empower the patient legally to acquire something which otherwise they could not.[89]

But this approach of looking for juridical powers that are accessory to the advisory relationship does not seem to solve the problem. First, there are probably some cases of advisory relationships where, try as we might, no legal power can be found. The doctor–patient relationship might be an example, but some lawyer–client relationships are also purely advisory. A second and more important reason is that focusing on some minor legal power, such as a power to

---

[86] See for example *Tate v Williamson* (1866) 2 Ch App 55 (LC); *Daly v Sydney Stock Exchange Ltd* (1986) 160 CLR 371; *Hodgkinson v Simms* [1994] 3 SCR 377; *Wingecarribee Shire Council v Lehman Brothers Australia Ltd (in liq)* [2012] FCA 1028, [743]–[745]. Three of the five judges in *Breen v Williams* (n 74) relied on *Daly* to hold that at least some aspects of the advisory physician–patient relationship are fiduciary (107–08 (Gaudron and McHugh JJ), 134 (Gummow J)), apparently in every case rather than based on an examination of the particular relationship.

[87] Civil Code of Québec, art 2130. The majority view in French law seems to be the same: Huet and others (n 29), 998–1001. Swiss law is different however: Werro (n 21), 13–28; there can be a mandate even to perform a purely factual task.

[88] Popovici (n 32), 217–21.

[89] In *Norberg v Wynrib* [1992] 2 SCR 226, the defendant physician prescribed drugs to the plaintiff, to which the plaintiff was addicted, in exchange for sex. The majority resolved the case using tort law. L'Heureux-Dubé and McLachlin JJ held that the relationship was a fiduciary one, referring (275) to factual power as well as the power to prescribe: 'He had the power to advise her, to treat her, to give her the drug or to refuse her the drug'.

communicate an offer, will never explain enough. It will never explain why in at least some relationships, the giving of advice itself is treated as akin to the exercise of a legal power. It is the giving of advice that must be done loyally, and that attracts obligations of disclosure, as well as the rules against conflicts and unauthorized profits.

The other way to understand these situations is as cases in which the law treats the giving of advice as sufficiently similar to the exercise of a legal power that the legal incidents of a relationship of administration should properly apply. The giving of advice needs to be distinguished from the giving of information, even though both may be part of the same conversation. Giving advice means telling someone what you think is *their* best course of action in the prevailing circumstances. Advice, properly given, is necessarily other-regarding. If you counsel someone to do something because it is good for *you*, you are not really giving them advice; you are asking for a favour, or perhaps trying to manipulate them.[90] But it remains true that not every case of giving advice can be compared to the exercise of legal powers held for and on behalf of another person. For example, an interior decorator might give excellent advice on the selection of curtains. That advice should properly be given in the client's interest; the decorator should recommend, not necessarily what *he* would choose if it were his house, but what he thinks will suit the client's tastes, preferences, budget, and so on. But the advice in this case does not have a very significant effect on the client's life. A court would not likely treat this as a relationship of administration. This is not only because the choice of curtains may not be the most momentous event in the client's life. It is also because the client in this case is likely to be able to exercise his or her own judgment, much more so than in the case of a patient who receives medical advice (including the prescription of medication and advice about treatments) from a physician.

In one common law case in which a financial advisor was held to be a fiduciary, both the majority and the dissenting judges quoted and approved an earlier decision which held that a crucial factor is the degree to which the client was independent from the advisor in relation to decision-making.[91] In that earlier decision it was said: 'The relationship of the broker and client is elevated to a fiduciary level when the client reposes trust and confidence in the broker and relies on the broker's advice in making business decisions'.[92] When the client

---

[90] Cf Julien Valiergue, *Les conflits d'intérêts en droit privé* (LGDJ 2019), 124, citing Thomas Hobbes' *Leviathan*, where we read in ch XXV that '... between counsel and command, one great difference is, that command is directed to a man's own benefit; and counsel to the benefit of another man'; and '... we may set down for the first condition of a good counsellor, *that his ends, and interests, be not inconsistent with the ends and interests of him he counselleth*' (emphasis in original; Thomas Hobbes, *Leviathan*, John CA Gaskin (ed) (OUP 2008) 132, 133).

[91] *Hodgkinson* (n 86).

[92] *Varcoe v Sterling* (1992) 7 OR (3d) 204 (Gen Div), 236. Reliance was also a factor in the decision in *Daly* (n 86), 377, 385, and in *Wingecarribee Shire Council* (n 86).

trusts the advisor, and relies heavily on the advice in the sense that it is likely to be followed in most or all cases, we are close to a situation in which the advisor actually makes the decision, at least in a practical sense.[93] It is not surprising that such relationships may also, in the common law, attract a presumption of undue influence.[94]

It may be going too far to treat the advisor as having enough power to effectively make the decision. The common law cases, although they look for trust and confidence, are willing to classify the relationship as fiduciary without finding that the advisor is the one effectively making the decisions. Another explanation for the common law's reasoning here may relate to the difficulty of unpacking human decision-making. In several contexts, the common law accepts that it is not possible to disassemble analytically all of the elements that go into the making of a decision. One context is the law of duress, where it has been held that if we know that some illegitimate pressure was a *factor* in the making of a decision, the law may treat that pressure as legally operative even if we cannot say with certainty that the pressure was *decisive*.[95] There are two other examples of this reasoning within the law governing relationships of administration. First, if an administrator uses their other-regarding power while in a conflict, the exercise is always voidable; this is simply because no one can know whether the holder's judgment was affected by an improper purpose.[96] It is never necessary to show that the conflict *actually* influenced the power-holder. The second example is seen in the context of the 'fair-dealing' rule, when a fiduciary deals with his own beneficiary.[97] The fiduciary—whether an advisory fiduciary or one holding a legal power—is obliged to disclose any information that he holds and that is potentially relevant to the beneficiary's decision-making process.[98] A breach of this duty allows the beneficiary to set aside the contract, or to recover loss of which the non-disclosure was a but-for cause, even where the loss was also

---

[93] On the role of trust in these advisory fiduciary relationships, see Arthur B Laby, 'Advisors as Fiduciaries' (2020) 72 Florida L Rev 953 and Andrew S Gold, 'Trust and Advice' in PB Miller and Matthew Harding (eds), *Fiduciaries and Trust: Ethics, Politics, Economics and Law* (CUP 2020) 35. Laby argues (997) that '[t]rust leads to clients' reliance on the advisor and to vulnerability with respect to matters related to the advice'. This is a description of a factual (not a legal) power held by the advisor.

[94] This presumption arises in all fiduciary relationships, but also in some other relationships like husband–wife. In the common law, the law on fiduciary relationships and on undue influence grew out of common roots: Julius Grower, 'From Disability to Duty: From Constructive Fraud to Equitable Wrongs', Doctor of Philosophy, University College London, 2021. They were not treated as fully separate until quite recently (eg *Geffen v Goodman Estate* [1991] 2 SCR 353, 81 DLR (4th) 211; cf *Lloyds Bank Ltd v Bundy* [1975] QB 326 (CA), in which the majority do not clearly distinguish undue influence from the fiduciary relationship and its duties of disclosure).

[95] *Barton v Armstrong* [1976] AC 104 (PC).

[96] See Chapter 4, especially section IV.

[97] In these cases, the fiduciary is not exercising a fiduciary power but only their own contractual capacity. See Chapter 4, section II.B.3.

[98] Chapter 5, sections VIII.D–E.

caused by a business failure or fall in the market.[99] Moreover, the Privy Council has held that once unlawful non-disclosure is established, it should be presumed unless proven otherwise that the claimant's loss was caused by the wrongful non-disclosure.[100] In all of these settings, the law recognizes the impossibility of unpacking the details of human decision-making. It is not surprising, then, that if an advisor can be seen to have had a material impact on the advisee's decision-making process, the law can rightly treat the advice as determinative in that process even if it might not be possible to prove conclusively that it was. This may explain why the law assimilates advice to a legal decision-making power even in cases where the advisee remains visibly involved in the relevant decision.

It has been argued also in the civil law that even where an investment advisor has no legal powers, advice may generate a de facto power that can justify characterizing the relationship as one of administration, attracting the regime of mandate or of the administration of the property of others.[101] Beyond the investment context, civilians have also developed more general accounts of factual powers to permit them to be assimilated them to legal powers where appropriate. One author develops a theory of *pouvoir matériel* or 'factual power', that includes the influence that may arise in an advisory relationship.[102] Another suggests that the giving of advice can in the right cases be classified as an 'intellectual power'.[103]

This analysis is supported by considering the category of 'shadow director' known in UK company law. This is a person who does not hold the office of director, but whose instructions are followed by the actual directors.[104] The shadow director is treated as being in a fiduciary relationship with the company.[105] Thus, a person whose factual powers can be equated to the legal powers of a director is treated by the law as owing all the obligations of an actual director.[106]

---

[99] ibid.
[100] *London Loan & Savings Co v Brickenden* [1934] 3 DLR 465 (PC), 469. The importance of the *Brickenden* principle has been recognized in Canada (*Southwind v Canada* 2021 SCC 28, [82]) and in Singapore (*Sim Poh Ping v Winsta Holding Pte Ltd* [2020] SGCA 35).
[101] Crête (n 29), 294.
[102] Thibault Douville, *Les conflits d'intérêts en droit privé* (Institut Universitaire Varenne 2014), 73–81.
[103] Valiergue (n 90), 123–36. Valiergue (73–74) disagrees with Douville (ibid) that factual powers attract the same regulation as juridical powers, but these authors have common ground inasmuch as both count the giving of advice as potentially regulated by the rules of administration. Valiergue counts intellectual powers (including the giving of advice) as juridical (not factual) powers on the view that the advisor is a co-author of the advisee's legal acts (123).
[104] Companies Act 2006, s 251(1): 'In the Companies Acts "shadow director", in relation to a company, means a person in accordance with whose directions or instructions the directors of the company are accustomed to act'.
[105] In addition to a number of provisions that specifically apply the Act to shadow directors, see s 170(5): 'The general duties [of directors, in ss 171–177] apply to shadow directors where, and to the extent that, the corresponding common law rules or equitable principles so apply'.
[106] In the next section we will consider the slightly different situation of 'de facto' directors. They also lack juridical powers. However they are treated as directors, not because their advice is routinely followed, but because they have themselves acted as if they hold a directorial position.

Some scholars resist the idea that purely factual powers can create a relationship of administration. Paul Miller, for example, would treat advisory relationships as regulated solely by the law of contract; this follows from his definition of the fiduciary relationship as one that includes legal power.[107] As we have seen above, though, this position does not square well with the positive law. In attempting to define a concept, it is usual to look for some essential feature or characteristic; for some concepts, we may articulate a list of features that are individually necessary and collectively sufficient for us to say that a posited candidate is an example of the concept. It is possible, however, that the case of advisors may help us to see that relationships of administration are not definable in the usual way. They may rather be 'cluster models' or 'cluster concepts'.[108] Often these are the result of semantic and conceptual evolution over time. In these cases, it is not possible to produce a list of features that are individually necessary and collectively sufficient. For example, in relation to one item on the list of features (which may in some cases be a list with only one entry), there may be two or more *alternatives*, each capable of allowing us to say that the posited candidate is an example of the concept (assuming any other items on the list of features are also present).[109] In this way, the other-regarding factual power that may exist in advisory relationships can qualify such relationships as relationships of administration, even in the absence of other-regarding juridical powers.

What happens when an advisory relationship is classified as a relationship of administration? Unlike in the exercise of a legal power, there is no possibility of 'setting aside' advice that was improperly given, because advice is not a legal construct like the making of a contract.[110] But other aspects of a relationship of administration are imported. For example, the administrator is accountable in the wide sense of that word, and so must disclose to the client all information relevant to the client's decision-making, including, but not limited to, any potential or actual conflict of interest.[111] In the case of an advisory relationship,

---

[107] Paul B Miller, 'The Fiduciary Relationship' in Andrew S Gold and Paul B Miller (eds), *Philosophical Foundations of Fiduciary Law* (OUP 2014) 63, 69–73 (fiduciary relationships always involve legal power held on behalf of another), 83–84 (advisory relationships as such are not fiduciary relationships).

[108] George Lakoff, *Women, Fire and Dangerous Things: What Categories Reveal about the Mind* (Chicago UP 1987), 74–76, arguing that 'mother' is a 'cluster model', so that there is no single essential list of characteristics that make someone a mother; Natalie Stoljar, 'Essence, Identity, and the Concept of Woman' (1995) 23 Philosophical Topics 261, arguing that 'woman' is a cluster concept, such that (264) '[t]here is no single set of features an individual must have in order to be a woman; she is a member of the type just in case she participates in the relevant resemblance structure'. I thank Carolyn McLeod for introducing me to cluster concepts.

[109] In some contexts, a cluster concept may be instantiated by the posited candidate where it possesses a sufficient number of a list of characteristics: Stoljar (ibid) 281–82.

[110] Chapter 3, section IV.F.

[111] Chapter 5, section VIII.C. There it was explained that this is wider than the disclosure of a conflict that may be necessary in order for an administrator's power to be exercised unimpeachably (which does not apply directly to advisors); a duty of disclosure arises when the *beneficiary* of the administrator has to make a decision, which is the core case in advisory relationships.

the client is inevitably making a decision in reliance on the advice, so the result is that conflicts must always be disclosed.[112] The failure to disclose relevant information to the beneficiary allows the beneficiary to set aside any contract made with the advisor.[113] In the presence of a duty to disclose, non-disclosure is a legal wrong.[114] Many cases arising out of advisory relationships of administration are cases in which the plaintiff client seeks damages for non-disclosure of a conflict.[115] In my view, the physician's obligation to disclose the risks of a procedure or treatment that is being advised is an obligation that arises precisely out of the other-regarding nature of this advisory relationship.[116] Again, it relates to information in the possession of the physician that is relevant for the patient in making their own decision. Information about risks is not information about a conflict, but it is information that is pertinent to the client's decision-making.[117] In the same category is information relating to past malpractice or error. Core private law administrators such as directors, mandataries, and agents must disclose their own breaches of duties.[118] The same is true of advisors who are in an administrative relationship, and for the same reasons: they are acting for and on behalf of the beneficiary.[119] The beneficiary cannot make an informed decision about their rights if they do not know what they are.

---

[112] This obviously includes any financial interest the advisor has in the course of conduct that is being advised, unless perhaps it is obvious. In the context of medical practice and research, the definitions of conflicts that have been elaborated are comparable to those that were used in Chapter 4, section III: Stephen R Latham, 'Conflict of Interest in Medical Practice' in Michael Davis and Andrew Stark (eds), *Conflict of Interest in the Professions* (OUP 2001) 279, 283; Bernard Lo and Marilyn J Field (eds), *Conflict of Interest in Medical Research, Education, and Practice* (National Academies Press 2009) ch 2. For discussion of some effects of undisclosed conflicts in medical practice, see Atul Gawande, 'The Cost Conundrum', *The New Yorker*, 25 May 2009.

[113] Chapter 5, section VIII.D. Valiergue (n 90), 195, discusses a decision of the *Cour de cassation* (1re civ, 13 avril 1983, Bull civ I 119, No 81-16.728) in which it applied by analogy art 1596 of the Civil Code to an advisor who did not have a legal power of representation, allowing the client to annul sales to advisors who bought the beneficiary's land through an intermediary. The article according to its text (see Chapter 4, section II.A) does not apply to advisors.

[114] Raymonde Crête and Cinthia Duclos, 'Les sanctions civiles en cas de manquements professionels dans les services de placement' in Raymonde Crête and others (eds), *Courtiers et conseillers financiers: encadrement des services de placement* (Éditions Yvons Blais 2011) 361, 385–89; Douville (n 102), 515–17, referring to this obligation in many advisory contexts.

[115] Lawyers: *Nocton v Lord Ashburton* [1914] AC 932 (HL); *London Loan & Savings Co v Brickenden* [1934] 3 DLR 465 (PC); *Canson Enterprises Ltd v Boughton & Co* [1991] 3 SCR 534; *Swindle v Harrison* [1997] 4 All ER 705 (CA). Financial advisors: *Hodgkinson* (n 86); see also *Merrill Lynch, Pierce, Fenner & Smith, Inc v Cheng* 901 F2d 1124 (DC Cir, 1990) (liability for non-disclosure that client had the right to reject unauthorized transactions). Physician: *Moore v Regents of University of California* 51 Cal3d 120, 793 P2d 479 (SC, 1990).

[116] In the common law, this duty of the physician is fully recognized but courts and commentators have struggled to explain it; Allan Beever, *A Theory of Tort Liability* (Hart 2016), ch 15. Some courts, however, tied it to the fiduciary nature of the physician–patient relationship (eg *Moore* (ibid)). In *Kenny v Lockwood* [1932] OR 141, [1932] 1 DLR 507 (CA), the Ontario Court of Appeal applied the fiduciary duty of disclosure recognized in *Nocton*, ibid, to an advising physician.

[117] We have seen that such information must be disclosed: Chapter 5, sections VIII.B-D.

[118] Chapter 5, section VII.B.3.

[119] Gerald B Robertson, 'When Things Go Wrong: The Duty to Disclose Medical Error' (2002) 28 Queen's LJ 353.

The rule against unauthorized profits should also apply to advisory administrators.[120] And although advice as such cannot be set aside, we have already seen that if the beneficiary contracts with their own fiduciary and the latter fails to disclose all relevant information that they hold, including but not limited to conflicts, the beneficiary will be able to set aside that contract.[121] This certainly applies to advisors.[122]

Thus in the right circumstances, an advisory relationship will be treated as a relationship of administration. The consequences will be the same as in other such relationships, with the necessary modifications arising out of the fact that in an advisory relationship, the administrator does not hold legal powers.

B. De facto relationships

The common law recognizes 'de facto' fiduciaries.[123] In most of the established categories of fiduciary relationship, it has been held that if a person *acts as if* they are in such a relationship, they will be treated as owing the obligations that apply to that relationship. The longest-established example may be that a person who acts as if he is an executor, without having been appointed as such, can be classified as an executor *de son tort*: that is, an executor by his own wrongful act.[124] In this context, a 'wrongful act' means not necessarily an unlawful act, but something done without authority. A person becomes an executor *de son tort* by doing or purporting to do an act that could only rightfully be done by an executor, such as purporting to pay the debts of the estate or to sell the deceased's assets. Such a finding will mean that the executor *de son tort* is potentially liable to third parties, such as creditors of the estate, and that all of the obligations of executorship in relation to the beneficiaries and creditors of the estate will arise.[125]

The same principle has since been applied to trustees, to corporate directors, and to agents. In relation to trustees, Lord Millett said:

---

[120] In *Breen* (n 74), it was suggested by two judges that the rules about conflicts and unauthorized profits apply to advising physicians (quoted above, n 77).

[121] Chapter 4, section V.C.

[122] Eg *Tate v Williamson* (1866) 2 Ch App 55 (LC); *McKenzie v McDonald* [1927] VLR 134; *Maguire v Makaronis* (1997) 188 CLR 449.

[123] Whether there is a corresponding category in the civil law tradition will be considered at the end of this section.

[124] *Coote v Whittington* (1873) LR 16 Eq 534, referring to a statute of Elizabeth I.

[125] *Loewen Funeral Chapel Ltd v Yanz* (1999) 136 Man R (2d) 318 (QB). In *Charron v Montreal Trust Co* [1958] OR 597, 15 DLR (2d) 240 (CA), relying on 18th century English authority, the Court held that if a defendant who is sued as an executor makes any plea other than denying that they are an executor, they become an executor *de son tort*.

They meant 'trustee de son tort'; that is to say, a person who, though not appointed to be a trustee, nevertheless takes it upon himself to act as such and to discharge the duties of a trustee on behalf of others.... Substituting dog Latin for bastard French, we would do better today to describe such persons as de facto trustees. In their relations with the beneficiaries they are treated in every respect as if they had been duly appointed. They are true trustees and are fully subject to fiduciary obligations. Their liability is strict; it does not depend on dishonesty.[126]

The same category exists in relation to corporate directors[127] and in relation to agents, where it is sometimes called a 'self-appointed agent'.[128]

The foundation of these de facto relationships is not always clear. We have already discussed how both the common law and the civil law protect those who rely in good faith on the appearance of authority even when authority is absent, using the ideas of 'ostensible authority' or 'apparent mandate' or, more generally, a 'theory of appearances'.[129] Those rules, however, are primarily concerned with the relationship between the third party outsider and the principal or mandatary who is responsible for the appearance of authority; and those rules are apt to create relationships between the principal or mandator and third parties. The result of a finding of self-appointed agency is different; such a finding creates a fiduciary relationship between the self-appointed agent and the principal.

In de facto directors, there may be some reference to holding out by the company. The effects of such holding out, in relation to third parties, could be understood on the same principles as those that govern apparent authority. But, as in agency, to find a fiduciary relationship between the de facto director and the company, it is not enough to look at what the *company* did in relation to third parties. The effects on the relationship between the de facto director and the company must be based on what the de facto director did. And it is the same with de facto trustees and executors *de son tort*, if the person is to be found to be in a fiduciary relationship with the beneficiaries.

In some of these cases, the de facto fiduciary, though lacking legal powers, may have had some factual power. This is sometimes said to be necessary for de facto trustees, and it is present in many cases of executors *de son tort*; for example, they may have paid debts of the estate using estate assets. But it is not clear that it is essential in either case, nor in the cases of self-appointed agents or de

---

[126] *Dubai Aluminium Co v Salaam* [2002] UKHL 48, [2003] 2 AC 366, [138].
[127] *Ultraframe (UK) Ltd v Fielding* [2005] EWHC 1638 (Ch), [1254]–[1257] (appeal as to costs dismissed, [2006] EWCA Civ 1660).
[128] *English v Dedham Vale Properties Ltd* [1978] 1 WLR 93; Michael Bryan, 'Boardman v Phipps' in Charles Mitchell and Paul Mitchell (eds), *Landmark Cases in Equity* (Hart 2012) 581, at 587–89.
[129] Chapter 3, section IV.F.3.

facto directors. One persuasive account of the governing principle is in *Gibson v Barton*.[130] The appellant was convicted of an offence of not complying with a duty imposed by statute on corporate directors and managers. He appealed, arguing in part that he was not appointed as either director or manager, even though he had so acted. The appeal was dismissed. One of the judges in the majority, Blackburn J, said:[131]

> The question, therefore, is, whether a person who is thus a manager de son tort,—a manager in his own wrong,—whether he can protect himself from the liability cast upon a manager under s 27, by saying, 'I am not manager de jure.' I think he cannot. There are many instances in which a person who de facto exercises an office cannot defend himself by saying, when he is called upon to bear liability in consequence of his wrong, 'I am not rightfully in the office, there is another man who may turn me out.' An executor de son tort is an instance in which a man incurs all the liabilities of an executor as to third persons, and he is not permitted to say, 'I am not executor; there is another man who may take out probate.' The answer is, 'Your liability as to a third person rests upon your being executor de son tort; you have usurped the office and must bear the liabilities.' So, if there was a disseisor in old times who turned out the rightful owner of the land and became freeholder by wrong, he could not, if he was indicted ratione tenuræ[132] for not repairing a bridge or not cleansing a harbour, say, 'Though I am in actual possession of the property I will prove that I am only a usurper; that the rightful heir, who is supposed to be dead, is alive, and I set up that as a defence, and say I am not a freeholder in law.' The answer would be at once, 'You are freeholder in your own wrong, and you must incur the liabilities so long as you are freeholder.' So, if a director were to set up in answer to a penalty under s 27, that he was not a director, that he was illegally elected, the answer would be, 'You have acted as director, and were a director in your own wrong.'

The governing principle is therefore arguably related to the principles in 'holding out' or apparent mandate, even though it is not exactly the same. In the holding out cases, there are three parties—or, two parties and the rest of the world. A holds out B, towards C or towards the world in general, as having some level of authority. Against C, or someone else in good faith, A cannot deny the truth of his earlier holding out of B. The principle with which we are concerned, however, applies where one holds *oneself* out. This holding out of oneself cannot bind anyone else, but as in ostensible authority, it binds the person who does the

---

[130] (1875) LR 10 QB 329 (DC).
[131] At 338.
[132] By reason of his tenure: the reference is to the situation in which the person having freehold tenure of land was, by that reason alone, subject to obligations to maintain a bridge or a harbour.

holding out. Thus, A holds out *A* as having a level of authority, and the result is that against someone in good faith, A cannot deny the truth of his earlier holding out of himself. So if you purport to act as an agent, a trustee, a director, an executor, then you are treated as what you purported to be, against outsiders and even against the beneficiaries of the fiduciary relationship so created.[133]

In the common law, the effects of 'holding out' have often been viewed as a kind of estoppel by representation, although this is theoretically awkward because holding someone out to the whole world cannot be directly compared to making a statement of law or fact to a person who relies upon it.[134] This may be why, even though the civil law does not have a general doctrine of estoppel by representation, nonetheless it has a well-established law of apparent mandate, which may be part of a wider theory of appearances. If this is correct, the common law's experience of de facto fiduciaries may well be one which could find a parallel in the civil law. One author, while showing that Quebec civil law does not have a doctrine of estoppel, noted:

> Indeed it must be an axiom, in the law of all civilized countries, that no party will be allowed to assume in an action before the courts an attitude contrary to that which he assumed at the transaction which is the cause of litigation.[135]

This idea seems to be attracting an increasing interest in the civil law tradition.[136] More recently, a leading author has discussed case law in Quebec that recognized that a person can become a de facto administrator of the property of others, with all of the obligations that this entails.[137]

The effect in these situations is that the person who assumed to act in a role is subjected to the same obligations to which he would be subject if he had been

---

[133] In *Re O'Reilly (No 2)* (1981) 28 OR (2d) 481, 111 DLR (3d) 238 (HC), aff'd (1981), 33 OR (2d) 352, 123 DLR (3d) 767n (CA), parties were held not to be de facto executors because they had not possessed the relevant land *as executors*, but had possessed it under colour of right as their own.

[134] Francis MB Reynolds, 'The Ultimate Apparent Authority' (1994) 110 LQR 21.

[135] ADP Heeney, 'Estoppel in the Law of Quebec' (1930) 8 Can Bar Rev 401 & 500, 508.

[136] Bénédicte Fauvarque-Cosson (ed), *La confiance légitime et l'estoppel* (Société de legislation comparée 2006). In the French report in this volume Denis Mazeaud, although focusing on contractual relationships, discusses a principle of French law that one may not contradict oneself to the detriment of another, and mentions (at 276) a decision of the *Cour de cassation* (1re civ, 6 juillet 2005, Bull civ I 302, No 01-15.912) which is founded upon 'la règle de l'estoppel'. In relation to German law on 'contrary behaviour', see the contribution of Florian Faust and Volker Wiese to the same volume, 115–18.

[137] Cantin Cumyn (n 22), 219–20, discussing *Kyprianou v Kyprianou* [2004] RJQ 293 (CS). Civil law in the French tradition knows a situation called *porte-fort* (which could be rendered in English as 'guarantee' in a non-technical sense). In *porte-fort*, A contracts with B on the basis that A is acting for C; both A and B know that A is without actual authority from C, but A undertakes to get from C a ratification of C to be bound to the contract with B. This is a kind of self-appointed mandate, but this legal institution is not what we are considering, because it is not capable of creating obligations between A and C without C's ratification.

properly appointed. These are all relationships of administration, and so this includes all of the rules that apply to such cases.[138]

V. Parents

There has been some controversy over whether parents can rightly be seen as being in a relationship of administration with their children. In common law, the relationship has been recognized as a fiduciary one by the Supreme Court of Canada[139] and by some US courts.[140] This has often been in cases involving incestuous sexual assault. The fiduciary status of the relationship may give rise to a longer limitation period. It may also create obligations of disclosure, the breach of which may be a separate wrong that prolongs the limitation period. These obligations have sometimes been used to explain the liability of the non-assaulting parent who knew of the abuse but did not alert the authorities.[141] Principles relating to conflicts of interest have also occasionally been applied.[142]

There are a couple of reasons why the relationship between a parent and child has only recently been seen as a relationship of administration. First, the older view was that parents had rights over their children. But this, in a way, is nonsense: you can have rights against a person, but not over them. So-called parental rights are not rights against children; they are prerogatives that allow parents to make decisions for and on behalf of their children, during the time that the children lack the maturity to make their own decisions.[143] In the terms of this book, no one would deny today that parents hold these powers for and on behalf of their children.[144] The law gives them to parents not for the benefit of the

---

[138] The rule against unauthorized profits was applied to self-appointed agents in *Boardman v Phipps* [1967] 2 AC 46 (HL) and in *English* (n 128).

[139] *M (K) v M (H)* [1992] 3 SCR 6, 96 DLR (4th) 289. The New Zealand Court of Appeal has also accepted that the relationship between a parent and their minor child is fiduciary: *D v A* [2022] NZCA 430. In a case involving a guardian, the Full Court of the Federal Court of Australia opined that such a claim was 'most unlikely to be upheld by Australian courts': *Paramasivam v Flynn* [1998] FCA 1711, 90 FCR 489, 160 ALR 203 (FCFCA), [79].

[140] *Evans v Eckelman* 265 Cal Rptr 605 (Cal App 1 Dist, 1990) (foster parent).

[141] *J (LA) v J (H)* (1993) 13 OR (3d) 306, 102 DLR (4th) 177 (Gen Div).

[142] *Ohio Casualty Insurance Co v Mallison* 223 Ore 406, 354 P2d 800 (1960); *Secretary, Department of Health and Community Services v JWB* (1992) 175 CLR 218 (judgment of McHugh J). For a more detailed discussion of parenthood as a fiduciary relationship, including whether and how the rule against unauthorized profits could apply in this context, see Smith (n 11).

[143] Henri Capitant, 'Sur l'abus des droits' (1928) 27 Revue trimestrielle de droit civil 365 observed in relation to parental authority (at 372–73): 'Cette autorité, qui impose des charges à celui qui en est investi, qui est organisé non en vue de son intérêt mais au profit d'une autre personne, ne ressemble en rien à un droit'. My translation: 'This authority, which imposes burdens on the one who holds it, which is structured not with eye on their interests but for the benefit of another person, bears no resemblance to a right'.

[144] The relationship of parenthood is therefore a crucial indicator that the presence of other-regarding powers is diagnostic of relationships of administration. An 'undertaking', while it may be

parents, but for the benefit of the children. The civilian terminology of 'parental authority' is a better way of capturing these powers than 'parental rights'. Second, even though parents have these legal powers, they are generally legal powers over non-financial or non-patrimonial interests, a category discussed above.[145] They include the power to make decisions relating to medical care, but also decisions relating to education, faith, discipline, and where the child shall live. It is also true that parents have substantial factual power over their children, also a category discussed above.[146] Whether the parent is giving advice or orders, their wishes are likely to be followed, regardless of the exact contours of the parent's legal powers. Thus the parent–child relationship partakes of two of the categories discussed earlier in this chapter, both of which are outside the core paradigm of powers to manage financial or patrimonial interests, the paradigm which was the concern of Section II.A.

Of course there *may* be a relationship of administration of financial interests, but this is atypical. In the normal case, the child's own assets are not large and the parent is constantly using his or her own resources for the benefit of the child. If, perhaps by inheritance or by being a talented artist, the child did have substantial assets, then a parent who managed those assets would be in a standard relationship of administration with respect to them. This has always been more obvious when the person holding parental authority is not the parent in the affective sense of the word. If someone is in the role of guardian or tutor of the child (and this might include the State, via some agency) then in respect of the child's assets, the guardian or tutor is obviously in a relationship of administration.[147]

But as we have seen, a relationship of administration can be founded on powers over non-financial interests, and such powers will always be present in relationship where one person holds parental authority over another. This juridical relationship is not necessarily an affective relationship; for example, the State may hold parental authority. The administrator in the relationship is thus not necessarily a biological parent, but is rather the person or persons who hold parental authority, because that authority contains the legal powers that found the relationship of administration. That relationship is separate from the duty of support, which can arise from biological parentage and can exist separately from parental authority. A person who owes support but has no parental authority is not in a relationship of administration.[148] Conversely, we can certainly imagine

important in many contexts (above, section II.A, and Chapter 2, section III.A.5), is not definitionally essential.

[145] Section III.
[146] Section IV.
[147] *Clay v Clay* (2001) 202 CLR 410.
[148] *Louie v Lastman (No 1)* (2002) 61 OR (3d) 449, 217 DLR (4th) 257 (CA).

that a de facto parent could be understood to be in a relationship of administration even if he or she did not have juridical parental authority over the child. As we have seen, in relation to other relationships of administration there is a systematic recognition of de facto versions of the relationship.[149]

Of course, the parent–child relationship has many differences from the other kinds of relationships that have been discussed in this chapter. The family is more complicated in its affective and juridical structure than other private law relationships. A parent cannot isolate his decisions regarding a child from those regarding another child, and since the parent is himself a member of the family, he or she must be able to take account of his own interests in some sense.[150] Moreover, the parent–child relationship is generally overlain with affective bonds of love which the law must respect, and must be reluctant to attempt to regulate. Another consideration is that in most relationships of administration, the administrator enters the relationship voluntarily; this is not true in the same way in relation to parenthood. Moreover, although it is legally possible to 'resign' from the role of parent, and indeed to be removed involuntarily from that role by a court, this is obviously a much more emotionally and legally complicated question than in relationship to pecuniary administration.

However, even though the law must be cautious about interfering in family life, it is clear that it must step in sometimes, and where this becomes necessarily, it seems impossible to deny that parental authority is held by the parent for the benefit of the child. In the case where parental authority is held by someone other than a biological parent, perhaps especially when it is held by the State, the role of the legal regulation of parental authority is more evident. But inevitably, it is also more evident when parents betray their children, and this may be why so many of the cases that have discussed the fiduciary nature of parenthood have been cases of parental sexual abuse.

---

[149] Section IV.
[150] This possibility is not unknown in relationships of a financial nature: see Chapter 3, sections IV.B.1. and V, and for explanation in more detail in the parental context, Smith (n 11), 446–51.

PART II.C

THE ENFORCEMENT AND SUPERVISION OF PRIVATE ADMINISTRATION

8
The Enforcement and Supervision of Private Administration

I. Introduction

Private law administration typically involves supervision and enforcement by the beneficiaries. The duties described earlier in this study, owed by administrators in relation to their administration, are owed to the beneficiaries, who have the power to enforce them.

There are two reasons for this short chapter on enforcement. One is simply to examine how, in some situations, enforcement is more complicated. The law has some systems to deal with these complications; in many cases these systems create another layer of private administration.

The other reason is to generate a vocabulary in relation to these systems of enforcement, which will be called upon later when we consider the enforcement of norms of public administration.

II. Rights and powers, and their enforcement and supervision

A. Rights and their enforcement

Standing in private law is usually uncomplicated inasmuch as it generally corresponds to the holding of rights. If someone has a right, they have a power to enforce it, whether it is a primary right, that arises by consent or otherwise without wrongdoing (such as a right to performance of a contract) or a secondary right, that arises via the breach of a primary right (such as a right to damages). Conceptually, however, the ability or power to enforce a right is separate from the right itself.[1] One illustration of this is that in both common law and civil law, there are legal rights that are unenforceable.[2]

---

[1] Timothy Liau, 'Privity: Rights, Standing, and the Road Not Taken' (2021) 41 OJLS 803.
[2] An example that operates in both traditions is a debt claim which has become unenforceable due to the passage of time: Stephen A Smith, *Rights, Wrongs, and Injustices* (OUP 2019), 284–86; Didier Lluelles and Benoît Moore, *Droit des obligations* (3rd edn, Thémis 2018), ¶¶ 12–19.1. Another

Another illustration is that, as we will see in this chapter, it is quite common in both traditions for a person other than the right-holder to have the power to enforce the right held by the right-holder. Such situations are frequently relationships of administration. This is not conceptually essential: it is possible to have the ability to enforce the right of another, and to have that ability for one's own benefit. If this seems strange, it is only necessary to think of the law relating to secured lending or execution of judgments: a creditor may have the power to sell their debtor's assets or to enforce the claims that their debtor has against third parties, and the creditor holds that power for their own benefit, in order to satisfy the debt owing to them.[3] The examples of enforcement by a person who is not the right-holder that we will see in this chapter are, however, mostly relationships of administration.

'Standing' could be defined simply as the power to enforce a right.[4] Others might confine 'standing' to situations where a person does not hold the right they are enforcing; still others might confine it to situations where a person does not simply *hold* a power of enforcement, but rather must seek the authorization of the court to enforce. In what follows I will not use 'standing' to refer to every power of enforcement. The power of enforcement that is held by the right-holder herself will be called 'direct enforcement'. In many situations, a person has the power to enforce a right that they do not hold, but the enforcing person does not need to seek any new authorization to do so, because they have already been granted that power by an agreement or by a court or in some other way. For example, a lawyer may have been authorized to start a lawsuit on behalf of their client. This will be called 'representative enforcement'. This will leave 'standing' with a narrower focus, which will appear to some extent in this chapter and to a greater extent when we turn to public law.[5]

B. Powers and their supervision

As we have seen, relationships of administration involve duties owed to the beneficiaries, but they also involve jural relationships that are not right-duty relationships.[6] This is because in relationships of administration, the

well-known example in the common law is that contractual claims may be unenforceable for want of writing under the *Statute of Frauds* and its descendants, but it is clear that such claims, although unenforceable, are valid in law: Smith, ibid 277–78.

[3] See also Chapter 1, section V.B.3.2 on the interaction of legal representation with mandate and agency.
[4] Liau (n 1), 805: '... standing is a power of enforcement'.
[5] Below I will introduce the terms 'proper person standing' (section III.C.2.c) and 'designated person standing' (section III.D).
[6] Especially Chapter 3, section IV.G; Chapter 4, sections II.B.4, V.

administrator holds legal powers; and typically, these powers are discretionary. This means that no one holds a *right* that the power be exercised, or be exercised with a certain outcome, or not be exercised. On the contrary, the administrator exercises judgment as to whether and when to exercise the power. Moreover, we have seen that when the power is exercised disloyally, or in a conflict situation, the exercise is liable to be set aside, subject to protections for third parties.

Consider the case in which a person, A, has entered into a contract under some serious mistake that was brought about by the other party, B. Even if B was acting perfectly innocently, A can probably set the contract aside. This power held by A does not arise because B did something unlawful.[7] It arises because consent is constitutive of a legal act, and consent is undermined by a serious mistake. In this case, it is so natural to give A the power to set aside such a contract that we do not think much about it. Some systems may also give such a power to B, which is perhaps a little less obvious.[8] But either way, the idea of a power of enforcement as separate from right-holding is evident here, since there is no relevant right but only a power.

This is also very important in relationships of administration. Where the powers of the administrator are discretionary, the beneficiary has no right that the power be, or not be, exercised. Moreover, the disloyal or conflicted exercise of a power by an administrator is not, by itself, a breach of duty.[9] Someone, however, must hold the power to have the exercise set aside. The beneficiary does, but as we will see later in this chapter, others may also.

III. Mechanisms of enforcement and supervision

A. Non-legal norms

Sometimes non-legal norms assist in enforcement. There can be, and there are, both legal and non-legal versions of the idea that we should keep our promises, and sometimes only the non-legal version is applicable, as where a

---

[7] Particularly in the civil law, but also in the common law, we might say that A holds a 'right' to have the contract annulled or avoided; see Chapter 1, section IV.A.2. In Hohfeldian terms it is a power, since there is no corresponding duty but only a liability.
[8] Civil Code of Québec, art 1420: 'The relative nullity of a contract may be invoked only by the person in whose interest it is established or by the other contracting party, provided he is acting in good faith and suffers serious injury therefrom...'
[9] Chapter 3, section IV.G; Chapter 4, Section V. 'By itself' because it may be accompanied by a breach of duty (such as one or more of the duties discussed in Chapter 6).

person promises to meet his friend for coffee. The same can be true in some contexts of private law administration. For example, some people may, by instinct or reflection, refuse to act in situations of conflict of interest, even though there may not be a legal norm that disqualifies them from acting. Conflict rules are quite pervasive in private law administration but one example in which non-legal norms might be relevant is the case in which an adult child is asked to make a decision about discontinuing life-supporting treatment for an elderly, unconscious, and seriously ill parent. If the child stands to inherit all of the parent's assets, they might not feel comfortable making such a decision.[10]

Since this study is concerned primarily with how we act for others in law, and with the legal regulation of acting for others, this non-legal aspect is noted but not further explored.

B. Criminal law

The most egregious violations of the norms with which we are interested may attract the sanctions of criminal law. An agent or mandatary may commit an offence by receiving a corrupt bribe, and the same may be true of a trustee who fraudulently takes trust property.[11]

These offences could be thought of as means to enforce sound administration, but they do not operate to the benefit of the beneficiary. Criminalization is called for when wrongful conduct is sufficiently serious to activate a *public* interest. There is a public interest in having a society in which people do not lie, cheat, and steal. Thus these crimes might be said to support the relationship of administration, by sanctioning some grievous infractions, in the same way that criminal law supports our right to bodily integrity by criminalizing serious infringements of that right. But even though a physical assault may be a crime, protecting the public interest in having a non-violent society, the victim still has their own private law right of action, protecting their own private interest. Putting an embezzling trustee in jail does not directly enforce their role as trustee. Separate steps, drawing on the law of private administration, would be needed to remove that person as a trustee; to appoint a new one if necessary; and, in an appropriate case, to order that the wrongdoing trustee replenish the trust fund.

---

[10] The case was discussed in Chapter 7, section III.B, where it was suggested that the naming of this person (whether by the court or by the parent earlier) is likely to be an implicit authorization to act in the conflict, thus disapplying the *legal* rule.

[11] To take the Canadian provisions as an example: *Criminal Code*, RSC 1985, c C-46, ss 426, 336.

C. Private law powers of enforcement and supervision

1. Direct enforcement

Typically, the beneficiary of administration holds rights that correspond to the duties of the administrator, duties that have been described earlier. Some of these rights might be called rights of supervision: for example, the administrator must produce accounts and certain other information, at the demand of the beneficiary and in some cases without being specifically asked.[12] This information allows the beneficiary to supervise the administration. The beneficiary holds a power of enforcement in relation to such rights.

The beneficiary can also enforce the rules about proper exercise of powers, and the rules about not exercising powers in conflict situations, by setting aside legal acts of the administrator. Here the beneficiary does not have rights in the strict sense, since they do not have a right that the administrator should exercise or not exercise the administrator's powers. The beneficiary holds a power of enforcement in relation to the proper exercise of the administrator's powers.

The beneficiary also holds a power of enforcement in relation to the rule against unauthorized profits; the beneficiary can demand that the administrator account for such profits to the beneficiary. The beneficiary can also enforce other duties, such as duties of careful administration, or duties to follow the terms of the particular administration. This may be through the accounting process or by other legal action against the administrator. For example, the accounting process might be used to disallow unauthorized expenditures. The duty of care and skill was historically enforced in English trust law by taking an account 'on the footing of wilful default' and 'surcharging' the account with what the trustees *would hold* in trust if they had not breached the duty.[13] Today, it might simply be framed as an action for damages.[14] To take another example, if a trust beneficiary is entitled to the income of the trust property and has not been paid, an action can be brought against the trustee to enforce this right.

2. Representative enforcement

Private law administration is often supervised and enforced through representative action. By this, I refer to the situation in which a person is empowered to enforce a legal right that does not belong to the person. This section aims to produce a typology of at least some of these situations, including some reference to the justifications for allowing representative enforcement and to techniques which may exist to make representative enforcement effective.

---

[12] Chapter 5, section VIII.
[13] *Bartlett v Barclays Bank Trust Co (Nos 1 and 2)* [1980] Ch 515.
[14] *Fales v Canada Permanent Trust Co* [1977] 2 SCR 302.

a) Delegated representation of a capacitated person

This is illustrated by a simple case of agency or mandate. A person engages a lawyer to launch a lawsuit on the person's behalf. The function of this kind of legal representation is to allow a fully capacitated person to act through another, in order to take advantage of the other's expertise, or possibly for reasons of convenience.[15] Representation of this kind is necessarily an administrative role. It is likely to be governed by contract, although whether or not that is the case, the representative is presumptively entitled to recover their properly incurred costs.

If the rights that are being enforced in the lawsuit are themselves rights relating to proper administration, then this creates a relationship of administration in respect of a relationship of administration. Imagine that an adult beneficiary of a trust engages a lawyer to sue the trustees, because the beneficiary believes that the trust is not being run properly. To the extent that the lawyer is the delegate who is enforcing the beneficiary's rights against the trustees, the lawyer is an administrator of the beneficiary's rights against the trustees; and those rights are rights to the due administration of the trust by the trustees.

b) Delegated or appointed representation of an incapacitated person

A person lacking full legal capacity may need another person to enforce their rights. A parent may have this role in relation to their child, and an incapacitated adult might also need a representative. Such guardians, tutors, or curators may be designated by the law (as parents may be for children), or be named by a court, or they may have been named by the incapacitated adult before they lost capacity. That is a kind of delegation in advance. Some of these roles are indefinite in scope or time frame, but in other cases a person may be a 'litigation guardian' to another, for the purposes of a particular legal proceeding.

This kind of representation is necessitated by the absence of full capacity on the part of the right-holder. It creates a relationship of administration, and once again the representative is presumptively entitled to recover their properly incurred costs. If the rights being enforced are rights to due administration (as where the child is a trust beneficiary suing the trustees), then again there will be a relationship of administration in respect of a relationship of administration.[16]

c) Appointed representation of a capacitated person

This is like the first category above inasmuch as the beneficiary is capacitated, but also like some parts of the second category inasmuch as the authority of the administrator does not come by delegation. An important example arises in a corporate representative action, sometimes called a derivative action. The rights

---

[15] On legal representation, see Chapter 1, section V.B.3.b.1.
[16] If the litigation guardian engages a lawyer, there may be three relationships of administration.

of business and other corporations are usually enforced through delegated representation, discussed above: the corporation takes steps to enforce its rights through its agents or mandataries, who are likely senior employees.

In the representative action, an interested person may seek, of their own motion, authority to represent the corporation in litigation. Very often, the context is that it is thought that the corporation has rights against one or more members of its own board of directors, or perhaps its upper managerial employees, for breaches of some of their duties. The board or the senior management typically hold the legal authority to decide whether the corporation shall pursue claims that it may have. Thus the classic problem in this situation is that the alleged wrongdoers may themselves have the power to decide whether they shall be called to account. This will be called the problem of self-supervision.

Of course, it is a kind of conflict of interest for a person to exercise a corporate power relating to litigation strategy when that person is the potential defendant. One way in which this has been addressed is by empowering the court to authorize the bringing of a representative action, allowing a shareholder (or perhaps some other interested party) to enforce the rights of the corporation. It is a temporary suspension of the normal rules of corporate governance; the justification for this must be found in an alleged misuse of power, or at least in the need for management of a conflict situation.[17] Inevitably the court that has this authority has the power to authorize that the costs of the litigation shall be borne by the corporation, since it is the corporation's rights that are being enforced and since the benefit of that enforcement, if any, will endure to the corporation.

This scenario brings in an important variation from the cases that have been discussed previously. The shareholder or other interested party—call them the applicant—does not automatically hold power of enforcement in relation to the rights of the corporation. The applicant has an interest, not a right, in relation to enforcement. This is one of the situations in which the language of 'standing' is typically used, because the applicant is not enforcing their own right (it is not direct enforcement), nor do they hold a pre-existing power of enforcement in relation to corporate rights (it is not simple representative enforcement). The applicant is presenting himself as a proper person to be *granted* a power of representative enforcement, on the basis of being qualified by an affected interest (not a right). This could be called 'proper person' standing.[18]

---

[17] We have seen that it is a well-known conflict management tool to temporarily disqualify the person or persons who are conflicted: Chapter 4, section VII.C.

[18] It goes without saying that if the applicant is granted the authority to bring the representative action, the applicant will be in a relationship of administration (in the common law, a fiduciary relationship) with the corporation.

d) Private law class action

A class action allows a particular kind of representative enforcement. The class representative or lead plaintiff is empowered, usually by the order of a court, to enforce the claims of all members of the plaintiff class. The lead plaintiff, however, is also a member of the class and so they are not *only* acting as a representative. This particular kind of representation usually depends upon legislative authority, since the members of the plaintiff class are generally capacitated, and yet they are represented without their having given any express authorization (although typically they are empowered to opt out).[19] A justification for such regimes is that the individual claims are too small to be economically viable, creating the risk that a defendant may not be held to account for large-scale wrongdoing.

Two aspects of the legal costs of such litigation are noteworthy. First, the quantum of the lead plaintiff's financial interest is unlikely to justify the risk for that person of bearing the legal costs of losing, or, one might say, even of winning, if costs are recovered by the winner but on less than a full indemnity basis (and a fortiori in systems, such as the general regime in the United States, where even a winning party is not typically awarded costs). This problem is inherent to this type of proceeding. This is why the action is generally feasible only on some kind of contingency arrangement, whether it is the lead plaintiff's lawyers or a third party that underwrites the risks. In some jurisdictions a public body may provide financial support.[20] In jurisdictions where a losing litigant pays the other side's costs, such arrangements may involve indemnifying the lead plaintiff against the risk of liability to pay the costs of the defendant.[21] Second, even if we set aside any concern about the lawyers' fees, there is a serious difficulty about whether any person would spend years litigating a claim that might be worth $25 to them even if they win. This is why, in some class action litigation in Canada and the United States, the lead plaintiff may be awarded extra compensation if the claim succeeds. In *Garland v Enbridge Gas Distribution Inc*,[22] a settlement of $22,000,000 was agreed in litigation that had been twice to the Supreme Court of Canada over twelve years. The lead plaintiff sought an award of $95,000, to be paid out of the portion of the award that was approved for his counsel's fees;

---

[19] However, in the common law tradition it was possible for something like a class action to occur even in the absence of legislation via the making of 'representative orders': see *Carnie v Esanda Finance Corp* (1995) 182 CLR 398, 427–29.

[20] Catherine Piché, 'Public Financiers as Overseers of Class Proceedings' (2016) 12 NYU J of Law and Business 776.

[21] Law Commission of Ontario, *Class Actions: Objectives, Experiences and Reforms: Final Report* (Law Commission of Ontario 2019) 80.

[22] (2006), 56 CPC (6th) 357. As a matter of disclosure, I note that I was a research consultant to the law firm engaged by the lead plaintiff.

he was awarded $25,000, in part because he acted in the public interest.[23] Such awards for lead plaintiffs are not automatic, nor are they usually so high.[24]

Although the compensation to the lead plaintiff was said to be based partly on the consideration that he had acted in the public interest, it is not clear that the interest of such a class, even though it is a large class, is always equivalent to the public interest. Vindicating the financial interests of a group of people is acting in their private interests, even if the group is a large one. But acting on behalf of the plaintiff class could be seen to justify an award of compensation out of funds that would otherwise go to the plaintiff class, without necessarily characterizing it as acting in the public interest. It can be justified as having benefited the private interests of the class members. The whole structure of class actions is designed in part to solve a collective action problem and to empower others—sometimes a judge, sometimes the lead plaintiff, sometimes the lead plaintiff subject to the approval of a judge—to make decisions for and on behalf of the plaintiff class. At the same time, one justification for class actions, as mentioned above, is that they help address the risk that a defendant may not be held to account for large-scale wrongdoing, and also to address the problems of access to justice that are particularly acute in relation to smaller claims. There is a public interest in access to justice and in having effective accountability for private wrongs, so that class actions could be said to have a hybrid public–private character.[25] In this sense, the class interest may correspond to a public interest. Even so, it seems right to say that the lead plaintiff's duties are to the members of the class; they are not public duties or duties to proceed in the public interest.

This leads us to notice that as in all the other examples of representation above, the relationship between a lead plaintiff and the plaintiff class is a relationship of administration. This follows inevitably from the fact that the lead plaintiff has been empowered by the court, when it certifies or authorizes the class action, to administer the litigation rights of the members of the class.[26] Thus where

---

[23] At [46]. His appeal against that decision was discontinued (2008 ONCA 13) when his lawyers agreed that he could have $95,000 out of the settlement funds that were approved by the court below for their fees.

[24] See Theodore Eisenberg and Geoffrey P Miller, 'Incentive Awards to Class Action Plaintiffs: An Empirical Study' (2006) 53 UCLA L Rev 1303. Some Canadian cases are collected in Warren K Winkler and Sharon D Matthews, 'Caught in a Trap—Ethical Considerations for the Plaintiff's Lawyer in Class Proceedings' (2008) online at https://www.ontariocourts.ca/coa/about-the-court/archives/caught/, text at notes 44–47, and Catherine Piché, *Fairness in Class Action Settlements* (Carswell 2011), 114–15.

[25] One way in which this has been evidenced in the United States and Canada is that often class action settlements are not even distributed to the class members (who may be impossible to contact), but rather to a charity that is thought to be related in some way to the litigation. This was done in *Garland*. See Jasminka Kalajdzic, 'The "Illusion of Compensation": Cy Près Distributions in Canadian Class Actions' (2013) 92 Can Bar Rev 173 and Law Commission of Ontario (n 21), 64–65, 91.

[26] See Piché (n 24), 109–15.

the class is asserting rights relating to administration, there are again multiple relationships of administration.[27] The basic claim in the lawsuit arises out of a relationship of administration, or an alleged one; but the rights of the plaintiff class are being administered by the lead plaintiff, and that person's rights, and powers as an administrator, are in turn to some extent administered through delegation to the lawyers whom the lead plaintiff has engaged.[28] One difference, however, from the examples discussed above is that almost any significant step that the lead plaintiff makes (such as settling or abandoning the action) may require the approval of the court, in a supervisory jurisdiction.[29] In a supervisory jurisdiction, the court does not act as a neutral arbiter but, acting like an administrator, attends to the best interests of one or more persons.[30] Thus this type of administration is more closely monitored than many others. Significant decisions are not only potentially reviewed after the fact if someone complains, but rather are reviewed in real time before they can take effect.

e) *Supervision and enforcement by beneficiaries and others on behalf of the class of beneficiaries*

Supervision and enforcement in the context of trusts and estates deserves its own attention. In some ways it operates rather like a class action, although without any machinery for the approval of a class action or of a settlement thereof.

In trusts and estates of deceased persons, any beneficiary has the standing to demand accounts, and to enforce the proper administration of the trust fund or the estate. This includes claims for loss caused by careless management, claims for unauthorized disbursements, and claims for unauthorized profits. Speaking generally, however, a successful claim of this kind does not put money directly into the pocket of the claiming beneficiary. In trusts, this is because the beneficiary may have no immediate right to *any* of the trust property; whether or not they do is determined by the terms of the trust, and may need to await future events.[31] For example, a beneficiary may be entitled to a share of the capital but only after some living person's death. Speaking generally, then, a successful claim

---

[27] As in *Alberta v Elder Advocates of Alberta Society* 2011 SCC 24, [2011] 2 SCR 261, a class action for breach of fiduciary duties.

[28] The lead plaintiff's lawyer is understood, like the lead plaintiff, to owe professional and private law duties to the whole class once the action is certified: Simone Degeling and Michael Legg, 'Fiduciary Obligations of Lawyers in Australian Class Actions: Conflicts between Duties' (2014) 37 UNSWLJ 914; Piché (n 24), 103–09. Piché notes (106) that in Quebec, however, it has been held that the lawyer's relationship is only with the lead plaintiff.

[29] Supervisory jurisdictions are discussed in Chapter 1, section V.B.3.d.

[30] Some US courts have said that the judge who is scrutinizing a proposed settlement should act as though they owed a fiduciary duty to the plaintiff class (eg *Kaufman v American Express Travel Related Services Co* 877 F3d 276 (7th CCA, 2017), 283).

[31] The same may be true in relation to the estate of a deceased person, as even in the absence of a testamentary trust the entitlement of a particular beneficiary may not be evident until some time after death, depending on the terms of the will and the complexity of estate administration.

will lead to an order against the trustee that aims to replenish or restore the trust fund, or that requires the trustee to hold an unauthorized profit as part of the trust fund. Depending on the facts, the trustee or executor may also be replaced, although that is a separate question. Whether the beneficiary who brought proceedings ever gets any of the trust fund is determined by other considerations.

A trust fund is not a legal person, and nor is the succession or the estate of a deceased person. Beneficiaries cannot therefore be seen as representing the trust or the estate, but any beneficiary can be seen as acting on behalf of the whole class of beneficiaries in asserting a common interest in the proper administration of the trust or estate.[32] Somewhat like a class action, then, this is a kind of self-appointed representative enforcement, by someone who is also personally interested.[33] If the integrity of the fund is maintained, then the interests of all beneficiaries are protected, including potential future beneficiaries; what each beneficiary ultimately obtains is determined by the terms of the trust or the will. Only if, in the events that have transpired, a beneficiary is currently entitled to some defined part of the fund will such a proceeding lead to an order that a sum of money be paid directly to the beneficiary.[34] There are, however, important differences from a class action; most obviously, a plaintiff beneficiary does not need to have the proceeding 'certified' by a judge, and cannot compromise the rights of another beneficiary. The normal course would be to ensure that all beneficiaries and potential beneficiaries have notice and the opportunity to participate in the litigation, which is likely to be more feasible than in the class action context.[35]

Even a person who is not a beneficiary in the strict sense may be able to assert rights of supervision and enforcement. Those who are only the 'objects' of discretionary powers do not, by definition, have any right to any trust property, and so they are not trust beneficiaries in the strict sense.[36] In the same way, they cannot demand that the powers of which they are objects be exercised in their favour;

---

[32] In the civil law, the succession of a deceased person may be seen as an independent patrimony; that is, a legal universality of rights and obligations. This is not a legal person, but it is a legal construct which an administrator can administer.

[33] It has been argued, by analogy to corporate derivative actions and to trustees' rights as administrators, that in appropriate cases beneficiaries should be able to secure an order that their legal costs be paid out of the trust property: Tang Hang Wu, 'Derivative Actions on Behalf of the Trust: Beddoe Orders for Beneficiaries' in Richard C Nolan, Kelvin FK Low, and Tang Hang Wu (eds), *Trusts and Modern Wealth Management* (CUP 2017) 221.

[34] *Boardman v Phipps* [1967] 2 AC 46 (HL).

[35] Indeed, if they choose not to do so, they may find that via notions such as abuse of process, they will not be permitted to start another proceeding relating to the same issues.

[36] The distinction is often difficult because trust instruments, lawyers, and judges often refer to objects of powers as 'beneficiaries'. The distinction was carefully drawn, however, in In *Grand View Private Trust Co v Wong* [2022] UKPC 47, [29], [33], [36]. On the terminology, see Lionel Smith, 'Massively Discretionary Trusts' (2017) 70 CLP 17, 18–29.

that decision belongs to the one who holds the power.[37] They do, however, have some supervision rights, at least to the extent of the proper exercise of the power of which they are objects.[38] This again is a kind of supervision on behalf of all the beneficiaries and indeed all of the objects of discretions as well: the whole class of those who will or may get trust property.

This representative supervision and enforcement sheds light on some other interesting features of the law of trusts and estates. For example, in the common law a co-trustee or co-executor, or a successor trustee or executor, has the power to enforce the obligations of the co-administrator or predecessor administrator.[39] That can only be a kind of representative enforcement, since a trustee or executor as such has no rights to any of the relevant property (except perhaps to recover expenses and for authorized remuneration).

Another representative enforcement mechanism in the common law and in Quebec civil law allows beneficiaries to enforce rights that they do not hold: in certain cases, beneficiaries may be allowed to enforce rights of trustees against third parties, where the trustees hold those rights for the benefit of beneficiaries but inexcusably fail to enforce those rights.[40] Similarly, beneficiaries of the estate of a deceased person, including creditors of the estate, can be allowed to enforce the rights of the executors against third parties.[41] This is a kind of representative enforcement in one's own interests, because the beneficiaries enforce the rights of the trustees, not for the benefit of the right-holder (the trustees) but for the benefit of the beneficiaries themselves. This is different from the more typical case of beneficiary enforcement with which this section began, because the rights discussed in that case—to information, or to enforce duties of care or the rule

---

[37] As discussed earlier (Chapter 3, section IV.A.2), this is why courts traditionally say that such powers must be exercised in the pursuit of the purpose for which they were granted.

[38] On the traditional view, objects can demand that trustees consider them as objects, and where trustees do not, can ask that trustees be replaced; in other words, their rights of supervision are limited to the supervision of the discretionary power of which they are objects. For discussion, see Smith (ibid), 400–01. It has been argued that Australian law grants objects full rights of supervision: Jessica Hudson, 'Mere and Other Discretionary Objects in Australia' in Ying Khai Liew and Matthew Harding (eds), *Asia-Pacific Trusts Law: Theory and Practice in Context* (Hart 2021) 19. One reason to be careful of this is that it seems to permit private trusts without beneficiaries (in the strict sense), but the common law does not traditionally allow such non-charitable purpose trusts.

[39] *Nelson v Larholt* [1948] 1 KB 339; *Young v Murphy* [1996] 1 VR 279 (CA); see also Donovan WM Waters, Mark Gillen, and Lionel Smith, *Waters' Law of Trusts in Canada* (5th edn, Thomson Reuters 2021) 1059–61. In *Turner v Turner* [1984] Ch 100 (ChD), trustees brought a proceeding to set aside their own improper exercises of power. The case is discussed in Chapter 3, section IV.F.1.

[40] Civil Code of Québec, art 1291; *Hayim v Citibank NA* [1987] AC 730 (PC), 747–79; *Parker-Tweedale v Dunbar Bank plc (No 1)* [1991] Ch 12 (CA), 19–20. In the common law the beneficiary issues proceedings against both the trustee and the third party, allowing the court to enforce the rights that the trustee holds against the third party as well as the beneficiary's rights against the trustee: *Harmer v Armstrong* [1934] Ch 65 (CA).

[41] This is what occurred in *Re Diplock* [1948] Ch 465, [1948] 2 All ER 318 (CA), affirmed *Ministry of Health v Simpson* [1951] AC 251; see the discussion in Lionel Smith, 'Unjust Enrichment, Property, and the Structure of Trusts' (2000) 116 LQR 412, 437–44. See also *Roberts v Gill & Co* [2010] UKSC 22, [2011] 1 AC 240.

against unauthorized profits—are held by the beneficiaries against the trustees. The fruits of those claims go to benefit all beneficiaries. Here the right is a right of the trustee against a third party; the beneficiary is allowed to enforce it, rather like a representative action in corporate law; again, the fruits of such claims go to benefit all beneficiaries.[42] One might think, as in corporate law, that this mechanism exists at least in part to address the problem of self-supervision.[43]

It is even more striking to find that non-persons sometimes have recognized rights and interests in trust law. Quebec law gives powers of supervision to as-yet unborn beneficiaries, who of course must be represented in this connection.[44] In the common law, when a court is considering an application to vary the terms of a trust under legislation that exists in most jurisdictions, it is empowered to consent to the variation on behalf of 'unborn persons' if it thinks the variation benefits them.[45] Speaking generally, in the common law and the civil law, a natural person is treated as coming into being for the purposes of criminal law, tort law or civil liability, and succession law when they are born alive, with some recognition of a foetus that is *en ventre sa mère* at the relevant time but is later born alive. In the case of 'unborn persons', by contrast, we are considering 'persons' who may never come into being. It is somewhat odd that they are treated as having justiciable interests and powers of enforcement. The logic again lies in viewing the beneficiaries as a class, a class which in some cases may have members added to it in the future.

D. Private purpose trusts: Powers of enforcement without rights

It has already been mentioned that in Quebec, there can be private purpose trusts without beneficiaries.[46] Moreover, even if a Quebec trust does have beneficiaries, it is arguably a private purpose trust, because the definition of the trust as a legal construct depends upon a purpose and not upon rights held by beneficiaries.[47]

If the trustee has legal duties relating to the trust, but there is no person who holds a corresponding right, then this is a rare example of undirected legal duties in private law. Such duties are common in public law, and the idea of undirected duties is explored in more detail in the next Part.[48] We have already seen that it

---

[42] The requirements and procedural mechanisms governing this recourse are not entirely clear, but leave of the court is almost certainly required.
[43] Above, section II.D.3.
[44] Civil Code of Québec, art 1289.
[45] For example, *Variation of Trusts Act*, RSO 1990, c V.1, s 1(1)(c).
[46] Chapter 1, section II.A; Chapter 3, section IV.A.2.
[47] Civil Code of Québec, art 1260: a trust arises when the settlor 'appropriates [property] to a particular purpose'.
[48] Chapter 10, especially section I.

is possible for someone other than a right-holder to have the power to enforce a right. In the case of an undirected duty, there is no right-holder, but it is still conceptually possible for someone to have a power of enforcement of the duty. To illustrate this, imagine that a trust existed for the purpose of erecting statues and towers to the glory of the deceased testator who established the trust.[49] The trustee's duty is to apply the trust property in the pursuit of the purpose of erecting towers and statutes. But no *person* holds a right that towers and statutes be erected; the trust does not give rights to beneficiaries. That is what makes it a purpose trust.

It is however conceptually possible to give one or more persons the power to enforce the trustee's duty, without giving those persons any right that corresponds to the trustee's duty. This is how undirected duties can be legal duties. Allocating a power of enforcement will be crucial in this regard, to avoid an obvious example of the problem of self-supervision. In Quebec, the 'settlor, the beneficiary or any other interested person' has the power to enforce a trust.[50] To use a term that was introduced above, we might say that anyone who presents themselves as an 'interested person' is seeking 'proper person standing' to enforce the trust.[51] By contrast, the settlor and the beneficiaries automatically have powers of enforcement. If we consider the case of the settlor, however, this is neither direct nor representative enforcement, because the settlor of a purpose trust does not have any right, owed to them, that the trust be performed.[52] The settlor has a power of enforcement in relation to an undirected duty. Not being any of direct enforcement, representative enforcement, or proper person standing, this could be called 'designated person standing'.[53]

In the common law, except where there is amending legislation, the only valid purpose trusts are charitable trusts. As we will see, these are examples of public law administration.[54] Here the enforcer is the Attorney General acting on behalf of the State (and thus of the public interest). This is another example of designated person standing.[55] The unreformed common law does not allow private purpose trusts even if the settlor designates an enforcer.[56] In other words, it does

---

[49] As in the Scottish case of *M'Caig v University of Glasgow* 1907 SC 231 (trust held invalid).

[50] Civil Code of Québec, art 1290; for analysis, see Alexandra Popovici, 'Droits de regard : la fiducie dans le *Code civil du Québec*' in Christine Morin and Brigitte Lefebvre (eds), *Mélanges en l'honneur du professeur Jacques Beaulne* (Wilson & Lafleur 2018) 225. The author questions whether the legislative solution effectively addresses the problem of self-supervision, because those who might have powers to enforce will generally lack any practical incentive to do so.

[51] Above, section III.C.2.c.

[52] This is further explained at the end of this section.

[53] This category is important in public law as we will see in Chapter 10.

[54] Chapter 9, section II.C.

[55] See Paul B Miller and Andrew S Gold, 'Fiduciary Governance' (2015) 57 Wm & Mary L Rev 513, 529, noting that in some US states the settlor has designated person standing to enforce charitable trusts.

[56] The 'material purpose' doctrine of US trust law prevents capacitated trust beneficiaries from ending a trust when there is an unaccomplished material purpose of the settlor, even if the settlor is

not allow the creation of undirected private duties.[57] The best explanation of this is that if this could be done in trust law, it would allow the creation of a privately oriented fund of rights that belonged, economically, to no one.[58] The settlor would be able to set the destiny of a fund, while depriving his creditors and heirs of it, and yet while giving it to no person. To do this for a charitable purpose is, by definition, to do something that is in the public interest. To do it for a private purpose is to try to escape from the law as a system for people.[59] The problem is of course exacerbated if the settlor continues to control the trustee, as this amounts to an attempt to implement conceptually inconsistent wishes: to keep, and to give away.[60]

Some legal systems do allow non-charitable purpose trusts. This includes not only Quebec, but also many jurisdictions traditionally called 'offshore', and now several states of the United States.[61] Typically, under such legislation the settlor may or must name a trust enforcer, and the legislation may provide for other or backup enforcers. The trust enforcers hold designated person standing; they hold a power of enforcement of the trust without holding any right, in the strict sense, that the trust be performed. This is because one who holds a right in the strict sense can always waive the right, making non-performance of the right lawful.[62] The enforcer of a purpose trust cannot do that.[63] The trustee's duties are undirected.

not a beneficiary. This is contrary to the law in other common law jurisdictions. I have argued that the doctrine effectively allows non-charitable purpose trusts (even though US common law purports not to allow them), since it allows the non-charitable purpose of the settlor to override the interests of the beneficiaries (Lionel Smith, 'Massively Discretionary Trusts' (2017) 70 CLP 17, 40).

[57] Paul Matthews, 'From Obligation to Property, and Back Again? The Future of the Non-Charitable Purpose Trust' in D Hayton (ed), *Extending the Boundaries of Trusts and Similar Ring-Fenced Funds* (Kluwer Law International 2002) 203; Kelvin FK Low, 'Non-Charitable Purpose Trusts: The Missing Right to Forego Enforcement' in Richard C Nolan, Kelvin FK Low, and Tang Hang Wu (eds), *Trusts and Modern Wealth Management* (CUP 2017) 486.

[58] Matthews, ibid 228–30; Lionel Smith, 'Give the People What They Want? The Onshoring of the Offshore' (2018) 103 Iowa L Rev 2155, 2167–72.

[59] For discussion of the implications, see Alexandra Popovici, *Êtres et avoirs: Les droits sans sujet en droit privé actuel* (Éditions Yvon Blais 2019).

[60] According to a maxim of customary French law: *donner et retenir ne vaut*.

[61] Smith (n 58), 2167, noting (in 2018) legislation in Delaware, Idaho, New Hampshire, South Dakota, and Wyoming.

[62] This is explored by Low (n 57). To illustrate: if A owes B a duty to build a house on B's land, it is not a 'purpose duty'; it is a duty owed to B, because B controls the duty. B can waive performance as well as demanding performance.

[63] The enforcer might be able to choose not to use the power of enforcement (particularly if the enforcer is *not* in a relationship of administration with someone, with respect to the power of enforcement). In principle, however, this would not diminish the trustee's duty. An enforcer who *could* waive performance of the trust would actually be the beneficiary, and then the trust would not be a purpose trust. A trust often requires certain conduct in relation to the trust property (such as investment or conversion) but this does not make it a purpose trust, because those obligations are for the benefit of the beneficiaries and the beneficiaries can waive them (see John H Langbein, 'Burn the Rembrandt? Trust Law's Limits on the Settlor's Power to Direct Investments' (2010) 90 BU L Rev 375; James Penner, 'Purposes and Rights in the Common Law of Trusts' (2014) 48 RJT 579).

PART III
ACTING FOR OTHERS IN PUBLIC LAW

9
Foundations of Public Law Administration

I. Structure, goals, and scope of this Part

A. Introduction

The previous Part II was focused on relationships of private administration: that is, relationships in which one person holds decision-making powers for the pursuit of a private mission in a private interest. This Part turns to how we act for others in public law. The overall goal is to identify both the common characteristics and the differences between the two domains.

Although the differences are profound, the commonality runs deep. The argument of this study is that there are legal norms that apply in both domains, which recognizably derive from common justificatory principles, precisely because both domains involve instances of acting for others in law.[1] The historical foundations of these norms in public law contexts are as deep as, or deeper than, they are in private law contexts.

The road to that goal has several steps. The remainder of this section I of this chapter aims to explain the structure of this Part of the book, and to explain the limited objectives of my argument in this Part. Section II of this chapter aims to explain how, for the purposes of this study, I distinguish between private administration and public administration. It presents a schema for distinguishing the different purposes for which people hold powers when they are granted those powers in order to pursue an other-regarding mission. Section III is a brief overview of which of the many problems that can arise in public administration are the primary focus of this study, and why.

The following Chapter 10 addresses a range mechanisms by which legal duties of public administration can be supervised and enforced. This discussion builds on the earlier analysis, in Chapter 8, of the mechanisms by which duties of private administration can be supervised and enforced. The goal is partly descriptive, but it also aims to disprove the idea that some holders of public powers—particularly

---

[1] On the idea of justificatory principles, see Chapter 1, section III.B.

The Law of Loyalty. Lionel Smith, Oxford University Press. © Lionel Smith 2023.
DOI: 10.1093/oso/9780197664582.003.0009

members of the executive branch of the government—are accountable politically but not legally for their exercise of power.[2]

Chapter 11 is a study of how the justificatory principles of sound administration are implemented, as legal norms, in the different contexts of public administration. As explained in Chapter 1, the principal justificatory principles are that other-regarding powers can only be rightly exercised in the pursuit of the purpose for which they were granted; that therefore they cannot generally be exercised in conflict situations; that an administrator is accountable for information and rights acquired in the course of administration; and that administration must be conducted with objectively reasonable care. The implementation of these principles in private law was explored in Part II. In this Part III, it will be shown that all of these justificatory principles are also implemented, albeit in different ways in different contexts, as legal norms in public administration.

In this respect, public and private administration can be seen as two manifestations of a juridical situation: acting for others in law. Moreover, in cases where public administration seems to lack legal norms to implement these justificatory principles, this allows a critical inquiry into why that is and what justifies such a situation. Hence this Part continues with an interpretive methodology, which is partly descriptive but which aims also to find an intelligible order in the law.[3] That enterprise makes room also for criticism of the positive law, where it fails to respect that intelligible order.

B. Structure and goals of this Part

Specialists in public law will find this Part to be incomplete and perhaps puzzling in its structure and orientation. Form follows function, and the goals of this Part explain its structure. They also explain its scope, about which more is said below when I explain the limits of the argument.[4]

The structure of Part III does not follow the structure of Part II. In Part II, separate chapters explained that other-regarding powers must be used loyally; that they should not generally be used in conflicts; that holders of such powers are accountable; and that other duties are attached to private administration. This allowed the demonstration of the implementation in the positive private law of the justificatory principles involved in acting for others. It also allowed

---

[2] Eg Samuel L Bray and Paul B Miller, 'Against Fiduciary Constitutionalism' (2020) 106 Virginia L Rev 1479, arguing that the only relevance of fiduciary norms in constitutional law is to 'political morality' and not to legal remedies.
[3] On this methodology, see Chapter 1, section III.A.
[4] Below, section I.C.

explanations to be offered for why those justificatory principles rightly apply when one is acting for others.

In this Part, those explanations are largely taken for granted as applying also, at least prima facie, in public administration. The next subsection of this chapter will outline that it is conceptually *possible* for someone to hold public power but to hold it for that person's own benefit; but this does not occur in the legal systems with which this study is concerned. On the contrary, as a matter of law (and here, as elsewhere, the law is not always complied with), public powers can only rightly be used for the purposes for which they were granted. The main concern in this Part is to see whether and how that is manifested in the positive law of public administration. Once a power can only rightly be used for some other-regarding purpose, the concerns raised by conflicts also present themselves. Those concerns, explored in Chapter 4, involve undetectable effects on human decision-making and the unconscious favouring of self-interest. These problems are equally present in public administration and they will not be rehearsed in this Part. Again, the main objective is to explore how they are given effect in the law governing public administration. Similarly, the idea of accountability that arises when we act for others in law, and its implications in relation to unauthorized profits and obligations of disclosure, were discussed in Chapter 5. These explanations will not be repeated in Part III. The objective is to see whether, how, and to what extent the idea of accountability that was examined in Chapter 5 is implemented in law in public administration.

C. Public trust and fiduciary government

1. Introduction

In the common law world, there are frequent references to State powers as held on 'public trust',[5] and more recently to the idea of 'fiduciary government'.[6] Some Australian judges have invoked the idea of 'Equity in public law'.[7] All of these

---

[5] Paul Finn has been a long-standing and eloquent advocate of a public trust model of State power. Among many papers: Paul D Finn, 'The Forgotten "Trust": The People and the State' in Malcolm Cope (ed), *Equity: Issues and Trends* (Federation Press 1995) 131; Paul D Finn, 'Fiduciary Reflections' (2014) 88 ALJ 127.

[6] Evan Fox-Decent, 'The Fiduciary Nature of State Legal Authority' (2005) 31 Queen's LJ 259; Evan Fox-Decent, *Sovereignty's Promise: The State as Fiduciary* (OUP 2011); Benjamin F Gussen, 'The State Is the Fiduciary of the People' [2015] Public Law 440; Evan J Criddle and others (eds), *Fiduciary Government* (CUP 2018). Other work will be cited in the pages that follow.

[7] Sir Anthony Mason, 'The Place of Equity and Equitable Doctrines in the Contemporary Common Law World' (1994) 110 LQR 238, 238, adopted by the majority of the High Court of Australia in *Bateman's Bay Local Aboriginal Land Council v Aboriginal Community Benefit Fund Pty Ltd* (1998) 194 CLR 247, [24]; Hon James J Spigelman, 'The Equitable Origins of the Improper Purpose Ground' in Linda Pearson, Carol Harlow, and Michael Taggart (eds), *Administrative Law in a Changing State: Essays in Honour of Mark Aronson* (Hart 2008) 147; Stephen Gageler, 'The Equitable

expressions resonate specifically in the common law tradition, particularly in relation to one part of it, the Court of Chancery.[8] The language of 'trust' and 'fiduciary' does not resonate in the civil law tradition, and 'equity' has a different connotation; this is one reason for the terminology of 'administration' adopted in this book.[9] But I am in agreement with what I understand to be the main claims implicit in the ideas of 'public trust', 'fiduciary government', or 'Equity in public law'. The main descriptive claim is that legal norms governing the proper exercise of other-regarding powers and of accountability (in a wide sense), which are recognizably similar to those seen in private administration, apply also in public administration. The main prescriptive or normative claim is that, roughly, this is as it should be. This could be unpacked as a claim that legal norms governing the proper exercise of other-regarding powers and of accountability (in a wide sense), which are recognizably similar to those seen in private administration, *rightly* apply in public administration; that they should have legal and not just political content; and, that they should have some effective enforcement mechanism. Hence, to the extent that one or more of these is not true in a legal system, there is ground for criticism unless some countervailing consideration is in play.

One goal of this Part is to show that descriptively, it is perfectly clear that the legal systems with which this study is primarily concerned do implement enforceable legal norms of public administration that are recognizably similar to the legal norms of private administration; and this, in a fairly thoroughgoing way. This, in my understanding, is why Finn said that it is a mistake to think that the idea of the public trust is merely a metaphor.[10]

It is not merely a metaphor. In my view, however, the word 'trust' in the phrase 'public trust' certainly is a metaphor.[11] The whole point of this Part is to show in what ways public administrators are subject to legal duties that are unsurprisingly similar to those applied to trustees and other private law administrators; but neither public administrators, nor the State itself, are typically trustees in the

---

Duty of Loyalty in Public Office' in Tim Bonyhady (ed), *Finn's Law: An Australian Justice* (Federation Press 2016) 126.

[8] By this I mean that the law of trusts and fiduciary relationships were developed and almost exclusively enforced in the Court of Chancery. Norms of sound administration, private and public, were however also enforced independently by the royal courts of common law long before the procedural fusion of law and Equity; see for example Chapter 11, section III.B.2.c.

[9] On this terminological choice, see Chapter 1, section IV.D.

[10] Finn, 'The Forgotten Trust' (n 5) 151; see also Finn, 'Fiduciary Reflections' (n 5), 128–31, discussing legal implementations of fiduciary principles in public law. Gageler (n 7) says (134) of Finn's project: '... much more would need to occur for the project to result in principles capable of being translated into concrete applications'. I find this mystifying inasmuch as Gageler's own paper, like Finn's work, is full of examples of concrete applications in the law of several common law countries.

[11] Finn, 'The Forgotten "Trust"' (n 5) himself signals this by putting inverted commas around the word 'trust' in his title.

technical sense of that word.[12] Trustee legislation does not apply to them, and nor does the Court's jurisdiction to appoint and remove trustees. One could multiply examples but the point is clear.

The most seemingly literal, or non-metaphorical, application of the idea must be US law's 'public trust doctrine'.[13] Although it is often said to derive from English law, the doctrine as it exists in the United States is not established in England or in most other common law jurisdictions.[14] In England and in common law countries that retain the Westminster state, the Crown is theoretically the owner of all land; citizens can only hold 'estates' as 'tenants' of the Crown, although the fee simple estate behaves much like civilian ownership (and not at all like a beneficial interest under a trust). In US law, privately held land is not held 'of' any feudal lord, even theoretically; but the States (or the federal State, the United States) do hold ownership of *public* land.[15] And it is to such land that the public trust doctrine applies. In this form, then, it is presented not as an idea about the powers of the State generally; it is a more particular concept, focusing basically on immovable property that belongs to the State and that has not been affected to some non-public use such as a government office building.[16] Characterizing the State as a trustee of such land, of course, is one way (but not the only way) of claiming that the State is in a fiduciary relationship (a relationship of administration) with the people in relation to that land. Like a private trustee, it must protect and preserve the property for benefit of the beneficiaries. Of course, private law trusts may leave a great deal of decision-making power in the hands of the trustee, and so presumably does the public trust doctrine as far as the powers of the State: it is the State that is empowered to decide what is in the best interests of the beneficiaries, the people. But it is difficult to understand how the State can be required to use its rights and exercise its powers in this setting as if it were a trustee, and yet not be required *in general* to use its rights and

---

[12] Not 'typically' trustees because it is certainly legally possible for the state, or some emanation of the state, to be a trustee in the strict sense.

[13] Allan Kanner, 'The Public Trust Doctrine, Parens Patriae, and the Attorney General as the Guardian of the State's Natural Resources' (2005) 16 Duke Env L & Policy Forum 57; *Juliana v United States*, 217 FSupp3d 1224 (D Or, 2016); Giorgio Resta, 'Systems of Public Ownership' in M Graziadei and L Smith (eds), *Comparative Property Law: Global Perspectives* (Edward Elgar 2017) 216, 240–43, with multiple citations to US literature.

[14] Resta (ibid), 241–42, gives examples of implementation in India, Kenya, and Uganda.

[15] It is somewhat paradoxical that the power of State expropriation is called 'eminent domain' in the United States but not elsewhere, since that phrase historically refers to the domain of the feudal lord that no longer exists in the United States: that is, the underlying ownership that in feudal logic co-exists with the tenant's 'useful domain'.

[16] When it is described as applying to 'natural resources', it may be said to cover wildlife (eg Kanner (n 13), 61, 90); but the background rule of the common law (and the civil law) is that no one owns wildlife at large (*Pierson v Post* 3 Cai R 175, 2 Am Dec 264 (NYSCJ, 1805)). The state cannot be a trustee (except metaphorically) of property that does not belong to it as trustee.

exercise its powers for the benefit of the population.[17] The public trust doctrine may allow citizens to control State action that does not comply with the public trust;[18] but this entire Part of the present study aims to explore the many ways in which citizens can control State action to ensure that it complies with the legal norms of public administration.

In this sense, it is not surprising that some more recent articulations of the public trust doctrine have taken it more widely, with the result that it is very difficult to see why it is not after all a theory that all public powers must be exercised for the proper public purposes.[19] When it extends also to resources in the form of art, on the basis that they are held for charitable purposes, it seems impossible to understand how it is not in fact a theory about the way in which all public powers must be used.[20] Indeed, this takes the doctrine even beyond State powers: speaking generally, charities act for public purposes but they do not exercise powers of the State.[21] So it seems that the 'trust' in 'public trust' is not a trust in the technical sense of trust law.

Depending entirely on one's definition of the word 'fiduciary', it may also be true that 'fiduciary government' is a metaphor. The term 'fiduciary' is highly debated and has no agreed definition;[22] it is perfectly defensible to confine it to private law relationships, or to the common law tradition, or both.[23] A majority of the Supreme Court of Canada has said:

> Public law duties, the performance of which requires the exercise of discretion, do not typically give rise to a fiduciary relationship . . . the Crown is not normally viewed as a fiduciary in the exercise of its legislative or administrative function.[24]

[17] See *Juliana* (n 13), 1252–53, linking the public trust theory to public powers generally, including the police power. The point about wildlife in the preceding note also points in the direction that the theory is really about public powers generally.

[18] Kanner (n 13), 75–81, noting that different states of the United States have different understandings of the extent to which the state can be subjected to this control.

[19] Eg Allison Anna Tait, 'Publicity Rules for Public Trusts' (2015) 33 Cardozo Arts & Ent LJ 421; Jennifer Anglim Kreder, 'The Public Trust' (2016) 18 U Pa J Const L 1425.

[20] Tait, ibid 424: 'That museums are public trusts is a truism in academic discourse and industry discussion.'

[21] Below, section II.A.

[22] For more on different understandings of 'fiduciary' within the common law, see Chapter 3, section I.B; Chapter 7, section III.C; Lionel Smith, 'Parenthood Is a Fiduciary Relationship' (2020) 70 UTLJ 395, 401–18.

[23] This is why I have avoided the word except when discussing the particular context of private law administration in the common law tradition: Chapter 1, section IV.D.

[24] *Guerin v R* [1984] 2 SCR 335, 13 DLR (4th) 321, 385 (SCR); see also *Swain v The Law Society* [1983] 1 AC 598 (HL), in which Lord Brightman said (618): 'The duty imposed on the possessor of a statutory power for public purposes is not accurately described as fiduciary because there is no beneficiary in the equitable sense.' In *Alberta v Elder Advocates of Alberta Society* 2011 SCC 24, [2011] 2 SCR 261, [37]–[38], and [49]–[50], McLachlin CJC said, for the Court: 'The government, as a general rule, must act in the interest of all citizens . . . No fiduciary duty is owed to the public as a whole, and

This is not, in my view, a statement that the Crown can use public powers for any purpose at all, or that such powers can rightly be exercised by someone in a conflict of interest, or that the holders of public powers are not accountable, or that they can extract unauthorized profits. It is a statement that in those legislative and executive roles, the Crown is not in a *privately enforceable* juridical relationship with particular beneficiaries. In this sense, with 'fiduciary' understood as term of private law, it must be the case that 'fiduciary government' is a metaphor.[25] Many advocates of fiduciary government argue to the contrary that on a proper understanding, the word 'fiduciary' applies to public powers as much as to private ones, so that its use in 'fiduciary government' is not metaphorical.[26] It is not necessary for me to take or defend a position on this terminological question. The substantive question—to what extent is public administration subject to a legal regime that clearly corresponds to that governing private administration?—is the concern of this entire Part III.

2. Limits of my argument

There are many versions of fiduciary government theories and my account does not correspond to some of them.

a) Not a theory of the State or of the source of State power

My account does not reach into political theory. It does not purport to ask, let alone answer, whether any particular State is legitimate or justified. In his groundbreaking work in this area, Evan Fox-Decent argues that the fiduciary nature of State power is constitutive of the authority of the State.[27] If this means that the fiduciary nature of State power *brings into existence* the legal authority of the State, I disagree.[28] Conceptually, powers can be other-regarding or not, and either way, the question where they come from is a different question from how

generally an individual determination is required to establish that the fiduciary duty is owed to a particular person or group'.

---

[25] Eg Bray and Miller (n 2).

[26] Eg the scholarship cited at n 6; see also Paul B Miller, 'Fiduciary Representation' in Evan J Criddle and others (eds), *Fiduciary Government* (CUP 2018) 21, arguing that private and public fiduciary relationships are unified analytically inasmuch as both are relationships of representation. I suggested earlier that his argument is compromised inasmuch as his understanding of 'representation' seems to include also some non-fiduciary relationships: Chapter 1, section V.B.3.b.3.

[27] Fox-Decent, 'The Fiduciary Nature of State Legal Authority' (n 6), 271; Fox-Decent, *Sovereignty's Promise* (n 6), 134–35 ('The state's subjection to this [fiduciary] duty empowers or authorizes the state to change the legal position of its subjects . . .').

[28] Antonia Waltermann, 'Book Review' (2013) 20 Maastricht J of Eur and Comp L 649, 651–52, suggests that such an argument would be circular. See also Paul B Miller, 'Principles of Public Fiduciary Administration' in Tsvi Kahana and Anat Scolnicov (eds), *Boundaries of State, Boundaries of Rights* (CUP 2016) 251, 253–55; response: Evan Fox-Decent, 'Challenges to Public Fiduciary Theory: An Assessment' in D Gordon Smith and Andrew S Gold (eds), *Research Handbook on Fiduciary Law* (Edward Elgar 2018) 379, 394–96.

they are held and how they may rightly be used. If Fox-Decent means that the authority of the State (the existence of which is otherwise explained) is always other-regarding in nature in a well-ordered State, then I agree, although this conclusion rests in part on other premises and is not analytically true.

I do not agree that one who holds authority over another (such as the State's authority over persons in it) is necessarily in a relationship of administration (or a fiduciary relationship) towards that other.[29] Employers have authority over their employees.[30] A mandator and a principal have authority over their mandatary and their agent, but the relationship of administration is in the other direction; the mandator/principal is the beneficiary.[31] A military commander may have the authority of life and death over those under her command, and while this power may be held for an other-regarding purpose, it is not held for the benefit of those who are subject to it; the commander is not in a relationship of administration with them.[32]

It does not seem to be the case that the powers of a sovereign are necessarily or conceptually held, according to the governing law, for an other-regarding purpose. As a descriptive matter, it is certainly not true historically, and although I cannot speak to all the world's legal systems, it seems quite possible to say that it is not true in some existing legal systems, being absolute monarchies or their functional equivalents. In the seventeenth century, the French theorist Jean Bodin described two modes in which the powers of a sovereign could be exercised: the 'seigneurial' and the 'lawful'.[33] In the former, the sovereign holds the power and the resources of the State as personal wealth; in the latter, that power must be exercised and those resources deployed according to the requirements of the law.[34] The two are extremes, and the history of many legal systems can be seen as a movement from one towards the other.[35] If the powers

---

[29] Evan Fox-Decent, 'Fiduciary Authority and the Service Conception' in Andew Gold and Paul Miller (eds), *Philosophical Foundations of Fiduciary Law* (OUP 2014) 363, 373–81.

[30] Fox-Decent (ibid 373 n 42) addresses this point by suggesting that authority with a contractual source may be different from authority granted by law. Note however that historically, parental authority included the authority of an employer-employee relationship (Smith (n 22), 424, arguing that the law has evolved away from this). That authority was granted by law, not by contract.

[31] On this feature of these relationships, see Chapter 1, section V.B.3.c.

[32] The case of prison guards, or an executioner, could also be invoked to make this point. They may owe some legal duties to the prisoners or the condemned, but they are not required to use their powers in what they perceive to be the best interests of the prisoners or the condemned.

[33] Daniel Lee, ' "Office Is a Thing Borrowed": Jean Bodin on Offices and Seigneurial Government' (2013) 31 Political Theory 409.

[34] Although the seigneurial mode is opposed to the lawful mode, the implication is not that the former mode is illegal or necessarily involves illegal action, but that under it the law of the State accepts that the sovereign's relationship to the wealth of the State is effectively one of ownership: ibid 413–15.

[35] Thus in English law, Magna Carta in 1215 marks an important moment of movement towards law, while still leaving the King with enormous personal powers; and even today, no law can be passed without the King's (formal) consent.

of a sovereign are held in the seigneurial mode, there is legal authority without any relationship of administration. The powers are held by the holder to use as they wish. The converse of this is that in a State that Bodin called lawful, the powers of the sovereign are held not for a selfish but for an other-regarding purpose; in this case, for the public purpose of the sound governance of the State. In these States, which include all those that this book is concerned with, public powers can only rightly be used for the pursuit of that public purpose. But the seigneurial mode shows that this is not conceptually true (and again, it may not be true at all in some places). It is true because the exercise of construing the grant of the power reveals that it is held for an other-regarding purpose. That is exactly what we saw in the private law context: first, one has to decide how the power is held; only if it is held for an other-regarding purpose does the regime of administration rightly apply.[36] The story of Bodin's classification shows that although it seems obvious that it is better for States to be 'lawful' than 'seigneurial', that is not because sovereign powers *can only* be held for an other-regarding purpose. Sovereign powers *are* so held as a matter of law *because* they are legally affected to an other-regarding purpose. And the reasons this seems obviously right lie outside of the norms of sound administration that are one of the consequences of this process of construction. The reasons include such ideas as the equal worth and dignity of all persons and the principle of non-domination.

Thus once we conclude, for reasons that stand apart from fiduciary norms or norms of administration, that the powers of the sovereign are other-regarding, it follows that the justificatory principles that apply to all other-regarding powers can potentially apply. Moreover, as Bodin noticed, once the powers of the sovereign are seen as other-regarding powers, it follows that they must be held through offices.[37] In a seigneurial State, the delegates of the sovereign can be removed at pleasure. In this, they are like agents and mandataries in private law: they do not hold offices, they can be removed by the principal or mandatary at any time for any reason, and no replacement need be named. While the agent or mandatary is an administrator, the principal or mandator acts in their own interest, like the seigneurial sovereign. In a lawful State, all public power is held for other-regarding purposes and this is mediated through offices which are regulated by law.[38] Officers

---

[36] Chapter 3, section III.B.
[37] Lee (n 33), 420–24.
[38] On offices, see Chapter 1, section V.B.3.d. In private administration, we noted that there is often a principle against delegation which may allow exceptions (Chapter 3, section IV.E). Public administration necessarily involves delegation; not every holder of public power is an office-holder and many are agents, employees, or both. But every such holder of public power is ultimately the delegate of an office-holder.

may be removable, but not at the bare will of someone who acts only in their own interest.[39]

b) Not even a theory of any part of the State

Ethan Leib and Stephen Galoob have tested some fiduciary government arguments in three domains of public law: judging, administrative governance, and international law.[40] In the title of their study, they frame the field of inquiry as belonging to political theory. In relation to administrative governance, they say:

> A theory of administrative governance provides standards for determining how governance by administrative institutions can (or cannot) be politically legitimate.[41]

It is not part of my ambition to provide a theory that satisfies this definition, nor of any cognate definition formulated so as to refer to any other branch of the State. This account does not aspire to political theory. I will aim to investigate the extent to which legal norms of sound public administration do apply to the organs of the State, and evaluate the positive law so described. The evaluative exercise is through the prism of the identified justificatory principles that are known to and implemented by the law.

c) Does not demand or rule out particular exercises of State power

Some versions of fiduciary government theory argue that the fiduciary nature of State power leads to conclusions as particular ways in which that power must be exercised.[42] In my understanding of the idea, this is not so.[43]

We have seen that as a matter of positive law, it is inherent to most examples of private law administration that the administrator has a great deal of decision-making autonomy.[44] Bound typically to act in *what she perceives to be* the best

---

[39] Voters in a democracy are the closest analogue to a principal/mandator; but even they have to wait for the next election and follow the relevant legal process.

[40] Ethan J Leib and Stephen R Galoob, 'Fiduciary Political Theory: A Critique' (2016) 125 Yale LJ 1820.

[41] ibid 1854. Leib and Galoob go on to evaluate the work of Evan Criddle on the basis that it aspires to meet this definition, but my reading is that at least one of Criddle's contributions is not political theory but an interpretive account of the law: Evan J Criddle, 'Fiduciary Foundations of Administrative Law' (2006) 54 UCLA L Rev 117, especially 123 where Criddle states that his account does not purport to address political legitimacy. See however Evan J Criddle, 'Fiduciary Administration: Rethinking Popular Representation in Agency Rulemaking' (2010) 88 Texas L Rev 441.

[42] Fox-Decent argues that the fiduciary conception of the State implies or entails that the State must provide a framework of human rights: *Sovereignty's Promise* (n 6), ch 9. See also Evan Fox-Decent and Evan J Criddle, 'The Fiduciary Constitution of Human Rights' (2010) 15 Legal Theory 301. Both accounts draw on Kant.

[43] In this respect I thus agree with Miller (n 26), 47–48.

[44] Chapter 3, section II.B.

interests of a beneficiary, she is nonetheless the one with decision-making authority. She must comply with the objective limits of that authority and with other objective limitations, but subject to those limits, she is the decision-maker and the law does not dictate the results of her decisions. The public law context is very similar in this respect. The claim that norms of sound administration apply to public law decision-makers is perfectly consistent with their having a very wide range of lawful decision-making authority.[45] The norms of sound administration require that public powers be exercised in certain ways, in the sense that they must be exercised for the right purposes and with due care and diligence; they do *not* require that they be used to bring about particular outcomes.

Thus the argument being made here is not a substantive political theory that is capable of dictating what is the best form of government; it purports to apply to any form of government that is 'lawful' and not 'seigneurial'. It is not capable of dictating how much tax should be levied and how many social services should be provided. It does not indicate which of our rights are so fundamental that they must be protected in private law or in the Constitution.[46] Just as corporate directors could lawfully make a series of bad decisions that cause the corporation to become insolvent, a state and its administrators could comply with the norms of sound public administration and still enact and enforce laws that were unjust according to other norms.[47] Other norms than the norms of administration are needed to argue for a particular form of government and for particular ways of running the State.[48] For the same reasons, the argument here does not involve any claim that judges, when enforcing sound norms of administration, will necessarily overstep their constitutional role because they will be deciding how State power should best be used.[49] Just as in private law, norms of administration constrain reasons for using powers, and they do not dictate particular results of their use.

3. Dicey and 'common law constitutionalism'

My account in this Part touches on aspects of the constitution, and since it is a legal account, some aspects of constitutional law, albeit at a very general of level. But, perhaps paradoxically, due to the ambitions of this study, the only part of the

---

[45] This reality is a large part of why courts may speak of deference to holders of State power. The matter of deference is addressed in Chapter 10, section II.A.2.

[46] Allan Beever, 'Our Most Fundamental Rights' in Andrew Robertson and Donal Nolan (eds), *Rights and Private Law* (Hart 2011) 63; Andrew Gold, *The Right of Redress* (OUP 2020), ch 6.

[47] Seth Davis, 'Pluralism and the Public Trust' in Evan J Criddle and others (eds), *Fiduciary Government* (CUP 2018) 281 argues that State oppression has often been justified in fiduciary terms.

[48] The arguments of Fox-Decent and Fox-Decent and Criddle (n 42) draw on Kant's philosophy; in my view that philosophy and the norms of administration are perfectly compatible but are not ineluctably connected to one another. A utilitarian could be a lawful administrator.

[49] This is an argument made against Fox-Decent in Matthew Lister, 'Book Review' (2012) 123 Ethics 150, 151.

constitution that I am interested in is the part that, I argue, is not uniquely constitutional. The justificatory principles relating to acting for others in law apply to private and public law alike.

When a court needs to decide whether a public power with a statutory source was used lawfully, it will rightly seek out the intention of the legislator that granted the power. Such an inquiry is certainly apt to reveal the objective limits on the power: what it empowers the holder to do. If a person purported to use it for something else, their act would be without legal effect; a power to revoke a restaurant's liquor licence does not empower the holder to revoke its licence to serve food. An inquiry into legislative intention is also apt to reveal whether the power is held by that person to do with as they wish, or—far more likely in the case of a public power—for the achievement of an other-regarding purpose. In the latter case, that inquiry is also apt to reveal what that purpose is, although some inference may be required as is often true in the interpretation of a text of law. Once the power is characterized as other-regarding, it can only be used unimpeachably when it is used for the pursuit of that purpose.

Albert Venn Dicey was preoccupied with the sovereignty of Parliament and his work gave rise to a view of the judicial supervision of State power that was very much concerned with the intention of Parliament.[50] If and to the extent that some purported exercise of public power was not authorized by Parliament on the proper interpretation of the relevant statute, then the purported exercise was ultra vires and void. But the intention of Parliament cannot solve every problem, as the case of prerogative powers reminds us: in the Westminster system, these are powers formerly held by the Crown and now by the executive, and which do not derive from legislation.[51] The source of such powers, one might say, lies in Crown sovereignty itself, although in this case it is an aspect of sovereignty that does not belong to Parliament, at least for the time being.[52] It is also true that powers arising out of a contract may in some cases be seen as public powers which can only be used for public purposes.[53] But the source of any legal power, whatever it may be, can be interrogated to construe the power. It may be construed as to its scope and limits;[54] it can also be construed to determine whether it is held for an other-regarding purpose, and if so, what that purpose is.

---

[50] Mark D Walters, *AV Dicey and the Common Law Constitutional Tradition: A Legal Turn of Mind* (CUP 2020).

[51] Those prerogative powers that exist in places with a written constitution, such as the US President's power to pardon, arise from a legal text, namely the Constitution.

[52] The qualification is necessary because in the Westminster system, once Parliament legislates on a matter formerly in the prerogative, it ceases to be part of the prerogative. The logic of this is that Crown is party to every Act of Parliament and so consents to the legislative regulation of the relevant power and the corresponding reduction in the prerogative (*Attorney-General v De Keyser's Royal Hotel Ltd* [1920] AC 508 (HL), 526).

[53] This is discussed below, section II.B.3.

[54] *Case of Proclamations* (1611) 12 Co Rep 74, 77 ER 1352.

Dicey's focus on the intention of Parliament thus leaves out of account the legal regulation of some public powers, those not deriving from a statute. Even in the realm of statutory powers, there is another difficulty with the pure ultra vires theory. The proper interpretation of a statute will usually reveal that Parliament's intention was to grant a power with articulable limits *and* to affect that power to some purpose. This allows us to draw a distinction between the absence of power and the misuse of power, just as we did in private law.[55] As in private law, this could have ramifications at the level of judicial remedies.[56] It might allow the conclusion that the improper use of a power that one holds is not necessarily wholly void; it may be valid but impeachable.[57] There is more to the regulation of public power and accountability than simply voidness. In at least some settings, as we will see, the law also forbids the use of public powers while their holder is in a conflict of interest or a conflict of duty and duty; and this, for exactly the same reasons that yield the same result in private law. In many settings also, the law may require that unauthorized profits derived from public office be surrendered, and that those who are charged with public administration must do so with a level of care and skill, just as in private law administration.

Dissatisfaction with Dicey's approach has led naturally to its evolution, and to the emergence of a contrasting approach which is often described as 'common law constitutionalism'.[58] Proponents of this view argue that separately from any finding of legislative intention as expressed in a statute, the common law itself imposes certain requirements in relation to the use of public powers (although the imposition of such requirements is itself subject to being overridden by expressed legislative intention, within the limits of the legislature's sovereignty).[59] In my view the label is not ideal. First, it implies something that is tied to the common law tradition. One might respond that 'common law' here means 'as opposed to statute law', not 'as opposed to civil law', and this seems clearly to be part of the idea of the label; and yet, some views of common law constitutionalism hold that it relies on norms that have evolved in the reasoned decisions made by common law judges.[60] This idea would tie it closely to the common law

---

[55] Chapter 3, section IV.F.2.
[56] David Feldman, 'Error of Law and Flawed Administrative Acts' (2014) 73 CLJ 275.
[57] There is some discussion of this in Chapter 11, section IV.A.2.
[58] Dawn Oliver, 'Is the Ultra Vires Rule the Basis of Judicial Review?' [1987] Public Law 543; Paul Craig, 'Competing Models of Judicial Review' [1999] Public Law 428; Adrian Vermeule, 'Common Law Constitutionalism and the Limits of Reason' (2007) 107 Col L Rev 1482; Evan Fox-Decent, 'Democratizing Common Law Constitutionalism' (2010) 55 McGill LJ 511.
[59] As discussed in Craig (ibid); see also Paul Daly, *A Theory of Deference in Administrative Law* (CUP 2012), 289–91, and literature cited there. Thomas Adams, 'Ultra Vires Revisited' [2018] Public Law 31 argues that both sides of the debate are correct in relation to different aspects of the judicial review of public power.
[60] Vermeule (n 58); Se-shauna Wheatle, 'Common Law Constitutionalism through Methodology' (2019) 65 McGill LJ 341, 347–51.

tradition; and yet French administrative courts were reviewing State action to ensure its use for lawful and proper purposes before Dicey published the first edition of his famous book on constitutional law in 1885.[61] But even if 'common law' in the name of common law constitutionalism is meant only to signal that the limits on the exercise of power do not derive from the construction of a particular statute or other legislative text, the name is not especially apt. To say a rule comes from the common law in this sense is to describe its formal source: that is, what makes it a legal rule.[62] It says nothing about what are the justificatory principles that underlie it. If one opened a book on tort law to seek enlightenment as to why some torts are actionable per se while others require proof of loss, or why the law of defamation may be different depending on whether the offending words were oral or written, one would not be very satisfied to read each time that this is what the common law says. It would be true, but it would be unhelpful.

On my account, 'constitutionalism' is also at least potentially misleading.[63] The norms of sound administration grow out of the juridical situation of holding powers in an other-regarding capacity.[64] They apply in private law as well as in constitutional law. Trustees' powers must be used for proper purposes, and cannot validly be used while in a conflict unless the conflict has been managed. Trustees cannot extract unauthorized profits from their role as trustees, and must act with prudence, diligence and care. Very few trust instruments say anything about any of that. The default rules apply unless they are disapplied, because they are inherent to the juridical situation of acting for others.[65] The same comment could be made about relationships of administration created by contract. The contract is the source of the relevant powers, but the conclusion that those powers are held for an other-regarding purpose is often a matter of interpretation that is not expressly provided for in the contract.[66] Similarly, the legal norms of private law administration that then apply are almost never provided for in the contract; they apply *because* the relationship is one of administration.[67]

There is no reason to think of public powers differently. For example, in some places there may be written rules against judges exercising their powers while in

---

[61] Roger Vidal, 'L'évolution du détournement de pouvoir dans la jurisprudence administrative' (1952) 68 RD public et de la science politique 275, 277–78.

[62] Lionel Smith, 'Sources of Private Rights' in Simone Degeling, Michael Crawford, and Nicholas Tiverios (eds), *Justifying Private Rights* (Hart 2020) 129.

[63] Voltaire quipped that the Holy Roman Empire was neither holy, nor Roman, nor an empire: Voltaire, *Essai sur l'histoire générale et sur les moeurs et l'esprit des nations, depuis Charlemagne jusqu'à nos jours*, 8 vols, vol 2 (new edn, Cramer 1761–63), ch 66, 239: 'Ce Corps qui s'appelait, & qui s'appelle encor [sic], le saint Empire Romain, n'était en aucune maniére [sic], ni saint, ni romain, ni empire'.

[64] I realize that common law constitutionalism may incorporate norms other than the norms of sound administration that are discussed here.

[65] Dawn Oliver, *Common Values and the Public-Private Divide* (reprint edn, CUP 2010) 194.

[66] See Chapter 7, section II.A.

[67] ibid.

a conflict; but statutory or written rules are not necessary.[68] Because the powers of a judge are other-regarding, they cannot be used in a conflict situation, unless the rules about conflicts have been explicitly disapplied for some reason. In the same way, a statute or a constitution could give someone a power to exercise as they chose without constraint; in that case, none of the norms of administration will apply. But if the legislator grants a power for the achievement of some mission or function, it can hardly have intended to authorize the use of that power for another purpose. If the power does need to be used for an other-regarding purpose, but the legislature has explicitly or implicitly authorized that it may be used in a conflict situation, then so it may be used. Otherwise, the rules about conflicts will apply; their applicability does not depend on any positive or express legislative intention; it arises from the juridical situation of holding powers for the pursuit of an other-regarding purpose.[69] Parliamentary sovereignty is respected inasmuch as Parliament can disapply those rules that will otherwise apply to such a situation.[70] The same logic is illustrated by a principle that is well-established in the common law: any exercise of State power that takes or destroys private property presumptively demands compensation.[71] That principle exists because the logic of the taking is that it is in the public good, and there is no good reason for the burden of it to fall on a single member of the public. Parliamentary sovereignty is respected inasmuch as a clear expression that no compensation is due will be effective (although in some places, like the United States, the Constitution excludes expropriation without compensation).

Overall, then, there are perfectly good reasons for applying those norms in the public sphere and this seems entirely consistent with respecting legislative sovereignty or the authority of a constitutional text. Of course, there are fundamental differences between the public law and private law settings, which will be explored in the following chapter and throughout this Part.[72]

---

[68] *Ex parte Pinochet (No 2)* [1999] UKHL 1, [2000] 1 AC 119, discussed in Chapter 11, section III.D.2.

[69] Compare Fox-Decent (n 28), 391–94, arguing that the recognition of public power as other-regarding justifies constraints on its exercise even in the absence of specific statutory creation of those constraints. See *Ainsworth v Criminal Justice Commission* (1992) 175 CLR 564, 575–76, holding that a duty of procedural fairness applied and that it was unnecessary to decide whether this was implied by the applicable statute or rather arose from the general law (and was not excluded by the statute).

[70] In respect of the relationship between Parliamentary sovereignty and the rule of law, Dicey placed great weight on the consideration that statues are not interpreted by Parliament itself, but by the courts: Walters (n 50), ch 10.

[71] *Attorney General v De Keyser's Royal Hotel Ltd* (n 52); *Burmah Oil Co v Lord Advocate* [1965] AC 75 (HL); *Manitoba Fisheries Ltd v The Queen* [1979] 1 SCR 101; *R v Tener* [1985] 1 SCR 533.

[72] See however the comment of Hon James J Spigelman, 'Foundations of Administrative Law: Toward General Principles of Institutional Law' (1999) 58(1) Australian Journal of Public Administration 3, 10, that 'Dicey may be proven right, after all'. What the author seems to mean (see also 7) is not that there is no such thing as administrative law or public law in the common law, but that the principles of sound public administration are not particularly a feature of public law, but are

II. The domain of public administration

A. Introduction

One might think that the dividing line between private administration and public administration is the source of the powers in question: Do they come from the State, or do they have a private source, being granted by some private person? There are however several difficulties with this starting point.

One is that word 'source' is very ambiguous in this connection. Imagine that you offer to sell me your car and I say 'I accept'. Now I have a legal obligation to pay you the price. What is the source? One person might say that the source was my acceptance, by which I performed a legal act that created (along with the offer) the contract.[73] A second person might say the obligation came from the law, because there is a general legal rule that an accepted offer creates a binding contract. A third might say that the source is in the authority of the legislature, because the legal rule is in the Civil Code.[74] In the same way, in a common law system one might say that a voluntary obligation is sourced in Equity (as in a trustee's obligations to beneficiaries), in the common law (as in general contract law), or in legislation (as in the case of a statute which lowered the age of majority, giving contractual capacity to a person who would not yet have it at common law). And a fourth person might say that the source of the legal obligation is the principle that seriously made promises should be binding.

In different ways, all four are correct; they are referring to different senses of the word 'source'.[75] The first person was referring to the 'material source': the operative facts in the world that brought the obligation into being. The second was referring to the 'normative source': the general legal rule which is activated by the occurrence of the material source. The third was referring to the 'formal source' of the legal rule that was the normative source: the pedigree that makes that rule a legal rule. The fourth was referring to the 'justificatory principle': the principle, itself not directly creative of legal relations, that explains the existence of the normative source in a justificatory way.

Thus we can see that the State is in some sense involved even in private grants of power, because the legal rule that allows the granting of such power is not itself privately created. This however is a fairly weak sense that relates only to the

common to private and public administration. I agree with that position, although I am not sure that this is what Dicey argued.

[73] On legal acts, see Chapter 1, section IV.A.2.
[74] Eg Civil Code of Québec, arts 1385–86.
[75] Benoît Moore, 'La théorie des sources des obligations: éclatement d'une classification' (2002) 36 Rev Juridique Thémis 689; Smith (n 62).

formal source. If we look at the material source, we will focus on whose actions led to the creation of the power; but this seems to be the wrong focus for this study. Compare two cases. An elderly parent, in advance of losing their capacity, executes a document giving their adult child the authority to manage the parent's assets; when the document comes into effect, there are legal powers held by the child and a relationship of administration. Another elderly parent neglects to execute a document before losing capacity; their child then commences a legal proceeding and the court names the child as a guardian of property, creating (let us assume) the same powers and the same kind of relationship of administration. In the dimensions with which I am concerned, there are no important differences in the legal characteristics of these two relationships. The fact that the power was *granted* by a part of the State—its judicial branch—does not change the legal norms applicable to the administration. Both cases are relationships of private administration.

For the same reasons, the fact that legislation may be the source of some or all of the relevant powers is not determinative. In the case of an intestacy, legislation (made applicable by a court appointment) grants powers to the liquidator of the succession or the administrator of the estate. But even where there is a valid will, legislation may grant powers to the liquidator or executor, just as it may grant powers to trustees of a privately created trust, powers greater than those found in the privately executed trust instrument. To identify the legislative source of such powers is only to identify the formal source, and does not of itself point towards different norms governing the administration.

Nor does the distinction between private and public administration turn on who holds the relevant powers. Sometimes the State itself, or an emanation of the State, takes on the role of private administration. Examples are the State or some emanation like a Public Trustee or Public Curator acting as guardian of a child, or as the trustee of a private trust. Speaking generally, the legal rules with which it must comply will be the same as those that apply to a private person acting in the same role.[76] In looking after a child, the State or its delegate is fulfilling a mission on behalf of a single person. In acting as a trustee, the State or its delegate is fulfilling a function in favour of the particular beneficiaries of the trust. Of course, there is a public interest in the State's fulfilment of these roles when no one else is able to act; but in these roles, the State must act, not in the general public interest, but in the interests of the particular beneficiaries.

We act for others when we hold powers, not for our own benefit, but in order to further a mission, assignment, function, or charge. The scope of this Part is defined by a difference in the mission. Private law administration is usually

---

[76] There may be minor differences; for example, a Public Trustee may have a legislative authority to charge fees that a private actor might lack.

directed towards the mission of furthering the individual interests (financial or non-financial) of another person, or a defined group of persons, or of a privately defined purpose. Those are the interests that must guide the decision-making of the administrator. Sometimes, as in a common law pension trust, it may be possible to articulate the mission in favour of persons so as to resemble a private purpose.[77] Even though this is often possible where the beneficiaries are very numerous, this remains a case of private administration, addressed to private interests, and enforceable by the beneficiaries or their representatives.

Sometimes there are true cases of private administration in which the mission is a private purpose.[78] This includes the trust in Quebec law, which is defined by a purpose set by the settlor.[79] In the common law, dispositive discretions held by trustees are also governed by a purpose set by the settlor; they cannot be interpreted as requiring the use of the power in the interests of either the objects of the discretion or of those who will take the property in default. And in some jurisdictions with trusts based on the common law model, legislation has validated non-charitable purpose trusts.[80] All of these cases may seem to be similar to public administration, because the administrator is not required to act in the interests of a person or persons, and supervision and enforcement of the administration requires structures that are similar to ones used in public administration.[81] These cases, however, involve powers of administration that must be used in the pursuit of a private purpose. The apparent similarity to public administration arises because the duties of the administrator are undirected. This is typical, as we will see, in public administration, but rare and unusual in private administration.

What distinguishes public law administration is that it is administration for a public purpose: for the benefit of the public or the public interest. Take the case of a judge, who has a wide range of powers related to the administration of justice. She can make rulings on the admissibility of evidence and make decisions about the law and, often, about disputed facts. She can make findings of liability or of criminal guilt, and can impose sanctions that may include compensation or punishment or other things, depending on the nature of the case. She holds none of these powers for herself. They are not hers to do with as she wishes. She holds them for the pursuit of a mission, assignment, function or charge: in this case, the administration of justice according to law. This mission is not directed towards a particular person or persons. The litigants in a particular case may have a particular interest in the proper performance by the judge of her functions

---

[77] Discussed in Chapter 1, section V.B.3.a.; and Chapter 3, section II.C.2.
[78] Discussed in Chapter 1, section V.B.3.a.; chapter 3, section IV.A; and chapter 8, section III.C.3.
[79] Civil Code of Québec, art 1260.
[80] Chapter 8, section III.C.3.
[81] ibid.

in *that* case; but the judge's duty is not to run the proceedings in the way that is best for them.[82] The judge's duty is a public duty.

Since there are at least some cases in private law of administrators whose mission is defined by an impersonal purpose, one cannot distinguish public administration from private administration by the sole consideration that public administration is for a purpose. In the same way, one cannot distinguish it by the observation that the administrator's duties are (or include) undirected duties, as this is also true in some cases of private law administration. Moreover, some cases of public administration may be for the benefit of a relatively small section of the public. I will argue in the next section that the administrators of a charitable entity are conducting public administration; but it is possible that a charity operates on a small scale, perhaps confined to a particular town, while some cases of private administration, such as pension trust or other collective investment trust, may have thousands or even millions of beneficiaries.

A signal that demarcates public administration from private administration is in a sense procedural, but it is a procedural distinction that rests on an important substantive point. Any case of administration is governed by legal rules and is subject to supervision and enforcement. Public administration, being administration in the public interest and on behalf of the public, involves undirected public duties, which are not owed to any particular person.[83] This is so even though it may simultaneously involve directed duties, possibly owed by administrators to a legal person through which the administration is carried out. The presence of undirected duties means that public administration is subject to a public regime of supervision and enforcement (although it may be subject also to other forms of supervision and enforcement).[84] This supervision and enforcement may be by the State, or some emanation of it; in different ways, it may also or at least sometimes be in the hands of members of the public. In the common law (and in Quebec, which has a common law system of public law), this is often through procedures for judicial review of administrative action.[85] In civil law jurisdictions with separate administrative courts, this is through proceedings in those courts. Enforcement of administration by the State, by the public, or both

---

[82] In the context of the court's supervisory jurisdiction in relation to office-holding administrators, the judge's duty may require her to do what she thinks is in the interests, or the best interests, of the beneficiary of the administration. In this role, however, the judge does not stand towards the beneficiary as a judge stands towards a litigant in a dispute. The judge acting in a supervisory role acts more like an administrator; this judicial function was discussed in Chapter 1, section V.B.3.d. Even here, however, the judge's duty is a public one and is not owed directly to the beneficiary.

[83] The idea of undirected public duties is addressed in more detail in Chapter 10, section I.

[84] This is explained and explored in more detail in Chapter 10.

[85] It will be shown in Chapter 11, section II.A., that there can be public enforcement of the administration of public trusts, and this has been occurring since long before the more recent creation of particular procedures for judicial review of administration action.

is a signal given by the positive law of the boundary between private administration and public administration.

But public supervision and enforcement of sound public administration cannot be both the consequence that administration is public and the test for determining whether it is. Some cases will always be on the borderline.[86] Some of these difficult cases are discussed below.[87] Ultimately, the question is whether the power in question can only *rightly* be exercised in the public interest.[88] If the answer is 'yes', then this generates undirected duties and activates public supervision and enforcement. The purpose for which a power can rightly be used is always determined by interpreting the terms on which the power was granted.

B. Beneficiaries of public administration

Some of those who challenge ideas of 'fiduciary government' do so on the basis that it is not possible to identify the beneficiaries of such a fiduciary relationship.[89] Defenders of those ideas have responded in various ways.[90] I agree with the most fundamental response: that when administration is directed to the furtherance of an impersonal purpose, there are no beneficiaries in the way that there are beneficiaries when administration is directed by service to someone's interests.[91] There are beneficiaries in a sense, of course: those who will benefit from sound administration. The word 'beneficiary' has both technical and non-technical senses.[92] The beneficiary of an insurance policy is not a trust beneficiary. More importantly, although a student who receives a scholarship from a charitable trust is a beneficiary of that trust in one sense, she is not a trust beneficiary in the technical sense. She does not, either before or after being awarded the scholarship, have a right to see the accounts or to sue the trustees in relation to an unauthorized profit. The trustees do not have to be guided by what is in her best interests.

---

[86] Spigelman (n 72), 5–7; Peter Cane, *Administrative Law* (5th edn, OUP 2011) 5–7, 268–70.
[87] Section II.D.
[88] This is not the same as the question whether the exercise of the power *affects* a wide range of persons. For a similar point in private administration, see Chapter 3, section IV.A.1.
[89] Seth Davis, 'The False Promise of Fiduciary Government' (2014) 89 Notre Dame L Rev 1145; Timothy Endicott, 'The Public Trust' in Evan J Criddle and others (eds), *Fiduciary Government* (CUP 2018) 306; Bray and Miller (n 2).
[90] Ethan J Leib, David L Ponet, and Michael Serota, 'Mapping Public Fiduciary Relationships' in Andew S Gold and Paul B Miller (eds), *Philosophical Foundations of Fiduciary Law* (OUP 2014) 388; Fox-Decent (n 69).
[91] See *Swain v The Law Society* [1983] 1 AC 598 (HL), in which Lord Brightman said (618): 'The duty imposed on the possessor of a statutory power for public purposes is not accurately described as fiduciary because there is no beneficiary in the equitable sense'; Paul B Miller and Andrew S Gold, 'Fiduciary Governance' (2015) 57 Wm & Mary L Rev 513 and Chapter 3, section IV.A.2.
[92] Lionel Smith, 'Massively Discretionary Trusts' (2017) 70 CLP 17, 21–29.

The absence of beneficiaries in the strict sense has two consequences. First, the administrator is not to be guided by the interests of any person or persons, but by the achievement of the purpose. Second, there is no one who has, as of personal right, powers to supervise and enforce the duties and liabilities of administration. Those duties and liabilities are undirected. This is why the mechanisms of enforcement must be different in public administration.[93] This is the subject of Chapter 10.

C. Examples of public administration

In public law administration the relevant powers are held for the benefit of the public, and not for the benefit of particular private persons. Such powers are usually held by the State itself, including its organs; by those holding offices in one of its branches, or their delegates; or by emanations of the State, such as corporate entities controlled by the State that act in a public role. However, there can also be (at least in some systems) powers for public law administration that originate at least partly in a private grant and that are held by private persons. In the common law and in Quebec civil law, it is possible to create, by private act, purpose trusts that do not have persons as beneficiaries. In many of these cases, the trustees' administration is public inasmuch as the purpose is, or includes, benefit to the public at large.

In common law charitable trusts, the powers of the trustees come from the terms of trust, which are usually set out either in a will or a deed of trust.[94] To this extent, the trust is a private creation. No registration or involvement of the State is required to bring it into being (although registration may be required to take full benefit of available favourable tax treatment). No common law trust can be charitable, however, unless it is for a charitable purpose *and* for the benefit of the public.[95] In this sense, every charitable trust has a public dimension which helps to explain why people are allowed to create them at all, why they can in principle last forever, and why they may receive favourable tax treatment.[96] This also explains why the powers of enforcement belong to the State,

---

[93] Enforcement is also one of the enduring puzzles of non-charitable private purpose trusts, which also feature undirected duties; see Chapter 8, section III.C.3.

[94] These powers may be supplemented, as in all trusts, by others in legislation.

[95] These are conceptually separate because the public benefit requirement dictates, not the purposes of the trust, but the width of the class of persons who may benefit. Moreover, the positive law imposes different requirements for public benefit in relation to different charitable purposes. See Donovan WM Waters, Mark Gillen, and Lionel Smith, *Waters' Law of Trusts in Canada* (5th edn, Thomson Reuters 2021) 767–825.

[96] Kathryn Chan, *The Public-Private Nature of Charity Law* (Hart 2016).

or to an emanation of the State; depending on the jurisdiction, it might be the Crown acting through the Attorney General, or a Charity Commission or similar public body.[97]

In Quebec civil law, public benefit is not a requirement of validity for purpose trusts, but it is certainly possible to create purpose trusts that benefit the public.[98] This, again, is a private creation but the trustees of such a trust are engaged in public administration on my definition.

D. Some borderline cases

As always, interpreting the grant of a power indicates for whose benefit it was given. This in turn tells us on whose behalf, or for what purposes, it must be used; it tells us which interests must be considered in exercising judgment as to the employment of the powers.

Part of the thesis of this book is that the principles that apply to acting for others in public law recognizably have significant features in common with those that apply to acting for others in private law. On this view, it is not surprising that the borderline between the two domains may be difficult to draw. This section considers some examples. As the next chapter will show, the formal difference in the structure of public and private duties necessarily means that the enforcement of the applicable legal norms may play out very differently as between public and private administration. To mention one concrete manifestation of that: if a power is held for the benefit of the public, then it is conceptually possible for a member of the public to challenge the exercise of that power, not as of right or because they hold a right, but on the footing that they are invoking the public interest.[99]

---

[97] Kathryn Chan, 'The Role of the Attorney General in Charity Proceedings in Canada and in England and Wales' (2010) 89 Can Bar Rev 373. Another example of a particularized notion of 'public trust' in US law (above, section I.B.1) is that the phrase is sometimes applied to charities in support of arguments that they should not be able to alienate works of art: Sara Tam, 'In Museums We Trust: Analyzing the Mission of Museums, Deaccessioning Policies, and the Public Trust' (2012) 39 Fordham Urban LJ 849. Every charitable trust is a public trust, and every charity (whether or not in the form of a trust) has a public mission; but I agree with Tam that this on its own does not generate a rule of inalienability.

[98] Civil Code of Québec, art 1270: 'A social trust is a trust constituted for a purpose of general interest, such as a cultural, educational, philanthropic, religious, or scientific purpose. It does not have the making of profit or the operation of an enterprise as its essential object.' This does not exactly track the common law definition of charity. However, in order to be registered as a charity and to receive the corresponding tax advantages, a Quebec charity must satisfy the common law definition that is applied by the federal taxation authority. For an argument that this is inconsistent with the goals of Canadian bijuralism, see Kathryn Chan, 'Taxing Charities/Imposer les organismes de bienfaisance: Harmonization and Dissonance in Canadian Charity Law' (2007) 55 Can Tax J 481.

[99] Chapter 10, section II.F.

1. Legal persons with private missions: Business corporations

There is a long-standing debate about whether business corporations should be managed only in the interests of their shareholders, or whether wider social concerns either can or must be taken into account. In the terms of the present chapter, this could be framed as a question whether the administrative powers of the directors and other managers are held for private or public purposes.

It seems clear that this is a case of private administration. The directors must be guided by what they perceive to be the best interests of the corporation.[100] A business corporation is a private and not a public person.[101] Commentators have frequently noted that the creation of a legal person, carrying protection for investors against unlimited liability, is a concession of the State, and in return for this concession the State can rightly demand something from those who benefit from the concession. This is true; indeed, the State does not necessarily need to grant concessions in order to make demands on citizens. But even if we look at corporate law this way, the reasoning does not entail that those administering a business corporation are required to act in the public interest. The State grants many privileges, including the privilege to drive a motor vehicle, to enter a national park, or to fish commercially. Some of these may be transferable but whether or not, these privileges may be very valuable.[102] Obligations are rightly imposed on those who hold them. But it does not follow that one must act in the public interest when driving, entering a national park, or fishing commercially.[103] One must comply with the obligations that are imposed, but one is free to act for oneself.

The argument rather must be one based on the proper interpretation of the powers granted by law to the corporation (or its administrators). For whose benefit are they held? When the legal rule is that the administrators must act in what they perceive to be the best interests of the corporation, it seems impossible to suggest that they are bound to act in the public interest.[104] One justification for articulating the mission of corporate directors in this way is that investors in business corporations do not typically invest as a means of contributing their

---

[100] In the United States, less care is taken about the separate personality of the corporation and it is often said that the managers must be guided by the best interests of the shareholders. In my view, this is technically incorrect but changes nothing in the current discussion. See Chapter 3, section II.C.2.

[101] The case of a corporation which exists for a public purpose or mission is very different and is touched on in the next subsection and explored in Chapter 11, sections II.B. and III.B.

[102] *Saulnier v Royal Bank of Canada* 2008 SCC 58, [2008] 3 SCR 166 (holding that a commercial fishing licence was 'property' for the purposes of bankruptcy and secured lending legislation).

[103] Those who practice a profession must take account of the public interest. Professions are discussed in Chapter 11, section V.

[104] Even if the duties of directors are viewed as owed to the shareholders (n 100), and even though in a widely held, publicly traded corporation, the shareholder class may be enormous and constantly changing, each shareholder at any given time has rights and interests precisely because they have invested in this particular enterprise, not as members of the public.

wealth to the public interest.[105] One clear signal of this in the positive law is that even in jurisdictions where the administrators of a business corporation derive most of their powers from a statute (which means, in most jurisdictions), their use of those powers is not treated as the proper subject matter of judicial review of administrative action. The corporation and its administrators are treated as private parties.

It does not follow from this, however, that the managers are not *allowed* to take account of interests other than the interests of the corporation. Still less does it follow that managers are duty-bound to choose the course of action that will have the greatest positive impact on the share price.[106] The reason is that corporate managers, when they are obliged to manage in the pursuit of the corporation's best interests, have as part of their job description the task of *deciding* what is in the corporation's best interests. In this, they are like every administrator.[107] It is true that they are subject to objective constraints;[108] but there is also a lot of flexibility. A business corporation is typically constituted for the financial benefit of its shareholders, but it depends upon its employees; it has need of creditors, consumers, and governments; and, like all of us, it cannot flourish in the absence of a healthful environment. Thus the interests of the corporation are typically intertwined with the interests of some or all of those others. It is not surprising that, for example, the Supreme Court of Canada has held that directors *may* consider all these interests;[109] but they may consider them, it should be remembered, as part of the process of deciding what they think is in the best interests of the corporation. That process also requires them to decide whether to think in terms of longer or shorter time horizons. In respect of all these factors, the law does not give an objective answer as to what they must do. Like all administrators, they have to decide for themselves, taking account of their mission. It should be remembered that corporate managers can always be removed and replaced by shareholders, although the details vary from one jurisdiction or another. That is, if shareholders do not like the way managers are managing, they can replace them. It does not follow that if shareholders do not like the way managers are managing, or if the market value of the shares goes down, the managers have done something unlawful.

---

[105] This is not true, or not entirely true, in the case of a 'benefit corporation'. Analysis of this vehicle is beyond the scope of this study, but they are mentioned below in the discussion of public–private partnerships (section II.D.4).

[106] This was called the 'one right answer' fallacy in Chapter 3, sections II.B and (in the corporate context) II.C.2.

[107] See the discussion in Chapter 3, section II.B, which explains this in jurisdictional terms.

[108] Chapter 3, section II.C.1.

[109] *BCE Inc v 1976 Debentureholders* 2008 SCC 69, [2008] 3 SCR 560, [40]; see the discussion in Chapter 3, section IV.B.1.

An extreme version of the mistaken view that managers must manage to maximize the share price is sometimes associated with the label 'shareholder primacy'. This tends to ignore the separate legal personality of the corporation, but that is not its most serious fault. Even if managers were obliged to manage in the best interests of the shareholders, it would not follow that this would require them to make every decision with an eye on the effect on the share price. History shows that overly short-term managerial thinking can lead to disastrous consequences. But there is no iron rule: sometimes, the short term is important. Nor does it mean that managers must necessarily do what shareholders *want* them to do, any more than elected politicians must do what the majority of the electorate wants them to do. This is another way of saying that managers have to do their jobs, jobs that involve making decisions and exercising judgment.

In sum, managers of business corporations must manage in the pursuit of what *they* perceive to be the best interests of the corporation. This is private administration, even though they may take account of the interests of others, such as employees or creditors. Those are natural factors to be considered in the making of complex decisions. But the interest to be pursued is a private interest.

2. Legal persons with public missions: Universities

McGill University is a legal person, constituted by a royal charter that was issued by King George IV in 1821 and re-issued by Queen Victoria in 1852.[110] It has officers and a Board of Governors who are ultimately responsible for everything the university does.[111] They operate within the framework of the royal charter that created the university, of the statutes and policies enacted thereunder, and of those provisions of the law of Quebec that govern universities and legal persons; these include some statutes that are particular to McGill, some that govern universities generally, and those provisions of the Civil Code that govern legal persons, particularly 'legal persons established in the public interest'.[112] The officers, and the members of the Board, hold their powers for an other-regarding purpose; but is it a public or private purpose?[113]

One could argue that this is a case of private law administration, in the sense that their mission is to do what is best for the particular legal person that is McGill University, even though the goals and objectives of the legal person are public in nature.[114] On this view, the administrators of the university have

---

[110] https://www.mcgill.ca/secretariat/charter-statutes/royal.
[111] The constitution of the Board and the principal offices are set out in the Statutes of the University enacted by the Board, under the authority of the Charter: https://www.mcgill.ca/secretariat/files/secretariat/statutes_of_mcgill_university.pdf.
[112] Civil Code of Québec, arts 298, 300, and following. For the relevant provincial statutes, see https://www.mcgill.ca/secretariat/charter-statutes/quebec.
[113] Peter Knight, 'So, Are Universities Public or Private?', The Guardian, 20 June 2006.
[114] Other examples of legal persons with public missions might be a civil law foundation, or in the common law any company or corporation with charitable purposes.

a private relationship with it, as do the directors of a business corporation. This does not deny that the university has a public mission. It was not brought into existence by investors to pursue their own financial interests. But this view might emphasize that the stated and legally binding objectives of the legal person exist to ensure that its public mission is pursued. These legally binding objectives or purposes are one example among many of how administration (whether private or public) can be constrained by objective limits.[115] In this case, the objective constraints rightly give the administration a distinctly public flavour. But, it might be concluded, the relationship of administration between the university and its administrators is one of private administration in the relevant sense.

The more natural view, however, is that the public nature of the mission of the legal person means that the administrators of that person are engaged in public administration. Their mission is a public one, even though it is mediated (and it may be, to some extent, enforced) by the duties that they owe to the legal person. Another way to put this is that even though their duties are primarily owed to a single legal person, that legal person is a public and not a private legal person; it exists for the pursuit of a public interest.[116] In the same way, we would say that a person exercising the public law powers of a police detective is exercising public powers, even if it so happened that the police department for which she worked was constituted as a legal person.

One way in which the public nature of the administration in these cases may become clear is through the enforcement mechanisms that are available. If the administration were private, the only person who could hold the officers of McGill University to account for unlawful administration would be the university itself, acting through one or more of its internal organs, possibly with other persons authorized to bring a derivative or representative action as in corporate law.[117] Even more than in a business corporation, however, one might be concerned about what was earlier called the problem of self-supervision,[118] and about the effectiveness of these mechanisms of enforcement.[119] Characterizing the administration as public, however, opens the door to other avenues of enforcement, because it means that in addition to the directed legal duties owed by the administrators to the university, those administrators also owe undirected legal duties. Because the university is a charity, the Attorney General of the

---

[115] Chapter 3, section II.C.1.
[116] Cf Pierre Issalys and Denis Lemieux, *L'action gouvernementale: Précis de droit des institutions administratives* (4th edn, Éditions Yvon Blais 2020) 567; Oliver (n 58), 549–51.
[117] Chapter 8, section II.C.3.
[118] Chapter 8, section II.C.3.
[119] See Natalie Brown, 'The Principal Problem: Towards a More Limited Role for Fiduciary Law in the Nonprofit Sector' (2013) 99 Virginia L Rev 879, addressing non-profit entities generally. Although her title suggests that there is a problem with the *norms* to which non-profit administrators are subject, in fact her argument is not about the norms as such but about the problems inherent in enforcing those norms.

province has standing to enforce the duties of its administrators.[120] The public mission of the university also makes supervision and enforcement by members of the public a possibility. For one thing, they may in the common law be able to take over the enforcement role of the Attorney General through the relator action.[121] More practically, exercises of power by university administrators may be the proper subject matter of judicial review of administrative action.[122] Outside of judicial review, common law courts have sometimes allowed members of the public to enforce the duties of administrators of charities.[123] 'Proper person' standing to bring such proceedings could in the proper case be granted (for example) to an employee or student, or even a graduate of the university who is not currently in any other relationship with it, although in any case it might be required that the person show that they were particularly affected by the decision or action in question.[124] The grant of standing permits a private person to enforce the public interest in sound administration.

A legal person 'established in the public interest' is not necessarily an emanation of the State. It may be independent in terms of governance, as is McGill University.[125] That is a separate question. As we have seen, the trustees of a common law charitable trust (which is not a legal person) are engaged in public administration. This is so even though the mission of the charity is selected by the settlor of the trust, and even though the decision-making of the trustees is generally independent of State control. Although the administrators of a charity are not subject to State *control* in their decision-making, their duties are enforceable by the State, and possibly by members of the public.[126] This is not affected by whether the charity is in the form of a trust or a legal person.

---

[120] That, at least, is the common law rule; the absence of a legal category of 'charity' in Quebec law may complicate this: Fabien Gélinas, 'Le *locus standi* dans les actions d'intérêt public et la *relator action*: l'empire de la common law en droit québécois' (1988) 29 Cahiers de Droit 657; Chan (n 98). But the fact that the University is a creation of the then-Imperial Crown (rather than of legislation) does not insulate it from the jurisdiction of the provincial Attorney General: *People's Holding Co v Attorney-General of Quebec* [1931] SCR 452.

[121] Chapter 10, section II.G.2.

[122] For example, *Shank v Daniels* (2002) 57 OR (3d) 559 (DC); see also Oliver (n 58), 549–51. In the old common law, now reformed in many jurisdictions, it was routine for courts to issue writs of *mandamus* not only against public officers but against charitable corporations: Stewart Kyd, *A Treatise on the Law of Corporations*, 2 vols, vol 2 (J Butterworth 1794), 291–394. *Mandaumus* lies (or lay) to enforce undirected public duties. In the common law tradition, a university or other charitable corporation may have a Visitor to resolve internal disputes. The courts will respect that person's jurisdiction (*Thomas v University of Bradford* [1987] AC 795 (HL); *Re CS* [2015] NIQB 36), but its exercise is judicially reviewable (ibid 825).

[123] See Chapter 11, section II.A.

[124] The term 'proper person standing' was introduced in Chapter 8, Section III.C.2.c; as it applies in public law, it is discussed in Chapter 10, section II.H.

[125] Conversely, most universities on the Continent of Europe are considered State entities, although the level of State involvement in governance is variable.

[126] See notes 121 and 123.

This naturally opens the question, what about a private university? This usually refers to an institution that receives no substantial direct State funding. It holds powers and privileges from the State: the power to grant degrees, for example.[127] We know, however, that every business corporation also gets some powers and privileges from the State, since in most jurisdictions no legal person can be created without the State's intervention; and we have already seen that a private business corporation is not generally considered to be an entity that exists in the public interest.[128] But where a private university is a charitable entity, this status will give it privileges in relation to taxation which are a form of State funding. Just as with charitable trusts, these privileges are, speaking generally, reserved to entities that are of benefit to some substantial section of the public. This pursuit of public benefit is usually inconsistent with a mission that exists for the benefit of investors, and reveals instead a public mission.

Thus even a private university which does not receive State operating funding is a public entity in my typology if it is a charitable entity, and those who administer it are exercising public powers.[129] This is not intended to suggest that such entities are or should be controlled by the State, as I have already explained. The practical implication is that it may, as discussed above, open the possibility of proper person standing, on the part of members of the public, to enforce the norms of sound administration.

3. Contractual powers held by public entities

The State or one of its emanations may hold contractual powers against a citizen; for example, the State may have leased land to the citizen, and may, following a breach of some term of the lease by the citizen, have the power to end the lease and evict the citizen. In the common law and in Quebec civil law, the rules of contract law are the same in public law as they are between citizens, with some adjustment for capacity and formalities in relation to some emanations of the State.[130] In French law this is not true: some contracts made by emanations of

---

[127] In some jurisdictions, however, not every institution with the word 'university' in its name is necessarily an institution that has the authority to grant degrees. The 'Trump University' existed under that name from 2005–2010 but was not a university in the generally accepted sense of that word.

[128] In the previous subsection.

[129] In some places there are for-profit degree-granting institutions: see Carol Everly Floyd, 'For-Profit Degree-Granting Colleges: Who are These Guys and What do They Mean for Students, Traditional Institutions, and Public Policy?' in John C Smart (ed), *Higher Education: Handbook of Theory and Research, vol XX* (Springer 2005) 539. It is arguable that the degree-granting power involves a public function, which might mean that a for-profit degree-granting institution is a kind of public–private partnership: see below, section II.D.4. But another view is that these are businesses constituted in a private interest, even if they have been granted certain powers that rightly call for regulation.

[130] *Communities Economic Development Fund v Candian Pickles Corp* [1991] 3 SCR 388; *Magical Waters Fountains Ltd v Sarnia (City)* (1992) 8 OR (3d) 689 (DC).

the State are governed, not by civil (private) law, but by administrative (public) law.[131] Although this dual structure is unknown in the common law tradition, it is interesting from the point of view of the current study, because one way to understand it is as addressing exactly the distinction being drawn here between private and public administration. When, in French law, a governmental contract is classified as 'private', it is governed by private law and justiciable in the civil courts; when it is classified as 'administrative', it is governed by administrative law and justiciable in the administrative courts. Not only are some rules of contract law different in the two systems, but the classification of a contract as administrative invokes all of administrative law, including the overarching principle that public powers must be used for proper purposes. The unitary court system of the common law tradition (a court system which exists also in Quebec), along with the longevity of the traditional Diceyan approach to public law (an approach that effectively denied or downplayed the separate existence of a body of public law rules that apply only to public entities), may have delayed the recognition that contractual powers may be public powers; but this certainly has been recognized.[132] Instead of a distinction between different court systems administering different bodies of private and public law, it may play out in part as a distinction between different court procedures: a proceeding for judicial review, instead of (or as an alternative to) a claim to enforce a right.[133]

4. Public–private partnerships

Another interesting case is a private entity involved in a 'public–private partnership'. A private company might not only design or build a public bridge or toll road, but might operate it and in one version might own the asset, if not forever then perhaps for some extended period of time. In terms of the present study, the most difficult aspects of such projects relate to powers that may need to be held by the private enterprise in order to carry out the project. If the State hires a private company to build a road, there are notorious vulnerabilities to corruption, typically involving a failure of public administration on the part of those *public* administrators responsible for granting and managing the contracts.[134] But the private company itself, although it may participate in wrongdoing if it offers a bribe for example, is not involved in public administration. It owes contractual duties to the State, but does not hold public administrative powers. Its duties are

---

[131] L Neville Brown and John S Bell, *French Administrative Law* (5th edn, Clarendon Press 1998) 141–43, 202–11. In general terms, this probably represents the norm in civil law systems.

[132] Oliver (n 58), 551–67; Cane (n 86); Nicolas Lambert, 'Effective Remediation in Public Procurement: Damages or Judicial Review?' (2020) 51 Ottawa L Rev 361.

[133] Cane (n 86), 258–63.

[134] For one example from Montreal, see the 2015 report of the *Commission d'enquête sur l'octroi et la gestion des contrats publics dans l'industrie de la construction*, online at https://numerique.banq.qc.ca/patrimoine/details/52327/2502593 (French only).

objective legal duties and if the public supervision of the project is not corrupted, it should be straightforward to decide whether those duties have been fulfilled.

In a public–private partnership, however, the opposite may be the case. In running a public bridge or highway, a private company is operating in some respects as an agent or mandatary of the State, not only in a political sense but possibly in a narrow legal sense as well.[135] This is especially clear in cases where a private company is given powers that can only be held or granted by the State itself. For example, a private company running a prison needs to be given powers relating to confinement and perhaps discipline that are themselves powers of the State. Such companies, even though they may be accountable to their investors, are also carrying out public administration. They are exercising powers that originate in the State, that the State holds for the benefit of all, and that the State has delegated in one way or another to the private 'partner'. This delegation is not capable of stripping these powers of their public character, because delegation does not change the purpose for which a power was created.[136] One clear signal of this is that the exercise of such public powers by a private entity is subject to judicial review of administrative action, even if the grant of the relevant powers to the entity is not done by way of a statute.[137]

There is an enormous literature on such arrangements.[138] In the terms of the current study, the private partner in these situations may well be an administrator who is charged with multiple conflicting missions.[139] On one view, which is certainly tenable as a juridical and not simply as a political position, this means that it may be very difficult to make these arrangements function according to the legal norms that properly govern them. A conflict of duty and duty arises where an administrator, in exercising judgment, must try to act in the pursuit of interests that are opposed to one another.[140] The general norms of private administration *forbid* an administrator from using their administrative powers in a

---

[135] Full privatization of control of the asset may not be legally or politically possible if some public control needs to be retained, as in the case of natural monopolies.

[136] It would be conceptually possible for the State to create powers and grant them to a private party that could be used by that party for private purposes. This would not be delegation and is unlikely to be the correct interpretation in the case of a public–private partnership.

[137] Cane (nn 86 and 132), 14–17.

[138] See Anne CL Davies, *The Public Law of Government Contracts* (OUP 2008), especially ch 8; Janet McLean, *Searching for the State in British Legal Thought* (CUP 2012), especially ch 8.

[139] Miller and Gold (n 91) use the term 'hybrid mandate' to refer to situations involving the combination of administration in pursuit of a purpose and in pursuit of the interests of a private person, but do not invoke this idea when they mention (533) public–private partnerships.

[140] Chapter 4, section IV.B. In that chapter it was noticed that the simple fact that an administrator may profit from the administration does not create a conflict of interest in the relevant sense (Chapter 4, section II); and, that every administrator must respect the *rights* (as opposed to the interests) of persons other than the beneficiary (Chapter 4, section IV.B). A conflict of duty and duty is separate from either of these situations.

conflict of duty and duty; an unauthorized conflict is considered to be an 'impossible position'.[141] And an authorized conflict is still a conflict.

Viewing the situation as inherently problematical would easily find deep foundations in the cultures of the law and of the civil service. This may have been the shared understanding among Western governments until public–private partnerships became more popular in the 1980s.[142] That a certain kind of economic thinking, holding that such arrangements can be beneficial to all, prevailed in some places was perhaps based not on any failure of economics, but on a failure to understand the law, and in this case of the law's moral and psychological foundations. It may be a perfect example of the view that we always act for ourselves in law, and that the only legal remedy needed to deal with conflicts is some kind of regime of incentives.[143] The thesis of this book is that this is profoundly mistaken: acting for others is qualitatively different from acting for oneself. In this perspective, it is not wise to invite a for-profit corporation to take up a position in which its managers are required, routinely, to decide whether to prioritize the financial interests of the corporation and its shareholders or rather the interests of the public on whose behalf it has been empowered to act.

Assuming that the conflict is authorized, how can it be managed? Where a for-profit corporation is also the administrator of its employees' pension plan, its management has conflicting private administration relationships: one with the corporation and its investors, and another with the pension plan members.[144] Here, the law regulates the conflict carefully and will require the administrators of the corporation to manage it so as to protect the interests of the beneficiaries of both private administrations.[145] It would be slightly absurd if any other solution were adopted when the private corporate interests conflicted, not with the private interests of pension plan members, but with the public interest that the corporation has been empowered to administer.

Unless there is a clear hierarchy between interests, it seems quite likely that the private actor will routinely be faced with situations in which the only way it can properly act with regard to one constituency will be by misusing its powers in relation to the other constituency.[146] The idea of a hierarchy, however,

---

[141] The phrase is from *Hilton v Barker Booth & Eastwood (a firm)* [2005] 1 WLR 567 (HL), [44]. For the private law prohibition see Chapter 4, section V; for the duties of disclosure that arise, see Chapter 5, section VIII.

[142] It may also explain why in most of the world, the idea of a for-profit university is an oxymoron.

[143] This view was introduced in Chapter 1, section II.B, and is also discussed in Chapter 5, section II.B.3.

[144] It might be more precise to say that the corporation is in a conflict of self-interest (in making profits) and duty (in acting as plan administrator). The directors are in a conflict of duty and duty inasmuch as they control the corporation in both its self-interested role and in its administrative role as plan administrator.

[145] *Sun Indalex Finance, LLC v United Steelworkers* [2013] 1 SCR 271, 2013 SCC 6.

[146] It is arguable that the same problem arises in the context of 'benefit corporations', which aim to produce profits for private investors while being obliged to take account of the public interest. This

seems untenable. It would of course have to be justified and understood by all stakeholders in advance. The State could not reasonably agree that in any conflict, the public interest shall be subordinated to the private interests of the corporation; that would not be public–private partnership, but full privatization. The investors in a private corporation would not likely be attracted to an arrangement in which, in the case of any conflict, the private interests of the corporation must be subordinated to the public interest.

Private administrators often have multiple beneficiaries, as where a business partner acts on behalf of all the partners, or a trustee acts for the benefit of all beneficiaries; such arrangements authorize, at least implicitly, any conflict of duty and duty. The question how it is to be managed still arises. Trustees whose beneficiaries have conflicting interests may be required to hold an 'even hand' between them.[147] In their study of how powers held for persons differ from, and may interact with, powers held for impersonal purposes, Paul Miller and Andrew Gold suggest that a related norm could be developed to address situations where there is a conflict between purposes that an administrator is required to pursue:

> fiduciaries could be held to standards of fair dealing, which require that they honestly and forthrightly serve the purposes attached to their mandates, and they not knowingly prejudice achievement of those purposes by disregarding some purposes or favoring conflicting purposes.[148]

The principle of holding an 'even hand', however, depends on the possibility of being able to characterize the beneficiaries as regularly having discernible common or shared interests, even if in other respects their interests diverge. The feasibility of the proposed adaptation of the principle to public–private partnerships is not obvious. If a corporation is running a prison, can its management routinely find common or shared interests between the corporation, whose capital comes from investors whose private financial interests must be considered, and the public, in whose interests the company holds delegated

---

may explain why this fairly new form of business association has not prospered: Ronald J Colombo, 'Taking Stock of the Benefit Corporation' (2019) 7 Texas A&M L Rev 73. The author anyway concludes (108–9) that the traditional business corporation gives directors wide latitude to pursue corporate social responsibility (a position with which I agree: Chapter 3, section IV.B.1). Miller and Gold (n 91, 579–80) discuss benefit corporations as situations in which directors have 'hybrid mandates', between the pursuit of a purpose and the promotion of a person's interests.

[147] This principle, known to the common law and Quebec law, was mentioned in Chapter 4, section VII.A.

[148] Miller and Gold (n 91), 64. This could presumably be adapted to a conflict between a requirement of pursuing the interests of a person (such as a business corporation) and of pursuing a public interest; Miller and Gold call this a 'hybrid mandate'.

public powers? Ultimately they will have to favour one side in relation to any particular decision.

The only way to make such arrangements consonant with sound public administration would seem to be with a clear statement and understanding that the proper use of public powers must prevail over investors' private interests; but as we have seen, this could make the role commercially unattractive. Moreover, to function properly it would require careful oversight by the State of the public administration part of the project. The State viewed as a whole may be a poor overseer, since those holding the power of oversight may be those who originated the idea of such arrangements and who therefore have a personal interest, not in showing their failures, but in trumpeting their success: still another conflict. The conflicts of those charged with oversight of administrators is a classic problem that can impair such oversight in both its private and its public dimensions. This is what was earlier called the problem of self-supervision.[149] For all these reasons, it is not surprising that public–private partnerships have not always achieved the benefits that were promised for them.[150]

III. Characteristics of public administration

A. The problems with which this study is concerned

Many things can go wrong in public administration, and as in private administration, this study is concerned more with some problems than with others. If a judge makes an error of law, there may be an appeal route. This recourse is based on the *correctness* of a legal holding, and the appeal system for ensuring correctness is outside of our concern with norms of public administration. Again, if a public decision-maker (judge or not) fails to adhere to correct procedures, such as making a decision without a required public consultation, the result may be that that the decision can be set aside. These procedural issues, while crucial in the day-to-day life of public administration, are not the focus of this study.

If any public administrator purports to do an act for which she lacks authority, that act will probably be void or voidable, as in private administration.[151] Similarly, if she refuses to do something which her position obliges her to do,

---

[149] Chapter 8, section II.C.3.
[150] Eyes *passim*. For those not familiar with this inside joke, it is a reference to the British journal *Private Eye*, which reports constantly on the systemic failure of public–private arrangements to deliver the promised benefits, and which uses this phrase to refer to discussion in its earlier issues when there are too many occurrences to list them all individually.
[151] 'Probably' because there may be rules that, in the name of reliance or some other interest, may validate or partially validate such actions (see the brief discussion in Chapter 11, section IV.A.2). Similar rules also exist in private administration (Chapter 3, section IV.F.3).

there will likely be some recourse to compel her to do the action. The discussion in the next chapter of standing to enforce norms of public administration is relevant to these problems, although a lack of authority and failure to act when required to do so are not the main focus of this study.

Our primary concern is with the proper exercise of public powers, in the sense of the legal constraints on the discretion that typically goes with such powers. When public powers are held for a mission, assignment, function, or charge, those powers must be used loyally: that is, in pursuit of that mission, assignment, function, or charge. We are therefore concerned with the misuse of power that consists of using it for an improper purpose. We are also concerned with the rules on conflicts; as we have seen, they aim to prevent the misuse of power, which in conflict situations may be unconscious. And we are also concerned with the rules that attribute information, profits, and opportunities acquired by an administrator to the beneficiary of that administration. As we have already seen, all of those rules flow directly from the other-regarding role of every administrator.[152]

Private law administrators presumptively owe a duty of care and skill, or a duty of prudence and diligence in more civilian terms. A breach of this duty may cause pure financial loss. The action or inaction of a public body may cause pure financial loss, or property damage or bodily injury, and there may be a recourse for the harmed citizen. This may be via the general law of private wrongs in some systems, and through public law procedures in others. This will be briefly explored in the following chapters.

B. Removal of public administrators

In private law, an administrator can always be removed from that role, although the details vary from one situation to another.[153] This is a characteristic of all situations of administration: the administrator's powers do not belong to them as a kind of wealth, but rather are assigned to them to carry out a mission. Thus it is also true of public administrators, although the removal mechanisms are different and may be indirect. In a democracy, those holding executive power are always accountable and removable in different ways. Secretaries or ministers may be removable by a President or a Prime Minister; that person, and in the Westminster system all ministers must periodically face the electorate. In some contexts, there may be a possibility of a 'recall' even before the end of the term of service. Those holding legislative office also acquire their powers by election and can have them removed in the same way.

---

[152] Chapters 3–7.
[153] Chapter 2, section III.B.

Every person, legal or natural, wielding public powers of the State acquires them through decisions of the executive (usually with some legislative framework) and can find them taken away. The same is true of those who wield public powers independently of State control.[154]

The case of judges is the most interesting in this regard. The independence of the judiciary from the executive branch has become a fundamental principle in relation to ensuring that the State and its emanations act lawfully. One solution to this is to have elected judges, as in many US states, although in the view of some the requiring of periodically facing the electorate may also interfere with judicial independence. Hence the typical system is that judges are appointed to a retirement age, or in some places for life. But even with the highest level of security of tenure, it is obvious that judicial powers are attached to an office and do not belong to the judge personally; and in extreme cases, with suitable safeguards, judges can be removed from office in most systems.[155] The rarity of such proceedings is a testament to the judges' understanding of their other-regarding role.

---

[154] This distinction is drawn in Chapter 11, sections II and III.
[155] For discussion of what might be called professional disciplinary sanctions against judges, see Chapter 11, section III.D.

10
The Enforcement and Supervision of Public Law Administration

I. Introduction: Dimensions of the enforcement and supervision of public administration

Private law administration typically involves supervision and enforcement by the beneficiaries, who have enforceable and actionable rights and powers of enforcement. In Chapter 8, we examined other mechanisms, including non-legal norms, the criminal law, and representative enforcement. The issue is less straightforward in public law administration, and the goal of this chapter is to articulate the problems and potential solutions.

Following Kit Barker, we can draw three different private–public distinctions that help us to understand enforcement.[1] The first is that between private law and public law. In our context, this is represented by the distinction between private administration and public administration. If the beneficiary of the administration is 'the public', or some section thereof, rather than one or more specified private persons, we are in the realm of public law and public administration.[2] This means that the duties and liabilities of the relevant administrator are not owed exclusively to particular persons, in a bilateral relationship, but rather are or include 'undirected' public duties and liabilities.[3] This concept will be explained immediately below and will be central in this Part of the book, which deals with public administration.

The second is between public and private interests. A judge holds her judicial powers in the role of a public law administrator. If the judge misuses them, say by taking a bribe to decide a case in a particular way, this is improper and unlawful. It infringes both a public interest and a private interest. It infringes

---

[1] Kit Barker, 'Modelling Public and Private Enforcement: The Rationality of Hybridity' (2018) 37 UQLJ 9.
[2] The line may not always be clear, as discussed in the previous chapter, section II.D, but penumbral cases do not prove that there is no valid distinction to be drawn. An important study has recently examined how the judicial review of both public and private administration reveals the law's aspiration to constitute public power as legitimate authority: Joanne Murray, 'Power-Conferring Principles and Authority', Doctor of Civil Law, McGill University, 2023.
[3] In Chapter 8, section III.C.3, we observed that there are also cases of undirected legal duties in private law.

the public interest in the administration of justice; in this sense, everyone has an interest in the problem, and this is why such conduct is probably a criminal offence, to say nothing of other public law sanctions such as removal of the judge from her position. But it also and differently infringes a private interest, namely the interest of the party who lost the litigation because of the bribe. That person's personal and private legal situation was wrongfully harmed in a way that no one else's was harmed. There is an analogy here to an indefensible physical assault: it violates the public interest in having a non-violent society, and so is a crime, but the same act violates the private interest of the victim, which is why some particular compensatory recourse (probably through private law, although possibly also through the criminal sentencing regime) is made available to the victim.[4]

The third distinction is between private and public enforcement. This is a distinction as to who is able to take action to challenge or contest the problem. Public enforcement is by the State, or some emanation of it. Private enforcement is by one or more private persons. It is possible to have situations in which the enforcement of the public interest is entrusted to private non-State persons. As we saw in the last chapter, it is also possible to have public enforcement of private administration, as where a Public Trustee intervenes in trust litigation to represent the interests of unborn future beneficiaries.[5]

All three of these distinctions are relevant when we look at how public administration can be monitored and its norms enforced. The function of this chapter is to describe various conceptual mechanisms for the enforcement of norms of public administration, the focus being on legal rules. Examples will be used to illustrate the different mechanisms that exist in positive law. This chapter aims to be comprehensive as to the various enforcement mechanisms. This chapter is not, however, arranged so as to explore systematically the different contexts of public administration to which such mechanisms may be relevant. Conversely, the next chapter is organized not by mechanisms but by categories or contexts of public administration. The function of that chapter is to examine the extent to which the norms of public administration are legally enforceable in those different contexts.

Before turning to the mechanisms, another distinction is needed. Private law rights are typically held *by* a person, and can be enforced or waived by that person, or by someone representing them. The right-holder is the one who controls the right, even if performance of the corresponding duty may benefit someone else.[6] On the other side of the relationship, a person owes the corresponding duty, and

---

[4] Barker (n 1), 11.
[5] Chapter 9, section II.A.
[6] Herbert LA Hart, *Essays on Bentham: Jurisprudence and Political Theory* (OUP 1982) 180–88.

that duty is owed *to* the right-holder, and no one else.[7] Public law is different, at least some of the time. *Some* rights held by or against the State (or some element or emanation of it) are like private law rights. I may owe $100 to the City of Montreal because I have not fully paid my property tax; the city may owe me $100, if I paid too much tax. But other public law relationships are not like this. I have a duty not to commit crimes, but it is not obvious to whom I owe this duty. The State can enforce it, but rights are often enforced by those who do not hold them.[8] Usually the one who holds a right can choose not to enforce it; although the State can usually pardon a criminal, it cannot authorize robbery in advance. We might say that the duty not to commit crimes is not owed *to* any one; it is an undirected duty.[9] There is no corresponding right in the strict sense. The State holds a power of enforcement in relation to a duty in respect of which it does not hold a right.[10]

My duty to pay the City of Montreal $100 is a directed, not an undirected duty. But although, for this reason, the city could *conceptually* waive it, it does not follow that it can lawfully waive it. The reason is that the city holds the benefit of the directed duty as an administrator, for the public good.[11] Waiving it is legally possible but would be unlawful unless done for some good public reason, such that the power to waive the right was used for a proper purpose.

The same considerations apply, slightly differently, to the State's power of enforcement in relation to undirected duties. As we saw in relation to private rights, when someone enforces a right for and on behalf of another, this is typically a

---

[7] Of course there can be multiple persons on either side, as in the case of joint debts.

[8] Similarly, considerations relating to the punishments that may be imposed do not entail that the State is the right-holder. A fine may be payable *to* the State, and imprisonment may be *by* the State, as may be the imposition of corporal or capital punishment in some places. None of these considerations show that it is accurate to call the State a right-holder, as opposed to the enforcer, of the original legal duty.

[9] The terminology is from Siegfried Van Duffel, 'The Nature of Rights Debate Rests on a Mistake' (2012) 93 Pacific Philosophical Q 104, 108. Paul B Miller and Andrew S Gold, 'Fiduciary Governance' (2015) 57 Wm & Mary L Rev 513 discuss how the powers of administrators may be held for purposes as well as for the benefit of persons, and explain (554–55) that in the former case, there is no beneficiary in the sense of one holding rights and powers of enforcement in relation to the administrator's duties. They use the terms 'standalone' and 'non-directed' duties. For another discussion that explores undirected legal duties, see Robert Stevens, 'Private Rights and Public Wrongs' in Matthew Dyson (ed), *Unravelling Tort and Crime* (CUP 2014) 111.

[10] Recent difficulties in Australian corporate law have arguably arisen because statutory duties imposed on directors may be ambiguous as to whether they are directed duties owed to the corporation (which may be waived) or undirected public duties (which may not). See Rosemary T Langford, 'Statutory Duties and Ratification: Untangling the Maze' (2021) 15 J of Equity 126.

[11] This is why, in French and Quebec law, the State and its emanations are said not to hold rights but rather powers; on this terminology, rights are only rights if held for the benefit of the holder. This point was discussed in Chapter 1, section IV.A.2.

relationship of administration, and entails that the administrator does not hold the enforcement power for their own benefit.[12] In the case of an undirected duty, such as my duty not to commit crimes, even though the State is not a right-holder and holds only a power of enforcement, it holds this power as an administrator: one that is bound to act, as the State usually is bound to act, in the public interest.

Similar considerations can apply to duties and liabilities owed *by* the State or its office-holders, delegates, or emanations. These include the legal duties and liabilities that accompany public administration.[13] Public administration generates undirected public duties and liabilities.[14] This is clearly illustrated by an expression from French administrative law: *contentieux objectif*. Translating it into English requires a consideration of the significance of undirected legal duties. *Contentieux* is straightforward: it refers to a contested legal proceeding. But *objectif* can only be understood by the distinction between *droit objectif* and *droit subjectif*. *Droit objectif* means 'the law' or the 'the legal order'. A *droit subjectif* is a legal right held by a particular person for their own benefit.[15] A subjective right always corresponds to a directed duty owed to the right-holder which can be enforced through a *contentieux subjectif*. Thus a *contentieux objectif*, by contrast, is a proceeding not to enforce a right, or a directed duty, but to enforce legality.[16] It is a way of enforcing undirected legal duties.

But as we have seen above, undirected duties are not (or not necessarily) unenforceable duties. This is just as true of undirected duties owed by the State as of undirected duties owed by individuals. Undirected duties owed by the State may be enforceable at the instance of (some other part of) the State, and potentially also at the instance of private persons. Unlike the State, however, private persons are not duty-bound administrators in relation to their potential ability to enforce such duties. These possibilities are explored below.

---

[12] Chapter 8, section II.A and *passim*.

[13] I refer here to 'duties and liabilities' because the requirement that legal powers be used for proper purposes is not a duty in the strict sense that it corresponds to any right held by another (Chapter 3, section IV.G). Where the power is used improperly, it is liable to be set aside, even though there may not have been any breach of a duty in the strict sense. Thus public administrators may have undirected liabilities (in relation to their powers) as well as undirected duties. I generally however refer to 'undirected public duties' with the intention to include also undirected public liabilities.

[14] Chapter 9, section II. As argued there, some cases of public administration may additionally generate directed duties. For example, a director of a corporate entity which exists to perform a public function owes directed duties to the entity, as well as undirected duties arising from the public nature of the administration. This is discussed below in section II.F.

[15] This is discussed briefly in Chapter 1, sections IV.A.2, V.B.2.a.

[16] Jean Waline, *Droit administratif* (26th edn, Dalloz 2016) 679: 'Dans ce dernier cas [*contentieux subjectif*], le demandeur invoque *son* droit; dans le premier [*contentieux objectif*], il défend *le* Droit' (italics and capitalization in original). My translation: 'In the latter [*contentieux subjectif*], the plaintiff invokes *his* right; in the former [*contentieux objectif*], he defends Legality'.

II. Mechanisms of enforcement and supervision

A. Non-legal norms

1. Introduction

We saw in Chapter 8 that private law administration can occasionally be supported by non-legal norms. These have more prominence in the public sphere. For example, the Australian Commonwealth government and the UK government have codes governing the conduct of cabinet ministers.[17] Among many other things, these codes cover financial conflicts of interest, including how interests should be declared and how conflicts may be managed. Contraventions, and potential or alleged contraventions, of the Code are serious matters that may lead to the dismissal or resignation of a minister. In February 2020, a minister of the Australian Commonwealth government resigned for a breach of the code.[18] But it remains the case that such a code is not law. It is not in an Act of Parliament but is a document generated by the executive branch of the government. It is government policy. Sanctions for its breach are political sanctions.

This study is concerned primarily with how we act for others in law, and thus with the legal regulation of acting for others. But it is important to notice that non-legal norms are still a significant part of the landscape in the public law sphere. One reason for this is precisely the public nature of the relationship. If a cabinet minister exercises her powers while in a conflict of interest, who has standing to complain? In a way everyone does, and this may mean that in a way no one does. Keeping the sanctions out of the legal sphere is one way of dealing with the difficulty of enforcement and also, perhaps, of accentuating the importance of the political (as opposed to legal) accountability of elected officials.

It is not the only way and it may not be the best way. Recent years have seen a trend towards increasing legal regulation, in place of political and other forms of non-legal regulation. Many of the mechanisms by which this can occur will be

---

[17] Australia: online at https://www.pmc.gov.au/resource-centre/government/statement-ministerial-standards; UK: online at https://www.gov.uk/government/publications/ministerial-code. In the UK, the Committee on Standards in Public Life has an advisory role; see Gillian Peele and Robert Kaye, 'Conflict of Interest in British Public Life' in C Trost and AL Gash (eds), *Conflict of Interest and Public Life* (CUP 2008) 155. The Canadian federal government also has such a code (online at https://pm.gc.ca/sites/pm/files/inline-files/oag_2015_english.pdf) but ministers and other holders of public powers are also governed in this regard by Canadian federal law, which will be discussed below.

[18] According to Rob Harris, 'Embattled McKenzie resigns from federal cabinet over "sports rorts" affair', *Sydney Morning Herald* (2 Feb. 2020), online at https://www.smh.com.au/politics/federal/embattled-mckenzie-resigns-from-federal-cabinet-over-sports-rorts-affair-20200202-p53wxm.html, the former minister said: 'At no time did my membership of shooting sports clubs influence my decision making'. This is another example of a classic and typical failure to understand the rationale for the rules against exercising other-regarding powers while in a conflict of interest: the rules are not about preventing conscious wrongdoing but rather are about excluding the unknowable effects of improper considerations. See Chapter 4, section IV.A.

examined in the remainder of this chapter. In the next chapter, we will look at particular public actors and the ways in which they are subject to legal norms of sound public administration.

One curious feature of the legal regulation of public administration is this: frequently the legal norms that are in place are referred to as 'ethical' rules, or as codes of 'ethics'.[19] One could say that they are *not* rules of ethics, or not only rules of ethics, inasmuch as they are rules of law. Conversely, if one thinks that these rules of law give legal effect to sound and important ethical principles, the same could be said of much of contract law, tort law, property law, family law, and other fields. One possibility for making sense of this 'ethical' terminology is that the use of the word 'ethics' in this context is based on a recognition that acting for others in law is different from acting for oneself.[20]

2. Reasons to resist legal norms governing public administration?

There is however an important point to be addressed in this section, which is this: If legal norms are better than purely political or otherwise non-legal norms in this context, why are these non-legal norms still so visible, particularly in relation to the executive branch of government? In the project of this book, which focuses on the law, it is easy to assume that law is better than non-law. But it is worth pausing to ask, what are the advantages and disadvantages of leaving at least some aspects of public administration to be governed by non-legal norms?

In administrative law there is always a background concern with overlegalizing the operation of government and of all of the functions that are delegated by government to boards, tribunals, and agencies. Of course these entities must operate within the law, but if this means that every act or omission can be challenged in court, it may be argued that the business of government becomes difficult to operate. The question whether some official even had the authority to do an act (or was obliged to do an act) must necessarily be a justiciable legal question. The more difficult questions arise around the norm of administration that powers must be used for the purposes for which they were granted. That is because this norm may allow a challenge to an action which the relevant official *did* have authority to do.

In relation to any exercise of state power that is justiciable, there is a question, often framed in terms of standing, as to who may bring proceedings; we

---

[19] To take two examples: the legal rules that govern the use of public powers by professionals, by legislators, and by judges may be referred to as rules of professional ethics, or as 'Codes of Ethics'; and a US federal statute covering similar issues for government employees of all branches and levels is called the Ethics Reform Act of 1989, Pub L No 101–194, 103 Stat 1716, codified in a range of chapters of the US Code. All of these are discussed in Chapter 11.

[20] Some reasons for the frequent failure to recognize this difference are discussed particularly in Chapter 1, section II.B; Chapter 5, section II.B.3.

will examine this later in the chapter. Here the focus is on whether some matters should rightly be left outside of any review by the courts.

In administrative law, the relationship between the courts and the State and its various emanations is sometimes described in terms of 'deference'. On one view, the courts should show some deference to the other branches, and not get caught up in, or try to control or supervise minutely, the running of the State. This seems like a mischaracterization, just as it is in private law administration.[21] Deference is a matter of choice, guided perhaps by respect. But the courts should not stay out of the decisions of other holders of public power out of choice or respect, but rather as a matter of legal jurisdiction.[22] The courts hear only legal arguments. They hear arguments that the government is acting unlawfully, not arguments that the government is making unwise choices.[23] When an argument for review fails, it is not because the court is 'deferential', but because the court has nothing to say except about legal questions.[24]

Where those holding the relevant power are elected, it could be argued that the most important form of accountability is at the polls.[25] But making the exercise of state power legally justiciable is hardly inconsistent with political accountability.[26] Moreover, the idea that democratic and political accountability are capable, on their own, of addressing improper exercises of power implies that any relevant action cannot be challenged, condemned, or set aside until the next election. It also presupposes that anything that the electorate does not react against should be allowed to stand. That is an inherently majoritarian view, and inconsistent with the ideal of the rule of law.

In English law, government power exercised under the royal prerogative was widely considered to be non-justiciable during the twentieth century.[27] The

---

[21] In the context of the so-called 'business judgment rule': Chapter 3, section II.B.

[22] See Trevor RS Allan, 'Judicial Deference and Judicial Review: Legal Doctrine and Legal Theory' (2011) 127 LQR 96, arguing that there is no independent legal doctrine of deference, but that it is embedded in jurisdiction and legal process. I would go further than him inasmuch as I doubt that what is called judicial deference rests on competence or expertise in the executive, separately from resting on jurisdiction. The reason is that judicial deference arising from jurisdiction should rightly apply *even if* the persons holding executive public powers were totally incompetent and even if judges could demonstrably do a better job. Until lawfully removed, the persons holding executive public powers are the ones who hold those powers. Paul Daly, *A Theory of Deference in Administrative Law* (CUP 2012), provides a comprehensive response, but it seems that most of what he characterizes as deference is what Allan understands to be a matter of spheres of jurisdiction.

[23] *Carltona Ltd v Commissioners of Works* [1943] 2 All ER 560 (CA), 563–55.

[24] A different idea of 'deference' may be in play if the courts conclude that the legislature has granted a non-judicial entity some authority to interpret the law. The courts may defer to the interpretation of the law made by that body, by applying a standard of whether its interpretation was reasonable, not whether it was correct (see *Canada (Minister of Citizenship and Immigration) v Vavilov* 2019 SCC 65). But even this 'deference' could be understood in jurisdictional terms.

[25] Stephen Gageler, 'The Equitable Duty of Loyalty in Public Office' in Tim Bonyhady (ed), *Finn's Law: An Australian Justice* (Federation Press 2016) 126, 131.

[26] *R (Miller) v Prime Minister* [2019] UKSC 41, [2020] AC 373, [33] (*Miller (No 2)*).

[27] In the Westminster tradition, the royal prerogative refers to the powers that were formerly exercised by the sovereign and now are usually exercised by the government in the name of the

House of Lords rejected this in 1984 and held that the exercise of such powers is potentially subject to judicial review, although there may be exceptions, including for matters touching national security.[28] In matters of security, Lord Fraser said: 'the Government alone has access to the necessary information, and in any event the judicial process is unsuitable for reaching decisions on national security'.[29] The implication is that in this context, non-justiciability arises out of an absence of legal accountability, in the narrow sense of having to provide reasons for actions taken. Thus although the government remains politically accountable, it does not have to explain itself in judicial proceedings, with the result that there will be no basis upon which to say that the actions were not proper. This is supported by the suggestion in another of the speeches that even powers relating to security can be reviewed when their exercise is completely unreasonable.[30] In such a case, one might say, the court can conclude on that basis alone that the power was misused, without investigation into the reasons behind the decision. The implication is that if the power was used in a way that is not completely unreasonable, the only accountability is political.

Another insight on the limits of saying that a power is not justiciable comes from an earlier case dealing with the powers of the Attorney General. *Gouriet v Union of Post Office Workers*[31] concerned in part the power of the Attorney General to authorize a relator action.[32] In the Court of Appeal, Lord Denning MR suggested that the Attorney General's decisions in this respect were subject

---

Crown, and that do not depend on legislation (which, where it exists as a source of power, itself grants and delimits the relevant power). In countries of that tradition, it generally includes the power to grant pardons, the conduct of international relations including defence, and other matters. See Thomas Poole, 'The Strange Death of Prerogative in England' (2018) 43 UWALR 42; Patrick F Baud, 'The Crown's Prerogatives and the Constitution of Canada' (2021) 3 J of Commonwealth L 219. Some few powers are still exercised not by the government but by the monarch or her representative, on the advice of the government, including the powers to dissolve Parliament and to grant honours.

[28] *Council of Civil Service Unions v Minister for the Civil Service* [1985] AC 374 (HL). The *Case of Proclamations* (1611) 12 Co Rep 74, 77 ER 1352 was important in establishing that the prerogative has legal limits and could not, for example, be used to change the law; the more recent development was that there could be judicial review of *intra vires* exercises of the prerogative power.

[29] ibid 402.

[30] Lord Scarman (406–07): 'Once the factual basis is established by evidence so that the court is satisfied that the interest of national security is a relevant factor to be considered in the determination of the case, the court will accept the opinion of the Crown or its responsible officer as to what is required to meet it, unless it is possible to show that the opinion was one which no reasonable minister advising the Crown could in the circumstances reasonably have held'. In the common law, that very high level of unreasonableness is understood to be evidence that the person must have misunderstood their powers or role (see also *NZ Council of Licenced Firearms Owners Inc v Minister of Police* [2020] NZHC 1456, [84]). *Vavilov* (n 24) can be read as saying that even apart from questions of interpretation of the law, a substantive decision made by one holding authority to make it can be overturned by a court if the decision was simply unreasonable. That seems to represent a confusion about jurisdiction.

[31] [1978] AC 435 (HL).

[32] Relator actions are discussed below, section II.G.2.

to judicial review; he also commented adversely on the fact that the Attorney General had refused to give his reasons for not allowing a relator action to proceed.[33] The House of Lords rejected this position. Viscount Dilhorne, who had been Attorney General from 1954 to 1962, compared the power over relator actions to the power over prosecutions:

> The Attorney General has many powers and duties. He may stop any prosecution on indictment by entering a *nolle prosequi*. He merely has to sign a piece of paper saying that he does not wish the prosecution to continue. He need not give any reasons. He can direct the institution of a prosecution and direct the Director of Public Prosecutions to take over the conduct of any criminal proceedings and he may tell him to offer no evidence. In the exercise of these powers he is not subject to direction by his ministerial colleagues or to control and supervision by the courts....
>
> In deciding whether or not to prosecute 'there is only one consideration which is altogether excluded,' Sir Hartley Shawcross said, 'and that is the repercussion of a given decision upon my personal or my party's or the Government's political fortunes.'[34]

Whether Viscount Dilhorne liked it or not, however, this implies that the Attorney General's decision *is* potentially justiciable, because the judge's position was that the power cannot lawfully be exercised for the improper purpose that he identified.[35] Thus if the exercise were known, by admission or otherwise, to have been used for that purpose, it would be revealed to be unlawful. The issue is a matter of procedure but also accountability: Who must prove that the purposes were proper or improper, and can the Attorney General be required to give reasons?

In more recent litigation that expanded the scope of justiciability, namely *Miller (No 2)*, the UK Supreme Court said very clearly that the presence of political accountability did not exclude justiciability.[36] It held that the prerogative power of the Prime Minister to ask the Queen to prorogue Parliament could only be used in a way that did not frustrate Parliament's constitutional role.[37] Whether

---

[33] [1977] QB 729 (CA), 752–53, 758–62.

[34] Nn 31, 487, 489, quoting John LJ Edwards, *The Law Officers of the Crown* (Sweet & Maxwell 1964) at 222–23. In this passage, Viscount Dilhorne directly adopted the argument of the Attorney General (at 453). As Attorney General, Viscount Dilhorne made a controversial decision to stop the prosecution of a medical doctor for murder.

[35] A more recent decision of the UK Supreme Court indicates that the power to end a private prosecution is indeed justiciable: *R (Gujra) v Crown Prosecution Service* [2012] UKSC 52, [2013] 1 AC 484.

[36] *Miller (No 2)* (n 26), [33]. In *Gouriet* the Attorney General's position was that he was accountable to Parliament but not to the courts: [1977] QB 729 (CA), 741–42.

[37] ibid [50].

or not that was the case could be determined by considering the explanation that the Prime Minister had given for the prorogation in question. But no such explanation had been given:

> no reason was given for closing down Parliament for five weeks.[38]
>
> It is impossible for us to conclude, on the evidence which has been put before us, that there was any reason—let alone a good reason—to advise Her Majesty to prorogue Parliament for five weeks, from 9 or 12 September until 14 October. We cannot speculate, in the absence of further evidence, upon what such reasons might have been. It follows that the decision was unlawful.[39]

This line of reasoning seems effectively to impose an obligation on the Prime Minister to give reasons. If we apply it to *Gouriet*, we might say that the Attorney General's powers over relator actions cannot be used for party political reasons but only for appropriate reasons; and if no reasons are given at all, the court cannot speculate on what the reasons were, and so must conclude that the decision was unlawful.[40]

In conclusion, the non-justiciability of some executive action seems not to be so much a principle but a consequence of the consideration that sometimes members of the executive cannot be required to explain their actions. Legality aspires to rationality, and the substantive review of the exercise of administrative powers depends on some assessment of the reasons for which they were exercised. If such reasons are unknown, one might conclude (as in *Gouriet*) that the exercise cannot be questioned. Another approach, apparently adopted in *Miller (No 2)*, is to conclude that an unexplained decision is an unlawful decision.

3. Problems with reliance on non-legal norms

Reliance on non-legal norms, norms which may be framed in terms of ethics and integrity, may be sufficient when such norms are widely shared and are felt to be binding in important ways by those holding public power. Both of those conditions may be less applicable now than they were in times past. Stephen Harper became Prime Minister of Canada in 2006, partly because of voters' dissatisfaction with the improper use of public funds by the previous government,

---

[38] ibid [58].
[39] ibid [61].
[40] See also *Padfield v Minister of Agriculture, Fisheries and Foods* [1968] AC 997 (CA, HL), at 1006–07, *per* Lord Denning MR: if a Minister gives no reasons, '. . . the court may infer that he has no good reason'. Lord Denning MR dissented in the Court of Appeal but the appeal was allowed. In the House of Lords, Lord Hodson (at 1049) indicated that a Minister would not necessarily escape judicial review by simply refusing to give reasons for not exercising a power. Compare the French decision of the Conseil d'État, 28 mai 1954, *Barel*, Rec 308, discussed in L Neville Brown and John S Bell, *French Administrative Law* (5th edn, Clarendon Press 1998) 255.

and Parliament enacted into law a wide range of rules of public administration that had previously been non-legal rules.[41] He was the head of a minority government, and remained so following another election in 2008. In December of that year, the opposition parties agreed to vote against the government on a motion of no confidence, which would have forced Harper to resign; Harper asked the Governor General to prorogue Parliament to avoid the vote's taking place. She did so, and there was no legal challenge to this, although it was certainly controversial. While Parliament had adopted his platform of turning some non-legal norms of public administration into binding law, his government was also characterized by an approach that was not greatly concerned with constitutional conventions and only considered itself bound by law.[42] To the extent that this mode of government is becoming more common, the legalization of norms of sound public administration becomes increasingly important.[43] As discussed above, it has now been held in UK law that the power to ask the head of state to prorogue Parliament may not be used for the improper purpose of preventing Parliament from functioning as such.[44] According to the logic of that decision, Harper's action was almost certainly unlawful, since a motion of no confidence is a central feature of the Westminster system of responsible government.

This approach to non-legal norms was also evident during the presidency of Donald Trump. Interestingly, one apparent consequence of Trump's approach to exercising power may be that the scope and extent of legal norms is being increasingly clarified. This is because Trump's actions generated a wave of lawsuits, some of which will be used as examples later in this chapter and in the next. This litigation clarified points of law that would never have been tested if executive power was used according to the conventions that had previously been respected. Similar comments could be made in relation to the powers of the federal Attorney General, if it is right to think, as was stated for English law in *Gouriet*, that those powers cannot lawfully be used for party political purposes.[45]

---

[41] *Conflict of Interest Act*, SC 2006, c 9, s 2. This will be discussed later in this chapter, section II.C.
[42] Another example is that in 2013, one of the seats on the Supreme Court of Canada reserved for judges from Quebec became vacant, and Harper appointed Marc Nadon, a supernumerary judge of the Federal Court of Canada. Nadon had been a Quebec lawyer before becoming a judge, but had not been a judge of a Quebec court, but rather of the Federal Court. This was the first time an appointment had been made from that Court to one of the Quebec seats. The Supreme Court of Canada held that the appointment was invalid: Reference re Supreme Court Act, ss 5 and 6 2014 SCC 21, [2014] 1 SCR 433.
[43] See the comment of 'Bagehot', the *Economist*'s anonymous columnist on British politics, *Economist*, 5 February 2022, 51: '... British politics relies on shame to function. The country still runs on the "good chap" theory of government: the idea that politicians abide by the invisible lines of the constitution. An absence of legal constraints requires an abundance of personal restraint ... A bad chap can go a long way'.
[44] *Miller (No 2)* (n 26).
[45] Lawrence Martin, 'William Barr: The Second-Most Dangerous Man in America', *Globe and Mail* (9 June 2020); Charlie Savage and Adam Goldman, 'Outsider Tapped in Flynn Case Calls Justice Dept Reversal a "Gross Abuse" of Power', *New York Times* (10 June 2020).

The Attorney General, in that role, must not act under political direction; he or she is a public administrator par excellence, one of whose duties is to enforce the claims of the State solely in the public interest.[46]

Of course, legal norms can be relied upon to ensure legality only if the judges who administer them are, themselves, above party political allegiances, as their judicial oaths require them to be.

B. Criminal law

The most egregious violations of the norms with which we are concerned may attract the sanctions of criminal law. For example, assume that a cabinet minister took a bribe to approve a project, or a legislator sold her vote on some question to a private person. Such cases might well be crimes.[47]

This might be considered an example of the enforcement of norms of public law administration, but I would argue that it is more of a supporting process than an enforcement process. Just as in private law administration, criminalization is better seen as a complementary measure that is called for when the conduct is sufficiently serious.[48] Criminal sanctions might be said to support relationships of administration, by sanctioning the most grievous infractions of the associated norms, in the same way that criminal law supports our right to bodily integrity by criminalizing serious infringements of that right.

Obviously criminal law is part of public law, but it does not follow that criminal sanctions in relation to public law administration must occupy the field of enforcement to the exclusion of more direct forms of enforcement. If we imagine a public administrator, such as a police chief, who takes a bribe, we can identify two different public interests. There is a public interest in having a public administration that is free from corruption, and this might be the justification for a criminal sanction. But there is a separate public interest in the proper conduct of public administration, indeed in the proper administration of this particular public police force. This interest is infringed by bribe-taking but it is also infringed by any conduct that does not meet the standards of good administration, whether or not it constitutes a crime. This calls for some enforcement

---

[46] See *Bateman's Bay Local Aboriginal Land Council v Aboriginal Community Benefit Fund Pty Ltd* (1998) 194 CLR 247, [38], and the study by Hon A Anne McLellan, *Review of the Roles of the Minister of Justice and Attorney General of Canada* (28 June 2019), online at https://pm.gc.ca/en/news/backgr ounders/2019/08/14/review-roles-minister-justice-and-attorney-general-canada. McLellan's report also notes that the best solution is not necessarily that all such decisions be made by someone who is independent of the government, because this will attenuate political responsibility for decisions that must be made in the public interest.

[47] Paul D Finn, 'The Forgotten "Trust": The People and the State' in Malcolm Cope (ed), *Equity: Issues and Trends* (Federation Press 1995) 131 cites examples at 145–47.

[48] Chapter 8, section III.B.

process in relation to the bribe, whether or not there is a criminal conviction. Thus there may be a non-criminal duty to surrender the bribe.

Criminal sanctions do not aim to rectify faulty administration, although they may aim to deter it, to denounce it, and to punish it. In the next subsection, we will see that some systems have non-criminal sanctions that have similar goals. The main focus in this section is on legal norms that aim to enforce sound public administration more directly. This includes by enforcing primary duties of administration, and by rectifying faulty administration, as in the case of setting aside decisions made for improper purposes.

The norms of criminal law create undirected duties.[49] So too do the supervision regimes discussed in the next subsection. There may be directed or undirected duties that exist to rectify faulty administration. In other words, the bribe-taking police chief may have a non-criminal duty to surrender the bribe, and it may be a directed duty (owed, perhaps, to the police force if it exists as a legal person) or an undirected duty. The rest of this chapter supplies examples of both.

C. Supervision with non-criminal denunciatory sanctions

In Canada's federal government, cabinet ministers including the Prime Minister, as well as many other federally appointed office-holders, are subject to a *Conflict of Interest Act*.[50] This statute includes all of the rules that characterize sound administration: rules on the misuse of public powers, rules on the avoidance of conflicts of interest, rules on disclosure, and a rule against unauthorized profits. The statute is administered by a Conflict of Interest and Ethics Commissioner.[51] The Commissioner is an 'officer of Parliament' who reports directly to Parliament.[52]

This is not a criminal regime but it shares some of the features discussed in the previous section. If, for example, the Commissioner finds that a Minister of the Crown exercised a power while in a conflict of interest, or acquired an unauthorized profit, the Commissioner can so declare.[53] For some violations, the

---

[49] For the terminology of directed and undirected duties and liabilities, see above, section I.
[50] SC 2006, c 9, s 2. Similar legislation exists in some provinces. The Act is discussed in Chapter 11, section III.A.1.d.
[51] The title is arguably inaccurate, since the Commissioner is charged with enforcing the law, not an ethical code, and since the norms include but go well beyond conflicts of interest. The Commissioner also, however, enforces the rules of the House of Commons that deal with the same issues and that apply to all Members of Parliament. These rules are not in a statute but a resolution of the House.
[52] Ann Chaplin, *Officers of Parliament* (Yvon Blais 2011). For the suggestion that officials of this kind represent a 'fourth branch of government', see Gageler (n 25) 133.
[53] *Trudeau II Report* (14 Aug 2019), online at https://ciec-ccie.parl.gc.ca/en/investigations-enquetes/Pages/TrudeauIIReport-RapportTrudeauII.aspx.

Commissioner can impose a monetary penalty.[54] These sanctions do not rectify the problems; like criminal law, they may denounce them and they may deter them in the future.

There are however other important elements to this regime. The Commissioner does not only react to complaints, but is available to counsel those subject to the regime on how to order their affairs. In this sense, the system may help to prevent faulty administration. Moreover, the Commissioner may, if made aware of a problem in advance, be able to make an order aimed at preventing it: for example, an order that someone recuse themself from a role.[55]

D. Enforcement by the State

Public administration, being directed towards a public purpose, creates undirected duties and liabilities in relation to the exercise of the powers of the administrator.[56] Undirected legal duties need one or more enforcers. Just as the State or some emanation of it enforces the undirected duties of private persons to obey the criminal law, so it can generally enforce undirected duties and liabilities of public administration. This is an example of what was earlier called 'designated person standing'.[57]

In the common law, the Attorney General can by default enforce the proper administration of charities, whether they are in the form of trusts or corporations.[58] This enforcement role includes rights to information and powers to supervise the proper exercise of powers, as well as rights arising from the rule against unauthorized profits. This enforcement power may in some places be given by statute to a governmental agency.[59]

Although they are engaged in public administration, charities have a large degree of autonomy and are not usually under the control of the executive. A great deal of other public administration is directly or indirectly under its control.[60] In this setting, the supervision of administration may involve the giving of instructions and the appointment and removal of administrators much more often than it may involve the enforcement of legal norms governing administration. But despite this control, it will sometimes be necessary for the State

---

[54] *Conflict of Interest Act* (n 50), s 52.
[55] ibid s 30.
[56] It may additionally create directed duties and liabilities. This is discussed below in section II.F.
[57] Chapter 8, section III.D.
[58] Miller and Gold (n 9), 529 note that in some US states, the settlor has standing to enforce charitable trusts. This is also true in all Quebec trusts, some of which have charitable status.
[59] In England and Wales there is the Charity Commission; Miller and Gold (ibid) refer to state agencies.
[60] The legislative and judicial branches of the government are self-regulating and not controlled or supervised by the executive (Chapter 11, sections III.C and III.D).

to intervene to correct misuses of power or other failures, and this may especially be so where the control is indirect. In many situations, these enforcement powers will be attributed to some department of government with oversight responsibility.[61]

In some well-known cases, the Attorney General has acted as the enforcer of the rule against unauthorized profits, against those holding public powers.[62] In a case brought in Jersey, the Federal Republic of Brazil recovered the proceeds of bribery from companies controlled by a corrupt municipal mayor. Under Brazil's constitution, the plaintiff was not an Attorney General but the State itself.[63] Other recent cases have seen State claims against third parties for receiving property that had been transferred by a public administrator, in breach of the administrator's public duties.[64]

E. The problem of self-supervision

The problem of self-supervision is ubiquitous in private and public administration.[65] We saw in the previous section that the State will generally have enforcement powers in relation to public administration that relates to the executive function of government. These enforcement powers may not always be used, for a range of reasons. The problem of self-supervision arises most where the person making the enforcement decisions is not sufficiently independent from the administrator.

Thus enforcement by the State or the Attorney General may be unrealistic when the administrator whose conduct is in question is also in a position of governmental power.[66] The US Constitution has a rule against unauthorized profits in the eighth clause of the ninth paragraph of Art I: '. . . no Person holding any Office of Profit or Trust under [the United States] shall, without the Consent of the Congress, accept of any present, Emolument, Office, or Title, of any kind whatever, from any King, Prince, or foreign State.' This is generally called the

---

[61] Miller and Gold (n 9), 552, 555 refer to Government Accountability Offices in the United States. In Canada, government-controlled corporations ('Crown corporations') usually report to a responsible minister.

[62] *Attorney-General v Edmunds* (1868) LR 6 Eq 381; *Reading v Attorney-General* [1951] AC 507 (HL); *Attorney-General for Hong Kong v Reid* [1994] 1 AC 324 (PC).

[63] *Federal Republic of Brazil v Durant International Corp* [2015] UKPC 35, [2016] AC 297. The judgment indicates ([1]) that the 'effective' plaintiff was the Municipality of São Paulo, but that Brazilian law requires that the State be a party to any action brought by a public authority outside of Brazil.

[64] *Arthur v Attorney General of the Turks & Caicos Islands* [2012] UKPC 30; *Akita Holdings Ltd v Attorney General of the Turks & Caicos Islands* [2017] UKPC 7, [2017] AC 590.

[65] For the introduction of this idea in relation to private administration, see Chapter 8, section II.C.3.

[66] *Bateman's Bay Local Aboriginal Land Council* (n 46), [38].

'foreign emoluments' clause.[67] One might think that the natural person to enforce it would be the Attorney General of the United States, but the difficulties are apparent if that person is not able or willing to make enforcement decisions independently from the President. There were attempts by others to enforce this clause in relation to Donald Trump, to which we will return below.

One way to address this problem this is to assign the enforcement role to a person with more independence from the person or persons being supervised. In the context of local government, an official such as an auditor may be charged with oversight of the exercise of public powers, and have standing to enforce proper administration.[68] It is immediately apparent that such roles cannot solve the problem of self-supervision unless there is some security of tenure for the supervisor, in relation to the authority held by those who must be supervised. Where those responsible for monitoring administration can simply be removed by executive fiat, they are unlikely to offer effective safeguards against the problem of self-supervision.[69]

The Canadian Conflict of Interest and Ethics Commissioner can be removed by the federal cabinet, but only on a vote of Parliament.[70] Under the Westminster system, however, in a majority government the governing party can typically control parliamentary votes. The potential weakness of this system is illustrated by an incident in the Canadian province of Alberta, which has similar legislation. The election commissioner was investigating whether members of the political party holding a majority government had broken campaign finance laws. The provincial legislature, controlled by the government, passed a statute abolishing the election commissioner's position. The province's Ethics Commissioner rejected a complaint that the members of the party who voted for the statute had been in a disqualifying conflict of interest. She found that a party's political interest was not a 'private interest' to which the legislation applied, and therefore did not create a conflict of interest in the relevant sense.[71] Although

---

[67] There is a 'domestic emoluments' clause in Art II, paragraph 1, clause 7 that applies only to the President: 'The President shall, at stated Times, receive for his Services, a Compensation, which shall neither be increased nor diminished during the Period for which he shall have been elected, and he shall not receive within that Period any other Emolument from the United States, or any of them'. Curiously, neither clause seems clearly to apply to benefits received from domestic non-governmental entities. This might be a case in which non-legal norms were assumed to be adequate.

[68] This was what happened in *Porter v Magill* [2002] 2 AC 357 (CA, HL), discussed in Chapter 11, section III.B.2.e.

[69] Jen Kirby, 'Trump's purge of inspectors general, explained', *Vox*, 28 May 2020, online at https://www.vox.com/2020/5/28/21265799/inspectors-general-trump-linick-atkinson.

[70] *Parliament of Canada Act*, RSC 1985, c P-1, s 82(1). The role of this person was introduced above, section II.C.

[71] Marguerite Trussler, Report of the Investigation under the *Conflicts of Interest Act*, 27 Apr 2020, online at http://www.ethicscommissioner.ab.ca/media/2491/april-27-2020-allegations-involving-bill-22.pdf. One member of the Assembly was found to have had a private interest in that he was actually under investigation by the election commissioner; he did not vote, but he was found to have breached the conflict-of-interest legislation by failing formally to declare his interest. The Ethics Commissioner recommended that he apologize to the Assembly. This underlines the point made in

she was bound to apply the governing legislation, it is not clear that the analysis was complete. It is true that members of a political party must be free to vote in favour of laws that advance the party's policies and agenda. It does not follow that any exercise of public power aimed at the retention of power by one's own party does not generate a conflict of interest. Quite the contrary: such reasoning has the potential to lead directly to misuse of power. The whole point of rules about conflicts is that a person with an irrelevant personal interest cannot be expected to exercise their judgment in the way that they would in the absence of that interest. Every politician no doubt thinks that the public interest will be best served by their re-election, but that is an assessment affected by a conflict of interest. The Canadian federal Conflict of Interest and Ethics Commissioner said in a report:

> private (or partisan) political interests, ones 'designed to protect or advance the retention of constitutional power by the incumbent government and its political supporters,' cannot be said to serve the general public.[72]

That seems like a better analysis.

F. Enforcement by claims of non-State bodies acting in the public interest against their own administrators

There is another available mechanism of enforcement of the norms of public administration where the relevant duties are owed directly to a right-holding entity (usually a legal person) that is carrying out a function in the public interest, whether or not it is an emanation of the State.[73] In those situations, rights of enforcement may be held by that entity. It is natural that the entity would be able to enforce the proper conduct of the relevant public administration. This is direct (not representative) enforcement, as it is enforcement by the entity to whom the duties are owed. Moreover, those duties are directed legal duties.[74]

I will give some examples from both of the categories mentioned in the previous paragraph. The first is emanations of the State. In the context of local

---

the previous subsection of this chapter, that these regimes cannot rectify problems except perhaps where they are able to act in advance.

[72] *Trudeau II Report* (14 Aug 2019), online at https://ciec-ccie.parl.gc.ca/en/investigations-enquetes/Pages/TrudeauIIReport-RapportTrudeauII.aspx.

[73] The term 'emanation of the State' is explained in Chapter 11, section III.B.1, but in the remainder of this section, I will give examples of both possibilities.

[74] For the terminology of directed and undirected duties and liabilities, see above, section I. Note that in the situations under discussion here, it is probable that there are *also* undirected duties and liabilities, opening the door to other mechanisms of enforcement, which are discussed briefly at the end of this subsection and elsewhere in this chapter.

government, claims have been brought by municipalities against their own administrators, for unauthorized profits.[75] These municipalities are legal persons, created by a legislature. To take another example, in Quebec, the *Société des alcools du Québec* is a Crown corporation, an emanation of the State that has a monopoly on the retail sale of liquor and decent wine in the province.[76] If a director of that corporation were to violate norms of sound administration by, for example, hiring a member of his own family, the *Société* would be able to annul this contract as improper.[77]

Similar mechanisms can apply to entitles that are not emanations of the State or controlled by it, but that are charged with acting in the public interest. A university is an example.[78] To take a similar problem, imagine that a professor, controlling public research funds, used those funds to employ a family member as a research assistant. The university would probably be able to challenge that exercise of juridical powers of administration, and to set aside the contract as having been made through a misuse of power or, at least, in a conflict of interest.[79]

These situations are cases of direct enforcement, not of rights and enforcement powers of the State as such, but of the rights and enforcement powers of legal persons with public missions. Although the State need have nothing to do with enforcement in these cases, we should not assume that it has no role to play in such a dispute. This may be important because all of these cases can raise the problem of self-supervision; for example, if the professor in the example in the previous paragraph was also a senior administrator of the university. In the case of a State-controlled corporation, the State will have both legal and practical rights as a sole shareholder. Even where this is not the case, as in the example of the university, in the common law the courts have a general supervisory jurisdiction over legal persons (at least those created by letters patent) and this is

---

[75] Eg *Bowes v Toronto (City)* (1858) 11 Moo PC 463, 14 ER 770. In *Edmonton (City) v Hawrelak* [1976] 1 SCR 387, the city brought a claim against its former mayor for acquiring an unauthorized profit. The claim was dismissed by a 3-2 majority, on the ground that the profit was acquired sufficiently independently from the mayoral role that it was not caught by the relevant rule. As far as the problem of self-supervision, it may be noted that the defendant mayor was out of office when the litigation began.

[76] *Act respecting the Société des alcools du Québec*, CQLR c S-13. The same statute creates the subsidiary corporation *Société québécoise du cannabis* (ss 23.1–23.43).

[77] In the absence of direct regulation in the governing statute of contracts made in conflict of interest, the annulment could be based on general provisions for legal persons in the Civil Code of Québec, arts 324, 326, at least if the offending administrator was a director. If not, the general law of mandate would apply (CCQ arts 2138, 2147), since anyone empowered to hire employees must be a mandatary (see Chapter 7, section II.B.1).

[78] Chapter 9, section II.D.2.

[79] The professor is unlikely to be a director or governor of the university, but if the employment contract of the research assistant is with the university, the professor empowered to hire the assistant must be in some sense a mandatary or agent of the university (see Chapter 7, section II.B.1). In many universities, there is in any event a conflict-of-interest policy that probably takes effect contractually and that would forbid such an appointment. Depending on the facts, the research assistant could conceivably invoke legal protections for third parties in good faith (Chapter 3, section IV.F.3).

also true in Quebec civil law.[80] Where modern business corporations' statutes are in place, they typically contain a thorough range of remedies for shareholders and other stakeholders. In the case of special act and charter corporations, the statute may not provide for such remedies. Here the court's supervisory jurisdiction may be important. In the case of corporations acting for public purposes, whether or not they are emanations of the State, the Attorney General could be expected to be considered a proper person to invoke the court's supervisory jurisdiction. And if, additionally, the legal person is a charity, as in the case of the university, in the common law the Attorney General has an independent right of enforcement that does not depend on the legal personality of the entity. On top of all that, members of the public may be able to enforce norms of administration, either through being authorized to enforce the rights of a legal person, through the relator action, or through 'proper person standing'.[81] This is because public administrators, even if they owe directed duties (say to a legal entity) also owe undirected public duties of sound administration.

G. Representative enforcement of claims of the State or its emanations

We have seen that in private law, rights that belong to one person are sometimes enforced by another; this was characterized as representative enforcement.[82] For example, the rights of an incapacitated person may need to be enforced by a guardian or tutor. Such guardianship is of course a kind of administration, since the guardian has the mission and duty of protecting and enforcing the rights of that incapacitated beneficiary.

In the public law contexts that we will now examine, we will see cases that could be described as the private enforcement of the public interest.

1. Delegated or appointed representative actions to enforce rights of a legal person with a public mission

Representative enforcement is typical in corporate law, where the representative is usually authorized as such by the corporation by delegation, but may be appointed by a court, particularly in cases where the alleged wrongdoers are the

---

[80] Franklin W Wegenast, *The Law of Canadian Companies* (Burroughs and Co 1931) 775–76; Roscoe Pound, 'Visitatorial Jurisdiction Over Corporations In Equity' (1936) 49 Harv L Rev 369; *Bateman's Bay Local Aboriginal Council* (n 46), [26]; for Quebec civil law, see *Code of Civil Procedure*, CQLR c 25.01, s 34; *Upton v Hutchison* (1899) 2 Que Practice Rep 300 (QB App Side), 304; *Laurent v Buanderie Villeray Ltée* [2001] JQ no 5796, JE 2002-3, 2001 CanLII 158 (CS).
[81] All three are discussed immediately below: sections II.G.1, II.G.2, and II.H respectively.
[82] Chapter 8, section III.C.2.

ones who otherwise control decisions about the enforcement of claims of the corporation (raising the problem of self-supervision[83]).

Such a recourse could certainly be deployed to enforce the rights of a legal person constituted in the public interest, perhaps to enforce its claims against its own administrators. In the last section we saw that while there may not be a detailed legislative regime governing representative actions in relation to such legal persons, the court's supervisory jurisdiction over legal persons might allow the court to appoint an interested member of the public to enforce the rights of a corporate entity that exists in the public interest.[84] The common law has some experience of allowing such representative enforcement in relation to the enforcement of the administrative duties of municipal politicians. Ratepayers have been allowed to bring claims as representatives of their municipality, which is a legal person.[85] This may be seen as another example of a solution to the problem of self-supervision.

2. Representative enforcement of the claims of the State

In the common law, a clear case of representative enforcement of claims of the State can occur via the relator action.[86] This can allow a private person to enforce some rights and enforcements powers of the State outside of the criminal context.[87] Typically this is in relation to undirected duties, since the State has enforcement powers in relation to such duties.[88] Examples include the enforcement of charitable trusts, the prosecution of public nuisance, the bringing of some prerogative writs against those holding public powers, and the denunciation of unlawful action by an emanation of the State.[89] In a relator action, a claim is brought by a private person called a 'relator', in the name of the Attorney General and

---

[83] Chapter 8, section III.C.2.c.
[84] N 80.
[85] An example is *Bowes* (n 75). At first instance, the defendant (the mayor of Toronto) vigorously resisted the plaintiff ratepayer's ability to bring the action in his own name, arguing that it had to be brought either by the city or the Attorney General. On the failure of that argument, the pleadings were amended to show the city as plaintiff. The story is told in more detail in Lionel Smith, 'Loyalty and Politics: From Case Law to Statute Law' (2015) 9 J of Equity 130, at 131–35.
[86] Geoffrey A Flick, 'Relator Actions: The Injunction and the Enforcement of Public Rights' (1978) 5 Monash U L Rev 133; Peter P Mercer, 'A Study and Evaluation of the Relator Action as a Vehicle of Public Interest Litigation' (Doctor of Philosophy, Cambridge University 1986); Fabien Gélinas, 'Le *locus standi* dans les actions d'intérêt public et la *relator action*: l'empire de la common law en droit québécois' (1988) 29 Cahiers de Droit 657; *Bateman's Bay Local Aboriginal Land Council* (n 46), [30].
[87] Some jurisdictions allow private prosecutions for crimes (see *Gujra* (n 35)); this is conceptually similar to the relator action, but we are not concerned with criminal sanctions here. Similar is the ability of an interested litigant to ask the court to impose sanctions on another litigant for contempt of court.
[88] For the terminology of directed and undirected duties and liabilities, see above, section I.
[89] *Attorney-General v London County Council* [1901] 1 Ch 781 (CA).

asserting some power or right of the latter. The litigation is always at the expense of the relator, which is one reason that the procedure may be unattractive to private persons.[90]

The proceeding requires the consent of the Attorney General, and is subject to being halted by that person, because the right or enforcement power in question belongs to the State.[91] In this sense, it is similar to a case of appointed representation. The individual relator in a sense appoints themself, but the Attorney General can refuse their self-appointment, or accept it and then discontinue it. Although one might think that the relator action might be used to address to some extent the problem of self-supervision, this may be undermined by the power of the Attorney General to discontinue the action.[92]

The relator action is not only about the enforcement of public administration, because not every claim held by the Attorney General is about the enforcement of public administration. Thus if a citizen uses a relator action to prosecute a claim of public nuisance, although they are enforcing undirected duties they are not enforcing norms of public administration, because the action is against a private person in relation to the nuisance.[93] But relator actions can be aimed at enforcing public administration, as where they are used to pursue charitable trustees or to enforce lawful behaviour by officials of the State.

---

[90] US law has some statutory versions of the relator action: see for example the False Claims Act, 31 USC § 3730. The statute authorizes civil claims by the State ('the government' or 'the United States' in the US terminology) and also allows claims by citizens to be brought, in the name of the government (as in the common law relator action). This statute, however, gives the citizen a right to a share of the proceeds of the action. Thus although the enforcement power belongs to the government, citizens are given a private interest in the *outcome* of the government's claim, as an incentive to take action. The citizen does not have to have had a private interest that was infringed by the defendant's conduct, nor does the citizen rely on a right of action held in his own capacity.

[91] In *Gouriet* (n 31) it was held that the Attorney General's refusal to consent, and their decision to discontinue, are non-justiciable, even while it was held that those powers cannot be used for a legally improper purpose. Those issues were discussed earlier (section II.A.3).

[92] Under 31 USC § 3730, the government's decision to take over or to halt the action is subject to the scrutiny of the court. This can be seen as a supervisory jurisdiction over a public office-holder (Chapter 1, section V.B.3.d).

Some US federal statutes authorize civil proceedings by citizens in relation to criminal and regulatory norms. See for example Clean Water Act, 33 USC § 1365; Racketeer Influenced and Corrupt Organizations Act, 18 USC § 1964. Here too the citizen must finance the litigation, but generally the State cannot halt it. This is because the conceptual structure is different: the citizen is not enforcing a right of the State, but rather has been granted a civil action by the statute. The right, and the power to enforce it (the right of action) thus belong to the citizen. Conceptually, this is not representative enforcement even though the granting of the private action is done to encourage lawsuits that will benefit the public. It is private enforcement of a private right that serves a private interest but which private right, one might say, has been created at least partly in the public interest. These 'statutory tort' claims, however, have little to do directly with public administration.

[93] Public nuisance can be a crime but it can be actionable by the Attorney General (or a relator) independently of that, as for example to secure an injunction to end the nuisance.

H. Private enforcement of undirected public duties and liabilities

1. Where private rights are affected

In much of administrative law, private persons are permitted to call into question the exercise of public powers. Public powers must be exercised in the public interest, not in any private interest, and so a private person is not owed a directed duty in respect of the use of those powers. A private person cannot say that the public powers must be exercised in the interests of that particular person, the way that trust beneficiaries can insist upon this in the exercise of trustees' powers. But where private *rights* are affected by the use of public powers, the holders of those rights will almost certainly be permitted to enforce the undirected duties and liabilities of the holders of those public powers.

Take the case of a probationary police constable whose position may be terminated at the sole discretion of his employer, without the need to show cause for dismissal.[94] The governing statute does not in terms require a hearing. Even so, it may well be held that the proper exercise of the public power to dismiss the constable requires 'procedural fairness', which in this case means giving the constable some opportunity to be heard and to present his case before a decision is reached.[95] The constable in this case does not have a right to keep his position; in this sense, his rights have not been infringed. Indeed, it is clear that the employer had the 'right' to dismiss him, if it had exercised its powers properly.[96] What the constable does have, however, is the power to enforce the undirected public liabilities of the employer. We may say that the constable had the 'right' to be heard before the decision was made.[97] More precisely, the power to dismiss him could not properly be exercised without hearing from him first.[98] And when the power was exercised improperly, the constable had a power to challenge that improper exercise of a public power.

Since the constable had no legal right to keep his position, his legal rights were not infringed by his termination. His legal rights were very substantially *affected* by his termination, in the sense that his employment came to an end, and therefore his private interests were also very substantially affected. This makes it easy to see why he should have the power to challenge the way public administration was conducted in his case. But it must be remembered that even if the termination had been conducted properly with a hearing, the same result might have occurred; and yet no such response to the constable's complaint could possibly

---

[94] *Nicholson v Haldimand-Norfolk Regional Police Commissioners* [1979] 1 SCR 311.
[95] This requirement is discussed briefly in Chapter 11, sections III.A.1.c and III.B.2.b.
[96] *Nicholson* (n 94), 328.
[97] ibid.
[98] If the decision had been *not* to dismiss him, no question of a 'right to be heard' could have arisen.

be admitted.[99] In other words, the whole proceeding rests not on proof that a right has been infringed, but on proof that a public power has been improperly exercised.

In a case like this, courts do not usually refer to someone like the constable as having 'standing' to challenge the decision of his employer. This, however, seems only because it is perfectly obvious that such standing must be granted to the person whose interests and indeed whose rights were most seriously affected by the decision, even though his rights were not infringed by it. In two famous recent cases, a British plaintiff secured rulings of the Supreme Court of the United Kingdom that the United Kingdom could not leave the European Union without parliamentary approval,[100] and that the Prime Minister's advice to the Queen to prorogue Parliament was unlawful.[101] In neither case, however, did the government dispute the question of standing.[102] In the first case, the Divisional Court expressed the view that everyone in the United Kingdom or holding British citizenship would have their rights affected (not infringed) by the United Kingdom's leaving the EU, and this suggested that every one of them had standing.[103]

It seems, therefore, that all of these cases are examples of 'proper person standing': a person is granted enforcement powers, who was not antecedently designated as holding such powers.[104]

Similar examples of this kind of enforcement can also be found outside of the area of traditional administrative law. If a judge has participated in the resolution of a case and it is seen afterwards that he was disqualified from acting by a conflict of interest, the parties to the litigation (and most obviously a party who was unsuccessful) have the power to take proceedings to set aside this improper use of public powers.[105] Here again, a private interest has obviously been engaged, and rights have been affected by the judge's decision; but the judge did not owe duties directly to the litigants, and so no private right was violated. The judge's

---

[99] *John v Rees* [1970] Ch 345 (ChD), 402.

[100] *R (Miller) v Secretary of State for Exiting the European Union* [2017] UKSC 5, [2018] AC 61 (*Miller (No 1)*).

[101] *Miller (No 2)* (n 26). Both *Miller* cases look as if the claim is representative, since the styles of cause suggest that the rights being asserted are those of the Crown; this however is misleading. They are not relator actions but proceedings for judicial review, which in other common law countries (as also in Scotland where parallel proceedings were taken in *Miller (No 2)* and later joined) would be brought in the name of the individual litigant. See *Practice Direction (Administrative Court: Establishment)* [2000] 1 WLR 1654 and now the *Administrative Court Judicial Review Guide 2019* at para 2.4, online at https://assets.publishing.service.gov.uk/government/uploads/system/uploads/attachment_data/file/825753/HMCTS_Admin_Court_JRG_2019_WEB.PDF. I thank Prof Mark Elliott for assistance on this point.

[102] I thank Lord Pannick QC for correspondence on this point.

[103] [2016] EWHC 2768 at [7].

[104] This term was introduced in Chapter 8, section III.C.2.c. and is opposed to 'designated person' standing.

[105] *Ex parte Pinochet (No 2)* [1999] UKHL 1, [2000] 1 AC 119.

public duties are undirected, and the litigants have a power to enforce those duties. They are clearly proper persons.

2. Where interests but not rights are affected

A private person is sometimes granted a power of enforcement in relation to an undirected duty of the State, or some emanation of it, or some other body engaged in public administration, even though that private person cannot point to any effect of the exercise of public power on their legal rights.[106] In such a case, they may be able to invoke only effects upon their private *interests*, or on the public interest, or both.

It is in this context that jurists are most likely to use the language of standing, or *locus standi*. Different systems take different views on the scope of the possibility of enforcing undirected public duties or, one might say, enforcing the public interest.[107] It is conceptually possible that it might not be allowed at all; but this could easily make a mockery of the idea that those engaging in the relevant public administration are subject to legal (as opposed to purely political) constraints on the use of their powers.

A system might say that a complainant will have standing only if some private interest (even if not a right) of their own was materially affected by the State action in question.[108] If my passport has been revoked, I can challenge the legality of the decision, even if I have no right in the strict sense to a passport. Here no one is likely to question my standing; but it is precisely because I have no right to a passport that my claim is effectively a claim to pursue the public interest in the legality of State action, as well as my private interest in having a passport. Such cases are not that different from those discussed in the previous subsection, where a right of the complainant was affected even if not infringed.

A less obvious case might be one in which there was a decision of the State, or some emanation of the State, to double the capacity of an airport. Standing to challenge the legality of that decision might be granted to someone who lives next to the airport and will be directly affected by the extra noise.[109] Again, this

---

[106] For the terminology of directed and undirected duties and liabilities, see above, section I.

[107] Denis J Galligan, *Discretionary Powers: A Legal Study of Official Discretion* (Clarendon Press 1986) 379–82.

[108] See, in Italian law, the distinction between a *diritto soggettivo* (subjective right, a legal right held for one's own benefit) and an *interresse legittimo* (legitimate interest, a private interest that is not protected as a legal right): Roberto Caranta, 'Public Law Illegality and Governmental Liability' in Duncan Fairgrieve, Mads Andenas, and John Bell (eds), *Tort Liability of Public Authorities in Comparative Perspective* (BIICL 2002) 271, 280. Caranta notes (281–87) that since 1999, Italian law has moved towards allowing claims against public authorities for loss caused by illegal action, which means that the line between subjective rights and legitimate interests is less sharp. In my terms, the public duties have moved from being undirected to being directed. Claims for loss caused are discussed in the next subsection of this chapter.

[109] See for example *Bateman's Bay Local Aboriginal Land Council* (n 46). The test set out in *Juliana v United States* 217 FSupp3d 1224 (D Or, 2016), 1242 (references omitted) is one developed by US

person complains not on the basis that a right of theirs was infringed, but as a member of the public. They seek private enforcement of the public interest, or of the undirected duties of the State and its organs. A standing limitation that requires at least that some private interest be engaged can be seen as a filter against what are sometimes called busybodies: those who have no genuine interest in the matter. Broader visions of standing, mentioned at the end of this section, obviously allow wider access to the courts.

Earlier I mentioned the foreign emoluments clause of the US Constitution. There were three proceedings against President Donald Trump that were based at least in part on this clause. One of them was brought by 215 elected members of Congress. The Court of Appeal for the District of Columbia ruled that they lacked standing, on the basis that as individuals they could not assert the interests of Congress as a whole; the Supreme Court of the United States refused to hear an appeal.[110] In another case, however, other plaintiffs were held to have standing by the Court of Appeal for the Second Circuit.[111] They were business persons who claimed financial losses resulting from the President's alleged violation of the Constitution.[112] The third case was brought by the Attorneys General of the District of Columbia and the State of Maryland. Even though they are law officers of their own jurisdictions, the Court of Appeals for the Fourth Circuit initially held that they lacked standing to enforce the federal Constitution against the President.[113] The same Court, however, later reheard the case *en banc* and held that those plaintiffs did indeed have standing.[114] On further appeals, the Supreme Court of the United States held that both the second and the third cases must be dismissed as moot as Trump was no longer President.[115]

It seems clear that the Attorney General of the United States would have standing to assert, against the President, a violation of the federal Constitution. As we have seen, in common law countries the Attorney General is the litigant most suited to enforce the rights of the State to lawful public administration. This, of course, forces us to confront the problem of self-supervision, as well as demanding a standard for the independence of the Attorney General that not

---

federal courts: 'To demonstrate standing, a plaintiff must show (1) she suffered an injury in fact that is concrete, particularized, and actual or imminent; (2) the injury is fairly traceable to the defendant's challenged conduct; and (3) the injury is likely to be redressed by a favorable court decision'.

[110] *Blumenthal v Trump* 949 F3d 14 (DCCA, 2020), cert denied, 141 SCt 553, 208 LEd2d 175 (2020).
[111] *Citizens for Responsibility & Ethics in Washington v Trump* 939 F3d 131 (2d CCA, 2019). The plaintiffs also invoked the domestic emoluments clause (n 67).
[112] The organization Citizens for Responsibility & Ethics in Washington, which was originally a plaintiff, did not appeal the first instance decision that it lacked standing (ibid at 138 n 1).
[113] *District of Columbia v Trump* 930 F3d 209 (4th CCA, 2019). The plaintiffs also invoked the domestic emoluments clause (n 67).
[114] *In re Trump* 958 F3d 274 (4th CCA en banc, 2020).
[115] 141 SCt 1262, 209 LEd2d 5 (2021).

every occupant of that office could attain. This arguably shows that a legal system that aspires to operate under the rule of law must grant standing to some citizens to assert the public interest in compliance with the legal norms of public administration. Judges' understanding of this has led to the evolution of proper person standing rules.

One feature sometimes seen in this kind of case is that a group may claim to speak for and on behalf of others similarly situated.[116] Peter Cane has called this associational standing.[117] To the extent that the claim is justified, the group can be understood as asserting that it is *more directly* enforcing the public interest and less to be acting in pursuit of a private interest, since it claims to speak for a group, being a section of the public.[118] There is an interesting analogy here with class actions. It is as if the plaintiff claims to speak on behalf of a class, but without the legislative framework for judicial approval of representation that exists in class actions.

A system that wished to be more generous to complainants might grant them standing to speak directly on behalf of the public interest even if no private interest of their own was directly affected. Particularly in civilian contexts, this possibility may be called an *actio popularis*: the people's action, to enforce the public interest directly.[119] English law has shown a wider recognition of standing than US law; one scholar has described this more generous approach as 'campaign litigation'.[120]

If a claim of this kind is successful, the most likely recourse will be in the nature of a declaration that something was not done properly, or is not being done properly, which may mean that some purported state action is seen to be invalid. Since a plaintiff's standing does not rest on the infringement of their own right,

---

[116] In *Citizens for Responsibility & Ethics in Washington v. Trump* (n 111), one plaintiff is described in the judgment (at 138) as 'a non-partisan, member-based organization of restaurants and restaurant workers'.

[117] Peter Cane, 'Standing Up for the Public' [1995] Public Law 276.

[118] As Cane notes (ibid 278), however, courts should not necessarily take the plaintiff's word that it speaks for and on behalf of a group. See also Carol Harlow, 'Public Law and Popular Justice' (2002) 65 MLR 1 (raising similar concerns and also apprehensions about intervenors); Kathryn Chan, 'Identifying the Institutional Religious Freedom Claimant' (2017) 95 Can Bar Rev 707.

[119] The term comes from Roman law, in which it was an action not to enforce public administration generally, but to vindicate land affected to public use: Giorgio Resta, 'Systems of Public Ownership' in M Graziadei and L Smith (eds), *Comparative Property Law: Global Perspectives* (Edward Elgar 2017) 216, 226–27. Today, it is more prominent in international law discourse than in domestic law. However, a domestic version of such a proceeding in Spain led to the ruling that Augusto Pinochet could be extradited from the United Kingdom: María del Carmen Márquez Carrasco and Joaquín Alcaide Fernández, 'In re Pinochet' (1999) 93 Am J of Int'l Law 690, 691; final ruling in the United Kingdom: *Ex parte Pinochet (No 3)* [1999] UKHL 17, [2000] 1 AC 147. The differences between this criminal manifestation of the *actio popularis* and a private prosecution (nn 35, 87) are that the *actio popularis* does not require the consent of the public prosecutor and that conceptually, the *actio popularis* is not confined to the enforcement of criminal law norms.

[120] Timothy Endicott, *Administrative Law* (5th edn, OUP 2021), 438-49; contrast *Lujan v Defenders of Wildlife* 504 US 555 (1992).

a claim of this kind will not lead, for example, to the recovery of compensatory damages. This brings us to the next category of enforcement.

I. Private claims for compensation

Private persons may be harmed, physically or financially, by acts or omissions of public administrators. This category is difficult to organize across legal systems, because these claims are conceptualized differently in different systems.[121] But the following general observations are warranted. Many of the differences between legal systems can be understood as differences as to the understanding of whether the public law duties of the State or its emanations are directed or undirected. If they are undirected, they may be enforceable through some procedure to enforce the public interest in lawful administration (as discussed in the previous subsection), but such procedures cannot give rise to a claim for individual compensation.[122] Where claims for compensation are allowed, the plaintiff can be said to have demonstrated that a directed duty was owed to the plaintiff by the State or some part of it.[123]

Some occurrences of harm are almost inevitable in the running of public administration. If a city passes a by-law that forbids attaching posters to any public property, a printing company may suffer a serious loss of business. While such a consequence might be a factor that should be considered in the decision to pass the by-law, one might think that a loss of this kind is not legally recoverable, if the process by which the by-law was passed was valid. In French administrative law, however, it is not always essential to prove fault or wrongdoing by the State to recover loss caused by public administration. In one well-known case, a valid law forbidding artificial cream drove out of business the only enterprise that was producing the product.[124] The company was awarded damages on the

---

[121] Valuable comparative studies can be found in Duncan Fairgrieve, Mads Andenas, and John Bell (eds), *Tort Liability of Public Authorities in Comparative Perspective* (BIICL 2002); Ken Oliphant (ed), *The Liability of Public Authorities in Comparative Perspective* (Intersentia 2016).

[122] Not discussed here is the law relating to State or Crown immunity for extracontractual liability, which has largely been abandoned. In the common law world, however, this is fairly recent and depends on statutory interpretation (P Hogg and PJ Monahan, *Liability of the Crown* (4th edn, Carswell 2011)); in the United States, the repeal of the immunity of the federal and state governments has been piecemeal: Helene M Goldberg, 'Tort Liability for Federal Government Actions in the United States: An Overview' in Duncan Fairgrieve, Mads Andenas, and John Bell (eds), *Tort Liability of Public Authorities in Comparative Perspective* (BIICL 2002) 521; Gregory C Sisk, 'A Primer on the Doctrine of Federal Sovereign Immunity' (2005) 58 Oklahoma L Rev 439.

[123] For the terminology of directed and undirected duties and liabilities, see above, section I.

[124] Conseil d'État, 14 janvier 1938, *Société anonyme des produits laitiers 'La Fleurette'*, 51.704; for more discussion of State liability without fault in French law: Waline (n 16), 546–65; Brown and Bell, *French Administrative Law*, 193–202.

basis that the law imposed a public burden in a manner that unfairly impacted the plaintiff.[125]

Generally, though, the claims discussed in this section are for loss caused by unlawful administration. Thus in the common law tradition, and in the law of Quebec, if the action was privileged, it generally follows that any harm caused is irrecoverable, even if the same action would have been unlawful if done by a private citizen.[126] In *Binsaris v Northern Territory*,[127] for example, the plaintiffs were harmed when officers in a youth detention centre used tear gas. The Court's analysis proceeds by asking whether the use of the gas was authorized by statute. If it had been, there would have been no liability; but because it was not, the officers committed the tort of battery. The use of physical force by law enforcement officers may be privileged, within limits, but if those limits are exceeded liability may follow, including vicarious liability of the entity employing the officer.[128]

The following is a rather pragmatic typology of cases where immunity is not applicable, in the light of the different conceptual structures that different legal systems employ.

1. Harm inflicted by abuse of public powers

This category addresses particularly egregious cases of misuse of public authority, and how they may be addressed in some systems.

In the common law, a plaintiff may be able to use the tort of misfeasance in public office, a tort that can only be committed by those holding public powers. A public officer will be liable if they acted with deliberate malice, or if they knew that the act was illegal and was likely to cause harm.[129] Recklessness as to illegality can also suffice, which means that the tort's scope is wider than truly intentional conduct. Even so, it is difficult to prove the tort. If it is proven, any consequential loss is recoverable, even if purely economic.

---

[125] One could draw a parallel to the principle of the common law that any exercise of State power that takes or destroys private property presumptively demands compensation: *Attorney-General v De Keyser's Royal Hotel Ltd* [1920] AC 508 (HL); *Burmah Oil Co v Lord Advocate* [1965] AC 75 (HL); *Manitoba Fisheries Ltd v The Queen* [1979] 1 SCR 101; *R v Tener* [1985] 1 SCR 533. Parliamentary sovereignty is respected inasmuch as a clear expression that no compensation is due will be effective: *NZ Council of Licenced Firearms Owners* (n 30) (although in some places, like the United States, the Constitution excludes this possibility).

[126] Robert Stevens, *Torts and Rights* (OUP 2007), 230–31.

[127] [2020] HCA 22.

[128] US law has been criticized for taking a very wide view of the immunity of police officers in the use of force: Avidan Y Cover, 'Reconstructing the Right against Excessive Force' (2016) 68 Fla L Rev 1773; *Jamison v McClendon* 476 F Supp 3d 386 (SD Miss, 2020).

[129] *Northern Territory v Mengel* (1995) 185 CLR 307; *Garrett v Attorney-General* [1997] 2 NZLR 332 (CA); *Three Rivers District Council v Bank of England (No 3)* [2003] 2 AC 1 (HL); *Odhavji Estate v Woodhouse* 2003 SCC 69, [2003] 3 SCR 263.

In some jurisdictions, malicious prosecution is also a tort aimed at addressing abuses of public prosecutorial powers.[130] The plaintiff must show that there were no reasonable grounds for the prosecution, and that the defendant was motivated by malice, in the sense of an improper purpose that amounts to a misuse of the criminal justice system.[131]

Quebec civil law, like French law, does not have named torts, but a general law of civil liability for loss caused by a fault. This has been used to address abuse of public power, most famously in *Roncarelli v Duplessis*.[132] The defendant Duplessis was the Prime Minister of Quebec, and also its Attorney General. At a time when the Catholic Church was very powerful in Quebec society, Duplessis was engaged in the repression of the Jehovah's Witnesses; many persons of that faith were charged with offences as a result of their efforts to distribute publications. The plaintiff was a restaurateur and a member of that faith, and he repeatedly provided surety so that other Witnesses could be released on bail. The relevant government agency refused the defendant's annual application to renew his licence to serve alcohol at his restaurant, which put the restaurant out of business after thirty-five years of operation by the defendant and his father before him. The Supreme Court of Canada found that the defendant had acted in bad faith and misused his authority in directing the licencing agency not to renew for wholly improper reasons. In the words of Rand J:[133]

> The act of the respondent through the instrumentality of the Commission brought about a breach of an implied public statutory duty toward the appellant; it was a gross abuse of legal power expressly intended to punish him for an act wholly irrelevant to the statute, a punishment which inflicted on him, as it was intended to do, the destruction of his economic life as a restaurant keeper within the province.

The majority of the Court held that Duplessis thus committed a fault, making him liable for any resulting damage under art 1053 of the then-in-force Civil Code of Lower Canada. This was the article governing the general law of wrongful harm; it is same article that would have been used between private parties, in a case of careless damage to property, or of defamation.[134] Although the form of the claim, being simply a claim for fault, would have been available against any defendant,

---

[130] In England and Wales, malicious prosecution is now available in relation to civil proceedings (*Willers v Joyce* [2016] UKSC 44). In those jurisdictions that confine the tort of malicious prosecution to defendants who wield public powers, the tort of abuse of process may be available in relation to the malicious use of civil litigation by private actors (eg *Oei v Hui* 2020 BCCA 214).
[131] *Miazga v Kvello Estate* 2009 SCC 51, [2009] 3 SCR 339.
[132] [1959] SCR 121.
[133] ibid 141, Judson J concurring.
[134] The current provision is Civil Code of Québec, art 1457.

the egregious abuse of power was essential to liability here because it was, itself, the fault. Had Duplessis done the same thing but in good faith and for proper purposes, there would have been no liability in Quebec law. Moreover, the abuse of power took away from Duplessis a public law procedural protection that would otherwise have immunized him.[135]

Quebec has a public law framework more closely based on the common law than on French law; there are no special rules for liability of the State or its officials.[136] In French administrative law, a claim for loss caused by an abuse of public powers would not be brought in the civil courts or under the civil code at all, but rather in an administrative tribunal.[137] We have already noticed that in French law, recovery of loss may be possible in some cases without the need to show fault or legal wrongdoing. Outside such cases, it is necessary to show a fault on the part of the administration.[138] Both French and Quebec law, however, use an idea of fault which does not generally distinguish between directed and undirected public duties for the purposes of identifying wrongdoing that may generate liability for loss caused.[139] A fault is typically constituted by a breach of duty, without regard to whether the duty is directed or undirected.[140] In French public law, '[a]s in French private law, mere illegality is in itself a fault capable of

---

[135] Art 88 of the Code of Civil Procedure required advance notice of the filing of the claim in the case of public officers, which had not been given. The majority held that Duplessis acted so far outside his proper functions that the provision did not protect him. Two judges dissented on this point.

[136] Quebec, however, not only has many statutory administrative tribunals like most common law jurisdictions; it has also created a statutory tribunal *(Tribunal administratif du Québec)* to hear appeals and complaints about a wide range of governmental decision-making: Patrice Garant, *Droit administratif* (7th edn, Éditions Yvons Blais 2017) 115. Like all administrative bodies in 'common law public law', however, it is in principle subject to the jurisdiction of the general courts (although as is well known, statutory techniques may aim to reduce the incidence of judicial review).

[137] Although in cases where the holder of public powers purported to use them in a way which was outside of their public role, that person may be liable in the civil courts or, sometimes, the plaintiff may have a choice of forum. In the most extreme cases, in which what was done by the holder of public powers could in no way be seen as lawful, the dispute may be ejected entirely from administrative law and into ordinary civil law, on the view that the administrator's actions had no foundation in lawful administration. See Waline (n 16), 515–18, 566–71, 630–35; Brown and Bell (n 124), 139–40, 186–90. In German law, by contrast, judicial review takes place in administrative tribunals, but claims for damages against public bodies are brought in the civil courts (Ralph-Andreas Surma, 'A Comparative Study of the English and German Judicial Approach to the Liability of Public Bodies in Negligence' in Duncan Fairgrieve, Mads Andenas, and John Bell (eds), *Tort Liability of Public Authorities in Comparative Perspective* (BIICL 2002) 355, 364). Italian law used to be like German law in this respect but now allows actions for damages in administrative tribunals: Caranta (n 108), 282–86.

[138] Waline (n 16), 534–45; Brown and Bell (n 124), 183–93. In some contexts, the plaintiff suing in public law must show *faute lourde* (grave or intentional fault).

[139] I do not imply that the rules of liability are same in French civil law and in French administrative law; as has been mentioned, the latter includes a range of cases in which liability arises without fault, as well as cases in which grave fault must be shown.

[140] France Allard and others, *Private Law Dictionary and Bilingual Lexicons—Obligations* (Les Éditions Yvon Blais 2003), sv 'fault[1]': 'Transgression of an obligatory juridical norm.' The bilingual civil law dictionaries of the Paul-André Crépeau Centre of Private and Comparative Law are available at https://www.mcgill.ca/centre-crepeau/.

giving rise to liability without more'.[141] In this context, the abusive use of public powers could well constitute a grave fault, which would allow liability for loss caused even where that higher level of fault is required.[142]

The reason that misfeasance in public office is somewhat mysterious in the common law can be explained as follows.[143] If it were available only where a private right had been infringed, it would hardly be necessary as a separate tort, because the infringement of any private right is generally actionable in tort, and this moreover does not require any form of malice or mens rea. If, however, it is distinctive precisely because it can only be committed by one wielding public powers, the question is why the public duties that accompany those powers are privately actionable.[144] In the common law, it is not, in general, the case that a private claim for damages can be founded on the failure by an official to comply with their undirected public duties. The restrictive terms of the tort, in particular the requirement of malice or recklessness, make this obvious.

Descriptively, the tort involves cases in which the abuse of public authority, which always infringes a public interest that is protected by an undirected duty, is found also to infringe on a private interest and to generate a private right of recourse for loss caused. Hence we could say that it reveals a private right, corresponding to a *directed* public duty, that public authority shall not be used maliciously or in bad faith.[145] Why, in these extreme cases, can a private claim for damages be founded on the failure by an official to comply with their (normally undirected) public duties? Donal Nolan argues that one way to make sense of this is to see the tort as protecting something like a human right: a right against the State, that its functionaries do not deliberately misconduct themselves in their public role, and whose infringement demands meaningful recourse.[146] Human rights often limit the competence of legislators and also the authority of governmental actors. In some systems, they may, when breached or when breached egregiously, give rise to a claim for damages.[147] These rights are rather

---

[141] Brown and Bell (n 124), 190; see also Caranta (n 108), 273–76.

[142] It might also engage the personal liability of the administrator (n 137).

[143] One could make a similar argument about malicious prosecution in jurisdictions where it is confined to public prosecutors (see n 130). However, in those jurisdictions there is a private law tort for abuse of the litigation process; thus although there are differences of detail, in a sense it is always tortious to litigate abusively.

[144] Donal Nolan, 'A Public Law Tort: Understanding Misfeasance in Public Office' in Kit Barker and others (eds), *Private Law and Power* (Hart 2017) 177.

[145] *Odhavji Estate* (n 129) [30]: '... the underlying purpose of the tort is to protect each citizen's reasonable expectation that a public officer will not intentionally injure a member of the public through deliberate and unlawful conduct in the exercise of public functions'.

[146] Nolan (n 144) 189–90. Nolan also notes (191–92) that English law has a category of exemplary damages where any tort is established and reveals an abuse of public powers.

[147] In Canada, as in many other places, a violation by the State of a protected constitutional right may generate a claim to damages: *Canadian Charter of Rights and Freedoms*, s 24(1) (Part 1 of the *Constitution Act, 1982*, being Schedule B to the *Canada Act 1982* (UK), 1982, c 11). For an example from US law, see Cover (n 128), showing however that the very wide immunities constructed by the

like rights to one's reputation or bodily integrity, inasmuch as they are usually not directly enforceable but rather create a right of action upon breach.[148] But the label 'human rights' is confined, at least in some systems, to rights exercisable only against the State or its emanations.

In summary, the tort of misfeasance in public office reflects a recognition by the common law that individuals have a right against the State, and against those who act for it, that they shall not maliciously exercise their powers or deliberately exceed them. If that right is violated and loss is caused, a private right of action is recognized. The common law system lacks a general doctrine of abuse of right; this tort can be seen as a particular recognition of the idea of abuse of right, in the context of public powers.[149] Although it addresses only cases of gross violations of the norms of public administration, it is an important touchstone because it shows that the common law is willing, in suitable cases, to generate private, non-representative rights of action out of the violation of undirected public duties of sound administration.

2. Unintended infliction of loss
a) Introduction

Just as they may be harmed by other private actors, citizens may suffer physical or economic harm through non-deliberate actions of the State or its agents in carrying out their functions of public administration. The law provides some recourse; however, it is not only the details, but also the conceptual categories that are variable across systems. This variability arises most obviously from the fact that in some civilian systems, State liability is governed by different rules than civil (private) liability, and that these different rules are applied by different courts. Apart from that institutional difference, we will examine four sources of variability. Three of these are the distinctions between directed and undirected duties; between acts and omissions; and between (on the one hand) personal injury and property damage, and (on the other hand) pure economic loss. The fourth is the acceptance in some systems of liability of the State without the need to show any wrongdoing. I will say a few words about each of these variables.

---

courts have reduced the effectiveness of the remedy created by Congress, as illustrated by *Jamison* (n 128).

[148] These are called 'personality rights' (as opposed to personal rights) in many civilian systems, where they may be characterized as 'extrapatrimonial' which implies that they are not alienable or available to creditors. Naturally, these rights also exist in the common law but do not have a consistent label. Birks called them 'superstructural' rights: Peter Birks, 'Definition and Division: A Meditation on *Institutes* 313' in Peter Birks (ed), *The Classification of Obligations* (Clarendon Press 1997) 1, 11–12, 24–25.

[149] So too can the torts of malicious prosecution and abuse of process (n 130).

First, we have already observed that the civil law may use a general idea of 'fault' which does not distinguish between whether the defendant breached a directed duty owed to the plaintiff, or an undirected duty such as is often owed by the State or its officials. The common law is less disposed to allow a private claim to be built on the breach of an undirected duty (hence the difficulty of understanding the tort of misfeasance in public office, discussed in the previous section). But there is variation between common law systems on this point.

Second, an omission is not generally actionable unless it was a breach of a duty to act. This is related to the first point, because agents of the State may have *undirected* duties to act (such as the duty of the police to investigate a crime) but not necessarily directed duties to act. An omission may therefore be a breach only of an undirected duty, and unless a breach of such a duty gives rise to a private right of action, that omission may not be privately actionable.

Third, although the law is always evolving, the common law tradition is generally committed to the position that there is an important difference between (on the one hand) personal injury and property damage, and (on the other hand) pure economic loss.[150] In that tradition, there is no general duty not to cause pure economic loss; one may deliberately drive a rival out of business (subject to public law rules on anti-competitive behaviour, which may be undirected penal rules, or directed duties, or both), and a fortiori it is not unlawful to do so carelessly.

Finally, as already mentioned, French law accepts that the State may be liable for economic loss that it has caused even through actions that are entirely lawful.[151] This particularity is useful as a reminder that the liability of the State can be understood according to principles that are quite different from those that apply to defendants who are private persons.

b) Harm to persons or property caused by State action
If the harm is to persons or property, then the systems converge somewhat. Systems that have a profound separation between civil law and administrative law will assign the majority of such cases to administrative law and administrative tribunals. In the common law, the citizen can in principle sue using any private cause of action, so long as the defendant was not immunized in some way. This could include trespass,[152] false imprisonment,[153] or battery.[154] Many cases

---

[150] If I am physically injured and unable to work, I may suffer *consequential* economic loss, consequential on the actionable physical injury. This is generally recoverable in the common law if the physical injury was actionable. The point of the word 'pure' in 'pure economic loss' is that it occurs in the absence of any property damage or personal injury.
[151] Discussed at n 124 and text.
[152] *Entick v Carrington* (1765) 19 St Tr 1029, 2 Wils KB 275, 95 ER 807 (KB).
[153] *R v Governor of Brockhill Prison, Ex p Evans (No 2)* [2000] UKHL 48, [2001] 2 AC 19.
[154] *Binsaris* (n 127).

will be brought in negligence.[155] The individual defendant is likely to be personally liable, and where State immunity has been abolished, the State will probably be vicariously liable.[156] Quebec law in this respect is rather like the common law inasmuch as the general law of fault found in the Civil Code will govern, along with vicarious liability.

There may however be important differences between systems in the applicable legal principles. In *Lapierre v Quebec*,[157] the plaintiff suffered catastrophic injury from a vaccination administered under a governmental program. The plaintiff could not establish liability on the part of the Crown because it could not establish fault; in common law terms, it could not establish any violation of the standard of care. The plaintiff unsuccessfully invoked the 'theory of risk', arguing that there should be liability for the consequences of a created risk, without the need to show fault. In French administrative law, this theory might have succeeded.[158]

In *Hill v Hamilton-Wentworth Regional Police Services Board*,[159] a person was imprisoned and charged with a crime; he was convicted at his first trial, but ultimately acquitted after an appeal and a second trial. The question was whether the police owed a directed duty of care to him to conduct the investigation carefully, and the court held by a majority that they did; although the conclusion was that the police in the particular case had acted with due care, and so there was no liability. In recognizing the tort of 'negligent investigation', the holding seems to make a nonsense of the tort of malicious prosecution (which the plaintiff also tried to establish in the courts below), a cause of action which can also be brought against police officers. As we have seen, that tort requires malice, which makes little sense if in any event there is a private law duty to take reasonable care in investigations. If the police *exceeded* their powers (in Hohfedian terms, their privileges)—for example, by imprisoning the plaintiff or using unlawful force on him—this would be actionable in tort, without any inquiry into malice. The new tort of negligent investigation therefore applies even if the police acted within their powers and privileges, and without malice or improper purpose. The result

---

[155] Cases are legion but one important landmark was *Home Office v Dorset Yacht Co* [1970] AC 1004 (HL).
[156] N 122. As noted there, in the United States the State entity may well be immune from tort liability. Even where the State or Crown is not liable, it may indemnify the agent or servant who is personally liable, although this use of public money of course requires legal authority.
[157] *Lapierre v Attorney General (Quebec)* [1985] 1 SCR 241.
[158] The theory of risk is a ground for establishing no-fault liability of the State or its emanations that is related to, but usually considered to be separate from, the unequal imposition of public burdens (n 124 and text). The idea is that the State may rightfully take such risks in the public interest, but that the burden of them should not necessarily fall on particular citizens. See Waline (n 16), 546–47; Brown and Bell (n 124), 193–202.
[159] *Hill v Hamilton-Wentworth Regional Police Services Board* 2007 SCC 41, [2007] 3 SCR 129.

is that *Hill* seems to turn the undirected public duties of the police—their duties to do their jobs properly—into privately actionable duties.[160]

c) *Pure economic loss caused by State action*
If the loss inflicted is purely financial, recovery is more difficult in the common law because there is no general duty not to cause financial loss to another. As was mentioned above, in business one can deliberately cause loss to a competitor. In the common law, a duty of care that extends to pure economic loss will require for its creation some extra factual elements, such as a voluntary undertaking to take care in relation to an opinion given.[161]

Although something like this distinction is found in German civil law, it seems less relevant in cases against public authorities.[162] The distinction is much less prominent in the civil law of France or Quebec.[163] In those systems, however, some such claims would anyway fail for other reasons. For example, in the case of one person driving another out of business, even if a fault on the part of the defendant were proven, it might be said that the proximate cause of the loss lay in the decisions of individual customers who chose to take their custom to the plaintiff's business.

It is important to remember that in private law administration in both common law and civil law, the primary claims that arise out of carelessness are for pure economic loss. This is because the relevant duties, say of corporate managers or of trustees, are not duties to avoid harming other peoples' bodies or property, but rather duties to manage with care and prudence the (usually) financial affairs of another person.[164] This is because the duty of care and skill, or of prudence and diligence, that is owed by a private administrator is not the same

---

[160] Bruce Feldthusen exempts the decision in *Hill* from his critique of the willingness of the Supreme Court of Canada to turn undirected public duties into directed and privately actionable duties: Bruce Feldthusen, 'Judicial Activism in the Supreme Court of Canada' (2016) 53 Alberta L Rev 955, 956 n 4. He suggests that the duty of care recognized in *Hill* is properly analogical to private law negligence claims recognized in relation to parents and custodial corrections officers. This seems difficult to follow; the duty recognized in *Hill* did not relate to a relationship of administration (which parenthood is in Canadian law: Chapter 7, section V) or a relationship of authorized physical detention; it arose out of public powers and duties of investigation.

[161] *Hedley Byrne & Co Ltd v Heller & Partners Ltd* [1964] AC 465 (HL); *Deloitte & Touche v Livent Inc (Receiver of)* [2017] 2 SCR 855, 2017 SCC 63; *Banca Nazionale del Lavoro SPA v Playboy Club London Ltd* [2018] UKSC 43, [2018] 1 WLR 4041.

[162] BGB § 823 (1) contains a list of legally protected interests whose wrongful infringement creates liability in private law, and pure economic loss is not in the list. Liability may arise in other ways, including via other statutes (through § 823 (2)), and such claims could extend to pure economic loss. The liability of public officials however is regulated in part by § 839 which refers simply to loss caused by breach of official duty, and so reaches to pure economic loss (with liability then attaching to the State or other relevant entity under the Constitution); see Surma (n 137), 364–73, and (for discussion of the liability of a prosecutor for pure economic loss) 382–84.

[163] Willem H van Boom, Helmut Koziol, and Christian A Witting (eds), *Pure Economic Loss* (Springer 2004).

[164] Chapter 6, section III.B.

as what might be called the ordinary tort law duty not to cause injury or property damage. The duty of an administrator is a duty of careful management, which necessarily includes a duty to take care not to cause pure economic loss.

Therefore, in the current setting of public administration, it could be argued that the main problem to be addressed is *not* the particular problem of whether a duty relates to pure economic loss, but is rather the problem, which we have already encountered in this chapter, of the private actionability of undirected public duties. The undirected public duties of a State administrator may relate to purely financial interests (as in the case of a financial services regulator) or to personal integrity and property (as in the case of the police). Thus in systems that allow private claims based on the breach of undirected public duties, claims against the State or its emanations for pure economic loss caused by carelessness are easily imaginable.[165]

There is a rather surprising decision of the Canadian Federal Court of Appeal which could be read as abolishing the common law of negligence as a relevant category for claims against the State or its emanations. In *Paradis Honey Ltd v Canada*,[166] the allegation was that an agency of the federal government had caused pure economic loss to the plaintiffs by the way it administered certain regulations. The claim was brought in a common law jurisdiction and was brought for damages, not for judicial review of any governmental action.[167] The trial judge allowed a motion to strike out the claim as disclosing no cause of action. The Court of Appeal allowed the appeal by a 2-1 majority. The majority refused to strike out the claim in negligence, and they also construed the pleadings as invoking a claim for 'monetary relief in public law', which they also refused to strike out. They said:

> Broadly speaking, we grant relief when a public authority acts unacceptably or indefensibly in the administrative law sense and when, as a matter of discretion, a remedy should be granted.[168]

The outcome seems to be a private claim for pure economic loss caused by unacceptable conduct, as in misfeasance in public office, but without the need for malice or anything similar, and without any inquiry into whether a directed duty was owed to the plaintiff. One could say that the requirement that the public

---

[165] Brown and Bell (n 124), 190; Donal Nolan, 'The Liability of Financial Supervisory Authorities' (2013) 4 J of European Tort Law 190.

[166] *Paradis Honey Ltd v Canada* 2015 FCA 89, [2016] 1 FCR 446, leave to appeal denied, 2015 CanLII 69423.

[167] The case arose in Alberta. In Canada there is no 'federal common law' and so the provincial common law governed.

[168] *Paradis Honey Ltd* (n 166) [132]. Following this, the Trial Division certified a class action (2017 FC 199, [2018] 1 FCR 275).

authority 'acts unacceptably or indefensibly' is precisely what all of the law of negligence aims to decide, including the legal doctrines found in the extensive and binding jurisprudence of the Supreme Court of Canada in relation to whether a directed duty of care of the relevant kind was owed. If this ruling takes hold, it implies that loss caused by public action, including pure economic loss, will be recoverable much more easily than under the general law of negligence or under the tort of misfeasance in public office.[169] This is perhaps somewhat mitigated by the assertion of wide curial discretion, but this itself is foreign to tort law doctrine. What the majority have introduced is much closer to French administrative law than to the common law.[170]

d) *Harm to persons, property, or financial interests caused by State omission*
A victim may suffer physical harm due to an unlawful failure to act on the part of some person or entity engaged in public administration. For example, the victim of a serial rapist may show that if the police had issued a warning or investigated more competently, she would not have been attacked.[171] To take a pure economic loss example, a plaintiff might show that a financial regulator failed to do its job diligently with the result that due to a lack of intervention, the plaintiff's investment was destroyed.[172] In this section I combine personal injury and property damage with pure economic loss, because the ways in which the common law stands apart on these issues—that is, in relation to the question of undirected public duties versus privately actionable ones—does not require those categories of loss to be examined separately.[173]

Whether this kind of omission can generate a private claim reveals a range of different approaches.[174] As we have already seen, in the civil law the distinction between a directed public duty and an undirected one may be less relevant, since

---

[169] In *Hughes v Liquor Control Board of Ontario*, 2018 ONSC 1723, [273]–[285], affirmed 2019 ONCA 305, the Court refused to give effect to what it called (at [3]) 'the freshly-invented tort of "Misconduct by a Civil Authority"'.

[170] This is all the more surprising given that Stratas JA, who authored the judgment, spoke publicly in 2016 about the importance of judicial respect for legal doctrine; the speech, 'Reflections on the Decline of Legal Doctrine', is available on youtube.com. Nadon JA, who concurred with Stratas JA in *Paradis Honey*, also styles himself as committed to legal doctrine: Sean Fine, 'Doctrine is "everything" for Marc Nadon, the outspoken conservative justice rejected by Canada's Supreme Court', *Globe and Mail* (2 Oct 2019) (see n 42).

[171] *Doe v Metropolitan Toronto (Municipality) Commissioners of Police* (1998) 39 OR (3d) 487 (Gen Div); *Carmichele v Minister of Safety and Security* 2001 (4) SA 938 (SA Constitutional Court) and 2004 (3) SA 305 (Supreme Court of Appeal).

[172] Nolan (n 165).

[173] For the terminology of directed and undirected duties and liabilities, see above, Section I.

[174] Note, 'Police Liability for Negligent Failure to Prevent Crime' (1981) 94 Harv L Rev 821; Duncan Fairgrieve, *State Liability in Tort: A Comparative Law Study* (OUP 2003), at 110–13; Peter Cane, 'Tort Law and Public Functions' in John Oberdiek (ed), *Philosophical Foundations of the Law of Torts* (OUP 2014) 148; Alistair Price, 'Negligence Liability for Police Omissions: A Golden Mean' (2018) 84 SCLR (2d) 131; Tom Cornford, 'The Negligence Liability of Public Authorities for Omissions' (2019) 78 CLJ 545.

the breach of any duty may be considered a 'fault' which, if it causes loss of any kind, is sufficient to trigger liability so long as the causal connection is established.[175] In some civilian systems, moreover, such claims may be governed by rules of public law, which in some contexts have more plaintiff-favourable rules than private law, including rules that do not require the proof of fault at all.[176]

In the common law of negligence, a defendant is not normally at risk of liability in negligence for omissions. The general tort law duty of care does not impose any positive duty to act, although particular circumstances (such as positive undertakings) may impose duties to act. But administration requires positive action. We have seen that the duty of care and skill, or of prudence and diligence, that is owed by a private law administrator does not allow the administrator to do nothing.[177] It is no surprise that the same is true in public law administration. The police, for example, do not fulfil their public law duties by doing nothing, and nor does a financial regulator.

The difficulty is whether a plaintiff can build a private law cause of action on the breach of a public law duty that is undirected and so not owed to the particular plaintiff. Some jurisdictions insist on the strict separation of undirected public duties and privately actionable duties, refusing to accept that an undirected public duty to act can form part of the foundation for a private claim.[178] On this approach, a privately enforceable duty to act must be found in legislation, or via the same elements that would support such a duty against a private defendant. Some common law courts, however, have held that in particular circumstances, the seemingly undirected public duty to act may be privately actionable, potentially creating a private law claim for at least some plaintiffs.[179]

In a study of cases reaching back to the 1970s, Bruce Feldthusen has identified five categories of 'unique public duties' recognized by the Supreme Court of Canada, in which public authorities have been found liable or potentially liable for failures to act.[180] They are unique inasmuch as they do not correspond to any analogous duty to act that may be owed by a private actor. His critique is not only that these directed duties of positive action have not been justified, but moreover that the Court seems largely to have ignored the drafting of Crown liability legislation in Canada, which often operates by making the Crown liable when a private actor would be liable.

---

[175] N 140 and text. For discussion of liability in German law of the police for omission, see Surma (n 137), 381–82.

[176] This was mentioned for French law above (n 124).

[177] Chapter 6, section III.B.

[178] Stevens (n 126), ch 7; *N v Poole Borough Council* [2019] UKSC 25.

[179] See the cases in n 171, from Canada and the Republic of South Africa. Both cases involved breaches of constitutional rights by the police. Some US courts allow recovery against the police where particular elements of proximity can be shown: Note (n 174), 824–28; David Basil, 'A Primer on the Public Duty Doctrine as Applied to Police Protection' (2005) 37 Urban Lawyer 403.

[180] Feldthusen (n 160).

III. Conclusion

One reflection that emerges from this chapter is whether the modes of enforcement of the norms of public administration can learn from experiences in private law, just as the reverse is also true. When private rights are enforced by a representative, there is often some possibility of relieving the representative from paying the costs of the litigation.[181] There are some parallels developing in public law in those common law jurisdictions where the courts have a discretionary authority related to costs. The usual rule in the United States is that each party pays its own costs, but in other common law jurisdictions the usual rule is that an unsuccessful litigant must pay a substantial portion of the winner's costs. When a plaintiff lost his case relating to environmental protection issues, the High Court of Australia reinstated the trial judge's order that each party should bear its own costs.[182] In litigation between certain First Nations and the Crown, the Supreme Court of Canada made an interim costs order in favour of the First Nations, in advance of the resolution of the case and without regard to its ultimate outcome.[183] In relation to judicial review proceedings brought in the public interest, UK courts have been willing to make 'protective costs orders' which cap the costs that may be awarded against the applicant should they lose, and generally also cap the amount of costs recoverable by that party should they win.[184] Legal aid is unlikely to be available to such litigants.[185]

Pushing further on the private law analogies, a plaintiff is sometimes given a financial reward for bringing and pursuing a class action, and this is justified at least partly because they have acted in the public interest.[186] Should such awards be made in favour of litigants who seek to vindicate the public interest in lawful government action, even if they are partly motivated by their private interest? Of course, in class actions there is an award or settlement out of which such a reward can be made to the representative plaintiff, and this will not be the case in litigation which goes only to legality of administrative action. Probably the most that a claimant could hope for in such a case is the protection of an advance costs order.

---

[181] Chapter 8, section III.C.2.
[182] *Oshlack v Richmond River Council* (1998) 193 CLR 72.
[183] *British Columbia (Minister of Forests) v Okanagan Indian Band* 2003 SCC 71, [2003] 3 SCR 371.
[184] Adrian Zuckerman, 'Protective Costs Orders: A Growing Costs-Litigation Industry' (2009) 28 Civil Justice Q 161; Aileen McColgan, 'Limiting the Costs of Litigation: Protective Costs Orders in the Court of Appeal' (2009) 28 Civil Justice Q 169; Endicott (n 120) 449–53. For some discussion of the reception of this idea in Canada, see Martin Twigg, 'Costs Immunity: Banishing the "Bane" of Costs from Public Interest Litigation' (2013) 36 Dalhousie LJ 193.
[185] In Canada the federal government funds an independently-administered program called the Court Challenges Program (https://www.canada.ca/en/canadian-heritage/services/funding/court-challenges-program.html) that finances litigation aimed at vindicating language rights and human rights. This litigation often challenges actions of the government, or the validity of legislation.
[186] Chapter 8, section III.C.2.d.

To address the problem of self-supervision in corporate law, the court and not the corporation decides who shall be allowed to bring a representative action. In public law, should control of relator actions be left so firmly in the hands of the Attorney General? There is arguably room for development on this point within the case law. The deferential approach of the House of Lords in *Gouriet*, as we have seen, has been called into question by *Miller (No 2)*.[187] At the very least, decisions to disallow or discontinue relator actions should be subject to judicial review, as are decisions to discontinue private prosecutions.[188] A plaintiff bringing a relator action and emboldened by the rules for representative actions in corporate law might go so far as to ask that the costs be borne by the Crown.

The norms of sound public administration, although they are sometimes only political, are increasingly rules of law. The juridification of these norms is happening through legislation and through developments in the courts. The mechanisms for the enforcement of those norms are not always perfect, but they are also developing. Rules of standing are more relaxed than they used to be. The argument that governmental decisions are not justiciable because the only accountability is political is less likely to be accepted by courts today than in the past. The ability of citizens to recover damages for loss they have suffered by unlawful State action or inaction is, perhaps, the most fluidly developing part of the law.

This chapter having reviewed enforcement mechanisms, the next chapter will look at how norms of sound administration regulate different aspects of public administration. Taking the two chapters together shows that Paul Finn's public 'trust' has not been forgotten, and that it is clearly not only a matter of political morality.[189]

---

[187] Section II.A.2.
[188] N 35.
[189] Finn (n 47).

11
Spheres of Public Law Administration

I. Introduction

The goal of this chapter is to explore the extent to which the norms of administration, which have been explored in detail in relation to private administration, also apply in public administration as legal rules. This includes whether there are legal rules that apply in public administration but that are not visible, at least in the same way, in private administration.

Who carries out public administration? Administration means the holding of powers that one has been granted for a mission, assignment, function, or charge. Public administration means administration where the mission, assignment, function, or charge is for the benefit of the public, rather than a particular person or a defined class of beneficiaries.

Most obviously, emanations of the State conduct public administration, but not only them. As we have seen, the definition of public administration is not coterminous with administration by the State or the government.[1] But the State is often present in public administration, even when the powers in question are not governmental powers. Depending on the context, the State may have a role in participating in the relevant public administration. It may also have a role in the mechanisms for the enforcement of the norms governing public administration. A range of mechanisms for the enforcement of those norms was examined in the previous chapter.

In this chapter, all of these issues—who holds the powers, what legal norms of administration apply, who is supervising, and how can the law be enforced—will be discussed in different contexts of public administration. The study here cannot be comprehensive. It aims to look at different categories of public administration, and to ask in each case to what extent the norms of sound public administration take effect as legal norms; and, to the extent that they do, how they are or may be enforced. It aims to be illustrative, rather than exhaustive.

But it does not aim only to give examples. By these examples, this chapter aims to show that the ideas of 'public trust' or 'fiduciary government' are not only metaphors.[2] It is not only as a matter of politics, or political theory, or political

---

[1] Chapter 9, section II.
[2] Although to some extent they are metaphors: Chapter 9, section I.C.1.

morality that those holding public powers must exercise them with loyalty, for the purposes for which they were granted; must avoid exercising them while in a conflict; must not derive unauthorized profits; and must act with reasonable care. The law demands these things.

II. Non-State holders of public powers

As we have noticed, there are many examples, mainly falling within what, in the common law world, is called the charitable sector.[3] That label is not directly applicable in the civil law world, but the terminological differences are not crucial for the purposes of this overview.

A. Trusts with public objects

Historically in the common law, charities were in the form of charitable trusts.[4] In this context, it is clear that all of the norms of administration are legally enforceable. The trustees of a charitable trust owe the same general duties of administration as the trustees of a private, non-charitable trust: they must use their powers for proper purposes; they may not exercise their powers while in a conflict; they may not acquire unauthorized profits; and they presumptively owe a duty of care and skill.

By definition, a charitable trust does not have trust beneficiaries who are entitled to the benefit of the trust property. It is a trust for the promotion of a purpose. In a private trust 'for persons', it is the beneficiaries who hold the powers to enforce due administration of the trust. In a charitable trust, the supervision and enforcement of those rights falls traditionally to the Attorney General.[5] The supervision of charities by the taxation authorities may actually be a more immediate form of control.[6] This is because charities receive favourable tax treatment, and it may be the responsibility of the taxation authority to ensure that this treatment is fully justified by the activities of the relevant charity. The taxation authority may take the role of ensuring that the charitable trust is run for

---

[3] Chapter 9, sections II.C and II.D.2.
[4] The basic categories of charitable purposes in the common law are education, the relief of poverty, and the promotion of religion. Analogical purposes are possible. In each case, there is a separate requirement that the range of potential beneficiaries be wide enough that the charity is for the public benefit. Thus even though the relief of poverty is a charitable purpose, one cannot create a charitable trust for the relief of poverty of a particular person.
[5] In some places, those powers of enforcement may be delegated, as to the Charity Commission in England and Wales.
[6] Kathryn Chan, *The Public-Private Nature of Charity Law* (Hart 2016).

its avowed charitable purposes, and in accordance with governing rules of taxation law. But even where the most immediate supervisor is the taxation authority, that authority is not directly concerned with the enforcement of the norms of administration.[7]

Thus even where a kind of de facto enforcement lies with a taxation authority, the role of the State is still relevant in the enforcement of common law charitable trusts. As we have seen, this also makes room for representative enforcement by a member of the public through the relator action, at least in the common law.[8] Such actions used to be very common in England in the nineteenth century.[9] It is even possible that members of the public as such may be allowed to bring proceedings, without the leave or consent of the Attorney General.[10] That can be seen as an example of public interest standing, in which the plaintiff is permitted to enforce the undirected duties of the trustees.[11]

In Quebec civil law, it is possible to create both public and private purpose trusts.[12] In any trust, the trustees will be subject to the same duties of administration. Those trusts that are registered as charities will be subject to the supervision of the taxation authorities and probably the Attorney General.[13] Whether or not the trust is charitable, or public or private, Quebec law grants wide standing to 'any interested person' to enforce trusts.[14]

One difficulty that was mentioned in relation to private law administration is that although administrators must act for proper purposes, they are generally not required to give reasons for the exercises of their discretionary powers.[15] This seems to square rather poorly with the idea of accountability, as it makes it largely a matter of chance whether the beneficiaries can find out what were the administrators' reasons for action. There is little sign that the law relating to

---

[7] It would be a very serious sanction for a charitable trust to lose its charitable status; but it is not clear that the taxation authority would be able, for example, to require a trustee to account for an unauthorized profit. That would fall to the Attorney General.
[8] Chapter 10, section II.G.2. For Quebec, see Fabien Gélinas, 'Le *locus standi* dans les actions d'intérêt public et la *relator action*: l'empire de la common law en droit québécois' (1988) 29 Cahiers de Droit 657.
[9] Chan (n 6) 86–88.
[10] ibid 89–92, discussing mixed case law. In a well-known case, *Re Beloved Wilkes's Charity* (1851) 3 Mac & G 440, 42 ER 330 (LC), the petitioners were members of the public who were disappointed in the decision of the trustees as to who should benefit from the charity. No point was taken about standing, and the implication is that members of the public have some powers of supervision over charitable trusts. See also, in England and Wales, Charities Act 2011, s 115(1), discussed in Chan (n 6) 94–97.
[11] See Chapter 10, sections I (undirected duties) and II.H.2 (public interest standing).
[12] Civil Code of Québec, arts 1260, 1268, 1270; Alexandra Popovici, *Êtres et avoirs: Les droits sans sujet en droit privé actuel* (Éditions Yvon Blais 2019).
[13] Gélinas (n 8).
[14] CCQ, art 1290; Alexandra Popovici, 'Droits de regard: la fiducie dans le *Code civil du Québec*' in Christine Morin and Brigitte Lefebvre (eds), *Mélanges en l'honneur du professeur Jacques Beaulne* (Wilson & Lafleur 2018) 225.
[15] Chapter 3, section IV.C.

charitable trusts attracts a different principle; indeed, the leading case that is still cited in the common law for this proposition, even in relation to private trusts, was a case involving a charity.[16] But there is an argument to be made that the relevant principles in relation to the giving of reasons by charitable administrators should be the ones that apply in public law.

B. Legal persons, that are independent of government, with public objects

Most charities are today in the form of legal persons. In such corporations, the classification as a charity is not necessary to secure the existence of the entity, as it is with a common law charitable trust. But it is necessary in order to attract the relevant taxation advantages; in Canada, as with a charitable trust, this requires proof of public benefit as well as of exclusively charitable purposes. In the case of a corporation, the determination of this status is made in relation to the legally binding objectives of the corporation. Although it is in the form of a legal person, such a corporation does not have share capital like a business corporation. It may or may not have members, depending on the applicable legal regime.[17]

There are innumerable examples of such corporations, corresponding to all of the categories of charitable and social purposes. In education, there are universities and privately run schools with legal personality; whether or not they receive public funding, they generally have charitable status and thus a public mission. The charitable category of education also includes museums and art galleries. Some emanations of organized religion may be organized as legal persons and be registered as charitable, since the promotion of any religion can be a charitable purpose in the common law. Other entities that work for the relief of poverty may also be constituted as legal persons. In all these cases, the legal person may be created under a general statute, or by a 'special act', that is, legislation particular to the legal person (supplemented by the general law on legal persons).[18]

In the civil law, a legal person with public objects may be called a *Stiftung* or a foundation, among other names.[19] It may run an art gallery, or it may help

---

[16] *Re Beloved Wilkes's Charity* (n 10).

[17] The difficulties that may arise in applying the principles developed in the context of charitable trusts to charitable corporations are evidenced in *Lehtimäki v Cooper* [2020] UKSC 33, [2022] AC 155.

[18] For example, *Act respecting the Montréal Museum of Fine Arts*, CQLR c M-42; *Royal Ontario Museum Act*, RSO 1990, c R.35.

[19] French law also has a *fonds de dotation* (endowment fund) with legal personality. In the common law, and in Quebec civil law, the word 'foundation' does not refer to any particular legal form; in those systems, a foundation can be a legal person or a trust. In most civil law systems, a foundation is a particular kind of legal person.

persons in need in various ways. Although it is impossible to generalize across a wide range of legal orders, it is often the case that if the entity's activities are for the public benefit, it receives advantageous tax benefits.

Sometimes the State has a role in the governance or decision-making of these legal persons, and sometimes not. Where the entity is controlled by the State, it falls outside of the current category of non-State entities.[20] The line between independence and State control is not always perfectly clear, but since on my account this only affects classification and not the legal regime, little turns on this for current purposes.[21] In most common law jurisdictions, even a publicly funded university is not considered a State entity as it is not controlled by the State; and yet, the State may have some involvement in governance. For example, some members of the governing board may be appointed by the government.[22] Conversely, in many civil law jurisdictions, the main universities are often emanations of the State itself, although private universities, similar in juridical status to universities in the common law world, may exist alongside the public ones.

Some State involvement in governance may be found also in the case of a museum or art gallery.[23] It may also be found in some civil law foundations. In most US states, the boards of publicly funded universities are appointed by the executive or elected by the legislature; in a minority of states, they are elected by the public.[24] Privately funded universities, and some publicly funded ones depending on the jurisdiction, may have processes for choosing board members that involve no governmental input. But to repeat, State participation in governance is not what makes the administration public; it is rather the objects of the administration. Just like a charitable trust, where an independent legal person has public objects, those who run it are carrying out public administration.

The applicability of legal norms of sound administration is just as clear here as in the case of charitable trusts, described in the preceding section. The

---

[20] These are discussed later in this chapter (section III.B.1.a).

[21] But the distinction may have significant consequences. In Canada, for example, the State and its emanations are subject to the *Canadian Charter of Rights and Freedoms*, but private persons are not. It has been that where an institution is independent of State control, it is not subject to the *Charter* (*McKinney v University of Guelph* [1990] 3 SCR 483 (university); *Stoffman v Vancouver General Hospital* [1990] 3 SCR 483 (hospital); however, where the executive appointed and could remove all the members of the board of a college, it was subject to the *Charter* (*Douglas/Kwantlen Faculty Assn v Douglas College* [1990] 3 SCR 570, followed in *Lavigne v Ontario Public Service Employees Union* [1991] 2 SCR 211).

[22] Eg *The University of Toronto Act, 1971*, SO 1971, c 56 (as amended), s 2(2)(c), online at https://governingcouncil.utoronto.ca/sites/default/files/import-files/ppdec1519784709.pdf.

[23] For example, *Act respecting the Montréal Museum of Fine Arts* (n 18), s 5. Cf *Royal Ontario Museum Act* (n 18), s 4(3)(a), providing that 15 of 21 'trustees' are appointed by the provincial cabinet. This is probably rightly classified as an emanation of the State (section III.B.1.a).

[24] Carolyn Waller and others, *Governance and Coordination of Public Higher Education in All 50 States* (North Carolina Center for Public Policy Research 2000), esp ch 8.

administrators of a legal person (including one with public objects) owe the same general duties of administration as all private law administrators, including the administrators of a business corporation: they must use their powers for proper purposes; they may not exercise their powers while in a conflict; they may not acquire unauthorized profits; and they owe a duty of care and skill.

The existence of a legal person inevitably has some effect on the legal analysis of the enforcement of duties of administration. One might say that the primary power of enforcement lies with the legal person, to whom the duties are owed; these are directed duties.[25] As in business corporations, however, this raises the spectre of the problem of self-supervision.[26] The implications were discussed in the previous chapter.[27] The law provides at least some solutions. Charitable corporations, like charitable trusts, are also subject to State supervision; in the common law, this is through the Attorney General.[28] This in turn raises the possibility of the use of the relator action.[29] As in private law, those who are, in some sense, members of the legal person may be able to obtain authorization to enforce its rights, according to the general law of legal persons.[30] Since these are cases of public administration, the administrators owe undirected public duties as well as those directed to the legal person. This means that in all of these cases, members of the public may be able to take legal action in the name of enforcing the public interest in sound administration, particularly if they could show that they were particularly affected by the actions in question.[31]

That is the theory. There are, however, serious practical issues relating to the enforcement of these duties.[32] The State may have limited practical interest in enforcement. As for the relator action, it is little known, and even if that were not the case, unlikely to be used except by those with extensive resources. It was widespread and unsupervised mismanagement in the charitable sector in the

---

[25] For example, *The University of Toronto Act, 1971* (n 22) s 2(3). An often-cited case on the duties owed by administrators of legal persons arose in the context of an educational institution (which later became one of the institutions that merged into Leeds University): *Bray v Ford* [1896] AC 44 (HL).
[26] Chapter 8, section III.C.2.c.
[27] Section II.E.
[28] As seen in *Lehtimäki* (n 17).
[29] For Quebec, see Gélinas (n 13).
[30] Chapter 10, section II.G.1.
[31] For example *Shank v Daniels* (2002) 57 OR (3d) 559 (DC). For this category of enforcement, see Chapter 10, section II.H. In the common law, a charitable corporation may have a Visitor whose role is to resolve internal disputes, and the courts will defer to the Visitor's proper exercise of jurisdiction (see *Thomas v University of Bradford* [1987] AC 795 (HL); *Re CS* [2015] NIQB 36). In the old common law, now reformed procedurally in many jurisdictions, it was routine for courts to issue writs of *mandamus* not only against public officers but against charitable corporations: Stewart Kyd, *A Treatise on the Law of Corporations*, 2 vols, vol 2 (J Butterworth 1794) 291–394. *Mandaumus* lies (or lay) to enforce undirected public duties.
[32] A gloomy picture is painted in Natalie Brown, 'The Principal Problem: Towards a More Limited Role for Fiduciary Law in the Nonprofit Sector' (2013) 99 Virginia L Rev 879.

nineteenth century that led to the establishment of the Charity Commission in England and Wales in 1853.[33]

In relation to many charities, especially smaller ones that may operate with little public scrutiny or even awareness, supervision by taxation authorities probably has an important role to play. Those authorities may have auditing powers as effective as the rights to see accounts that are held by the Attorney General or other enforcer. If we turn to larger entities like universities, there is the paradox that those most affected by failures of administration—students, faculty, staff, and alumni—may have no legal standing in their own right to enforce the duties that senior administrators owe to the university. Large boards with multiple constituencies may be well-intentioned, but large boards whose members have no financial interest in the enterprise may lose sight of their governance responsibilities. As in many business corporations, decision-making power is more often exercised by those in executive roles than by the board. This is one reason why the university's traditional ideals of transparency, collegiality, and academic freedom are unfortunately sometimes honoured more in rhetoric than in the actual exercise of power behind closed doors.

III. The components of the State, and its emanations

A. The executive and its delegates

The powers of the executive, in all its manifestations, are powers of public administration. This is so whether the powers are held directly, as in the case of the members of the executive government themselves, or by delegation, as in the case of those who are agents or mandataries or employee-functionaries of the holders of executive offices.

What follows is only a survey of some examples. It begins with those who hold executive power in their own hands, and then to those who hold it by delegation or legislation. One very important issue in administrative law is not addressed here: the standard of review which courts will apply to decisions of administrative entities—including tribunals—as to what the law is. The theoretical and practical importance of this question are evident, but it is outside of the concerns of this study.

---

[33] Chan (n 6) 42–45.

1. Members of the executive
a) The use of powers for proper purposes

Members of the executive branch of the government hold the powers of their offices not for their own benefit, but in order to further a mission, assignment, function, or charge: namely, the running of the apparatus of the State according to law.[34] Of course, it is a fact that in some places and times, this ideal may not be met. Holders of powers may misuse them, for their own benefit. This study aims to analyse what the law requires, focusing on a small number of legal systems; this can certainly lead to conclusions about how the law, and its effectiveness in practice, can be improved.

We begin with the basic norm that powers may only be used for the purposes for which they were granted.[35] The misuse of power by members of the executive may constitute a crime. Even former Attorney General William Barr, who took an extremely wide view of presidential authority,[36] expressed the view under oath that the use by the President, for an improper purpose, of the power to pardon can be a crime.[37] As explained in the previous chapter, this study is not primarily concerned with criminal sanctions, nor with purely political ones.[38] The first impeachment and trial of Donald Trump for abuse of power in 2019–2020 partook of both. It was not purely political inasmuch as it was formally a juridical proceeding founded on the Constitution that led to a kind of trial. But the trial itself, in the Senate, was political, inasmuch as senators did not address the charges as they would have done in a criminal trial in which they were the jurors. The sanction, had Trump been convicted, would have been removal from office. As with criminal law sanctions, this is not the direct enforcement of sound administration, but the indirect enforcement of a general public interest in sound administration.

The direct enforcement of the basic norm that powers may only be used for the purposes for which they were granted would be one that led to the setting

---

[34] In Chapter 9, section I.B.2.a, it was observed that in some places, powers of government may not be legally constrained in this way. Those are absolute monarchies or their equivalents.

[35] Denis J Galligan, *Discretionary Powers: A Legal Study of Official Discretion* (Clarendon Press 1986) 6–8, 30.

[36] See Memorandum from William Barr to Deputy Attorney General Rod Rosenstein and Assistant Attorney General Steve Engel, Re: Mueller's "Obstruction" Theory, 8 June 2018, online at https://www.wsj.com/public/resources/documents/BarrMueller.pdf.

[37] Senate Hearing 116-65, *Confirmation Hearing on the Nomination of Hon William Pelham Barr to Be Attorney General Of The United States*, 15–16 January 2019, online at https://www.congress.gov/116/chrg/CHRG-116shrg36846/CHRG-116shrg36846.htm: Senator Leahy: 'Do you believe a President could lawfully issue a pardon in exchange for the recipient's promise to not incriminate him?' William Barr: 'No. That would be a crime.' Also available in video form online at https://www.c-span.org/video/?456626-1/attorney-general-nominee-william-barr-confirmation-hearing beginning 1:23:06.

[38] Chapter 10, sections II.A–II.B. For the political nature of sanctions on British cabinet ministers, see Gillian Peele and Robert Kaye, 'Conflict of Interest in British Public Life' in C Trost and AL Gash (eds), *Conflict of Interest and Public Life* (CUP 2008) 155, 174–77.

aside, in law, of misuses of power. It seems clear that this applies in principle to members of the executive, all the way to the highest levels.[39] Some people may find that claim controversial; I will qualify it below, noting certain aspects of curial deference. But courts have been willing to declare unlawful the actions of members of the executive when they have been shown or admitted to have been exercised for an improper purpose. In *Roncarelli v Duplessis*,[40] the defendant was the Premier of Quebec (another name for the Prime Minister in the Westminster system) and also the Attorney General. In the latter role, it seems clear that he had the legal power to direct the liquor licencing authority not to renew the plaintiff's liquor licence. But he could not do so for the improper purpose of taking a kind of revenge on the plaintiff. In *Gouriet v Union of Post Office Workers*,[41] the House of Lords made it clear that that powers of the Attorney General in relation to the administration of justice cannot lawfully be used for party political ends. And in *Miller (No 2)*,[42] the UK Supreme Court held that the Prime Minister could not ask the Sovereign to dissolve Parliament for an improper reason. Similar recourses have existed in French administrative law since the nineteenth century.[43]

In a 1988 decision, the House of Lords quoted with approval a textbook on administrative law:

> Statutory power conferred for public purposes is conferred as it were upon trust, not absolutely—that is to say, it can validly be used only in the right and proper way which Parliament when conferring it is presumed to have intended.[44]

Gouriet and *Miller (No 2)*, to name only those, show that this legal norm applies whether or not the power in question derives from a statute. If the power in

---

[39] Cf Andrew Kent, Ethan J Leib, and Jed H Shugerman, 'Faithful Execution and Article II' (2019) 132 Harv L Rev 2111.

[40] *Roncarelli v Duplessis* [1959] SCR 121. The case is discussed in Chapter 10, section II.I.1.

[41] *Gouriet v Union of Post Office Workers* [1978] AC 435 (HL) The case is discussed in Chapter 10, section II.A.2.

[42] *R (Miller) v Prime Minister* [2019] UKSC 41, [2020] AC 373 [(*Miller (No 2)*)].

[43] Jean Waline, *Droit administratif* (26th edn, Dalloz 2016), 695–700; L Neville Brown and John S Bell, *French Administrative Law* (5th edn, Clarendon Press 1998), 245–50, 254–56. As in common law, review for 'error of law' sometimes means a conclusion that the decision was taken for improper reasons.

[44] *R v Tower Hamlets London Borough Council, Ex p Chetnik Developments Ltd* [1988] AC 858 (HL), 872 *per* Lord Bridge (with whom the other judges concurred), quoting William Wade, *Administrative Law* (5th edn, Clarendon Press 1982) 355. See also Sir Anthony Mason, 'The Place of Equity and Equitable Doctrines in the Contemporary Common Law World' (1994) 110 LQR 238, 238: 'modern administrative law . . . from its earliest days, has mirrored the way in which equity has regulated the exercise of fiduciary powers' and Hon James J Spigelman, 'The Equitable Origins of the Improper Purpose Ground' in Linda Pearson, Carol Harlow, and Michael Taggart (eds), *Administrative Law in a Changing State: Essays in Honour of Mark Aronson* (Hart 2008) 147. The passage from Mason's text was adopted by the majority of the High Court of Australia in *Bateman's Bay Local Aboriginal Land Council v Aboriginal Community Benefit Fund Pty Ltd* (1998) 194 CLR 247, [24].

question is, however, derived from a statute, then it may be the case that on the proper interpretation of the statute, there are certain factors that the holder of the power must take into account, or must not, or perhaps both.[45] This is exactly parallel to private administration.[46] It is a conclusion that the holder of the power was not merely required to act in the public interest, but was also bound by various additional and objective constraints that were inherent in the power because they were built into the grant of the power. The characterization of a decision as indefensible because it was 'irrational' can be understood as a conclusion that the decision-maker could not possibly have considered the proper factors.[47]

Of course, the courts will inevitably show some deference to the executive.[48] This can have several dimensions. The first is that the wider is the relevant power, the less likely are the courts to construe its grant as constrained to certain purposes. This ultimately is a matter of the correct construction of the grant of the power.[49] But as demonstrated by *Roncarelli*, *Gouriet*, and *Miller (No 2)*, in relation to even the widest power, some purposes will be improper. Another dimension of deference, which applies also in private law administration, is that there is a subjective element to all administration which is not subjected to legal constraint.[50] It arises precisely because the power is a discretionary power, and the discretion—the exercise of judgment—belongs to the holder of the power. If a member of the executive honestly believes that a certain course of action is in the public interest, or in the case of a more constrained power, believes that a certain course of action is the proper way to pursue the narrower purpose of the empowering legislation, then that action is properly taken, and it is not for the court or the law or anyone else to gainsay the decision. As in private administration, this is not so much a question of deference as simply a recognition of to whom the relevant power has been granted. Just as in private law, difficult questions may arise when proper and improper purposes are both present.[51] Some solutions to this problem will, in effect, be more deferential than others.[52]

---

[45] For example, *Padfield v Minister of Agriculture, Fisheries and Foods* [1968] AC 997 (CA, HL).
[46] Chapter 3, especially sections II and IV. For discussion in the public law context, see Galligan (n 35), 30–33.
[47] See Galligan (n 35), 140–42. In the same way, rationality may be invoked in relation to powers of private administration; see *Re Manisty's Settlement* [1974] Ch 17, 26.
[48] For the suggestion that deference is largely a matter of jurisdiction, see Chapter 10, section II.A.2.
[49] For an example: *NZ Council of Licenced Firearms Owners Inc v Minister of Police* [2020] NZHC 1456, [87]–[96].
[50] For the private law administration discussion, see Chapter 3, section II.B.
[51] For discussion in private law, see Chapter 3, section IV.B.
[52] See the discussion in Spigelman (n 44), 156–60.

b) Reasons

Another dimension of deference may lie in the extent to which a member of the executive must provide the reasons for their decision or action. Whether or not reasons have to be given for decisions made by public law administrators is a difficult and context-specific question, discussed in all books on administrative law. As in private law, reasons may be essential to accountability, as they may be the only way to tell whether the power was exercised for proper purposes, including whether irrelevant matters were considered or relevant matters were ignored.[53] As with all norms of administration, a duty to provide reasons can be understood to arise out of the relationship of accountable administration, without the need for a legislative basis.[54]

In Switzerland, a crucial decision relating to an application for citizenship is made by the commune (roughly, town or municipality) where the person is applying. This is not a power delegated by the executive government; it is rather a constitutional allocation of power, and so the communes can set their own requirements and procedures.[55] In some communes, decisions were traditionally made by secret ballot, which generated no reasons at all. Switzerland is famous for its direct democracy, and this process could be seen as one in which citizens are the ones who make the commune's decision in each case. The absence of any reasons in cases of refusal, however, could be seen to be problematical, particularly where the applicant's photograph was a required part of the application.[56] In 2003, the Federal Tribunal held that the secret ballot process was unconstitutional.[57] This was because the absence of reasons violated the right to a fair hearing in administrative decision-making,[58] and exposed people to unconstitutional discrimination.[59]

But even if reasons need to be given where a person's personal interests are gravely affected, there probably cannot be a duty to give reasons for every exercise of public power. If a member of the executive is not obliged to give reasons, then this could be described as a kind of deference. This has to be qualified in

---

[53] Peter Cane, *Administrative Law* (5th edn, OUP 2011) 88; Galligan (n 35), 275–77; Waline (n 43), 449–50, also describing in the following pages the strong movement in French administrative law since the 1970s towards the obligation to give reasons.

[54] Paul Craig, 'The Common Law, Reasons and Administrative Justice' (1994) 53 Cambridge LJ 282. It was argued earlier (Chapter 9, section I.C.3) that legislative sovereignty is not threatened by such a process of reasoning, so long as the legislature is free to exclude a duty that would otherwise arise.

[55] A person must become a citizen of a commune and of the canton (roughly, province) in which the commune is located in order to become a Swiss citizen (*Constitution fédérale de la Confédération suisse*, art 37^1).

[56] Jonathan Steinberg, *Why Switzerland?* (3rd edn, CUP 2015) 91.

[57] BGE 129 I 217 and BGE 129 I 232; see Felix Uhlmann, 'Switzerland: Naturalization Process Presents Conflict between Democracy and the Rule of Law' (2004) 2 Int'l J of Constitutional Law 716.

[58] *Constitution fédérale de la Confédération suisse*, art 29^2.

[59] ibid, art 8^2.

three ways. First, a decision-maker may disclose their reasons voluntarily, as in *Roncarelli*. Second, even without formally imposing an obligation to give reasons, the same effect may arise if the courts adopt the position that in the absence of reasons, an inference can be drawn that there was no good reason. As has been discussed, this was part of the reasoning in *Miller (No 2)*.[60] Third, in some cases the substantive unreasonableness of a decision may itself allow a court to draw an inference that there were improper reasons, or some other juridical defect in the decision. Traditionally this was limited to the case of wholly unreasonable decisions.[61] Some courts seem to have widened this principle to require simply that decisions be reasonable, although this arguably impinges on the principle that the decision-maker, and not the court, holds the decision-making power.[62]

Where reasons do have to be given, it must be remembered that courts do not have to believe everything they are told. A recent example comes from the attempt by the US federal Secretary of State to add a question about citizenship to the 2020 United States census. This proposal was challenged and the US Supreme Court ruled that although the Secretary had the power to add such a question, this statutory power could only be used for a proper purpose.[63] Even though it adopted a deferential attitude towards the review of his decision,[64] the Court simply disbelieved the government's allegations as to the purposes of the Secretary. The judgment of the Court concludes:

> Our review is deferential, but we are 'not required to exhibit a naiveté from which ordinary citizens are free' [citation omitted]. The reasoned explanation requirement of administrative law, after all, is meant to ensure that agencies offer genuine justifications for important decisions, reasons that can be scrutinized by courts and the interested public. Accepting contrived reasons would defeat the purpose of the enterprise....
>
> We do not hold that the agency decision here was substantively invalid. But agencies must pursue their goals reasonably. Reasoned decisionmaking under the Administrative Procedure Act calls for an explanation for agency action. What was provided here was more of a distraction.[65]

---

[60] As discussed in Chapter 10, section II.A.2, noting also similar suggestions in *Padfield* (n 45) and in French administrative law.

[61] In such a case, '. . . the Court infers that the decision-maker must have misunderstood their powers, or otherwise erroneously applied them . . .': *NZ Council of Licenced Firearms Owners Inc* (n 49), [84].

[62] *Minister for Immigration and Citizenship v Li* [2013] HCA 18, 249 CLR 332; *Canada (Minister of Citizenship and Immigration) v Vavilov* 2019 SCC 65.

[63] *Department of Commerce v New York* 139 S Ct 2551, 204 L Ed 2d 978 (2019).

[64] ibid, 2569 (S Ct).

[65] ibid, 2575–76 (S Ct). The parallel with *Miller (No 2)* is striking.

We live in an era of increasing freedom of information, however imperfect these systems may be, and as we have seen, obligations to provide information are part of the idea of accountability that applies to every administrator.[66] In this sense, freedom of information legislation is a direct implementation of the norms of sound public administration. Even so, most people would agree that the State needs some measure of confidentiality in relation to at least some matters in order to function well.[67] But the examples above show that the law governing public administration seems to be moving in the direction of the increasing recognition that as a general proposition, accountability requires transparency.

c) *Procedural fairness*
Audi alteram partem—'hear the other side' before deciding—is a fundamental principle of procedural justice. It applies however to some, but not all, exercises of public power.[68] In some systems or contexts, its applicability may be regulated by statute or by constitutional provision. In litigation, whether criminal, civil, or administrative, it is almost always essential. The extent to which procedural fairness is required in settings of non-litigious public administration is a very important issue.[69] Procedural fairness can be tied to the requirement that public powers can only be exercised for proper purposes by considering that where the law requires that an affected party be heard before decision, it is stipulating that a decision made without any input from that party will necessarily have been made without considering factors that needed to be considered. We have already seen that a decision so made is liable to be set aside, in public administration as in private administration. As Megarry J once said:

> It may be that there are some who would decry the importance which the courts attach to the observance of the rules of natural justice. 'When something is obvious,' they may say, 'why force everybody to go through the tiresome waste of time involved in framing charges and giving an opportunity to be heard? The result is obvious from the start.' Those who take this view do not, I think, do themselves justice. As everybody who has anything to do with the law well knows, the path of the law is strewn with examples of open and shut cases which, somehow, were not; of unanswerable charges which, in the event,

---

[66] Chapter 5, section VIII.
[67] Gabriel Schoenfeld, *Necessary Secrets* (WW Norton & Co 2010).
[68] For some discussion related to private administration, see Chapter 3, section IV.D.
[69] In *Ainsworth v Criminal Justice Commission* (1992) 175 CLR 564, 576, the majority said that '... a duty of procedural fairness arises, if at all, because the power involved is one which may "destroy, defeat or prejudice a person's rights, interests or legitimate expectations". Thus, what is decisive is the nature of the power, not the character of the proceeding which attends its exercise.' The majority's quotation is from *Annetts v McCann* (1990), 170 CLR 596, 598.

were completely answered; of inexplicable conduct which was fully explained; of fixed and unalterable determinations that, by discussion, suffered a change.[70]

d) Conflicts and unauthorized profits

What of the rules about conflicts and unauthorized profits? Since public powers can only be used properly in the pursuit of the purposes for which they were granted, the concerns raised by conflicts of self-interest and duty, and conflicts of duty and duty, are just as problematical in public administration as they are in private administration.[71] Concerns about conflicts in public administration are often framed in terms of corruption.[72] But as in private administration, conflicts are problematical even for those acting in good faith. They have unmeasurable effects on the exercise of judgment, and make it unknowable whether improper considerations have affected that exercise. As for unauthorized profits, the concern in public administration is again the same as in private administration: the administrator is acting in an other-regarding role, not acting for themselves, and they should not be able to extract unauthorized personal benefits from that role.

There is a range of legal approaches. Bribery of a member of the executive is likely a crime of both the briber and the bribee, but again criminal sanctions are not the direct enforcement of sound administration.[73] And not all unauthorized profits are bribes, in public administration just as in private administration.

In some systems, the norms about conflicts and unauthorized profits (outside of criminal offences) are purely political, leading only to political consequences. Thus in some places, there is a code of conduct, and violation may lead to a minister's being forced to resign.[74]

In the United States, there is a 'foreign emoluments clause' in the federal Constitution, that applies to anyone 'holding any Office of Profit or Trust under [the United States]'.[75] There is also a 'domestic emoluments clause' that applies only to the President.[76] Both of these clauses can be seen as legal implementations

---

[70] *John v Rees* [1970] Ch 345 (ChD), 402.

[71] These were discussed in Chapter 4, section IV, where illustrations were drawn from the case of judges, who exercise public administration.

[72] World Bank, OECD, and UN Office on Drugs and Crime, *Preventing and Managing Conflicts of Interest in the Public Sector* (2020), online at https://www.unodc.org/documents/corruption/Publications/2020/Preventing-and-Managing-Conflicts-of-Interest-in-the-Public-Sector-Good-Practices-Guide.pdf.

[73] Chapter 10, section II.B.

[74] Chapter 10, section II.A.1. In Canada, a Royal Commission was set up by the federal government in the 1980s to inquire whether a Minister of the Crown had infringed a ministerial code of conduct: Hon William D Parker, *Commission of Inquiry into the Facts of Allegations of Conflict of Interest Concerning the Honourable Sinclair M Stevens* (Minister of Supply and Services Canada 1987), concluding that he had. The Commissioner formulated definitions of 'conflict of interest' comparable to those set out earlier for private law administration: Chapter 4, section III.

[75] Art I, paragraph 9, clause 8.

[76] Art II, paragraph 1, clause 7.

of the rule against unauthorized profits. In relation to the President, there are some difficulties of enforcement, as the natural enforcer is the federal Attorney General who is unlikely to take proceedings. It has been left to others to commence public interest litigation.[77]

US federal law also has very comprehensive legal norms that apply to members, officers, and employees of all three branches of the federal government.[78] This regime is basically a regulatory statute with penalties. It imposes requirements of disclosure and strictly limits the receipt of gifts and of earned outside income. The law also addresses conflicts of interest; in this context this often refers to the taking of private sector employment too soon after the end of public service, but it also applies to the exercise of State power in a conflict situation.[79] The penalties for violation of this statute can be very severe. The law is administered by an Office of Government Ethics, and individual agencies can supplement the statutory rules with their own regulations.

In Canada, the federal level and some provinces have legal rules that reach up to the executive imposing rules for public administration. These laws have extensive disclosure requirements. The federal statute directly forbids the exercise of public powers for an improper purpose, and their exercise while in a conflict of interest, and requires at least some unauthorized profits to be surrendered to the State. Senior officials may be required to divest themselves of certain investments, or place them in a blind trust to avoid conflicts of interest.[80] These are some provisions, dealing with conflicts, misuse of power, and unauthorized profits:[81]

4. For the purposes of this Act, a public office holder is in a conflict of interest when he or she exercises an official power, duty or function that provides an opportunity to further his or her private interests or those of his or her relatives or friends or to improperly further another person's private interests.
5. Every public office holder shall arrange his or her private affairs in a manner that will prevent the public office holder from being in a conflict of interest....

---

[77] Enforcement of these provisions is discussed in Chapter 10, section II.H.
[78] The Ethics Reform Act of 1989, Pub L No 101–194, 103 Stat 1716, codified in a range of chapters of the US Code; see Mark A Adams, Jeremy W Barber, and Hildy Herrera, 'Ethics in Government' (1993) 30 Am Crim LJ 617; Bruce E Cain, Alison L Gash, and Mark J Oleszek, 'Conflict-of-Interest Legislation in the United States: Origins, Evolution, and Inter-Branch Differences' in Christine Trost and Alison L Gash (eds), *Conflict of Interest and Public Life* (CUP 2008) 101.
[79] 18 USC §208.
[80] A 'blind trust' in this context refers to a trust in which the beneficiary does not know what assets are held in trust at any given time. Obviously, it can only work as a conflict management strategy if the trustees have the authority to change the assets held in the trust without the knowledge or consent of the beneficiary.
[81] *Conflict of Interest Act*, SC 2006, c 9, s 2. For some discussion of the history, see A Stark, 'Conflict of Interest in Canada' in C Trost and AL Gash (eds), *Conflict of Interest and Public Life* (CUP 2008) 125.

9. No public office holder shall use his or her position as a public office holder to seek to influence a decision of another person so as to further the public office holder's private interests or those of the public office holder's relatives or friends or to improperly further another person's private interests....

11. (1) No public office holder or member of his or her family shall accept any gift or other advantage, including from a trust, that might reasonably be seen to have been given to influence the public office holder in the exercise of an official power, duty or function.

   (2) Despite subsection (1), a public office holder or member of his or her family may accept a gift or other advantage

   (a) that is permitted under the Canada Elections Act;

   (b) that is given by a relative or friend; or

   (c) that is received as a normal expression of courtesy or protocol, or is within the customary standards that normally accompany the public office holder's position.

   (3) When a public office holder or a member of his or her family accepts a gift or other advantage referred to in paragraph (2)(c) that has a value of $1,000 or more, the gift or other advantage is, unless otherwise determined by the Commissioner, forfeited to Her Majesty in right of Canada.

12. No minister of the Crown, minister of state or parliamentary secretary, no member of his or her family and no ministerial adviser or ministerial staff shall accept travel on non-commercial chartered or private aircraft for any purpose unless required in his or her capacity as a public office holder or in exceptional circumstances or with the prior approval of the Commissioner.

The interesting thing about s 11(3) is that it is a rule of attribution, not a sanction for doing something wrong.[82] Even though, according to s 11(2)(c), the public office-holder is allowed to accept the gift, nonetheless it is forfeited to the State.[83]

Generally, however, this legislation only leads to minor fines for non-compliance, or even simply to statements that the rules have been violated. In 2018, Prime Minister Justin Trudeau was fined $100 by the Conflict of Interest and Ethics Commissioner for accepting a gift of sunglasses without declaring it as required by law.[84] The year before, he was also found to be in more serious

---

[82] In this it is like the rule against unauthorized profits in private law: Chapter 5, section II.B.4.

[83] It is curious that the same result does not follow on a violation of s 11(1). It is unclear whether the Conflict of Interest and Ethics Commissioner could enforce s 11(3) on behalf of the Crown. If enforcement belongs to the Attorney General, then in theory citizens should be able to enforce via a relator action, although the Attorney General must approve such an action and can discontinue it (see Chapter 10, section II.G). For discussion of whether those decisions are subject to judicial review, see Chapter 10, section II.A.2.

[84] The notice (18 June 2018) is here: http://prciec-rpccie.parl.gc.ca/EN/PublicRegistries/Pages/Declaration.aspx?DeclarationID = 728a6ef2-3573-e811-99fe-000e1e07bde8.

breach of the legislation in relation to accepting more significant hospitality.[85] Still more seriously, in 2019, another investigation led to the conclusion that the Prime Minister intervened inappropriately in the decision-making process of the federal Attorney General in relation to whether a corporate entity should be criminally prosecuted.[86] The Prime Minister was found to have violated s 9, set out above, a provision of the legislation that basically forbids misuse of public power.

Thus, paradoxically, although the norms have been made into legal rules, under this legislation their violation does not necessarily lead to the natural consequences: that the exercise of a power for an improper purpose, or in a conflict, situation, can be set aside. The Commissioner does not have that authority. Similarly, the far-reaching US federal statute is basically criminal law. To set aside governmental action for the improper use of executive power, private persons must resort to judicial review.

There is an interesting contrast in the legislation of the Canadian province of Manitoba. There, executive actions taken in violation of the rules on conflicts of interest are voidable at the instance of the Crown or relevant agency.[87] Although this raises the problem of self-supervision, it provides at least the possibility of the direct enforcement of the norm that executive power should not be used in conflict situations. Even more strikingly, this statute provides for its enforcement through the courts, and gives standing to members of the public to enforce its provisions.[88] This relates partly to the enforcement of penal sanctions: the court can order that a cabinet minister in violation of the statute be disqualified, suspended, or fined. However, the court can also order, even in the case of an inadvertent breach, the surrender to the Crown of unauthorized profits. This, again, is the direct enforcement of a norm of public administration, combined with an unusually generous enforcement mechanism.[89] This legislation is, however, going to be replaced by new statute which lacks these features.[90]

Interestingly, quite apart from any legislative framework, the Judicial Committee of the Privy Council has recently treated the public duties of a

---

[85] See the report (20 Dec 2017) here: https://ciec-ccie.parl.gc.ca/en/publications/Documents/InvestigationReports/The%20Trudeau%20Report.pd.

[86] The report (14 Aug 2019) is here: https://ciec-ccie.parl.gc.ca/en/investigations-enquetes/Pages/TrudeauIIReport-RapportTrudeauII.aspx.

[87] *Legislative Assembly and Executive Council Conflict of Interest Act*, CCSM c L112, s 10. This provision does not appear in the replacement legislation which will take effect after the next election *(Conflict of Interest (Members and Ministers) Act*, CCSM c C171). For a similar provision to s 10, see British Columbia *Members' Conflict of Interest Act*, RSBC 1996, c 287, s 12.

[88] *Legislative Assembly and Executive Council Conflict of Interest Act*, ibid, ss 20–22; see also s 29.

[89] Under s 20, ibid, a member of the public bringing a proceeding must pay $300 as security for costs and may forfeit this.

[90] Under the *(Conflict of Interest (Members and Ministers) Act* (n 87), s 52, persons 'affected' by an unauthorized profit may go to court to seek its surrender. The general standing to enforce the statute is not present in this legislation.

Minister of the Crown in the Westminster system as exactly equivalent to private fiduciary duties in terms of the remedies that they generate. The Minister's public duties were treated as directed duties whose violation gave rise to remedies enforceable by the Attorney General, in private law categories but for the benefit of the Crown.[91]

e) Liability for loss caused

If gross abuse of executive power causes loss, there may be a private claim for damages.[92] In French administrative law, administrative action may allow recovery of private loss without the need to prove any fault at all.[93] But in the common law, and in Quebec civil law, merely careless infliction of harm by the executive is unlikely to generate recovery. This is because, although those holding executive power are legally duty-bound to exercise it with care, skill, diligence, and prudence, this is an undirected public duty.[94]

2. Delegates from the executive

Those who hold office in the executive part of the government cannot possibly perform all of their functions personally. Delegation is essential. This is often done through the creation of legal persons which are juridically separate from the government but controlled by it. These are discussed below.[95] Where there is direct delegation within the government to employees or functionaries, their acts in exercising public powers are considered in law to be the acts of the delegator.[96] The private law categories of agency and mandate may not be directly applicable, but the logic is similar. The public power being exercised is the executive authority of the delegator, the office-holder wielding executive power, and it can be challenged for its lawfulness as if that person acted personally.

In the same way, if an employee of the State who is administrator were to take an unauthorized profit, he should rightly be accountable for it to the State.[97]

---

[91] *Arthur v Attorney General of the Turks & Caicos Islands* [2012] UKPC 30; *Akita Holdings Ltd v Attorney General of the Turks & Caicos Islands* [2017] UKPC 7, [2017] AC 590. In both cases the claim was against a third party but the foundation in both was the Minister's breach of fiduciary duty. For the terminology of directed and undirected duties, see Chapter 10, section I.

[92] *Roncarelli* (n 40); in the common law this may be via the tort of misfeasance in public office. Both are discussed in Chapter 10, section II.I.

[93] This is discussed in Chapter 10 at the beginning of section II.I., where a parallel is drawn to the presumptive requirement in the common law to compensate for property taken or destroyed by lawful State action.

[94] The unprecedented Canadian decision in *Paradis Honey Ltd v Canada* 2015 FCA 89, [2016] 1 FCR 446, leave to appeal denied, 2015 CanLII 69423, which is discussed in Chapter 10, section II.I.2.c, points however in the direction of the recovery of economic loss caused by mere carelessness of the State or its emanations. It is not clear whether this decision will be followed.

[95] Section III.B.1.a.

[96] *Carltona Ltd v Commissioners of Works* [1943] 2 All ER 560 (CA).

[97] *Attorney-General v Edmunds* (1868) LR 6 Eq 381.

The public administration version of the rule against unauthorized profits is also revealed in cases of bribery, where it has been applied in the common law to delegates of the State. It is clearly an example of that rule, because the State recovers the bribes, regardless of whether the State suffered any loss. A member of the armed forces (a servant of the Crown) who obtained bribes from smugglers to assist them in avoiding detection had to give up the profits to the Crown.[98] This holding was confirmed more recently when a Director of Public Prosecutions, also a Crown servant with public powers, had to surrender bribes to the Crown.[99]

3. Conclusion

Any legal system which respects the rule of law will insist that executive power can only be used for proper purposes. This can be enforced by judicial review, which will require consideration of standing and proof of improper purposes. Through such proceedings, the exercise of power is liable to be set aside.

Although there may be non-legal norms that forbid the exercise of executive power by a person who is in a conflict, in the absence of statutory intervention it is not obvious that there is a legal norm (as there is in private administration) that such an exercise can be set aside, in the same way as can be the exercise of a power for a proved improper purpose; or, that conflicts can disqualify a person in advance from acting. Here, the law may need improvement, with due care paid to the need to allow the government to function. Conflict of interest legislation that generates fines and bad publicity may be better than nothing, but it still does not allow the setting aside of the exercises of power by those who should not have acted in the particular case, nor does it require recusal in advance in order to insulate exercises of power from being subject to challenge.

The legal implementation of the rule against unauthorized profits is uneven in relation to members of the executive. Gross cases may be criminalized. The US Constitution has some text on the issue, although the law is unclear as to who can enforce it. US federal law has extensive regulation of gifts and outside income. Some Canadian legislation aims to implement a rule of attribution, as in private law, although it applies only to some unauthorized profits. The general principles of attribution have been applied in the common law to persons *below* the members of the executive in the hierarchy of government.[100] It is a question for the future whether they will be applied also to those at the highest levels. There seems no sound reason why they should not be. If they are, the problem

---

[98] *Reading v Attorney-General* [1951] AC 507 (HL). The defendant had no authority to do what he was doing, but as a member of the armed forces he held some public powers (derived from the Crown prerogative) which apparently justified treating him as an administrator.
[99] *Attorney-General for Hong Kong v Reid* [1994] 1 AC 324 (PC).
[100] See the subsection immediately above.

of self-supervision may mean that members of the public will need to be granted standing to enforce the public interest in sound public administration.

B. Emanations of the State

1. Scope of the term

This section discusses some examples of 'emanations of the State'. They exercise powers of public administration, but not by direct delegation from the executive; rather, they typically hold their powers under legislation. The first category, which is large and varied, contains entities which are not under the direct control of the executive in the way that employees of the executive branch are. They are however subject to substantial, if indirect, control of the executive, as where the executive can appoint and remove those who control the entity or make its decisions.[101] In this sense they are emanations of the State. The other three categories are created by legislation or by prerogative power, but are not under the control of the executive. These are emanations of the State not in virtue of being controlled by the executive, but in virtue of carrying out the functions of the State.

a) Legal persons controlled by the State

Public powers of administration are often exercised on behalf of the State by legal persons that are controlled by it. To take one example, in Quebec the sale of many alcoholic beverages is the monopoly of the *Société des alcools du Québec*.[102] Although this legal person is juridically separate from the Crown in right of Quebec, it is entirely controlled by it; all of its board members are appointed by the government.[103] Such entities may be called 'Crown corporations' in the Westminster tradition, or more generically, 'State-owned enterprises'. Crown corporations are sometimes formally designated as agents or mandataries of the Crown, which underlines the level of governmental control.[104] Not all of them are in business of any kind: dairy commissions, licencing commissions, police forces, and many other bodies may be legal persons of this kind. Such entities are found also in the cultural sector; for example, the boards of the National Gallery

---

[101] In this, they differ from the non-State entities discussed above, section II. As mentioned there, different systems may view similar entities in different ways. In Continental systems, a university might well be considered an emanation of the State of the kind described in this section.

[102] *Act respecting the Société des alcools du Québec*, CQLR c S-13.

[103] ibid s 7.

[104] ibid s 4. If this designation was taken literally, one might think that such legal persons could and would bind the Crown to any contracts made by the legal person. In fact, the point of this designation is to confer on the legal person *immunities* that the Crown enjoys: P Hogg and Wade K Wright, *Constitutional Law of Canada* (5th looseleaf edn, Carswell 2007–) §§ 10.2–10.4.

of Canada and the Canadian Museum of History are entirely appointed by the government of Canada.[105]

These entities have a lot in common with the category discussed above, of legal persons that have a public mission.[106] The difference is that the legal persons described here not only have a public mission; they are moreover controlled by the State, which is why they can be called emanations of the State. In common with the earlier discussion, however, the duties of their administrators are prima facie owed to the legal person.[107] The mechanics of enforcement could therefore be similar: the corporation in question has the right to enforce the duties. These situations may share some enforcement difficulties with business corporations in relation to the problem of self-supervision.[108] If the State itself seeks to hold administrators to account, however, those difficulties will be easier to overcome in this context. Since the governance of these entities is entirely in the hands of the State, this means that if the State's wishes in relation to enforcement were not being followed by the corporation, its management could relatively easily be changed and the ousted persons pursued if that was desired. Members of the public have at least the possibility to take action to enforce the public interest in the performance of the undirected public duties of administration, at least if some private right or interest has been affected.[109]

The use of State-controlled corporations is simply one way to perform certain functions that might otherwise be directly performed by some branch of the executive. It creates some distance from the executive in terms of governance, but not full independence.

b) Administrative tribunals

This phrase is meant to capture tribunals that are established by legislation in the pursuit of a public purpose, but which are not built into the constitutional order. Thus French administrative *courts*, although they are tribunals in a sense, are not 'administrative tribunals' of the kind discussed here. The last century has seen a proliferation of such administrative tribunals as part of the rise of the 'administrative State'. The motivation may include a desire to have some disputes resolved by specialists without the need for recourse to the courts. Indeed, legislative attempts to restrict the judicial review of the decisions of such tribunals has been part of the development of administrative law in common law countries the last

---

[105] *Museums Act*, SC 1990, c 3, s 19. Note also s 26 providing that each museum is an agent (mandatary in the French text) of the federal Crown.
[106] Section II.B.
[107] As in business corporations, not only the directors or governors are administrators in my sense, but all of those who hold legal powers on behalf of the legal entity. Thus officers, who are agents or mandataries, are administrators even if they are not directors.
[108] Chapter 8, section III.C.2.c.
[109] Chapter 10, section II.H.

decades.[110] The members of tribunals of this kind typically have a much higher degree of independence than the kinds of legal persons that were discussed in the previous subsection. Those members are not under the control of the executive, and it may not be possible for them to be removed before the end of their term. This greater degree of independence might be thought to make the label 'emanation of the State' less apt. But if we remember that if these tribunals did not exist, the disputes they address would fall to the courts—the judicial branch of the government—then it is easier to see them as part of the State.[111]

c) Commissions of inquiry

Commissions of inquiry are a feature of the Westminster system. They are established by the executive and given a mandate and a budget, but they operate independently of the executive. Again, they are not 'emanations' in the sense of being controlled by the State; but they are created and their mission assigned by the executive. These commissions are not courts nor are they tribunals that resolve a dispute between parties. Their findings, however, can have very significant effects on persons involved. The exercise of these public powers is clearly subject to judicial review.[112]

d) Local political units

A city, town, or municipality may be in the form of a legal person, that holds more or less wide legal powers. In some systems, these entities are parts of the State, inasmuch as their existence is provided for in the constitution.[113] In common law countries, they may however be the creation of a statute. These statutory political units are constitutionally more precarious, inasmuch as they exist only by virtue of ordinary legislation. They are not controlled by the executive, since the legislation will provide for the election of executive members of the local political unit by its residents. But these units are legal persons that exist for public purposes, and moreover they perform State functions, typically pursuant to the idea that some such functions are best run at the local level. In the common law,

---

[110] Patrice Garant, *Droit administratif* (7th edn, Éditions Yvons Blais 2017), 499–510.

[111] I have not classified as emanations of the State some legal persons (like universities) that pursue a public purpose but are independent of State control (above, section II.B). If university education were viewed as a State responsibility—as it is in some countries—then even independent universities might rightly be considered emanations of the State. My categorization of some but not all entities with public powers as emanations of the State is largely a matter of convenience, since it is argued above (section II) that even those that are not so classified must comply with the norms of public administration and are legally accountable in that respect.

[112] For example, in Canada a Royal Commission was set up by the federal government in the 1980s to inquire whether a Minister of the Crown had infringed a ministerial code of conduct; the Commissioner concluded that he had (Parker (n 74)). Years later this finding was quashed on jurisdictional grounds: *Stevens v Canada (Attorney General)* 2004 FC 1746.

[113] Such as communes (municipalities) in many civil law countries.

the Attorney General has a power of enforcement against such entities in relation to the norms of public administration, and this power may be invoked by private persons using the relator action.[114]

2. Legal norms of sound administration

Those who exercise public powers, in any of these categories, are exercising public administration. It is not surprising that the norms of administration apply. These norms can apply not only to momentous decisions of a member of the executive, but also to the exercise of more modest powers.

a) The use of powers for proper purposes

Police forces may be constituted in different ways, for example as commissions or as legal persons. Shortly after the Second World War, the English courts made it clear that police officers must use their public powers for the right purposes.[115] In the case, the power was a legislative power to demand an identity card, a power granted under a state of emergency based on a threatened invasion. The threat had passed but the legal regime had not been altered. The accused refused to produce his card, and as a result was convicted of an offence that, the court thought, should never have been pursued against him. Although convicted, he was given an absolute discharge. This means that the exercise of the police power was not considered to be void in law. The police had the power but misused it. In this case, no police action was legally set aside; the misuse served the accused as a kind of defence, in relation to sentencing.

But when public powers are not used for the right purposes, the courts routinely set aside such exercises of power, or indeed find them to be void. Such review is routinely applied to the huge range of administrative agencies, boards, tribunals, and other entities that are created to exercise functions of the State. The legal regulation of such entities is a core function of administrative law. In every legal system, the details of this field of law are very complex. The broad outlines of the legal regulation of other-regarding power, however, are plainly visible in this field. It is clear that these entities must use their powers for the right purposes. Frequently, by an interpretation of the grant of such powers, courts will articulate lists of factors which much, or may, or may not be considered in the exercise of these powers. This elaboration of objective constraints is also seen in private law administration,[116] and, as discussed above, in the interpretation of the powers held by members of the executive themselves.[117] A court may set

---

[114] *Attorney-General v London County Council* [1901] 1 Ch 781 (CA). The relator action is discussed in Chapter 10, section II.G.1.
[115] *Willcock v Muckle* [1951] 2 KB 844 (DC).
[116] Chapter 3, section II.C.
[117] Section III.B.1.a.

aside a decision of an emanation of the State on the basis that it considered a matter that, on a proper interpretation of the statute that empowered the entity, should not have been considered; conversely, that the entity failed to consider a matter that, on a proper interpretation of the statute, should have been considered. That is nothing more or less than a conclusion that the power was used improperly. In French administrative law, the conclusion is that there has been a *détournement de pouvoir*, which has been translated as 'abuse of power', rather than absence of it.[118] Standing to challenge such decisions was discussed in the previous chapter.[119]

It is not surprising that the approach of the courts to the work of State entities exercising public powers reveals an attitude sometimes described as deference. There is a constant tension between the need to ensure that these agencies act lawfully, and the recognition by courts that agencies have the rightful ability to exercise the powers and authority that have been granted to them. This tension is inherent in the legal regulation of all kinds of administration, both public and private. The tension is perhaps more evident in relation to the examination of whether or not a power was exercised for the right purposes than whether the power existed at all. This is partly because this inquiry is more subjective than the simple and objective question whether the relevant power allowed the person holding it to do some particular action. It may also be partly because the judiciary, in interpreting the grant of the relevant power, may conclude that a power was implicitly subject to certain constraints which may not be obvious on the face of the legislation or other grant.

b) Reasons and procedural fairness

As we have seen, the ability of an affected person to demand reasons for a decision that affects her is a difficult and context-specific question. It is obviously more difficult to allege that a decision was taken for improper reasons if one does not know the reasons, and yet it seems clear that not all entities exercising public powers could be obliged to provide the same kinds of reasons in all settings. This too has parallels in private law administration.[120] In general, the courts are more likely to require that emanations of the State give reasons for their decisions than they are to impose that obligation on members of the executive itself.[121] This is particularly true of tribunals, or those making a decision after hearing from the affected person. Just as with the exercise of power by the executive, the

---

[118] Brown and Bell (n 43), 245–50, with the translation at 246; Waline (n 43), 695–97. 'Misuse of power' might be better.
[119] Chapter 10, sections II.F–II.H.
[120] Chapter 3, section IV.C.
[121] David J Mullan, *Administrative Law* (Irwin Law 2001), 306–18; Garant (n 110), 752–62; Christopher Ellis, 'Reasons and the Record—Reconsidering *Osmond* and Constitutional Perspectives' (2015) 82 Australian Institute of Administrative Law Forum 55.

courts may draw their own inferences about the purposes for which powers were exercised if no reasons are given, or reasons that seem contrived.

Procedural fairness is also a central concern of administrative law, and one whose demands must also vary according to context. Again, a tribunal resolving a bilateral dispute must just about universally observe the principle of *audi alteram partem*.[122] The suggestion above was that this principle is closely related to the requirement that powers be exercised for the right purposes. A requirement to hear representations from a party can be construed as a decision that the views and submissions of those most affected are matters which must be considered in the exercise of the power. Sound procedures exist to improve the prospects of sound outcomes.

c) Conflicts

Delegates of the executive may hold very wide powers of many different kinds. Those who are directly part of the administration or civil service may well be subjected to the legislation that was discussed above for the executive itself, governing such things as disclosure of interests, recusal and other strategies for managing conflicts, and rules aimed at preventing unauthorized profits. As we noticed in that section, however, most of these regimes impose sanctions after the fact, rather than allowing attacks on exercises of power that were made in violation of the relevant norms.[123]

Just as in private law administration, however, the regulation of conflicts does not necessarily depend on a statute. Those who think that in the common law tradition, norms about conflicts of interest are particularly related to the legacy of the Court of Chancery would do well to remember *Dr Bonham's Case*,[124] decided by the common law Court of King's Bench long before the famous Chancery decisions on fiduciary duties in the eighteenth and nineteenth centuries. The case is understood to have laid a foundation for the judicial review of the validity of legislation in the United States, because Sir Edward Coke suggested that even an act of Parliament would be void if it was 'against common right or reason'. The defect of the statute in that case was that it made the College of Physicians competent to judge and fine physicians, while providing that any fines so imposed were payable to the College. In other words, in making the College into a kind of administrative agency, it placed the College in an institutional conflict of interest: it was the judge in the same causes in which it had a financial interest.[125]

---

[122] As with courts, temporary orders made in urgent circumstances may allow an exception.
[123] US federal law criminalizes acting while in a conflict under 18 USC §208; but the exemptions in that statute effectively create a system governing the proper management of conflicts, for example through disclosure and approval; recusal is of course another way to avoid committing the offence.
[124] *Bonham v College of Physicians* (1610) 8 Co Rep 107, 77 ER 638 (KB).
[125] My point is not that there is any such constraint on the sovereignty of the UK Parliament; Coke is understood to have retreated from this position: John H Baker, *An Introduction to English Legal History* (5th edn, OUP 2019) 223–24. My point is only that Coke, applying the common law and not

In the common law, the problem of a conflicted public law decision-maker is often labelled 'bias' instead of 'conflict of interest'.[126] Some commentators argue that the rules have different foundations in public law and in private law. In public law, it may be said, the function of the rules on bias is to maintain public confidence in public institutions.[127] It is not clear that this reveals a difference between private and public law. As we have seen, the problem with decision-making in conflict situations is that the decision-maker may favour their own self-interest, not only invisibly but unconsciously and while trying not to.[128] In other words, the *reality* of the problem is the same in both situations. In the light of this, it seems redundant to try to justify the rules in terms of appearances. Were conflicted decision-making allowed, the resultant loss of confidence in public institutions would be based not on appearances but on reality.[129] By analogy from the rules governing judges, a doctrine of 'necessity' can allow a conflicted decision-maker to act when there is no one qualified who is unconflicted.[130]

d) Unauthorized profits

Emanations of the State, and those who work for them, are not entitled to extract unauthorized fees from the public for the work that they do.[131] A breach of this principle entitles the affected person to recover the unauthorized exaction. That in itself is not a direct illustration of the rule against unauthorized profits; it is rather an illustration of the importance of legality of State action.

In private law, an employee as such is not an administrator because she does not, as an employee, hold legal powers to act for and on behalf of the employer;

Equity, thought that the principle against conflicts, at least in this setting, was so fundamental as to be a matter of 'common right or reason'. Baker notes that other judges agreed.

[126] Lionel Smith, 'Conflict, Profit, Bias, Misuse of Power: Dimensions of Governance' in PB Miller and Matthew Harding (eds), *Fiduciaries and Trust: Ethics, Politics, Economics and Law* (CUP 2020) 149.

[127] See Matthew Conaglen, 'Public-Private Intersection: Comparing Fiduciary Conflict Doctrine and Bias' [2008] Public Law 58 and Remus Valsan, 'The No-conflict Fiduciary Rule and the Rule against Bias in Judicial Review: A Comparison' (2019) 6 European J of Comparative Law and Governance 1.

[128] Chapter 4, section IV. For an application of the same considerations to the public administration context, see Eyal Zamir and Raanan Sulitzeanu-Kenan, 'Explaining Self-Interested Behavior of Public-Spirited Policy Makers' (2018) 78 Public Administration Rev 579.

[129] To repeat a quotation that appears in Chapter 3: 'It is obvious—everybody knows it who has any knowledge of life—that when a man has a pecuniary interest, his mind is naturally warped in favour of his own interest. It is human nature, and no one can doubt it.': *Re Lamb* [1894] 2 QB 805 (CA), 820.

[130] Ian Leigh, 'Bias, Necessity and the Convention' [2002] Public Law 407. The rule as it relates to judges is mentioned below, section III.D.2. The case discussed by Leigh involves bias allegedly arising not from any financial interest but from not coming to the case with an open mind. This also applies to judges, and it is argued below that it can be seen as a species of conflict.

[131] For some discussion of United States law, see Cain, Gash, and Oleszek (n 78), 107–8. There is a review of older cases on office holders in *Woolwich Equitable Building Society v Inland Revenue Commissioners* [1993] AC 70; see also *Kingstreet Investments Ltd v New Brunswick (Department of Finance)* [2007] 1 SCR 3, 2007 SCC 1.

but many employees do hold such powers.[132] Government employees may have legal powers that no private employee has. Consider the person who examines candidates for drivers' licences. This person might not be considered an agent or mandatary since he does not make contracts that bind the State or deal with its property. In a sense, however, he is, since the public power to grant or withhold the licence is delegated to him. This person might also be called a 'functionary' since it is his job, or part of it, to exercise a function of the State. If he were to take an unauthorized profit, he should rightly be accountable for it to the State or the relevant emanation of it.[133]

In the common law, the rule against unauthorized profits has long been applied to elected members of local governments, like town or city councils. They hold their authority by delegation through a statute, and so are not directly members of a sovereign legislature. In the common law, they have been treated as trustees for the purpose of this rule.[134] In a similar way, the Federal Republic of Brazil recovered a bribe from companies controlled by the bribee, who was the mayor of a city.[135]

e) *Liability for loss caused*
A public administrator who causes loss to their beneficiary by careless or deliberate conduct of their role or function is potentially liable, like any administrator to their beneficiary. In public administration, directed duties may be owed to the emanation of the State which the administrator serves. A striking example from municipal law is found in *Porter v Magill*.[136] The House of Lords upheld the finding of an auditor that city councillors who had misused their powers in pursuit of electoral advantage were personally liable for loss thereby caused to the local authority, exceeding £26 million. The decision was expressly based on the use of public powers for an improper purpose. Lord Bingham said:

---

[132] Chapter 7, section II.B.

[133] So held in *ICBC v Dragon Driving School Canada Ltd* 2005 BCSC 1093, where a driving examiner had received $175,000 in bribes to issue drivers' licences without testing the candidates. Subsequent proceedings (2006 BCCA 584; 2007 BCSC 389) concerned the liability of a driving instructor who had received much larger amounts from the candidates. The instructor, who was also held liable for his gains, was not an administrator but was a corrupt participant in the unlawful scheme.

[134] *Bowes v Toronto (City)* (1858) 11 Moo PC 463, 14 ER 770; *Edmonton (City) v Hawrelak* [1976] 1 SCR 387; *Toronto Party v Toronto (City)* 2013 ONCA 327, 115 OR (3d) 694; contrast *How Weng Fan v Sengkang Town Council* [2022] SGCA 72. See Lionel Smith, 'Loyalty and Politics: From Case Law to Statute Law' (2015) 9 J of Equity 130 and Nadav Shoked, 'The American Law of Local Officials as Fiduciaries' in Evan J Criddle and others (eds), *Fiduciary Government* (CUP 2018) 258.

[135] *Federal Republic of Brazil v Durant International Corp* [2015] UKPC 35, [2016] AC 297. The judgment indicates ([1]) that the 'effective' plaintiff was the Municipality of São Paulo, but that Brazilian law requires that the State be a party to any action brought by a public authority outside of Brazil.

[136] *Porter v Magill* [2002] 2 AC 357 (CA, HL).

It follows from the proposition that public powers are conferred as if upon trust that those who exercise powers in a manner inconsistent with the public purpose for which the powers were conferred betray that trust and so misconduct themselves.[137]

The obligation to compensate the authority for loss caused by 'wilful misconduct' was in the governing statute, which itself treated the councillors rather like trustees in this respect.[138] In the case of employees of emanations of the State (rather than elected councillors), such claims are probably rare, just as private sector employers would only rarely sue their employees for loss caused by carelessness. Termination is more likely.

More difficult is the question whether a private person can sue a public entity, such as a police force, for loss caused the careless performance of their duties. The duty to perform the function with care, skill, prudence, and diligence is a duty of sound administration; but whether loss caused by a breach raises difficulties in several dimensions. French law uses different courts, and different legal rules, for administrative law and civil (private) law. The common law does not, but it typically draws a distinction between the undirected duties of public officials, and directed duties that are owed to persons. A police officer may owe a directed duty to private persons not to cause physical harm or property damage, of the kind that every private person may owe to others (although the police officer may have some statutory immunity). But the police officer's duties, for example, to use care in investigating crimes and in trying to prevent them may be seen as undirected duties, which are less likely to be privately actionable. If a private person is complaining about *inaction*, the duty is perhaps more likely to be seen as undirected. The common law also typically uses different rules for duties not to cause pure economic loss and duties not to cause personal injury or property damage (which may result in consequential, not pure, economic loss). The matter was discussed in outline in the previous chapter.[139]

f) Conclusion

Those who hold public powers as emanations of the State are often subject to the same norms of sound administration that apply in private law administration. Powers can only be validly used in the pursuit of the purposes for which they were granted, and cannot be unimpeachably exercised by a person who is in a conflict situation. Those who extract unauthorized profits from their administrative role

---

[137] ibid, 463.
[138] See also *Roberts v Hopwood* [1925] AC 578 (HL), a controversial decision which treats councillors as trustees for those who pay property taxes, not for those who have the right to vote. For a similar trend in US law, see Shoked (n 134), 262–64.
[139] Chapter 10, section II.I.

can be forced to account for them to the State. The State itself, possibly through some emanation, can enforce these norms. Members of the public may also be able to do so.[140] Public administrators who, in carrying out their public administration, cause personal loss to members of the public may be directly liable to them, although the law here is complicated and is variable across systems, for a range of reasons.

C. Legislators

Those who hold the power to pass legislation obviously hold a power that exists for a public purpose. Individual legislators may not have executive authority, although in Westminster systems, members of the executive are also elected legislators. But in many ways the power to change the law may be even more significant, and this is the foundation of the lobbying industry that can at one and the same time be perceived as an example of the proper consultative role of a legislative body, or as a rank swamp of influence peddling.

In the United States, the Ethics Reform Act[141] applies to the federal Congress. Implementing it, the US House of Representatives has a comprehensive Ethics Manual,[142] as well as a Code of Official Conduct,[143] which is part of the Rules that the House has adopted to govern itself. These rules are administered by the House itself, through its Ethics Committee. Such codes are not always drafted with precision. Rule XXXVII of the Senate of the United States is entitled 'Conflict of Interest' and provides:[144]

> 1. A Member, officer, or employee of the Senate shall not receive any compensation, nor shall he permit any compensation to accrue to his beneficial interest from any source, the receipt or accrual of which would occur by virtue of influence improperly exerted from his position as a Member, officer, or employee.

Despite the title, what is forbidden by this Rule is not a 'conflict of interest' but rather corrupt influence peddling. In the terms used in this study, this norm describes a combination of an unauthorized profit and the misuse of public power. Calling it a 'conflict of interest' is like characterizing a gangland killing

---

[140] As discussed in Chapter 10, section II.H.
[141] N 78.
[142] Online at https://ethics.house.gov/sites/ethics.house.gov/files/documents/2008_House_Ethics_Manual.pdf.
[143] Online at https://ethics.house.gov/publications/code-official-conduct.
[144] Online at https://www.ethics.senate.gov/public/index.cfm/conflictsofinterest, under 'Authorities'.

as a 'failure to take proper care with a firearm'. The same is true of another paragraph of the same Rule:

> 4. No Member, officer, or employee shall knowingly use his official position to introduce or aid the progress or passage of legislation, a principal purpose of which is to further only his pecuniary interest, only the pecuniary interest of his immediate family, or only the pecuniary interest of a limited class of persons or enterprises, when he, or his immediate family, or enterprises controlled by them, are members of the affected class.

Again, this does not forbid a conflict of interest; it forbids the misuse of public power. More seriously, as going to substance and not just terminology, the Senate Ethics Committee focuses on the repeated use of the word 'only' in that paragraph to take the position that a Senator *may* use his official position to aid in the passage of legislation that significantly furthers his pecuniary interest, as long as a public interest is also involved.[145] In other words, he may act while in a significant conflict of interest.[146]

In many Canadian provinces, members of the provincial legislative assemblies are also subject to the legislative regimes that were discussed earlier in this chapter in relation to the executive.[147] The sanctions are generally quasi-penal in nature. Speaking generally, the provincial legislation is often even more toothless than the Canadian federal legislation.[148] This is because the administering official only recommends a sanction for breach; the assembly makes the actual decision.[149] In a majority government this may mean that members of the governing party are unlikely to be sanctioned. The Manitoba legislation is unusual in providing enforcement through the courts, and giving standing to members of the public to bring action; but as was noted earlier, that legislation has been replaced by a more typical statute that is scheduled to come into force after the next provincial election.[150]

---

[145] Donna M Nagy, 'Congressional Officials and the Fiduciary Duty of Loyalty: Lessons from Corporate Law' in Evan J Criddle and others (eds), *Fiduciary Government* (CUP 2018) 233, 253. The paper as a whole shows that members of Congress do not hold themselves to the same standards as those that apply to administrators in corporate law. See also Cain, Gash, and Oleszek (n 78), 116–20.

[146] See the discussion in Chapter 3, section IV.B.2, on mixed purposes, where it is argued that the logic of the rules on conflicts, which forbid the use of power where an improper purpose *may* be involved, must imply that a power cannot be properly exercised where it is known that an improper purpose is involved.

[147] Eg Alberta: *Conflicts of Interest Act*, RSA 2000, c C-23; BC: *Members' Conflict of Interest Act*, RSBC 1996, c 287; Ontario: *Members' Integrity Act, 1994*, SO 1994, c 38.

[148] On which see above, section III.A.1.d.

[149] See the discussion in Chapter 10, section II.E of the Alberta investigation in Marguerite Trussler, Report of the Investigation under the *Conflicts of Interest Act*, 27 April 2020, online at http://www.ethicscommissioner.ab.ca/media/2491/april-27-2020-allegations-involving-bill-22.pdf.

[150] Text at n 87 and following.

Legislatures are conscious of the need to use their public powers properly, but a sovereign legislature is perhaps the clearest illustration of the falsity of the 'one right answer' fallacy.[151] Administrators hold powers for an other-regarding purpose and are legally bound so use them, but at the same time, the law recognizes the power-holder as the decision-maker. A trustee must use their powers in what they perceive to be the best interests of the beneficiaries, but in many cases, it is for the trustee to decide what is in their best interests. Even stronger is the case of a sovereign legislature: it must act in the public interest, but it decides, itself, what is in the public interest. Legislatures are also jealous of their historical privileges as self-regulating entities. Those privileges have insulated them from challenge in courts of law.[152] For this reason, the relevant norms may be found in their own resolutions, which are under their own control and are distinct from legislation. This is the case for the Canadian federal House of Commons and Senate.[153] Legislative privileges may lead the courts to refuse to hear a complaint that the body did not follow correct procedures or otherwise behaved unlawfully.[154] This is not an example of deference as such, but rather a lack of jurisdiction. One way to put this is that the undirected duties owed by legislators in this respect are not part of the general legal order; they are owed, perhaps, to the legislature itself. As a result, it seems impossible to contemplate enforcement by a member of the public, even using the representative methods discussed in the previous chapter. This may seem to imply that these legislators are above the law, but the better characterization, in line with the long tradition of the privileges of legislative bodies, is that they regulate their own affairs. This includes the regulation of norms of sound public administration, including such questions as whether a legislator's powers were used for an improper purpose or in a conflict, or whether a legislator is devoting adequate effort, care, and skill to their role. For such failings, the remedy for the general public lies in the ballot box.[155]

The US House of Representatives has an investigative role which is ancillary to its legislative role. In the performance of this investigative role, a committee of

---

[151] This was discussed in the context of private administration in Chapter 3, section II.B.

[152] Smith (n 134), 142–46.

[153] See the *Conflict of Interest Code for Members of The House of Commons*, online at https://www.ourcommons.ca/about/standingorders/appa1-e.htm; *Ethics and Conflicts of Interest Code for Senators*, online at https://seo-cse.sencanada.ca/en/code/ethics-and-conflict-of-interest-code-for-senators/.

[154] *Duffy v Senate of Canada* 2020 ONCA 536, application for leave to appeal dismissed 11 February 2021 (SCC).

[155] D Theodore Rave, 'Politicians as Fiduciaries' (2013) 126 Harv L Rev 671, argues that laws passed in conflicts of interest (in particular, relating to the drawing of constituency boundaries) should be voidable by the courts on general fiduciary principle, when it is combined with rights protected by the US federal Constitution. The use of independent commissions to draw such boundaries may be a difficult goal to reach, but it is another way to deal with this conflict of interest. See the response at Ethan J Leib, David L Ponet, and Michael Serota, 'Translating Fiduciary Principles into Public Law' (2013) 126 Harv L Rev Forum 91.

the House demanded financial information by subpoena from then-President Trump's bankers and accountants. For the President, it was argued that the subpoenas were invalid because they lacked a 'proper legislative purpose'. This argument failed in the courts below.[156] In the US Supreme Court, the case was remanded to the trial judge to be reconsidered in the light of the Supreme Court's guidance on the law.[157] The Supreme Court agreed that the power had to be used for proper purposes, and laid out a legal test for evaluating that requirement in this particular context.[158] The decision confirms the legal norm that powers of public administration held by legislators must be used for proper purposes. In this, such powers are no different from powers held by the executive or the judiciary.

One final issue that may arise with legislators is the definition of the public purpose which they are required to seek to advance in the use of their public powers. Legislators often represent a constituency. Is their mission to act in what they perceive to be the interests of the people in their constituency? Or is it to act in what they perceive to be the interests of the entire country, state, province, or other unit for which they legislate?[159] They were elected by people in their constituency; but their authority to exercise public power extends over everyone in the political unit. It is certainly conceivable that in a particular case, a legislator could feel that the different formulations point in different directions. It would be quite defensible, given the logic of constituency representation, for the legislator to prioritize the pursuit of the interests of the people in their constituency. It would also be quite defensible for the legislator to act in what they perceived to be the wider interest of the whole polity of which their constituency forms a part. They are in a dual role, that has the potential to create a conflict of duty and duty; but the conflict has been authorized in advance by the design of the political system. The mediation between these potentially conflicting missions, both of which are proper considerations in the deliberations of the decision-maker,

---

[156] See *Trump v Deutsche Bank AG* 943 F3d 627 (2d CCA, 2019) and *Trump v Mazars USA LLP* 940 F3d 710 (DCCA, 2019), rehearing denied 941 F3d 1180 (DCCA, 2019).

[157] *Trump v Mazars USA, LLP* 140 SCt 2019, 207 LEd 2d 951 (2020).

[158] The application of this test by the Circuit Court of Appeal led to an order that some, but not all, aspects of a subpoena were valid: *Trump v Mazars USA LLP* 39 F4th 774 (DCCA, 2022). Following separate litigation by the Committee against the Treasury Department (ending with *Trump v Committee On Ways And Means, United States House of Representatives* 143 SCt 476 (2022)), the former President's tax returns were made public in late 2022.

[159] This is addressed in detail in Ethan J Leib, David L Ponet, and Michael Serota, 'Mapping Public Fiduciary Relationships' in Andew S Gold and Paul B Miller (eds), *Philosophical Foundations of Fiduciary Law* (OUP 2014) 388. Those authors frame the question in terms of who are the beneficiaries of public administration, with particular reference to the constituency issue for legislators (398–402). Some of the issues they discuss are resolved if this kind of public administration is seen not as one involving directed duties to identifiable beneficiaries, but rather undirected public duties. But the question as to which public interest is to be pursued remains. In relation to local governments, see n 138 for the suggestion that power-holders in that context must act in the interests of property tax payers.

therefore lies in the judgment of the individual decision-maker. This is another example of the law not giving a single answer to how an administrator must act.

D. Judges

1. Introduction

Judges are independent from government and from legislatures, but they exercise their functions as part of the State. They exercise public powers for a public purpose, which could be described generally as the administration of justice according to law.[160]

In classical Roman law, under the formulary system, judges were private citizens and so the trial was something like an arbitration. The judge's task was assigned to him by the formula, which was the document, issued to the plaintiff by a State official, that authorized the trial. In this setting, judges who acted improperly could be personally sued for a number of reasons, including incompetence, acting without authority, and so on.[161]

The professionalization of the judiciary and its regularization as part of the apparatus of the State, along with the emergence of the crucial principle of the independence of the judiciary from the other elements of that apparatus, has changed this dramatically. Rather like the legislators discussed in the previous section, judges operate within a sphere that is generally privileged from legal recourse. A legislator cannot be sued for libel for something said in the chamber; no more can a judge, for her pronouncement in court or in a judgment that a witness is not credible.

For this reason, a concern that a judge acted improperly or incompetently is unlikely to give rise to any proceeding for recourse, apart from an appeal to a higher court. An appeal is of course a step in the same proceeding that challenges, usually, the first judge's understanding of the law, or perhaps their application of the law under the circumstances. As with legislators, only cases of extreme misconduct will generate separate proceedings. Judges are of course subject to the criminal law.

---

[160] Ethan J Leib, David L Ponet, and Michael Serota, 'A Fiduciary Theory of Judging' (2013) 101 Cal L Rev 699, addressing (723–28) the case of elected judges and concluding this does not affect the analysis. I agree: the consideration that some electors may be the material source of the judge's authority is quite separate from the question how that authority is properly exercised. The latter is determined, as always, by construing the purposes for which the power was given, and in the case of elected judges it is obviously not given to pursue the interests of those who elected the judge.

[161] Peter BH Birks, 'A New Argument for a Narrow View of Litem Suam Facere' (1984) 52 Tijdschrift voor rechtsgeschiedenis (Legal History Review) 373. Some of the source texts on the liabilities of judges are Justinian, *Digest*, 5.1.15–17, 50.13.6; Justinian, *Institutes*, 4.5; *Theodosian Code*, 1.20, 2.2; Justinian's *Codex*, 3.5.1.

In another parallel with legislators, judges are usually self-regulating, and it is possible that a duly constituted disciplinary body may sanction a judge for misconduct. This kind of self-regulation has much in common with the self-regulation of professions, which is discussed below.[162] First, the disciplinary rules are of a public law nature, imposing penalties for misconduct rather than directly enforcing sound administration at the behest of the beneficiary. Second, and unlike the self-regulation of sovereign legislatures, judicial self-regulation is (like professional self-regulation) itself subject to legal regulation and to the norms governing the proper exercise of public powers. In Canada, the Canadian Judicial Council is constituted under federal legislation to investigate complaints into the conduct of federally appointed judges. A judge in Ontario, Mr Justice Patrick Smith, took a leave of absence in order to take on the role of Acting Dean at the law faculty of Lakehead University, whose dean had resigned in contested circumstances. The judge had received permission from the Chief Justice of his court and clearance from the federal Minister of Justice. Even so, and in the absence of any complaint from the public, the Canadian Judicial Council found in 2018 that he had acted unlawfully and unethically by taking on this non-judicial role that might draw him into public controversy, and by improperly using the prestige of his judicial office to bolster the law school. This proceeding was challenged by Smith J in the Federal Court of Canada, which quashed the decision of the Canadian Judicial Council and declared that the findings against him could not stand.[163]

2. Use of powers for proper purposes, and conflicts

Rare is the case in which it is proven that a judge has used their powers for an improper purpose. In 2002 a judge of the New York Supreme Court was convicted of taking a bribe to approve a settlement in a civil case.[164] It goes without saying that the use of the judicial power to approve the settlement in these circumstances was improper. A judge's duties of sound administration are undirected; they are not owed directly to litigants.[165] But clearly any party to that litigation would have standing to demand that the settlement be set aside, and a new judge be appointed to review it. Although the duty is an undirected public duty, in this case the effect on the rights and interests of the parties would be so obvious that standing would go without saying.

---

[162] Section V.
[163] *Smith v Canada (Attorney General)* 2020 FC 629.
[164] He was imprisoned and disbarred: *In re Barron* 302 AD2d 81, 751 NYS2d 563 (App Div, 2002).
[165] For the terminology of directed and undirected duties, see Chapter 10, section I. When a judge is acting in a supervisory jurisdiction (on which see Chapter 1, section V.B.3.d), she will use her powers in what she perceives to be the best interests of some person or persons. Even here, however, the judge does not owe a directed duty to those persons; she is not in a relationship of accountability to them.

Conflicts of interest can have a similar effect even in the absence of proven misconduct. This is because, as we have seen, conflicts have unknowable effects on human reasoning and create the serious possibility that a power might be used for an improper purpose, even unconsciously.[166]

The inappropriateness of judging while in a conflict of interest was well-known in Roman law: '... if one of the litigants has made the judge heir to all or part of his estate, another judge must of necessity be appointed, because it is unfair to make someone judge in his own affairs'.[167] As in all contexts of administration, there is a *de minimis* threshold for concerns about conflicts.[168] In this context, a doctrine of 'necessity' holds that conflicted judges may act when there is no one qualified who is unconflicted.[169]

As in all contexts, conflicts may be financial or non-financial.[170] In the United Kingdom, extradition proceedings against Augusto Pinochet, the initial decision of the House of Lords was in favour of extradition to Spain on some charges.[171] Counsel for Pinochet then brought a proceeding to have the first judgment set aside, on the ground that one of the judges had non-financial personal connections with a party (an intervenor) in the case.[172] The first decision was indeed set aside on that ground, on the footing that the court's inherent power to regulate its own affairs gave it the jurisdiction to make this order. Finally on a third hearing, judgment was given in favour of extradition on a smaller set of charges.[173] There is obviously a strong argument that elected judges should recuse themselves from proceedings involving persons who have financially supported them in their election campaigns.[174]

---

[166] Chapter 4, section IV, where some situations involving judges are discussed.

[167] D.5.1.17 (Ulpian), translation from Alan Watson (ed), *The Digest of Justinian*, 4 vols (revised edn, U of Pennsylvania Press 1998).

[168] *Locabail (UK) Ltd v Bayfield Properties Ltd* [2000] QB 451 (CA).

[169] Commentators agree that this exception should be confined as much as possible: Thomas Mckevitt, 'The Rule of Necessity: Is Judicial Non-Disqualification Really Necessary?' (1996) 24 Hofstra L Rev 817; Luc Huppé, 'Les conflits d'intérêts institutionnels au sein de la magistrature' (2007) 38 RDUS 127.

[170] In the United States, standards for recusal of federal judges are statutory: 28 USC §455. See also in Quebec the *Code of Civil Procedure*, CQLR c C-25.01, ss 201–5.

[171] *Ex parte Pinochet (No 1)* [1998] UKHL 41, [2000] 1 AC 61.

[172] *Ex parte Pinochet (No 2)* [1999] UKHL 1, [2000] 1 AC 119.

[173] *Ex parte Pinochet (No 3)* [1999] UKHL 17, [2000] 1 AC 147. The government, which had the final say, declined to extradite Pinochet.

[174] Vernon V Palmer and John Levendis, 'The Louisiana Supreme Court in Question: An Empirical and Statistical Study of the Effects of Campaign Money on the Judicial Function' (2008) 82 Tul L Rev 1291; Vernon V Palmer, 'The Recusal of American Judges in the Post-Caperton Era: An Empirical Assessment of the Risk of Actual Bias in Decisions Involving Campaign Contributors' (2010) https://ssrn.com/abstract = 1721665; Morgan LW Hazelton, Jacob M Montgomery, and Brendan Nyhan, 'Does Public Financing Affect Judicial Behavior? Evidence From the North Carolina Supreme Court' (2015) 44 American Politics Research 587; Neel U Sukhatme and Jay Jenkins, 'Pay to Play? Campaign Finance and the Incentive Gap in the Sixth Amendment's Right to Counsel' (2020) 70 Duke LJ 775.

A judge may also be disqualified by prior participation in the proceedings. Although it used to be normal in the English courts of common law for a judge to sit in the court reviewing a decision of that same judge, there is now a very strict rule against this.[175] It might be said that this is not exactly a conflict of interest, but rather a concern that the judge does not come to the new proceeding with a completely open mind. It is arguable, however, that this is an example of a conflict of self-interest and duty, since any judge who cares about his or her job does not like being overturned on appeal.[176]

Judges may not like being asked to recuse themselves, whether it be on the ground of conflict of interest or of 'apparent bias'.[177] They may feel that their integrity is being attacked, even though this is not at all the point of the rules about conflicts.[178] For this reason, institutional design needs attention. It may be appropriate for the initial request for recusal to be presented to the judge in question; but it would be a mistake for that person to have the final decision on their own recusal. The principle that one may not be judge in one's own cause is 'the first and most fundamental principle of natural justice'.[179] No greater conflict could be imagined, and this is precisely the situation that was described by Sir Edward Coke as 'against common right or reason'.[180] It is curious that the practice of the Supreme Court of the United States on a motion for recusal is that the motion is decided by the judge in question, with no possibility of appeal.[181]

3. Unauthorized profits

Bribery of judges is fortunately relatively rare, and when it occurs the criminal sanctions may include a fine aimed at least partly at taking away the profits, thus leaving little room for civil proceedings. But not all unauthorized profits are bribes, in public administration just as in private administration. In principle, just as with the case of a person employed by the executive, it seems logical that a judge should be accountable to the State for unauthorized profits extracted from their judicial role.[182] It is not clear that this proposition has ever been tested.

---

[175] *R v Stubbs* [2018] UKPC 30, [2018] 1 WLR 4887. For discussion of the difficulties that this can give rise to in long-running cases with multiple sequential rulings, see *Otkritie International Investment Management Ltd v Urumov* [2014] EWCA Civ 1315.

[176] See Smith (n 126), 168–70.

[177] For the suggestion that apparent bias is usually just another way of describing conflicts of interest, see Smith (ibid).

[178] ibid 159; for an example, see *Cheney v United States Dist Court for the District of Columbia* 541 US 913 (2004), discussed in Chapter 4, section IV.A.

[179] *Report of the Committee on Ministers' Powers* (1932) Cmd 4060, 76.

[180] N 124.

[181] For an attempt to defend this, which in my view is unconvincing, see Chief Justice John G Roberts, Jr, '2011 Year-End Report on the Federal Judiciary', online at www.supremecourt.gov/publicinfo/year-end/2011year-endreport.pdf, 7–10.

[182] Section III.B.2.d.

A norm barring unauthorized profits may be found in the relevant ethical code.[183] In the United States, federal legislation applies to federal judges, but the wording of the legislation and the regulations under it arguably have the effect of making the norm much narrower than the rule known in private law administration.[184]

4. Duties of care and skill, or of prudence and diligence

The principle of judicial independence makes it highly unlikely that anyone can directly enforce the norm that a judge must do their job carefully and diligently. For litigants, appeal routes may be one way in which the norm is indirectly enforced. Since a judge is not a normal employee, any recourse for failure in this respect will not be a claim for loss caused, but in extreme cases it might lead to professional disciplinary consequences.[185]

5. Conclusion

The position of judges is particular, because their independence from other branches of government, and from political influence, are essential to their role in a society governed by law. Despite this, all of the norms of sound administration are rightly applicable to the role of the judge. In some cases, however, the norms are effected by way of the availability of appeals. In other cases, they are effected by professional discipline. The rules about conflicts, however, can be invoked by those whose private rights or interests are affected or potentially affected. In the most extreme cases, it is possible for judges to be removed from office for serious misbehaviour.

---

[183] The document *Ethical Principles for Judges* (1998), online at https://cjc-ccm.ca/cmslib/general/news_pub_judicialconduct_Principles_en.pdf, published by the Canadian Judicial Council, does not have a general rule about unauthorized profits (although rule E.18, which permits a judge to act as an executor of the estate of a close friend or relative, indicates that this should be done gratuitously). A new version (2021), however, online at https://cjc-ccm.ca/sites/default/files/documents/2021/CJC_20-301_Ethical-Principles_Bilingual_Final.pdf has a rule (5.B.19) against taking gifts 'that give rise to a reasonable apprehension of bias'.

[184] See the critique in Sung Hui Kim, 'The Supreme Court's Fiduciary Duty to Forego Gifts' in Evan J Criddle and others (eds), *Fiduciary Government* (CUP 2018) 205.

[185] An English judge resigned after the Court of Appeal severely criticized him for a twenty-month delay in giving judgment: *Goose v Wilson Sandford & Co* [1998] EWCA Civ 245, [112]. *Ethical Principles for Judges* (n 183) has a section (section 4) on diligence. It refers also the *Judges Act*, RSC 1985, c J-1, s 55, which requires that a judge devote themself exclusively to their judicial duties. This was the provision that Patrick Smith J was found to have violated by the Canadian Judicial Council (n 163). The draft of the new version of *Ethical Principles for Judges* (n 183) has a section (section 3) on Diligence and Competence.

IV. The State itself as holder of public powers

A. Is the State an administrator towards all persons in it?

1. Undirected, not directed duties

The argument in the preceding chapters, and in this one, is that those who hold powers for the benefit of the public are engaged in public administration when they exercise those powers. They are acting for and on behalf of everyone, or at least on behalf of a sector of the public that is so wide that it cannot be meaningfully delimited. It seems to follow that the State itself, seen as a legal person, is always acting as a public administrator. Such an idea underlies a flourishing body of scholarship which argues that the State is a fiduciary towards the people, using the traditional language of the common law tradition for private law administration.[186]

There are a number of issues here, which may come out differently depending on whether one is conducting a legal analysis or one of political theory. Juridically, to say that the State is in a relationship of administration with private persons is different from saying that the people who run the apparatus of the State are public administrators acting for and on behalf of the State. Such public administrators owe legal duties which may be directed or undirected. They may owe directed duties to a legal person which has been constituted for a public interest, whether or not that legal person is an emanation of the State in the sense of being controlled by it.[187] In those cases, a violation of one of the norms of good public administration potentially generates a legal recourse available to the relevant legal person. These public administrators may also owe undirected public duties. These are legal duties that are not owed *to* a particular person; but they are enforceable in various ways.[188] Importantly, individual persons may be able to take action in both situations.[189] This may be by the representative enforcement of a right of the State; more typically, it is by the enforcement of the public interest in State legality, in the absence of a right; this allows members of the public to enforce undirected duties. Sometimes, it is through the enforcement of a private right in cases where the failure of administration creates such private rights of action. Of course, any such recourse may be subject to the various limits that have been described, including the privileges of judges and legislators, and the jurisdictional deference that is rightly owed to public administrators just as it is owed to private law administrators.

---

[186] Eg Evan Fox-Decent, *Sovereignty's Promise: The State as Fiduciary* (OUP 2011); Evan J Criddle and others (eds), *Fiduciary Government* (CUP 2018).
[187] Chapter 10, section II.F.
[188] For the terminology of directed and undirected duties, see Chapter 10, section I.
[189] As explored in Chapter 10.

From this perspective, what would be added by saying that the State itself owes legal duties of administration to persons within it? If these were legal duties owed to each person, then everyone in the polity would have the right to enforce these obligations of the State—not an interest which might give them standing, but a right to demand information, to intervene in doubtful exercises of power, and presumably to recover unauthorized profits. This would turn administrative law on its head.[190]

The State as public administrator towards the people can, however, be understood juridically if we see the State as owing undirected duties of public administration. In a previous chapter we considered the situation in which a legal person itself acts in a role of public administration: for example, a university.[191] I argued that even though the university's administrators owe directed duties of administration to the university, there is more to the picture: because the university is itself carrying out a public mission, those administrators can be seen as also owing undirected public duties of administration. What is more, the university itself can also be seen as owing undirected public duties of administration in relation to the pursuit of its public purposes. This example arguably maps fairly well onto the administration of the State. Because the State is the public administrator par excellence, its administrators can be seen as owing undirected public duties which may be enforceable by the public. And there is nothing to stop us from saying that the State itself owes undirected public duties in relation to its use of its public powers. The people subject to the powers of the State do not hold corresponding legal rights; but they may have mechanisms to enforce the undirected legal duties of the State.

2. Who acts unlawfully?

The juridical analysis of this problem arguably opens up a crucial distinction between not having a discretionary power, and having a discretionary power but using it improperly. If an official has no discretion, it may be that they were obliged to act, or not to act. A private person may be allowed to enforce this duty even though it is undirected.[192] The more conceptually difficult case is where there is a discretionary power. If some official has a discretionary power, but has attempted to do something that the power does not authorize, then the attempt is void in law.[193] Now consider the case in which the official has purported to use

---

[190] Timothy Endicott, 'The Public Trust' in Evan J Criddle and others (eds), *Fiduciary Government* (CUP 2018) 306.

[191] Chapter 9, section II.D.2.

[192] Mullan (n 121) 411; Brown and Bell (n 43), 244–45, 253–54.

[193] Cf Herbert LA Hart, *The Concept of Law* (3 edn, 2012), 69–70, discussing legislative power. However, except perhaps in extreme cases, for various reasons the official's act might be treated as one that needs to be set aside by judicial declaration: Brown and Bell (n 43), 240–42; Paul Craig, *Administrative Law* (8th edn, Sweet & Maxwell 2016) ch 24.

the power to do something that the power *does* authorize, but has used the power for an improper purpose; or, used it while in a conflict situation, which at least in private law attracts the same recourse.[194] If every defect in the exercise of a public power were to be an example of a person's acting ultra vires or without lawful authority, the result would be the same in this case. The State on this view has done nothing. Any liability for loss wrongfully caused would attach to the official (although the State may be authorized to indemnify the official, or it may in any event be vicariously liable).

This seems overly simplistic.[195] A person can *have* a power but misuse it or abuse it. This space—where the power exists but has been misused—is recognized in private law by saying that the exercise of the power is voidable but not void, or, in civil law, is relatively null but not absolutely null or non-existent.[196] If a public administrator misuses a public power that the person holds, we could certainly say that the State power *has* been exercised, albeit in a way that is liable to be set aside. It is not simply a case in which some official stepped entirely out of their official role and acted in a way that had no legal effect. Rather, the State itself has acted improperly through its official. Take the case in which a person's commercial fishing licence is revoked by a State agency, but for improper reasons. In the ultra vires view summarized in the previous paragraph, we would have to say that the State agency did nothing in law; some official purported, on its behalf, to revoke the licence but did not actually do so. This seems unnecessary and artificial, at least in the case of a power that exists but was misused. In this example, the State has not necessarily breached a legal duty in the strict sense, not even an undirected duty. The result can be explained, rather, by the consideration that the State failed to fulfil the law's requirements for the fully valid exercise of the power.[197] This corresponds to the similar problem that arises in private law administration, when powers are not used for the right purposes; the problem is not a breach of duty in the strict sense.[198]

---

[194] Chapter 4, section V.B.

[195] See also the discussion in Chapter 9, section I.C.3 of theories of ultra vires and 'common law constitutionalism'.

[196] Chapter 3, section IV.F.2. Whether a corresponding distinction exists in public law is affected by concerns about reliance that may not apply in the same way in private law (see n 193). Be that as it may, in French public law, there is a clear distinction between absence of power and misuse *(détournement)* of power: Waline (n 43), 691–97; Brown and Bell (n 43), 240–44, 245–50.

[197] For this distinction, see Hart (n 193); Lionel Smith, 'Can We Be Obliged to be Selfless?' in Andew S Gold and Paul B Miller (eds), *Philosophical Foundations of Fiduciary Law* (OUP 2014) 141.

[198] Chapter 3, section IV.G. The mechanisms of enforcement, of course, may be different in public law. As we saw in Chapter 10, such mechanisms may include a challenge by a legal person constituted in the public interest, in the case that the public power-holder was in a relationship of administration with such a person (section II.F); by the State itself against the power-holder, whether or not their administration is mediated by a legal person constituted in the public interest (sections II.D, II.G); or by a citizen who directly asserts the public interest in sound administration (section II.H).

There are practical and conceptual reasons for paying attention to the difference between this approach and the ultra vires approach that was outlined earlier. A practical reason is that it may change how proceedings are framed. In the example of the revocation of the fishing licence, the ultra vires view implies that the nature of the proceeding against the relevant State agency should not allege that agency did anything in law; it should allege that some individual purported, without effect, to do so, so that in law the complainant still holds the licence. On the other view, which accepts that the State and its emanations are capable of acting outside of the requirements of the law while remaining State actors, the proceeding could allege that the agency revoked the licence for improper reasons. At a conceptual level, the ultra vires view seems to imply that even if the State is a public administrator, *it* can never do anything that amounts to a failure to comply with the law. On this view, any such failure would involve individual persons stepping outside of their official roles (and possibly making themselves personally liable).[199] If that were right, any conclusion that the State does owe legal duties (albeit undirected) in relation to sound administration would seem rather empty.[200]

In an important English case, a Minister had defied a court order.[201] It was held that it was possible for government officials to be personally liable when they had acted without legal authority; this is perfectly in line with the ultra vires approach. More interestingly for present purposes, it was also held that a government department, or Minister of the Crown in his *official* capacity only, could be found in contempt of court. This seems entirely inconsistent with a binary view that supposes that State actors either act with legal authority and so officially and lawfully, or, if they exceed their authority, step out of their official role and (apart from the possibility of vicarious liability) act for no one but themselves.

B. The State's obligations towards Aboriginal persons

This leads to a difficult and controversial topic which cannot be treated here in the detail that it deserves: the State's fiduciary obligations towards Aboriginal persons. Such duties have been recognized in Canada[202] and in New Zealand[203]

---

[199] A strand of Catholic theology apparently takes the position that the Church itself cannot sin, even when its officials sin, because '[w]hat is sinful in each member is, necessarily, outside the church': Jeremy M Bergen, *Ecclesial Repentance: The Churches Confront Their Sinful Pasts* (T & T Clark International 2011) 210.

[200] This would not, however, imply that the State could not be liable or responsible, because depending on the context, the State may well be vicariously liable for actions taken by its officials. That possibility typically extends to cases in which an official acted without authority (although, just as in private law, the attribution of responsibility does have some limits).

[201] In *Re M* [1994] 1 AC 377 (HL).

[202] *Guerin v R* [1984] 2 SCR 335, 13 DLR (4th) 321.

[203] *Proprietors of Wakatū v Attorney-General* [2017] NZSC 17, [2017] 1 NZLR 423.

and, under the label of the 'Indian trust doctrine', in the United States.[204] The difficult question is how these obligations can be squared with the State's relationship to other persons. To say that the State is in a fiduciary relationship with Aboriginal persons is to say, in the language of this study, that it is in a relationship of administration for their benefit. This imposes on the Crown a 'duty to act with respect to the interest of the aboriginal peoples with loyalty, good faith, full disclosure appropriate to the subject matter and with "ordinary" diligence in what it reasonably regarded as the best interest of the beneficiaries'.[205]

The difficulty that arises is how to analyse this duty in relation to the legal requirement that the State use its public powers for the benefit of all persons.[206] This problem has come to the fore in different contexts. In Canada, it has been held that so long as it meets constitutional requirements including consultation, the Crown can extinguish aboriginal rights.[207] But how can one extinguish the rights of persons towards whom one stands in a fiduciary relationship? Is it because there is a fiduciary relationship towards all persons? If that were, true it would seriously undermine the significance of the recognition of a fiduciary obligation towards Aboriginal persons.

The best way to make sense of this, as has been argued by Kirsty Gover and Nicole Roughan, is that the fiduciary obligation owed to Aboriginal persons is qualitatively different from the relationship between the State and the general public.[208] We have already seen that the State can be the trustee of a private trust.[209] In the same way, they argue that when the Crown is (for example) dealing with the reserve land of a First Nation, it can be understood to be in relationship of *private* administration with the First Nation.[210] This does not entail a position that a First Nation is no different to some group of persons who benefit from a trust; indeed, it leaves room for an understanding of the Crown–First Nation relationship as a nation-to-nation relationship.[211]

---

[204] Mary Christina Wood, 'Indian Land and the Promise of Native Sovereignty: The Trust Doctrine Revisited' [1994] Utah L Rev 1471; Seth Davis, 'American Colonialism and Constitutional Redemption' (2017) 105 Cal L Rev 1751. For perspectives in other settler states: Camilla Hughes, 'The Fiduciary Obligations of the Crown to Aborigines: Lessons From the United States and Canada' (1993) 16 UNSWLJ 70; Kent McNeil, 'Indigenous Territorial Rights in the Common Law' in M Graziadei and L Smith (eds), *Comparative Property Law: Global Perspectives* (Edward Elgar 2017) 412.
[205] *Wewaykum Indian Band v Canada* 2002 SCC 79, [2002] 4 SCR 245, [97].
[206] Kirsty Gover and Nicole Roughan, 'The Fiduciary Crown: The Private Duties of Public Actors in State–Indigenous Relationships' in Paul B Miller and Matthew Harding (eds), *Fiduciaries and Trust: Ethics, Politics, Economics and Law* (CUP 2020) 198, 210.
[207] *Tsilhqot'in Nation v British Columbia* 2014 SCC 44, [2014] 2 SCR 257, [71], [77]–[88].
[208] Gover and Roughan (n 206).
[209] Chapter 9, section II.A.
[210] Or, perhaps, with its members.
[211] Gover and Roughan (n 206), 202–3. The jurisprudence of the Supreme Court of Canada, at least, is however a long way from this. See John Borrows, *Recovering Canada: The Resurgence of Indigenous Law* (University of Toronto Press 2002); Joshua Nichols, *A Reconciliation Without Recollection: An Investigation of the Foundations of Aboriginal Law* (University of Toronto Press 2020).

As Gover and Roughan note, the Supreme Court of Canada, when it has used the language of 'fiduciary duties' in relation to the Crown–First Nation relationship, has characterized such duties as being in the nature of private duties.[212] In the terms of this study, it might be better to say that the duty is public but is directed, so that there is a corresponding right (and power of enforcement) in those to whom it is owed. Conversely, when the Court has spoken of the public law relationship between the Crown and the public at large, it has deprecated the label 'fiduciary':

> Public law duties, the performance of which requires the exercise of discretion, do not typically give rise to a fiduciary relationship ... the Crown is not normally viewed as a fiduciary in the exercise of its legislative or administrative function.[213]

This analysis provides a conceptual toolbox for understanding the characteristics of different relationships, such as the relationship between the Crown and a First Nation with whose land or rights the Crown is dealing, and the relationship between the Crown and the people generally. In my terms, the Crown may owe directed fiduciary duties to a particular First Nation in relation to the Crown's dealing with the particular assets of that Nation. Its duties to the entire polity are undirected public duties. These are still legal duties, as we have seen, but undirected duties do not correspond to legal rights in another.

In a phrase that creates an arresting mental image, Binnie J said, 'The Crown can be no ordinary fiduciary; it wears many hats and represents many interests, some of which cannot help but be conflicting.'[214] In the language of this study, this analysis indeed implies that the Crown will often be in a conflict of duty and duty when its directed duties to a First Nation conflict with its undirected, but still juridical, duties towards the public in general. The constitutional tests that have been elaborated by the Supreme Court of Canada for the infringement or extinguishment of Aboriginal rights or title can be understood to be a legal standard for reconciling such conflicts.[215]

---

[212] *Guerin* (n 202), 385 (SCR): 'The Crown's obligation to the Indians with respect to that interest is therefore not a public law duty. While it is not a private law duty in the strict sense either, it is nonetheless in the nature of a private law duty.' See also *Wewaykum* (n 205), [74].

[213] *Guerin* (n 202), 385 (SCR); see also *Alberta v Elder Advocates of Alberta Society* 2011 SCC 24, [2011] 2 SCR 261, [37]–[38].

[214] *Wewaykum* (n 205), [96].

[215] *R v Sparrow* [1990] 1 SCR 1075; *Tsilhqot'in Nation* (n 207). This is not to say that the tests are necessarily satisfactory, only that they perform this function.

V. The widening reach of public administration: Professionals

This section looks briefly at some people who could be considered to be engaged in public administration in their professional role. We will explore a range of situations, from professionals in a strict sense to those who are professionals in a wider and less technical sense.

A. Introduction

Many professionals, like lawyers and physicians, are in a relationship of private law administration with their clients.[216] This section asks whether professionals are also public administrators, at least for some purposes, and how these two roles can be reconciled.

The concepts of a profession and a professional are clearly defined in some legal systems, and less so in others. The idea of a profession is in constant evolution. Historically, its conceptual independence might be thought to rest on the propositions that a person carrying on a profession is not an employee of her clients, and yet nor is she in business or trade. This may be less obvious today, as firms of lawyers and accountants may operate globally, and large enterprises may employ qualified lawyers and other professionals; but it retains at least a grain of truth. When laws were first passed in England allowing a bankrupt to be discharged and so released of their debts, they were restricted to those in business or 'traders', who, it was thought, might become insolvent without fault of their own through the hazards and risks involved in commerce.[217] That logic had no application to a professional, who—at least it was thought at that time—could not possibly become insolvent unless they acted irresponsibly. Even today, there are some legal systems in which it is juridically impossible for a professional to become bankrupt.[218] Something like the same logic explains why in many legal systems, only individuals, and not corporations, are allowed to exercise a profession: a professional must stand behind his work, not disclaim responsibility for the consequences.[219]

---

[216] At least, as advisors: Chapter 7, section IV.A. Lawyers may also be administrators as agents, trustees, or executors.
[217] Louis E Levinthal, 'The Early History of English Bankruptcy Law' (1919) 67 U Penn L Rev 1, 18–20.
[218] For example, Luxembourg: Michele Graziadei, Ugo Mattei, and Lionel Smith, *Commercial Trusts in European Private Law* (CUP 2005) 318. It is always possible for a person to become insolvent, which is a state of fact, but bankruptcy is here used in the strict sense of a legal status.
[219] In some jurisdictions, professionals have persuaded legislators to allow them to avoid this principle through the statutory creation of limited liability partnerships.

But as a definition, it is not satisfactory to say that a professional is neither in business nor employed. One way to distinguish a profession analytically from business and from the general law of employment is that a professional can be said, as such, to owe duties to the public at large.[220] When professionalism is defined in this way, it is possible for a professional to be employed and still be a professional. In terms we have used earlier, the distinctive character of 'professional duties', whether or not they are formally codified and enforced by a professional order, is that they are undirected duties.[221]

B. Professionals in a strict sense

The strictest sense of a profession might be one in which there is a self-regulating professional order. This implies that the order makes its own decisions about admission, and about discipline up to and including disqualification, and that it develops, promulgates and enforces rules of professional conduct that bind its members. Later we will look at wider ideas of what it means to be a professional.

The rules of professional conduct impose undirected duties of a public nature, in the sense that they are associated with various penal sanctions for the protection of the public.[222] Why are these special duties imposed? It is not merely because professionals are empowered by the State to do things that others cannot do: practise dentistry, represent people in court, and so on. As we have seen, some but not all persons are licenced by the State to drive motorcycles or fly airplanes; it does not follow that they must do so in the public interest.[223]

The decision that some callings should be professions in the strict sense can only be explained as a decision that it would not be in the public interest if those callings were treated simply as businesses. The types of calling to which this logic applies have varied over time. Medieval guilds, for example, of silversmiths, were granted monopolies rather like those of modern professions, and perhaps for similar motivations. This might include the protection of the public, although sceptics will point to the private interest of those in the calling in excluding competition. This has always been a challenge that professions in the strict sense have to meet.

Today, at least, we might describe self-regulating professions—professions in the strict sense—in the following way. They hold authority from the State to

---

[220] Evan J Criddle and Evan Fox-Decent, 'Guardians of Legal Order: The Dual Commissions of Public Fiduciaries' in Evan J Criddle and others (eds), *Fiduciary Government* (CUP 2018) 67.
[221] For the terminology of directed and undirected duties, see Chapter 10, section I.
[222] The enforcement of undirected duties often falls to the State or some emanation of it; in this case, it falls to the professional order.
[223] Chapter 9, section II.D.1.

regulate their calling; this authority can only be justified as being in the public interest. That is, it is in the public interest that persons who wish to practise the calling must meet certain standards of qualification, skill, knowledge, and perhaps character. In turn, the justification for a self-regulating structure (as opposed, for example, to the system under which driving or firearm licences are granted) can only be justified on the basis that those who are learned in the profession are best able to regulate it. And if, in turn, the whole justification for this closed system is that it is in the public interest (as opposed to a free market in the relevant calling), then it follows quite naturally that the profession may be subject to undirected public duties that are different from the undirected public duties owed by everyone else, in order to protect the public interest that the monopoly exists to support.[224]

Professional duties can be said to be of two kinds. Some are public law versions of the private law duties that grow out of a relationship of administration. Every private administrator is required by private law to exercise their powers loyally, and not to exercise them while in a conflict of interest. Undirected professional duties may replicate these directed private duties. To take one example, in Quebec, under the *Code of Ethics of Physicians*, physicians owe duties of loyalty and diligence to their patients, and must avoid acting in a conflict of interest.[225] Unauthorized profits may also be addressed, for example, by rules against 'fee-splitting' which describes a practice in which a referring physician receives part of the fee billed to the patient by the treating physician.[226] A breach of these undirected duties can be sanctioned by the professional order, although in the case of

---

[224] It might be argued that the administration of justice (to take the example of lawyers) simply could not work if lawyers had no public duties; if, for example, they were allowed to mislead the courts and to ignore communications from other lawyers. In extreme cases, such misbehaviour can attract judicial as well as professional sanctions: *King v Whitmer* 556 FSupp3d 680 (ED Mich, 2021), in which the lawsuit is described in the first sentence of the judgment as 'a historic and profound abuse of the judicial process'. But these considerations, on their own, seem to point only to the system we have for drivers' licences: the roads would not be safe if people could drive however they wished; those who drive are thus subject to all sorts of undirected public duties that apply while driving; but we do not apparently see the need for a profession of drivers. It is arguable, however, that these pragmatic considerations play a supporting role in justifying professional obligations.

[225] CQLR c M-9, r 17, arts 5, 63. For evidence of how conflicts of interest may affect the professional judgment of physicians, see Ashley Wazana, 'Physicians and the Pharmaceutical Industry: Is a Gift Ever Just a Gift?' (2000) 283(3) JAMA 373; David Grande and others, 'Effect of Exposure to Small Pharmaceutical Promotional Items on Treatment Preferences' (2009) 169(9) Arch Intern Med 887; Susan F Wood and others, 'Influence of Pharmaceutical Marketing on Medicare Prescriptions in the District of Columbia' (2017) 12(10) PLoS ONE e0186060, online at https://doi.org/10.1371/journal.pone.0186060 ; see Chapter 4, section VI.B.

[226] This was described as a 'vicious and unethical practice' in *Henderson v Johnston* [1957] OR 627, 11 DLR (2d) 19 (CA), 638 *per* Roach JA for the Court, affirmed [1959] SCR 655. Roach JA quoted the prohibition against fee-splitting in the then-current code of ethics of the Canadian Medical Association. The decision upheld the by-law of a hospital board that forbade the practice. See also Atul Gawande, 'The Cost Conundrum', *The New Yorker*, 25 May 2009.

unauthorized profits the undirected nature of the duty may make it may difficult to attribute the profits to any particular person.[227]

This doubling of professional duties can be understood as rather like the case in which the same action, such as striking someone, may be both a crime and a civil wrong.[228] Both the private interest and the public interest are protected by legal duties, one private and directed, and one public and undirected. But some professional duties are *opposed* to the professional's private law duties.[229] To take a classic problem from the legal profession, a lawyer may possess, or know the whereabouts of, evidence that incriminates her client who has been charged with a crime. The lawyer's private duties to her client would point in the direction of suppressing that evidence, but this would be a violation of her professional duties that support the administration of justice.[230]

I will call the public duties that are opposed to the professional's private law duties 'client-opposed public duties'. In the terms of this study, a question is whether these client-opposed public duties are duties that relate to a kind of public administration. Alternatively, we might think that they are simply rules of public law that constrain the professional. The answer seems to be that they are a bit of both. Let me explain. A medical professional may learn that her patient is about to harm herself or another, and may come under a (public) duty (that would not apply to a non-professional) to notify the police, regardless of the wishes of the patient. This is a difficult situation, but it seems clear that the public duty must be complied with. We have seen that those exercising administration must always comply with legal duties.[231] If this was the only kind of client-opposed public duty owed by professionals, we might not think of them as

---

[227] In *Centre de santé et de services sociaux de Laval v Tadros* 2015 QCCA 351, a medical supplier paid money over six years to the defendant surgeon and others in proportion to the number of medical devices purchased from the supplier. The defendant was disciplined by the College of Physicians and this proceeding was now brought by the hospital where he had practiced, seeking to recover the profits. The claim failed; the argument that the defendant was a mandatary of the plaintiff was rejected (as was an argument based on unjust enrichment); an argument based on good faith and on *Bank of Montreal v Kuet Leong Ng* [1989] 2 SCR 429 (discussed in Chapter 7, section II.B.1) failed on the ground that the plaintiff was found to have been aware of, or wilfully blind to, the unauthorized profits.

[228] Kit Barker, 'Modelling Public and Private Enforcement: The Rationality of Hybridity' (2018) 37 UQLJ 9, 11.

[229] Criddle and Fox-Decent (n 220) call the private duties 'first-order' duties and the public duties 'second-order' duties, even though the second-order duties often take precedence. They do not distinguish systematically between those public duties that replicate private duties and those that may contradict them.

[230] Suppression may even be criminally unlawful as an obstruction of justice: Christopher D Clemmer, 'Obstructing the Bernardo Investigation: Kenneth Murray and the Defence Counsel's Conflicting Obligations to Clients and the Court' (2008) 1 Osgoode Hall Review of Law and Policy 137. For some other examples where public duties may override private ones outside of the criminal law setting, see David Luban, 'Fiduciary Legal Ethics, Zeal, and Moral Activism' (2020) 33 Georgetown J of Legal Ethics 275.

[231] Chapter 3, section II.C.1.

carrying out public administration. Merely having obligations does not constitute administration; rather, one must have powers that are affected to a mission, charge, assignment, or function.

But this example does not exhaust the possibilities, because in many cases the professional may indeed have a kind of power in relation to their public role. Take the case of the lawyer whose client, charged with a crime, reveals to the lawyer the location of crucial evidence in the case. The lawyer has a public duty to make the authorities aware of that evidence; but the lawyer does not simply have a duty to call the police and tell them where it is. There are different ways for them to fulfil the public duty, and so it is more like a discretionary power.[232]

A professional is privileged in a Hohfeldian sense: he or she is legally enabled to do things that others may not. We have seen that this in itself does not engage the public interest.[233] But in the case of professionals, we have also seen that there are independent reasons for obliging them to act in the public interest, since the restriction of their professional activities to members of the profession exists precisely to protect a public interest. In this sense, one could say that a professional in the strict sense, in exercising the privileges that they hold as a member of the profession, is required to do so in the public interest. This explains both their client-opposed public duties, and their client-aligned public duties. And it implies that at least some of their public duties are duties of public administration, being duties relating to the proper exercise of their public powers.

This conclusion also, however, clearly has the capacity to generate a conflict of duty and duty, most obviously when the professional's private law duties to their client (and thus probably their client-aligned public duties) point in a different direction to their client-opposed public duties. It is not surprising that the literature, and the practise, of professional ethics is extremely preoccupied with these situations and how they can be managed. Such conflicts are likely to be very difficult to resolve. The ones that arise most regularly are likely to be specifically addressed in rules of professional conduct. Earlier we noted that courts have described a conflict of duty and duty as an 'impossible situation'.[234] It is impossible if there is no way to prioritize the competing duties. It is not impossible if one duty always prevails; and it is not blameworthy to be in such a conflict if the professional was not the one who created it. This kind of conflict is never easy, but in general if there is a client-opposed public duty, it must prevail.[235] The challenge—which again, is one with which the study of professional ethics is

---

[232] See the scholarship cited in n 230.
[233] N 223.
[234] Chapter 4, section IV.B; see also Chapter 9, section II.D.4.
[235] Whether or not there is such a public duty in a particular situation may not always be obvious, as discussed by Luban (n 230).

rightly preoccupied—is often how to comply with the public duty in a way that least impinges on the private interests of the client.

C. Professionals in a wider sense

1. Teachers and professors

In some jurisdictions, teachers constitute a profession in the strict sense, being a self-governing order.[236] In many places, they are not, and so far as I know, university professors are nowhere members of a profession in the strict sense.[237] In that setting, whether one is willing to think of teachers and university professors as professionals depends, of course, on one's definition.[238] They are employees. There are of course credentials required, but this is true of airline pilots and long-haul truck drivers. If one were to define 'professional' in a wide sense as a skilled calling, then all of these could be considered professions.

If one takes the presence of legal duties to the public as way of defining a profession, then one can generate an intermediate sense, narrower than 'skilled calling' but wider than 'member of a self-regulating profession'. It is this sense that is used, perhaps, when people consider teachers and professors to be professionals. Both are employees; the question is whether the only duties that they owe are owed to their employers.[239] Those who work in these fields are perhaps more likely to think in terms of duties owed to their students than duties owed to the public. A professor or teacher has very significant authority and power (both factual and legal) over their students. Assigning marks and grades is an obvious example. Even if the only legally recognized relationship were the one between the teacher or professor and their employer, most teachers and professors would instinctively think of the discretionary powers that they hold in relation to the students as held for benefit of the students, not the employer. It would probably be more precise to say that these powers are held for the purpose of furthering the students' education.

The reason for suggesting this can be illustrated by thinking about the power to assign grades. A professor who held that power *for the benefit* of each particular student, in the sense of private law administration, would have to use it in the way that the professor thought was in the best interests of the student. That

---

[236] *Ontario College of Teachers Act, 1996*, SO 1996, c 12.

[237] In the Continental tradition, university teachers must often qualify through a national examination process and may be employees of the State.

[238] Robert Runté, 'Is Teaching a Profession?' in Gerald Taylor and Robert Runté (eds), *Thinking about Teaching: An Introduction* (Harcourt Brace 1995) 288.

[239] In England it has been held that a university professor is not in a fiduciary relationship (a relationship of private administration) with the university: *University of Nottingham v Fishel* [2000] EWHC 221 (QB); see Chapter 7, section II.B.2.

is obviously not the right analysis, any more than a judge must exercise her judicial powers in the best interests of the particular litigants before her. Rather, the power is held for a purpose, and in this case the purpose is a public one. We have already seen that the *administrators* of a university, although they are in a relationship of private administration with the university, are properly seen as conducting public administration, because the mission of the university is a public one.[240] In the same way, teachers and professors, even if they are not administrators of their institution, are entrusted with some of the powers of that institution, powers that exist in order to advance its public mission. In this sense, every teacher and professor is engaged in public administration.[241] The recognition of professional duties is one way to give effect to this and to try to secure compliance with the norms of public administration.[242]

This part of the law has certainly evolved in recent decades. This can be illustrated with two examples. A university professor typically has the authority to decide which book or books shall be required reading in a course that they are teaching. Although they cannot legally oblige the students to buy a book, this is a kind of factual power. It would seem to go without saying, moreover, that it is a power held for the furtherance of the students' education, not as a kind of asset held by the professor. On that analysis, it should be used in the way that best advances that purpose. If a professor requires that a book be purchased which generates financial reward for the professor, then the professor is in a conflict of interest, since their financial self-interest conflicts with the requirement that they use the power in an other-regarding way. The conflict is present even if the professor honestly believes that this is the best book for the course.[243] This is a conflict that can be managed in various ways, for example, by voluntary disgorgement of the royalties generated, either to the students who buy the book or perhaps to a charity. Some professors do this purely voluntarily. The duty that they feel in this respect might then be described as a moral rather than a legal duty.[244]

---

[240] Chapter 9, section II.D.2.

[241] For similar reasons, a professor is engaged in public administration when he or she disburses research funds that exist for the pursuit of the university's public mission: Chapter 10, section II.F.

[242] Judicial review is another possible avenue for securing that these public powers are used properly. In *Shank* (n 31), a student successfully sought judicial review of the use of a disciplinary power of a university administrator.

[243] Chapter 4, section III. If the professor recommended their own book when they actually thought that another book (or no book) was better, this would not be a conflict but an actual misuse of power: Chapter 3, section II.A.

[244] Anyone who thinks that the professor who requires students to buy the professor's own book is in a conflict of interest must think that the professor is constrained in *some* other-regarding way in respect of their power to choose the course text; you cannot be in a conflict in relation to a power that you hold to do with as you please. Moral duties can create moral conflicts of self-interest and duty.

Some characterize it as a professional duty.[245] A duty owed to the students in one's class from time to time might seem difficult to see as a public duty, as it is not owed to the public as a whole. As we have seen, however, the duty is better understood as relating to a power held for a public purpose; the students in the class from time to time are not the beneficiaries of the duty in the strict sense, although they are the ones whose private interests are most affected by it. It is not a directed duty owed to them, but an undirected public duty. In some universities, there may be a formal policy that governs the specific case of book recommendations, or conflicts of interest generally.[246] In this case, the duty will be given effect to as a term of the contract of employment, and it will be a directed legal duty owed to the university. Even here, however, the university does not stipulate these policies for its own pecuniary benefit; it stipulates them in the furtherance of its public mission. This contractual manifestation of the professors' 'professional' duties is a way in which the university can supervise, with legal recourse if necessary, the use by professors of the powers that they hold for the furtherance of the university's mission.[247]

The other example, far more grave, is the question of intimate relationships between professors and students.[248] Decades ago, this was more common and one justification for it was that university students are adults. This justification left out of account the tremendous power inequality which is inherent in the relationship and which calls into question true, enlightened consent on the part of the student. This imbalance creates a kind of factual power, which can be subject to legal control as much as a legal power.[249] Even when this type of intimate relationship was more common, it was generally considered unprofessional: another example of an instinctive inference that some duties—duties that could be characterized as professional duties, even if not legal duties—apply in this context. If the professor is seen as holding a factual power, then one could say that the power is used here for an improper purpose, or used in a conflict of interest, or both.

Just as with pecuniary conflicts of interest, these duties are increasingly being turned into legal ones. Universities, like schools, have increasingly adopted

---

[245] Tim Wu, 'How Professors Help Rip Off Students', *New York Times*, 11 Dec 2019, online at https://www.nytimes.com/2019/12/11/opinion/textbook-prices-college.html: 'Teaching is a profession with its own ethical duties: students are both our charges and a captive market'.

[246] Eg McGill University *Regulation on Conflict of Interest*, online at https://www.mcgill.ca/secretariat/files/secretariat/conflict-of-interest-regulation-on_0.pdf.

[247] In just the same way, and according to the same logic, these policies will control the use by professors of research funds which, whether they come from public or private sources, are affected to the pursuit of the university's public mission.

[248] This arises for teachers as well: *Ontario College of Teachers v Lewis* 2017 ONOCT 94 (Disc Ctee, Ontario College of Teachers). In the light of the younger age of these students, it is likely to be rarer and may well be criminally unlawful.

[249] Cf Chapter 7, section IV.

policies that forbid or regulate intimate relationships between professors and students.[250] In relation to professors and other employees, these take effect as contractual terms of employment. Somewhat like rules of professional conduct, the enforcement of these policies is unlikely to be entirely in the hands of the people whom they aim to protect; just as a professional body disciplines its members, these policies are administered by universities and schools in relation to their professors, teachers, and other employees. But these policies turn what were non-legal norms into legal norms. They perform an important expressive or signalling function about the seriousness of the problem, and that the university takes seriously the protection of its students. And when they are well-crafted, they ensure that students who are affected by professorial misconduct have paths to seek assistance and recourse.

If the duties of teachers and professors are considered professional duties, then they are increasingly moving from moral duties into legal ones.

2. Journalists

Journalism is not a profession in the sense of having a self-regulating professional order. But journalists consider themselves to owe duties to the public and to be bound by ethical standards in this respect. On the wider view of professional outlined above, therefore, journalism can be seen as a profession.

Journalists can be seen to act on behalf of the public in at least two distinct but overlapping ways. One is as securing information on behalf of the public, information that is necessary to hold to account the government and other powerful actors. When Stephen Harper was the Prime Minister of Canada (2006–2015), he rarely answered questions from the press. His successor called a press conference the day after taking office. One journalist expressed her relief in terms of recovering her ability to ask questions as a 'proxy' for the public, which she viewed as one of her roles as a journalist.[251] Similarly, Peter Cane has written of 'the quasi-constitutional role of the media in a free society in maintaining the flow of information to the public about the activities of government'.[252] Here he was addressing the justification for the granting of standing to a journalist

---

[250] Eg McGill University *Policy against Sexual Violence*, online at https://www.mcgill.ca/secretariat/files/secretariat/policy_against_sexual_violence.pdf, section 8.

[251] Marsha Lederman, 'If the media is the message, the Harper government wasn't listening', *Globe and Mail*, 23 Oct 2015, online at https://www.theglobeandmail.com/opinion/if-the-media-is-the-message-the-harper-government-wasnt-listening/article26963017/: 'Journalists at the very least act as a proxy for citizens; we have access—or should—to those in power. In order to hold governments to account, reporters require access to those governments. This is how journalists can expose bad behaviour—systemic or individual . . .—and effect change. When journalists are cut off, society suffers'.

[252] Peter Cane, 'Standing Up for the Public' [1995] Public Law 276, 284; see also Cane (n 53), 132–33.

to challenge a decision that certain information would not be made public by a branch of government.

The other role is as an advisor to the public, since advising can also be a kind of administration.[253] Some kinds of journalism partake of a function that involves information filtered through an exercise of judgment, and that comes fairly close to advising the public, or at least helping them to make decisions. As we have seen, the idea of a conflict of interest only makes sense when a person is exercising judgment on behalf or for the benefit of another, or for an other-regarding purpose. When journalists have been accused of being in a conflict of interest, it is usually because they have derived private benefits that might call their objectivity into question.[254] It seems clear that the duty that was seen to be in conflict with their self-interest was not simply a private duty to the employer, but rather a duty to the public to provide unbiased reporting.

Some journalists, like persons in all walks of life, may seek to have it both ways. They may take the view that they have no obligations towards the public, and therefore need not be concerned about conflicts of interest. Traditionally this view was understood to be more justifiable in relation to editorial content, which is not presented as purporting to be objective or unbiased; but in some contexts, it may be taken in relation to news content as well. To take another example, Conrad Black, a business person and a journalist and biographer, published a book about Donald Trump in 2018 entitled *A President Like No Other*.[255] If Black had been subject to any norms about conflicts of interest, he would have been in one in relation to any parts of the book that purported to be factual or unbiased, since Black hoped (correctly, as it turned out) that Trump would grant Black a pardon from Black's US felony convictions.

The inevitable consequence of failing to draw any line between information and opinion must be a loss of confidence in the reliability of the journalist or the organization to which they belong, in relation to any part of their reporting that purports to be objective. Most journalists, of course, understand this, and they understand that their credibility turns on their professionalism.

3. Conclusion

In these contexts of teachers, professors, and journalists, the norms of public administration may take effect as moral and not as legal norms; or, perhaps, as legal rules in the contract of employment. This may simply be another way of saying

---

[253] Chapter 7, section IV.A.

[254] Canadian Press Agency and Globe and Mail Staff, 'Evan Solomon scandal joins long list of TV news's ethical imbroglios', *Globe and Mail*, 10 June 2015, online at https://www.theglobeandmail.com/arts/television/evan-solomon-scandal-joins-long-list-of-tv-newss-ethical-imbroglios/article24891488/.

[255] Conrad Black, *A President Like No Other: Donald J Trump and the Restoring of America* (Encounter Books 2018). By providing the reference to this book I do not imply that I have read it.

that these are professions only in an extended sense. If they were professions in the strict sense, those obligations to act in the public interest would take effect as enforceable (undirected) legal duties. Even where they do not, the consensus that some duties (even if not legal) of a public nature are owed in these situations reflects a consensus that persons in these callings are bound to act in an other-regarding way.

VI. Conclusion

A huge range of persons are engaged in public administration. This includes every branch of the government, as well as non-governmental entities that have public missions.

The legal implementation of norms of sound administration is variable across this wide landscape. But aspects of these norms are reflected, in law, in every single context, and in relation to all three branches of government, and in relation to non-governmental entities that have public missions.

Professionals, in the strict sense, can be understood to be engaged in a kind of public administration, one that may come into tension with their relationship of private law administration with their client. In some settings, an extended idea of professionalism can be seen, in which concerns about conflicts of interest serve as a flag that the relevant actors are not free to behave selfishly, even if the governing norms may be non-legal.

PART IV
CONCLUSION

12
Conclusion

This study set out to establish that there are particular legal principles that apply when we act for others in law, including acting for an other-regarding purpose.

These are what I have called justificatory principles. A justificatory principle is not a legal rule that operates directly on facts that have occurred; it is a higher-level idea that explains and justifies one or more legal rules.[1] Such principles are not directly enforceable as legal duties or legal requirements. They explain and justify the legal duties and requirements that apply in these situations. The legal duties and requirements are not identical in all of the situations in which we act for others; the justificatory principles are implemented differently in different settings.

The justificatory principles are these:

A power that is given to a person, not for their own benefit but to allow them to fulfil a mission, charge, function or assignment, can only rightly be used for the pursuit of that mission, charge, function or assignment. That is the requirement of loyalty.

The exercise by that person of the power for an improper purpose is impeachable. Any legal act created by such use is liable to be set aside. That is the consequence of a failure of the requirement of loyalty.

Subject to objective constraints that may be imposed, and to other legal rules and duties, the person who holds a discretionary power is the one who decides how best to pursue the mission, charge, function or assignment. That is the autonomy of the power-holder. The law does not give any single answer to how the power must be used.

Because the human mind cannot systematically exclude the influence on reasoning of self-interest, an other-regarding discretionary power should not be exercised in a situation of conflict between self-interest and the duty to exercise the power for proper purposes. Such conflicts can be managed in various ways, but otherwise the exercise of such a power while in a conflict is treated as an improper exercise.

The same result follows on parallel reasoning where an other-regarding discretionary power is used in a situation in which the holder of the power has

---

[1] Chapter 1, section III.B.

a conflicting other-regarding duty owed to another person or purpose. The power-holder cannot be certain of avoiding favoring the interests of one over the other. Unless the conflict is managed, the exercise of a power in such a situation is treated as an improper exercise.

Whenever a person is acting for and on behalf of another, both the burden and the benefit of their actions while acting in that role are attributed to that other. This means (a) that they can recover expenses properly incurred; (b) that they must account for any benefit derived from so acting; (c) that they must divulge any information so acquired that is relevant to the decision-making process of the person for whom they were acting.

Whenever a person is acting for and on behalf of another, they must presumptively do so with care, skill, prudence, and diligence. They cannot rightly ignore their mission and do nothing, nor can they act without due care and attention to their mission.

Any person holding other-regarding powers is subject to being stripped of them. Those powers are not a form of wealth held by the person and they can be relieved of their mission and of the powers that they were granted for the accomplishment of that mission.

There is no hierarchy among these. They are a set, and they are presumptively applicable, all together, in the juridical situation where a person is empowered to act for others. Some of them may be disapplied, either in the original grant of the power or where the beneficiaries of the administration, being fully capacitated, waive their rights. The first two, however, are different in this respect because they are definitional of the juridical situation. If a person is able to use a power for whatever purpose they wish, then the relationship is not a relationship of administration.

The implementation of these principles as legal rules is variable in different contexts. In particular, there is a deep division between public administration and private administration. Private administration is typically characterized by directed private duties and liabilities; public administration is typically characterized by undirected duties (although it is often also characterized by directed duties, as where the administration is through a legal person). The duties and liabilities are therefore fundamentally different in terms of their formal structure, and this in turn generates important differences in the mechanisms of their enforcement. It remains true, however, that private and public administration are examples of acting for others in law.

In some situations, perhaps more so in public administration, the justificatory principles do not take effect as legal rules or duties, or do so only incompletely. In any such situation, and in situations where there are legal rules and duties but they lack effective enforcement (for example, due to the problem of self-supervision), some people will take advantage of those failings, for example, to misuse their powers or to extract unauthorized profits. Unless there are sound and articulable reasons for an absence of legal regulation, this means that the law needs reform.

The contexts across which this study has ranged are widely variable, and it may be asked the following: What is gained by seeing all of them as a unity? We have trust law, where the use of trustee powers for improper purposes is subject to judicial scrutiny; and we have judicial review of administrative action, where the use of public powers for improper purposes is subject to judicial scrutiny; but the rules are different, as are the interests at stake. This is true; and some people may be more interested in difference than in commonality.

In my view, the commonality is enlightening. It helps us to understand both private law and public law better; and it helps us to see that acting for others in law has a logic and a unity. The legal duties and requirements that are applied to people who hold legal powers for public purposes are not worked out by analogy from the legal duties and requirements that are applied to people who hold legal powers for private purposes. Conversely, the legal duties and requirements that are applied to people who hold legal powers for private purposes are not worked out by analogy from the legal duties and requirements that are applied to people who hold legal powers for public purposes. The legal duties and requirements that are applied to people in either situation are worked out from the underlying justificatory principles, which are the same in both contexts.

If this unity exists, why do we not see it? Some people do see it. In at least some parts of the civil law, private lawyers have been arguing since the 1980s that the control of powers that developed in administrative law over many decades can rightly be applied in private law.[2] In the common law, the scholarship of Paul Finn has prompted a flourishing of 'fiduciary government' scholarship, with a wide range of approaches and understandings.[3]

Why, then, was it not seen earlier? Viewed against the long histories of the civil law and the common law, the deep division between public law and private law is relatively recent.[4] But deep it is in the modern world: in our books, in our legal educations, and in our legal procedures.

In private law, apart from relationships of administration, people act for themselves. When they hold legal prerogatives, like rights, powers, privileges,

---

[2] Michel Storck, *Essai sur le mécanisme de la représentation dans les actes juridiques* (LGDJ 1982); Emmanuel Gaillard, *Le pouvoir en droit privé* (Economica 1985); Madeleine Cantin Cumyn, 'Le pouvoir juridique' (2007) 52 McGill LJ 215; Madeleine Cantin Cumyn, 'The Legal Power' (2009) 17 European Rev of Private Law 345.
[3] See especially Chapter 9, section I.C.
[4] Dawn Oliver, *Common Values and the Public-Private Divide* (reprint edn, CUP 2010) esp chs 1, 11; Allan Beever, 'Our Most Fundamental Rights' in Andrew Robertson and Donal Nolan (eds), *Rights and Private Law* (Hart 2011) 63.

immunities, they can do more or less what they wish with them, so long as they do not infringe the rights of others. Their subjective motives are largely irrelevant, except perhaps in extreme cases that may amount to abuse of right. Their legal prerogatives cannot be taken away from them. Speaking generally, they are liable outside of contract law only when they infringe upon the rights of others.[5]

As a result, when many private law thinkers turn to the fields that are covered by this study, they do not have a toolbox that helps them to understand it. They do not understand that powers can be linked existentially to particular purposes, such that those powers can only be exercised properly in the pursuit of those purposes. Remedies are even more confusing. Why would a person be liable to give up a gain that belongs to them? Why would a person not be allowed to act when their own self-interest is implicated in the transaction? They must have done something wrong, or must have made a promise, or perhaps both. When acting for others is properly understood, those instincts are revealed to be incorrect. And the most fundamental illustration that acting for others is not like acting for oneself is that the powers that one holds to act for others can always be taken away.[6]

It may be that many public lawyers have also failed to perceive the unity between acting for others in private and in public law. Public lawyers do not have any difficulty in seeing public powers as held for particular purposes. The debate in the common law world between the ultra vires approach and 'common law constitutionalism' is, however, illuminated by looking to private law.[7] The private law rules on the control and supervision of other-regarding powers shows that a statutory foundation is not needed for such rules, even if a sovereign legislature may have the power to override them.

In the common law tradition, much of the elaboration of the law in this field took place in Equity, leading to the development of a range of legal concepts for apprehending relationships of administration.[8] But the common law made its own contributions, with a long history of enforcing accountability, and more recently with the elaboration of many norms of public administration. And the same principles are well known in the civilian tradition, where a dual legal system never existed; equity in the Aristotelian sense is known in civil law, but the rules of administration are rules of law.

---

[5] 'Speaking generally' because liabilities in family law, for example, are not based on wrongdoing; nor are liabilities to make restitution.
[6] Chapter 2, section III.B.
[7] Chapter 9, section I.C.3.
[8] Lionel Smith, 'Equity Is Not a Single Thing' in Dennis Klimchuk, Irit Samet, and Henry Smith (eds), *Philosophical Foundations of the Law of Equity* (OUP 2020) 144.

The justificatory principles of administration, implemented as legal rules in different ways in different contexts, do not belong exclusively to the common law or to the civil law. Nor do they belong exclusively to public law or to private law. They belong, rather, to the *ius commune,* because they grow out of the nature of administration as the pursuit of an other-regarding mission.

Bibliography

Books

Allard, France, M-F Bich, J-M Brisson, É Charpentier, P-A Crépeau, M Devinat, Y Emerich, P Forget, and N Kasirer, *Private Law Dictionary and Bilingual Lexicons – Obligations* (Les Éditions Yvon Blais 2003)
American Law Institute, *Restatement of the Law Third: Agency*, 2 vols (ALI 2006)
Aristotle, *Nicomachean Ethics*, trans Terence Irwin (2nd edn, Hackett Publishing Co 1999)
Ashdown, Michael, *Trustee Decision Making* (OUP 2015)
Baker, John H, *An Introduction to English Legal History* (5th edn, OUP 2019)
Bean, Gerard MD, *Fiduciary Obligations and Joint Ventures* (Clarendon Press 1995)
Beaulne, Jacques, *Droit des fiducies* (3rd edn, Wilson & Lafleur 2015)
Beever, Allan, *Forgotten Justice: Forms of Justice in the History of Legal and Political Theory* (OUP 2013)
———, *A Theory of Tort Liability* (Hart 2016)
Bentham, Jeremy, *The Works of Jeremy Bentham*, John Bowring (ed), 11 vols, vol 3 (William Tait 1843)
———, 'An Introduction to the Principles of Morals and Legislation' in JH Burns and HLA Hart (eds), *The Collected Works of Jeremy Bentham* (OUP 1995)
Bergen, Jeremy M, *Ecclesial Repentance: The Churches Confront Their Sinful Pasts* (T & T Clark International 2011)
Birks, Peter, *An Introduction to the Law of Restitution* (Clarendon Press 1985)
Black, Conrad, *A President Like No Other: Donald J Trump and the Restoring of America* (Encounter Books 2018)
Borrows, John, *Recovering Canada: The Resurgence of Indigenous Law* (University of Toronto Press 2002)
Brown, L Neville, and John S Bell, *French Administrative Law* (5th edn, Clarendon Press 1998)
Buckland, William W, and Peter Stein, *A Text-Book of Roman Law* (3rd edn, CUP 1963)
Campbell, Lord, *Lives of the Lord Chancellors*, John A Mallory (ed), 13 vols, vol 6 (R Carswell 1876)
Cane, Peter, *Administrative Law* (5th edn, OUP 2011)
Cantin Cumyn, Madeleine, *L'administration du bien d'autrui* (Éditions Yvon Blais 2000)
Cantin Cumyn, Madeleine, and Michelle Cumyn, *L'administration du bien d'autrui* (2nd edn, Éditions Yvon Blais 2014)
Chambers, R, *Resulting Trusts* (Clarendon Press 1997)
Chan, Kathryn, *The Public-Private Nature of Charity Law* (Hart 2016)
Chaplin, Ann, *Officers of Parliament* (Yvon Blais 2011)
Clarry, Daniel, *The Supervisory Jurisdiction Over Trust Administration* (OUP 2019)
Conaglen, Matthew, *Fiduciary Loyalty: Protecting the Due Performance of Non-Fiduciary Duties* (Hart 2010)

Craig, Paul, *Administrative Law* (8th edn, Sweet & Maxwell 2016)
Criddle, Evan J, and Evan Fox-Decent, *Fiduciaries of Humanity* (OUP 2016)
Dabin, Jean, *Le droit subjectif* (Dalloz 2008 [1952])
Daly, Paul, *A Theory of Deference in Administrative Law* (CUP 2012)
Davies, Anne CL, *The Public Law of Government Contracts* (OUP 2008)
De Page, Henri, and René Dekkers, *Traité élémentaire de droit civil belge*, vol 5 (2nd edn, Bruylant 1975)
Douville, Thibault, *Les conflits d'intérêts en droit privé* (Institut Universitaire Varenne 2014)
Dufour, Julien-Michel, *Code civil des français, avec les sources où toutes ses dispositions ont été puisées*, 4 vols, vol 3 (Lenormant 1806)
Easterbrook, FR, and DR Fischel, *The Economic Structure of Corporate Law* (Harvard UP 1991)
Edwards, John LJ, *The Law Officers of the Crown* (Sweet & Maxwell 1964)
Endicott, Timothy, *Administrative Law* (5th edn, OUP 2021)
Fairgrieve, Duncan, *State Liability in Tort: A Comparative Law Study* (OUP 2003)
Ferran, Eilís, *Company Law and Corporate Finance* (OUP 1999)
Finn, Paul, *Fiduciary Obligations: 40th Anniversary Republication with Additional Essays* (Federation Press 2016)
Finn, Paul D, *Fiduciary Obligations* (Law Book Co 1977)
Fox-Decent, Evan, *Sovereignty's Promise: The State as Fiduciary* (OUP 2011)
Gaillard, Emmanuel, *Le pouvoir en droit privé* (Economica 1985)
Galligan, Denis J, *Discretionary Powers: A Legal Study of Official Discretion* (Clarendon Press 1986)
Garant, Patrice, *Droit administratif* (7th edn, Éditions Yvons Blais 2017)
Gardner, John, *Law as a Leap of Faith* (OUP 2012)
Godbout, Jacques, and Alain Caillé, *The World of the Gift*, trans Donland Winkler (McGill-Queen's UP 1998)
Gold, Andrew, *The Right of Redress* (OUP 2020)
Goldberg, John, and Benjamin Zipursky, *Recognizing Wrongs* (Harvard UP 2020)
Graziadei, Michele, Ugo Mattei, and Lionel Smith, *Commercial Trusts in European Private Law* (CUP 2005)
Guillouard, Louis V, *Traités des contrats aléatoires et du mandat* (2nd edn, A Durand & Pedone-Lauriel 1894)
Häcker, Birke, *Consequences of Impaired Consent Transfers* (Mohr Siebeck 2009; Hart 2013)
Hart, Herbert LA, *Essays on Bentham: Jurisprudence and Political Theory* (OUP 1982)
———, *The Concept of Law* (3rd edn, 2012)
Hayton, D, P Matthews, and C Mitchell, *Underhill and Hayton: Law Relating to Trusts and Trustees* (19th edn, LexisNexis 2016)
Hobbes, Thomas, *Leviathan*, John CA Gaskin (ed) (OUP 2008)
Hogg, P, and PJ Monahan, *Liability of the Crown* (4th edn, Carswell 2011)
Hogg, P, and Wade K Wright, *Constitutional Law of Canada* (5th looseleaf edn, Carswell 2007–)
Hohfeld, Wesley N, *Fundamental Legal Conceptions as Applied in Judicial Reasoning* (Yale UP 1964)
Horder, Jeremy, *Ashworth's Principles of Criminal Law* (9th edn, OUP 2019)
Huet, Jérôme, Georges Decoq, Cyril Grimaldi, and Hervé Lécuyer, *Les principaux contrats spéciaux*, Jacques Ghestin (ed), Traité de droit civil (3rd edn, LGDJ 2012)

Issalys, Pierre, and Denis Lemieux, *L'action gouvernementale: Précis de droit des institutions administratives* (4th edn, Éditions Yvon Blais 2020)
Kahneman, Daniel, *Thinking, Fast and Slow* (Farrar, Straus & Giroux 2011)
Kerr, Michael, Richard Janda, and Chip Pitts, *Corporate Social Responsibilty: A Legal Analysis* (LexisNexis 2009)
Kyd, Stewart, *A Treatise on the Law of Corporations*, 2 vols, vol 2 (J Butterworth 1794)
Lakoff, George, *Women, Fire and Dangerous Things: What Categories Reveal About the Mind* (Chicago UP 1987)
Law Commission of Ontario, *Class Actions: Objectives, Experiences and Reforms: Final Report* (Law Commission of Ontario 2019)
Lepaulle, Pierre, *Traité théorique et pratique des trusts en droit interne, en droit fiscale et en droit international* (Rousseau et Cie 1932)
Lluelles, Didier, and Benoît Moore, *Droit des obligations* (3rd edn, Thémis 2018)
Locke, John, *Two Treatises of Government: [. . .]* (A Churchill 1690)
Markesinis, Basil S, Hannes Unberath, and Angus Johnston, *The German Law of Contract: A Comparative Treatise* (2nd edn, Hart Publishing 2006)
McLean, Janet, *Searching for the State in British Legal Thought* (CUP 2012)
Mullan, David J, *Administrative Law* (Irwin Law 2001)
Nichols, Joshua, *A Reconciliation without Recollection: An Investigation of the Foundations of Aboriginal Law* (University of Toronto Press 2020)
Normand, Sylvio, *Introduction au droit des biens* (3rd edn, Wilson & Lafleur 2020)
Oliver, Dawn, *Common Values and the Public-Private Divide* (reprint edn, CUP 2010)
Parker, Hon William D, *Commission of Inquiry into the Facts of Allegations of Conflict of Interest Concerning the Honourable Sinclair M Stevens* (Minister of Supply and Services Canada 1987)
Pétel, Philippe, *Les obligations du mandataire* (Litec 1988)
Piché, Catherine, *Fairness in Class Action Settlements* (Carswell 2011)
Pont, Paul, *Commentaire-traité des petits contrats et de la contrainte par corps*, 2 vols, vol 1 (Cotillon 1864)
Popovici, Adrian, *La couleur du mandat* (Les Éditions Thémis 1995)
Popovici, Alexandra, *Êtres et avoirs: Les droits sans sujet en droit privé actuel* (Éditions Yvon Blais 2019)
Rotman, Leonard I, *Fiduciary Law* (Thomson/Carswell 2005)
Schoenfeld, Gabriel, *Necessary Secrets* (WW Norton & Co 2010)
Scott, Austin W, William F Fratcher, and Mark L Ascher, *Scott and Ascher on Trusts*, vol 1 (4th edn, Aspen Publishers 2006)
———, *Scott and Ascher on Trusts*, vol 2 (4th edn, Aspen Publishers 2006)
Shepherd, JC, *The Law of Fiduciaries* (Carswell 1981)
Smith, Lionel, *The Law of Tracing* (Clarendon Press 1997)
Smith, Stephen A, *Contract Theory* (OUP 2004)
———, *Rights, Wrongs, and Injustices* (OUP 2019)
Steinberg, Jonathan, *Why Switzerland?* (3rd edn, CUP 2015)
Stevens, Robert, *Torts and Rights* (OUP 2007)
Stoljar, Samuel J, *The Law of Agency: Its History and Present Principles* (Sweet & Maxwell 1961)
Storck, Michel, *Essai sur le mécanisme de la représentation dans les actes juridiques* (LGDJ 1982)
Thomas, G, *Powers* (2nd edn, OUP 2012)

Troplong, Raymond-Théodore, *Du mandat* (Charles Hingray 1846)
Valiergue, Julien, *Les conflits d'intérêts en droit privé* (LGDJ 2019)
Voltaire, *Essai sur l'histoire générale et sur les moeurs et l'esprit des nations, depuis Charlemagne jusqu'à nos jours*, 8 vols, vol 2 (new edn, Cramer 1761–63)
Wade, William, *Administrative Law* (5th edn, Clarendon Press 1982)
Waline, Jean, *Droit administratif* (26th edn, Dalloz 2016)
Waller, Carolyn, Ron Coble, Joanne Scharer, and Susan Giamportone, *Governance and Coordination of Public Higher Education in All 50 States* (North Carolina Center for Public Policy Research 2000)
Walters, Mark D, *AV Dicey and the Common Law Constitutional Tradition: A Legal Turn of Mind* (CUP 2020)
Waters, Donovan WM, Mark Gillen, and Lionel Smith, *Waters' Law of Trusts in Canada* (5th edn, Thomson Reuters 2021)
Watson, James A, *The Duty to Account: Development and Principles* (Federation Press 2016)
Watts, Peter, and Francis MB Reynolds, *Bowstead and Reynolds on Agency* (22nd edn, Sweet & Maxwell 2020)
Wegenast, Franklin W, *The Law of Canadian Companies* (Burroughs and Co 1931)
Welling, Bruce, *Corporate Law in Canada: The Governing Principles* (3rd edn, Scribblers 2006)
Welling, Bruce, Lionel D Smith, and Leonard I Rotman, *Canadian Corporate Law: Cases, Notes & Materials* (4th edn, LexisNexis Canada 2010)
Werro, Franz, *Le mandat et ses effets* (Éditions Universitaires Fribourg 1993)
Wicker, Guillaume, *La notion du patrimoine* (Les Éditions Thémis 2015)
World Bank, OECD, and UN Office on Drugs and Crime, *Preventing and Managing Conflicts of Interest in the Public Sector* (2020)

Edited Books

Note that this list only includes books which the main work cites as a whole; see also the list of Book Chapters, below.

Bonell, Michael J, and Olaf Meyer (eds), *The Impact of Corruption on International Commercial Contracts* (Springer 2015)
Corniot, S (ed), *Dictionnaire de droit*, 2 vols, vol 2 (2nd edn, Dalloz 1966)
Criddle, Evan J, Evan Fox-Decent, Andrew S Gold, Sung Hui Kim, and Paul B Miller (eds), *Fiduciary Government* (CUP 2018)
Criddle, Evan J, Paul B Miller, and Robert H Sitkoff (eds), *The Oxford Handbook of Fiduciary Law* (OUP 2019)
Dannemann, Gerhard, and Reiner Schulze (eds), *German Civil Code: Bürgerliches Gesetzbuch (BGB)*, 2 vols, vol I (CH Beck 2020)
Fairgrieve, Duncan, Mads Andenas, and John Bell (eds), *Tort Liability of Public Authorities in Comparative Perspective* (BIICL 2002)
Fauvarque-Cosson, Bénédicte (ed), *La confiance légitime et l'estoppel* (Société de legislation comparée 2006)
Hondius, Ewoud, and André Janssen (eds), *Disgorgement of Profits: Gain-Based Remedies Throughout the World* (Springer 2015)
Lo, Bernard, and Marilyn J Field (eds), *Conflict of Interest in Medical Research, Education, and Practice* (National Academies Press 2009)

Oliphant, Ken (ed), *The Liability of Public Authorities in Comparative Perspective* (Intersentia 2016)
van Boom, Willem H, Helmut Koziol, and Christian A Witting (eds), *Pure Economic Loss* (Springer 2004)
Watson, Alan (ed), *The Digest of Justinian*, 4 vols (revised edn, University of Pennsylvania Press 1998)

Journal Articles

Anonymous note, 'Police Liability for Negligent Failure to Prevent Crime' (1981) 94 Harv L Rev 821
Adams, Mark A, Jeremy W Barber, and Hildy Herrera, 'Ethics in Government' (1993) 30 Am Crim LJ 617
Adams, Thomas, 'Ultra Vires Revisited' [2018] Pub L 31
Allan, Trevor RS, 'Judicial Deference and Judicial Review: Legal Doctrine and Legal Theory' (2011) 127 LQR 96
Bant, Elise, 'Causation and Scope of Liability in Unjust Enrichment' [2009] Restitution L Rev 60
Barker, Kit, 'Modelling Public and Private Enforcement: The Rationality of Hybridity' (2018) 37 UQLJ 9
Basil, David, 'A Primer on the Public Duty Doctrine as Applied to Police Protection' (2005) 37 Urban Lawyer 403
Baud, Patrick F, 'The Crown's Prerogatives and the Constitution of Canada' (2021) 3 J Commonwealth L 219
Birks, Peter, 'The Content of the Fiduciary Obligation' (2000) 34 Israel LR 3
Birks, Peter BH, 'A New Argument for a Narrow View of Litem Suam Facere' (1984) 52 Tijdschrift voor rechtsgeschiedenis (Legal Hist Rev) 373
Bray, Samuel L, and Paul B Miller, 'Against Fiduciary Constitutionalism' (2020) 106 Virginia L Rev 1479
Bridge, Michael, 'The Exercise of Contractual Discretion' (2019) 135 LQR 227
Brodie, Douglas, 'The Employment Relationship and Fiduciary Obligations' (2012) 16 Edinburgh L Rev 198
Brown, Natalie, 'The Principal Problem: Towards a More Limited Role for Fiduciary Law in the Nonprofit Sector' (2013) 99 Virginia L Rev 879
Cane, Peter, 'Standing Up for the Public' [1995] Pub L 276
Cantin Cumyn, Madeleine, 'Le pouvoir juridique' (2007) 52 McGill LJ 215
———, 'The Legal Power' (2009) 17 European Rev of Private Law 345
———, 'L'obligation de loyauté dans les services de placement' (2012) 3 Bulletin de droit économique 19
Capitant, Henri, 'Sur l'abus des droits' (1928) 27 Revue trimestrielle de droit civil 365
Chambers, Robert, 'The End of Knowing Receipt' (2016) 2 CJCCL 1
Chan, Kathryn, 'Taxing Charities/Imposer les organismes de bienfaisance: Harmonization and Dissonance in Canadian Charity Law' (2007) 55 Can Tax J 481
———, 'The Role of the Attorney General in Charity Proceedings in Canada and in England and Wales' (2010) 89 Can Bar Rev 373
———, 'Identifying the Institutional Religious Freedom Claimant' (2017) 95 Can Bar Rev 707

Clemmer, Christopher D, 'Obstructing the Bernardo Investigation: Kenneth Murray and the Defence Counsel's Conflicting Obligations to Clients and the Court' (2008) 1 OHRLP 137

Colombo, Ronald J, 'Taking Stock of the Benefit Corporation' (2019) 7 Texas A&M L Rev 73

Conaglen, Matthew, 'Public-Private Intersection: Comparing Fiduciary Conflict Doctrine and Bias' [2008] Public Law 58

Cooter, Robert, and Bradley J Freedman, 'The Fiduciary Relationship: Its Economic Character and Legal Consequences' (1991) 66 NYU L Rev 1045

Cornford, Tom, 'The Negligence Liability of Public Authorities for Omissions' (2019) 78 CLJ 545

Cover, Avidan Y, 'Reconstructing the Right against Excessive Force' (2016) 68 Fla L Rev 1773

Craig, Paul, 'The Common Law, Reasons and Administrative Justice' (1994) 53 Cambridge LJ 282

——, 'Competing Models of Judicial Review' [1999] Pub L 428

Criddle, Evan J, 'Fiduciary Foundations of Administrative Law' (2006) 54 UCLA L Rev 117

——, 'Fiduciary Administration: Rethinking Popular Representation in Agency Rulemaking' (2010) 88 Texas L Rev 441

Cullity, Maurice, 'Judicial Control of Trustees' Discretions' (1975) 25 UTLJ 99

Davis, Michael, 'Conflict of Interest' (1982) 1 Bus Prof Ethics J 17

——, 'Conflict of Interest Revisited' (1993) 12 Bus Prof Ethics J 21

Davis, Seth, 'The False Promise of Fiduciary Government' (2014) 89 Notre Dame L Rev 1145

——, 'American Colonialism and Constitutional Redemption' (2017) 105 Cal L Rev 1751

Degeling, Simone, and Michael Legg, 'Fiduciary Obligations of Lawyers in Australian Class Actions: Conflicts between Duties' (2014) 37 UNSWLJ 914

DeMott, Deborah A, 'Breach of Fiduciary Duty: On Justifiable Expectations of Loyalty and Their Consequences' (2006) 48 Arizona L Rev 925

——, 'Disloyal Agents' (2007) 58 Alabama L Rev 1049

——, 'Corporate Officers as Agents' (2017) 74 Wash & Lee L Rev 847

Devinat, Mathieu, and Édith Guilhermont, 'Enquete sur les théories juridiques en droit civil québécois' (2010) 44 RJT 7

Edelman, James, 'When Do Fiduciary Duties Arise?' (2010) 126 LQR 302

Eisenberg, Theodore, and Geoffrey P Miller, 'Incentive Awards to Class Action Plaintiffs: An Empirical Study' (2006) 53 UCLA L Rev 1303

Elliott, Steven B, and Charles Mitchell, 'Remedies for Dishonest Assistance' (2004) 67 MLR 16

Ellis, Christopher, 'Reasons and the Record – Reconsidering *Osmond* and Constitutional Perspectives' (2015) 82 AIAL Forum 55

Feldman, David, 'Error of Law and Flawed Administrative Acts' (2014) 73 CLJ 275

Feldthusen, Bruce, 'Judicial Activism in the Supreme Court of Canada' (2016) 53 Alberta L Rev 955

Finn, Paul D, 'Fiduciary Reflections' (2014) 88 ALJ 127

Fleischer, Holger, 'Legal Transplants in European Company Law – The Case of Fiduciary Duties' (2005) 2 Eur Co & Financial L Rev 378

Flick, Geoffrey A, 'Relator Actions: The Injunction and the Enforcement of Public Rights' (1978) 5 Monash U L Rev 133

Fox-Decent, Evan, 'The Fiduciary Nature of State Legal Authority' (2005) 31 Queen's LJ 259

———, 'Democratizing Common Law Constitutionalism' (2010) 55 McGill LJ 511

Fox-Decent, Evan, and Evan J Criddle, 'The Fiduciary Constitution of Human Rights' (2010) 15 Legal Theory 301

Frazer, A, 'The Employee's Contractual Duty of Fidelity' (2015) 131 LQR 53

Galoob, Stephen, and Ethan J Leib, 'Fiduciary Loyalty, Inside and Out' (2018) 92 S Cal L Rev 69

Gardner, John, 'Legal Positivism: 5½ Myths' (2001) 46 Am J Jurisprudence 199

Gélinas, Fabien, 'Le *locus standi* dans les actions d'intérêt public et la *relator action*: l'empire de la common law en droit québécois' (1988) 29 Cahiers de Droit 657

Gold, Andrew S, 'The New Concept of Loyalty in Corporate Law' (2009) 43 UC Davis L Rev 457

———, 'Purposive Loyalty' (2017) 74 Wash & Lee L Rev 881

Graham, Toby, and Thomas Beasley, 'Trust the State: The Relevance of Principles of Public Law in Trust Law and Practice' (2019) 25 Trusts & Trustees 841

Graham, Toby, David Russell, and Tom Williams, 'Is the Genuine Transaction Rule Really So Genuine?' (2022) 28 Trusts & Trustees 156

Grande, David, Dominick L Frosch, Andrew W Perkins, and Barbara E Kahn, 'Effect of Exposure to Small Pharmaceutical Promotional Items on Treatment Preferences' (2009) 169(9) Arch Intern Med 887

Grantham, Ross, 'The Powers of Company Directors and the Proper Purpose Doctrine' (1994–95) 5 KCLJ 16

Gretton, George, 'Trusts Without Equity' (2000) 49 ICLQ 599

Grundmann, Stefan, 'Trust and Treuhand at the End of the 20th Century – Key Problems and Shift of Interests' (1999) 47 Am J Comp Law 401

Gummow, William M, 'Review: *Fiduciary Obligations*' (1978) 2 UNSWLJ 408

Gussen, Benjamin F, 'The State is the Fiduciary of the People' [2015] Pub L 440

Harlow, Carol, 'Public Law and Popular Justice' (2002) 65 MLR 1

Harris, Daniel, 'The Rival Rationales of Vicarious Liability' (2021) 20 FSU Business L Rev 49

Hazelton, Morgan LW, Jacob M Montgomery, and Brendan Nyhan, 'Does Public Financing Affect Judicial Behavior? Evidence from the North Carolina Supreme Court' (2015) 44 Am Politics Res 587

Heeney, ADP, 'Estoppel in the Law of Quebec' (1930) 8 Can Bar Rev 401 & 500

Hoover, Earl R, 'Basic Principles Underlying Duty of Loyalty' (1956) 5 Cleveland-Marshall L Rev 7

Hudson, Jessica, 'One Thicket in Fraud on a Power' (2019) 39 OJLS 577

Hughes, Camilla, 'The Fiduciary Obligations of the Crown to Aborigines: Lessons from the United States and Canada' (1993) 16 UNSWLJ 70

Huppé, Luc, 'Les conflits d'intérêts institutionnels au sein de la magistrature' (2007) 38 RDUS 127

Iacobucci, Edward, 'Indeterminacy and the Canadian Supreme Court's Approach to Corporate Fiduciary Duties' (2009) 48 CBLJ 232

Kalajdzic, Jasminka, 'The "Illusion of Compensation": Cy Près Distributions in Canadian Class Actions' (2013) 92 Can Bar Rev 173

Kanner, Allan, 'The Public Trust Doctrine, Parens Patriae, and the Attorney General as the Guardian of the State's Natural Resources' (2005) 16 Duke Env L & Policy Forum 57

Kent, Andrew, Ethan J Leib, and Jed H Shugerman, 'Faithful Execution and Article II' (2019) 132 Harv L Rev 2111

Kershaw, David, 'Corporate Law's Fiduciary Personas' (2020) 136 LQR 454

Kreder, Jennifer Anglim, 'The Public Trust' (2016) 18 U Pa J Const L 1425

Kuntz, Thilo, 'Transnational Fiduciary Law: Spaces and Elements' (2020) 5 UC Irvine J Int'l Transnat'l & Comp L 47

Laby, Arthur B, 'Advisors as Fiduciaries' (2020) 72 Florida L Rev 953

Lambert, Nicolas, 'Effective Remediation in Public Procurement: Damages or Judicial Review?' (2020) 51 Ottawa L Rev 361

Langbein, John H, 'Mandatory Rules in the Law of Trusts' (2004) 98 Northwestern U L Rev 1105

———, 'Questioning the Trust Law Duty of Loyalty: Sole Interest or Best Interest?' (2005) 114 Yale LJ 929

———, 'Burn the Rembrandt? Trust Law's Limits on the Settlor's Power to Direct Investments' (2010) 90 BU L Rev 375

Langford, Rosemary T, 'Best Interests: Multifaceted but Not Unbounded' (2016) 75 Cambridge LJ 505

———, 'Statutory Duties and Ratification: Untangling the Maze' (2021) 15 J Equity 126

Le Breton-Prévost, Caroline, 'Loyalty in Québec Private Law' (2014) 9 J Civ L Stud 329

Lee, Daniel, '"Office Is a Thing Borrowed": Jean Bodin on Offices and Seigneurial Government' (2013) 31 Political Theory 409

Leib, Ethan J, and Stephen R Galoob, 'Fiduciary Political Theory: A Critique' (2016) 125 Yale LJ 1820

Leib, Ethan J, David L Ponet, and Michael Serota, 'A Fiduciary Theory of Judging' (2013) 101 Cal L Rev 699

———, 'Translating Fiduciary Principles into Public Law' (2013) 126 Harv L Rev Forum 91

Leigh, Ian, 'Bias, Necessity and the Convention' [2002] Pub L 407

Leow, Rachel, 'Understanding Agency: A Proxy Power Definition' (2019) 78 CLJ 99

Leslie, Melanie B, 'In Defense of the No Further Inquiry Rule: A Response to Professor John Langbein' (2005) 47 William & Mary L Rev 541

Levinthal, Louis E, 'The Early History of English Bankruptcy Law' (1919) 67 U Penn L Rev 1

Liau, Timothy, 'Privity: Rights, Standing, and the Road Not Taken' (2021) 41 OJLS 803

Licht, Amir N, 'Farewell to Fairness: Towards Retiring Delaware's Entire Fairness Review' (2020) 44 Del J Corp L 1

Lister, Matthew, 'Book Review' (2012) 123 Ethics 150

Luban, David, 'Fiduciary Legal Ethics, Zeal, and Moral Activism' (2020) 33 Georgetown J Leg Ethics 275

MacIntosh, Jeffery, 'BCE and the Peoples' Corporate Law: Learning to Live on Quicksand' (2009) 48 CBLJ 255

Márquez Carrasco, María del Carmen, and Joaquín Alcaide Fernández, 'In re Pinochet' (1999) 93 Am J Int'l Law 690

Mason, Sir Anthony, 'The Place of Equity and Equitable Doctrines in the Contemporary Common Law World' (1994) 110 LQR 238

McCamus, J, 'Prometheus Unbound: Fiduciary Obligation in the Supreme Court of Canada' (1997) 28 CBLJ 107

McColgan, Aileen, 'Limiting the Costs of Litigation: Protective Costs Orders in the Court of Appeal' (2009) 28 Civil Justice Q 169

McKevitt, Thomas, 'The Rule of Necessity: Is Judicial Non-Disqualification Really Necessary?' (1996) 24 Hofstra L Rev 817

Miller, Paul B, 'A Theory of Fiduciary Liability' (2011) 56 McGill LJ 235

——, 'Justifying Fiduciary Remedies' (2013) 63 UTLJ 570

——, 'Regularizing the Trust Protector' (2018) 103 Iowa L Rev 2097

Miller, Paul B, and Andrew S Gold, 'Fiduciary Governance' (2015) 57 William and Mary L Rev 513

Millett, Peter, 'Bribes and Secret Commissions' [1993] RLR 7

Millett, Lord, 'Bribes and Secret Commissions Again' (2012) 71 CLJ 583

Mitchell, Charles, 'Equitable Compensation for Breach of Fiduciary Duty' [2013] CLP 307

——, 'Stewardship of Property and Liability to Account' [2014] CPLJ 215

——, 'Good Faith, Self-Denial and Mandatory Trustee Duties' (2018) 32 Trust L Int'l 92

Moore, Benoît, 'La théorie des sources des obligations: éclatement d'une classification' (2002) 36 Rev Juridique Thémis 689

Moore, Don A, and George Loewenstein, 'Self-Interest, Automaticity, and the Psychology of Conflict of Interest' (2004) 17 Soc Justice Res 189

Moore, Don A, Lloyd Tanlu, and Max H Bazerman, 'Conflict of Interest and the Intrusion of Bias' (2010) 5 Judgm Decis Mak 37

Morin, Michel, 'La compétence parens patriae et le droit civil québécois: un emprunt inutile, un affront à l'histoire' (1990) 50 Rev du Barreau 827

Motulsky, Henri, 'De l'impossibilité juridique de constituer un Trust anglo-saxon sous l'empire de la loi française' (1948) 37 Rev critique de droit international privé 451

Müller-Freienfels, Wolfram, 'Legal Relations in the Law of Agency: Power of Agency and Commercial Certainty' (1964) 13 Am J Comp Law 193 and 341

Nicholls, Lord, 'Trustees and Their Broader Community: Where Duty, Morality and Ethics Converge' (1995) 9 Trust L Int'l 71

Nolan, Donal, 'The Liability of Financial Supervisory Authorities' (2013) 4 J Eur Tort L 190

Nolan, Richard, 'Controlling Fiduciary Power' (2009) 68 CLJ 293

Oliver, Dawn, 'Is the Ultra Vires Rule the Basis of Judicial Review?' [1987] Pub L 543

Ost, Suzanne, 'Breaching the Sexual Boundaries in the Doctor-Patient Relationship: Should English Law Recognize Fiduciary Duties?' (2016) 24 Medical L Rev 206

Palmer, Vernon V, 'The Recusal of American Judges in the Post-Caperton Era: An Empirical Assessment of the Risk of Actual Bias in Decisions Involving Campaign Contributors' (2010) https://ssrn.com/abstract=1721665

Palmer, Vernon V, and John Levendis, 'The Louisiana Supreme Court in Question: An Empirical and Statistical Study of the Effects of Campaign Money on the Judicial Function' (2008) 82 Tul L Rev 1291

Penner, James, 'Distinguishing Fiduciary, Trust, and Accounting Relationships' (2014) 8 J Equity 202

——, 'Purposes and Rights in the Common Law of Trusts' (2014) 48 RJT 579

Perell, Paul M, 'Remedies for the Victims of a Bribe' (1999) 22 Advocates' Q 198

Piché, Catherine, 'Public Financiers as Overseers of Class Proceedings' (2016) 12 NYU J L Bus 776

Pollard, David, 'The Short-form "Best Interests Duty" – Mad, Bad and Dangerous to Know' (2018) 32 Trust L Int'l 106 and 176
Poole, Thomas, 'The Strange Death of Prerogative in England' (2018) 43 UWALR 42
Pound, Roscoe, 'Visitatorial Jurisdiction Over Corporations in Equity' (1936) 49 Harv L Rev 369
Pratte, Caroline, 'Essai sur le rapport entre la société par actions et ses dirigeants dans le cadre du Code Civil du Québec' (1994) 39 McGill LJ 1
Price, Alistair, 'Negligence Liability for Police Omissions: A Golden Mean' (2018) 84 SCLR (2d) 131
Rave, D Theodore, 'Politicians as Fiduciaries' (2013) 126 Harv L Rev 671
Raz, Joseph, 'Voluntary Obligations and Normative Powers' (1972) 46 Proc Aristot Soc, Suppl Vol 79
Reid, Kenneth GC, 'Patrimony Not Equity: The Trust in Scotland' (2000) 8 Eur Rev Priv L 427
Rendleman, Doug, 'Commercial Bribery: Choice and Measurement within a Remedies Smorgasbord' (2017) 74 Wash & Lee L Rev 369
Reynolds, Francis MB, 'The Ultimate Apparent Authority' (1994) 110 LQR 21
Robertson, Gerald B, 'When Things Go Wrong: The Duty to Disclose Medical Error' (2002) 28 Queen's LJ 353
Russell, David, and Toby Graham, 'Protector Questions' (2020) 26 Trusts & Trustees 709
Sales, Philip, 'Use of Powers for Proper Purposes in Private Law' (2020) 136 LQR 384
Scheer, Richard K, 'Intentions, Motives, and Causation' (2001) 76 Philosophy 397
Scott, Austin W, 'The Fiduciary Principle' (1949) 37 Cal L Rev 539
Sealy, Len S, 'Fiduciary Relationships' [1962] CLJ 69
———, 'Fiduciary Obligations, Forty Years On' (1995) 1 J Contract L 37
Seymour, John, 'Parens Patriae and Wardship Powers: Their Nature and Origin' (1994) 14 OJLS 159
Shepherd, JC, 'Toward A Unified Concept of Fiduciary Relationships' (1981) 97 LQR 51
Sisk, Gregory C, 'A Primer on the Doctrine of Federal Sovereign Immunity' (2005) 58 Oklahoma L Rev 439
Sitkoff, Robert H, 'An Agency Costs Theory of Trust Law' (2004) 69 Cornell L Rev 621
Smith, D Gordon, 'The Critical Resource Theory of Fiduciary Duty' (2002) 55 Vanderbilt L Rev 1399
———, 'Contractually Adopted Fiduciary Duty' [2014] U Ill L Rev 1783
Smith, Lionel, 'Fiduciary Relationships — Arising in Commercial Contexts – Investment Advisor: Hodgkinson v Simms' (1995) 74 Can Bar Rev 714
———, 'Unjust Enrichment, Property, and the Structure of Trusts' (2000) 116 LQR 412
———, 'Can I Change My Mind? Undoing Trustee Decisions' (2009) 27 ETPJ 284
———, 'Simplifying Claims to Traceable Proceeds' (2009) 125 LQR 338
———, 'Trust and Patrimony' (2009) 28 ETPJ 332
———, 'Deterrence, Prophylaxis and Punishment in Fiduciary Obligations' (2013) 7 J Equity 87
———, 'Scottish Trusts in the Common Law' (2013) 17 Edinburgh L Rev 283
———, 'Fiduciary Relationships: Ensuring the Loyal Exercise of Judgement on Behalf of Another' (2014) 130 LQR 608
———, 'Loyalty and Politics: From Case Law to Statute Law' (2015) 9 J Equity 130
———, 'The Duties of Trustees in Comparative Perspective' (2016) 6 Euro Rev Priv L 1031
———, 'Massively Discretionary Trusts' (2017) 70 CLP 17; reprinted (2019) 25 Trusts & Trustees 397

———, 'Give the People What They Want? The Onshoring of the Offshore' (2018) 103 Iowa L Rev 2155
———, 'Prescriptive Fiduciary Duties' (2018) 37 UQLJ 261
———, 'Parenthood is a Fiduciary Relationship' (2020) 70 UTLJ 395
———, 'A Tale of Two Patrimonies: Limits on the Flexibility of Trust Law' (2021) 40 ETPJ 139
Spigelman, Hon James J, 'Foundations of Administrative Law: Toward General Principles of Institutional Law' (1999) 58(1) Aust J Publ Admin 3
Stoljar, Natalie, 'Essence, Identity, and the Concept of Woman' (1995) 23 Philos Top 261
Strine Jr, Leo E, LA Hamermesh, RF Balotti, and JM Gorris, 'Loyalty's Core Demand: The Defining Role of Good Faith in Corporation Law' (2010) 98 Georgetown LJ 629
Sukhatme, Neel U, and Jay Jenkins, 'Pay to Play? Campaign Finance and the Incentive Gap in the Sixth Amendment's Right to Counsel' (2020) 70 Duke LJ 775
Tait, Allison Anna, 'Publicity Rules for Public Trusts' (2015) 33 Cardozo Arts Ent LJ 421
Tam, Sara, 'In Museums We Trust: Analyzing the Mission of Museums, Deaccessioning Policies, and the Public Trust' (2012) 39 Fordham Urban LJ 849
Tan, Weiming, 'Peering through Equity's Prism: A Fiduciary's Duty of Care or a Fiduciary Duty of Care?' (2021) 15 J Equity 181
Taoka, Eriko, 'Shaping and Re-shaping the Duty of Loyalty in Japanese Law' (2019) 14 Asian J Comp Law S119
Twigg, Martin, 'Costs Immunity: Banishing the "Bane" of Costs from Public Interest Litigation' (2013) 36 Dalhousie LJ 193
Uhlmann, Felix, 'Switzerland: Naturalization Process Presents Conflict Between Democracy and the Rule of Law' (2004) 2 Int'l J Const L 716
Valsan, Remus, 'Directors' Powers and the Proper Purposes Rule' (2016) 27 KCLJ 157
———, 'Fiduciary Duties of Credit Brokers' (2016) 20 Edinburgh L Rev 99
———, 'Fiduciary Duties, Conflict of Interest, and Proper Exercise of Judgment' (2016) 62 McGill LJ 1
———, 'The No-conflict Fiduciary Rule and the Rule against Bias in Judicial Review: A Comparison' (2019) 6 Eur J Comp Law Gov 1
Valsan, Remus, and Lionel Smith, 'The Loyalty of Lawyers: A Comment on *3464920 Canada Inc v Strother*' (2008) 87 Can Bar Rev 247
Van Bever, Aline, 'When Is an Employee a Fiduciary?' (2014) 18 Can Lab Emp LJ 39
Van Duffel, Siegfried, 'The Nature of Rights Debate Rests on a Mistake' (2012) 93 Pacific Philos Q 104
Vermeule, Adrian, 'Common Law Constitutionalism and the Limits of Reason' (2007) 107 Col L Rev 1482
Vidal, Roger, 'L'évolution du détournement de pouvoir dans la jurisprudence administrative' (1952) 68 RD public et de la science politique 275
Waltermann, Antonia, 'Book Review' (2013) 20 Maastricht J Eur Comp L 649
Watson, Susan, 'Conceptual Confusion: Organs, Agents and Identity in the English Courts' (2011) 23 Singap Acad LJ 762
Watterson, Stephen, 'An Account of Profits or Damages? The History of Orthodoxy' (2004) 24 OJLS 471
Watts, Peter, 'Authority and Mismotivation' (2005) 121 LQR 4
Wazana, Ashley, 'Physicians and the Pharmaceutical Industry: Is a Gift Ever Just a Gift?' (2000) 283(3) JAMA 373

Weinrib, Ernest J, 'The Fiduciary Obligation' (1975) 25 UTLJ 1

Wheatle, Se-shauna, 'Common Law Constitutionalism through Methodology' (2019) 65 McGill LJ 341

Wood, Mary Christina, 'Indian Land and the Promise of Native Sovereignty: The Trust Doctrine Revisited' [1994] Utah L Rev 1471

Wood, Susan F, Joanna Podrasky, Meghan A McMonagle, Janani Raveendran, Tyler Bysshe, Alycia Hogenmiller, and Adriane Fugh-Berman, 'Influence of Pharmaceutical Marketing on Medicare Prescriptions in the District of Columbia' (2017) 12(10) PLoS ONE e0186060

Worthington, Sarah, 'Corporate Governance: Remedying and Ratifying Directors' Breaches' (2000) 116 LQR 638

Wu, Ying-Chieh, 'Trusts Reimagined: The Transplantation and Evolution of Trust Law in Northeast Asia' (2020) 20 Am J Comp Law 1

Yip, Man, and Kelvin FK Low, 'Reconceptualising Fiduciary Regulation in Actual Conflicts' (2021) 45 Melbourne U L Rev 1

Zamir, Eyal, and Raanan Sulitzeanu-Kenan, 'Explaining Self-Interested Behavior of Public-Spirited Policy Makers' (2018) 78 Public Adm Rev 579

Zuckerman, Adrian, 'Protective Costs Orders: A Growing Costs-Litigation Industry' (2009) 28 Civil Justice Q 161

Book Chapters

Barrière, François, 'The French *fiducie*, or the Chaotic Awakening of a Sleeping Beauty' in Lionel Smith (ed), *Re-imagining the Trust: Trusts in Civil Law* (CUP 2012) 222

Beever, Allan, 'Our Most Fundamental Rights' in Andrew Robertson and Donal Nolan (eds), *Rights and Private Law* (Hart 2011) 63

Birks, Peter, 'Definition and Division: A Meditation on *Institutes* 313' in Peter Birks (ed), *The Classification of Obligations* (Clarendon Press 1997) 1

Bryan, Michael, '*Boardman v Phipps*' in Charles Mitchell and Paul Mitchell (eds), *Landmark Cases in Equity* (Hart 2012) 581

Cabrillac, Remy, 'Les conflits d'intérêts en droit civil' in Centre français de droit comparé (ed), *Les conflits d'intérêts: fonction et maîtrise* (Société de législation comparée 2013) 236

Cain, Bruce E, Alison L Gash, and Mark J Oleszek, 'Conflict-of-Interest Legislation in the United States: Origins, Evolution, and Inter-Branch Differences' in Christine Trost and Alison L Gash (eds), *Conflict of Interest and Public Life* (CUP 2008) 101

Cane, Peter, 'Tort Law and Public Functions' in John Oberdiek (ed), *Philosophical Foundations of the Law of Torts* (OUP 2014) 148

Cantin Cumyn, Madeleine, 'De l'administration des biens à la protection de la personne d'autrui' in Barreau du Québec – Service de la Formation continue (ed), *Obligations et recours contre un curateur, tuteur ou mandataire défaillant 2008*, vol 283 (Yvon Blais 2008) 205

Caranta, Roberto, 'Public Law Illegality and Governmental Liability' in Duncan Fairgrieve, Mads Andenas, and John Bell (eds), *Tort Liability of Public Authorities in Comparative Perspective* (BIICL 2002) 271

Chevrette, François, and Hugo Cyr, 'De quel positivisme parlez-vous?' in Louise Rolland and Pierre Noreau (eds), *Mélanges Andrée Lajoie* (Éditions Thémis 2008) 33

Chugh, Dolly, Max H Bazerman, and Mahzarin R Banaji, 'Bounded Ethicality as a Psychological Barrier to Recognizing Conflicts of Interest' in Don A Moore, Daylian M Cain, George Loewenstein, and Max H Bazerman (eds), *Conflicts of Interest: Challenges and Solutions in Business, Law, Medicine, and Public Policy* (CUP 2005) 74

Crête, Raymonde, 'Les manifestations du particularisme juridique des rapports de confiance dans les services de placement' in Raymonde Crête, Mario Naccarato, Marc Lacoursière, and Geneviève Brisson (eds), *Courtiers et conseillers financiers: encadrement des services de placement* (Éditions Yvons Blais 2011) 275

Crête, Raymonde, and Cinthia Duclos, 'Les sanctions civiles en cas de manquements professionels dans les services de placement' in Raymonde Crête, Mario Naccarato, Marc Lacoursière, and Geneviève Brisson (eds), *Courtiers et conseillers financiers: encadrement des services de placement* (Éditions Yvons Blais 2011) 361

Criddle, Evan J, and Evan Fox-Decent, 'Guardians of Legal Order: The Dual Commissions of Public Fiduciaries' in Evan J Criddle, Evan Fox-Decent, Andrew S Gold, Sung Hui Kim, and Paul B Miller (eds), *Fiduciary Government* (CUP 2018) 67

Cumyn, Michelle, 'L'encadrement des conflits d'intérêts par le droit commun québécois' in Denis Mazeaud, Benoît Moore, and Blandine Mallet-Bricout (eds), *Les conflits d'intérêts* (Dalloz 2013) 49

Davern, Raymond, 'Impeaching the Exercise of Trustees' Distributive Discretions: "Wrong Grounds" and Procedural Unfairness' in D Hayton (ed), *Extending the Boundaries of Trusts and Similar Ring-Fenced Funds* (Kluwer Law International 2002) 437

Davis, Michael, 'Introduction' in Michael Davis and Andrew Stark (eds), *Conflict of Interest in the Professions* (OUP 2001) 3

———, 'Conflict of Interest' in Ruth Chadwick (ed), *Encyclopedia of Applied Ethics* (2nd edn, Elsevier 2012) 571

Davis, Seth, 'Pluralism and the Public Trust' in Evan J Criddle, Evan Fox-Decent, Andrew S Gold, Sung Hui Kim, and Paul B Miller (eds), *Fiduciary Government* (CUP 2018) 281

DeMott, Deborah A, 'The Fiduciary Character of Agency and the Interpretation of Instructions' in Andrew S Gold and Paul B Miller (eds), *Philosophical Foundations of Fiduciary Law* (OUP 2014) 321

———, 'Fiduciary Principles in Agency Law' in Evan J Criddle, Paul B Miller, and Robert H Sitkoff (eds), *The Oxford Handbook of Fiduciary Law* (OUP 2019) 23

Edelman, James, 'The Role of Status in the Law of Obligations' in Andrew S Gold and Paul Miller (eds), *Philosophical Foundations of Fiduciary Law* (OUP 2014) 21

Endicott, Timothy, 'The Public Trust' in Evan J Criddle, Evan Fox-Decent, Andew S Gold, Sung Hui Kim, and Paul B Miller (eds), *Fiduciary Government* (CUP 2018) 306

Finn, Paul D, 'The Fiduciary Principle' in Timothy G Youdan (ed), *Equity, Fiduciaries and Trusts* (Carswell 1989) 1

———, 'The Forgotten "Trust": The People and the State' in Malcolm Cope (ed), *Equity: Issues and Trends* (Federation Press 1995) 131

Floyd, Carol Everly, 'For-Profit Degree-Granting Colleges: Who Are These Guys and What do They Mean for Students, Traditional Institutions, and Public Policy?' in John C Smart (ed), *Higher Education: Handbook of Theory and Research, vol XX* (Springer 2005) 539

Fox-Decent, Evan, 'Fiduciary Authority and the Service Conception' in Andew Gold and Paul Miller (eds), *Philosophical Foundations of Fiduciary Law* (OUP 2014) 363

———, 'Challenges to Public Fiduciary Theory: An Assessment' in D Gordon Smith and Andew S Gold (eds), *Research Handbook on Fiduciary Law* (Edward Elgar 2018) 379

Gageler, Stephen, 'The Equitable Duty of Loyalty in Public Office' in Tim Bonyhady (ed), *Finn's Law: An Australian Justice* (Federation Press 2016) 126

Gelter, Martin, and Geneviève Helleringer, 'Constituency Directors and Corporate Fiduciary Duties' in Andrew S Gold and Paul B Miller (eds), *Philosophical Foundations of Fiduciary Law* (OUP 2014) 302

———, 'Fiduciary Principles in European Civil Law Systems' in Evan J Criddle, Paul B Miller, and Robert H Sitkoff (eds), *The Oxford Handbook of Fiduciary Law* (OUP 2019) 583

Getzler, Joshua, 'Duty of Care' in P Birks and A Pretto (eds), *Breach of Trust* (Hart 2002) 41

———, 'Rumford Market and the Genesis of Fiduciary Obligations' in Andrew Burrows and Lord Rodger of Earlsferry (eds), *Mapping the Law: Essays in Memory of Peter Birks* (OUP 2006) 577

Gold, Andrew S, 'The Loyalties of Fiduciary Law' in Andrew S Gold and Paul B Miller (eds), *Philosophical Foundations of Fiduciary Law* (OUP 2014) 176

———, 'Trust and Advice' in PB Miller and Matthew Harding (eds), *Fiduciaries and Trust: Ethics, Politics, Economics and Law* (CUP 2020) 35

Goldberg, Helene M, 'Tort Liability for Federal Government Actions in the United States: An Overview' in Duncan Fairgrieve, Mads Andenas, and John Bell (eds), *Tort Liability of Public Authorities in Comparative Perspective* (BIICL 2002) 521

Gover, Kirsty, and Nicole Roughan, 'The Fiduciary Crown: The Private Duties of Public Actors in State–Indigenous Relationships' in Paul B Miller and Matthew Harding (eds), *Fiduciaries and Trust: Ethics, Politics, Economics and Law* (CUP 2020) 198

Graziadei, Michele, 'Diritto soggettivo, potere, interesse' in Rodolfo Sacco (ed), *Trattato di diritto civile; La parte generale del diritto civile 2, Il diritto soggetivo* (Utet 2001) 1

———, 'Virtue and Utility: Fiduciary Law in Civil Law and Common Law Jurisdictions' in Andrew S Gold and Paul B Miller (eds), *Philosophical Foundations of Fiduciary Law* (OUP 2014) 287

Harpum, Charles, 'Fiduciary Obligations and Fiduciary Powers—Where Are We Going?' in P Birks (ed), *Privacy and Loyalty* (Clarendon Press 1997) 145

Hayton, David, 'The Irreducible Core Content of Trusteeship' in Anthony Oakley (ed), *Trends in Contemporary Trust Law* (OUP 1996) 47

Helms, Tobias, 'Disgorgement of Profits in German Law' in Ewoud Hondius and André Janssen (eds), *Disgorgement of Profits: Gain-Based Remedies Throughout the World* (Springer 2015) 219

Ho, Lusina, 'Trust Laws in China' in Lionel Smith (ed), *Re-imagining the Trust: Trusts in Civil Law* (CUP 2012) 183

Hudson, Jessica, 'Mere and Other Discretionary Objects in Australia' in Ying Khai Liew and Matthew Harding (eds), *Asia-Pacific Trusts Law: Theory and Practice in Context* (Hart 2021) 19

Kim, Sung Hui, 'The Supreme Court's Fiduciary Duty to Forego Gifts' in Evan J Criddle, Evan Fox-Decent, Andew S Gold, Sung Hui Kim, and Paul B Miller (eds), *Fiduciary Government* (CUP 2018) 205

Latham, Stephen R, 'Conflict of Interest in Medical Practice' in Michael Davis and Andrew Stark (eds), *Conflict of Interest in the Professions* (OUP 2001) 279

Lawson, Frederick H, 'Rights and Other Relations in Rem' in Ernst von Caemmerer, Walter Hallstein, FA Mann, and Ludwig Raiser (eds), *Festschrift für Martin Wolff* (Mohr Siebeck 1952) 103

Leib, Ethan J, David L Ponet, and Michael Serota, 'Mapping Public Fiduciary Relationships' in Andew S Gold and Paul B Miller (eds), *Philosophical Foundations of Fiduciary Law* (OUP 2014) 388

Low, Kelvin FK, 'Non-Charitable Purpose Trusts: The Missing Right to Forego Enforcement' in Richard C Nolan, Kelvin FK Low, and Tang Hang Wu (eds), *Trusts and Modern Wealth Management* (CUP 2017) 486

Matthews, Paul, 'From Obligation to Property, and Back Again? The Future of the Non-Charitable Purpose Trust' in D Hayton (ed), *Extending the Boundaries of Trusts and Similar Ring-Fenced Funds* (Kluwer Law International 2002) 203

McNeil, Kent, 'Indigenous Territorial Rights in the Common Law' in Michele Graziadei and Lionel Smith (eds), *Comparative Property Law: Global Perspectives* (Edward Elgar 2017) 412

Miller, Paul B, 'The Fiduciary Relationship' in Andrew S Gold and Paul B Miller (eds), *Philosophical Foundations of Fiduciary Law* (OUP 2014) 63

———, 'The Idea of Status in Fiduciary Law' in Paul B Miller and Andrew S Gold (eds), *Contract, Status and Fiduciary Law* (OUP 2016) 25

———, 'Principles of Public Fiduciary Administration' in Tsvi Kahana and Anat Scolnicov (eds), *Boundaries of State, Boundaries of Rights* (CUP 2016) 251

———, 'Fiduciary Representation' in Evan J Criddle, Evan Fox-Decent, Andrew S Gold, Sung Hui Kim, and Paul B Miller (eds), *Fiduciary Government* (CUP 2018) 21

Mitchell, Charles, and Stephen Watterson, 'Remedies for Knowing Receipt' in Charles Mitchell (ed), *Constructive and Resulting Trusts* (Hart 2010) 115

Nagy, Donna M, 'Congressional Officials and the Fiduciary Duty of Loyalty: Lessons from Corporate Law' in Evan J Criddle, Evan Fox-Decent, Andrew S Gold, Sung Hui Kim, and Paul B Miller (eds), *Fiduciary Government* (CUP 2018) 233

Nolan, Donal, 'A Public Law Tort: Understanding Misfeasance in Public Office' in Kit Barker, Simone Degeling, Karen Fairweather, and Ross Grantham (eds), *Private Law and Power* (Hart 2017) 177

Nolan, Richard, '*Regal (Hastings) Ltd v Gulliver*' in Charles Mitchell and Paul Mitchell (eds), *Landmark Cases in Equity* (Hart 2012) 499

Nolan, Richard, and Matthew Conaglen, 'Good Faith: What Does It Mean for Fiduciaries and What Does It Tell Us About Them?' in Elise Bant and Matthew Harding (eds), *Exploring Private Law* (CUP 2010) 319

Peele, Gillian, and Robert Kaye, 'Conflict of Interest in British Public Life' in Chrisitne Trost and Alison L Gash (eds), *Conflict of Interest and Public Life* (CUP 2008) 155

Penner, James, 'Is Loyalty a Virtue, and Even If It Is, Does It Really Help Explain Fiduciary Liability?' in Andrew S Gold and Paul B Miller (eds), *Philosophical Foundations of Fiduciary Law* (OUP 2014) 159

Perkins, David N, 'Reasoning as It Is and Could Be: An Empirical Perspective' in Donald M Topping, Doris C Crowell, and Victor N Kobayashi (eds), *Thinking Across Cultures: The Third International Conference on Thinking* (L Erlbaum Associates 1989) 175

Popovici, Adrian, 'Le mandat apparent, une chimère?' in Anne-Sophie Hulin, Robert Leckey, and Lionel Smith (eds), *Les apparences en droit civil* (Éditions Yvon Blais 2015) 3

Popovici, Alexandra, 'La fiducie québécoise, re-belle infidèle' in Alexandra Popovici, Lionel Smith, and Régine Tremblay (eds), *Les intraduisibles en droit civil* (Thémis 2014) 129

——, 'Droits de regard: la fiducie dans le *Code civil du Québec*' in Christine Morin and Brigitte Lefebvre (eds), *Mélanges en l'honneur du professeur Jacques Beaulne* (Wilson & Lafleur 2018) 225

Popovici, Alexandra, and Lionel Smith, 'Lepaulle Appropriated' in Remus Valsan (ed), *Trusts and Patrimonies* (Edinburgh University Press 2015) 13

Resta, Giorgio, 'Systems of Public Ownership' in Michele Graziadei and Lionel Smith (eds), *Comparative Property Law: Global Perspectives* (Edward Elgar 2017) 216

Runté, Robert, 'Is Teaching a Profession?' in Gerald Taylor and Robert Runté (eds), *Thinking About Teaching: An Introduction* (Harcourt Brace 1995) 288

Shoked, Nadav, 'The American Law of Local Officials as Fiduciaries' in Evan J Criddle, Evan Fox-Decent, Andew S Gold, Sung Hui Kim, and Paul B Miller (eds), *Fiduciary Government* (CUP 2018) 258

Smith, Henry E, 'Why Fiduciary Law is Equitable' in Andrew S Gold and Paul B Miller (eds), *Philosophical Foundations of Fiduciary Law* (OUP 2014) 261

Smith, Lionel, 'Constructive Fiduciaries?' in Peter Birks (ed), *Privacy and Loyalty* (Clarendon Press 1997) 249

——, 'The Motive, Not the Deed' in Joshua Getzler (ed), *Rationalizing Property, Equity and Trusts: Essays in Honour of Edward Burn* (LexisNexis Butterworths 2003) 53

——, 'Philosophical Foundations of Proprietary Remedies' in Robert Chambers, Charles Mitchell, and James Penner (eds), *Philosophical Foundations of Unjust Enrichment* (OUP 2009) 281

——, '*North-West Transportation Co Ltd v Beatty*' in Charles Mitchell and Paul Mitchell (eds), *Landmark Cases in Equity* (Hart 2012) 393

——, 'Can We Be Obliged to Be Selfless?' in Andew S Gold and Paul B Miller (eds), *Philosophical Foundations of Fiduciary Law* (OUP 2014) 141

——, 'Contract, Consent, and Fiduciary Relationships' in Paul B Miller and Andrew S Gold (eds), *Contract, Status and Fiduciary Law* (OUP 2016) 117

——, 'What Is Left of the Non-Delegation Principle?' in Birke Häcker and Charles Mitchell (eds), *Current Issues in Succession Law* (Hart 2016) 209

——, 'Droit et pouvoir' in Anne-Sophie Hulin and Robert Leckey (eds), *L'abnégation en droit civil* (Éditions Yvon Blais 2017) 109

——, 'Powership and Its Objects' in Andrew Steven, Ross Anderson, and John MacLeod (eds), *Nothing So Practical as a Good Theory: Festschrift for George L Gretton* (Avizandum 2017) 223

——, 'Civil and Common Law' in Andrew S Gold, John CP Goldberg, Daniel B Kelly, Emily Sherwin, and Henry E Smith (eds), *Oxford Handbook of the New Private Law* (OUP 2020) 228

——, 'Conflict, Profit, Bias, Misuse of Power: Dimensions of Governance' in PB Miller and Matthew Harding (eds), *Fiduciaries and Trust: Ethics, Politics, Economics and Law* (CUP 2020) 149

——, 'Equity Is Not a Single Thing' in Dennis Klimchuk, Irit Samet, and Henry Smith (eds), *Philosophical Foundations of the Law of Equity* (OUP 2020) 144

——, 'Sources of Private Rights' in Simone Degeling, Michael Crawford, and Nicholas Tiverios (eds), *Justifying Private Rights* (Hart 2020) 129

Smith, Lionel, and Jeff Berryman, 'Disgorgement of Profits in Canada' in Ewoud Hondius and André Janssen (eds), *Disgorgement of Profits: Gain-Based Remedies Throughout the World* (Springer 2015) 281

Smith, Stephen A, 'The Deed, Not the Motive: Fiduciary Law Without Loyalty' in Paul B Miller and Andrew S Gold (eds), *Contract, Status and Fiduciary Law* (OUP 2016) 213

———, 'Intermediate and Comprehensive Justifications' in Simone Degeling, Michael Crawford, and Nicholas Tiverios (eds), *Justifying Private Rights* (Hart 2020) 63

Spigelman, Hon James J, 'The Equitable Origins of the Improper Purpose Ground' in Linda Pearson, Carol Harlow, and Michael Taggart (eds), *Administrative Law in a Changing State: Essays in Honour of Mark Aronson* (Hart 2008) 147

Stark, Andrew, 'Comparing Conflict of Interest Across the Professions' in Michael Davis and Andrew Stark (eds), *Conflict of Interest in the Professions* (OUP 2001) 335

———, 'Conflict of Interest in Canada' in Christine Trost and Alison L Gash (eds), *Conflict of Interest and Public Life* (CUP 2008) 125

Stevens, Robert, 'Private Rights and Public Wrongs' in Matthew Dyson (ed), *Unravelling Tort and Crime* (CUP 2014) 111

———, 'Not Waiving but Drowning' in Andrew Dyson, James Goudkamp, and Frederick Wilmot-Smith (eds), *Defences in Contract* (Hart 2017) 125

Surma, Ralph-Andreas, 'A Comparative Study of the English and German Judicial Approach to the Liability of Public Bodies in Negligence' in Duncan Fairgrieve, Mads Andenas, and John Bell (eds), *Tort Liability of Public Authorities in Comparative Perspective* (BIICL 2002) 355

Weinrib, Ernest, 'The Juridical Classification of Obligations' in Peter Birks (ed), *The Classification of Obligations* (Clarendon Press 1997) 37

Weller, Matthias, 'Who Gets the Bribe? – The German Perspective on Civil Law Consequences of Corruption in International Contracts' in Michael J Bonell and Olaf Meyer (eds), *The Impact of Corruption on International Commercial Contracts* (Springer 2015) 171

Welling, Bruce, 'Individual Liability for Corporate Acts: The Defence of Hobson's Choice' in Lionel Smith (ed), *Ruled by Law: Essays in Memory of Mr Justice John Sopinka* (LexisNexis Butterworths 2003) 55

Wu, Tang Hang, 'Derivative Actions on Behalf of the Trust: Beddoe Orders for Beneficiaries' in Richard C Nolan, Kelvin FK Low, and Tang Hang Wu (eds), *Trusts and Modern Wealth Management* (CUP 2017) 221

Theses

Grower, Julius, 'From Disability to Duty: From Constructive Fraud to Equitable Wrongs', Doctor of Philosophy, University College London, 2021

Mercer, Peter P, 'A Study and Evaluation of the Relator Action as a Vehicle of Public Interest Litigation', Doctor of Philosophy, Cambridge University, 1986

Motta, Madeline, 'Fiduciary Obligations of the Physician Scientist in a Post Hippocratic Era', Doctor of Civil Law, McGill University, 2008

Murray, Joanne, 'Power-Conferring Principles and Authority', Doctor of Civil Law, McGill University, 2023

Valsan, Remus, 'Understanding Fiduciary Duties: Conflict of Interest and Proper Exercise of Judgment in Private Law', Doctor of Civil Law, McGill University, 2012

Newspaper and Newsmagazine Stories

Canadian Press Agency and Globe and Mail Staff, 'Evan Solomon scandal joins long list of TV news's ethical imbroglios', *Globe and Mail*, 10 June 2015, online at https://www.theglobeandmail.com/arts/television/evan-solomon-scandal-joins-long-list-of-tv-newss-ethical-imbroglios/article24891488/

Fine, Sean, 'Doctrine is "everything" for Marc Nadon, the outspoken conservative justice rejected by Canada's Supreme Court', *Globe and Mail*, 2 October 2019

Gawande, Atul, 'The Cost Conundrum', *The New Yorker*, 25 May 2009

Harris, Rob, 'Embattled McKenzie resigns from federal cabinet over "sports rorts" affair', *Sydney Morning Herald* (2 February 2020), online at https://www.smh.com.au/politics/federal/embattled-mckenzie-resigns-from-federal-cabinet-over-sports-rorts-affair-20200202-p53wxm.html

Knight, Peter, 'So, Are Universities Public or Private?', *The Guardian*, 20 June 2006

Lederman, Marsha, 'If the media is the message, the Harper government wasn't listening', *Globe and Mail*, 23 October 2015, online at https://www.theglobeandmail.com/opinion/if-the-media-is-the-message-the-harper-government-wasnt-listening/article26963017/

Martin, Lawrence, 'William Barr: The Second-Most Dangerous Man in America', *Globe and Mail*, 9 June 2020

Savage, Charlie and Adam Goldman, 'Outsider Tapped in Flynn Case Calls Justice Dept Reversal a "Gross Abuse" of Power', *New York Times*, 10 June 2020

Wu, Tim, 'How Professors Help Rip Off Students', *New York Times*, 11 December 2019, online at https://www.nytimes.com/2019/12/11/opinion/textbook-prices-college.html

Index

For the benefit of digital users, page references are to the entire paragraph in which the indexed term appears. For this reason, where a page reference spans two pages (e.g., 52–53), the indexed term may appear on only one of those pages.

accountability
    contractual 177–78, 220–28
    meanings of 10–11, 212–15
    public administration, in 301–2, 311, 339, 340–44, 385–87
    as a remedy for wrongdoing 199, 214–15, 227–28, 257–58
    as source of duties of disclosure 122, 212–14, 228–38
    for unauthorized profits 192, 207, 216–20, 257–58
administration
    definition 28–30
administration, relationships of
    duties and rules arising in (*see* conflicts of duty and duty; conflicts of self-interest and duty; duties of disclosure; duties of prudence and diligence; duty of care, skill and diligence; duty of commitment; duty of good faith; fair-dealing rules; loyalty; self-dealing rules; unauthorized profits, rule against)
    fiduciary relationships, as examples of 27–29
    private law
        ad hoc 248–60
        constitution 65–71
        generally 63–65
        factual powers 22–23, 60–61, 264–76, 423–24, 425
        legal powers 60–61, 63–64
        non-financial interests 260–64
        termination 71–75 (*see also* administrators: removal of)
    public law
        generally 319–31
        termination 332–33 (*see also* administrators: removal of)
administrators. *See also* administration, relationships of
    employees, may be simultaneously 252–54
    removal of (including recusal)
        private law 73, 74–75, 152n.33, 179–80
        public law 332–33, 335–36, 348–49, 382
advisory relationships
    as relationships of administration 70–71, 148n.20, 233, 236–37, 264–72, 427
agency costs 145–46
agents
    administrators, as 5, 18, 26, 32–33, 79, 101
    duties and rules applying to (*see* conflicts of duty and duty; conflicts of self-interest and duty; duties of disclosure; duties of prudence and diligence; duty of care, skill and diligence; duty of commitment; duty of good faith; fair-dealing rules; loyalty; self-dealing rules; unauthorized profits, rule against)
    employees, may simultaneously be 252–54
appearances, theory of 131, 132n.230, 273, 275
    See also representation; third parties, protection of
Attorney General
    as enforcer of undircted public duties 42, 294–95, 349, 381, 388–89
    independence of 345–46, 382
    relator action 134–35, 324–25, 342–43, 344, 352–53, 354–55, 357n.101, 374, 377, 380–81, 396–97
    self-supervision, and the problem of 374, 388–89
authority
    misuse of, distinguished from absence of 8–9, 129, 413–15
    parental 6, 53–54, 55n.195, 68, 70, 74, 116–17, 260–61, 276–78
    private law 5, 6, 31, 41, 48–49, 50–51, 52, 54, 55n.195, 81–82, 85, 93–95, 98–99n.80, 100, 105, 110, 129–32, 208–10, 249–50, 252–53, 254, 260–61, 272–75, 276–78, 287

456 INDEX

authority (*cont.*)
    public law 54, 55–56, 305–9, 340, 342n.30, 362–66, 392, 398, 401, 406–7, 407n.160, 413–14, 415, 419–20, 423, 424
    relationship to other-regarding power 21, 32, 33–34, 50–51, 54, 305–8
    See also authorization
authorization
    conflicts, informed consent to 172, 175–76, 207, 230–31, 262
    conflicts, prior authorization of 173–75
    disapplying rules about unauthorized profits, as 207, 220
avoidance. *See* setting aside of legal acts

bailment 241
beneficiary
    definition, for the purposes of this book 28–29
    ambiguity of term 112–13, 134–35, 175n.127, 229n.184, 291–92
benefit corporation 116, 322n.105, 329–30n.146
business judgment rule 88, 341n.21

charitable organizations, as public administration 7–8, 134–35, 294–95, 319–20, 323–26, 348–49, 354–55, 376–81
    See also trusts: charitable
class actions
    class counsel, as administrator 289–90
    enforcement on behalf of class of trust beneficiaries, contrasted 290–93
    enforcement of undirected duties, contrasted 360, 373
    lead plaintiff, as administrator 288–90
    supervisory jurisdiction of judge 289–90
cluster concepts 23n.67, 270
common law constitutionalism 309–13, 434
companies. *See* corporations
conflict of duty and duty
    apparent 167–68
    authorization 173–75
    conflict of self-interest and duty, contrasted 143–44, 159–63
    definition 159–63
    de minimis 171–73
    effects 163–67
    informed consent 175–76
    management of 154–55, 165, 169, 171, 172, 173–80
    potential 168–71
    recusal 176–79
    as a rule about the exercise of administrative powers rather than a duty in the strict sense 146–50, 151–52, 159–63
conflict of interest. *See* conflict of self-interest and duty; conflict of duty and duty; conflict of interests
conflict of interests
    definition, vs conflict of self-interest and duty 144–46
conflict of self-interest and duty (conflict of interest)
    apparent 167–68
    authorization 173–75
    conflict of duty and duty, contrasted 159–63
    conflict of *interests*, contrasted 144–49
    de minimis 171–73, 409
    definition 152–54
    effects 163–67, 388–92, 399–400, 403–4, 408–10
    informed consent 175–76
    management of 154–55, 165, 169, 171, 172, 173–80
    potential 168–71
    prior involvement in process, as a kind of 194–95, 410
    psychological research in relation to 156–59
    public administration
        executive 347–48, 388–92, 399–400
        judges 408–10
        legislators 403–7
        professionals 420–21, 422–23, 424–26, 427, 428
    recusal 72, 121, 157, 163–64, 165, 176–79, 348, 393, 399, 409–10
    as a rule about the exercise of administrative powers rather than a duty in the strict sense 146–50, 151–52, 155–59
contentieux objectif and *contentieux subjectif* 338
corporate social responsibility 115–17, 139–40, 321–23
corporations
    benefit corporation (*see* benefit corporation)
    business corporations, as private administration 43–44, 115–17, 321–23
    business judgment rule (*see* business judgment rule)
    charitable corporations, as public administration 323–26, 378–81
    Crown corporations, State-controlled corporations, and State-owned enterprises, as public administration 53, 351–53, 394–95

INDEX 457

costs, in public interest litigation 373
criminal law, as indirect enforcement of norms of administration
   private law 284
   public law 335–36, 346–48
Crown corporations, State-controlled corporations, and State-owned enterprises, as public administration 53, 351–53, 394–95

damages 64, 167n.97, 218, 236, 244, 258, 270–71, 285, 360–62, 364–66, 370–71, 374, 392, 401–2
   distinguished from setting aside legal acts for disloyal use of powers 128n.211
   punitive, for breach of administrator's duty of good faith 243–44
deference. *See* jurisdiction
decision-making, inscrutability of
   and advisory relationships 267–68
   and conflicts 155–63
   and mixed purposes 117–21
delegation
   private law relationships of administration 124–25, 261, 286, 289–90
   public law relationships of administration 307–8, 315, 328, 353–54, 381–94
'deliberative exclusivity', not always essential to relationships of administration 115–17, 138–40
deposit (civil law nominate contract) 241
directors (corporate/company)
   as administrators 5, 18, 25–26, 79, 101
   business corporations, of, are private not public administrators 321–23
   business judgment rule (*see* business judgment rule)
   de facto 272–74
   duties and rules applying to (*see* conflicts of duty and duty; conflicts of self-interest and duty; duties of disclosure; duties of prudence and diligence; duty of care, skill and diligence; duty of commitment; duty of good faith; fair-dealing rules; loyalty; related-party transactions; self-dealing rules; unauthorized profits, rule against)
   employees, directors who are also employees are subject to wider rules about unauthorized profits 220–25
   generally administrators of the corporate person, not of a purpose 111–12, 321–23
   may consider other interests in assessing corporation's interests 97–99, 115–17, 322
   not, as such, agents or mandataries 5
disgorgement. *See* gain-based remedies for wrongdoing
discretion
   fettering 124–25
   meaning 23, 88
   not essential to a relationship of administration 15–16, 23–25, 106–9, 206–7
doctors. *See* physicians
duties
   directed vs undirected 336–38, 367, 370, 371–72, 432
   disclosure, of (*see* duty of disclosure)
   enforcement of
      direct enforcement 282, 285, 351–53, 382–83, 391
      representative enforcement 111n.134, 133n.232, 282, 285–93, 294, 353–55, 377, 412
      standing, designated person 282, 294–95, 348, 357n.104
      standing, proper person 282, 287, 294, 324–25, 326, 352–53, 357, 359–60
      State, by the 317–18, 325, 336, 348–50
   fiduciary (*see* fiduciary relationships)
   prudence and diligence (*see* duty of care, skill and diligence; duty of prudence and diligence)
   undirected
      definition 336–37
      private administration 293–95
      public administration 42, 316–18, 324–25, 335, 336–38, 348, 354–55, 356–61, 366–67, 368–69, 370, 371–72, 377, 380, 392, 395, 402, 405, 408, 412–13, 417, 419, 420–21, 425
duty of care, skill and diligence (common law) 16, 34–35, 64, 90–91, 128n.211, 138, 147, 218–19, 222, 230–31, 240–43, 312, 332, 369–70, 372, 392
duty of commitment 239, 244
duty of disclosure
   private administration 64, 108, 150, 161–62, 166–67, 171, 177–78, 199, 228–38, 270–71, 276
   public administration 347, 385–87, 389, 398–99
duty of good faith. *See* good faith

duty of prudence and diligence (civil law) 16, 34–35, 64, 90–91, 128n.211, 138, 147, 218–19, 222, 230–31, 240–43, 312, 332, 369–70, 372, 392

embezzlement
  as breach of administrator's duty of good faith 137, 243–44
  as crime 284
employees
  corporate stakeholders, as 97–99, 110–11, 115–17, 139–40, 322–23
  directors who are also employees are subject to wider rules about unauthorized profits 220–25, 258
  duty of loyalty, different from that of administrators 256–58
  may simultaneously be administrators 252–54, 400–1, 423
  not as such administrators except in US law 47n.160, 254–55
enforcement
  private law
    derivative 44, 286–87, 291n.33
    direct (*see* duties: enforcement of: direct enforcement)
    representative (*see* duties: enforcement of: representative enforcement)
  public law
    designated person standing (*see* duties: enforcement of: standing: designated person)
    proper person standing (*see* duties: enforcement of: standing: proper person)
    standing 324–25, 339, 340–41, 350, 357, 358–61, 374, 377, 381, 391, 393–94, 404, 408, 426–27
Equity
  private law administration 61, 128–29, 131, 211, 314, 434
  public law administration 301–2, 383, 399, 434
ethical investment 36–37, 96–97
ethics 152–54, 159, 340, 344–45, 347–48, 388–92, 403–4, 420–21, 422–23
even hand rule 174, 330–31
executive branch of government
  as subject to norms of public administration 53, 305, 385–88, 392–93
  conflicts 305, 388–92, 393, 399
  unauthorized profits 305, 388–94
  use of powers for proper purposes 53, 305, 382–84, 393

executors
  as administrators 65, 101, 176, 221–22, 273–74
expropriation 303–4, 312–13, 361–62

factual power. *See* power: factual
fair-dealing rules (contract between an administrator and beneficiary) 149–50, 177n.137, 177n.138, 234n.208, 234n.215
fallacy, 'one right answer'. *See* 'one right answer' fallacy
fiduciary duties. *See* fiduciary relationships
  different definitions of 27–28, 79–80
fiduciary government 301–13, 318–19, 433
fiduciary relationships
  duties and rules arising in (*see* conflicts of duty and duty; conflicts of self-interest and duty; duties of disclosure; duties of prudence and diligence; duty of care, skill and diligence; duty of commitment; duty of good faith; fair-dealing rules; loyalty; related-party transactions; self-dealing rules; unauthorized profits, rule against)
  relationships of administration, as 27–29, 101
fraud on a power
  as disloyal use of a power 81n.14, 137n.253

gain-based remedies for wrongdoing 199, 214–15, 227–28, 257–58
See also unauthorized profits, rule against
good faith
  administrators, duty of 79–80, 112–13, 127, 230–31, 243–44, 253n.32, 259, 363–64, 415–16
  irrelevant to operation of profit and conflict rules 154–55, 157n.58, 159, 163, 164, 184, 194, 388
  outside of relationships of administration 27n.77, 48n.167, 103–4, 253n.32

improper purposes. *See* proper purposes
'inadequate deliberation'
  as a failure of loyalty in the use of a power 106n.113, 128, 129n.218
indemnity, right of administrator to. *See* reimbursement, right of administrator to
information, rights to. *See* duty of disclosure
informed consent. *See* authorization

interests, as opposed to rights, as foundation for enforcement of duties
   private law 282–83, 285, 287, 288, 290–95
   public law 336–38, 348–49, 352–55, 356–61
journalists
   as professionals 426–27
judicial branch of government
   as subject to norms of public administration 62–63, 312–13, 316–17, 333, 346, 407–11
   conflicts 157, 312–13, 409–10
   duties of care, skill, prudence, diligence 411
   unauthorized profits 410–11
   use of powers for proper purposes 316–17, 408
jurisdiction, as frequently underlying deference
   private administration 87–93, 115–21
   public administration 309n.45, 341, 382–83, 384, 385–86, 398, 405, 412
justificatory principles
   definition, for purposes of this book 14–15
   generally 13, 15–16, 24–25, 27, 28–29, 33, 42, 59–60, 299, 300–1, 307–8, 309–10, 314, 431–35
   one kind of source of obligations, as 16, 314

legal act
   definition 20–21, 126
   null 128–29, 130, 141–42, 164n.85
   void or voidable
      private administration 105, 126–30, 133–35, 137, 164n.85, 217, 283, 285
      public administration 331–32, 391, 405n.155, 414
legal positivism 12–13
legislative branch of government
   as subject to norms of public administration 8–9, 18, 28n.80, 304–5, 310, 403–7, 417
legitimate expectations, in natural justice 123–24, 387n.69
loyalty
   conflicts (*see* conflict of self-interest and duty; conflict of duty and duty)
   consequences of disloyal use of administrative powers
      private administration 126–30, 164–66
      public administration 42, 382–83, 397–98, 399, 408
   definition, for purposes of this book 30–32, 79–81
   definitions of, various 79–80

'duty of' 30, 31, 32, 79–80, 136–38, 192–93, 227n.180, 243
employees, different meaning of loyalty from administrators 256–58
improper purposes, as a failure of loyalty 81–82 (*see also* proper purposes)
'inadequate deliberation'
   as a failure of loyalty in the use of a power 106n.113, 128, 129n.218
natural justice, relation to
   private administration 122–24
   public administration 356, 385, 387–88, 410
objective definition of mission to which administrator must be loyal 86, 88, 90, 93–99
'one right answer' fallacy (*see* 'one right answer' fallacy)
to persons and to purposes 5–9, 95–99, 109–14, 315–19, 327–31, 406–7
as a requirement for the exercise of administrative powers rather than a duty in the strict sense
   private administration 32, 33–34, 81–82, 85–93, 99–100, 109–38
   public administration 312–13, 382–83, 397–98, 408
sole interests vs best interests 120n.170
subjective nature of 33–34, 87–93, 341, 384, 386, 398
unauthorized profits (*see* unauthorized profits, rule against)

malicious prosecution 362–66, 368–69
mandataries
   as administrators 5, 52, 101, 131–32, 180, 220, 221n.161, 248–49, 253–54, 270–71, 307–8, 395n.107
mandate (civil law contract)
   as source of rules on administration 19–20, 101–2n.88, 141–42, 181–86, 251n.18
misfeasance in public office 362–66, 370–71
mission, other-regarding 3, 8–9, 10–12, 15, 22, 25, 41–43, 47, 63, 67, 70–72, 75, 82, 101–4, 106, 125, 126, 247, 306–7, 310, 312–13, 435
motive 33–34, 82–84, 87n.32, 92, 99–100, 107–8, 363, 373, 433–34
   mixed 115–21, 404
   See also proper purposes

natural justice
   private administration 122–24
   public administration 356, 387–88, 398–99, 410

negligence, of public authorities, liability for 366–72
non-charitable purpose trusts. *See* trust: non-charitable purpose
non-intervention, principle of (trust law) 88
nuisance, public 354–55
nullity 128–30, 137
  absolute 128–29, 130
  relative 128–29

office
  concept 32–33, 53–56
  in private law 68–69, 71–72, 73, 74–75
  in public law 300–1, 307–8, 319, 323, 324–25, 332, 347, 362–66, 382–84, 388–90, 394–95, 408, 411
'one right answer' fallacy
  business corporations 89n.41, 98–99n.80, 322
  legislators 405
  loyalty, subjective nature of 33–34, 88–90, 98–99, 155
  See also business judgment rule; non-intervention, principle of (trust law)
opportunism 189, 190
organs, decision-making, of a legal person 5, 52, 66, 123, 177, 319, 324–25

parens patriae 54–55, 69
parents
  as administrators 6, 53–54, 68, 70, 74, 116–17, 260–61, 276–78
patrimony
  patrimonial vs extrapatrimonial rights 39–41, 44–45, 60–61, 68, 247, 260–64, 265–66, 276–77, 366n.148
physicians
  as advisory administrators 6, 233, 263–65, 266–67, 270–71, 272n.120
  as professionals 418, 420–21
political accountability. *See* accountability: in public administration
positivism, legal. *See* legal positivism
power
  autonomous 46, 52, 55, 66n.30
  discretionary, or not 106–9, 206–7
  distinguished from right 21–22
  factual 6, 22–23, 24–25, 247, 264–77, 424, 425
  misuse of distinguished from absence of 8–9, 129, 413–15 (*see also* loyalty)
  misuse by non-use 135–36
  organic 52, 66

other-regarding 10–11, 15, 18–20, 23–24, 28–29, 32, 81–82, 103–4, 105, 126–27, 138, 143–44, 148, 149, 150, 152–53, 166–67, 169, 171, 177–78, 190–91, 192–93, 194–95, 200–1, 218–19, 300, 301–2, 307–8, 397–98, 432, 434
representation, of 19–20, 44–49, 92, 131–32, 149, 264–65
professions
  public administration, as a case of 418–28
  self-regulating 408, 419–20, 423, 426
  strict and wider senses 419–28
professors
  not generally private administrators 254–55, 423
  as professionals 423–26
profits, unauthorized (*see* unauthorized profits, rule against)
proper purposes
  administration, in relationships of 10–11, 81–82, 101–2, 103–4, 105–6, 311–12, 326–27, 338n.13, 376, 377–78, 382–84, 385, 387, 393, 397–98, 405–6, 408–10, 431, 433
  administration, outside of relationships of (good faith) 102–4, 105–6
  improper purposes, as defective use of power
  private administration 83–84, 87, 92, 99–100, 102, 105, 106n.113, 115, 117–21, 122, 125, 126, 127–30, 133, 137
  public administration 382–84, 385–86, 389–91, 393, 397–99, 401–2, 405, 408, 409, 413–14, 425
  mixed purposes 115–21, 404
  See also loyalty; motive
protectors, of trusts, as administrators 259–60
public authorities, liability of 361–72
public–private partnerships 327–31
'public trust' 7–8, 35–36, 124n.191, 301–13, 317n.85, 320n.97, 375–76
purposes
  improper (*see* proper purposes: improper)
  motives (*see* motive)
  other regarding (*see* mission, other regarding)
  proper (*see* proper purposes)

rationality 103–4, 105, 116, 156, 158–59, 344, 383–84
reasonable expectation, in tort of malicious prosecution 365n.145
reasons for the use of administrative powers
  private administration 33–35, 84, 85–86, 91, 118, 119–20, 128, 204, 219
  giving of reasons 122, 377–78

public administration 309, 363, 385–87, 398–99, 414–15
  giving of reasons 341–44, 377–78, 385–87, 398–99
recusal 72, 74n.67, 121, 157, 163–64, 165, 176–79, 348, 393, 399, 409–10
rescission. *See* setting aside of legal acts
reimbursement, right of administrator to 45n.149, 46–47, 198–99, 208, 288–89
  as converse of rule against unauthorized profits 181–83, 187–88, 198–99, 200–1, 209, 218–19, 228, 432
related-party transactions 165n.90, 173–74, 177n.138
  See also fair-dealing rules; self-dealing rules
relator action. *See* Attorney General: relator action
remedies
  attribution of profits (*see* unauthorized profits, rule against)
  damages (*see* damages)
  rescission (*see* setting aside of legal acts)
  setting aside (*see* setting aside of legal acts)
  for wrongdoing, gain-based (*see* gain-based remedies for wrongdoing)
representation
  legal 44–52, 55, 65–66, 131–32, 264–65, 286
  political 49–51, 65–67, 145–46
representative enforcement 99n.82, 110–11, 133n.232, 282, 285–93, 353–55, 377, 412
rule against unauthorized profits. *See* unauthorized profits, rule against
rules against exercising administrative power while in a conflict. *See* conflict of duty and duty; conflict of self-interest and duty

self-dealing rules 141–44, 149–50, 177–78, 234
  See also conflict of self-interest and duty
self-supervision, problem of 287, 292–93, 324–25, 331, 349–51, 352–54, 355, 359–60, 374, 380, 391, 393–94, 395, 432–33
setting aside of legal acts 10–11, 34, 53, 64, 81, 91n.49, 92, 106n.113, 117–21, 126–30, 133–35, 137, 150, 154–55, 164–66, 171, 200–3, 234, 236, 270–72, 282–83, 292n.39, 331, 338n.13, 352, 357–58, 387, 391, 393, 397–98, 408, 409, 413–14, 431
  distinguished from damages for breach of duty 128n.211
shareholders
  'shareholder primacy' 88–89, 323

stakeholders, and 115–17, 139–40, 321–23, 329–30, 352–53
source, of rights and other legal relations
  ambiguities of 16n.40, 311–12, 314–15
standing
  'designated person' standing 294–95, 348
  direct enforcement 282
  private law 74–75, 110–11, 134–35, 138–39, 164–65, 178, 229n.184, 281–82, 287, 290–91, 294–95
  'proper person' standing 287, 294, 324–25, 326, 352–53, 357–58
  public law 339, 340–41, 350, 357, 358–61, 374
  representative enforcement (*see* representative enforcement)
State-owned enterprises, State-controlled corporations, and Crown corporations, as public administration 53, 351–53, 394–95
status 32–33
supervisory jurisdiction 8n.13, 53–56, 68–69, 135–36, 175–76, 179, 259, 289–90, 317n.82, 352–53, 354, 355n.92, 408n.165

teachers
  as professionals 423–26
third parties, protection of
  reliance by third parties 130–32, 201, 273, 274–75
trust
  charitable 3, 7–8, 36–37, 43, 97n.71, 114, 124n.191, 134–35, 294–95, 318, 319–20, 326, 348n.58, 354–55, 376–78
  non-charitable purpose 7n.8, 7n.11, 73n.63, 114n.144, 292n.38, 294–95n.56, 295
  'public trust' (*see* 'public trust')
  Quebec 45, 67n.34, 73, 102n.90, 114, 134, 175n.126, 197n.75, 293, 316, 319, 320, 348n.58
  supervisory jurisdiction 54–56, 175–76, 179, 259
trustees
  as administrators 6–8, 18, 25–26, 32–33, 79, 101
  duties and rules applying to (*see* conflicts of duty and duty; conflicts of self-interest and duty; duties of disclosure; duties of prudence and diligence; duty of care, skill and diligence; duty of commitment; duty of good faith; loyalty; unauthorized profits, rule against)

unauthorized profits, rule against
  basis of 188–200
  contractual duties, distinguished from 185–88, 220–22, 223–28, 233n.205
  as converse of administrator's right to reimbursement 181–83, 187–88, 198–99, 200–1, 209, 218–19, 228, 432
  as a primary rule of attribution rather than a remedy for breach of duty 181–200, 209–10
  public administration 376, 379–80, 388–94, 400–1, 402–4, 410–11, 420–21
  scope of 216–20

undertaking theory 69–71, 250, 276–77n.144
universities 323–26, 378–81
unselfish
  meaning other-regarding 7, 33–34, 236

visitor, jurisdiction of 55n.194, 325n.122, 380n.31
void/voidable
  private law 85, 127, 128–30, 133–34, 164–66, 217, 234
  public law 331–32, 391, 397–98, 399, 405n.155, 413–14
  See also setting aside of legal acts
vulnerability 110, 249–50, 255